Information Technology Entrepreneurship and Innovation

Fang Zhao
RMIT University, Australia

 **INFORMATION SCIENCE REFERENCE**

Hershey · New York

Acquisitions Editor:	Kristin Klinger
Development Editor:	Kristin Roth
Senior Managing Editor:	Jennifer Neidig
Managing Editor:	Jamie Snavely
Assistant Managing Editor:	Carole Coulson
Copy Editor:	Larissa Vinci
Typesetter:	Carole Coulson
Cover Design:	Lisa Tosheff
Printed at:	Yurchak Printing Inc.

Published in the United States of America by
Information Science Reference (an imprint of IGI Global)
701 E. Chocolate Avenue, Suite 200
Hershey PA 17033
Tel: 717-533-8845
Fax: 717-533-8661
E-mail: cust@igi-global.com
Web site: http://www.igi-global.com

and in the United Kingdom by
Information Science Reference (an imprint of IGI Global)
3 Henrietta Street
Covent Garden
London WC2E 8LU
Tel: 44 20 7240 0856
Fax: 44 20 7379 0609
Web site: http://www.eurospanbookstore.com

Library of Congress Cataloging-in-Publication Data

Information technology entrepreneurship and innovation / Fang Zhao, editor.

p. cm.

Summary: "This book presents current studies on the nature, process and practice of entrepreneurship and innovation in the development, implementation, and application of information technology worldwide, as well as providing academics, entrepreneurs, managers, and practitioners with up-to-date, comprehensive, and rigorous research-based articles on the formation and implementation of effective strategies and business plans"--Provided by publisher.

Includes bibliographical references and index.

ISBN 978-1-59904-901-4 (hbk.) -- ISBN 978-1-59904-902-1 (e-book)

1. Information technology. 2. Electronic commerce. 3. Technological innovations. 4. Entrepreneurship. I. Zhao, Fang

T58.5.I5377 2008

004.068--dc22

2007037398

British Cataloguing in Publication Data
A Cataloguing in Publication record for this book is available from the British Library.

All work contributed to this book set is original material. The views expressed in this book are those of the authors, but not necessarily of the publisher.

Table of Contents

Section I
Information Technology Innovations

Simrn Kaur Gill, National University of Ireland Galway, Ireland
Kathryn Cormican, National University of Ireland Galway, Ireland

Jari Tammela, Spiral Business Services Oy, Finland
Vesa Salminen, Lappeenranta University of Technology, Finland

Shamsuddin Ahmed, Bang College of Business, KIMEP, Almaty, Kazakhtan
Francis Amagoh, Department of Public Administration, KIMEP, Almaty, Kazakhtan

Section II
IT Management and Corporate Governance

Fang Zhao, RMIT University, Australia
Adela J. McMurray, RMIT University, Australia
Mark Toomey, Infonomics Pty Ltd., Australia

Section V
Innovation and Knowledge Management

Section VI
Innovation Process

Detailed Table of Contents

Section I
Information Technology Innovations

Chapter I

> *Simrn Kaur Gill, National University of Ireland Galway, Ireland*
> *Kathryn Cormican, National University of Ireland Galway, Ireland*

This chapter introduces the concept of ambient intelligence (AmI), a new concept in the area of information and communication technology (ICT), from a systems development perspective in the manufacturing environment. To create an AmI environment requires the use of a combination of technologies. The AmI environment can be enabled through the use of computers that are embedded into everyday objects and through the use of wireless communication. The interaction between these embedded devices and the human user is improving through advancements in the area of natural interaction.

Chapter II

> *Jari Tammela, Spiral Business Services Oy, Finland*
> *Vesa Salminen, Lappeenranta University of Technology, Finland*

This chapter is focusing on interoperability and providing a concept in order to speed up common innovation of the products and services in open semantic infrastructure. This includes identification of solution boundaries and innovation partners. Operative challenge is how to decompose the requirements across the boundaries of different companies in different branches and in different role in the value and innovation network. There is also challenge on how to manage evolving technologies to satisfy customers' existing and future expectations.

Chapter III

Shamsuddin Ahmed, Bang College of Business, KIMEP, Almaty, Kazakhtan
Francis Amagoh, Department of Public Administration, KIMEP, Almaty, Kazakhtan

This chapter presents the design of a heritage tourism Web portal. Factor analysis is used to identify how the navigation tools are to be grouped. Correlation analysis additionally identifies methods of grouping the navigation functionalities to substantiate the decision. Statistical analysis lends support to the reliability of the data used in the study. Examples are given about how heritage portal navigation functionality can be developed as hierarchical layered portal pages. Additionally, the perceptual map shows the layout and proximity of the portal functionalities.

Section II
IT Management and Corporate Governance

Chapter IV

Effectiveness of Information Technology Governance:

Fang Zhao, RMIT University, Australia
Adela J. McMurray, RMIT University, Australia
Mark Toomey, Infonomics Pty Ltd., Australia

In today's business world, most organisations depend on information technology (IT) for their day-to-day activities and the achievement of their future strategies. However, the track record of IT initiatives in many organizations is not strong, and many fail—particularly when measured against the outcomes they were intended to produce. This chapter examines practices and frameworks for effective IT governance in industry and business. Utilizing a mixed research methodology of survey and interview, 20 board directors' and senior mangers' perceptions of IT governance and management were sought and analysed. The findings show there is a need and opportunity for improvement in IT governance and that in most organizations, Australian Standard AS8015-2005—provides a sound foundation for such improvement.

Chapter V

Donglin Wu, RMIT University, Australia
Fang Zhao, RMIT University, Australia

This chapter identifies the challenges, features, and drivers of performance measurement (PM) in the SMEs in the IT industry and introduces a PM framework based on the system theory and business excellence model for SMEs. This study finds that a dynamic and flexible PM framework is more suitable to SMEs than a mechanized PM model. By examining the PM features and key success factors in SMEs in the IT industry, this study concludes that traditional PM theories and tools are not suitable for SMEs, which is supported by many recent studies on PM in SMEs.

Section III
IT Entrepreneurship and E-Business

Brychan Thomas, University of Glamorgan Business School, UK
Christopher Miller, University of Glamorgan Business School, UK
Gary Packham, University of Glamorgan Business School, UK
Geoff Simmons, University of Ulster, UK

This chapter introduces the role of Web sites and e-commerce in the development and growth of global higher education start-ups. The extant concepts, research, and experiences the chapter builds on is the literature concerning e-commerce and small and medium-sized enterprises (SMEs) together with published research on global start-ups. It argues that the key results, evidence and experience, from the empirical case study research, highlight clear and precise reasons for the development of Web sites and e-commerce by the global start-ups. There are important implications of the study for entrepreneurs, policy makers, practitioners, researchers, and educators for the specific field of e-commerce developments for global start-ups.

Alemayehu Molla, RMIT University, Australia
Richard Duncombe, The University of Manchester, UK

Small and medium size enterprises (SMEs) innovativeness to use e-commerce has received significant research attention. This chapter continues with this tradition and offers a theoretically grounded and deeper insight into the e-commerce innovation process in SMEs. This is achieved by proposing a motivation-ability based four-state developmental framework. Each of the four states is then described in terms of organisational readiness, organisational capability, e-commerce capability, e-commerce motivational factors, and commodity chain position. SME mangers can use the framework as a decision making tool to critically stock-take their innate state and to set realistic goals and expectations with regards to future e-commerce investments. The utility of the framework is demonstrated through case studies of 14 small-scale enterprises located in the Indian state of Karnataka.

Tobias Kollmann, University of Duisburg-Essen, Germany

The constant and rapid development of Internet-related technologies in the accompanying Net Economy has inevitably had a significant influence on various possibilities for developing innovative online business concepts and realizing these by establishing entrepreneurial ventures. The term "e-entrepreneurship" respectively describes the act of founding new companies that generate revenue and profits independent from a physical value chain. With this in mind, this article focuses on the process of creating electronic customer value within the net economy as well as the success factors and development phases of electronic ventures.

The chapter discusses the use of business strategies for pure Internet firms. It separates the strategic choices and directions used for idea generation, during start-up, and beyond business or brand establishment. Corroborating much of the literature, it argues that traditional notions of strategy might be inappropriate for some dotcom firms due to the high level of complexity, speed of change and competitiveness characteristic of the Internet environment. As has been observed by research, idea generation on the Internet can involve prospecting and reacting quickly to markets to a greater extent than amongst traditional businesses. Likewise, start-up strategies often appear to involve flexibility and an openness to strategic change in response to the fast dynamic nature of the online market. The chapter suggests alternative strategy models that might be useful in our understanding of Internet business creation and development.

Section IV
Networks and Partnerships

The Internet has reached a stage of maturity where its innovative adoption and implementation can be a source of competitive advantage. Supply chains are one of the areas that has reportedly benefited greatly, achieving optimisation through low cost, high efficiency use of the Internet, almost seamlessly linking global supply chains into e-supply networks. This field is still in its academic and practical infancy, and there is a need for more empirical research to build a robust theoretical foundation, which advances our knowledge and understanding. Here, the main aims and objectives are to highlight the importance of information flows in e-supply chains/networks, and the need for their standardisation to facilitate integration, legality, security, and efficiency of operations. This chapter contributes to the field by recommending a three-stage framework: the development of standardised Internet technology platforms (e-platforms), integration requirements, and classification of information flows.

Chapter XI

This chapter describes an in-depth analysis of the methods to increase the effectiveness of virtual teams in health care using the Northern Alliance Hospital Admission Risk Program (HARP) Chronic Disease Management (CDM) Program as the test case. A conceptual framework of the specific components required for virtual team effectiveness and a survey tool to examine a team's performance (based on virtual team member perception) with each of these components is presented. The proposed Conceptual Framework of Virtual Team Effectiveness categorises the determinants influencing the effectiveness of virtual teams into four key frames of leadership, team components, organisational culture, and technology. An empirical survey of 38 virtual team members within the Northern Alliance HARP CDM Program demonstrates high levels of agreement with Leadership and some Team components, however, limited Agreement with the organisational culture and technology components.

Chapter XII

There is a general consensus that networks and community interaction provide a critical mechanism for innovation. However, methods for the analysis of social networks have yet to better understand knowledge dynamics of innovation. It is argued for the need to (i) switch the unit of analysis from individuals' ideas to social construction of knowledge and (ii) use the Deleuzo-Guattarian rhizomic view on networks to reveal not only the dynamics of meaning creation, but also those of meaning disruption, both essential conditions for the emergence of new concepts. A new approach, Rhizomic Network Analysis (RNA) is explored, which aims to move analysis beyond mere description of relationship structures towards enabling the differentiation of the type of knowledge dynamics emergent. An example of an entrepreneurial business network is used to illustrate this approach.

Chapter XIII

This chapter develops and underlines the concept of continuous improvement teamworking approach in a major Australian banking organization. The study develops a model, which is a virtuous CTIO circle, reflecting the concern (issue), task (action), interaction (involvement and connection), outcome (result) phases. It illustrates the new evolving consultative, participative, and interactive virtuous teamworking approach. The findings from the participant observation conducted for the present study has shown that synchronous conferencing, internet online functional services, continuous improvement and team meetings form the essential four core elements of the CTIO model. The adoption of a continuous improvement teamworking approach is assisting in better running of retail banking operational activities and in achieving better performance. This study is important to senior managers and managers in improving the operational activities of their businesses to be more competitive.

Chapter XIV

This study presents the regional development of universities aiming to increase their external impact on their environment. The purpose is to show that the activities of regional development and quality assurance at universities are important means of promoting the development of ICT in the region. Regional development is analysed in this study using the approach of quality assurance, which provides a general framework to analyse the cooperation between universities and enterprises operating in information and communication technology. The study contributes to the knowledge and practice of regional development in higher education and presents how educational institutions can support their regional engagement and incorporate the regional development in its activities. Regional cooperation between a higher education institution and ICT enterprises is illustrated with examples. Conclusions and recommendations are drawn based on the findings.

Chapter XV

The swift sharing of sensitive information is a major source of competitive advantage in today's age and is not possible without trustworthy relationships of top management with external as well as internal customers (employees) of a business. Islam is the second biggest religion in the world with over 1/4th of the world's population as its followers. Where traditional literature believes that long-term relationships result in trust development, Islam considers that trust development results in building and maintaining long-term relationships. This chapter is specifically meant to highlight the role of trust from an Islamic perspective in a leader-followers relationship as well as a leader-customers relationship.

Section V
Innovation and Knowledge Management

Chapter XVI

Managing knowledge for innovation in an extended enterprise (EE) environment is a key issue. This in turn requires effective utilisation of information and communication technologies (ICT). This chapter addresses the application of ICT for knowledge management (KM) needed for innovation in industry. An ICT based KM system to support innovation process in EE environment, i.e. to support mastering of the innovation process is presented. The main objective of the new AIM System is to provide the means of stimulating the creation of innovative ideas in general, and specifically on potential product/process improvements and on problem solving. The AIM system supports collection of such ideas throughout EE from people involved with the products and processes, as well as a development of the collected ideas into innovations.

Chapter XVII

Andrew Creed, Deakin University, Australia
Ambika Zutshi, Deakin University, Australia
Jane Ross, University of Maryland—University College, USA

This chapter discusses how the independent nature of entrepreneurs, combined with the enabling features of digital information technology (IT), may lead to a situation where paper-based and campus-specific classroom education is at best uncomfortable and at worst almost meaningless. The purpose of the chapter is to define and capture the latest thinking in applied education and relate this to the mindset of the emerging generation of entrepreneurs. To this end, industry and business education cases are drawn upon to illustrate key points, and a framework is provided for better understanding knowledge management in the emerging global context of e-learning technologies.

Chapter XVIII

Cecilia Hegarty, University of Ulster, UK

Entrepreneurial knowledge and innovation resonates with positive views, hence the need to tell everyone about entrepreneurship and give students the opportunity to learn more about it. Internet-based education and distance learning are commonly known as e-learning. E-learning provides a method of reaching high volumes of students within a culturally rich virtual workspace. It is arguable that e-learning has become a cornerstone tool in entrepreneurship delivery. This chapter aims to stimulate debate among practitioners on the use of information technology in the process of entrepreneurial learning. Learning activity, pedagogical shifts within the wider disciplines of entrepreneurship education and the spin-off effects for entrepreneur training programs are all considered. The application of information technology through entrepreneurship e-learning packages is shown to have magnified the entrepreneurship potential in wider society.

Section VI
Innovation Process

Chapter XIX

James Perotti, Rochester Institute of Technology, USA

This chapter asserts that process models are an excellent platform for a continuous stream of innovations. Such models can illuminate opportunities for new products and services and for new ways of distributing products and services. These dynamic models make it possible to coordinate the efforts of multiple business partners in order to better serve customers with quality, speed, and responsiveness to their needs. There is increasing evidence that businesses using these models to discover opportunities have achieved a sustainable advantage over their competitors.

This chapter introduces a new approach for performance measurement in product development and innovation processes. It shows that there is a great need in practice to increase the efficiency of product development processes because existing approaches are not sufficient to give enough information about a running project. These approaches both from science and industry are analysed and a new attempt is introduced that aims at the integration of concrete project data with information about the product by using semantic Web technologies. Furthermore, the chapter shows that there is an emerging gap between productivity increase and the complexity of product development processes. This will be a challenge in the future and has high potential for research that has to be done in close cooperation with industry.

Innovation is seen by many organizations as the next frontier to be managed in order to gain a competitive advantage and remain sustainable. Current psychometric tests used to test for innovation or creativity often do little more than identify various personality traits or characteristics which can be used to suggest an individual who might be suitable to fill a recognized gap in the organization. This chapter offers an approach, building on the authors' work along psychological lines with tacit knowledge measurement in the ICT domain that seeks to capture responses to real scenarios experienced by recognized innovators and entrepreneurs. These scenarios and responses are used to evaluate the degree to which the respondent can be considered an innovator and to suggest what areas of personal or professional development may be needed.

This chapter develops a set of seven dimensions, which may be applied to each sovereign nation as a guide to allow for systematic consideration and comparison of opportunities and challenges across borders. Under the assumption that innovation itself requires a unique set of skills or opportunistic settings, the chapter then explores each dimension's applicability to situations particularly associated with innovation in technology. Using current research and examples from world business, the chapter moves to a brief discussion of projected future developments in the field and related research needs.

Chapter XXIII
Roman Boutellier, ETH Zurich, Switzerland
Andreas Biedermann, ETH Zurich, Switzerland

Technologies are praised initially as problem solvers and frequently evolve into problem causers themselves. Affected companies are facing the threat of technological obsolescence and fundamental change
processes. A framework of the social environment and the value chain helps the management to better
understand the relevant mechanisms. Using a case of lead-bearing solders, the chapter illustrates the
far-reaching consequences of the forced phase-out of these alloys, which have been used since the beginning of industrial electronics production. Lead bearing solders are one example of many technologies,
which are candidates to become controversial. Increased awareness of side-effects, globalization and
intensified use of single technologies indicate that this management task will gain momentum in the
electronics industry and others.

Preface

It has become a widely recognized fact that entrepreneurs and information technology (IT) have become the backbone of the world economy. The increasing penetration of IT in society and in most of industries/businesses, and the joining forces of entrepreneurship, innovation, and IT in the knowledge-based economy re-enforce the need for a leading and authoritative forum to disseminate frontier research results about entrepreneurship, innovation, and IT from an international perspective. The primary purpose of this book is to present and explore current trends and changes in the nature, process, and practice of entrepreneurship and innovation in the development, implementation, and application of information technology.

THE CONCEPT OF ENTREPRENEURSHIP

There has been no consensus in defining entrepreneurship and innovation in the exiting literature (Zhao, 2006). Some studies have dealt with entrepreneurship and innovation by investigating the personality and psychology of entrepreneurs and innovators (Caird, 1988; Casson, 1982; Littunen, 2000). Others have talked of the nature of entrepreneurship and innovation in organizations (Goffin & Pfeiffer, 1999; Martin, 1994).

"Entrepreneurship, in its narrowest sense, involves capturing ideas, converting them into products and or services, and then building a venture to take the product to market" (Johnson, 2001, p. 138). A noticeable trend in the study of entrepreneurship in recent years has been away from the subject of small business *per se* toward the concept of entrepreneurship (Chell, 2001; Cornwall & Perlman, 1990). The book reflects this trend by emphasizing the concept of entrepreneurship itself, rather than the personality or psychology of small business entrepreneurs.

Entrepreneurship represents organizational behavior. The key elements of entrepreneurship include risk-taking, proactivity, and innovation (Miller, 1983). However, Slevin and Covin (1990, p. 43) have argued that the three elements are not sufficient to ensure organizational success. They maintained that "a successful firm not only engages in entrepreneurial managerial behavior, but also has the appropriate culture and organizational structure to support such behavior." The book adopts a similar approach and treats entrepreneurship as organizational behavior that is related to change and innovation.

It should be noted that entrepreneurs are different from small business owners. Garland, Hoy, Boulton, and Garand (1984) and Steward, Watson, Garland, and Garland (1998) argued that small business owners were concerned primarily with securing an income to meet their immediate needs and that they did not usually engage in innovation, whereas entrepreneurs had higher achievement motivation and risk-taking, and were inclined to innovation and change. This book presents a related perspective in arguing that entrepreneurship and innovation are closely related and complementary in the development, implementation and application of information technology.

THE CONCEPT OF INNOVATION

For more than half a century, research and development (R&D) has been closely associated with technological innovation (Miller & Morris, 1999). But invention is the narrowest definition of innovation. Drucker (1994) maintained that there are seven basic sources of opportunities to innovate. Only one of them is to do with inventing something new. Innovation is thus more than invention, and does not have to be technical. There are numerous examples of social and economic innovations (Drucker, 1994). Innovation is a proposed theory or design concept that synthesises extant knowledge and techniques to provide a theoretical basis for a new concept (Bright, 1969; Sundbo, 1998). Innovation thus has many facets and is multidimensional. The most prominent innovation dimensions can be expressed as dualisms—(1) radical vs. incremental; (2) product vs. process; and (3) administrative vs. technological (Cooper, 1998).

In this book, innovation is defined broadly to include new information technologies and products, new processes including business, managerial and production processes, new services (including new uses of IT and other established products, processes and services), new forms of organization, new markets, and the development of new skills and human capital.

INTEGRATION OF IT WITH ENTREPRENEURSHIP AND INNOVATION

Studies show that industries and businesses have varied considerably in terms of their IT performance. According to a McKinsey study, "after spending $7.6 billion on IT between 1995 and 2000, the lodging industry experienced no increase in revenue and no increase in productivity" (cited in King, 2007, p. 2). On the contrary, some businesses and industries are making significant improvement in productivity through IT and achieving new revenue streams and competitive advantage (King, 2007). Although there are a number of factors contributing to the success and failure of IT investment and performance, entrepreneurship and innovation play a key role for driving the success. Increase in spending on IT does not warrant superior performance in productivity and profitability if there is a lack of entrepreneurial capacity to identify and seize market opportunities and a lack of innovative use of IT. An integration of entrepreneurship, innovation, and IT presents new opportunities and challenges to today's managers in gaining competitive advantage in this digitalized and more dynamic world.

This book deals with the interactions and interfaces of entrepreneurship, innovation, and IT at both a macro level, which concerns the mega environmental drivers of entrepreneurship, innovation, and IT as well as a micro level, which concerns the contextual factors underpinning the practices of the three. The book in its entirety demonstrates that business successes are inextricably linked to a combination of entrepreneurship, innovation, and IT, and that the three are enablers and key drivers of business sustainability. The book provides readers with up-to-date, comprehensive and rigorous research-based chapters in the topical areas. The book will help entrepreneurs, managers and other practitioners formulate and implement effective strategies and business plans in the development, implementation and application of information technology. The book also provides an in-depth insight into critical issues in IT applications in a wide range of industries and in different geographical areas around the world. Furthermore, as the book is based upon both empirical and theoretical research, it will be a rich and valuable resource for researchers and students in the study fields.

ORGANIZATION OF THE BOOK

The book containing XXIII chapters is grouped into six sections based upon the dominant themes of each chapter. **Section I**, consisting of three chapters, presents some of the most recent research into IT innovations. This section captures and raises some of the key issues in the development and application of IT innovations as shown below.

Chapter I introduces the concept of ambient intelligence (AmI), a new concept in the area of IT, from a system development perspective in the manufacturing environment. To create an AmI environment requires the use of a combination of technologies. The AmI environment can be enabled through the use of computers that are embedded into everyday objects and through the use of wireless communication. The interaction between these embedded devices and the human user is improving through advancements in the area of natural interaction.

Chapter II is focusing on interoperability and providing a concept in order to speed up common innovation of the products and services in open semantic infrastructure. This includes identification of solution boundaries and innovation partners. Operative challenge is how to decompose the requirements across the boundaries of different companies in different branches and in different role in the value and innovation network. There is also challenge on how to manage evolving technologies to satisfy customers' existing and future expectations.

Chapter III presents the design of a heritage tourism Web portal. Factor analysis is used to identify how the navigation tools are to be grouped. Correlation analysis additionally identifies methods of grouping the navigation functionalities to substantiate the decision. Statistical analysis lends support to the reliability of the data used in the study. Examples are given about how heritage portal navigation functionality can be developed as hierarchical layered portal pages. Additionally, the perceptual map shows the layout and proximity of the portal functionalities.

Section II pursues managerial innovation in the management of IT and IT companies. In today's business world, most organizations depend on IT for their day-to-day activities and the achievement of their future strategies. However, the track record of IT initiatives in many organizations is not strong, and many fail—particularly when measured against the outcomes they were intended to produce.

Chapter IV looks at the importance of good corporate governance of IT to the success of IT investment. It examines practices and frameworks for effective IT governance in industry and business. Utilizing a mixed research methodology of survey and interview, 20 board directors' and senior mangers' perceptions of IT governance and management were sought and analyzed. The findings show there is a need and opportunity for improvement in IT governance and that in most organizations, Australian Standard AS8015-2005 provides a sound foundation for such improvement.

Chapter V develops a performance measurement framework for SMEs specifically in the IT industry based upon the system theory and business excellence model to fill a knowledge gap in the study field. This chapter identifies the challenges, features, and drivers of performance measurement (PM) in the SMEs in the IT industry and finds that a dynamic and flexible PM framework is more suitable to SMEs than a mechanized PM model.

Section III focuses on entrepreneurs and entrepreneurship in the development and growth of IT and e-business enterprises in different sectors. The challenges and crucial issues in the process of entrepreneurship are explored and discussed with a number of in-depth case studies and working examples.

Chapter IV introduces the role of Web sites and e-commerce in the development and growth of global higher education start-ups. It argues that the key results, evidence, and experience, from this empirical case study research, highlight clear and precise reasons for the development of Web sites and e-commerce by the global start-ups. There are important implications of the study for entrepreneurs, policy makers, practitioners, researchers, and educators for the specific field of e-commerce developments for global start-ups.

Chapter VII offers a theoretically grounded and deeper insight into the e-commerce innovation process in SMEs. This is achieved by proposing a motivation-ability based four-state developmental framework. Each of the four states is then described in terms of organizational readiness, organizational capability, e-commerce capability, e-commerce motivational factors, and commodity chain position. The utility of the framework is demonstrated through case studies of 14 small-scale enterprises located in the Indian state of Karnataka.

Chapter VIII focuses on the process of creating electronic customer value within the net economy as well as the success factors and development phases of electronic ventures. The constant and rapid development of Internet-related technologies in the accompanying net economy has inevitably had a significant influence on various possibilities for developing innovative online business concepts and realizing these by establishing entrepreneurial ventures. The term "e-entrepreneurship" respectively describes the act of founding new companies that generate revenue and profits independent from a physical value chain.

Chapter IX discusses the use of business strategies for pure Internet firms. It separates the strategic choices and directions used for idea generation, during start-up, and beyond business or brand establishment. Corroborating much of the literature, it argues that traditional notions of strategy might be inappropriate for some dotcom firms due to the high level of complexity, speed of change and competitiveness characteristic of the Internet environment. The chapter suggests alternative strategy models that might be useful in our understanding of Internet business creation and development.

Section IV tackles specific issues in inter and intra organizational partnerships involving IT innovation. E-supply chain networks, virtual teams, and entrepreneurial business partnerships are the foci of the discussion. Technology issues such as system integration and e-platforms as well as people issues such as trust, culture, and communication in the partnerships are investigated and explored.

Chapter X studies the importance of information flows in e-supply chains/networks, and the need for their standardization to facilitate integration, legality, security, and efficiency of operations. The chapter contributes to the field by recommending a three-stage framework: the development of standardised Internet technology platforms (e-platforms), integration requirements, and classification of information flows.

Chapter XI aims to enhance the effectiveness of virtual teams in the health care industry. A conceptual framework of the specific components required for virtual team effectiveness and a survey tool to examine a team's performance (based on virtual team member perception) with each of these components are presented. The proposed conceptual framework of virtual team effectiveness categorises the determinants influencing the effectiveness of virtual teams into four key frames of leadership, team components, organizational culture, and technology.

Chapter XII studies the dynamics of online business networks where large numbers of entrepreneurs sign up. It introduces and explores a new approach, Rhizomic Network Analysis (RNA) to move analysis of networks and community interaction beyond mere description of relationship structures towards enabling the differentiation of the type of knowledge dynamics emergent. An example of an entrepreneurial business network is used to illustrate this approach.

Chapter XIII develops and underlines the concept of continuous improvement teamworking approach in a major Australian banking organization. The study develops a model, which is a virtuous CTIO circle reflecting the concern (issue), task (action), interaction (involvement and connection), and outcome (result) phases. It illustrates the new evolving consultative, participative, and interactive virtuous teamworking approach. The adoption of a continuous improvement teamworking approach is assisting in better running of retail banking operational activities and in achieving better performance.

Chapter XIV presents the regional development of universities aiming to increase their external impact on their environment. The purpose is to show that the activities of regional development and quality assurance at universities are important means of promoting the development of IT in the region. Regional cooperation between a higher education institution and IT enterprises is illustrated with examples. Conclusions and recommendations are drawn based on the findings.

Chapter XV highlights the role of trust from an Islamic perspective in a leader-followers relationship as well as a leader-customers relationship. The swift sharing of sensitive information is a major source of competitive advantage in today's age and is not possible without trustworthy relationships of top management with external as well as internal customers (employees) of a business. Where traditional literature believes that long-term relationships result in trust development, Islam considers that trust development results in building and maintaining long-term relationships.

Section V discusses the use of IT for knowledge management (KM). Some KM tools and KM systems are explored and the advantages and issues in innovative adoption and implementation of KM technologies are identified and analyzed critically. This section also gives sufficient space to e-learning and e-learning technologies in developing entrepreneurship and entrepreneurs.

Chapter XVI addresses the application of IT for knowledge management (KM) needed for innovation in industry. An IT based KM system to support innovation process in extended enterprise (EE) environment (i.e., to support mastering of the innovation process) is presented. The main objective of the new AIM System is to provide the means of stimulating the creation of innovative ideas in general, and specifically on potential product/process improvements and on problem solving.

Chapter XVII discusses how the independent nature of entrepreneurs, combined with the enabling features of digital information technology, may lead to a situation where paper-based and campus-specific classroom education is at best uncomfortable and at worst almost meaningless. The purpose of the chapter is to define and capture the latest thinking in applied education and relate this to the mindset of the emerging generation of entrepreneurs.

Chapter XVIII aims to stimulate debate among practitioners on the use of information technology in the process of entrepreneurial learning. Learning activity, pedagogical shifts within the wider disciplines of entrepreneurship education and the spin-off effects for entrepreneur training programs are all considered. The application of information technology through entrepreneurship e-learning packages is shown to have magnified the entrepreneurship potential in wider society.

Section VI examines the fundamental issues and complex process of technology innovation, which goes beyond information technology innovation. How to prepare for and deal with the dynamics of technology innovation as a whole is a main theme of the section. New product development and innovation processes, which lead to technological obsolescence and fundamental change process, are examined in-depth. Working models, instruments and case studies are provided to illustrate the theoretical concepts presented and/or implement them in the real world contexts.

Chapter XIX asserts that process models are an excellent platform for a continuous stream of innovations. Such models can illuminate opportunities for new products and services and for new ways of distributing products and services. These dynamic models make it possible to coordinate the efforts of multiple business partners in order to better serve customers with quality, speed, and responsiveness to their needs. There is increasing evidence that businesses using these models to discover opportunities have achieved a sustainable advantage over their competitors.

Chapter XX introduces a new approach for performance measurement in product development and innovation processes. The new approach aims at the integration of concrete project data with information about the product by using semantic Web technologies. The chapter shows that there is an emerging gap between productivity increase and the complexity of product development processes.

Chapter XXI offers an approach, building on the authors' work along psychological lines with tacit knowledge measurement in the IT domain that seeks to capture responses to real scenarios experienced by recognized innovators and entrepreneurs. These scenarios and responses are used to evaluate the degree to which the respondent can be considered an innovator and to suggest what areas of personal or professional development may be needed.

Chapter XXII develops a set of seven dimensions, which may be applied to each sovereign nation as a guide to allow for systematic consideration and comparison of opportunities and challenges across borders. Under the assumption that innovation itself requires a unique set of skills or opportunistic settings, the chapter then explores each dimension's applicability to situations particularly associated with innovation in technology.

Chapter XXIII, the last chapter of the book, uses a case of lead-bearing solders to illustrate the far-reaching consequences of the forced phase-out of technologies, which have been used since the beginning of industrial electronics production. Lead bearing solders are one example of many technologies, which are candidates to become controversial. Increased awareness of side-effects, globalization and intensified use of single technologies indicate that this management task will gain momentum in the electronics industry and others.

REFERENCES

Bright, J. R. (1969). Some management lessons from technological innovation research. *Long Range Planning, 2*(1), 36-41.

Caird, S. (1988). *A review of methods of measuring enterprising attributes.* Durham University Business School.

Casson, M. (1982). *The entrepreneur: An economic theory.* Oxford: Martin Robertson.

Chell, E. (2001). Entrepreneurship: Globalization, innovation, and development. *International Journal of Entrepreneurial Behavior Research, 7*(5), 206-206.

Cooper, R. J. (1998). A multidimensional approach to the adoption of innovation. *Management Decision, 36*(8), 493-502.

Cornwall, R. J., & Perlman, B. (1990). *Organizational entrepreneurship*. Boston: IRWIN.

Drucker, P. F. (1994). *Innovation and entrepreneurship: Practice and principles*. London: Heinemann.

Garland, J. W., Hoy, F., Boulton, W. R., & Garand, J. C. (1984). Differentiating entrepreneurs from small business owners: A conceptualization. *Academy of Management Review, 9*(2), 354-359.

Goffin, K., & Pfeiffer, R. (1999). *Innovation management in U. K. and German Manufacturing Companies*. York: Anglo-German Foundation.

Johnson, D. (2001). What is innovation and entrepreneurship? Lessons for large organizations. *Industrial and Commercial Training, 33*(4), 135-140

King, W. R. (2007). IT strategy and innovation: The IT deniers versus a portfolio of IT role. *Information Systems Management, 24*(2), 197-200, Boston: Spring 2007.

Littunen, H. (2000). Entrepreneurship and the characteristics of the entrepreneurial personality. *International Journal of Entrepreneurial Behaviour and Research, 6*(6), 295-309.

Martin, M. (1994). *Managing innovation and entrepreneurship in technology-based companies*. New York: John Wiley & Son.

Miller, D. (1983). The correlates of entrepreneurship in three types of firms. *Management Science, 29*, 770-791.

Miller, W., & Morris, L. (1999). *Fourth generation R & D: Managing knowledge, technology, and innovation*. Chichester: John Wiley & Son.

Slevin, D. P., & Covin, J. G. (1990). Juggling entrepreneurial style and organizational structure—How to get your act together. *Sloan Management Review*, Winter Issue, 43-53.

Sundbo, J. (1998). *The theory of innovation: Entrepreneurs, technology, and strategy*. MA: Edward Elgar.

Steward, W. H., Watson, W. E., Garland, J. C., & Garland, J. W. (1998). A proclivity for entrepreneurship: A comparison of entrepreneurs, small business owners, and corporate managers. *Journal of Business Venturing, 14*(2), 189-214.

Zhao, F. (2006). *Entrepreneurship and innovation in e-business: An integrative perspective*. Hershey, PA: Idea Group Publishing.

Acknowledgment

The production of this book would not have been possible without the assistance of the institutions and people to whom I am grateful. I am greatly indebted to the School of Management of Royal Melbourne Institute of Technology University, Australia, for its support in the course of editing of the book. I am immensely grateful to all the chapter authors for their hard work and insightful and rigorous contributions to the book and the study fields. Special thanks go to all the reviewers of the book chapters for their invaluable comments and expert advice.

A further special note of thanks goes to the IGI Global, its publishing team, in particular, Ms. Kristin Roth and Ms. Deborah Yahnke for helping me keep the project on schedule.

Finally, I wish to dedicate this work to my late beloved mother, Quo Deming, for her intellectual passion and extraordinary determination, which propelled me to complete this enormous task while juggling with multiple duties and jobs. My heartfelt gratitude goes to my father, Zhao Peishen, and beautiful daughter, Kelly, for their steadfast love and encouragement.

Section I
Information Technology
Innovations

Chapter I
Ambient Intelligent (AmI) Systems Development

Simrn Kaur Gill
National University of Ireland Galway, Ireland

Kathryn Cormican
National University of Ireland Galway, Ireland

ABSTRACT

This chapter introduces the concept of ambient intelligence (AmI), a new concept in the area of information and communication technology (ICT), from a systems development perspective in the manufacturing environment. To create an AmI environment, requires the use of a combination of technologies. The AmI environment can be enabled through the use of computers that are embedded into everyday objects and through the use of wireless communication. The interaction between these embedded devices and the human user is improving through advancements in the area of natural interaction. The aim of the chapter is to provide a better understanding of AmI. To this end the following tools are presented, an AmI definition, typology, and taxonomy. The typology solidifies the understanding of AmI by highlighting the elements that need to be considered when developing an AmI system. The taxonomy shows the evolution of technologies towards development of AmI.

INTRODUCTION

The manufacturing environment has changed greatly over the last 20 years and is set to advance even more in the coming years. The Society of Manufacturing Engineers (Koska & Romano, 1988) commissioned a survey in 1988 to con-

sider the changes that would occur in the area of manufacturing in the 21st century. They identified a number of trends. One of these trends was that products would become more sophisticated and the methods used to produce them would become equally as complex. Another was that manufacturing would become more human centred and a shift in manufacturing towards the customer would occur. These changes that were highlighted in the report are at present taking place in the manufacturing environment. This change process is supported by advancements in the area of information communication technology (ICT).

Ambient intelligence (AmI), a new paradigm in the area of ICT allows for user centred developments and adaptability. However, traditional ICT systems are not capable of this level of accommodation, and as a result a user centred approach that provides adaptability and flexibility is needed. AmI is an advancement of ICT that places the human user at the centre of the technology enabled and embedded environment. The user does not have to make an effort to understand the technologies that occupy the environment but rather the embedded technologies need to be able to express themselves in a way that the user can understand (speech, graphical representation, light, music, and heat). In turn, the embedded technologies need to be able to understand the human (gesture, speech, and body language) as well. Therefore, the AmI system in essence caters for the needs and wants of the human user that occupies the AmI environment. To achieve this level of interaction the AmI system has to possess an understanding of the context and information regarding the user and the environment in which it co-exists. To create this environment, the AmI system therefore needs to have knowledge of the user, process, and environment. The need to incorporate all these elements creates a complex system with elements of hardware and software that need to interact together seamlessly. For the AmI system to be achieved requires the advancement of traditional ICT.

No single technology creates an AmI environment, therefore, a combination of different technologies are used to create the AmI environment. Each technology has unique features and characteristics that it brings to the AmI environment. With this level of diversity in technology comes with it a complexity. There are numerous technologies that can be utilized; the challenge lies in which combination of the technology creates the desired AmI environment. AmI has many potential benefits as highlighted in the Information Society Technologies Advisory Group (ISTAG) report *Scenarios for Ambient Intelligence 2010* (Ducatel, Bogdanowicz, Scapolo, Leijten, & Burgelman, 2001). The scenarios cover everything from the social, work and home environments in which AmI will exist. In the area of AmI manufacturing, this will involve products and services becoming human-centred, and users will have far greater involvement in the design and development process. Products will be intelligent and they will be able to interact with other technologies, but the human user will control the level of interaction. AmI will allow for the human worker in the manufacturing environment to come to the centre of the production process. Through accomplishing this it will empower the human worker by giving them greater autonomy over their work and environment. The use of AmI will improve decision-making and utilization of resources to enhance efficiency and effectiveness. Therefore, all aspects of manufacturing will be built around the human user.

The aim and objective of this chapter is to provide a better understanding of the AmI concept and by doing so develop tools that can be used in the assistance of its development. To accomplish this, a review of literature in the area of AmI is provided. This reviews the concept, definitions and technologies that enable developments in the area as well as some of the socio-technical implication of the AmI environment. The findings from the literature review led to the development of typologies that can be used in explaining the concept and can be in developing an AmI system. The example of the manufacturing environment is given. The discussion then moves to the future trends in the area of AmI and the impact that this will have on the research that is imparted. Finally a conclusion of the discussion provides a review of key findings.

AMBIENT INTELLIGENCE

This section will explore the evolution of ICT in relation to the development of the AmI paradigm. The three elements that make up AmI are discussed and examined. This section reviews relevant literature relating to AmI definitions from key authors. This allows for the development of an AmI definition that supports the research that is presented in this chapter. The development of the concept that AmI is built on is discussed. The socio-technical implications of AmI are examined. The key findings and conclusion of the section are presented at the end.

This section will discuss the evolution of ICT and the developments that have been made in the area towards achieving the information society and the AmI paradigm. The evolution of ICT begins with the design of the first computer by Charles Babbage during the 1840s; however, it was never built. The development was based on his vision that the science of numbers could be mastered by mechanisms (Swade, 2000). The design was known as the "analytical engines" it was a general purpose machine capable of being programmed by the user (Swade, 2000) and

could execute programs through the use of cards. It was a decimal digital machine and had many similar features to modern computers. However, these ideas lay forgotten for over a century but they did lay the foundation for the evolution of the computer age in the 1960s.

The computer age of the 1960s led to the automation of processes in design and manufacturing and computer aided manufacturing. This evolution in computing has led to advancements of telecommunications, electronic engineering, and computer and control science. These developments have led to a gradual shift away from a focus on the computers, to the user instead. This shift is changing the way people interact with each other. It has led to the emergence of blogs and wikis as the modern way of sharing information. This has involved the meeting and merging of technologies from the areas of telecommunications, electronic engineering, and computer and control science (see Table 1). The area of telecommunications enables the flexibility to communicate through the use of various media from both remote and local locations. Electronic engineering involves the use of sensors and microelectronics. The sensors can provide real-time information regarding the user, process, and environment. The microelectronics enables the integration of technology into everyday objects. In the area of computer and control science the assimilation of information can provide decision support.

Table 1. The emerging ICT trends adapted from Riva (2005)

Technology	Electronic Engineering	Computer & Control Science	Telecommunications
Features	- Sensors - Microelectronics	- Tele-operators - Expert Systems - Computer Vision	- Mobile Communication - Telecommunication Network - Signal Processing

The advancement of telecommunications, electronic engineering, and computer and control science can be viewed in relation to the development of a European information society. A survey conducted by SIBIS (2002), compared the advancements that have been made in Europe and the U.S. toward an information society. Their goal was to create a benchmark for the development of a European information society.

The study looked at the uptake of ICT in Europe during 2002 and compared it to that in the U.S. The findings of the study cover areas from telecommunication and access to e-government. It found that on many of the indictors Europe was behind the U.S., this can be demonstrated by the fact that Europeans are less likely to have Internet access at home about 40% compared to 60% of Americans. This trend continues in the usage of the Internet on a regular basis and the uses made of the Internet. One of the reasons for this is the slow roll out and uptake of faster broadband services. On some indicators the Europeans were ahead of their U.S. counterparts. It was found that the Dutch are more likely to be involved in eWork (at least one day a week) than their American counterparts. Since 2002, there has been an improvement in Internet access. Household Internet access ranges between 23% in Greece to 80% in the Netherlands and nearly "half of the individuals in the 25 EU states used the Internet at least once a week in 2006" (Eurostat, 2006, p. 1).

The developments in the areas of telecommunications, electronic engineering, and computer and control science are furthered in their accessibility by development in three core areas. These areas are in the embedding of computers into everyday objects (ubiquitous computing), allowing for these technologies which are embedded in everyday objects to communicate (ubiquitous communication), and an interface that allows for ease of use and access for the user to interact with these embedded technologies (intelligent user friendly interface). These three elements, ubiquitous computing, ubiquitous communication, and intelligent user-friendly interfaces, are discussed in greater detail in the following subsection.

Ubiquitous Computing

Ubiquitous computing is defined by Alcaniz (2005) as being an "integration of microprocessors into everyday objects like furniture, clothing, white goods, toys even paints" (p. 3). The term ubiquitous computing was coined by Mark Weiser in a 1991 article in Scientific America. Weiser (1993) described ubiquitous computing to have "as its goal the non-intrusive availability of computers throughout the physical environment, virtual, if not effectively, invisible to the user" (p. 71). Therefore ubiquitous computing can be defined as computers embedded into the social, home, and work environments that are invisible to the user. These computers are at the disposal of the users in the specific environment. The computers can perform predetermined action with or without the user having direct interaction with it (Alcaniz, 2005; Sørensen & Gibson, 2004; Weiser, 1993, 1999).

Ubiquitous computing is described as the third wave of computing. The first wave can be described as one computer and many people using it. The second wave is the era of the personal computer and the third wave is one person with many computers interacting with them.

Therefore, for ubiquitous computing to be made a plausible reality "near-zero telecommunications costs and seamless interoperability of devices across networks" (Blackman, 2004, p. 261) is needed. Some examples of ubiquitous computing devices are the Philips TV mirror that can show weather and television reports all in one device and be used as mirror. It can also recognize the user by weight and height if used in a bathroom. The device can present information related to news and weather that is tailored to the preferences of the user. Another device is the ambient orb developed by Ambient. The device can be configured to monitor stocks and shares as well as the weather. It changes color depending on how the stock and shares are moving. The following section describes the area of ubiquitous communication, which provides the ubiquitous computing devices with the ability to communicate with other devices creating a system that is omnipresent.

Ubiquitous Communication

Ubiquitous communication allows the ubiquitous computer devices "to communicate with each other and the user by means of ad-hoc and wireless networking" (Alcaniz, 2005, p. 3). There are various different types of communications and technology networks, which depend on the type of communication that is necessary. The communications and technology network is best described in Figure 1 (Friedewald & Da Costa, 2003), which shows the communications networks that surround the user in a ubiquitous computing environment. This communication network provides the ability for different technology devices

to communicate with each other over varying distances depending on the communication technology that they operate on. The spheres of communication distance are discussed below.

The five spheres surrounding the user are:

- **Body area network (BAN):** BAN provides the link between the user and the technology (Ducatel et al., 2001). The BAN may be used in mobile telephones that can both send and receive telephone calls as well as transmitting physiological data to the system to monitor heart rate for example. It will communicate over a distance of 1 to 2 metres (Friedewald et al., 2003).
- **Personal area network (PAN):** Wireless PAN is in use at present as Bluetooth. It is used at present in mobile telephones and PDA's (Personal Digital Assistant) (Friedewald et al., 2003). The range is up to 10 metres. New Bluetooth versions are being developed that will allow for increased data transfer rates (Raisinghani et al., 2004). Only when Bluetooth capable devices come into

Figure 1. Multi sphere reference model of communication and network technologies adapted from (Friedewald et al., 2003)

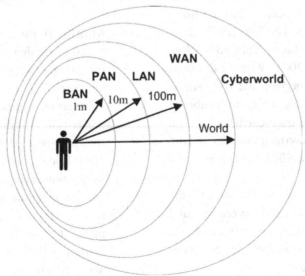

range of one another do they communicate either exchanging data or one controls the other. Due to this fact it is well suited to various technologies (Diegel, Bright, & Potgieter, 2004).

- **Local area network (LAN):** Wireless LAN or WiFi as it is more commonly known is commercially available at present. WiFi can be extended over entire building or production floors through the introduction of multiple access points (Friedewald et al., 2003; Raisinghani et al., 2004). It can be used to allow for the seamless interaction of devices that are located in opposite ends of a production floor, which are of distance less than 100m.

- **Wide area network (WAN):** Wireless metropolitan area networks (WMAN) are commercially available but it is still undergoing further development and will be used more extensively in the future. (Friedewald et al., 2003; Raisinghani et al., 2004). WAN has the ability to span the world and can be used by intelligent agents to search databases that are dispersed across continents for information that is pertinent to the user.

- **Cyber world:** Cyber world is the seamless interaction into cyberspace. To facilitate seamless interaction and the adoption of more interoperable technologies the Internet is changing too. The Internet Protocol version 4 (IPv4) is being replaced by IPv6 (Friedewald et al., 2003). With the development of the semantic Web, the Web will be given meaning in that it will be capable of accommodating smarter search engines and providing information to the user that is more tailored to their specific requirements.

Ubiquitous communication is the enabler of the ubiquitous computing. It is also the concept that transforms intelligent user friendly interfaces to allow for seamless interaction between computer to human and vice versa.

Intelligent User Friendly Interface

Intelligent users friendly interface "enables the inhabitants of the ....environment to control and interact with the environment in a natural (voice, gesture) and personalized way (preference, context)" (Alcaniz, 2005, p. 3). In essence this is done to provide an improved level of communication between the human and computer and visa versa. To achieve this, the interface adds increased functionality by making the system more intuitive, efficient, and secure. This allows the system to have a greater awareness about the user i.e. the situation, environment, and context that the user is in (Raisinghani et al., 2004). This is accomplished through the characteristics of the interface (Alcaniz, 2005; Friedewald et al., 2003; Raisinghani et al., 2004):

- Ease of use
- Ability to personalize
- Adapts automatically to user behavior
- Adapts automatically to different situations

This level of adaptation is achieved in developments in three areas that are discussed by Friedewald et al. (2003), multilingualism, multisensorial, and multi-modality.

- **Multilingualism** will provide the user with the language that they prefer to be used when they interact with the system. This creates a number of challenges for multilingualism. An example of this is an application that operates using multilingual text input or speech interpretation (Alcaniz, 2005; Ducatel et al., 2001; Friedewald et al., 2003).

- **Multi-sensorial** (sight, hearing, touch) is the concept that numerous sensors can be used to collect input from the user in the environment. These sensors collect information that is used by the system to adapt to the needs and wants of the user. This is an example of collecting information implicitly from the environment that the user occupies to allow the system to adapt. This is related to context awareness (Alcaniz, 2005; Ducatel et al., 2001; Friedewald et al., 2003).

• **Multi-modality** (speech, touch, expression, gesture) interfaces need to use multiple modals to take advantage of the fact that humans communicate in numerous ways at the same time. Human users can use gestures, body language, and speech for example to express and communicate ideas and thoughts. By having a system that takes advantage of this level of interaction improves the natural interaction element of the system (Alcaniz, 2005; Ducatel et al., 2001; Friedewald et al., 2003).

Intelligent user-friendly interfaces have the potential to create a more natural interaction between humans and computers. It will also allow for complex tasks to be completed quickly and with ease. The system also manages the information and knowledge that it provides to the user. This may be accomplished through the use of

tailored information being provided to the user. This information can be presented in the most efficient way for each user. In the example of a maintenance technician who needs his or her hands free to complete the task, the system may present the information in spoken format. This accomplishes a more user friendly environment where the user does not feel out of place and instead it will improve the satisfaction that user has for the system.

The Next Evolution

The integration of the three elements, ubiquitous computing, ubiquitous communication, and intelligent user friendly interface has led to the development of the AmI paradigm. Emiliani and Stephanidis (2005) describe the paradigm as being developed on the principles of invisible computing and intelligent mobile devices. The integration of these elements in the users environment will have a profound effect on the "type, content, and functionality of emerging products and services, as well as on the way people will interact with them, bringing about multiple new requirements

Figure 2. AmI evolution

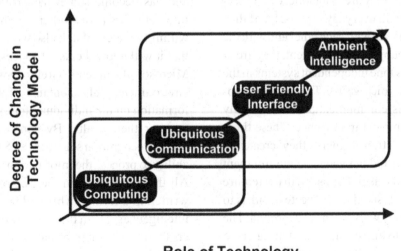

for the development of information technologies" (Emiliani et al., 2005, p. 605). ISTAG (Ducatel et al., 2001) explains the usage of the technology in relation to the vision statement of AmI "on convergence humans will be surrounded by intelligent interfaces supported by computing and networking technology which is everywhere, embedded in everyday objects such as furniture, clothes, vehicles, roads and smart materials even particles of decorative substances like paint" (p. 11). The convergence of these technologies is demonstrated in Figure 2. The x-axis represents the role of technology as an enabler and a transformer. The enabler technologies facilitate the advancement of technology at a technical level. The transformer technologies permit the advancement of the technology at a more human centric level. The y-axis represents the degree of change in the technology model as tactical and strategic. The tactical change represents the approach taken to overcome a specific problem. The strategic change is a part of a long-term plan that will achieve the overall goals. They have been built on each other and enhance the technology further. This provides us with an appreciation of where it came from and what it is built on.

This diagram also shows two groupings of the technology. The first is ubiquitous computing and communication. These two technologies are linked together as they are symbiotic. Computers can be integrated in everyday objects, but if they cannot communicate with each other and with the humans that occupy the environment, they are of no real benefit as lone independent systems in the modern world in which we live. The second grouping is ubiquitous communication, user-friendly interface, and ambient intelligence. These three technologies are transformers; they create an easily accessible and navigateable environment that will benefit the user. The user will not require the ability to understand the intricate detail as to how the technology works in the background. The user only needs to know that the system caters to their needs as it comes into contact with the user.

In the ideal scenario, the user may be interacting with twenty or more devices embedded into their environment without realising it. The AmI concept and definitions are examined further in the following section.

Concept of Ambient Intelligence

This section will explore the concept of AmI. A review of relevant literature relating to AmI definitions from key authors is presented. This allows for the development of an AmI definition that supports the research that is presented in the following sections.

The easiest way to convey the concept of AmI is through the use of an example:

An executive vice president in her office in Dublin could ask for an up to the minute efficiency report from one of their facilities in Chile for her board meeting. If she also requested that the efficiency report should be added to her presentation for the board meeting in five minutes. That would seem completely normal. Except that she was talking not to her secretary but to her mobile phone.

This could be one of the plausible scenarios for AmI in the years to come. The mobile phone has evolved from what we know it to be today and has become somewhat of a hybrid. It can interact with many other computing devices within 10 meters of it. It also works like a PDA in that it will allow the user to access for example, Microsoft documents wirelessly within a secure environment. It also contains all the relevant information on the individual, for example, it may monitor their health. By containing advanced speech recognition software (SRS) it now has the ability to process the information that it receives. All the information in the electronic devices is written in a format, which allows for the use of intelligent agents in this case searching the servers for the relevant information to the request and then presenting the information in an appropriate format for the presentation. This is accomplished by the fact that the AmI has learned how the vice president presents her work and will format the presentation to comply with this request (Ducatel et al., 2001; Friedewald et al., 2003).

Defining

The previous scenario describes an AmI environment which humans inhabit. The AmI concept that was presented in the previous section will be further developed in this section with a focus on the definitions of AmI from key authors in the area. Various definitions are outlined and the important aspects of AmI are summarized. A definition of AmI is presented that aligns with the research in this chapter.

Definitions are fundamental to the understanding of AmI as they illustrate the properties of AmI and they explain the term in relation to related terms. They lay the foundation of our understanding of this new concept.

The concept of ambient intelligence is made up of two words "ambient" and "intelligence." Ambient is described as the environment in which we inhabit. Morville (2005) defines ambient as being an "encircling" and "completely enveloping" (p. 6) environment. In essence the physical ambient environment becomes the user's interface in a digital world. Providing only the necessary information that the user requires tailored to the users specific needs and level of knowledge.

Intelligence is more elusive, Hofstadter (1980) suggests that certain characteristics denote intelligence. He represents intelligence as the ability:

- "To respond to situations very flexibly.
- To take advantage of fortuitous circumstances.
- To make sense out of ambiguous or contradictory messages.
- To recognize the relative importance of different elements of a situation.

- To find similarities between situations despite differences which may separate them.
- To draw distinctions between situations despite similarities which may link them.
- To synthesize new concepts by taking old concepts and putting them together in new ways.
- To come up with ideas which are novel" (p. 26).

The descriptions of ambient and intelligence that are presented create an environment where technology is all encompassing and has the ability to adapt and learn. This leaves the task of programming intelligence into a computer. Computers by their nature are inflexible and rule following. They also lack the desire to show initiative. The characteristics above describe intelligence and the description of ambience illustrates the environmental interaction that is needed to achieve ambient intelligence. A number of definitions of ambient intelligence have been put forward over the last few years. A selection of these definitions are discussed and analyzed.

Ambient intelligence is lauded to be "a digital environment that is aware of" human "presence and context and is sensitive, adaptive, and responsive to their needs, habits, gestures, and emotions" (ITEA, 2003, para. 1). Ambient intelligence is a pervasive and proactive technology that is omnipresent. Horvath (2002) develops the definition further in practical terms, "this means we will be surrounded by intelligent interfaces embedded in everyday objects such as furniture, clothes, vehicles, and roads" (para. 2). He also highlights the fact that the technology will be omnipresent and learn "these interfaces register our presence, automatically carry out certain tasks based on given criteria, and learn from our behavior in order to anticipate our needs" (para. 2). Lindwer et al (2003) delves more into the human actors interactions with the AmI system and defines it as a technology that is "invisible, embedded in our natural surroundings, present whenever we need it," the technology is easily "enabled by simple and effortless interactions," that are "attuned to all our senses, adaptive to users and context and autonomously acting" (p. 10). The ISTAG (Ducatel et al., 2001) definition is the most comprehensive for ambient intelligence as it describes the "seamless environment of computing, advanced network technology, and specific interfaces" (p. 11). It also communicates the interaction that is envisioned with the user, "aware of the specific characteristics of human presence and personalities, taken care of needs and is capable of responding intelligently to spoken or gestured indications of desire, and even can engage in intelligence dialogue" (p. 11). ISTAG further articulates the environment in which the technology will exude, "unobtrusive, often invisible; everywhere and yet in our consciousness - nowhere unless we need it" (p. 11). The interactions with the users "should be relaxing and enjoyable for the citizen, and not involve a steep learning curve" (p. 11).

For the purposes of this discussion, the author defines ambient intelligence as a people centred technology that is intuitive to the needs and requirements of the human actor. They are non-intrusive systems that are adaptive and responsive to the needs and wants of different individuals.

The following section reviews some of the socio-technical implications of ambient intelligence on the human user.

Socio-Technical Implications of Ambient Intelligence

AmI by its very nature that has been discussed in earlier sections is centred on the user. Due to this fact, it has socio-technical implications. The following subsection will discuss the implication of AmI with regard to monitoring of users which highlights issues regarding trust, safety, security, and privacy. The next subsection will review the

impact that an AmI environment could possibly have on the knowledge worker. With Europe moving towards an information society the knowledge worker becomes more prevalent on the landscape and their use of the AmI environment is crucial to the success of the paradigm.

Monitoring: Trust, Safety, Security, Privacy

Aarts (2004) states "The opportunities of ambient intelligence also comes with threats" (p.18). One of the key factors to ensuring the successful integration of AmI into the environment is the trust of the user in the system. The core function of AmI is to monitor the environment which the user occupies waiting for the right moment to assist the user. A number of concerns are raised with regards to such an environment, the safety and security of users. Some of these include Casal, Burgelman, and Bohlin (2004), Raisinghani et al. (2004), and Wright (2005):

- Such an open system could be susceptible to influences by outsiders (i.e., hackers or viruses).
- The system will be storing large amounts of personal information, which could threaten privacy and security.
- The personal response that the system will give to each user requires the recording of the user behavior, which leads to privacy issues.
- The users will co-exist in an environment that contains technologies that are capable of making autonomous decisions.
- If these technologies become uncontrollable this could create a serious concern.

Some of these concerns are prevalent today; radio frequency identification (RFID) technology is causing unease among customers who buy products that contain RFID tags. RFID is the successor to bar coding. This technology can provide information on location and movements. It is made up of a small tag, which contains an integrated circuit chip and an antenna. The chip and the antenna give the tag the ability to recognize and respond to radio waves which are transmitted from a RFID reader (Kiritsis, Bufardi, & Xirouchakis, 2003; Potter, 2005). If the tags are not disabled, they are capable of being used to track customers. A RFID tag that is designed to be read up to 30cm away, could be read by an invader approximately 30m away. The invader could also manipulate the data on the tag. To subjugate this problem some retailers replace the information of the tag to random data when it is sold. With random data stored in the tags it is no longer linked to information in the retailers database (Potter, 2005). Another method that is discussed by Potter (2005) is the KILL command. This command when received by the RFID stops it responding to RFID readers.

Concerns regarding trust, safety, security, privacy of personal users of the AmI environment are crucial to a successful introduction of the system and the acceptance of the users of the system. If the users do not have faith in the system and use it, the system will become redundant and the development will have been a waste of time, effort, and expense.

Ambient Intelligence and the Knowledge Worker

The technologies that enable AmI will have a dramatic increase with regard to the availability and ease of access that knowledge workers will have to data and computing facilities. Davis (2002) described knowledge work as being "cognitive rather than physical" (p.68). The knowledge worker is for example a professional, an accountant, manager, programmer, or lawyer. They output evaluations, instructions, or arguments. This is all based on the mental capabilities of the worker to develop information and knowledge from training they received, or data that they have

been given. In completing this form of work the knowledge worker accesses the data and computing facilities. With the introduction of the AmI environment the knowledge worker will have far greater access to the information at any time and at any location. This will be accomplished thought availability of embedded devices in the surrounding environment. The knowledge worker will be released from their office environment and from fixed working hours.

The benefits and the drawbacks of knowledge workers having access to computing facilities at all times and at any location are discussed by Davis (2002), Drury and Farhoomand (1999), and Kidd (1994). This discussion leads to the possible benefits, the first being the elimination of constraints on communication. The location, time, and environment in which the knowledge worker inhabits in AmI will not constrain the ability of the knowledge worker to communicate. The AmI environment can provide information and data in a timely manner that is tailored to the user's particular requirements. The second is the ability of the knowledge worker to work in conditions and at times that they are most productive. An example of this could be an engineer who has an idea in the middle of the night of how to solve the productivity problem on an assembly line and has access to the information so that the problem can be solved from home before production starts at 8 o'clock in the morning. The third is an improvement in the knowledge with regard to the location of people. As the knowledge worker has access to information and analysis at anytime, the result is more prudent responses to requests and critical information being exchanged more efficiently among key stakeholders. The final benefit is for example the improvement in the information that is gathered regarding the company. This may include the availability of real-time information from the shop floor in relation to production or quality. This allows managers to access information and solves problems as they arise (Davis, 2002; Kidd, 1994).

The possible drawbacks are discussed, first being the management of the individual. The level of distractions that enter the realm of the knowledge worker will increase. The knowledge worker will require guidelines and training with regard to how best to manage their time. This can be demonstrated by the use of e-mail; the norm is now to respond to all e-mails immediately, which takes away from productivity. The second is a possible reduction in boundaries between personal and work life. As the knowledge worker is always contactable there may occur an invasion of the knowledge workers private space. Finally the access to unlimited information may result in decisions being made in haste without an adequate level of thought been exerted on the problem resulting in a quick fix. This may lead to a larger problems in the long term. The information that is provided needs to be filtered and analysed prior to action being taken. (Davis, 2002; Drury et al., 1999)

Discussed above are only possibilities, it is not known how the users will react to the AmI environment. It is important to consider the benefits and the drawbacks of such an environment in the development of an AmI system. This needs to be facilitated so that some of these issues can be solved and considered in the design, which is the least costly phase to make changes to a system and also the least complex.

Summary of Key Findings

The concept of AmI is obscure. The AmI concept involves a complex combination of elements that together create the AmI environment. Each definition that was presented in the literature review highlights slightly different aspects of the concept as being of greater importance than others. Therefore a comprehensive definition and explanation to support the concept is needed. The AmI environment is about breaking down boundaries and making information and knowledge accessible to all. This idea is wonderful in theory but in practice

boundaries are an essential part of every day life. Particularly in businesses, boundaries to access to sensitive information, work and personal time are needed as within the AmI environment users are accessible at all time.

There are numerous technologies that can be used in combination to create an AmI environment. No single technology incorporates the characteristics of the AmI environment. Only when combined seamlessly with other enabling technologies is the concept realized. In designing and implementing an ambient intelligence system that caters to the needs of the user, the requirements of the user need to be gathered. This gathering of information gives the designer a better understanding of the present environment in which the user operates and the type of AmI environment that will meet the needs of the user. This will require the user to be involved in a collaborative process with the designers and developers of the system with regard to both technical and knowledge of the system. The benefits of developing an AmI system need to be outlined to the user as well as the drawbacks. To create the environment requires cross-functional involvement by multidisciplinary team in the development process. In the following section a typology and taxonomy are presented that support the development of an AmI system. AmI is an inspiring concept and with its introduction will change the way that we work and live our lives.

TOWARDS A FRAMEWORK FOR AMBIENT INTELLIGENCE

This section examines the need for a structure to help developers of AmI systems develop systems that are AmI and user centred, it incorporates the research that is presented in the previous sections. In doing so it presents various elements of research, a typology, and a taxonomy that help to further the developers understanding of interacting elements of an AmI system. The typologies

Figure 3. Evolution of manufacturing

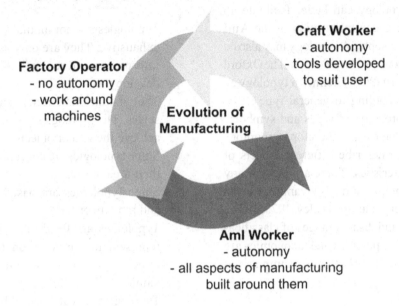

that are presented have been developed by Gill and Cormican (2006). The first element is a typology for AmI that incorporates the tasks and skills that the system needs to be cognisant of. The second element is the taxonomy that reflects the development of technologies in the AmI environment. The elements outlined are interrelated and this relationship is highlighted with AmI system development structure. The manufacturing environment is used to demonstrate the implications of the typology and taxonomy.

Over the last 200 years, the manufacturing environment has come full circle (Figure 3). Prior to the industrial revolution, there were craft workers who through the use of their skills had autonomy over their work and conditions. The tools that they used were developed and tailored to their specific needs. They were entrepreneurs and mainly sole traders who passed on the skills to their children. During the industrial revolutions machines became the driving force of evolution and development. In the earlier years, they were

crude, but over time developed into high precise pieces of machinery. The production process no longer revolved around the human; instead, the human was required to meet the needs of the machines. As the machines became more efficient, the human was in many cases designed out of the system and their role was taken by robots and other machines during the automation of production processes. AmI reverses the trend and gives the human more autonomy by creating an environment where all aspects of manufacturing are built around him.

Ambient Intelligence System

Typologies and taxonomies are classification techniques. Classification is the act for placing order on units to form groups and classes purely on the basis of similarity (Bailey, 1973, 1994; Rich, 1992). It lays the foundation for language, speech, mathematics, statistics, data analysis, and conceptualizations (Bailey, 1973, 1994; Rich,

1992). In essence it is both the process and the end result. A typology can better facilitate an understanding and communication of the AmI concepts and philosophy. A typology may also be known as a taxonomy or classification. The Oxford English Dictionary (2005) defines a typology as "classification according to general type... the study and interpretation of types and symbols" (para. 1). Typologies are therefore groupings of models, which describe different aspects of the same characteristics. There are as with any technique advantages and disadvantages to its use and later interpretation (Bailey, 1973, 1994). The advantages and disadvantages of classification in relation to typologies and taxonomies are discussed by Bailey (1994), they are summarized in the following:

Advantages (Bailey, 1994):

- It is the foremost descriptive tool. A good classification provides the user with an extensive array of types.
- It helps to reduce complexity by providing a very frugal explanation of the concept being demonstrated.
- It allows for the grouping and identification of similarities.
- It allows for the difference within cases to be identified.
- Typologies and taxonomies need to show all the types and dimensions that are possible. They also necessitate the inclusion of the relationship between both the types and dimensions.
- It allows for use as a quick reference and for quick comparison between types.
- It provides the research with the tools needed to know the position of any type and to also know which types are in use for analysis.
- Typologies may be used not only for describing but also in some cases to explain the relationships between cases.

Disadvantages (Bailey, 1994):

- Typologies are not mutually exclusive and exhaustive. They are only as useful as the information and research that was used to develop them.
- They should not be seen as an ends in themselves. The typologies are used as a tool to achieve the aim or objective.
- Some typologies are not concise enough for their area of use.
- Some typologies are based on subjective and random criteria.
- Typologies are fixed or static. They only represent the information that was used to develop them. As such they are not dynamic.
- Typologies are categorized by mainly their differences rather than their similarities.
- Typologies can at times be treated as objects rather than as concepts.
- Typologies tend to be more descriptive rather than explanatory or predictive.

In literature many models and theories can be found, some examples of these are Hellenschmidt and Kirste (2004) developed a topology for AmI middleware and Riva et al. (2005) presents the development of the technology that has led to AmI. These models and theories however do not take a combined view of the characteristic of what an AmI system should include. They look at the technological areas that AmI has evolved from and the technologies that can be used to initiate an AmI system. With regard to this the typology that is presented will help in outlining; what constitutes an AmI system, what are the unique characteristics and how it differs from other technologies and if not AmI what characteristics it must have to achieve AmI. The typologies below have been developed to assist in the understanding and the development of an AmI system. In particular to help to remove the ambiguity around what constitutes AmI. The first is an AmI system typology and the second is AmI taxonomy. The AmI system typology illustrates the tasks and the skills that an AmI system must have. The AmI taxonomy shows the evolution of the technology in relation to three areas: mobility, pervasive intelligence, and human and computer interactions in comparison to technology complexity and the development of higher value products for the end user.

Ambient Intelligence System Typology

AmI is centred on the human actors, because of this there are two main areas that together define what is and what is not an AmI system. The outer ring of Figure 4 represents the tasks that the AmI system needs to respond to and the inner ring has the skills that AmI system should contain. The tasks are person orientated, in that they represent the human characteristics that the AmI has to be aware of, in other words they represent the human characteristics that the system needs to recognize and needs to respond to. The skills are

technology orientated, in that they represent AmI characteristics that the technology must have to interact with the human actors. They represent what the technology must innately accomplish as its aptitudes. Both are inseparable, interlinked and interdependent, the link between them is shown in Figure 4.

The tasks are:

- **Habits:** A habit is something that we do often. The AmI system should recognize the users' habits and adapt to suit them. These habits may include the customs, routines, practices, traditions, conventions, patterns, tendencies, inclinations, likes, and preferences of a person.
- **Needs:** A need is something that humans have to have to survive. The AmI system in a home may learn that one of the occupants is allergic to nuts and if food was brought into the home that contains nuts, it would inform the occupants. As such, it could

Figure 4. Ambient intelligence system (Gill et al., 2006)

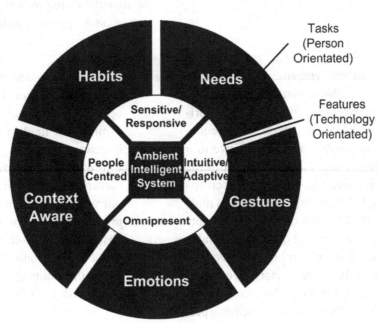

recognize requirements, wants, necessities, the things we cannot do without, our must haves, essentials, and prerequisites.

- **Gestures:** This is the movement of body parts to convey feelings. AmI systems will be able to sense changes in humans from their body language and learn to adapt and respond to it. The gestures could be for example a motion, wave, shrug or a nod.
- **Emotions:** Emotions are feelings that one has. These feelings could be sadness, joy, boredom, etc. The AmI technology should be able to recognize the outward manifestations of the various emotions that humans experience.
- **Context aware:** The AmI is required to recognize the difference between, for example crying for joy and crying for sadness. The two would require a completely different response from an AmI system. This could be achieved through a combination of speech recognition software (SRS) and sensors that recognize differences in the human reactions, the AmI system should be able to recognize the context in which the human actor is communicating.

The skills are:

- **Sensitive/responsive:** The system needs to be tactful and sympathetic in relation to the feelings of the human actor, has to react quickly, strongly, or favorably to the various situations it encounters. In particular, it needs to respond and be sensitive to a suggestion or proposal. As such, it needs to be responsive, receptive, aware, perceptive, insightful, precise, delicate, and most importantly finely tuned to the requirements of the human actor and quick to respond.
- **Intuitive/adaptive:** AmI needs to be able to adapt to the human actor directly and instinctively. This should be accomplished without being discovered or consciously per-

ceived therefore it needs to be accomplished instinctively (i.e., able to be adjusted for use in different conditions). The characteristics it is required to show are spontaneity, sensitivity, discerning, insightful, and at times shrewd.

- **People centred:** AmI's most basic requirement is that it must be focused on the human actor. If a systems focal point is not the human actor then it is not an AmI system.
- **Omnipresent:** The AmI will have to be seemingly present all the time and everywhere. As such, it will have to be ubiquitous.

Now that we have reviewed the elements of the AmI system we will discuss in detail the application of these principles to the manufacturing industry

AmI is human centred therefore the AmI system in the manufacturing industry can only exist in its interaction with the human user. In this case, it is the human operator. In reviewing the information that is presented in the earlier section a deduction is made of what the AmI concept is and how it can be manifested. The system in the manufacturing industry environment needs to possess a minimum of three of the following characteristics:

- Ease of interaction through an appropriate level of multimodality with the human operator, this may include both or just one, explicit and implicit (inputs and outputs) interaction.
- Information and knowledge of the manufacturing environment and the human operator based on models which provides prior knowledge or history and sensory observations to collect information on the ambience environment and ease of interaction with the human operator. The collection of dynamic knowledge on the following:

o   Human operators (e.g., location, context, her/his intensions, etc.)

o   Process environment in which the human operator is working and interaction among the human operators and process environment

o   The system itself and its interaction with the environment, which provides a level of context surrounding its use.

• Providing support to the human operator with regard to processes, this may include supplying a tailored task execution list to each human operators requirements. The functionality can be imparted by using the systems intelligence. This can be based on the knowledge on the ambience environment related to each unique human operator that is involved in the business processes.

• The implicit actions in processes, these actions are not visible to the human operator.

• The implicit actions in ambience, these actions are not visible to the human operator. They involve the system adapting to the needs of the human operator.

There are some addition characteristics that are identified by the DG Information Society (2004) and include following:

• The ability of the system to develop its own rules on how best to interact with near by systems and the human operator. At the same time continuously trying to progress the development of its own tasks and the interaction, which it has with the environment.

• The system needs to have the ability to be dynamic. It should have the ability to configure and reconfigure under varying and even unpredictable conditions.

• It is essential that the system be resilient and able to recover from events that may cause some of its parts to malfunction.

• The system is required to be trustworthy as to handle issues of safety, security and privacy.

• The system should be traceable.

These conclusions are used in the refinement of the taxonomy that is presented in the following subsection.

Ambient Intelligence Taxonomy

The AmI taxonomy (Figure 5) shows the evolution of the technology in relation to three areas; mobility, pervasive intelligence and human and computer interactions in comparison to technology complexity and the development of higher value products for the end user. The taxonomy for example can be viewed in respect to the evolution of mobile communications. The x-axis represents the technology complexity and the y-axis the higher value of the technology to the user. The technology complexity can be explained as the evolution of the technology; it becomes more complex as we continue to add on more options, requirements, applications, etc. The higher value of the technology refers to the user friendliness and improved usability of the technology or system, which increases the value of the product in the eyes of the end user. The elements of the taxonomy are as follows:

• **Mobility:** At a basic level, for example a pager that gives only mobility; there is no nice user interface.

• **Pervasive intelligence:** Mobile phones for example that can interact seamlessly and invasively with technologies around them are an example of pervasive intelligence. This could be a mobile phone with Bluetooth technology that can interact with other mobile phones and with other technologies that have Bluetooth. The technology therefore begins to encompass and envelop the human actor and by doing so becomes omnipresent.

Figure 5. AmI Taxonomy (Gill et al., 2006)

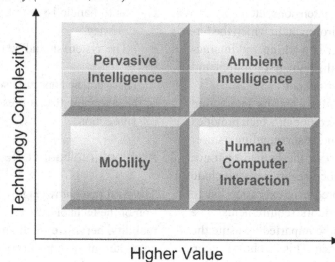

- **Human and computer interactions:** A mobile phone that has a user-friendly interface and which allows one to track personal goals and as such has all the functions of a PDA. It can make connections and exchange data on your behalf.
- **Ambient intelligence:** A combination of both the human and computer interactions that makes the technology user friendly and feel safe in the customers hands. The pervasive intelligence allows the technology to work unobtrusively in the background.

The definition, typology, and taxonomy that have been previously presented are tools to be used in the development of an AmI system. They have been designed to incorporate a holistic approach to the development of the system. The typologies that are presented will help in outlining, what an AmI system is and what characteristics are needed to achieve an AmI system. They are not a means to an end in themselves but are tools to assist developers, analysts, and potential user in their understanding of the concept.

FUTURE TRENDS

AmI is an evolving concept and research in the area covers numerous areas. AmI is built on the research and work in the areas of ubiquitous computing, ubiquitous communication and intelligent user-friendly interface. These areas are developing from theories in the laboratory to real world applications.

The real question is whether or not AmI will be adopted out side of Europe. For an AmI society to emerge certain developments need to be in place. These include some technology requirements. These technology requirements for achieving an AmI system are listed in the ISTAG report 'Scenarios for Ambient Intelligence in 2010' (Ducatel et al., 2001) are:

- "Very unobtrusive hardware.
- A seamless mobile or fixed Web-based communication infrastructure.
- Dynamic and massively distributed device networks.

- A natural feeling human interface.
- Dependability and security" (p. 9).

In achieving these requirements there needs to be an amalgamation of the fundamental developments in the area of ICT which will assist in the development of AmI. These developments include (Ducatel et al., 2001; Friedewald et al., 2003; ISTAG, 2000):

- Human Machine Interface (HMI) which may involve humans commanding machines and an improvement in robotic usability;
- The introduction of networked products through the use of wireless technology in the monitoring of product lifecycles; advancements of adaptability and reconfigurable production lines allowing for mass customisation and wireless shop floor configuration;
- The enhanced modelling of supply chain process and the long term monitoring of the behavior of products in their working life;
- Supporting knowledge creation and development by reducing the factors that hinder the transfer of knowledge across teams and organisations;
- The ability to develop integrated and co-operative design of products, processes and services with suppliers, end users and strategic partners;
- The ability of equipment software to become context aware through the use of sensors and actuators to grow into becoming self-correcting and the raise of research into nano-technology.

These developments in the area of ICT are fuelled by the need for advanced ICT services. It is not clear yet how the AmI environment will be created, but Emiliani et al. (2005) and Ducatel et al. (2001) discuss the evolution being based on the present development trends. This will involve:

- Services becoming dynamic and reconfigurable to suite the needs of users.
- Use of multiple devices to communicate and interact with various systems that occupy the user environment.
- Interaction in the system is multimodal and is completed on a more graphical basis.
- Problem solving may occur between human users in a more dynamic way due to increase in resources or between agents that have been granted a specific level of trust.
- Communication is spread to encompass social groups and not just person to person communication.

These developments in ICT and service trends can utilize the typologies that have been presented in the chapter to choose enabling technologies. Technologies that compliment each other and that provide the key characteristics that create an AmI environment for the user.

The typologies that have been developed and presented can be used in the alignment of these developments with the AmI paradigm. They will need to evolve and adapt to encompass new research in the area of AmI.

CONCLUSION

To survive the changing business environment, companies must be able to innovate and become more flexible. Companies need to be able to change and innovate more effectively and efficiently. To adapt to the fluctuating business environment, business's need to have an ICT system that is flexible and adaptive to their changing needs and requirements. This will involve developing real-time information systems that can adapt to changing technical, manufacturing and organisational structures. AmI can be used as a conduit to achieve this.

To create an AmI environment, requires the use of a combination of technologies. The AmI environment can be enabled through the use of computers that are embedded into everyday objects and through the use of wireless communication. The interaction between these embedded devices and the human user is improving through advancements in the area of natural interaction. As with all new developments there are some negative aspects that need to be considered and discussed with all potential users. These aspects relate to the omnipresent nature of the technology and the level of data collected by the system. These aspects of the system may inadvertently collect and record information that may violate the privacy of the individuals that are interacting with the system. If this data is recorded and stored it must be secure and only accessible to authorized users of the system.

AmI is a people centred technology that is intuitive to the needs and requirements of the human actor. They are non-intrusive systems that are adaptive and responsive to the needs and wants of different individuals. The typologies presented facilitate an understanding and communication of the AmI concepts and philosophy. These typologies should assist the developers, by having an improved understanding of the AmI paradigm. It will allow for the development of enhanced AmI systems. The typologies are new models as they are based on the human side of the AmI, as previous models in literature concentrated on the technologies that enable the AmI system. The typologies are not panaceas. They will only assist in the development of AmI systems. The typologies will also help in defining what AmI is and what it is not.

REFERENCES

Aarts, E. (2004). Ambient intelligence: A multimedia perspective. *IEEE Multimedia, 11*(1), 12-19.

Alcaniz, M. (2005). New technologies for ambient intelligence. In G. Riva, F. Vatalaro, F. Davide, & M. Alcaniz (Eds.), *Ambient intelligence: the evolution of technology, communication, and cognition towards the future of human-computer interaction*. IOS Press.

Bailey, K. D. (1973). Monothetic and polythetic typologies and their relation to conceptualization, measurement, and scaling. *American Sociological Review, 38*(1), 18-33.

Bailey, K. D. (1994). *Typologies and taxonomies: An introduction to classification techniques* (Vol. 07-102). Thousand Oaks, CA: Sage Publications.

Blackman, C. (2004). Stumbling along or grave new world? *Towards Europe's Information Society Foresight, 6*(5), 261-270.

Casal, C. R., Burgelman, J. C., & Bohlin, E. (2004). Prospects beyond 3G. *Info, 6*(6), 359-362.

Davis, G. B. (2002). Anytime/anyplace computing and the future of knowledge work. *Communications of the ACM, 45*(12), 67-73.

Diegel, O., Bright, G., & Potgieter, J. (2004). Bluetooth ubiquitous networks: Seamlessly integrating humans and machines. *Assembly Automation, 24*(2), 168-176.

Drury, D. H., & Farhoomand, A. (1999). Knowledge worker constraints in the productive use of information technology. *Computer Personnel, 19/20*(4/1), 21-42.

Ducatel, K., Bogdanowicz, M., Scapolo, F., Leijten, J., & Burgelman, J. C. (2001). *Scenarios for ambient intelligence in 2010* (ISTAG 2001 Final Report). IPTS, Seville: ISTAG.

Emiliani, P. L., & Stephanidis, C. (2005). Universal access to ambient intelligence environment: Opportunities and challenges for people with disabilities. *IBM Systems Journal, 44*(3), 605-619.

Eurostat. (2006). *Internet usage in the EU25.* News release.

Friedewald, M., & Da Costa, O. (2003). *Science and technology roadmapping: Ambient intelligence in everyday life (AmI@Life)*. Seville, Spain: JRC-IPTS/ESTO.

Gill, S. K., & Cormican, K. (2006). *Support ambient intelligence solutions for small to medium size enterprises: Typologies and taxonomies for developers*. Paper presented at the 12th International Conference on Concurrent Enterprising.

Hellenschmidt, M., & Kirste, T. (2004, November 8-11). A generic topology for ambient intelligence. Paper presented at the Ambient Intelligence: The 2nd European Symposium, EUSAI Eindhoven, The Netherlands.

Hofstadter, D. R. (1980). Gödel, Escher, Bach : An eternal golden braid (1st ed.). Harmondsworth: Penguin Books Ltd.

Horvath, J. (2002). *Making friends with Big Brother?* [Electronic Version]. Telepolis. Retrieved December 6, 2005.

ISTAG. (2000). *Recommendations of the IST Advisory Group for Workprogramme 2001 and beyond "implementing the vision": ISTAG.*

ITEA. (2003). *The Ambience Project*. Retrieved September 21, 09, 2005, from http://www.extra.research.philips.com/euprojects/ambience

Kidd, A. (1994). *The marks are on the knowledge worker*. Paper presented at the Conference on Human Factors in Computer Systems.

Kiritsis, D., Bufardi, A., & Xirouchakis, P. (2003). Research issues on product lifecycle management and information tracking using smart embedded systems. *Advanced Engineering Informatics, 17*(3-4), 189-202.

Koska, D. K., & Romano, J. D. (1988). *Profile 21 issues and implications, countdown to the future: The manufacturing engineer in the 21st Century*. Dearborn, MI: Society of Manufacturing Engineers.

Lindwer, M., Marculescu, D., Basten, T., Zimmermann, R., Marculescu, R., Jung, S., et al. (2003). *Ambient intelligence vision and achievement: Linking abstract ideas to real-world concepts*. Paper presented at the Design, Automation, and Test in Europe Conference and Exhibition.

Morville, P. (2005). *Ambient findability* (1st ed.). Sebastopol, CA: O'Reilly.

Oxford English Dictionary. (2005). *Compact Oxford English Dictionary*. Retrieved December 1, 2005, from http://www.askoxford.com/?view=uk

Potter, B. (2005). RFID: Misunderstood or untrustworthy? *Network Security, 2005*(4), 17-18.

Raisinghani, M. S., Benoit, A., Ding, J., Gomez, M., Gupta, K., Gusila, V., et al. (2004). Ambient intelligence: Changing forms of human computer interaction and their social implications. *Journal of Digital Information, 5*(4).

Rich, P. (1992). The organizational taxonomy: Definitions and design. *The Academy of Management Review, 17*(4), 758-781.

Riva, G. (2005). The psychology of ambient intelligence: Activity, situation, and presence. In G. Riva, F. Vatalaro, F. Davide, & M. Alcaniz (Eds.), *Ambient intelligence: The evolution of technology, communication, and cognition towards the future of human-computer interaction*. IOS Press.

Riva, G., Vatalaro, F., Davide, F., & Alcaniz, M. (2005). *Ambient intelligence: The evolution of technology, communication, and cognition towards the future of human-computer interaction*. IOS Press.

SIBIS. (2002). *Towards the information society in Europe and the US: SIBIS Benchmarking Highlights 2002*. Bonn: Emipirca.

Sørensen, C., & Gibson, D. (2004). Ubiquitous visions and opaque realities: Professionals talking about mobile technologies. *Info, 6*(3), 188-196.

Swade, D. (2000). The cogwheel brain: Charles Babbage and the quest to build the first computer (1st ed.). London: Little, Brown and Company.

Weiser, M. (1993, October 1993). Ubiquitous computing. *IEEE Computer*, 71-72.

Weiser, M. (1999, 9-12 May 1999). *How computers will be used differently in the next twenty years*. Paper presented at the Symposium on Security and Privacy Oakland, CA, USA.

Wright, D. (2005). The dark side of ambient intelligence. *Info, 7*(6), 33-51.

Chapter II
Interoperability Concept
Supporting Network Innovation

Jari Tammela
Spiral Business Services Oy, Finland

Vesa Salminen
Lappeenranta University of Technology, Finland

ABSTRACT

*Innovation capability in creating new offering and new business models by distributed communities is becoming more important. Competitive advantage can be achieved by knowledge communities. Increasing share of the innovation process is taking place outside the company. This is due to **increasing complexity** of products and services containing multiple technologies that are not developed inside the company. Also shortened product life cycle and time to market force companies to focus on their key technologies and looking for partners to cover the supporting technologies. This interdependency organizes companies to the networks where innovation capability success is emerging property of the network. This chapter is focusing on interoperability and providing a concept in order to speed up common innovation of the products and services in open **semantic infrastructure**. This includes identification of solution boundaries and innovation partners. Operative challenge is how to decompose the requirements across the boundaries of different companies in different branches and in different role in the value and innovation network. There is also challenge on how to manage evolving technologies to satisfy customers' existing and future expectations.*

INTRODUCTION

Knowledge intensive business is in continuous **co-evolution**. Nowadays competitive advantage can be achieved by open innovation in **knowledge communities**. Increasing share of the innovation process is taking place outside the company. In the global scale the information is available anywhere when there is internet connection available. The community shares the same information at the same time. The question is how to integrate and synchronize knowledge, technology, competences, and processes, especially when making something new.

Shortened product life cycle and time to market force companies to focus on their key technologies and looking for partners to cover the supporting technologies. Innovation is not only developing new technology and capabilities, but it is also connecting existing capabilities in creative new way. Network environment is a platform for making the connections efficiently.

Complexity is increasing when number of elements to be managed and the connections are increasing. If the network is concentrating around the one strong company where number of smaller companies is in close relationship, the participating companies can partly adopt the leading partner's processes. This is typical in manufacturing industry. If the network is peer to peer type having similar size of the companies, where no one is taking the leading role, the question is what mechanism is then leading the network in order to focus on right things.

The interdependency organizes companies to the networks where innovation capability success is **emerging property** of the network. Innovation needs a focus that is provided by flow of requirements in the network. The requirements are understood as an explicit semantic description derived from the end customer's existing and future needs across the boundaries.

Innovation collaboration in open network environment is efficient if the network have common **semantic infrastructure, knowledge interface**, and network processes. Together this creates dynamics that activate the network to innovate. Knowledge is increasing in the network by learning process on every boundary. The **management of complexity** on boundaries is controlled by interface definition. The focus for innovation on every stage is based on decomposition of the end customers' requirements.

In this article is presenting *interoperability concept* for speeding up innovation in open system environment by using **knowledge communities**. This concept is explained in the chapter: "**Interoperability Concept**." The open innova-

tion is crossing company and technical systems boundaries. Increasing dynamics and interaction on the boundaries is boosting innovation. The **interoperability concept** is providing a framework that allows bidirectional dialogue and exchange of knowledge at the boundaries in structured way. This is explained in chapter: "**Innovation Boundaries**."

The chapter: "**Knowledge Interface** and **Punctual Innovation**" focuses on innovation content creation. *Punctual innovation* is mechanism to focus the network innovation. The innovation process that is distributed to network and having to multiple dialogues over the boundaries is difficult to manage. **Punctual innovation** creates coherence in discrete activities of innovation process to act in same direction, which is customer value. The **interoperability concept** as a modeling tool of network competences is presented through case study in chapter: "**Innovation Network** Environment, Case Medical Healthcare."

INTEROPERABILITY CONCEPT

Innovation Process and Theoretical Background

The logics of closed innovation were working quite well until the end of 1990 decade. Now the efficiency of that approach is disappearing and it is partially replaced by the logics of open innovation (Chesbrough, 2003). The idea of open innovation is to use external and internal ideas in product development. Figure 1 illustrates the systematic approach of open innovation. The difference to closed innovation is to systematize the analyzing and use of business intelligence coming from various knowledge and information sources. Integration of external innovations means validating and integrating the information into internal innovation process.

Succeeding in open innovation requires excellent collaboration between knowledge sources

Figure 1. The process for open innovation (Chesbrough, 2003)

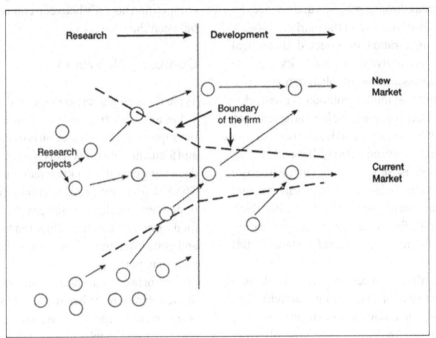

and integration of them into internal innovation process. During the research project LIIMA (see Acknowledgement), a framework was created for managing the interoperability between partners of innovation and **value networks**. It was made a deep literature analysis to create solid theoretical basis for the framework.

Developed **interoperability concept** is based on commonly known theoretical considerations by integrating them in a hybrid system. One of the basic considerations is that information is a flow of messages, while knowledge is created by that very flow of information and is anchored in the beliefs and commitment of its holder (Nonaka & Nishiguchi, 2001). Chesbrough (2003) declares innovation practices over the enterprise boundaries and in **value networks** by open innovation. In the open innovation model, the boundary between a firm and its surrounding environment is more porous, enabling innovation to move easily between the two. (Miller & Langdon, 1999) has introduced how to manage dominant design by

managing platform, product, and process innovation in continuous cycles. Dominant design in his article means the same as disruptive innovation. Innovation process is becoming spiral.

Interoperation is supported by infrastructure model, which includes common semantics and semantics infrastructure (Pallot, Salminen, Pillai, & Kulvant, 2004). Network dynamics forms the corner stones creating breeding environment (Camarinha-Matos, 2004) in new knowledge economy. Florida (2002) states that diverse and open communities have compelled competitive advantage in stimulating creativity, generating innovations and increasing wealth and economic growth. The heart of innovation is therefore the capability to learn, or generate and manage knowledge (McGrath & Iansiti, 1998). The key to achieving innovation speed and productivity is in the automation, leveraging, and expanding an organization's ability to manage the knowledge required completing an innovation. Knowledge management without innovation management means that the company is unable to continuously make new breakthrough products and services by which it can differentiate in the market (Pyötsiä, 2001). The integration of selected theoretical considerations has given an opportunity to create model of business innovation collaboration in open infrastructure and implementation framework.

In full concept creation, we have adapted open innovation (Chesbrough, 2003) system modeling and spiral innovation process (Miller et al., 1999). Interoperation is supported by infrastructure model, which includes common semantics and semantics infrastructure (Pallot et al., 2004). Network dynamics forms the corner stones creating breeding environment (Camarinha-Matos, 2004) in new knowledge economy (Florida, 2005).

Interoperability concept is a framework for a community to establish innovation activity. The driving force for innovation is business growth that is achieved by introducing new offering. Technology is an enabler to comply customers' value. Applying technologies and developing new products, services companies strive their own success and same time they are connected

to each others' success. On a market there is a competition not only between companies but also between the networks.

Company Networks

Typically companies manage and organize the **value network** (i.e., supply chain) to 1st and 2nd tier suppliers. The interaction is transaction based and focusing deliveries. This type of collaboration does not generate the knowledge in daily work. The dialogue happens in exceptions (i.e., problems in delivery, quality, or design). In that case, the focus is on solving the problem as fast as possible and quite often in negative atmosphere. The supplier may participate in customer's development projects or taking care of autonomous development of the subsystem. When the development project is started the targets are already set by the main contractor and suppliers' innovativeness is limited in internal solutions of the subsystems.

The **value network** (Figure 2) is not providing a sustainable environment for creating innovations in a community. It is centered on assets and

Figure 2. Value network

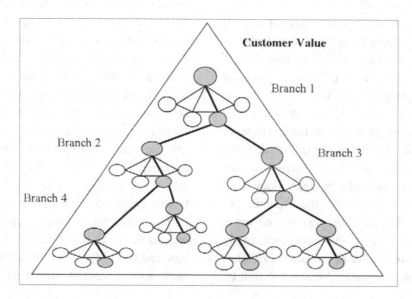

Figure 3. Innovation network

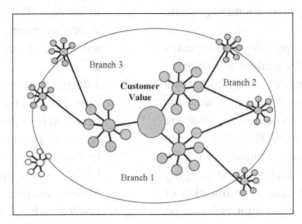

material flow and by the hierarchical structure it filters the knowledge from the network. At the best it can manage incremental innovation and bring value by driving down operative costs in existing business. Radical innovations are possible but most likely come outside the network. The structure itself is not systematically supporting totally new approaches.

Innovation network (Figure 3) that is centered on customer's value broads the scope for innovation. New integrated products and services or business concepts can be innovated. The difference how **innovation network** operates is in network topography and the type of connection. **Value network** is structured to exchange messages and data, where **innovation network** is dialogue and exchange of knowledge. There needs to be a different mechanism to support this activity that is called a *knowledge interface*. The current weak points in **innovation networks** are that they are usually closed and mainly work in tacit knowledge. This may lead to ineffective process and limit the interaction. Companies may invest money to technology development that can be commercially already available.

The purpose of creating an **interoperability concept** has three main targets. First target is to define open network environment that organize available capability around customer's value and provide method to generate the knowledge. Second target is to speed up the innovation by doing right things. Third target is related to the nature of innovation and presence of coincidence or serendipity. Good ideas can prompt anywhere from the network and result of the collaboration. One dimension in effective network innovation is to exploit as much as possible ideas that are driven from the customer needs. The last target is property of the network as a whole.

Interoperability Concept

Innovation collaboration in open environments can be summarized as *interoperability concept* where:

1. **Network infrastructure enhance network dynamics:** Network dynamics is easy connecting/disconnecting to network and its processes. Also number of interactions (dialogues, groups) and content is sign of the dynamics. The dynamics is achieved by common **semantic infrastructure** for products, services, and business processes. *Knowledge interface* is for connecting to the network and enabling the exchanging of the messages. Value proposition is needed to evaluate technical and economical risks

in order to prioritize activities. Network dynamics speed up innovation and generate new knowledge.

2. **Identification of capability gaps by mapping requirements against offering:** In customer driven innovation the company's offering is constantly evaluated against customers' requirements because also they are changing continuously. By understanding what requirements are the most valuable for the customers now and in the future bring the focus for innovation. Identification of the new business opportunities based on customer's future requirements and expectations reveals also the lack of competence and capability in company's structure. Gaps point out what capability company needs to develop or adapt in order to win in the competition. The identification of the gaps is two stage processes. First the company identifies its own capability to meet the requirements. When the gap is identified the second stage is to find out if the capability exists in the network. The common semantics in the network infrastructure provide the method to describe the gaps explicitly as new set of

requirements for the community. In open innovation all the companies that have the capability can participate and suggest their solution and start the dialogue with the company.

3. **Filling of the gaps by revising the offering:** The common **semantic infrastructure** makes it possible to model products, services, processes, competences, tools, methods, and explicit knowledge. Capability is configuration of these elements. When managing the key elements in the layered architecture, it is possible to route and combine existing capability in creative new way. Filling the missing capability gaps can be done by creating new competence or by combining existing elements with creative new way. The first option is bringing totally new offering on market and generates competitive advance in the long perspective. The second solution is effective way to revise the offering. Both the solutions are needed, and customer experience of the new and valuable can be achieved. The new capabilities as well as the gaps are described using common semantics. The new offering is communicated to network.

Figure 4. Spiral process (Nonaka & Takeuchi, 1995)

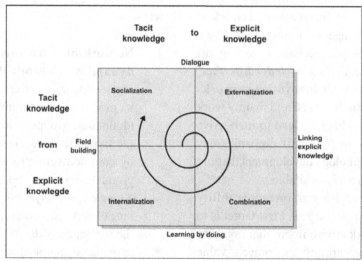

4. **Generate new knowledge by spiral process:** The innovation network is for connecting and disconnecting the capability. The driving force for collaboration is business growth and the success is achieved trough customer value. In each connection, there is an intention for creating new knowledge in order to understand the customers' value and market better. The knowledge is realized as new offering and capabilities. The knowledge and new capabilities can be created in the network processes.

Network process is the sum of the multiple discreet dialogues. When the theme in a dialogue evolves, a new knowledge can emerge out of it. The systematic approach to enhance the knowledge creation and learning in community is spiral process, where the knowledge increase in four consecutive steps that can be repeated. Network dialogues can take advantage of spiral process to create new offering (Figure 4). The dialogue is possible. The network dialogues through **knowledge interface** support innovation when concentrating on the value and development capabilities. Information is processed to knowledge and turn it to intellectual capital of the network and hence to innovations and success of the community.

INNOVATION BOUNDARIES

Creating an innovation is crossing several boundaries where the most important are company boundaries and technical system boundaries. Company boundaries are reflecting to **value network** that is enabler for realization and commercializing the innovation. When creating new, it always has influence to the **value network**. There need to be adaptability in the network to re-organize the activities. The flow and quality of information improve the understanding what is expected from each supplier.

Company Boundaries

The **value network** works efficiently based on information (items) that already is in systems. The contractor and the supplier know exactly what they are ordering by knowing the identifier code for an item. The business critical information is how many, when, where and what price. In case of innovation and developing something new there are many open issues. Problem is how to make a dialogue with the **value network** in order to optimize the solution. The traditional approach to the problem is the concurrent engineering, but as closed system it does not take advantage of the full potential of the innovation capability.

Company boundaries are working as a damper for customer requirements. Many technical details can be important for customer value or brand image. If the supplier is far in value chain the original customer requirement is filtered to a request for the modification. At that point is difficult to know, if this is new business opportunity or additional cost and chaos. It is important to make information to flow and create network platform that enable bidirectional dialogues across the boundaries. The information architecture and structure can improve the common understanding.

Layered architecture in common **semantic infrastructure** of the network is supporting modeling of products and services as well as business processes. This provides tool that is rich enough to model the image of the innovation objects. The semantics is powerful tool for messaging, because it expands the bandwidth of communication to cover any critical elements that is critical for innovation value, requirements, capabilities, offering, competences, knowledge, etc.

The common **semantic infrastructure** can support the information flow across the company boundaries (Figure 5). A company that is offering goods and services to end user market is constantly fitting the offering to customers needs. Internally these needs can be described as a set of requirements and refined to the solution as a

Figure 5. Information flow a cross the company boundaries

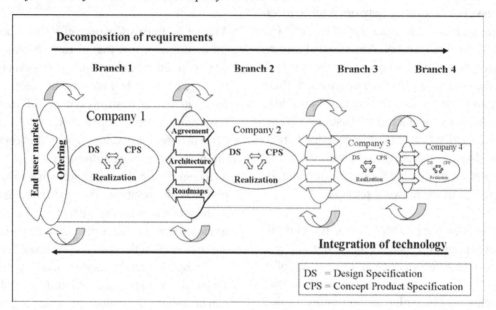

Figure 6. Requirements flows across the technical system boundaries

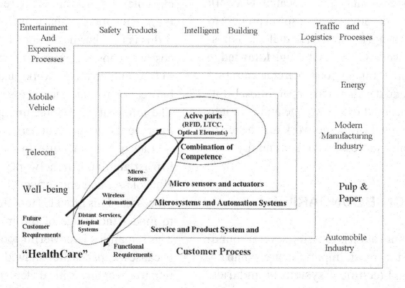

design specification (DS). This solution can be divided to the smaller entities and subsystems that can be expressed as conceptual products and services (CPS). The realization of the solution covers the capabilities, internal processes and gives the cost structure. Solution can be partly shared to the partner network where conceptual product and service description is design specification for partner's design activities. The partner network is open but long-term relationship requires also collaboration processes that include agreement process, information architecture definition, and road map to express long-term direction.

Technical System Boundaries

The technical system boundaries are important for managing knowledge. There also has to be a bidirectional flow of the requirements across system hierarchy. At each boundary, customer requirements are reflected against functionality. Going deeper in the system the core technology can be applied in multiple markets. New business opportunities can be found by adapting new requirements on existing capability. The boundaries are also important because there are source for the innovation. Shared knowledge and dialogue around customer value and capabilities create an environment to emerge something new. The innovation capability and speed in the community is increasing by enhancing the dynamics in boundaries (Figure 6).

Interrelated Technology Innovation and Network Topologies

The semantic offering description reflects the processes and the knowledge in the company. Typically there are explicit descriptions of the processes and knowledge in the company (work instructions, QA systems, ERP, PDM, etc.). The next step further is that processes and knowledge are mapped to the semantic description of offering. Finally, when customer specifies its needs using standard documents, this customer semantics can be mapped against the offering. As result the requirements are transcribed and mapped to the internal processes. This leads to an exact list of the processes and capabilities involving of the customer's request. Identification of gaps comes out in detailed analysis of listed processes.

Gap analysis gives the estimation of the development effort to comply customer's request.

Figure 7. Interrelated technology innovation and network topologies

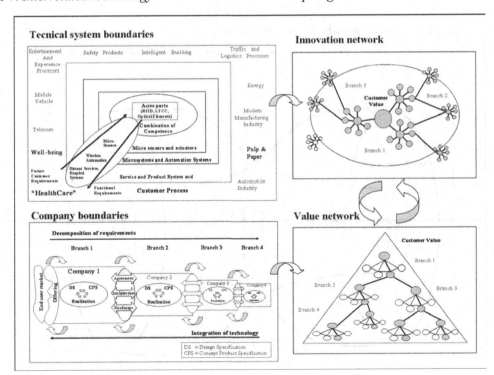

This also is helping to make business decision and control the risk. Gap analysis propagates also converted requests to its own partner network. Gap need to be described as a formal specification that may look different than original request. This usually happens when going over technical system boundaries. The interrelation between networks when crossing the boundaries is shown in Figure 7.

Scope of Innovation

The scope of the innovation (Figure 8) is broad. Main dynamics is between the market and technology **co-evolution**. By integrating technology and knowledge, it is possible to provide new products and services to the certain market segment. Markets are driven by customers' needs and requirements. Technology development is constantly in evolving state and there is strong relationship between the markets and technology development. New technology enables new functionality or replaces existing

technologies. Market requirements can direct technology development in certain direction.

Innovation in network is not limited for fulfilling the requirements around the products and services. Re-organizing network activities can provide possibilities for new business. New core technology may lead to new industry and even new economic system. The question is what drives the network to re-organize itself and commercialize innovations in the new way? There have to be a customer's value that can be evaluated against investments and cost of change in the network. Management of economical and technical risks is important as well as win-win situation among the partners.

The substance in the network is knowledge and capability, which is activated when the customer requirements are decomposed. In order to manage economical and technical risks the new innovation should be evaluated as a value for customer and network partners. Effective method of decomposing the requirements reveals precisely

Figure 8. Scope of the innovation and co-evolution of business

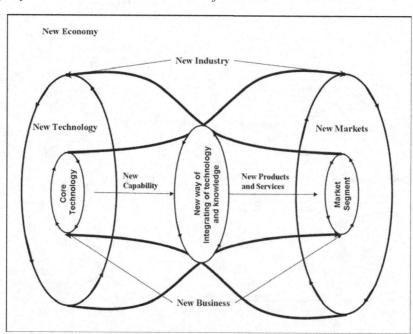

in the network what gaps needs to be filled. This partly lowers the economical risk for each level of activities when most of the risk is then known and estimated in terms of costs, investments, and timeframe. The most attractive innovation is when recognized customer value is high with low risk. In practice, this means creative re-combination of existing capability to create new functionality or value to customer. This point of view makes the service innovation look interesting.

KNOWLEDGE INTERFACE AND PUNCTUAL INNOVATION

The interface definition creates a node point in the network. The connection is the capability for dialogue through the interface. Normally this dialogue is exchange of the messages. The

same message based on common **semantic infrastructure** can be routed to multiple nodes and each having its own meaning and content. The message triggers the internal processes through the interface. The message itself is not modeling the knowledge but it refers to the objects or the processes inside the node. The reply for message releases the knowledge for use of the network. It also activates the appropriate nodes to take advantage of shared knowledge. The interpretation of the knowledge depends on the role of the node in the network topography (right side of Figure 7). Interoperability in the network creates new knowledge by combining and cumulating existing knowledge which catalyses open innovation.

The customer's requirements can be distributed and converted using messages while it is breaking down to the core technology or n^{th} tier supplier (left side of Figure 7). The messaging

Figure 9. Knowledge interface for routing innovation

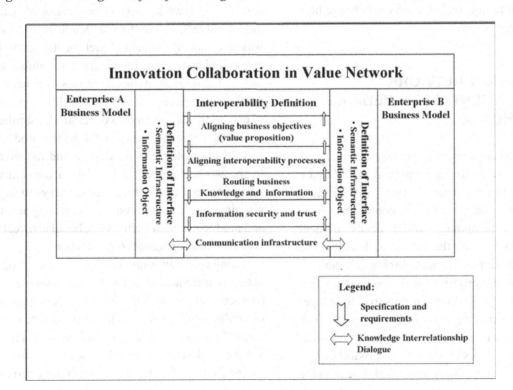

of requirements together with shared knowledge enables the *punctual open innovation.* The most critical elements are **knowledge interface** and common **semantic infrastructure** for messaging and knowledge sharing.

In the manufacturing industry supplier network infrastructure is typically dominated by logistic business processes and **innovation network** typically is not structured so systematically. There is need for defining the interface that can simultaneously serve both networks. The problem is **increase of complexity**. Therefore, the **knowledge interface** definition should have layered architecture (Figure 9).

The network environment is also possible to organize into a common platform. By joining to community platform, a company is building a **knowledge interface**. The **knowledge interface** ground the different business models of the different companies together. Working in the platform environment is really doing a business and leading real business activities. The platform without **knowledge interface** is additional channel to communicate, but it does not change how the network operates.

INNOVATION NETWORK ENVIRONMENT, CASE MEDICAL HEALTHCARE

The case company is contract manufacturer of the medical devices, for main company in healthcare business. The company's strength is in injection molding of plastics. The key competence is in production technology, which needs to meet strictest norms of the public authorities and quality standards. The outsourcing is becoming a business opportunity for the company, when the customer is seeking partners to deliver lager entities—full equipments including design. The new situation requires the company to develop their competences in new areas as product design and engineering. The new network role in value

chain is main supplier, which requires also a capability to act as an integrator. Commitment to one customer does not bring the all the targeted business growth. The seeking of new customer and business is necessity.

The company manages several technologies (Figure 10) that have been refined to its capabilities. There is also knowledge involved in integration phase. Part of the technology, capability, and design knowledge is developed outside the company (company boundary). The company's end product has system hierarchy and it is part of the customer's product (system and company boundaries). The weak point is currently the offering. The company can show what type of products they manufacture, but their offering is actually knowledge and processes including their partner network. In order to communicate this to their potential new customers and start up the dialogue they should make semantic description of their capabilities.

The case approach was two-dimensional. First identify what existing competences are in-house and in the network using same developed data model and architecture for competences. Second was to establish the data model for the product using architecture based on functional modularity. Idea of the product architecture was to generalize the description as much as possible in order to extend the description to cover all the similar products. The dependency between the product and the competences was studied and modeled in the work. Applying same data architecture analyzing second and third product very quickly visualize the company's competences, companies, and products in their own layers, but also reveals how they are connected to each other.

Using common general architecture for products, competences, and companies (customers, partners) also give general view to company's capability and business. The value is that core technology and market segment have an explicit structured description and the knowledge can be routed from the front end to the company and its

Figure 10. Content mapping and identification of gaps

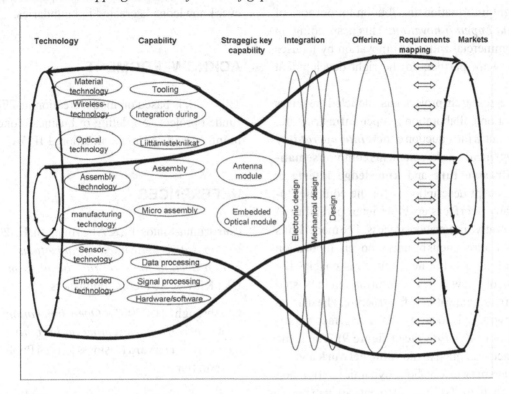

network. This also helps to identify potential new business (Figure 8 and Figure 10).

The real business generates the dynamics in the network. When new customer is asking quote for a new product, the first questions are "Do we have the capability to make it and what commercial and technical risks are involved?" Breaking down the product to functions reveal the gaps in capability and understanding the how much is new there really is new for the company or partners. Technical and economical risks are recognized and isolated for decision-making. ***Punctual innovation*** is filling the gap by taking new partners and/or developing new capability. Also targets for long-term technology development is aligned to market needs.

CONCLUSION

Open innovation process requires the definition of interoperability in order to achieve a critical level of network dynamics to create new products and services. It is important to recognize solution boundaries on various systems. This enhances self organizing structure in open innovation. Various kinds of boundaries should be recognized: technical system boundaries and company boundaries. The difference in network topographies leads to different network dynamics. Interrelation happens when commercializing the innovation. The common **semantic infrastructure** supporting modeling of products and services as well as business processes is speeding up the commercialization of innovation. The use of common semantics leads the right information distribution for purpose of *punctual open innovation.* This is speeding up the commercialization of innovation by focuses the network partners to the right development activities.

The research project has modeled business innovation collaboration in open infrastructure. The result is introduction of new *interoperability concept* including key elements common **semantic infrastructure** and **knowledge interface**. The concept description is for the company-to-company interfaces enabling interoperability in collaborative innovation process. The model links together autonomous business models, innovation network, and **value network**. This enables the routing of knowledge and information in trusted way in communication infrastructure. The sharing of knowledge is focusing in the interface definition *knowledge interface* (Figure 9). The same interface is applied to the **value network** and **innovation network** enabling dynamic interrelation between them. The other elements are gap filling processes and spiral learning processes that are taking place simultaneously and parallel. The gap filling process means mapping the incoming requirements against existing offering and identifies gaps in capability. The effective way to fill the gaps is creatively combine something that already exists in the network. The gaps need to be defined using common **semantic infrastructure** and communicate to the network as a new set of the requirements.

The architectural elements of the concept provide the basis for network environment. Network dynamics is possibility to connect or disconnect in different roles according to specific customer derived requirements. The spiral learning process is dialogue across the **knowledge interface**. The network infrastructure needs to support the decomposition of the requirements across the boundaries of different companies in different branches and in different position and role in the

value network. Learning takes place in when ever knowledge is created in boundaries.

ACKNOWLEDGMENT

This work is based on model creation in TEKES funded project "Modeling of business concepts in innovation commercialization, LIIMA."

REFERENCES

Camarinha-Matos, L., & Afsarmanesh, H. (2004). *Collaborative networked organizations—A research agenda for emerging business models.* UK: Kluwer Academic Publishers

Chesbrough, H. (2003). *Open innovation: The new imperative for creating and profiting from technology.* Harvard Business School Publishing Corporation.

Florida, R. (2002). *The rise of the creative class.* New York: Basic Books.

Florida, R. (2005). *The flight of the creative class: The new global competition for talent.* New York: Harper Collins.

McGrath, M.E. & Iansiti, M. (1998). Envisioning IT-enabled innovation. *PRTM Insight Magazine.*

Miller, W., & Langdon, M. (1999). *Fourth generation R&D: Managing knowledge, technology, and innovation.* Canada: John Wiley & Sons Inc.

Nonaki, I. & Nichiguchi, T. (2001). *Knowledge emergence: Social, technical, and evolutionary dimensions of knowledge creation.* Oxford University Press.

Nonaka, I., & Takeuchi, H. (1995). *The knowledge-creating company.* New York: Oxford University Press.

Pallot, M., Salminen, V., Pillai, B., & Kulvant, B. (2004). Business semantics: The magic instrument enabling plug & play collaboration? *ICE 2004, International Conference on Concurrent Engineering*, Sevilla, June 14-16.

Pyötsiä, J. (2001). Innovation management in network economy. *186JP IAMOT Conference*, Lausanne, 19-22 March 2001.

Tammela, J., & Salminen, V. (2006). *Modeling business innovation collaboration in open infrastructure.* In K. D. Thoben, K. S. Pawar, & S. Terzi (Ed.), *ICE 2006, 12th International Conference on Concurrent Enterprising*, Milan, Italy 26-28 June 2006: Innovative products and services through collaborative networks (pp. 283-290). Nottingham: Centre for Concurrent Enterprise Nottingham University Business School.

Chapter III
Heritage Tourism Portal Web Page Design with Factor and Correlation Analysis

Shamsuddin Ahmed
Bang College of Business, KIMEP, Almaty, Kazakhstan

Francis Amagoh
Department of Public Administration, KIMEP, Almaty, Kazakhstan

ABSTRACT

This chapter presents the design of a heritage tourism Web portal. Factor analysis is used to identify how the navigation tools are to be grouped. Correlation analysis additionally identifies methods of grouping the navigation functionalities to substantiate the decision. Statistical analysis lends support to the reliability of the data used in the study. Examples are given about how heritage portal navigation functionality can be developed as hierarchical layered portal pages. Additionally, the perceptual map shows the layout and proximity of the portal functionalities.

INTRODUCTION

This chapter demonstrates the design of a heritage Web portal through the use of factor and correlation analysis. Such design approach is used to sequence heritage portal Web pages, and enhances Web browsing with orderly layered portal pages in a manner that reduces information access time. The main purpose of such a design is to enhance the growth of the tourism industry through the design of an efficient Web navigation portal. The portal functionality related data is collected through **survey** instrument given to tourists and it is used to develop Web portal pages. Factor analysis is applied to group the portal **functionalities** and correlation analysis validates the grouping. Additionally, perceptual mapping using the factor components shows the layout of the navigation tool.

Of the various forms of tourism, the growth in **heritage/ecotourism** has continued to receive intense attention because of its potential impacts on the environment due to lack of a coherent plan to adequately manage such growth (Sorice, Shafer, & Ditton, 2006). Even though some scholars recommend that **ecotourism** be integrated with cultural/heritage tourism, there is a slight difference between the two. While heritage tourism involves traveling to experience the places, artifacts, and activities that authentically represent the stories and people of the past and present (Hill, Etienne, & Trotter, 2006), **ecotourism** is aimed at the appreciation of both the natural world and the traditional cultures located in natural areas (Neto, 2003; Rugendyke & Son, 2005). Heritage tourism comprises of such items as local handicrafts, language, art and music, architecture, sense of place, historic sites, festivals and events, and many others (Bastmeijer & Roura, 2004). **Ecotourism** is widely perceived as a nature-based form of alternative tourism that embodies the visitor's traits that mass tourism supposedly lacks (Hill, Etienne, & Trotter, 2006).

As with all industries, the use of electronic commerce is essential in facilitating the growth of the tourism industry and optimizing its benefits. Consequently, **e-commerce/e-government** is an important field of application for providing electronic public services. Heritage electronic-tourism concerns the use of electronic media for promotion, site development, interpretation, visitor services, and economic development, and uses historical, cultural, and environmental settings that already exist for **heritage/ecotourism** development (Lu & Lu, 2004; Sorice et al., 2006). With the rapid growth of the tourism industry in recent years, it is necessary for government and the industry to make appropriate use of the Web in facilitating and optimizing the various components of tourism activities. However,

while **e-commerce** initiatives show that tourism information is one of the most accessed data on the Web, a high number of Web users experience long delays in accessing relevant tourism information (Wu & Chang, 2005). It is therefore important to develop user-friendly portals with a focus on usability and easy-to-use requirements (Wimmer & Holler, 2003).

The remaining sections of this chapter are organized as follows: In Section 2, we review the current literature on issues of importance to Internet **portal design, e-tourism**, and consumer Web shopping behavior. Section 3 discusses portal function. Section 4 presents the methodology used in the study. In Section 5, we discuss the metric for **portal design**. Section 6 explains how factor analysis is used in design of heritage tourism portal navigation tool. Similarly, Section 7 presents the design of heritage portal navigation tool with correlation analysis. Section 8 discusses future prospects in the tourism industry. Section 9 is the conclusion.

LITERATURE REVIEW

There is almost universal agreement that Web users are more interested in portals with user-friendly interfaces that provide needed information in a timely manner. It is also widely acknowledged that the use of information technology in the tourism industry enhances the provision of goods and services both by government and the private sector. A number of studies have been conducted on issues of relevance to Internet portals, **e-commerce** initiatives, Internet privacy, and other aspects of consumer Web shopping behavior relevant to the tourism market. For example, Chou, Hsu, Yeh, and Ho (2005) propose a framework for designing efficient portals, and for evaluating industry portal performance through the use of analytical hierarchical process. The framework incorporates both expert's and users' judgments into the performance evaluation process, and was tested by using an industry portal project developed by small and medium enterprises (SMEs) administration, Ministry of Economic Affairs, Taiwan. Their results suggest that the three objectives for performance evaluation for Internet portals include data quality, technological acceptance, and knowledge distribution.

Law and Hsu (2005) investigated the perceived importance of dimensions and attributes on hotel Web sites from the perspective of travelers. Through personal interviews with 304 travelers who had previously visited hotel Web sites in the past year, the extent to which various hotel Web site dimensions and attributes were perceived as important were examined. Empirical results show that respondents viewed reservation information as the most important dimension, and room rates as the most important attribute. In addition, these dimensions and attributes were more important on Web sites of up-scale hotels than on Web sites of economy hotels.

Privacy issues and the safeguard of personal information are major concerns for Web users, and consequently the governance of Web portals. Flavian and Guinaliu (2006) investigated the effects of privacy and the level of trust shown by users of Internet portals. Their study shows that an individual's loyalty to a Web site is closely linked to the level of trust. This suggests that trust in an Internet portal is influenced by the perceived security by users regarding the handling of their personal data. On the issue of trust in government, Elovici, Glezer, and Shapira (2005) propose a model of privacy-enhanced catalogue search system (PECSS) in an attempt to address privacy threats to consumers who search for product and services on the Web. The model extends an agent-based architecture for electronic catalogue mediation by supplementing it with a privacy enhancement mechanism.

An understanding of Web shopping behavior and consumer loyalty is essential in enhancing the growth of any industry. So, Wong, and Sculli (2005) used principal **component** analysis

and structural equations to investigate the Web shopping behavior of consumers in Hong Kong through a Web-based **questionnaire survey**. Their findings suggest that Web-shopping intentions are directly affected by Web-search behavior and Web-shopping adoption decisions. Web search behavior was a stronger factor than adoption decision in terms of influencing Web shopping intentions. Chiou and Shen (2006) developed and empirically tested a model to examine the antecedents of consumer loyalty toward Internet portals by collecting data based on an Internet **survey** in Taiwan. Results show that attributive satisfaction is very important in affecting consumers' overall satisfaction toward an Internet portal, which in turn affects consumer's loyalty intention toward an Internet portal. Lee and Lin (2005) developed a model to examine the relationship among e-service quality dimensions and overall service quality, customer satisfaction and purchase intentions. They conclude that the dimensions of Web site design, reliability, responsiveness, and trust affect overall service quality and customer satisfaction.

The use and standardization of best practices is important in improving the image of the tourism industry, while taking into account regional- and country-specific factors. Hwang and Lockwood (2006) studied barriers to the application of best practices in hospitality and tourism in the UK. Results suggest a model identifying seven key capabilities that underlie the adoption of best practices and six barriers to their implementation. The seven key capabilities are customer focused goals, planning and control, partnering and networking, internal and external **communication,** achieving consistent standards, strategic workforce management, cash flow and performance management.

Functional frameworks and design processes can be used to support tourism activities. The rapidly growing Web technologies and electronic commerce applications have stimulated the need for personalized and group decision support

functionalities in e-tourism intermediary systems. Woess and Dunzendorfer (2002) suggest an adapter concept, which allows uniform and homogeneous data interchange between a Web-based client application and several distributed heterogeneous tourism information systems. A major advantage of this concept is that both the client adapter and the server adapter are designed as add-on modules, and therefore their installation causes only low adaptation effort with regards to existing applications.

Clustering mechanism for tourism data can facilitate the effectiveness and accessibility of information for tourists. The **clusters** group tourism data of similar functions or activities under the same category. For example, information that relates to dining activities - such as restaurants, bars, etc. would be grouped under the same **cluster**, while information that relates to natural sites, lakes, mountains, etc. would be under a different **cluster**. Wickramasinghe, Amarsin, and Alahakon (2004) conducted a study that proposes a multi-agent system with enhanced capabilities obtained through a hybrid of intelligent techniques. Two types of agents, namely, a distributed agent and a central administrator agent, handle the processing of the model. Localized processing at the individual agents is carried out using mathematical techniques and genetic algorithms. The central administrator agent obtains information about the problem domain from the Internet and maintains a knowledge pool using a **clustering** technique called the growing self-organizing map. Distributed agents communicate with the central administrator agent if they need further knowledge about the problem domain to provide solutions to user-defined tasks. The approach integrates traditional mathematical, data mining, and evolutionary techniques with a multi-agent system. The system is implemented as a travel optimizer application for the **e-tourism** domain. Such a technique can be integrated with currently available e-tourism applications to provide tourists with enhanced solutions.

In an effort to address the problem of fragmented data sources, Puhretmair and Woess (2001) propose a system that extensively uses maps for data presentation, and federation of multiple structured and semi-structured tourism information sources on the Web. Touristic maps are generated dynamically, including data resulting from database queries. This concept allows a clear and meaningful representation of up-to-date tourism information embedded in a geographical context. The integration of distributed data sources has great impact on the quality of tourism information systems.

Most tourism information systems offer a variety of sharp query **functionalities** with some relaxation mechanisms that provide vague results or alternatives to users. To address this problem, Puhretmair, Rumetshofer, and Schaumlechner (2002) present two methodological approaches to support the tourist. The first is a case-based reasoning approach, which provides answers to tourists by deriving individual travel suggestions from previous cases stored in the knowledge base. The second approach is a visual method through maps that identifies locations of elements of tourism sites or activities. This gives tourists a good impression of the location of objects, and enables them to decide which of the resulting objects is best located regarding their needs and interests.

Menczer (2004) used a number of empirical approaches to evaluate two general conjectures utilized in the design of Web portals. The first conjecture is that a page is similar to other pages that link to it, while the second conjecture states that pages about the same topic are clustered together. Conditional probability calculations were used to directly estimate the semantic (relevance) similarity between pages in any topic in a Web portal, and to characterize how this relationship decays as one crawls away from the start page. Vector analysis was used to make connections between lexical and link relationships. Conditional probability was used to test the assumption that portal user searching for pages about a topic would hit a relevant page within a certain time. Additionally, the author used nonlinear least square fit to analyze the decrease in the reliability of lexical content inferences with distance from the topic page in link space through a family of exponential decay models. The resulting similarity decay fit curve provides a rough estimate of how far in link space one can make inferences about the relevance of pages. This result can be useful in the design of search engines as well as topical crawling algorithms that prioritize links based on the textual context in which they appear.

Ozer (2005) used fuzzy c-means **clustering** to study the relevance and **clustering** of information in Internet portals. The study indicates that there are meaningful **clusters** among potential users of an Internet portal that offers business-related information. This suggests that fuzzy c-means **clustering** can be an important tool in the design of efficient internet portals, by determining and grouping homogeneous groups of people, and offering specific information to each group. Finally, Chakrabarti, Joshi, Punera, and Pennock (2002) used various page-sampling strategies to examine the correlation between pages across links in an Internet portal.

PORTAL FUNCTION

The portal Web site contains pages that are organized by navigation tools. The navigation tool is designed such that the access page, consisting of logically nested layered Web pages, gives users access to desired information in a single location. Navigation tools have a hierarchical relationship to each other. A well-designed portal contains resources and **functionalities** that can be made easily available to a user. The tourism portal is a reliable interface that serves as a valuable information resource for the travel industry. The entry screen or the presentation layer provides the portal user precise information. This layer is tailored based on the necessities of the user (Bhatt & Emdad, 2001; Javalgi & Ramsey, 2001).

The heritage tourism portal supports commercial, government, and tourism activities with broad diversity of information, data, tourism events, and value added functions between two or more parties (Rayport & Jaworski, 2000). The features of the tourism portal comprise of transaction processing, collaboration, searching, Web links, activities, event, and all necessary tourism related information. It provides systematic Web surfing and reduces random searches for specific information. Portals are a subset of Web sites, but the overall domain of Web sites does not form a portal. They assist clients by providing them a good understanding of the products or services through a variety of information retrieved through direct links to the Internet (Lee, 2001).

METHODOLOGY

The prime objective of this empirical study is to determine the sequencing of the important functionality dimensions for heritage/eco tourism portal. The study is undertaken to collect primary data from UAE tourists from different parts of the UAE to avoid bias. The designed **questionnaires** were extracted from Table 1 with appropriate scale and were distributed to 150 foreign tourists. Forty-seven items are defined under eight functionality dimensions for the **questionnaire** and **survey** purpose. The functionality dimensions are grouped as: I=Information, A=Accommodation, S=Activity, H=Heritage, W=User interface, V=Variety of Information, O=Online Reservations, and F=Additional Function. These groupings are derived as follows: From Table 1, items such as aa, ab, ac, ad, ae, and af are classed as "A or Accommodation Related information." Similarly, items fa, fb, fc, and fd are clased as "F or Additional function." The classification continues in this way until all the items in the **survey** results are classified into eight dimensions. These dimensions serve as the instrument for sequencing the Web pages and grouping the portal functionality. The data is represented in a

Figure 1. Activity oriented portal functionality responses (mean and standard deviations)

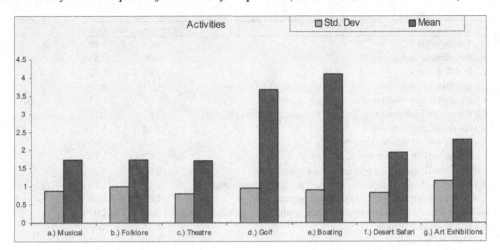

Figure 2. Activity oriented portal functionality responses (mean and standard deviations)

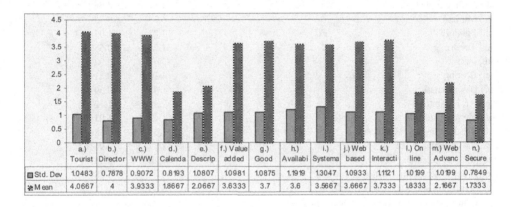

	a.) Tourist	b.) Director	c.) WWW	d.) Calenda	e.) Descrip	f.) Value added	g.) Good	h.) Availabi	i.) Systema	j.) Web based	k.) Interacti	l.) On line	m.) Web Advanc	n.) Secure
Std. Dev	1.0483	0.7878	0.9072	0.8193	1.0807	1.0981	1.0875	1.1919	1.3047	1.0933	1.1121	1.0199	1.0199	0.7849
Mean	4.0667	4	3.9333	1.8667	2.0667	3.6333	3.7	3.6	3.5667	3.6667	3.7333	1.8333	2.1667	1.7333

scale of 1 to 5, with 5 being highest and 1 being the lowest in any item. The five-point scaling technique used for gathering data was as follows. 5=strongly agree, 4=fairly agree, 3=agree, 2=neutral, and 1=strongly disagree. The tourists returned 97 **survey** instruments and only 55 responses are found acceptable for analysis, a response rate of 57%. Using the information from the **questionnaires**, the data is analyzed for validity using **ANOVA**. Factor analysis is used to provide exploratory measure in order to group the portal **functionalities.** Correlation analysis is used to validate the **functionalities'** groupings.

The mean scores of the factors as shown in Table 1, thus, represent the respondents' average position based upon this scaling technique. The measures of the response in **variance** with respect to the mean response would define the reliability of the data. Using the information from the **questionnaire,** the data is analyzed for internal validity using **ANOVA**, correlation analysis, and factor analysis. The **ANOVA** validates these constructs

Table 1. Item analysis with mean and variance

Item	Average	Variance
Ia.) Tourist guide	4.07	1.10
ib.) Directories of attractions	4.00	0.62
ic.) WWW guide	3.93	0.82
id.) Calendar of events	1.87	0.67
ie.) Descriptions of local features	2.07	1.17
if.) Value added features (map, distance, news, currency information)	3.63	1.21
ig.) Good still images/photos	3.70	1.18
ih.) Availability of web cam and images	3.60	1.42
ii.) Systematic link to other web sites	3.57	1.70
ij.) Web based inquiry form or order (gifts, product…)	3.67	1.20
ik.) Interactive features (currency converter, weather, current event…)	3.73	1.24
il.) On line customer support, FAQ, search engines,,,,	1.83	1.04
im.) Web Advanced features (e-mail updates, multimedia, chat, forum)	2.17	1.04
in.) Secure on line payment	1.73	0.62
aa.) Hotel information	4.00	1.03
ab.) Accommodation information, price, features of rooms, facility	3.90	0.78
ac.) Restaurant guide	2.43	1.50
ad.) Price guide	3.50	1.02
ae.) Contact information	3.97	1.27
af.) On-line reservation	4.17	0.76
sa.) Musical	1.73	0.75
sb.) Folklore	1.73	1.03
sc.) Theatre	1.70	0.63
sd.) Golf	3.67	0.92
se.) Boating	4.10	0.81
sf.) Desert Safari	1.93	0.69
sg.) Art Exhibitions	2.30	1.32
ha.) Heritage attractions	1.77	1.01
hb.) Castle, Museum, Monuments	1.63	0.38
hc.) Parks, Fauna, Flora	1.87	0.95
wa.) Easy to access the web	4.20	0.58
wb.) Easy to access information in this web	4.07	0.88
wc.) Format of site is consistent (font/color..)	3.83	1.11
wd.) Multiple way to access information in web	3.97	1.21
we.) Interface for help, guide, information	4.27	0.69
va.) Simplicity & clear direction	3.43	1.22
vb.) Information are up to date, current	2.73	0.82
vc.) Comprehensive coverage, more information	3.33	1.13
vd.) Hyperlink to related web	4.10	0.71
oa.) Easy Booking facility with the web/portal	3.97	1.00
ob.) Payment system is on-line	0.70	0.22
oc.) Payment system by email	0.23	0.19
od.) Payment system by telephone	0.30	0.22
fa.) Education Center	3.93	0.82
fb.) Business Center	3.90	0.99
fc.) Address - Resources	3.77	0.81
fd.) Passport - Visa	4.30	0.56

with the F-statistics, **variance**, and p-values. Factor analysis provides exploratory measure to group the information validated through correlation measures. Figure 1 and 2 show the mean and standard deviation measures of the responses of portal **functionalities**.

METRIC FOR PORTAL DESIGN

The service quality of heritage portal **e-tourism** is measured by metrics, such as response time, throughput, reliability, and availability. Response time is measured at the server side. From the user's side, the essential components of time are browser time, network access time at the client side, ISP time, Internet time, network access time at the server side, and server response time. Throughput is measured in requests per second or transactions per second, and determines the rate at which the system can adequately respond to requests. If the response time is high, the user may quit the session or wait if they have to use the system (Duffy & Dale, 2002). This implies that customers may leave the site and use other Web sites for information, thereby reducing the efficiency of the portal. The "quickness" of a Web site has an impact on the site's overall functionality (Ryan & Valverde, 2006).

Portal workloads consist of sessions. A session is defined as a sequence of requests made by a customer during a single visit to a site. Examples of requests made by an online shopper are browse, search, book flight and hotel room, register, and pay. An online trader may make requests, such as review hotel information, compare features and tariffs, gather flight information, review special events, and cultural information.

The **portal design** format can be classified as *basic, intermediate, standard, comprehensive,* and *integrated.* In *basic* information presentation layer, items such as company name, physical address, contact details, and area of business are provided. The *intermediate* level contains

items, such as annual report, e-mail contact, information on company activities, and basic product catalogs. The *comprehensive* Web portal includes hyperlinks to other online services, online enquiry features, chat rooms, discussion forums, multimedia, newsletters, and updates by e-mail services. The *integrated* format for a portal contains product catalogs, customer support, and value-added features like site map, secure online transactions, reservation status, and tracking. A **tourism portal** ideally should contain internal and external links for supplementary information to integrate value-added features. An example of such characteristic of the tourism industry includes location, map, climate, weather, currency converter, time zone information, itineraries, news and media releases, and photo gallery.

Portal Navigation Tool Design with Factor Analysis

In heritage **tourism e-portal**, factor analysis aims to reduce the number of Web **functionalities** or Web links in a system, and to detect structure in their relationships (Kostoff & Block, 2005). Correlations are computed, and highly correlated groups (factors) are identified. Factor analysis begins with **covariance** and correlation information between items or factors and attempts to identify compact set of items or factors that are interrelated. The factor analysis assumes that the **variance** of an item is integral of components of three **variances**: namely, by the contribution by one or more common factor or item that appear in more than one factors or items; the unique factor or item itself; and by the error **variance** due to measurement difficulty. The other assumption is that the correlations between two items or factors are equal to the sum of the cross product of their common-**factor loadings**.

In factor analysis, an un-rotated principal **components** define the general pattern of interaction in the data but the rotated principal **components** identify distinct **clusters** of associations. Table

Table 2a. Factor analysis of the portal functionality (Factor Loading)

Category of Portal Information	1	2	3	4	5
aa.) Hotel information	0.14	0.15	-0.15	0.13	0.55
ab.) Accommodation information, price, features of rooms, facility	-0.14	0.60	0.17	-0.32	-0.32
ac.) Restaurant guide	-0.37	0.12	0.44	0.04	-0.17
ad.) Price guide	0.62	0.06	0.10	-0.09	-0.27
ae.) Contact information	0.13	0.16	0.57	-0.04	-0.29
af.) Online reservation	0.55	0.27	-0.26	0.04	-0.28
fa.) Education Center	-0.12	-0.19	-0.10	-0.25	0.60
fb.) Business Center	-0.03	-0.01	0.30	-0.44	-0.22
fc.) Address - Resources	-0.04	0.46	-0.55	-0.06	0.12
fd.) Passport - Visa	0.20	0.03	0.05	0.08	0.06
ha.) Heritage attractions	-0.26	-0.08	-0.28	0.70	0.21
hb.) Castle, Museum, Monuments	0.19	-0.61	-0.12	-0.07	-0.18
hc.) Parks, Fauna, Flora	-0.36	-0.31	0.11	0.44	0.18
ia.) Tourist guide	0.41	-0.09	0.29	-0.34	0.08
ib.) Directories of attractions	-0.06	-0.17	-0.07	0.11	-0.11
ic.) WWW guide	0.62	0.01	0.17	0.09	0.19
id.) Calendar of events	-0.27	-0.10	0.10	0.15	0.56
ie.) Descriptions of local features	-0.26	0.01	0.03	-0.17	0.49
if.) Value added features (map, distance, news, currency information)	0.70	0.41	-0.08	-0.15	-0.18
ig.) Good still images/photos	-0.01	-0.04	0.00	0.63	-0.13
ih.) Availability of Web cam and images	0.20	0.29	0.35	0.00	0.12
ii.) Systematic link to other Web sites	0.10	0.33	0.51	0.13	-0.07
ij.) Web based inquiry form or order (gifts, product...)	0.46	0.47	-0.25	-0.10	-0.09
ik.) Interactive features (currency converter, weather, current	0.23	0.26	-0.15	-0.31	0.47
il.) On line customer support, FAQ, search engines,,,,	-0.76	-0.23	-0.16	0.22	-0.25
im.) Web Advanced features (e-mail updates, multimedia, chat,	-0.31	-0.50	0.03	0.23	0.08
in.) Secure on line payment	-0.19	-0.09	-0.28	-0.37	0.50
oa.) Easy Booking facility with the Web/portal	0.06	0.19	0.71	-0.04	-0.28
ob.) Payment system is online (yes/no)	0.15	-0.08	0.52	-0.51	0.18
oc.) Payment system by e-mail (yes/no)	-0.56	0.14	0.11	0.55	-0.03

continued on following page

Table 2a. continued

od.) Payment system by telephone (yes/no)	-0.18	0.50	-0.20	-0.16	-0.01
sa.) Musical	-0.43	0.02	-0.05	0.08	0.09
sb.) Folklore	-0.75	-0.04	-0.23	0.26	0.04
sc.) Theatre	-0.39	-0.11	0.54	0.20	0.31
sd.) Golf	0.04	-0.73	0.19	-0.06	0.22
se.) Boating	0.03	0.57	-0.18	0.00	0.10
sf.) Desert Safari	-0.05	-0.39	0.51	-0.13	0.27
sg.) Art Exhibitions	-0.10	-0.09	0.22	0.70	-0.20
va.) Simplicity & clear direction	0.06	0.17	-0.12	-0.17	0.63
vb.) Information are up to date, current	-0.18	0.24	0.52	-0.21	0.29
vc.) Comprehensive coverage, more information	0.11	-0.09	0.69	-0.03	0.13
vd.) Hyperlink to related Web	0.21	0.61	-0.19	0.29	0.28
wa.) Easy to access the Web	0.56	-0.10	-0.23	0.43	0.29
wb.) Easy to access information in this Web	0.27	0.48	-0.09	0.27	0.51
wc.) Format of site is consistent (font/color..)	0.05	0.03	-0.38	-0.69	0.14
wd.) Multiple way to access information in Web	-0.02	0.61	0.36	-0.26	0.16
we.) Interface for help, guide, information	0.14	0.71	0.15	-0.19	0.05

2a shows the factor **loading** results and Table 2b shows the results from the **varimax** orthogonal rotation of the components. The columns define the factors; the rows refer to variables. In the intersection of row and column is given the **loading** for the row variable on the column factor. The axes of the components are rotated to maximize the **variance** of the squared **loading** in each column. The objective of rotation is to identify distinct factors. The orthogonal rotation helps to minimize the number of variables that have high **loadings** on a factor to identify pattern among the factors. A clear grouping emerges from the rotation method as seen in Table 2b.

Factor analysis accounts for random error and invalidity to disentangle complex interrelationships into major and distinct regularities (Basilevsky, 1994). If we believe that portal functionality is interrelated in a complex fashion, then factor analysis can untangle the linear relationships into separate sub-patterns. Each pattern will depict a distinct **cluster** of interrelated portal **functionalities**. The ability to group browsing preferences into distinct categories and classify similar characteristics or features is the main idea behind the portal functionality layout design (Norm & Yaun, 2000). We utilize this approach to analyze interrelationships among different portal **functionalities** in order to account for those **functionalities** that are common in characteristics or preferred more favorably while browsing a portal.

Logically, applying factor analysis in the design of heritage **tourism portal** helps in constructing **clusters** in portal **navigation** tools. The information from factor analysis gives us an indication about how different heritage **tourism**

Table 2b. Factor analysis of the portal functionality (Varimax rotation)

Category of Portal Information	h²	Components				
		1	2	3	4	5
ad.) Price guide	0.53	0.62				
af.) Online reservation	0.42	0.55				
fd.) Passport - Visa	0.16	0.20				
hb.) Castle, Museum, Monuments	0.49	0.19				
ia.) Tourist guide	0.38	0.41				
ic.) WWW guide	0.25	0.62				
if.) Value added features (map, distance, news, currency info)	0.72	0.70				
sd.). Golf	0.57	0.04				
wa.) Easy access to the Web	0.61	0.56				
ab.) Accommodation information, price, features of rooms, facility	0.58		0.60			
ij.) Web based inquiry form or order (gifts, product, ...)	0..53		0.47			
se.) Boating	0.21		0.57			
vd.) Hyperlink to related Web	0.46		0.61			
wd). Multiple ways to access information in Web	0.63		0.61			
od.) Payment system by telephone	0.39		0.50			
we.) Interface for help, guide, information	0.58		0.71			
ac.) Restaurant guide	0.39			0.44		
ae.) Contact information	0.44			0.57		
fb.) Business center	0.29			0.30		
ih.) Availability of Web cam and images	0.28			0.35		
ii.) Systematic link to other Web sites	0.36			0.51		
oa.) Easy Booking facility with the Web/portal	0.65			0.71		
ob.)Payment system is online	0.44			0.52		
sc.) Theatre	0.55			0.54		
sf.) Desert safari	0.41			0.51		
vc.) Comprehensive coverage, more information	0.55			0.69		
vb.) Information are up to date, current	0.33			0.52		
ha.) Heritage attractions	0.62				0.70	
hc.) Parks, Fauna, Flora	0.45				0.44	
ib.) Directories of attractions	0.12				0.11	
ig.) Good still images/photos	0.53				0.63	
il.) Online customer support, FAQ, search engines,	0.69				0.22	
im.) Web Advanced features (e-mail updates, multimedia, chat, forum)	0.44				0.23	
oc.) Payment system by e-mail	0.54				0.55	
sa.) Musical	0.20				0.08	
sb.) Folklore	0.73				0.26	

continued on following page

Table 2b. continued

sg.) Art Exhibitions	0.53				0.70	
aa.) Hotel information	0.33					0.55
fa.) Education Center	0.33					0.60
fc.) Address - Resources	0.48					0.12
id.) Calendar of events	0.48					0.56
ie.) Description of local features	0.41					0.49
ik.) Interactive features (currency converter, weather, current evnt.)	0.45					0.47
va.) Simplicity & clear direction	0.42					0.63
wb.) Easy to access information in this Web	0.21					0.51
wc.) Format of site is consistent (font/color,....)	0.57					0.14
in.) Secure online payment	0.51					0.50

items are grouped. The process begins by finding a linear combination of heritage portal functionality as a **component** that accounts for as much variation in the identified portal functionality. Next, it identifies a dominant functionality or **component** that accounts for as much of the other preferences, but uncorrelated with the previously grouped functionality or **component**. The method continues in this way to account for as many remaining **functionalities** as possible to group from the original list.

In Table 2a, a total of 47 items are listed as portal functionality. In this application, five **cluster** components are defined as location guides (component 1), web accessibility (component 2), leisure sports (component 3), nature artifacts (component 4), and information resources (component 5).

These **clustered functionalities** describe the heritage portal **functionalities** under different groups. The first column shows the **communality** (h^2) that explains the amount of common **variance** in that item extracted by the factor analysis. For example, the item "ab" (accommodation information, price, features of rooms, facility) has 58 percent of **variance** extracted in that item due to

all five components. On the same row, component 2 shows factor **loading** with correlation of 0.6. It is the correlation between the second component, defined as **Web** accessibility and the item accommodation information. Alternatively, it is estimated that this **loading** alone accounts for 62 percent, computed as $0.6^2/0.58$; of the unique variance extracted in item "ab." The other unaccounted **variance** can be termed as error **variance** due to unreliability of the data gathering. As a matter of fact the **communality** can be expressed as $h^2 = \sum (\text{Loading})^2$. In this analysis, we include all the factor scores into considerations, since the objective here is to develop the portal **navigation Web** page sequence for all the factor **components**.

The first component, denoted as "location guide" is most highly correlated with the following information: price guide (ad), online reservation (af), passport-visa (fd), castle, museum, monuments (hb), tourist guide (ia), www guide (ic), value added features (if), and easy Web access to the Web (wa). While the interest in golf (sd) also belongs to this component, however, it has a very low correlation (0.04).

The second component, denoted as "Web accessibility" is most highly correlated with the following information: accommodation information (ab), Web based inquiry form (ij), boating (se), hyperlink to Web (vd), multiple Web access (wd), and Web interface (we).

In the third component "leisure sports," the information that are most highly correlated are restaurant guide (ac), contact information (ae), business center (fb), Web cam (ih), links to other Web (ii), booking facility (oa), online payment (ob), theatre (sc), desert safari (sf), and information-coverage (vc). It has been said that in the first component, golf has poor cluster membership due to a low score of 0.04. This could be merged with the third component, since similar functionality, theatre (sc), has a high score of 0.54. Also, it is logical to put boating (se) functionality with a high score of 0.57 belonging to second component to be merged in this group. This suggests that the navigation tool layout design would group the ecotourism related portal functionality in the third component.

The fourth component is denoted as "**nature artifacts**" and contains the following information:

heritage attraction (ha), park, fauna, flora (hc), directories of attraction (ib), images, photos (ig), online support (il), Web advanced features (im), electronic payment system (oc), musical (sa), folklore (sb), and art exhibition (sg). However, due to poor score for musical (sa) of 0.08, it is better to group this functionality in the third component. Since folklore (sb) is of similar functionality, it is also recommended to move it to third component.

Finally, the fifth component, "information resources," comprises of hotel information (aa), education center (fa), address (fc), calendar events (id), local features (ie), interactive features (ik), clear direction (va), easy access (wb), and format consistently (wc).

Figure 3 is a perceptual map developed using information of two factor loading bases on factors from component matrix. The figure shows portal functionalities placed in four sections namely A, B, C, and D. From the preceding analysis, it is seen that portal functionalities are grouped into five components. Observe that component number

Figure 3. Perceptual map of the portal functionality (Derived using two components)

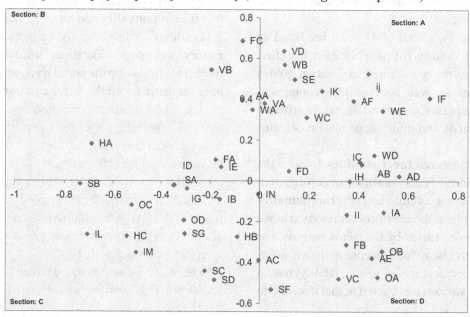

2 is placed in section A. Also, component 4 is placed in section C, except portal functionality HA is resting in Section B as an outlier. Similarly, component 3 is condensed in Section D except the functionality SC is an outlier in Section C, while component 5 is resting in Section A and B. Finally component 1 is scattered namely in Section A and D and few outliers in Section C. This perceptual map reveals that the portal functionalities are grouped in a manner of browsing preference and to the proximity of easy navigations.

Correlation Analysis to Support Portal Navigation Tool Design

Correlation refers to the degree of linear association between two or more portal **functionalities**. Two functionalities are positively correlated if both portal functionalities simultaneously move in same direction. On the other hand, if both variables tend to move in opposite direction, they are negatively correlated. Hence, if a higher preference in a portal functionality is identified with higher inclination for other **functionalities**, then the association between the two **functionalities** varies positively, and we denote this situation as positive **covariation** or **positive correlation**, even if the **functionalities** show weak correlation. The second possibility is that two portal **functionalities** vary inversely or oppositely. In this case, higher preference in one the functionality is associated with a lower preference against another, and vice versa. We denote this situation as negative covariation or **negative correlation**. The direction of association, therefore, provides guidelines to determine if two portal **navigation tools** should be identified together or apart. We deduce that if two portal **functionalities** are correlated, then the access to one influences the affinity to browse the other. The most common measure of association in this regard is the correlation, which measures the degree to which the relationship between the portal functions occurs (Basilevsky, 1994).

Using the correlation information, we would be confirming the results found in factor analysis in grouping the **navigation tools**. This is illustrated by looking into the correlation Table 3, which identifies negative and positive **correlations** between two or more navigation tools. In the remaining portion of this section, we will analyze the **correlation** results and demonstrate if the results support that found in factor analysis.

For instance from factor analysis results in Table 2b, it is found that the *tourist guide (ia), www guide (ic),* and *value added features (if)* items have *loading* 0.41, 0.62 and 0.7 respectively. These items are classed Location Guide or Component 1. The *correlation* in Table 3 suggests that the corresponding items, *www guide* (ic) and *tourist guide* (ia) are correlated positively with value 0.26. It is likely that a *Web* visitor would prefer that these two portal *functionalities* not only be in same access page but also browsing the related pages in sequence. Further, the items *Web advance features* (im) and *online customer support* (il) reveals a **correlation** of magnitude 0.36. Again, these two items are grouped into Component 4, defined as nature artifacts, with factor *loading* of 0.23 and 0.22 respectively as shown in Table 2b. Consequently, these two portal **functionalities** are *clustered* and browsed in sequence.

In Table 3, the sample segment of the portal functionality **correlation** at 0.05% significance level is listed. The correlation information is used to identify the inclination of a heritage portal user as to how the portal pages are to be sequenced and grouped. By observing the correlation information, potential portal layout functionality navigation tool position is suggested. For instance, if the portal function provides the *www guide (ic),* the portal user may not browse the *directories of attraction (*ib) because of the negative **correlation** between the two. Thus, while designing the navigation tool, it is undesirable to group the two *functionalities* together. It is also expected that the user would not browse the *directories of at-*

Table 3. Correlation of sample segment of heritage portal functionality (Significance 0.05%)

	a.) Tourist guide	b.) Directories of attractions	c.) WWW guide	d.) Calendar of events	e.) Descriptions of local features	f.) Value added features (map, distance, news, currency information)	g.) Good still images/photos	h.) Availability of web cam and images	i.) Systematic link to other web sites	j.) Web based inquiry form or order (gifts, product...)	k.) Interactive features (currency converter, weather, current event...)	l.) On line customer support, FAQ, search engines,...	m.) Web Advanced features (e-mail updates, multimedia, chat, forum)	n.) Secure on line payment	a.) Hotel information	b.) Accommodation information, price, features of rooms, facility	c.) Restaurant guide	d.) Price guide	e.) Contact information	f.) On-line reservation	a.) Musical	b.) Folklore	c.) Theatre	d.) Golf	e.) Boating
a.) Tourist guide	1.00																								
b.) Directories of attractions	-0.25	1.00																							
c.) WWW guide	0.26	-0.05	1.00																						
d.) Calendar of events	0.01	-0.11	-0.01	1.00																					
e.) Descriptions of local features	0.18	-0.12	-0.14	0.24	1.00																				
f.) Value added features (map, distance, news, currency information)	0.05	-0.08	0.46	-0.55	-0.30	1.00																			
g.) Good still images/photos	-0.22	0.20	-0.16	-0.09	-0.25	-0.04	1.00																		
h.) Availability of web cam and images	0.30	-0.15	0.39	0.23	-0.17	0.17	-0.10	1.00																	
i.) Systematic link to other web sites	0.27	0.13	0.27	-0.09	-0.20	0.08	0.12	0.42	1.00																
j.) Web based inquiry form or order (gifts, product...)	0.23	-0.04	0.08	-0.32	-0.18	0.53	0.23	0.19	0.06	1.00															
k.) Interactive features (currency converter, weather, current event...)	0.13	-0.24	0.15	0.00	0.10	0.28	-0.35	0.31	-0.06	0.24	1.00														
l.) On line customer support, FAQ, search engines,...	-0.36	0.17	-0.53	-0.11	0.01	-0.52	0.08	-0.23	-0.13	-0.39	-0.22	1.00													
m.) Web Advanced features (e-mail updates, multimedia, chat, forum)	-0.01	0.09	-0.32	0.28	-0.04	-0.56	0.20	-0.17	-0.23	-0.23	-0.26	0.36	1.00												
n.) Secure on line payment	0.06	-0.28	-0.12	-0.27	-0.02	0.00	-0.34	-0.19	-0.18	-0.19	-0.20	0.33	-0.24	1.00											
a.) Hotel information	-0.10	0.00	0.22	0.21	0.22	0.00	-0.16	-0.09	0.05	0.06	0.27	-0.27	0.10	-0.43	1.00										
b.) Accommodation information, price, features of rooms, facility	0.08	0.10	-0.09	-0.07	-0.10	0.17	-0.14	0.12	0.32	0.21	-0.06	-0.17	-0.21	0.01	-0.04	1.00									
c.) Restaurant guide	-0.16	0.21	-0.41	-0.28	-0.13	-0.13	0.39	-0.09	0.21	0.01	-0.32	0.31	0.30	-0.16	-0.17	0.17	1.00								
d.) Price guide	0.46	-0.04	0.11	-0.33	-0.38	0.42	-0.02	0.32	0.30	0.47	0.22	-0.32	-0.28	0.09	-0.27	-0.02	-0.04	1.00							
e.) Contact information	0.06	-0.16	0.07	-0.12	0.09	0.21	-0.12	0.19	0.15	-0.20	-0.03	-0.15	-0.20	0.07	0.00	0.24	0.09	0.11	1.00						
f.) On-line reservation	0.06	0.10	0.19	-0.30	-0.16	0.43	-0.13	0.10	-0.09	0.28	0.01	-0.24	-0.07	-0.03	0.12	-0.20	0.10	0.04	1.00						
a.) Musical	-0.13	0.20	0.06	0.05	-0.05	-0.29	-0.09	0.16	0.17	-0.02	0.17	0.42	0.17	-0.01	0.00	-0.04	0.15	-0.12	-0.36	-0.12	1.00				
b.) Folklore	-0.44	0.17	-0.32	0.20	0.02	-0.65	0.08	-0.18	0.01	-0.33	-0.22	0.69	0.31	0.04	0.17	0.01	0.18	-0.57	-0.37	-0.18	0.50	1.00			
c.) Theatre	-0.22	0.06	-0.08	0.15	0.27	-0.25	0.13	0.09	0.14	-0.32	0.02	0.28	0.06	-0.30	-0.13	-0.19	0.42	-0.19	0.10	-0.47	0.38	0.15	1.00		
d.) Golf	0.23	0.14	0.05	0.25	0.16	-0.25	-0.07	-0.06	-0.04	-0.37	-0.05	0.01	0.27	-0.12	0.04	-0.24	0.17	0.07	0.05	-0.34	-0.15	-0.17	0.18	1.00	
e.) Boating	-0.16	-0.15	-0.33	-0.03	0.21	0.23	-0.04	-0.02	-0.17	0.30	0.31	-0.06	-0.02	-0.11	0.34	0.23	0.09	0.02	0.22	0.34	-0.24	-0.13	-0.21	-0.28	1.00

traction (ib), while visiting the *calendar of events (id)*. Hence, when assigning the navigation tool in portal layout, these two *functionalities* should be separated. It should be noted that due to multicollineraity, there are some weak **correlation** among certain items. This does not prevent us to use these items in sequencing the pages. When a browser is navigating a *Web* page, the next expected page in hit sequence would be identified by a positive **correlational** measure in our study. Weak **correlational** measure would not deter us from concluding that these pages in hit sequence are uncorrelated, as long as the **correlation number** is positive.

A customer's requirement need for www guide (ic) links may make one to browse the value-added features (if) because of the positive correlation between the two. If a Web cam is available, then the customer may need to get more information from the systematic link to other Web sites (ii). More portal-based customer inquiry is expected from value-added features (if). If value-added features (if) are browsed, this means that there is less preference to browse calendar of events (id). This can be explained by the fact that the information available in value-added features (if) satisfies some of the requirements for calendar of events (id). We can also see that once the Web-based inquiry form or order (ij) is downloaded, the portal user is expected to browse the tourist guide (ia) as well. This implies that additional information is needed to fill the form. A customer is expected to navigate the calendar of event (id) portal page when accessing the description of local feature (ie) information because of the positive correlation between the two. The hotel information (aa) and secure online payment (in) show negative correlation with a value of -0.43; hence, some customer may not opt for Secure online payment (in) due to personal reservation. As a result, these navigation tools should not be in close proximity. The portal information price guide (ad) together with value-added feature (if) and Web-based inquiry form or order (ij) are correlated with values of 0.42 and 0.47 respectively. It is most likely that a potential customer would like to get more information about the Web based inquiry form or order (ij) with the value-added features (if) since the correlation is 0.53. This suggests that a user would browse the two pages in sequence. However, due to lack of confidence in secure online payment (in), there is also negative correlation with Web-based inquiry form or order (ij) with a correlation of −0.19. Further consideration in such behavior, a portal designer would tend to put this navigation tool in a different page. Additionally, price guide (ad) show negative correlations with online customer support (il) and with Web advance features (im) with values of −0.32 and −0.28 respectively. Consequently, there is reluctance to visit these pages in sequence. These examples illustrate the layout design principles of the portal navigation functionality tool. Table 2b shows how the factors are grouped along five components, after varimax rotation and the grouping of the functionalities are supported by correlation analysis. By combining the results of the correlation and factor analysis, this study provides us a more efficient way of sequencing the heritage tourism portal Web pages. From this analysis it is clear how the Web pages for the portal of heritage tourism are developed. This configuration or layout of Web navigation tool makes Web browsing easy, well organized, and convenient. The average predilection of a Web browser is incorporated in this analysis and design method. The ANOVA results, as shown in Table 4 suggest that the F-value (43.63) and P-value (almost 0) are significant and, therefore,

the data is reliable in this experiment. It is evident that the low magnitude of item variances and the mean support the reliability of the data (Table 1, Figure1, and Figure 2).

In factor analysis, we are regrouping the portal **functionalities** using the *survey* information. This implies that our initial logical grouping of eight components may change their association. Consequently, factor analysis regroups the *survey* information into five components, which are then redefined. The **correlation** analysis provides the internal and functional relationships among the constructs. **Correlation** (positive and negative) association between the portal **functionalities** is used to validate our results from factor analysis. Additional internal validity measures would be structural equation modeling, which is equivalent to confirmatory factor analysis in addition to other reliability measures.

FUTURE PROSPECTS

The future direction of tourism **portal design** is important for the continued growth of the tourism market. The design of **portal design** with structural equation modeling appears to be an attractive alternative area to explore (Wallgren & Hanse, 2007; So et al., 2005). Alternatively, the **clustering** (Menczer, 2004) and **perceptual map** methodology would be another way to design a portal. The potential exists among portal designers to apply innovative approaches in developing heritage tourism portals. For example, fuzzy c-means **clustering** (Ozer, 2005) has been shown to be efficient in grouping categories of people, and targeting specific information relevant to each group. As in the present study, heritage tourism portal designers should incorporate information given by tourists in their designs. Such an approach was successful in the design of an educational portal for middle school students by Large, Beheshti, and Cole (2002). The children's evaluation criteria of what constitutes an efficient

Table 4. ANOVA result with the portal dataset (Significance 0.05%)

Source of Variation	SS	df	MS	F	P-Value	F-criti.
Between Groups	1837.573	40	39.9473	43.6332	5.8E-233	1.37528
Within Groups	1245.112	1360	0.91552			
Total	3082.691	1400				

children's educational portal was integrated into the design. Additionally, conceptual models can be utilized in heritage tourism **portal design**, in order to enhance the effectiveness of information retrieval. Chen, Magoulas, and Dimakopoulos (2005), give such an example, which integrates users' cognitive styles (field dependent and field independent) in organizing subject categories, presentation of results, and screen layout in an Internet portal. These design measures will be useful in producing an ideal set of **functionalities** from which an optimal heritage tourism portal can be developed. It will also facilitate the projected growth of the tourism market, which is expected to reach 1.6 billion international arrivals by 2020 (WTO, 2006).

CONCLUSION

This study illustrates how to design portal navigation tools for the heritage tourism industry. A **survey** instrument identifying the major heritage *Web* **functionalities** is developed. Data from the **survey** instrument is used to group related **portal functionalities** using factor and correlation factor analysis. The factor analysis results provide information about the **functionalities'** groups and the correlation values in Table 3 helps in sequencing the portal navigation tools. The factor **loadings** from Table 2b provide the **functionalities'** groupings. From the initial groupings of eight functionality dimensions from the **survey** instrument, factor analysis identifies five major components from the **survey** items. **Correlation** analysis

indicates how two **functionalities** are related with each other based on available information, and hence how the pages of a heritage tourism portal should be sequenced. Consequently, **factor** and **correlation** analysis show how the *Web* navigation tool is designed. **ANOVA** analysis supports the reliability of the data used in the study. Additionally, a perceptual map is used to validate the groupings of the functionalities in the study. These results provide a clear picture of how the heritage tourism Web pages should be sequenced.

The goal of a tourism **portal design** is to increase the effective dissemination of information to potential visitors or tourists, in order to attract them to a country and make their visit as trouble free as possible, while contributing to local economic development. Implementation of e-government and **e-commerce** policies is an indication of innovative governance that enhances the delivery of goods and services to citizens (Wimmer et al., 2003). A coherent tourism policy should ensure that governments and the tourism industry design heritage tourism portals that are user friendly and easily accessible by users. **Portal design** that clusters relevant tourism information enhances user-friendliness and effective retrieval of information. Such measures would assist tourists in their planning and decision making process.

Since tourism, and especially **heritage/eco-tourism**, is a major source of income for governments around the world, any effort to facilitate its development should be part of governments' strategic plan towards economic, social, and cultural development (Koh, Prybutok, Ryan, &

Ibragimova, 2006). Most studies indicate that privacy of personal information rank among the top issues that concern *Web* users (see Flavian et al., 2006; Graeff & Harmon, 2002). Thus, it is essential that stringent policies be put in place regarding the use and dissemination of personal information of users of *Web* portals.

A heritage portal aims to be a means of attracting visitors to a country by host governments. Thus, governments need to ensure that visitors have a comfortable experience during their stay in the country. Governments should establish a code of practice for the tourism industry to ensure that the industry operates within the bounds of norms and the law. Such a measure calls for adequate training of all heritage tourism operators on issues ranging from customer relations to business ethics. Additionally, heritage tourism operators should be required to carry enough liability insurance coverage for potential injuries or fatalities of tourists that may be in their care. Injuries and fatalities among participants of certain tourism activities, such as adventure, heritage, **ecotourism**, have the potential to seriously impact on a country's tourism industry (Bentley, Page, & Laird, 2000; Hsieh, Lai, & Shi, 2006). Furthermore, the heritage tourism industry should develop its own sets of voluntary self-regulatory practices (a self-imposed code of conduct) that strive to make the industry as efficient as possible. While government regulatory approach may be necessary, it is also advisable for the industry to establish "best practices" that reflect the goals of the industry to enhance the experience of visitors (Sorice et al., 2006), and encourage return visits by tourists. Positive tourist experience is a good marketing tool that adds value by improving the image of the tourism industry (Forsyth, 1997; Hwang et al., 2006; Rugendyke et al., 2005).

To ensure that high standards are met, strict quality control measures should be put in place for all elements of business activities included in the portal. This may include periodic checks or audits on facilities or businesses that are part of

the tourism industry to ensure proper compliance. Successful tourism development in emerging locations is predicated on a range of issues, such as clear tourism objectives, integration of these into national plans, local investment and control, and tourism entrepreneurship (Dieke, 2003; Font, Tapper, & Cochrane, 2006; Neto, 2003; Yasin, Alavi, Sobral, & Lisboa, 2003).

REFERENCES

Basilevsky, A. (1994). *Statistical factor analysis and related methods: Theory and applications.* New York: John Wiley.

Bastmeijer, K, & Roura, R. (2004). Regulating antarctic tourism and the precautionary principle. *The American Journal of International Law, 98*(4), 763-781.

Bentley T, Page, S., & Laird, S. (2000). Safety in New Zealand's adventure tourism industry: The client accident experience of adventure tourism operators. *Journal of Travel Medicine, 7*(5), 239-246.

Bhatt, G., & Emdad, A. (2001). An analysis of the virtual value chain in electronic commerce. *Logistics Information Management, 14*(1), 78-85.

Chakrabarti, S., Joshi, M., Punera, K., & Pennock, D. (2002). The structure of broad topics on the Web. In D. Lassner, D. De Roure, & A. Iyengar (Eds.), *Proceedings of the 11th International World Wide Web Conference* (251-262), New York: ACM Press.

Chen, S., Magoulas, G., & Dimakopoulos, D. (2005). A flexible interface design for Web directories to accommodate different cognitive styles. *Journal of the American Society For Information Science And Technology, 56*(1), 70-83.

Chiou, J., & Shen, C. (2006). The effects of satisfaction, opportunism, and asset specificity on consumers' loyalty intention toward internet portal sites. *International Journal of Service Industry Management, 17*(1), 7-22.

Chou, T., Hsu, L. Yeh, Y., & Ho, C. (2005). Towards a framework of the performance evaluation of SMEs' industry portals. *Industrial Management and Data Systems, 105*(4), 527-544.

Dieke, P. (2003). Tourism in Africa's economic development: Policy implications. *Management Decision, 41*(3), 287-295.

Duffy, G., & Dale, B. (2002). E-commerce processes: A study of criticality. *Industrial Management and Data Systems, 102*(8), 432-441.

Elovici, Y., Glezer, C., & Shapira, B. (2005). Enhancing customer privacy while searching for products and services on the World Wide Web. *Internet Research, 15*(4), 378-399.

Flavian, C., & Guinaliu, M. (2006). Consumer trust, perceived security, and privacy policy: Three basic elements of loyalty to a Web site. *Industrial Management and Data Systems, 106*(5), 601-620.

Font, X., Tapper, R., & Cochrane, J. (2006). Competitive strategy in a global industry: Tourism. *Handbook of Business Strategy, 7*(1), 51-55.

Forsyth, T. (1997). Environmental responsibility and business regulation: The case of sustainable tourism. *The Geographic Journal, 163*(3), 270-280.

Graeff, T., & Harmon, S. (2002). Collecting and using personal data: Consumers' awareness and concerns. *Journal of Consumer Marketing, 19*(4), 302-318.

Hill T., Etienne, N., & Trotter, D. (2006). Small-scale, nature-based tourism as a pro-poor development intervention: Two examples in Kwazulu-Natal, South Africa. *Singapore Journal of Tropical Geography, 27*(2), 163-175.

Hsieh, C., Lai, F., & Shi, W. (2006). Information orientation and its impacts on information

asymmetry and e-business adoption: Evidence from China's international trading industry. *Industrial Management and Data Systems, 106*(6), 825-840.

Hwang, L., & Lockwood. A. (2006). Understanding the challenges of implementing best practices in hospitality and tourism SMEs. *Benchmarking: An International Journal, 13*(3), 337-354.

Javalgi, R., & Ramsey, R. (2001). Strategic issues of e-commerce as an alternative global distribution system. *International Marketing Review, 18*(4), 376-391.

Koh, C., Prybutok, V., Ryan, S., & Ibragimova, B. (2006). The importance of strategic readiness in an emerging e-government environment. *Business Process Management Journal, 12*(1), 22-33.

Kostoff, R., & Block, J. (2005). Factor matrix text filtering and clustering. *Journal of the American Society for Information Science and Technology, 56*(9), 946-968.

Large, A., Beheshti, J., & Cole, C. (2002). Information architecture for the Web: The IA matrix approach to designing children's portals. *Journal of the American Society For Information Science And Technology, 53*(10), 831-838.

Law, R., & Hsu, C. (2005). Customers' perceptions on the importance of hotel Web site dimensions and attributes. *International Journal of Contemporary Hospitality Management, 17*(6), 493-503.

Lee, C. (2001). An analytical framework for evaluating *e-commerce* business Models. *Internet Research: Electronic Networking Applications and Policy, 11*(4), 349-359.

Lee, G., & Lin, H. (2005). Customer perceptions of e-service quality in online shopping. *International Journal of Retail and Distribution Management, 33*(2), 161-176.

Lu, J., & Lu, Z. (2004). Development, distribution, and evaluation of online tourism services in China. *Electronic Commerce Research, 4*(3), 221-239.

Mastny, L. (2002). *Ecotourism* trap. *Foreign Policy, 42*(133), 94-96.

McDavid, H., & Ramajeesingh, D. (2003). The state and tourism: A Caribbean perspective. *International Journal of Contemporary Hospitality Management, 15*(3), 180-183.

Menczer, F. (2004). Lexical and semantic clustering by Web links. *Journal of the American Society for Information Science and Technology, 55*(14), 1261-1269.

Moon, M., & Norris, D. (2005). Does managerial orientation matter? The adoption of reinventing government and e-government at the municipal level. *Information Systems Journal, 15*(1), 43-60.

Munoz, M. (2005). Executive insights on globalization: implications for hospitality managers in emerging locations. *International Journal of Contemporary Hospitality Management, 17*(4), 365-371.

Neto, F. (2003). A new approach to sustainable tourism development: Moving beyond environmental protection. *Natural Resources Forum, 27*(1), 212-222.

Norm A., & Yuan, Y. (2000). Managing business-to-business relationships throughout the *e-commerce* procurement life cycle. *Internet Research: Electronic Networking Applications and Policy, 10*(5), 385-395.

Ozer, M. (2005). Fuzzy c-means clustering and Internet portals: a case study. *European Journal of Operational Research, 164*(3), 696-714.

Priskin, J. (2003). Issues and opportunities in planning and managing nature-based tourism in the Central Coast Region of Western Australia. *Australian Geographical Studies, 41*(3), 270-286.

Puhretmair, F., & Woess, W. (2001). XML-based integration of GIS and heterogeneous tourism information systems. *Lecture Notes in Computer Science*, 2068, 346. Heidelberg: Springer Publishing.

Puhretmair, F., Rumetshofer, H., & Schaumlechner, E. (2002). Extended decision- making in tourism information systems. *Lecture Notes in Computer Science*, 2455, 57. Heidelberg: Springer Publishing.

Rayport, J., & Jaworski, F. (2000). *E-Commerce.* New York: McGraw-Hill/Irwin.

Rugendyke, B., & Son, N. (2005). Conservation costs: Nature-based tourism as development at Cuc Phuong National Park, Vietnam. *Asia Pacific Viewpoint, 46*(2), 185-200.

Ryan, G., & Valverde, M. (2006). Waiting in line for online services: A qualitative study of the user's perspective. *Information Systems Journal, 16*(2), 181-211.

So, W., Wong, T., & Sculli, D. (2005). Factors affecting intentions to purchase via the internet. *Industrial Management and Data Systems, 105*(9), 1225-1244.

Sorice, M., Shafer, C., & Ditton, R. (2006). Managing endangered species within the use preservation paradox: The Florida manatee (trichechus manatus latirostis) as a tourism attraction. *Environmental Management, 37*(1), 69-83.

Thomas, R., & Thomas, H. (2006). Micro politics and micro firms: A case study of tourism policy formation and change. *Journal of Small Business and Enterprise Development, 13*(1), 100-114.

Wallgren, L., & Hanse, J. (2007). Job characteristics, motivators and stress among technology consultants: A structural equation modeling approach. *International Journal of Industrial Engineers, 37*(1), 51-59.

Wickramasinghe, L., Amarasin, R., & Alahakon, L. (2004). A hybrid intelligent multiagent system for e-business. *Computational Intelligence, 20*(4), 603-623.

Wimmer, M., & Holler, U. (2003). Applying a holistic approach to develop user-friendly customer-oriented e-government portal interfaces. *Lecture Notes in Computer Science, 2615,* 167-178. Heidelberg: Springer Publishing.

Woess, W., & Dunzendorfer, A. (2002). Homogeneous EDI between Web-based tourism information systems. *Lecture Notes in Computer Science, 2455*(1), 183. Heidelberg: Springer Publishing.

World Tourism Organization (WTO). (2006). *Tourism highlights: 2006*. Madrid: WTO.

Wu, J., & Chang, Y. (2005). Towards understanding members' interactivity, trust, and flow in online travel community. *Industrial management and Data Systems, 105*(7), 937-954.

Yasin, M., Alavi, J., Sobral, F., & Lisboa, J. (2003). Realities, threats, and opportunities facing the Portuguese tourism industry. *International Journal of Contemporary Hospitality Management, 15*(4), 221-225.

Section II
IT Management and Corporate Governance

Chapter IV
Effectiveness of Information Technology Governance:
Perceptions of Board Directors and Senior Managers

Fang Zhao
RMIT University, Australia

Adela J. McMurray
RMIT University, Australia

Mark Toomey
Infonomics Pty Ltd., Australia

ABSTRACT

IT governance is viewed as a managerial innovation, which responds to the needs of strong leadership, strategic direction, and control from the highest level within an organization. In today's business world, most organizations depend on information technology (IT) for their day-to-day activities and attainment towards their future business strategies. However, despite improved project management, according to KPMG the track record of IT initiatives in many organizations is not strong, and many fail—particularly when measured against the outcomes they were intended to produce. Recent studies have found "an IT attention deficit" at board level, despite calls for directors to consider a wide range of IT matters including governance. This chapter examines practices and frameworks for effective IT governance in industry and business settings. Utilizing a multi-method research approach comprised of survey and interview techniques, 20 board directors' and senior mangers' perceptions of IT governance and management were sought and analyzed. The findings show there is a need and opportunity for improvement in IT governance and that in most organizations, Australian Standard AS8015-2005—provides a sound foundation for such improvement.

INTRODUCTION

Today's leading companies embrace information technology not as a means of cost-cutting, but as a tool for generating innovation, business success, and sustainability. Innovation is viewed as an essential element in the entrepreneurial process (Schaper & Volery, 2003) and creates benefits to the organization, which often manifest themselves in an economy's wealth creation. Innovation is linked to knowledge and learning and is frequently viewed as an organization's capability, knowledge asset and resource, which, in a global marketplace, provide new platforms for competitive advantage that others find difficult to replicate (McMurray & Dorai, 2003).

Studies show that the key success factor of information technology (IT) use is strongly linked to effectiveness of **IT governance** (Toomey, 2006). The IT literature is predominantly focused on outcomes addressing tangibles such as key performance indicators and innovation. International competitiveness, innovation capacity, and sustainability of industry and business are significantly influenced by the ability to develop and harness the power of IT. While IT has created abundant business opportunities, it has also rendered many traditional business management models obsolete. For example, IT requires digital transformation and profound changes in corporate governance, organizational internal and external business structure, including strategy (Zhao, 2006) and furthermore require an organizational culture embracing such values, attitudes, and beliefs to become embedded in and move across traditional organizational boundaries (McMurray, Cross, & Caponecchia, 2007). Recent proposed new initiatives under development to promote best practice in corporate governance of investment projects involving IT in Australia are evidenced in Australian Standard AS8015:2005 (Standards Australia, 2005).

This study examines directors' and senior managers' perceptions of IT governance in terms of effective structures, systems, processes for corporate monitoring, and the governance of IT in their organizations. The findings of the study may be used to inform organizational policies, procedures, and practices that will lead to the development of sustainable business practices through responsible IT governance that reflect the interests of all stakeholders. The study is significant given the current global trend of the booming e-business and IT economy and the increasingly dominant roles that IT plays in helping organizations improve the efficiency and productivity of their business. The study assists board directors and senior managers to formulate and implement effective strategies to align and integrate technology, operation, strategy, structure, culture, and human resources in IT governance. The findings provide a greater understanding of the important issues involved in IT governance and management within industry and business contexts.

LITERATURE REVIEW

IT Governance Definition Issues

Australian Standard AS8015-2005 (Standards Australia, 2005, p6) defines: "Corporate governance of information and communication technology is the system by which an organization's current and future use of IT is directed and controlled. It involves evaluating and directing the plans for the use of IT to support the organization and monitoring this use to achieve plans. It includes the strategy and policies for using IT within an organization." The definition provides a straightforward and clear meaning of IT governance, linking it explicitly to the common definition of corporate governance originally credited to Sir Adrian Cadbury. The AS8015 definition makes explicit reference to a "system." A system is comprised of processes, people (including structure and skills), and tools, or technology.

Thus, an organization's system of governance for IT would include processes, roles and tools to enable the organization to plan, control and monitor its use of IT.

However, there has been no consensus on the definitions of IT governance in industry and academia (Webb, Pollard, & Ridley, 2006). A number of definitions refer to the role of the board and top management whilst other definitions focus primarily on the role of management, and technology managers. This lack of shared understanding and clarity has created confusion in both the literature and the workplace. The confusion is compounded when service and product companies use the words "governance" and "management" interchangeably. In reality, much of what is referred to as governance is in fact a management responsibility, which may be overseen by the governing body as part of an overall system of governance (Toomey, 2006). For example, a director of a large Australian government agency made the following remarks in reference to IT governance:

Effective IT governance is a key to the effective delivery of IT to our organization. The purpose of IT governance is to ensure that all IT endeavours are effectively managed and that IT's performance meets the following objectives:

- *IT is aligned with the business*
- *IT enables the business to maximise benefits*
- *IT resources are used responsibly*
- *IT risks are managed appropriately.*

The Need for IT Governance

The role of the board of companies (particularly public listed companies) is under increasing scrutiny and hence subject to new legislated demands and increasingly subject to regulatory intervention. Understandably there has been a growing demand from various quarters for boards to be involved in governing their organization's use of IT. These demands are driven by the long-term failure of organizations to resolve poor performance in the delivery of IT projects, combined with increasing dependence on IT for their day to day operations. Project failures mean that money spent on the projects is wasted, and that the expected rewards of the investment are not realized (Auditor-General, 2003). In many cases, operational failures have significant financial consequences (Luciw, 2004) as in some organizations IT accounts for approximately 50% of their capital spending (PRO:NED, 2007). Therefore, some failures have life-or-death consequences for the company and for people (Australian Pharmaceutical Industries, 2006).

Studies show that industries and businesses have varied considerably in terms of their IT performance. According to a McKinsey study, "after spending $7.6 billion on IT between 1995 and 2000, the lodging industry experienced no increase in revenue and no increase in productivity" (cited in King, 2007, p. 2). On the contrary, some businesses and industries are making significant improvement in productivity through IT and achieving new revenue streams and competitive advantage (King, 2007). Many consulting organizations and researchers have explored the frequency, cause, and impact of IT failures, and particularly IT projects. KPMG state that despite improved project management, failure rates remain constant. Furthermore, Gartner estimated that in 2001, US$500 billion was wasted on failed IT initiatives (Gartner Group, 2002). The long-running Standish Chaos Report stated that only 16.2% of projects were successful in 1994 (on time and on budget) (Standish Group, 1994). In 2004, Standish detailed 28% were successful, a reduction from 34% in the previous year (cited in Hayes, 2004). One should note that there is an inconsistency in the Standish reporting of these figures where in one case the averages were reported as high yet careful reading uncovered that during the IT investment downturn, fewer and less adventurous projects were undertaken and there was an expectation that performance would deteriorate again as investment rates ramped up. Hence inconsistencies in the reporting of the averages of these figures should be viewed with caution. Moreover, KPMG clearly state that the measure of success is shifting from "on time, on budget" as assessed by Standish, to "achievement of intended outcomes," which the authors believe Standish overlook.

KPMG (2005) assert "Failure rates are still appalling," and "Many organizations do not focus on realising or measuring benefits." Huff, Maker, and Munro (2006) researched the extent to which boards actually understand and address IT issues. They found an "IT attention deficit," with boards attending only to IT risk and mostly failing to address IT in the context of vision, strategy, competitive advantage, effectiveness, and major project decisions. KPMG recommended board level governance as essential: "The key element (that makes some organizations more successful) appears to be an appropriate governance framework—to complement planning and prioritisation of activities and to help ensure execution controls are in place until benefits are realized." Their nomination of board responsibility was direct and explicit: "The board must put in place, through management, a rigorous oversight framework to monitor achievement of budgets, the meeting of timelines and to help ensure that the agreed benefits are realized. To achieve this, the board must receive the right information at the right time."

KPMG's assertions are entirely consistent with the findings of Weill and Ross (2004), that organizations with effective IT governance produced not only better success rates for IT, but also better overall corporate performance. Consequently, there is a growing trend towards boards undertaking a much higher level of governance relating to their IT investment (PRO:NED, 2007, p. 1).

The importance of IT governance has led to a series of publications by interested parties and regulative bodies to address the need for directors and their managers to better understand the need for, and nature of IT governance. The international IT Governance Institute (ITGI) publishes a range of papers including the "*Board Briefing on IT Governance*" (IT Governance Institute, 2007). CPA Australia published "*IT Governance: A Practical Guide for Company Directors and Corporate Executives.*" Standards Australia published AS8015-2005: Corporate Governance of Information and Communication Technology.

Key Themes of Australian Standard AS8015-2005

Australian Standard AS8015-2005 was developed with a view to improving the performance of organizations in their use and delivery of information and communication technology—areas where there are historically significant levels of underperformance across many organizations in both private and public sectors. AS8015 provides guidance to directors and to those who advise directors—typically the members of the executive management team, but also members of steering groups, specialists, suppliers and service providers, auditors, and other advisors.

AS8015 recommends that directors (the members of the most senior governing body of an organization) should evaluate, direct, and monitor the organization's use of IT. This would be supported by PRO:NED (2007). It also notes that directors may delegate their responsibility, but not their accountability (Standards Australia, 2005). In the normal course of events, the detail of governance processes is invariably the responsibility of managers within the organization. But the directors should always be aware of IT governance, and assure themselves that the processes are delivering the required outcomes.

It should be noted that AS8015 is designed to provide guidance rather than to define rigid rules for compliance. It is therefore open to the directors and managers of organizations to determine exactly how they will implement their approach to the corporate governance of IT.

The introduction to AS8015 describes a set of broad characteristics of good IT governance practice. AS8015 presents a framework of three key tasks for governing IT:

- Evaluate the use of IT
- Direct preparation and implementation of plans and policies
- Monitor conformance to policies and performance against the plans

There are six principles in AS8015 to guide directors and the executive in the conduct of these tasks as follows:

1. Establish clearly understood responsibilities for IT
2. Plan IT to best support the organization;
3. Acquire IT validly
4. Ensure that IT performs well, whenever required
5. Ensure IT conforms with formal rules
6. Ensure IT use respects human factors (Standards Australia, 2005)

Many of these processes would be viewed as the domain of management. The role of the board would be defined as part of the system of governance for IT, but it would not typically require the board to participate in the detail of the system. Within this system model, it is critical that there are appropriate and effective channels of communication between the overseeing body (the board) and management. If the channels are inadequate, management may not be aware of strategy and policy, and the board may not have adequate visibility of what is happening. The design of the communication channels, and many of the processes in the system, will depend significantly on the overall nature of the organization. For example, in smaller organizations, as reflected in the experience of a small government agency, the emphasis in governance may be quite

different to that of a larger organization, and the actual role of the executive and board may vary from one of significant engagement to one of quite high level oversight. As Weill et al. (2004) found, any design can be quite effective. What is important is that the chosen design works, and that, at the top of the governance model, there is sufficient oversight to ensure that the system is functioning appropriately.

The context for the application of AS8015 in terms of **entrepreneurship and innovation** is critical in the way an organization considers which IT innovations facilitate their competitive performance and hence advantage in the market place through competition, economic welfare and hence overcoming market monopoly (Teece, 2002). Many established methodologies and management standards concentrate on the processes for delivering an organization's IT capability whereas AS8015 focuses on the macro picture of the management system in which the organization determines how it will use IT i.e. demand drives supply and is the dominant focus of the standards to date.

From the brief overview of the purposes and coverage of AS8015, the standard should be a recommendable performance measurement and problem diagnostic instrument for IT governance. This study employed the AS8015 framework in developing its survey tool and some of its interview questions. Further detail and the results of the study are discussed in the following sections of the chapter.

RESEARCH METHOD

This study implemented a multi-method research design comprised of a questionnaire and supported by semi-structured interviews so as to capture a wider spectrum of views and in-depth insights into IT governance. A multi-method research design not only overcomes the weaknesses of each of the individual approaches, but also enhances theory building, hypothesis testing, and generalizing (McMurray, Pace, & Scott, 2004).

In 2005, a 32 item questionnaire was designed by Infonomics and was based on AS8015, so as to elicit director, chief executive and other executive views on the governance systems in place within their organizations. The 32 items were designed to collect both quantitative and qualitative data where the items were anchored to a numerical scale of 6 and included opportunities for inserting open ended comments. Since its inception two years ago, the questionnaire has been administered to more than 230 clients in numerous industry sectors.

As this was a preliminary study, a systematic random sample size of sixty respondents, drawn from a networked list of 175 companies, was deemed as being a sufficient number to conduct this exploratory research. The sixty questionnaires were mailed to a random population sample comprised of non-executive directors, chief executives, senior executives, and chairmen employed in both public and private sectors.

A 30% response rate yielded 20 responses, which, according to the literature, is more than an acceptable response rate in postal survey research method techniques (Hair, Anderson, Tatham, & Black, 1998). The respondents consisted of 11 non-executive directors, four chief executives, five other senior executives (none of whom has a CIO type responsibility), and one non-executive director (a chairman). The nineteen organizations represented in the survey ranged from a small research and development company to major national and trans-national organizations. The list included privately held, listed and government-owned enterprises, substantial not-for-profit organizations, local government, a statutory authority, banking and insurance, logistics, business services, and education. The survey data was analyzed utilizing descriptive statistics.

To add depth and richness to the survey data, a series of seven, semi-structured, one-hour interviews were conducted. Of the seven male interviewees, five were managers and/or executive directors and two were non-executive directors of the board. The seven interviewees were from six various organizations of which three were large, two were medium-sized, and one was small. The key questions asked in the interviews were concentrated on the following areas which are consistent with the aims of this study:

- Effectiveness of IT governance
- Effective IT governance and management structure, process and system
- IT governance and IT management
- Implementation of AS8015-2005

The qualitative data was content analyzed, which gave greater weight to the analysis of latent content and the larger discourse themes conveyed through the participants' responses to interview schedules, rather than on literal characteristics of content. A summary of results are presented and discussed in terms of the main themes drawn from the content analysis of the interview transcripts.

FINDINGS AND DISCUSSION

This section summarizes and discusses the key findings from the 20 surveys and 7 interviews. The results of the survey present the current IT governance status and performance of the organizations studied against AS8015-2005, while the interview findings identify and portray some frameworks and good practices in terms of effective governance of IT.

Survey Findings

Performance Against IT Governance Indictors

The respondents ranked their organizations' performance against the Australian Standards

AS8015-2005 twelve IT governance indicators, which identify the outcomes that should be produced by an effective system in pursuit of IT governance. The 12 indicators are:

- IT governance system
- Management compliance with the system
- Effective protection against the likelihood of IT failures
- Informing & engaging managers and directors in key IT decisions
- Dependence of ongoing business operations on IT understood
- Continuity & sustainability of business through IT use
- Alignment of IT capability to business need
- IT resource allocation
- Appropriate use of IT in business innovation
- Demonstrated investment value of IT
- Capability to deploy new IT initiatives
- Control of IT related business risks.

In this study, the overall ranking of organizational performance against the 12 indicators of IT governance was just above basic, as detailed in Figure 1. The survey found that, while directors placed a great deal of reliance on management, the formal systems of management were often inadequate. Only five respondents claimed a well-developed system of governance for IT, and only six confirmed that management complied with the system. Despite these weaknesses, many felt that management and directors were properly engaged and informed. Perhaps surprisingly, the high score suggests that respondents were most comfortable regarding the risks their organizations took with IT, despite their being less certain about whether they had effective protection against failures and whether IT was used appropriately to protect business continuity and sustainability.

Considerable scope exists for organizations to deliver more value from investing in IT and using it for business innovations. These improvements, along with better IT business alignment, better allocation of resources, and demonstrated

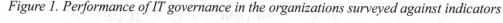

Figure 1. Performance of IT governance in the organizations surveyed against indicators

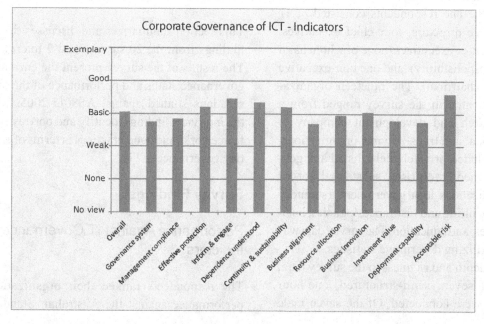

capacity to successfully deploy new initiatives should correspond to the development of more effective systems of governance, in which all managers understand and perform their appropriate IT roles.

Performance Against IT Governance Principles

The Australian Standard AS8015-2005 defines six IT governance principles which relate to responsibility for IT (responsibility); proper planning IT use (plan); How IT is acquired (acquire); performance of IT in business use (perform); IT conformance with regulations and policies (conform); and how the relationship between IT and people is managed (human factors).

The principles do not prescribe approach to IT, but instead specify matters that should be addressed effectively in any system of governance. The standard is addressed to directors as the members of the most senior governing body of the organization, and those informing, assisting and advising the directors. This includes the organization's management and committees or groups formed by management to oversee the use and delivery of IT.

One of the aims of AS8015 is to provide a basis for objective evaluation of the corporate governance of IT (Standards Australia, 2005). The authors used AS8015 as the basis for the survey—an 18 point test of the extent to which the respondents thought that their organizations were effective in evaluating, directing and monitoring the use of IT in respect to the six principles. As shown in Figure 2, the overall performance against the AS8015 principles is consistent (ranking marginally lower) with that established against the "indicators."

Again, the responses suggest considerable scope for improvement. Even the strongest area—acquiring IT validly, requires improvement. Comments made by a number of the respondents include:

- Rational grounds for commitments to invest in IT considering risk, priority, capacity, and value for money
- Proper disciplines with complete audit trails and documentation for acquiring and developing IT assets

Figure 2. Performance of IT governance in the organizations surveyed against principles

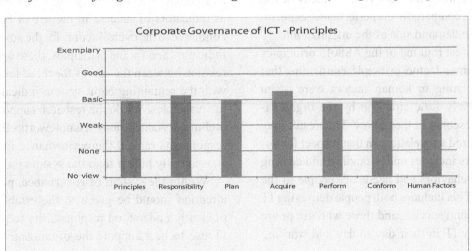

Figure 3. Comparison of IT governance and IT performance for 19 organizations

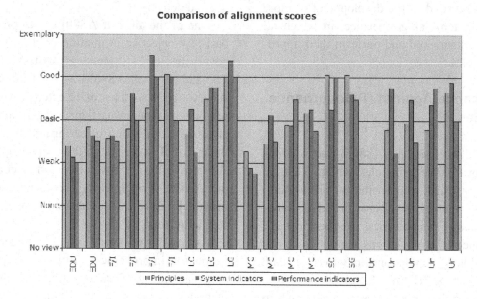

Assurance that the organizations long term interests are protected

It is remarkable that, while IT service organizations frequently invest heavily in performance measurement and management of systems and infrastructure, the survey responses scored the Perform principle second lowest overall. As respondents to the survey were virtually all business executives and directors, this suggests that a gulf remains between the performance focus of the supply side, compared to the performance expectations of the demand side of the organization.

The lowest ranking of the AS8015 principles was the human factors principle, confirming that aspects relating to human factors were given comparatively little attention by the organizations represented in the survey. This result may be considered a revelation, in that respect for human factors includes understanding and dealing with the behaviors and needs of "people in the process." This includes both people delivering IT capability and service, and those who use or are affected by IT in their day to day and working

lives. A failure to attend to human factors would include, for example, a failure to attend to proper business process change management to complement a new IT system.

IT Performance and Governance Performance

Four of the governance indicators (business alignment, business innovation, investment value, and deployment capability) may be considered as indicators of success in the use of IT. When compared to the overall scores for the governance indicators and for the principles, there was a correlation between the scores for these four points with the remaining eight system indicators and the principles. While the research supports only preliminary conclusions, it is noteworthy that three respondents ranked the performance indicators substantially higher than the system indicators.

Within the system of governance, particular attention should be given to the establishment of clearly understood responsibility to planning IT use to best support the organization, being more deliberate and precise in deciding to invest in IT, ensuring that IT performs well whenever required, ensuring that IT conforms with formal rules and, most particularly ensuring that human factors, including communication, engagement, training, and support are appropriately considered. Improving IT governance ought to begin with a sound understanding of the role of IT in the organization's business. Furthermore, it should clearly establish the role of the board where the directors establish the overall tone of the governance system by emphasising its goals.

While the survey provides some initial insight into the IT governance of nineteen diverse organizations, it ought to be noted that the view of the individual respondents may not in all cases be an accurate reflection of the status of the corresponding organizations. More comprehensive surveys within a single organization generally provide stronger insight into the organization's reality, taking into account the broad spectrum of views from a representative sample.

Interview Findings

The fundamental research question underpinning this study was "What is an effective IT governance framework?" Table 1 summarizes the views of the directors and senior managers that were interviewed about what key attributes they perceived as being important elements within an effective IT governance framework. The summary is illustrated by key quotes elicited from the interviews and lays the foundation for the theme category analysis in this study.

Table 1. Directors' and senior managers' perceptions on an effective it governance framework

Theme	Success Factors and Good Practices
Role of the board	• Providing strategic directions to IT management. • Closely monitoring IT performance in meeting business objectives. • Appreciation of financial implications and risk of IT for business. • Basic understanding and knowledge of IT and IT procedures. • Risk management. • Aligning and integrating IT with an organization's overall business strategy. • Ensuring transparencies and accountabilities of financial information, IT operations, IT projects.
Process	• Streamlining IT governance and management structure and responsibility. • Board involvement in all the significant IT projects and having a board level committee chaired by a board member who has IT background. • Transparent process of IT budget planning and execution. • Effective measurement systems and key performance measures in place. • Engaging or commissioning an independent evaluation of IT system and performance to assist in identifying and detecting issues and gaps.
Structure	• Clear line of responsibilities of the board and the management. • Two groups in IT governance: one strategy group at the board level and one steering group at the business unit. • An IT governance infrastructure where the committee is chaired by a CEO. The committee reports to a sub-committee of the board. In addition steering committees in each of the divisions within an organization.
System	• Effective performance measurement system in place. • Risk management system in place.
Strategy	• Risk management strategy in place. • IT policy and IT strategy in place, which should be adapted to the changing operational environment.

Effectiveness of IT Governance

The participants expressed their views about the board's role in ensuring and improving the effectiveness of IT governance. The following key attributes of the board were identified:

- The ability to provide strategic directions to IT management, as stated by an interviewee:
  The effectiveness of IT governance would be the ability of senior management and the board, to be ale to direct IT activity, to focus on the strategic directions of the institution.
- The ability to closely monitor the performance of IT groups, projects, and operations in meeting business objectives. An executive director stated in his interview:
  Their (the Board's) role would be to get involved in the evaluation of the project business case, to validate estimates of value within the business case. Their role would also be monitoring the project to ensure the IT is meeting its obligations and also assessing the objectives completion, to ensure business benefits were actually delivered.
- The ability to understand the financial implications and the risk of IT for business.
- A basic understanding and knowledge of IT and IT procedures. The board should make decisions on IT strategy rather than delegate its responsibilities because of lack of IT knowledge and skills. Several executive directors and managers interviewed felt very strongly that the board should be IT literate in today's information technology era as illustrated below:

Part of my role as a CIO is to educate not only the executives, but also the board in terms of what is important and might be important and so on. There's a growing awareness among all directors of the need to understand more about IT and not treat it as a black-box. A lot of them still look at it as a black-box. A lot of them still don't understand what IT does. They just see that as a big cost and don't see any value or minimum value. They only see value when it stops all of a sudden.

IT is too technical for the old gentlemen at the board level. The board generally doesn't have the intellectual talent to understand the IT procedures.

If you can't read a balance sheet on the board, then you are really not a good director. So if you can't understand what an IT system is supposed to give you, then you can't criticize it.

Most of the staff, including the CFO and the CEO, are very computer savvy. So I think that influences the board—if they can do the three-dimensional computer graphic of a combustion system, they must be good at other things that computers give you. And I think that's mostly the case for small companies.

However, the participants expressed a different view about whether the board ought to be IT savvy. One of the executive directors believed that board members do not have to know the technical side of IT but should set performance indicators for IT management and monitor IT management performance:
The function of the board basically is a high-level direction setting. So the board will make some assessment based on recommendations. For example, I (CIO) might take on IT strategy if it's around the state of our current IT assets. So if I go to the board and say 'our IT asset is in a poor state, we need to make some significant investment, a couple of investments to bring them up to a sustainable level of performance for the

future', and the board agrees, then the board wants to make sure that actually happens. So the board looks at issues like risks, security, sustainability, and performance and so on. That's their key role from a governance standpoint. And as CIO, I go to the board to make sure that we keep the doors open.

- The ability of risk management;
- The ability of aligning and integrating IT with an organization's overall business strategy; and
- Transparencies and accountabilities of financial information, IT operations, IT projects, IT applications, etc. A senior manager stated:

Defining effectiveness of IT governance to me is much about transparency of critical information that the business needs to know or understand. So the effectiveness of IT governance is the transparency, whether it's financial information, IT operations, IT projects, IT applications and so on.

The key themes drawn from the effectiveness of IT governance data demonstrated the awareness and comprehension of the directors and senior managers towards the key issues concerning good corporate IT governance. The data uncovered the issues with IT governance and the disappointment of executive officers and managers at the ways that IT was governed in their organizations. This led to the question "What is a responsive and effective governance and management structure, process and system?" and is addressed below.

Effective IT Governance and Management Structure, Process, and System

The following framework for IT governance and management in organizations was perceived important by the seven directors and senior managers

and embraced various aspects of IT governance, management structure, process, and system.

- There ought to be a clear line of responsibilities of the board and the management including CEO, CFO, and CIO.
- Effective measurement systems and key performance measures are in place to evaluate and monitor the performance of IT systems.
- There ought to be two groups in IT governance: one strategy group at the board level and one steering group at the business unit level as one participant stated:

That steering group would have responsibilities to receive the directions from the strategic group in terms of implementation and, also providing the information to the overarching strategy group to help it plan.

- An IT governance committee should be established and chaired by a CEO. The committee reports to a sub-committee of the board. There are also steering committees in each of the divisions within an organization. Membership of that committee is drawn from every department within the division. The committees should have strategies and charters which specify clear roles and responsibilities of the committees.
- The board ought to become involved in all the significant IT projects and should have a board level committee chaired by a board member who has an IT background.

A participant who was a CEO stated:
I have a technology strategy steering committee, which comprises the heads of the major businesses [in the organization], plus myself, plus the deputy CEO. That committee meets monthly. And it's an ongoing governance body [that was set up] for the implementation of the technology strategy. That also results priority conflicts. So if business A wants something which is opposite

*to business B, we will have that committee
sit until it determines which is important.*

- A risk management system and strategy
  ought to be in place.
- IT policy and IT strategy ought to be in place
  and adapted to the changing operational
  environment.
- Engaging or commissioning an independent
  evaluation of an IT system and performance
  may assist in identifying and detecting issues
  and gaps earlier.
- The process of budget planning and executing the budget plan needs to be transparent.
  As one CEO explained:

*One of the first things would be to create a
definitive budget which will be published,
and each major item on that budget will have
a business case which would be observed on
the company's intranet. So everybody would
be able to see the budget and everybody
would be able to see the business cases that
support the budget. Every project that wants
to involve IT will have to submit a business
case to the governance committee, and that
project will be described and the business
case will be documented, Again, each of
these projects would be available on the
intranet, so all staff across the company
will see what type of projects IT is working on and the underpinning value that is
extracted from them: i.e. why we're doing
it, who's going to benefit from, in what time
frame, and so on.*

IT governance and management structure
and responsibility should be streamlined. One
participant provided the following example.

*Within the IT group of the 18 staff, I created 4
teams. I created a team leader position for each of
them. And again they formed part of the cascad-
ing levels of responsibility: from the board to the
strategy committee and to the steering committee,*

*and then within the IT group, to the IT manager
and to the team leaders. In addition, there is a
performance and development review for each
staff member. They (staff) would be required to
commit up to 5 key goals for the year, and that
goal would be linked to the overall strategy.*

Compared with the key elements of effective
IT governance frameworks found in the existing
IT governance literature, this study uncovered
that the frameworks identified by the participants
generally confirmed those found in the literature.
The commonly referred five important elements
in the IT governance framework were:

- Strategic alignment
- Delivery of business value through IT
- Performance management
- Risk management
- Control and accountability (Webb et al.,
  2006)

However, it was apparent that there was confusion and discrepancy in the perceptions among
the participants over whether senior management
and the board should take IT governance above
the project and operational level. According to
Australian Standard AS8015-2005 and PRO:NED
(2007), corporate governance of IT should be
the responsibility of senior management and the
board, as IT governance is a subset of corporate
governance.

In terms of structures and control and monitoring systems for IT governance, the interview
findings tended to favour a centralized control
system. The current literature shows that there
are other primary structures and systems that
are popular in IT governance in organizations,
such as, decentralized and federal modes. The
decentralized mode delegates IT decision-making
authority to division or line managers while the
federal mode distributes the authority between
corporate and divisional management. Regardless of what structure and system an organization

adopts, there should be a clear line of responsibilities and authority. This view was shared amongst the interviewees.

In regards to the process of IT governance, the effective framework identified by the interviewees concentrated on control and accountability, risk management, and performance measurement. However, the identified process overlooked an important component, in particular, aligning IT process with key business processes of its corporate governance with the aim of achieving better business value through IT investment. In addition, a well-established strategic planning process ought to be part of the IT governance process.

TRIANGULATION

The quantitative data generated by the questionnaire's closed questions, combined with the qualitative data generated by the questionnaire's open questions and interviews, provided a triangulation approach to the merging of the study's findings. The quantitative data showed that while directors placed a great deal of reliance on management, the formal systems of management were often inadequate in dealing with IT governance. The interview data confirmed this finding with the participants showing an inconsistent view of who was responsible for IT governance, and the required structures to support IT governance in their organization. In addition, many participants were not aware of or understood AS8015. Furthermore, a number of the participants noted that many industry sectors outsource their IT entirely and if not, then there should be two groups addressing IT governance: one strategy group at the board level and one steering group at the business unit level where,

...the steering group would have responsibilities to receive the directions from the strategic group in terms of implementation and, also providing

the information to the overarching strategy group to help it plan.

It is no surprise that the human factor rated the lowest on the six IT governance principles. The qualitative data supported this finding and offered several explanations. A number of participants cited the technical language of IT as creating a barrier when communicating with others who were not IT educated or literate. For example, often management left this task to the IT department and then "ran away." The participants suggested that the rewriting of manuals and procedures in everyday language would assist in dismantling this communication or language barrier and hence facilitate with the inclusion of the human factor in IT governance within an organization. Education at both the upper and lower levels of the organizational management structure was a consist theme that was associated with assisting in the effective integration of IT governance across the organization.

The limitations in IT governance performance, despite organizations having worked for years to improve their IT's internal processes, reflect a failure to recognize that controlling the use of (or demand for) IT is different to controlling the supply of IT. It is viewed that IT is a tool of business, employed to enable new business capability, to provide a foundation stone for innovation, and to contain and reduce organizational costs. As a tool of business, it is vital to understand that it is the management of the business who are responsible for making effective use of IT. The essential missing elements of IT governance largely relate to effective planning of how IT is to be used as part of business strategy (Thorp, 2005) and how IT implementation is an integral part of organizational transformation when new business systems are put in place (Toomey, 2005). A vivid example of failure in IT governance as part of organizational transformation was the disastrous implementation of the Australian Customs Service Cargo Management System Imports Module in

October 2005. Because customs failed to govern the overall organizational transformation of the entire imports industry, many organizations were unprepared, and the resulting problems in use of the new system caused severe impact on the national supply chain (Australian National Audit Office, 2007).

Board directors do not need to know technical details of IT in order to govern, any more than directors of mining companies need to be geologists and metallurgists in order to test the development and operation of major mines. But directors do need to be certain that there are adequate and effective systems of control in place, covering both the supply of, and demand for IT and supported by appropriate behaviours upon which to base decisions.

The quantitative and qualitative data showed that IT governance and innovation may be considered as either a tangible organizational outcome or as a process through which new ideas; objects and practices are created, developed, or reinvented. Both the quantitative and qualitative data confirmed that IT governance is context specific as is innovation in an organization's unique culture. Supporting statements ranged from processes such as *"clear lines of responsibilities of the board and the management";* and outcomes such as *"effective measurement systems and key*

performance measures to evaluate and monitor the performance of IT systems."

The convergence of the quantitative and qualitative data shows that organizational culture plays a significant role in managerial innovation when managing IT governance. Hence an effective governance framework would embrace an organization's human resource capital that is composed of values attitudes and beliefs committed to IT governance. The themes drawn from the IT governance and management structure, process and system data provide exemplary practices of effective IT governance in the views of the directors and managers. The authors believe that the framework is insightful and comprehensive as a whole, and could be used as a reference and/or guide, depending on the specific situation or state of each organization.

The research to date highlights that in many organizations, there are clearly discernable gaps in their governance of IT, with inconsistent expectations regarding clarity of roles and responsibilities, risk management, strategic alignment, and business cases.

While many organizations have sought to formalize their IT governance through adoption of formal, structured models for the management processes, it remains that many have not formalized their approach to IT management—and many

Figure 4. An effective IT governance framework—AS8015:2005

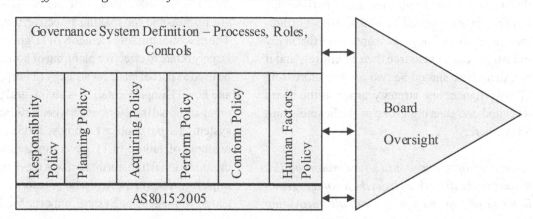

have left IT as a "black box" shrouded in mystery. Indeed, as highlighted by one of the interviewees, it is the perception of mystery that inhibits many directors from asking pertinent questions about IT. In most cases, they believe that if they do ask a question, they may not understand the answer.

As Weill et al. (2004) pointed out, having a well defined approach to IT governance is a significant factor in having effective governance. As this study found, many organizations did not have an adequately defined system of governance, with clearly defined (and appropriate) responsibilities. Directors who wish to ensure that managers are performing their roles effectively would find value in a well-defined system of governance, as this could provide them with a clear and consistent basis for evaluation of the management performance. If governance systems are rated as generally inadequate, specific attention to assessing and improving the governance systems may reap rewards for the organization.

AS8015 provides a strong core strategy for organizations that wish to improve their use of IT. The six principles provide guidance toward a foundation of six core policies to guide the development of a governance system and all future decisions regarding IT (see Figure 2). For example, a responsibility policy would provide clarity on who is responsible for IT. It would address responsibility from the point of view of using IT in a business context as well as for the supply of IT capability and services. The policy would explain who is responsible for understanding and controlling the business risks associated with the use of IT, and who is responsible for ensuring that the organization's IT meets its business need.

CONCLUSION

IT governance is a relatively new concept, which responds to the need for strong leadership, strategic direction, and control from the highest level of an organization. This study contributes to

the existing body of international literature by presenting an Australia study in the context of Australian Standard AS8015-2005.

The survey and interview findings from this empirical study suggest that whilst many organizations have considerable dependence on IT, their systems of governance for IT are not of the standard they should be in today's organizational contexts. The findings relating to governance performance and the AS8015-2005 principles point to opportunities for considerable improvement in the approach to governance. These improvements will be in the way that directors engage in IT governance and in the overall design of the system of IT governance. The spin-offs from such improvements are that there are benefits and improved value realized from investments in IT, better alignment of IT to business need hence increased business innovation, greater confidence and reduced organizational risk.

Any initiative to improve IT governance requires underpinning by a sound understanding of why governance of IT is important, and of who should be involved in the process. The fundamental, question is: "What is the real dependence of the organization on IT for its current and future operations?" Organizational dependence on IT means that directors and executives ought to be similarly served by a well-defined system of IT Governance, with audits confirming the efficacy of the system, the organization's conformance with the rules defined in the system and the conformance of the system with established laws, regulations, and good practice.

It may not be necessary or appropriate for non-executive directors to be deeply involved in their organization's financial management. It is no more necessary or appropriate for them to be deeply involved in planning and delivery of IT. But, the readily acknowledged dependence on IT in contemporary organizations suggests that directors ought to have confidence in their organization's IT use and controls. That confidence would be through an effective system of governance, which provides appropriate information to the board. The information may be audited and facilitates in directors asking appropriate and timely questions.

Just as systems of financial governance are founded on key rules and standards, it is appropriate for the system of IT governance to be founded on sound principles, such as those expressed in AS8015-2005. In order to improve their performance, organizations would do well to first check that they have policies in place that reflect the guidance of the AS8015 principles.

Finally, the value of this study lies in its practical application where the findings facilitate in raising senior management's awareness to develop, disseminate, and operationalize effective strategies to align and integrate technology and human factors in the management of IT in their workplace. Innovation, management, and IT governance are context specific and unique to each organization's culture. However, embedding IT philosophy into the organization's culture so that it becomes a measurable objective is a challenge and requires management to address the integration of human resource processes and outcomes simultaneously. The redressing and management of human resources in organizational IT governance is viewed as one of managerial innovation in managing an organization's IT that results in the implementation of strategies to enhance and optimize workplace innovation. Organizations may improve IT governance by identifying the costs of their own limitations such as failed projects, uncertain or lost benefits, missed opportunities or disruption and inconvenience. An appropriately designed and executed IT governance improvement initiative would reduce these costs and show a clear linkage between organizational processes being altered to achieve desired innovative organizational outcomes that are unique to the organization and its entrepreneurial endeavours and activities. As with any preliminary study, there are limitations that should be considered and addressed in future IT governance research. In this case, future studies would benefit from a larger and more gender balanced population sample.

ACKNOWLEDGMENT

The authors wish to thank the School of Management of the Royal Melbourne Institute of Technology University for the generous financial support to conduct the study. We gratefully acknowledge the assistance of Ms. Ling Deng and Mr. Donglin Wu, our PhD candidates, in the data collection process of this project. Finally, we are deeply indebted to the study's participants for their valuable insights into IT governance.

REFERENCES

Auditor-General. (2003). Review of Sydney Water's customer information and billing system. *Auditor-General's Report to Parliament 2003* (Volume One). Retrieved June 20, 2007, from http://www.audit.nsw.gov.au/publications/reports/financial/2003/vol1/SpecialRevSydneyWaterCIBS.pdf

Australian National Audit Office. (2007). *Audit Report no 24 2006-07, Customs' Cargo Management Re-engineering Project*. Canberra, Australia: Australian National Audit Office.

Australian Pharmaceutical Industries. (2006). Australian Pharmaceutical Industries and Its Controlled Entities ABN 57 000 004 320 *Annual Report,* 30 April 2006.

Gartner Group. (2002). *Gartner Says 20 Percent of Corporate IT Budgets Wasted Globally in 2001 on Inefficient Information Communication Technology Spending*. Gartner Group Press Release, Egham, UK, 14 March 2002. Retrieved March 15, 2007, from http://www.gartner.com/5_about/press_releases/2002_03/pr20020314a.jsp

Hair Jr., J. F., Anderson, R. E., Tatham, R. L., & Black, W. C. (1998). *Multivariate data analysis.* (5th ed.). NJ: Prentice-Hall.

Hayes, F. (2004). *Chaos is back.* November 08, 2004 Retrieved March 7, 2007, from http://www.computerworld.com/managementtopics/management/project/story/0,10801,97283,00.html

Huff, S. L., Michael Maher, P., & Munro, M. C. (2006). Information technology and the board of directors: Is there an IT attention deficit? *MIS Quarterly Executive, 5*(2), [electronic version]. Retrieved January 10, 2007, from http: www.misque.org/V0502-03.pdf

IT Governance Institute. (2007). *Board briefing on IT governance.* Retrieved March 7, 2007, from www.itgi.org.

King, W. R. (2007). IT strategy and innovation: The IT deniers versus a portfolio of IT role. *Information Systems Management, 24*(2), 197-200, Boston: Spring 2007.

KPMG. (2005). *Global IT project management survey—How committed are you?* Retrieved March 7, 2007, from http://www.kpmg.com.au/aci/issues.htm#105

Luciw, R. (2004). *RBC extends bank hours.* Retrieved June 20, 2007, from http://www.theglobeandmail.com

McMurray, A. J., & Dorai, R. (2003). Workplace innovation scale: A new method for measuring innovation in the workplace. The *5th European Conference on Organizational Knowledge, Learning and Capabilities (OKLC 2003).* Barcelona, Spain April.

McMurray, A. J., Cross, J., & Caponecchia, C. (2007, August 3-8). *Business continuity plan practices within the risk management profession.* Presented at the Academy of Management Meeting, Philadelphia, Pennsylvania.

McMurray, A. J., Pace, R. W., & Scott, D. (2004). *Research: A commonsense approach.* Melbourne: Thomson Learning Social Science Press.

PRO:NED. (2007). *Non-Executive Directors' Survey Report 2007.* IBM:NSW.

Schaper, M., & Volery, T. (2003). *Entrepreneurship and small business: A Pacific Rim perspective.* Brisbane: John Wiley.

Standards Australia. (2005). *AS8015-2005—Australian Standard for Corporate Governance of Information and Communication Technology.* Sydney.

Standish Group. (1994). *The CHAOS Report.* Retrieved March 7, 2007, from http://www.standishgroup.com/sample_research/chaos_1994_1.php

Teece, D. J. (2002). *Managing intellectual capital* (pp. 183). Oxford: Oxford University Press.

Toomey, M. (2005). *A catastrophe in governance of IT: Australian customs integrated cargo system.* Melbourne, Australia: Infonomics Pty. Ltd.

Toomey, M. (2006). Achieving business sustainability: Director's perceptions of information technology investment, corporate, monitoring, and governance. *Infonomics Newsletter Report.*

Toomey, M. (2007, August 13-25). Achieving business sustainability: Director's perceptions of information technology investment, corporate monitoring, and governance. *Presented at itSMF Australia National Conference, Melbourne, Australia.*

Thorp, J. (2005, September 7). Meeting the challenge for IT-enabled change: A strategic governance approach. *Presented at the Committee for Economic Development of Australia (CEDA) Luncheon.* Melbourne, Australia.

Weill, P., & Ross, J. (2004). *IT governance: How top performers manage IT decision rights for superior results.* Boston: Harvard Business School Press.

Webb, P., Pollard, C., & Ridley, G. (2006). Attempting to define IT governance: Wisdom or folly? *Proceedings of the 39ᵗʰ Hawaii International Conference on System Sciences.* Retrieved April 26, 2007, from http://ieeexplore.ieee.org/iel5/105 48/33368/01579684.pdf?arnumber=1579684

Zhao, F. (2006). *Maximize business profits through e-partnerships.* Hershey, PA: Idea Group Publishing.

Chapter V
Performance Measurement in the SMEs in the Information Industry

Donglin Wu
RMIT University, Australia

Fang Zhao
RMIT University, Australia

ABSTRACT

This chapter identifies the challenges, features, and drivers of performance measurement (PM) in the SMEs in the IT industry and introduces a PM framework based on the system theory and business excellence model for SMEs. This study finds that a dynamic and flexible PM framework is more suitable to SMEs than a mechanized PM model. By examining the PM features and key success factors in SMEs in the IT industry, this study concludes that traditional PM theories and tools are not suitable for SMEs, which is supported by many recent studies on PM in SMEs.

INTRODUCTION

During the last two decades, many **performance measurement (PM)** theories and tools were introduced. Most of these **performance measurement** frameworks are developed for large organizations. Up until now, there is no consen-sus on whether these theories and tools apply to small- and middle-sized firms (SMEs). Some scholars (Abouzeedan & Busler 2005; Hudson, Smart & Bourne 2001; Hvolby & Thorstenson 2000) believe that **PM** in SMEs is quite different from that in the large enterprises. It is believed that **PM** in SMEs has its special characteristics and cannot be regarded simply as a small version of that in big enterprises.

The issue of **PM** in SMEs has been addressed by different approaches based on the features of SMEs. Hvolby et al. (2000) analyzed the use of balanced score card (BSC) and suggested that the choice of indicators for PM in SMEs has to be highly prioritized because of strongly constrained resources. They believed that the use of a very limited number of performance indicators might have some further advantages in SMEs. Hudson et al. (2001) compared different PM models. They found that SMEs always have limited resource with a dynamic, emergent strategy, which implies limitation of the existing **PM** models that require intensive resource and are strategically oriented. Therefore, the performance model in SMEs should be very resource effective and be dynamic and flexible enough to accommodate the strategic changes. Abouzeedan et al. (2005) used a series of failure prediction model and decision making model to discuss the issue of PM model. They found that none of the models specifically address the SMEs area. Through studying the use of quantitative and qualitative measurement in small firms, Jarvis, Curran, Kitching, and Lightfoot (2000) found that small firms pursue a range of goals rather than profit. Small business also uses a variety of measures and indicators to assess business performance. In particular, cash flow indicator was considered to be critical and the quality of inputs and outputs is often used. Besides, the use of ISO9000 certification in SMEs has been studied (Mulhaney, Sheehan, & Hughes, 2004; Rahman, 2001). All the previously mentioned studies agree that SMEs are different from big enterprises in terms of their tightly constrained resources; therefore, SMEs have not enough resource and time to conduct a PM system that is issued by large enterprises. Furthermore, there is hardly any study that was done from a holistic perspective of **PM.**

From another aspect, as a fast growing industry in the new economy, information technology (IT) industry has many special characteristics, which are different from the traditional industry.

Hence, the performance measurement in IT industry is always a challenging issue. Cumby and Conrod (2001) mentioned that historic financial data is not enough to satisfy the performance measurement in the new economy. They stated that sustainable shareholder value is driven by non-financial factors such as customer loyalty, employee satisfaction, internal processes, and the organization's innovation. In the new economy, financial reports are of limited use in predicting shareholder value. For the standard and poor 500, only 10% to 15% of market value is captured by traditional accounting measures (Webber, 2000). Particularly, for the high technology enterprise, multi-various performance methods, which include financial and non-financial and other performance measure methods, are indispensable. There is also some empirical research on the IT industry. For example, Wright, Smith, Jesser, and Stupeck (1999) analyzed the correlation between information technologies, process reengineering and performance measurement in the Compaq Computer Corporation using the balanced scorecard. However, in spite of many PM studying on the IT industries, the literature review shows that there is little research on the IT industry's performance measurement from a comprehensive and holistic perspective.

In this chapter, based on a comprehensive literature review of performance measurement in SMEs, the **key success factors** in SMEs in the IT industry were investigated through a qualitative study. Then the features of performance measurement in IT SMEs were discussed. This chapter concludes with a proposed performance measurement framework for SMEs in the IT industry.

In this study, the following terms are used and defined for the purpose of the study:

Small- and medium-sized firms (SMEs): This study agrees with the European Union (EU)'s definition that SMEs are those enterprises with employees between 10 to 250 persons and the turnover is 40 millions EUC (UN-ECE 1996).

The information technology (IT) industry: According to the Information Technology Association of America (ITAA), the information technology (IT) industry includes computer hardware, software, telecommunications, Internet, e-business, e-education, computer services, and more.

LITERATURE REVIEW

Performance Measurement Features in SMEs

Based on reviewing the relevant literature, Garengo, Biazzo, & Bititci (2005) identify five common characteristics of PM in SMEs:

1. SMEs are difficult to be involved in performance measurement projects. Furthermore, the SMEs that take part in PM projects rarely continue on to the last phase.
2. SMEs either do not use any PM model or use models incorrectly.
3. SMEs rarely implement PM through a "holistic approach."
4. PM in SMEs is informal, not planned and does not base on a model; performance measurement is introduced to solve specific problems rather than as a result of planning.
5. SMEs have limited resources for data analysis.

Various Approaches to Implementing PM in SMEs

It is generally acknowledged that **PM** tools can help enterprises identify the weakness in their management, clarify their objectives and strategies, and improve their management processes. Therefore, measuring SMEs' performance is a critical issue, especially for investors. Many important studies into implementation of a variety of PMs in SMEs have been conducted. These studies address issues of PM in SMEs from different aspects.

Balanced Scorecard (BSC)

BSC is initiated by Kaplan and Norton (1992). It is perhaps the most well known PM framework. The objectives and measures of BSC are derived from an organization's vision and strategy. It incorporates financial and non-financial measures in one measurement system and provides executives with a comprehensive framework that translates a company's vision and strategy into a coherent set of performance measures. The BSC is a strong strategy management tool (Kaplan & Norton, 1992, 1996, 2001).

Research shows that there exist a number of problems when BSC is applied to SMEs (Kaplan et al., 1992, 1996, 2001; McAdam, 2000). These problems can not be alleviated by simply reducing the rigor in BSC. First, the BSC's mechanization and inflexibility does not fit the flexible environment of SMEs. BSC focuses on a long-term measure; in contrast, SMEs always change their operations according to their market situation. Second, SMEs often keep a closer relationship with their customers, compared with large organization. A large number of employees in SMEs have direct customer contacts. It thus seems that measuring customers' satisfaction is an 'adding bureaucracy'. Third, the processes within SMEs are much more temporal and less defined than those in large organizations. The formalized process of large organizations might restrict the rapid and spontaneous cross functional process in SMEs.

Business Excellence Model and Total Quality Management (TQM)

The typical business excellence models are **EFQM model** and **Baldrige criteria**. The **EFQM excellence model** is a non-prescriptive framework to help guide an organization to improve its performance. The model includes nine measure criteria that were divided into two groups: enables and results. The logic interrelation between the "results" and "enablers" is "results" are caused by "enablers" and "enablers" are improved by using feedback from "results." The **Baldrige criteria** for performance excellence framework are designed to help an organization to manage performance using an integrated approach. Similar to EFQM, the Baldrige performance criteria consist of seven categories, which are divided into two triads: leadership triad and result triad.

Stephens (2000) evaluated the implementation of Baldrige criteria in SMEs. His study identifies the importance of the Baldrige criteria to small firms and to what extent these criteria were used by small businesses. It is shown that small business leaders rate the importance of underlying management practices from least moderately important to highly important; the strategy development process and leadership were ranked higher than other items. Usually, the operational items are ranked high, which might comes from the fact that managers in small firms spend more time on day-to-day operations; small firms implement all practices to some extent. But none of the practices were used to full extent because of resource constraint.

Rahman (2001) studied TQM implementation and organizational performance of SMEs in Western Australia, with and without ISO 9000 certification. His research shows that the TQM approach based on the Australia Business Excellence (ABE) framework is a valid and reliable instrument to assess organizational performance for SMEs. However, there is no significant difference between the impacts of TQM practices on organizational performance for firms with and without ISO 9000 certification. Ahire and Golhar (1996)'s research shows that TQM implementation leads to better product quality regardless of the firms' size in the auto parts industry.

The Approach of System Theory

Jackson (2000) believes an organization can be taken as a system made up of interrelated parts. Each part contributes to the system and ensures its survival and continuity. To achieve this objective, managers have to understand the various parts of their organization and the relationship between the parts and with the external environment. Based on this assumption, Ali (2003) constructed a PM model for SMEs. In his model, the performance measure is divided into two categories: end-result indicators and input factors that influence end-results indicators. A company's final **PM** framework is determined by sensitivity analysis.

Similarly, Australian CSIRO (Barnes et al. 1998) introduces the organizational performance measurement (OPM) system for both SMEs and large enterprise based on open system theory and zones of management. The OPM divides the PM into three levels: strategic, tactical, and operational. The open **systems theory** considers enterprises as systems located within a larger system-environment. A dynamic relationship exists between an enterprise and its environment.

The Approach of Activities Based on Costing (ABC)

The main idea of **ABC** is to measure the cost of resource used to perform organizational activities directly and then to link the activity costs to outputs. Laitinen (2002) introduced a dynamic integrated performance system (IPMS) specifically designed for SMEs based on the theory of **ABC**. His proposed IPMS consists on seven main factors and a causal chain connecting these factors. The factors are classified into two external factors (financial performance and competitiveness) and five internal factors (costs, production factors, activities, products, and revenues). In the causal chain, the factor at any point along the chain is regarded as a determinant of the factor that succeeds it.

Table 1. Companies and people interviewed

Company	Main Business Activities	Interviewees
Company A	Internet Security Company	CEO, CTO
Company B	Education software design and consulting	CEO
Company C	Electronic design and consulting	CEO
Company D	System control and telecommunication solution	Founder Manager
Company E	Online human resource company	General Manager
Company F	Telecommunication products research	Project Manager
Company G	Telecommunication products research	Senior Sale Manager
Company H	IT consulting and training	Founder Manager
Company I	IT service and consulting	Sales Manager
Company J	Telecommunication	Founder Manager
Company K	IT technical consulting, planning, mentoring, and training	Sales Manager
Company L	Technical consulting and implementation services	Managing Director
Company M	Electronics company	Managing Director
Company N	Online marketing service company	CEO

RESEARCH METHODOLOGY

Following a comprehensive and extensive literature review of PM theories and models as previously shown, this research mainly employed a qualitative methodology. Fifteen semi-structured interviews were conducted with 14 SMEs in the IT industry to collect the ideas about performance measurement. The interviewees include four CEOs, three founder managers, one CTO, one general manager, one R&D project manager, three senior sales manager, and two managing directors. The sample companies include different sized SMEs at different developing stages in the IT industry. The information about sample companies and interviewees are presented in the Table 1. To collect the perceptions of SMEs' performance measurement from investors, three senior investment managers were also interviewed. They work with three venture capital companies whose main investment area is in the IT industry.

In the interviews, key success factors were investigated and the current PM used by these companies was studied, including the PM structures, the key performance indicators employed, and the weakness of the performance measurement. Furthermore, how to modify current PM was also discussed.

FINDING & DISCUSSION

This study is based upon some special features of SMEs in the IT industry, including:

*   First, due to rapid development of technologies, the performance of SMEs often depends on their understanding and grasping of the technological trend.
*   Second, the shortness of resource is a critical factor that impacts the performance of SMEs. Obtaining resource in time and utilizing resource effectively are the key success factors for SMEs in the information industry.

- Third, many entrepreneurs in the information industry are technological specialists. Many of them focus on the technology and have not got enough business experience and skills. This influences the SMEs' performance significantly.

Given the previous features, the PM in SMEs is facing its specific issues. This section discusses the key issues from our findings as follows.

PM in SMEs in the IT industry

This study found that measuring SMEs' performance is a challenging issue. SMEs have a short operating history and the performance information is not easy to be collected. Hence, traditional financial measures of performance are often unavailable (Brush & Vanderwerf, 1992; Chandler & Hanks, 1993; Wang & Ang, 2004). Financial data is difficult to be interpreted in SMEs. Misleading conclusion will be obtained if the traditional measure criterion is used. This is because SMEs usually have small starting base, enormous and erratic growth rate and uneven record keeping (Sapienza & Grimm, 1997). Most SMEs focus on day-to-day operation. There is not enough resource to execute comprehensive PM measurement. The decision-making processes in SMEs are always not formalized and their strategies are poorly planned, which influences the standard PM system employed in SMEs. Because of above challenges, the **PM** in the SMEs in the IT industry presents the following features:

1. According to the interviews for this study, SMEs have rarely applied institutional **PM** system to measure performance. The reasons may be that the managerial structure is simple and the business does not need a complex process to support.
2. Most SMEs apply several **key performance indicators** to measure performance. However, the indicators vary according to the

companies and the business stages. It seems that no universal indicator system can be employed by SMEs in the information industry.
3. Many executives in the SMEs reject a formal **PM** system. For example, executives in SMEs in the IT industry, most of which are invested by venture capital companies, think that there is too much paper work for the report required by the venture capital companies.
4. As previously mentioned, the traditional financial measuring is always lagging. In contrast, the development of IT companies and its environmental is rapid. Furthermore, traditional financial measures of performance are often unavailable in SMEs. Therefore, using only traditional financial indicators cannot capture the real performance in the SMEs. SMEs are apt to use the growth and intangible indicators to measure performance.
5. The **PM** in the SMEs is often objectives-orientated, i.e. the PM is often used to deal with some specific work objectives rather than ongoing measures for long-term strategic goals. Some companies even use the project management instead of the performance management.

Key Success Factors in SMEs in the IT Industry

All enterprise factors would influence a company's performance (Executive F).

A company's performance is determined by many factors. Every factor that is related to an enterprise would influence the company's performance. According to system theory (Jackson 2000), a company is a system which operates in a larger systemic environment. The systems interact with each other and exchange the factors. Therefore, every internal and external factor would influence a company's performance. However, what are the key factors that influence a company's performance? Based on this qualitative research, the following factors influence a small and medium IT company's performance significantly:

A Highly Competent and Competitive Team

SMEs in the IT industry face a very strong competitive environment. Almost all the executives interviewed believe that a high-quality team is a crucial factor that influences a company's performance.

I think the most important factor is the team, which includes senior managers and ordinary employees (Executive F).

According to Executive F, a high-quality team should involve all employees and leaders:

Employees have the same expectation and value. The culture is upward and active. The senior managers understand the detailed business and can work out appropriate business models. At the same time, the team should be a learning organization, because IT companies compete with each other strongly. The team should have strong ability to adapt to the environment." To build a competitive team, "First, the leader is very important, who can influence, motivate other team members. Second, emphasizing on team building and building a culture that can be aligned with work.

Executive D also agrees that building a perfect working environment is a critical factor for performance.

In a small company, the key factor of performance- we want to create the environment here where people are happy to work, and they gain satisfaction from their work (Executive D).

In company C, it is believed that it is important to set upward culture and expectations.

In the small company, the directors of the business were very much involved in the day-to day operation of the business. So it is very connected to kind of environment. We have total staff of 50; about half of them are here. We see interaction of all of the staff, so I think it's an important aspect of setting culture and expectations, kind of lead to how we like things done, how we like to conduct and treat each other, and treat our customers (Executive C).

First, for a company to go, people have to like each other. They have to be compatible. And the management is different when you put a lot of very clever, creative people together. They actually manage themselves very well. If you put a team of ordinary people together, you'll put management at a higher rank like a big company. Every team of a big company has a manager who reports to a higher manager. But that's not work for small creative teams. They make much more freedom, creativity. And because of the sort of people who are very good at holding new things, and very individual, they do not like other people to disturb them. Small teams are very important to work together. And not the traditional sort of management that applies to IBM, all the things you know about product development. Small business is quite different (Executive A).

They all change. So this is why you need an atmosphere in your company that looks for change, it is always critical (Executive A).

Since we're a small company, all the employees should be involved. This is a team, they should work together. And the company will work better if the communication works better. In fact, they are very smart people, you should respect them. That is the intelligent asset. You can't measure it by money, you measure by the people. It's not an accounting business (Executive A).

The company had employed nearly 40 NPD fellows. Among them, 15 employees are PhD. This kind of structure did not help the company accelerate its R&D; on the contrary, it slows down the speed of NPD seriously. The team manager has not enough power to manage the NPD team. The team manager has no right to recruit new team members and has no right to refuse team member. The management in NPD is poor. The structure of team members influences the collaboration in the NPD team. Each team member has an idea for the technological direction. They always quarrel with each other. It is short of a long-term design and long-term objectives. Management skill is quite poor. All employees came from the technological background. Poor management leads to poor performance. The significant weakness was presented on human resource management (Executive G).

You have to have an environment where people are happy working, where they cooperate well, interact well. If you have problems in the way people work, it could terribly affect the performance (Executive B).

The previous statements indicate that valuing people and a high efficient team are the first **key success factors** for the performance of SMEs in the IT industry. A high performance team for SMEs has the following characteristics:

1. The team is made of smart and creative people.
2. The team should keep an appropriate personnel structure. Even though the team members' average educational levels in the IT industry are higher than those in many other industries, it is still hard to achieve the excellent performance if the manage-

ment cannot lead such an organization in the right direction.
3. The team should be made up of the people with different features. It needs not only leadership, but also people who keep criticizing - it is crucial to embrace new challenge and changes.
4. In a SMEs' team, the requirements for a team leader are different from those for leaders of a traditional team. The leader should be familiar with the business and hold detailed technological knowledge besides the managerial skill and knowledge. The leader can influence, motivate other team members and build a compatible and upward team culture.
5. Building a compatible and upward culture in the team is very important. This means every team member has the same expectation and the same value. The team members like work with each other and enjoy the friendly atmosphere in work.
6. Management is quite different in a team of SMEs. The traditional sort of management that applies to big organization does not fit to the small team of R&D. However, as the company grows up, the standard and normative management will become more and more important.
7. The team should be a learning organization because of the heavy competition in the IT industry. The members should be sensitive to the change of technology, track the right technology direction and be adapted to the changing external environment.

Right Strategy

A company's strategy is the second key factor that influences SMEs' performance in the IT industry. In the IT industry, the changes of technology are so rapid that tracking right technology direction is very important. Therefore, making a good strategy based on the companies' own competence and the external environment is the key factor for the SMEs' future performance.

In a R&D company, most is spent on research. So you really need to match your R&D outcome to product development. And product development needs to strategically in line with market. So you need to position the product in the market. If you begin a product not suitable to the market, which we've done a few times, then you are burning your resources that could be useful for other projects. So if you get in a wrong product, then you get stuffed at trouble (Executive C).

Based on the interview data, every SMEs in the IT industry has its 3-5 years strategic objectives. Every executive agrees with that choice of strategy would influence the company's survival. It is shown that the start-up firms usually have a blurry strategy. With the growth of the company, the developing strategy would become more and more clear and explicit. In the companies that have achieved good performance, their strategies usually have following characteristics:

• First, they have an in-depth understanding of the industry and the technology development direction.
• Second, they know their own advantages and core competences. The company's competence should be aligned with the strategy.

I think if you have good R&D, you can control your intellectual base, and you can match that against your strategic plan. And if that strategy plan is in line with the market expectation, then that components will be well matched usually by having good key stuff, well trained and strategically well placed, which provides the company with its core-competence. And I guess the direction is in the right strategy. So you need to make

sure that the competence is in line with the strategy (Executive C).

• Third, they know where the competitors are, and are aware of the competitors' process. In this aspect, how to grasp the development of technology and collect competitive information is always a risk for the SMEs.
• Fourth, they understand what resources they need and how to get the resources to achieve their strategic objectives.
• Finally, the companies can position themselves in a right place of the industry and market. They usually cooperate with strategic partner in the industry.

I think may be the best thing to do is to be in line with the big companies. It's like to have a big brothe. But the problem is that the big brother will choke you as well. If you grow to threat their propagation, they will try to cut you. It is very hard to be independent. But you need strategic partners. And if you can broaden that base, then you are strategic to avoid other company controlling your company (Executive C).

Based on the discipline of market leadership (Treacy & Wiersema, 1995), a company's strategy can be categorized into: operational excellence, product leadership, and customer intimacy. However, most SMEs in the IT industry usually choose two different strategies. One is to be partnership with the big companies, find its own position in the industry, and set up a strategic partnership. The other one is to develop original technology and lead the market when there are few competitors.

This study found that most SMEs in the IT industry use the first strategy due to the consideration of their limited resources. In terms of second strategy, it has a higher risk and needs more resources. Only a few SMEs with advanced technology resources choose the later. In fact, the above two strategies are not in conflict. In the IT industry, a company that has no original technology would not find a partner in the industry. Indeed, it is basic that a company has original technology and exclusive competitive advantage for the company to get the "pass" to align with the giant of the industry.

In the IT industry, it is a strategic trap that many SMEs chase an ambitious strategy regardless of their resource and core competence. To attract investment, a number of SMEs make very ambitious strategic objectives. This often leads to their future failure.

Developing Core Competency Aligning with Strategy

Every executive agrees that the company's competence is very important to the company's performance.

The company's competence influence the performance very much, very lots. Well, I think our directors have strong competence in computing technology, communication technology, and I think in the business and reform process. I think in the business sector, we are very strong in these areas, our external directors; his core competence is in strategy planning business, finance and overall company governance. So we've got some well-potential external directors that stand on us. Now the gentleman on our board is the former chairman of the major director of an investment bank. So in terms of competency at the board level, we are fairly sound in that area, and the board are very much focusing on growth strategy, on the managed basis, whereas we have lots of opportunities (Executive D).

From the previous statement we can see that the executives in SMEs realized that a company's competence include many perspectives besides the technological capability. According to their experience, a company's core competences include:

First, the research development capability; most founders in SMEs in the IT industry are technology specialists. They believe that their core competence is the technology development capability.

Second, the managerial skill; the smart SMEs pay attention to building a network to improve their resource network, strategic planning, and managerial capability. They look for smart persons from funding organization and the managerial experts to help them build the network. A familiar method is to invite external directors and independent board members to join their company.

Third, a core competence often means that the company can get exclusive resource. This kind of companies is less influenced by external environmental factors. For example, company D has held the historical data of open-water channels in Australia. This is their core-competence because they have the exclusive resource. In future, any research institute that wants to enter this area should collaborate with this company. This kind of exclusive resource is usually formed through two routes. The first is through some special operation history, for example, company D starts up from a government-owned research institute. Because of some historical operation, it has gathered the long-term technological data in this area. The second route is to build a barrier to other companies through the base technology. This is a dream for many companies. But the success rate is very low for most SMEs in the IT industry. The companies who choose the original technology with few competitors usually belong to this category. They hope to achieve their core competence through the exclusive technology.

From the data collection, we identified that the core-competence of a company should be aligned with the company's strategy. For successful SMEs, their competences were developed according to their strategy. On the other hand, SMEs also need to make correct strategy according to their own core competence.

Competitive Advantages

Whether a company achieves a technology advantage is also a key factor that influences a company's performance.

So the key factor is to really have a unique product and to address unique challenges (Executive D).

First, that product of your design should be the original and basically without much competition (Executive A).

To measure a company's performance from technological aspect, it mainly checks whether the technology has competitive advantages or not (Executive A2).

Even though these executives stated that products and technology should be unique and with competitive advantages, in the IT industry, since the technology changes rapidly, it is very hard to identify the competitive advantage of one technology. And for the SMEs, how to track the right technology direction is always challenging. Compared to big companies in this industry, SMEs can only apply some simple methods to collect technology information. They have no designated departments and persons to collect and analyze the competitive intelligence.

Yes, it is always a risk. We get the information from the Internet, search the products release information. It often happened that other companies released their products when we get the product concept. There is a benefit that we can test our idea through other companies' product release (Executive A2).

For SMEs, to communicate with customers and to design products according to market expectation are very important. At the same time, SMEs should pay attention to the competitors' progress.

First, communicate with customers. Second, from market, you should always focus on the competitors; you should know the progress of competitors. For our small companies, there is no special person to do this job (Executive A2).

Furthermore, SMEs in the IT industry should understand their products' position in the market and make appropriate marketing plans.

Focus on Customers

Generally, scholars believe that focusing on the customer is a key performance factor. However, it is strange that not every SME notices that. It is perhaps that most small companies contact directly with customers, they do not think communication with customers is an issue. But the leading enterprise realized that the growth in terms of customer is the key factors for long-term performance.

Obviously we're not going into business in the long term if we don't have an underlying financial framework in place. But growth in terms of customer is obviously key factors for us in moving forward (Executive D).

Managing Internal Process

In the SMEs studied for this project, it seems that the internal process is not as important as that in the big organizations. Most executives believe that internal process is simple in SMEs. But the leading SMEs have realized that the internal process would be more important than the external business environment to a company's performance.

Certainly internal process is really a key factor to make a long going business. And we've internally adapted the role and responsibilities of the company directors over the last 6 months, where my role is more formally on overseas market. We're traditionally involved in Australian market. So I think the internal process really is a critical factor and in terms of us, it's probably more important to external business environment (Executive D).

The issue of internal process in SMEs is always around the cost management, i.e. to have the thing done within the scheduled time and the limited budget.

Well, internal process is generally very loose. They really evolved around the balance sheet. How much money have I got? How much more can I do? How much more that I can find at the moment? When we had a lot of people and a lot of money, we have a lot of issues. The more money we have, the more issues we could have. When revenues start running out, you have to start cutting projects. I guess in terms of internal processes, you need to have money (Executive C).

Many executives understood that the internal processes are mainly on the project management (e.g., how to manage a team and manage a research project). Therefore, the internal process is simpler compared to that in the large organizations.

That depends on what process you mean. There is a technical process, and there's a financial process. It's obvious the financial reporting has to be good. As far as management type, in a small company like us is concerned, it's just commonsense. So the most management is the management of the technological building. Because it is research, everything should be properly documented. It has to be done in a very scientific manner; so managing that process to make sure the thing is done well. Not managing reporting. It's just being very material and working together to make

sure it's done right, tested. So it's a team process. We have a guy working on that. But we don't call him CTO, we call him the team leader. He leads the team and helps the discussions and helps management. So the concept of management role is again different than in a company, which sells products (Executive A).

Optimizing Resources

"Resource is something an organization has access to even if that access is temporary. Resource can be either "tangible" or "intangible." Tangible resources are relatively obvious; examples include buildings, plant, equipment, exclusive licenses, patents, stocks, land, debtors, and employees. Intangible resources include skills, experience and knowledge of employees, advisers, suppliers, and distributors and so on" (Mills, Platts, Bourne, & Richards, 2002). For SMEs, resources usually include funding, technologic specialist, managerial expert, strategic analyzer, and marketing and sales channels.

Resource is obviously a key issue for small companies. Many executives agreed with this. In SMEs, many executives' main job is looking for adequate resource to realize the companies' plans. Some executives believe that resource is the key to excellent performance.

We've largely been a company that's grown organically. So we've found developments in our products as we've won jobs for sell, but we've implemental built for capabilities of our products. So certainly that's probably the most challenging area for a small company, -to have resources available to build their dream. Obviously, a market strategy and then developing a product to match the strategy can be your reasonably academic consider. But if you haven't got the balance sheet to found it, ever though you have the best idea in the world, and you have the best to implement it, but you can't pay their wages, you are not going to set there. So resource is obviously a key issue for small company (Executive D).

On the other hand, other executives believe that although resource is a key factor for performance, there is no direct correlation between performance and resource. They think resource is a necessary factor, but it is not a sufficient factor to achieve excellent performance.

Capital is important. It is a main resource. However, there are other necessary conditions to achieve excellent performance. Resource is very important, but it is not the key factors (determinant). It is mainly a marketing strategy (Executive F).

In SMEs, resource utilization is a very important topic. Resource is usually very limited in SMEs. Wasting resource often leads to failure because the SMEs have no second chance to correct their mistake.

Well, you can't waste your resources. You must use it efficiently. Because you are inefficient, the other companies become more efficient than you are. You then lost your strategic advantages. So you need to make sure you are efficient in using your resource (Executive C).

Organizational Agility

This study found that environmental factors strongly influence SMEs' performance. There are interesting comments made by people interviewed.

Yes, because you are doing R&D, you're doing the future, which is affected by the economy, by technological changes, by people, by all sorts of things. So for a company it's important to be aware of the changes and to catch the important information in it and change with it. If you're going in a wrong way, you have to stop. To catch all these kinds of change, we have a board director to talk about it. And we talk to other people, and we read. In our company, this is not one person's

job, everybody does it. And this way is much better. It's not that' your job is research officer, you do what you should. '–That's what they do in big companies (Executive A).

The environmental factors influence the performance. For example, the Internet users increased year by year, the broad-band widely spread; the competitive environment in employment brings many opportunities to our company. We often consider how we can do if the economy slows down and the enterprise does not recruit new employee (Executive F).

Business environment is very important. Because here is Australia, we've been quite removed from overseas market. So it's very difficult to get market penetration. A lot of the environment factors are actually external. Probably the most influential I guess is the competition environment (from other companies, overseas, whatever) (Executive C).

The business environment is external for small companies. Most threats come from external sources. A lot of threats come from very big circle strategic companies as well. They may decide they are going to go into your strategic wish and just do those themselves (Executive C).

From previous statements, we can identify that the environmental influences come from:

1. **Economic factors:** The economic influence depends on the products and service that SMEs provide. For example, some SMEs claim that they were greatly influenced by economic factors. On the other hand, some SMEs argue that they are not influenced by economic factors. This is partly because the companies have some exclusive resource. *Well, we're probably being a bit insulated in terms of what other things are going on in economy. That probably doesn't matter too much to us, whether the resource industry*

is booming or whether it is not (Executive D).

2. **Technology changes:** Most SMEs in the IT industry are specializing in R &D. Technology changes obviously influence their performance. The issue is whether the SMEs can catch and track the technology changes.

3. **The industry changes:** The influence of a SME on the industry is very weak; on the other hand, SMEs should follow the industry changes.

4. **The strategic partners:** For SMEs, one big challenge is how to find the market penetrative point, enter the industry successfully, and play with the Giants in the industry. In the companies interviewed, one company claims that they have to constrict their business because their strategic partners cancel the collaboration.

5. **Competitors:** The competitive environment influences SMEs' performance significantly. The competitive factors include the number of competitors in the market segment; the entering barriers and so on.

6. **Geographic factors:** It is interesting that every SMEs in Australia believe that the Australia is not close to global market from geographic aspect. They believe Australia is a small market, which influences their performance significantly. Therefore, every SME in Australia is eager to enter global market.

Compared to large companies, SMEs have a smaller influence on the market. They cannot lead the technology and market as some giants in the industry do. Therefore, for SMEs, the big challenge is how to be adapted to the external environment. According to the statement from the executives, the key is that a SME can catch the changes of external factor and adjust the company's strategies in time. At the same time,

SMEs need apply flexible methods to realize market penetration.

The smaller you are the smaller influence you have in the market, and the less ambitious you are going to be. So you need to set small step changes to give you high profit-return. So you have to pick small influential products in your market position, but usually that are low-profit (Executive C).

For a company, it's important to be aware of the changes and to catch the important information in it and change with it (Executive A).

Proposed PM Framework for SMEs in the IT Industry

Through previous analysis of **PM** features and the **key success factors** in SMEs in the IT industry, we believe that the traditional financial measurement, the traditional **PM** tools and framework that are used in large organizations actually do not fit the SMEs, especially the SMEs in the IT industry. The present qualitative research shows that a practical PM framework for SMEs in the IT industry needs to meet following requirements:

1. The **PM** framework should include both financial and non-financial measurements. In the SMEs that are at the initial developing stage, the non-financial and intangible performance indicators are often more important than the financial indicators.

2. The measures should reflect both current performance and future performance because the rapidity of changes. Therefore, evaluating performance determinant factors is also very important.

3. SMEs' performance is influenced by environment significantly. SMEs can be taken as small systems in the environmental system. Therefore, the PM system should not only measure the internal factors, but also measure external factors.

Figure 1. PM components for SMEs

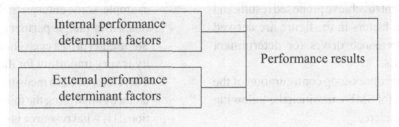

Figure 2. A proposed PM framework for SMEs

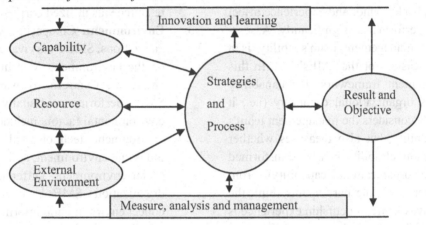

4. In different SMEs, the importance of performance factors is different. Therefore, the framework should be a dynamic one, which can be adjusted according to specific factors.

5. The institutional PM framework is not suitable to SMEs since most SMEs have not enough resource to carry out a complex performance measurement system. The measures should be tailored and reflect the SMEs' performance validly and reliably. Using **key performance indicators (KPIs)** to measure performance is hence a good choice for constructing the PM framework in SMEs.

Based on the literature review and previous analysis, we suggest that measuring SMEs' per-

formance needs evaluating three components: internal performance determinant factors, external performance determinant factors and performance results (as shown in Figure 1). According to the features of current **PM** frameworks, we believe that the structure of **Business Excellence Models** is valid and reliable for SMEs. However, more study is needed to test whether the indicators in this framework are suitable for SMEs. The **System Theory** is a useful approach to constructing a PM system for SMEs because of the uncertain prospect of SMEs and their performance being significantly influenced by environment. In summary, PM in SMEs can be constructed based on the **Excellence Business models** and **System Theory** as shown in Figure 2.

SMEs' performance depends on whether entrepreneurs can adopt appropriate strategies and process to align the internal/external resource with environment to achieve proposed results and objectives. The factors in the figure are derived from the performance drives (or determinant factors) in SMEs.

This is a 2-feedback-loop configuration of the PM framework for SMEs, in which the following factors are considered:

1. **Capability:** It is shown that entrepreneurs' ability, background, and experience affect SMEs performance significantly. Assessing the management team's ability is a basic measure for the SMEs' PM. In this measurement framework, the capability stresses organizational capability (i.e., it not only considers the management team's static ability, but also measures whether the personnel ability can be transformed into the organizational capability). From our interviews, the participants think the executives' entrepreneurship experience is not very important; however, the organizational managerial capability, as well as the marketing capability, the technological capability, is very important to the performance of SMEs in the IT industry.

2. **Resource:** Resource is always restraining SMEs' development. To achieve better performance, an enterprise must hold enough resources, which includes human resource, financial resource, social resource (government or community support), technological and physical resource and so on. From our interviews, it is found that most SMEs regard human resource as the most important performance factors. They believe that employees in the IT industry are creative persons, and organizing a highly efficient team is the critical factor to achieve excellent performance. Financial and technological resources are also very important for SMEs in the IT industry. The interviews also show that enterprises at different development stages have different resource needs. For example, some enterprises believe corporation with strategic partner is very important. Some enterprises even claim physical facility is very important for their performance. Therefore, one can measure SMEs' resource factor by answering the following three questions: (1) what resource is needed to achieve the proposed performance results? (2) What resource can be obtained? (3) Whether the resource was utilized correctly?

3. **Environment:** Comparing with large organizations, SMEs' survival depends more on the environment. Measuring business environment is an effective way for assessing SMEs' performance. Usually, the business environmental factors include competitive environment, technological environment, industrial environment, and economic and social environment. Different from large organizations, SMEs have no advantage to collect environmental information systematically and incorporate the information into their strategy making. However, all interviewees agree that environmental factors influence their performance significantly. They believe that technological factors and competitive factors are very important. Understanding and learning customers' need is also important. But they do not think that measuring customers' satisfaction periodically is needed. This is because SMEs has no resource to conduct customer satisfaction surveys, and their employees have regular direct contact with customers that they need not conduct special customer satisfaction surveys.

4. **Strategies and process:** SMEs' strategies are derived from an enterprise's vision and objectives. They are also decided by the enterprise's capability, resource, external environment, and the interaction of the above factors. Process guarantees that the SMEs' strategies can be executed and the proposed

performance results can be achieved. It is interesting to find that SMEs think that a clearly defined strategy is very important, but a few of them have a structured internal process and measurement system to ensure the realization of the strategy. Compared with large enterprises, SMEs emphasize less on process.

5. **Performance results and objectives:** Performance results are the result of past activities. The performance objectives are the expected performance targets based on the current situation. In SMEs, the performance results and objectives cannot be mechanized; in contrast, they should be flexible. There exist some key performance indicators, which vary according to specific SMEs. Generally, SMEs in the information industry prefer growth indicator and technological progress indicators to measure performance. In SMEs, performance measurement is often used to measure the realization of scheduled objectives rather than as a managerial tool to help realize strategic goals.

6. **Two feedback loops:** Finally, there are two feedback chains involved in the PM framework. One is that the capability can be improved through innovation and learning, based on the feedback of performance results and objectives. The other feedback loop means that strategies and process can be developed through measurement, analysis and management, based on performance results/objectives and the changes of performance determinant factors.

The following benefits can be obtained by implementing this framework in SMEs.

First, it provides a comprehensive and holistic framework to look into SMEs' performance. To achieve excellent performance, a SME should keep sight of all of performance determinant factors (i.e., improving organizational capability, obtaining resources and utilizing resources effec-

tively, adapting to environment, choosing correct strategy based on internal and external factors, and modify internal process continually).

Second, this framework suggests SMEs not only measure performances results, but also evaluate the internal and external performance determinant factors. It fits the features of SMEs in the IT industry. The IT industry is a rapidly developing industry; lagging performance results do not often reflect a SME's real performance. To overcome this shortage, assessing and improving the performance determinant factor are the key measures. Indeed, the performance determinant factors not only influence the short-term performance results but also affect the long-term performance results.

Third, this framework can also be used as a performance and strategy management tool. For example, after setting a performance objective, a SME needs first to think about the correct strategies; then assess whether the internal process provide enough reliability to achieve the objective and strategies. After that, the SME needs to count its own capability and resource and identify the changes of environment. The above process can be accomplished by running the framework step by step. In fact, this process can also be used in business unit, work team, and on every employee.

Fourth, this framework combines both performance objectives setting and executing processes. As we mentioned before, most SMEs' strategic plan is not formal. This framework helps SMEs set up their performance objectives and strategies based on their capabilities, resources, and environment. Furthermore, the bi-direction process helps SMEs conduct the strategies correctly across the whole organization.

Finally, this framework provides great flexibility. It suits the SMEs' feature of resource constraint. Because of resource constraint, it is impossible for SMEs to improve all aspects of performance. This framework helps SMEs focus on one or several performance aspects at a time to improve their performance whilst it provides SMEs a comprehensive view on PM.

Implementation of PM Framework in IT SMEs

This study found that very few SMEs applied structured performance measurement frameworks to measure performance. In our research sample companies, there is only one company that executed the ISO9000 quality management system in their factory because they have a factory with 50 employees. Most of them applied only several key indicators in PM. Only one company employed systematic KPIs performance measurement.

Based on the proposed performance measurement framework, the performance measurement process in SMEs can be divided into two sub-processes: the performance objectives setting and performance results measurement.

The performance objectives setting: The performance objectives setting is based on the company's vision and strategies. The version and strategies are built on the company's core capabilities, resources, and external environment. The performance objectives can be translated by several **key performance indicators (KPIs)**. These **KPIs** can be quantitatively measured and can lead to the realization of vision and strategies. After setting **KPIs**, SMEs analyze the capability needs, the resource needs, and the environmental changes to realize the **KPIs** and then identify the gaps between their current status and the needs. Some of these gaps can be overcome through learning and innovations. Therefore, the intangible performance objectives can be set based on the learning and innovation targets. Figure 3 and Figure 4 show the performance objectives setting.

Performance measurement: performance indicators vary from company to company. It is very hard to find a set of indicators for every SMEs in the information industry. The following

Figure 3. Performance objectives setting (KPIs)

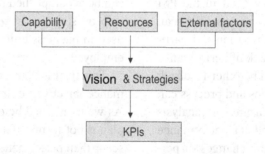

Figure 4. Intangible performance objectives setting

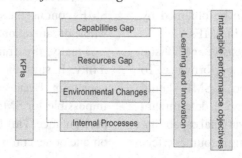

financial and non-financial indicators are often used in SMEs in the IT industry.

Key financial indicators:

1. **Profit:** Profit is the key indicator for SMEs. Many SMEs measure it. But for some companies that are specializing on R&D and have no products selling in the market, using this indicator to measure is always impossible.
2. **Growth indicators:** Growth indicators were most important in SMEs. The key growth indicators include: sales growth, income growth, profits growth, cost growth, and margin growth.
3. **Cash flow:** There are a few SMEs that noticed the importance of the measurement of cash flow. For the companies that have operated for several years, especially for the companies that have temporary financial frustrations, cash-flow is taken as a very important indicator.

The non-financial indicators: The measurement of non-financial indicators varies with different companies. The non-financial indicators that are often used can be categorized as follows:

1. **Customer orientation:** Customer service calls, sales volume from single customer, the growth of customer number, the distribution of customer, the important customers recruit.
2. **Market orientation:** Market penetration (like the market you've got, captured), new market entry, etc.
3. **Product orientation:** The products are original with competitive advantage; others cannot provide.
4. **Project management orientation:** Match R&D outcome to product development; the goals in the project plan.
5. **Staff orientation:** How many staff the company has; the specialists in the board; the culture building in the team; the atmosphere

of the working team; the employee's morale, etc.

6. **Intellectual property orientation:** The number of IP a company has; the protection of IP; the value of the IP.

CONCLUSION

This chapter identifies the challenges, features, and drivers of PM in the SMEs and introduces a PM framework based on the **system theory** and **business excellence model**. Our present study shows that a dynamic and flexible PM framework is more suitable to SMEs than a mechanized PM model. Many managers in SMEs in the IT industry claim that the mechanized PM model does not suit their organizations and it brings in much paper work. Interpreting the PM information in SMEs requires special skills. Using traditional measurement will end with misleading conclusions. Prioritizing their measurement efforts on a small number of key operational and strategic areas, we found that employing several **key performance indicators** to measure performance is a good choice for SMEs Measuring external factors is very important for SMEs' survival. Growth indicators are far more important than absolute scales, such as sales volume, revenue, etc.

Through investigating the success factors in small and medium sized IT companies, we believe that focusing on internal and external performance determinant factors and tailored **key performance indicators (KPIs)** is a good solution to performance measurement in small and medium sized IT companies. If SMEs are willing to take on an integrated PM model, the model should be resource effective and flexible, which follows the strategic changes in the companies.

REFERENCES

Abouzeedan, A., & Busler, M. (2005). ASPEM as the new topographic analysis tool for small and medium-sized enterprises (SMEs) performance models utilization. *Journal of International Entrepreneurship, 3*(1), p. 53.

Ahire, S. L., & Golhar, D. Y. (1996). Quality management in large vs small firms. *Journal of Small Business Management, 34*(2), p. 1.

Ali, I. (2003). *A performance measurement framework for a small and medium enterprise.* Unpublished thesis, University of Alberta, Canada.

Barnes, M., Coulton, L., Dickinson, T., Dransfield, S., Field, J., & Fisher, N. (1998). *A new approach to performance measurement for small to medium enterprises.* Paper presented to Conference Proceedings Performance Measurement - Theory and practice conference, Cambridge.

Brush, C. G., & Vanderwerf, P. A. (1992). A comparison of methods and sources for obtaining estimates of new venture performance. *Journal of Business Venturing, 7*(2), 157-70.

Chandler, G. N., & Hanks, S. H. (1993). Measuring the performance of emerging businesses: A validation study. *Journal of Business Venturing, 8*(5), 391-408.

Cumby, J., & Conrod, J. (2001). Non-financial performance measures in the Canadian biotechnology industry. *Journal of Intellectual Capital, 2*(3), 261.

Garengo, P., Biazzo, S., & Bititci, U. S. (2005). Performance measurement systems in SMEs: A review for a research agenda. *International Journal of Management Reviews, 7*(1), 25.

Hudson, M., Smart, A., & Bourne, M. (2001). Theory and practice in SME performance measurement systems. *International Journal of Operations & Production Management, 21*(8), 1096.

Hvolby, H. H., & Thorstenson, A. (2000, April). Performance measurement in small and medium-sized enterprises. *The 3ʳᵈ Conference on "Stimu-*

lating Manufacturing Excellence in Small and Medium Enterprises." Coventry, UK.

Jackson, M. C. (2000). *Systems approaches to management.* New York, London: Kluwer Academic/Plenum.

Jarvis, R., Curran, J., Kitching, J., & Lightfoot, G. (2000). The use of quantitative and qualitative criteria in the measurement of performance in small firms. *Journal of Small Business and Enterprise Development, 7*(2), 123-34.

Kaplan, R. S., & Norton, D. P. (1992). The balanced scorecard - measures that drive performance. *Harvard Business Review,* January-February, 71-9.

Kaplan, R. S., & Norton, D. P. (1996). *The balanced scorecard: Translating strategy into action.* Boston: Harvard Business School Press.

Kaplan, R. S., & Norton, D. P. (2001). *The strategy-focused organization: How balanced scorecard companies thrive in the new business environment.* Boston: Harvard Business School Press.

Laitinen, E. K. (2002). A dynamic performance measurement system: Evidence from small Finnish technology companies. *Scandinavian Journal of Management, 18*(1), 65-99.

McAdam, R. (2000). Quality models in an SME context: A critical perspective using a grounded approach. *The International Journal of Quality & Reliability Management, 17*(3), 305.

Mills, J., Platts, K., Bourne, M., & Richards, H. (2002). *Competing through competences.* Cambridge, UK: Cambridge University Press.

Mulhaney, A., Sheehan, J., & Hughes, J. (2004). Using ISO9000 to drive continual improvement in a SME. *The TQM Magazine, 16*(5), 325.

Rahman, S. U. (2001). A comparative study of TQM practice and organisational performance of SMEs with and without ISO 9000 certification. *International Journal of Quality & Reliability Management, 18*(1), 35-49.

Sapienza, H. J., & Grimm, C. M. (1997). Founder characteristics, start-up process, and strategy/structure variables as predictors of shartline railroad performance. *Entrepreneurship Theory and Practice*, vol. Fall, 5-24.

Stephens, P. R. (2000). *Small business and high performance management practices.* Unpublished doctoral dissertation, The University of Cincinnati.

Treacy, M., & Wiersema, F. (1995). *The discipline of market leaders: Choose your customers, narrow your focus, dominate your market.* Reading, MA: Addison-Wesley Pub. Co.

UN-ECE. (1996). *Small and medium-sized enterprises in countries in transition: Government policy, legislation, statistics, support institutions.*

United Nations Economic Commission for Europe. Retrieved June 14, 2007, from http://www.unece.org/indust/sme/review96.htm

Wang, C. K., & Ang, B. L. (2004). Determinants of venture performance in Singapore. *Journal of Small Business Management, 42*(4), 347.

Webber, A. M. (1999). New math for a new economy. *Fast company*, I *31*, 214. Retrieved on May 21, 2006, from http://www.fastcompany.com/magazine/31/lev.html

Wright, W. F., Smith, R., Jesser, R., & Stupeck, M. (1999). Information technology, process reengineering and performance measurement: A balanced scorecard analysis of Compaq Computer Corporation. *Communications of AIS (Association for Innovation System), 1*(8), 1-61.

Section III
IT Entrepreneurship and E-Business

Chapter VI
The Role of Web Sites and E-Commerce in the Development of Global Start-Ups

Brychan Thomas
University of Glamorgan Business School, UK

Christopher Miller
University of Glamorgan Business School, UK

Gary Packham
University of Glamorgan Business School, UK

Geoff Simmons
University of Ulster, UK

ABSTRACT

This chapter introduces the role of Web sites and e-commerce in the development and growth of global higher education start-ups. The extant concepts, research, and experiences the chapter builds on is the literature concerning e-commerce and small- and medium-sized enterprises (SMEs) together with published research on global start-ups. It argues that the key results, evidence, and experience, from the empirical case study research, highlight clear and precise reasons for the development of Web sites and e-commerce by the global start-ups. The limitations of the results are that they report early stage development of Web sites and e-commerce by global start-ups. The authors plan to undertake "follow-up" interviews in future years to develop a longitudinal study. Furthermore, there are important implications of the study for entrepreneurs, policy makers, practitioners, researchers, and educators for the specific field of e-commerce developments for global start-ups.

INTRODUCTION

This chapter considers the growth of global higher education start-ups and the role of Web sites and **e-commerce** in their development. The chapter builds on the extant concepts, research, and experiences of the literature concerning e-commerce and SMEs together with published research on **global start-ups**. It has been recognised that e-commerce is revolutionising business transactions. In fact, e-commerce is changing the way businesses of all sizes operate in terms of their interaction with customers and suppliers. In addition, it is contended that the rapid adoption of e-commerce by many firms is also providing the catalyst for societal change. Through e-commerce, it is possible to market products and services to customers around the World. While there is no internationally accepted definition of e-commerce, the UK Department of Trade and Industry proposed the following working definition to the organisation for economic cooperation and development (OECD):

Using an electronic network to simplify and speed up all stages of the business process, from design and making to buying, selling, and delivery. E-commerce is the exchange of information across electronic networks, at any stage in the supply chain, whether within an organisation, between businesses, between businesses and consumers, or between the public and private sectors, whether paid or unpaid. (Inland Revenue, 1998, p.1)

E-commerce continues, however, to present a significant challenge to regional and central governments alike, in terms of policies and programmes. In this sense, it is argued that businesses will need to adopt a proactive approach if they are to benefit from this new medium. Moreover, it is submitted that unless firms develop their own procedures and systems to keep pace with electronic developments, they are likely to be left behind and fall by the wayside as the e-economy gathers momentum.

Ever since the early 1970s, smaller firms have been recognised by economists and governments throughout the western world as being essential to economic development in terms of wealth creation and employment. SMEs make substantial contributions to national economies and are estimated to account for 80% of global economic growth (Jutla, Bodorik, & Dhaliqal, 2002). Within the extant literature, there is no single uniformly acceptable definition of a SME. For example, while the EU defines small businesses as having up to 50 employees and medium-sized businesses having up to 250 employees, the U.S. defines small businesses as having up to 500 employees. The most widely accepted definition of a SME is still one based on the ideas of the Bolton committee (1971). They identify three important factors that constitute the essence of a smaller firm:

- They have a relatively small share of their marketplace
- They are managed by owners or part owners in a personalised way, and not through the medium of a formalised management structure
- They are independent, in the sense of not forming part of a larger enterprise

Developments in information technology have ceaselessly had profound marketing implications for smaller businesses. None more so in recent years than the ever-prospering forum of the Internet, which poses both tremendous opportunities and challenges for SMEs globally. Despite the widespread acceptance of Internet use in corporate environments the extent of Internet use continues to vary widely among small businesses (Sadowski, Maitland, & van Douyer, 2002). The opportunities presented by e-commerce participation for SMEs relates to the leveraging of inherent strengths to create competitive advantage. The size of SMEs enables them to be more adaptable and responsive to changing conditions than larger organisations and to further benefit from the speed and flexibility that the electronic environment offers (Stockdale & Standing, 2004). E-commerce, for many SMEs, is manifested in Web sites, which are viewed as providing the most value within an inherently marketing-driven context (McCue, 1999; Pflughoeft, Ramamurthy, Soofi, Yasai-Ardekani, & Fatemah, 2003; Quinton & Harridge-March, 2003; Raymond, 2001; Sellitto, Wenn, & Burgess, 2003; Sparkes & Thomas, 2001; Standing, Vasudavan, & Borbely, 1998). Many SMEs initially adopt the Internet for business use as a tool for e-mail and surfing the World Wide Web. However, Web site adoption takes this Internet adoption to a higher level by requiring the SME to register a URL and develop a Web site, which can be accessed by visitors globally. This Web site adoption, in turn, will be at different levels at any particular point in time in terms of its sophistication and relevance to target customers.

SMEs are adopting e-commerce for marketing, promoting, buying and selling of goods and services electronically. In particular, this is carried out as a new way of transacting business and encompasses various aspects of Internet use. This involves virtual store fronts that are sites for shopping and making purchases, exchange of data and e-mail. There is also business-to-business buying and selling and the need for the security of data handling and transactions (Van Ketel & Nelson, 1998). In these terms, Forrester Research (1998), which is an independent research firm, defines e-commerce as "the trading of goods and services in which the final order is placed over the Internet" (p. 1). It is evident that a growing number of SMEs are accessing the Internet for their business and to reach new customers. It may seem intuitive to conclude that larger companies with greater levels of expertise and resources would appear to be in a much stronger position to implement e-commerce strategies. Indeed, Smyth and Ibbotson (2001) found that smaller businesses

exhibited much lower rates of e-commerce adoption than larger companies. Development of appropriate skills, investment in staff training and poor knowledge of the Internet adoption process have been identified as central barriers to **e-commerce** diffusion (Smyth et al., 2001). However, SME Internet competencies have been identified and studied by McGowan, Durkin, Allen, Dougan, and Nixon (2001). They contend that Internet technology can be a facilitator of SME relationships through its ability to transfer information between them and other firms in a network. By creating Internet-based competencies, a SME can potentially transcend traditional business barriers such as physical distance between markets and thus allowing more effective and efficient interactions within the network. To facilitate this process, McGowan et al. (2001) postulate that a broad range of skills will be essential in enabling it to happen. Knowledge of the medium will be important as well as the vision to predict its usefulness in future business strategies, and the ability to translate the vision into actual proactive business practice. Technological awareness of how Internet technology operates will also be essential within the process. A survey, conducted by the Arthur Anderson Enterprise Group and the National Small Business United (1998), reported that e-mail and research are the most popular use of the Internet amongst SMEs. In the survey it was found that SMEs used a Web site in order to reach new and potential customers (78%), sell goods and services (65%), provide information more efficiently (62%), reach new prospective employees (13%) and expand globally (17%).

Potential entrepreneurs can be discouraged from setting up ventures in the global market place because of the many complexities and barriers that appear to reduce their chances of success. Through the use of Web sites many of these barriers can be overcome. By performing case study interviews this chapter provides a detailed understanding of the role of Web sites and e-commerce for global higher education spin-offs. There is an identification of the specific problems encountered and the key Internet factors, which have helped them to succeed, based upon the university and regional support available. The six case study interviews, described, lasted about one hour each and were centred on three key elements:

1. **The company:** Profile and background of the spin-off's Web site, e-commerce development and major milestones
2. **The university:** Analysis of the technology transfer office (TTO) in the development of the Web site, e-commerce and internationalisation
3. **The region:** Regional infrastructure Web site and e-commerce support and internationalisation

The key results, evidence, and experience from the empirical case study research highlight clear and precise reasons for the development of Web sites and e-commerce by the **global start-ups**. The limitations of the results are that they report early stage development of Web sites and e-commerce by global start-ups. It is planned to undertake follow-up interviews in future years to develop a longitudinal study. There are important implications of the study for entrepreneurs, policy makers, practitioners, researchers, and educators for the specific field of e-commerce developments for global start-ups.

BACKGROUND

The increasing importance and role of Web-based technologies to support company operations (e-business) is widely acknowledged by both practitioners and academicians. A number of studies have appeared in the management literature, trying to describe and better understand the e-business phenomenon. One of the key points that have been clarified is that the concept of e-business itself is rather wide, since it includes a number of different applications and uses of the Internet technology.

Among the possible classification dimensions, a relevant one is based on the process supported by Internet tools. For example, supply chain management refers to the management of different processes, such as customer relationship management, customer service, demand management, order management, production and material flows, and purchasing (Lambert, Cooper, & Pagh, 1998). In this context, e-business could be classified as:

- **E-commerce (Brynjolfsson & Smith, 2000):** Support to sales, distribution and customer service processes
- **E-procurement (De Boer, Harink, & Heijboer, 2002):** Support to sourcing, procurement, tendering, and order fulfilment processes
- **E-manufacturing (Kehoe & Boughton, 2001):** Supporting demand and capacity planning, forecasting and internal supply chain integration

Three phases of Internet use, which SMEs go through as their **e-commerce** involvement develops, are described as connectivity, customer relations, and commerce (Ng, Pan, & Wilson, 1998; YG, 1998;). The three phases are seen as the building blocks of e-commerce (Williams & Phillips, 1999), as shown in Figure 1 (based on von Goeler, 1998).

The three phases towards e-commerce can be described as follows:

- **Brochure-ware sites:** Enterprises use their Web sites for product/service advertisement, gather information, and improve services through customer feedback forms. Such enterprises need to install electronic technology to sell goods over the World Wide Web.

Figure 1. Phases in the development of e-commerce for SME Web sites (Adapted from von Goeler, 1998)

Phases		Information exchange		Web site development
Connectivity		Product/Service and Enterprise Information Customer Feedback Forms		Brochure-ware sites
Customer Connections		Online catalogue		Pre E-Commerce sites
E-Commerce		Online ordering Online payment		Simple E-Commerce sites

- **Pre-commerce sites:** Enterprises are able to provide information on price for immediate orders from their Web sites. But they do not carry out online point-of-sale transactions, although they keep their site current.
- **Simple e-commerce sites:** Enterprises accept orders and payments over the Web.

Customers have developed a behavioural sequence to online shopping. Indeed, Forrester Research (1998) has divided the online retail market into the three categories of convenience items, replenishment goods, and research purchases. Convenience items are low cost discretionary items such as books, clothes and music. Replenishment goods are medium cost high frequency purchases like groceries. Research purchases are information driven and cost more than the other two categories and include planned purchases such as cars, computers and airline tickets. The Forrester Research study (1998) found that first time buyers usually bought convenience items and that it took around one year for online shoppers to move to a further category.

Internet sales have shown a fast growth in books, cars, computers, and software (USDoC, 1998). Important players in this growth are **online entrepreneurs** (Simons, 1999). Whereas some SMEs have been early adopters of e-commerce,

others have lagged behind in establishing the ability to sell their products and services over the Internet (Williams et al., 1999). In fact, SMEs have been slower than large businesses in embracing e-commerce (Mehling, 1998). Even though the number of SMEs using the Internet is rising there are a number of obstacles to their use of e-commerce. Specifically, SMEs are particularly constrained by resource factors, and are therefore more sensitive than larger organisations to **e-commerce** adoption costs (Lewis & Cockrill, 2002; Smith & Webster, 2000). If there is no clear benefit in Web site adoption, for example, within resource constraints, SMEs will be more constrained in adoption than a larger company who will have more latitude to experiment (Jones, Muir, & Benyon-Davies, 2004). However, on a more cautionary note, Sadowski et al. (2002) argue that over-concentration on perceived costs/barriers has prevented many SMEs from properly exploring the benefits which could be extracted from e-commerce adoption, resulting in adoption which is opportunistic, rather than being based on a clear perception of its potential value. Essentially, by clearly exploring both the benefits and the barriers, a SME can more effectively perceive the value of e-commerce within their business context. Quayle (2001), who explores perception and level of implementation of e-com-

Figure 2. The e-commerce stairway

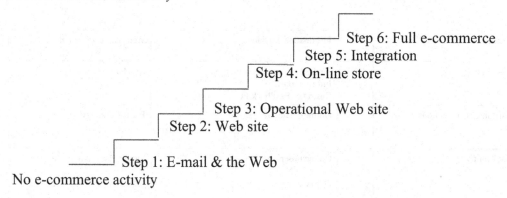

merce, has eloquently described the e-commerce challenge for SMEs. Results of a survey of 298 small firms were used to identify barriers faced by these enterprises and he suggests paths, which might be followed in seeking to achieve best in class performance for e-commerce. In order to overcome the barriers to e-commerce, the e-commerce ladder has been developed which involves step 0 (not started), step 1 (using e-mail and the Web), step 2 (basic Web site), step 3 (an effective Web site), step 4 (an online store), step 5 (integration), and step 6 (advanced e-commerce) (Opportunity Wales, 2007). In relation to this the chapter proposes the **e-commerce stairway** as a method of measuring the type of e-commerce adopted by case companies (Figure 2).

SMEs rely on knowing customer needs and build business processes and quality control around communications. A major concern is that the loss of customer contact may lead to a lower quality of service, and there may be customer resistance to product price at the point of transaction. Low technology enterprises, in contrast to **high tech businesses**, will have concerns about online sales and e-commerce (von Goeler, 1998). Most SMEs recognise the importance of selling on the Internet as being important in the future (Williams et al., 1999). It is the proposition of this chapter that, because of the increasing importance of SMEs being able to sell their products and ser-

vices over the internet, it is necessary for regional governments to develop an e-commerce policy, particularly as affects **global start-ups**, to ensure the future competitiveness of their regions.

GLOBAL START-UPS' WEB SITES AND E-COMMERCE

Rialp-Criado, Rialp-Criado, and Knight (2002) noted several key driving forces behind the emergence of global start-ups as well as their age, industry affiliation, export behaviour and performance, geographic distribution, (rise in) number and size. In addition, international operations from the start-up of the business have been seen to be important. General consensus has provided that the underlying notion and theoretical definition of the global start-up phenomenon perceives them as young entrepreneurial firms engaged in international business from inception (Rialp-Criado et al., 2002). On the one hand, researchers have considered a six-year period as the standard in measuring international operations from the start-up of the business (Oviatt & McDougall, 1997). On the other hand, academics have selected other criteria to empirically define the **global start-ups** being analysed. Rennie (1993) has reported that firms began exporting two years after foundation on average and realised 76% of their total sales by exporting. Other authors have defined this according to foreign sales of 25% or more after starting exporting activities and within three years of birth (Knight & Cavusgil, 1996; Madsen, Rasmussen, & Servais, 2000; Servais & Rasmussen, 2000). By describing, understanding, and interpreting the reasons behind the emergence of global start-ups it is possible to gain insight into their needs for IT support provision. Interestingly, according to Rialp-Criado et al. (2002), much of the present literature about global start-ups has been assumed to be concerned with **high tech businesses**, considering the globalisation aspects present in sectors within which these firms compete (Autio & Sapienza, 2000; Autio, Sapienza, & Almeida, 2000; Bell, 1995; Burgel & Murray, 2000; Coviello & Munro, 1995; McDougall & Oviatt, 1996; Roberts & Senturia, 2000; Zahira, Ireland, & Hitt, 2000).

According to Rialp-Criado et al. (2002), the top ten characteristics considered as critical success factors (CSFs) for global start-ups (not in rank order) are:

- *Managerial global vision from inception.*
- *High degree of previous international experience on behalf of managers.*
- *Management commitment.*
- *Strong use of personal and business networks (networking).*
- *Market knowledge and market commitment.*
- *Unique intangible assets based on knowledge management.*
- *High value creation through product differentiation, leading edge technology products,* **technological innovativeness** *(usually associated with a greater use of IT), and quality leadership.*
- *Niche focussed, proactive international strategy in geographically spread lead markets around the World from the very beginning.*

- *Narrowly defined customer groups with strong customer orientation and close customer relationships.*
- *Flexibility to adapt to rapidly changing external conditions and circumstances* (Rialp-Criado et al, 2002, p. 25-26).

Further to this, Rialp-Criado et al. (2002) from their research into twenty seven of the most important studies in the decade 1993-2002, which consider global start-ups amongst other forms of these types of businesses, say that having identified, examined and critically assessed these studies they have been able to formulate an adequate observation of the state of the art of this important research area within the field of **international entrepreneurship** (IE).

According to Wakkee, van der Sijde, and Kirwan (2003), global start-ups are described in the literature as perfect examples of entrepreneurial ventures and therefore need to be investigated from an entrepreneurial perspective. They go on to say that, the concept of global start-up was first mentioned in a paper by Mamis (1989). At about the same time, Ray (1989) undertook four cases for which the term global start-up was used. Following this, the term global start-up was defined by Oviatt and McDougall (1994) "as one that seeks to derive significant competitive advantage from extensive co-ordination along multiple organisational activities, the location of which is geographically unlimited" (p. 59-60). Wakkee et al. (2003) add that, these firms do not only respond to global market conditions, they also act to acquire resources and sell wherever in the World there is the largest value. Since Oviatt and McDougall (1994, 1995) the term global start-up has been referred to by Harveston (2000), Madsen and Servais (1997), and Saarenketo (2002). Furthermore, Rasmussen and Madsen (2002) have suggested that they are the only type of international new venture. Wakkee et al (2003) have said that "a global start-up is the most radical manifestation of the international new venture"(pp. 6-7). According to Wakkee et al (2003), from their discussion of the literature on the definition of a **global start-up**, five relevant characteristics are apparent, and these are:

1. *The diversity or scope of the international activities*
2. *The company age*
3. *The timing of international activities (time to entry)*
4. *The global diversity of the international activities*
5. *The purpose of the international activities (strategic choice)* (Wakkee et al., 2003, p. 13).

In fact, they say that the nature of the opportunity differences global start-ups from other types of start-ups since the opportunity is a global one. From this, Wakkee et al. (2003) define a global start-up as:

A new venture that from its inception ("opportunity recognition") seeks to pursue opportunities wherever they arise (i.e., global or in an unlimited number of countries around the world), it coordinates multiple activities in the value chain through the interaction with network actors around the World. The entrepreneur(ial team) leading the firm is internationally experienced and skilled. (Wakkee et al., 2003, p. 14).

They go on to say that global start-ups are characterised by high levels of **entrepreneurial orientation** (EO) although originally developed by Lumpkin and Dess (1996) and Lumpkin (1998) for established firms when considered for global start-ups they exhibit high levels of EO. In these terms, Wakkee et al. (2003), bring together the descriptions of global start-ups and, describe them as "an entrepreneurial firm that literally from its inception is involved in a variety of international activities around the World" (Wakkee et al., 2003, p. 28).

The case studies selected are spin-offs, from a new university, which are believed to have global potential and exhibit differing states of **technological innovativeness**. Those that have been selected are university spin-offs operating in the global market or with a global potential. Founders, closely involved with the spin-offs from establishment until now, have been interviewed. No restrictions have been placed with regard to the spin-off age and industry. Although, it is the case that spin-offs running for a number of years will provide more valuable information about their IT development than those only recently founded. For spin-offs in existence for many years it may be difficult to find a founder who has been involved with the business since the original idea. It might also be more difficult for these people to remember the specific problems encountered in the early stages of the IT development of the spin-off. The spinout managers (see http://www.spinoutwales. co.uk/man.html) identified the interesting spin-off cases and provided contact names for interviews. They also approached the companies in the first instance to gain their support. The stages of development of the case study companies have been measured against the **e-commerce** ladder (Opportunity Wales, 2007).

GLOBAL START-UPS: CASE STUDIES

Described next are the six global start-up case studies, which were investigated, and these reveal different characteristics and aspects for Web site development and e-commerce activity. Perhaps the main limitation is that most of the companies are in the early stage of IT and business development, but it is envisaged that this work will be developed into a longitudinal study, which will show interesting evolutionary Web site and e-commerce dynamics in future years. Due to the sensitive nature and stage of their development all the companies have been referred to anonymously.

Consultancy Services

Profile and Background to the Company's Web Site and E-Commerce Development

The consultancy services (CS) company founded in January 2004 as a University spinout, commenced trading in January 2005 to assist organisations access European Union (EU) funding in order to implement specific projects in accordance with regulations accompanying the use of funds. In particular, the Internet has been used to interact with organisations who, as the customers, need to access EU funds. This has been taken into account in the company's overall marketing strategy and e-business strategy. Services involve a range of training courses that cover all aspects of European Union (EU) funded projects, including State Aid Rules and Public Procurement Directive. CS has a team of Prince 2 practitioners and freelance consultants. Table 1 summarises the profile and background of the company.

The company has grown on an incremental basis and this followed a long period of time to receive approval with the University. The construction of the Web site took six months and this was achieved on 1st March 2005. The company has won a number of contracts and this has therefore not been an issue. It has also been important to have clients returning and to draw on their exper-

tise. There are six current clients including public sector and voluntary organisations.

Development of the Web Site and E-Commerce

To a large extent the company has relied on public support, through the Spinout programme, in its early stage development. The founder has been satisfied with the university support that has been provided and the company has received £30,000 from its activities, which has included grant aid to pay for the Web site and employees' wages that have been subcontracted from the University Commercial Services Company to carry out work. Whilst these staff have been undertaking this work the company has been making money and this has been found to be a good arrangement. Support through the Spinout programme to set up the business plan was slow and it was not proactive. This could have been undertaken in a month, rather then six or seven months, if more advice had been provided at the start. As part of the business plan the Founder is hoping to recruit a partner to drive the business forward off campus so that he can retain his position on campus.

Web Site and E-Commerce Support

A spinout loan has been secured and there has been an undergraduate working with the company

Table 1. Profile and background: Consultancy services

Brief overview of the firm's activities, its mission and focus	
Industry	European Project Management
Technology	Project Management software
Product/service	Training and consultancy
Market and targeted customers	Wales, Romania, Poland, Hungary, Lithuania, Bulgaria and other European countries
Company's current mission and focus	To develop the company at a European level over the next three years.

for 10 weeks. Additionally, the company has been assigned a mentor to develop a strategy to make a first contact and receive a contract in Poland.

The company has also received grant aid to develop the Web site. There has been an additional £750 provided for a Web site psychologist to attract customers through the Web site. Regarding the potential role played by the Internet, since the company has been trading for less than two years, it is yet to be seen if the results of the company, in terms of revenue, profit, numbers of staff and customers, generated through its Web site, are on target when compared with the original business plan. In terms of the **e-commerce** ladder, the company is at step 3 of development.

Energy Management Systems

Profile and Background to the Company's Web Site and E-Commerce Development

Energy management systems (EMS) was launched in January 2005 as a spinout company. The focus of the company is to reduce utility costs and to provide customised online utility information regarding these costs and to ensure that they remain low. The company works with customers to provide a full energy/utility service ranging from fuel purchasing, meter installation, advanced monitoring and targeting to project engineering and information technology (IT) solutions. In its

early stages the company received public support through the Spinout programme and more recent developments have been resourced by the foudners. In addition to IT and software developments, EMS undertakes remote analysis of customers' consumption patterns and works closely with clients to achieve reduced costs. The company aims to be a professional service provider by establishing trust through building personal relationships with customers over the Internet. This has been included in the firm's overall marketing and e-business strategy. Through this trust it enables EMS to work with customers, employing the most appropriate technology to gain outstanding results. The products and services provided include metering hardware and connectivity; IT support, hosting, VDN and networking; installation of metering hardware and network cabling; installation of gas, water and steam meters; Web design, Web development and consultancy. Table 2 summarises the profile and background of the company.

Development of the Web Site and E-Commerce

The reasons why customers have chosen EMS for their energy system requirements are because they have energy bills over £100,000, require a rebate, have experienced a large rise in energy bills, want to improve their bottom line for little capital outlay and are concerned about the environ-

Table 2. Profile and background: Energy management systems

Brief overview of the firm's activities, its mission and focus	
Industry	Energy
Technology	Energy management technology
Product/service	.Net Web management system
Market and targeted customers	Public, private and leisure organisations
Company's current mission and focus	To maintain and consolidate company activities over the next five years.

ment. Additionally, technical reasons for choosing EMS include their unique and advanced .Net Web management system, advanced statistical process control and proactive alarming, secure VPN data connectivity to each company, customisable reporting, visualisation, and an exceptional range of business patterns and support. Also, the company is one of the few organisations that offer a full energy management service remotely. So far there have been four pilot customers.

Web Site and E-Commerce Support

With the company Web site, it is possible to log on from anywhere and it provides online real-time monitoring. Through the Web site it will be possible to market the company internationally. Due to the importance of this, the founders have allocated money in the business plan to update the site since it will be the main marketing tool. Again, since the company has been trading for less than two years it is yet to be seen if the results of the company in terms of revenue, profit, numbers of staff and customers, generated through its Web site, are on target. According to the **e-commerce** ladder, the company is again at step 3 of development.

Literary Book Publishing

Profile and Background to the Company's Web Site and E-Commerce Development

Literary Book Publishing (LBP) was launched and registered, as a limited company in May 2001 as a spinout company from the university with public support through the Spinout programme. The company publishes short stories by authors in a small book format and provides retailing through coffee shops, tearooms, restaurants, and hotels. The books are being marketed, over the Internet, to customers in the United Kingdom (UK), United States (U.S.) initially and the English speaking world due to the co-founders' business partner being American. This role of the Internet has been included in the company's overall marketing and e-business strategy. Other markets and languages will be considered later. There is a three-year business plan targeting sales in the UK and USA for the first three years. The spin off is linked to the University since both of the co-founders are graduates of the English Department Centre for Creative Writing. This provides a link with academics and a network of authors. The co-founders are MPhil students from the University. Table 3 summarises the profile and background of the company.

Table 3. Profile and background: Literary book publishing

Brief overview of the firm's activities, its mission and focus	
Industry	Book Publishing
Technology	Book publishing graphic design technology
Product/service	A6 pocket sized books
Market and targeted customers	UK, USA and the English speaking world
Company's current mission and focus	To develop the company in the book publishing trade over the next three years.

Development of the Web Site and E-Commerce

The initial markets are in the UK and U.S. to be followed internationally. Work with partners is finite for international distribution. Once the product is proved LBP will approach international chains such as Marks and Spencer. As a small start-up company they are not ready to sell to Marks and Spencer who have 6 warehouses and 140 coffee shops in the UK. The large international chain stores will consider the product once it is proven. A contact for London and Cambridge has taken the books to shops that are willing to pay a higher price. The product will sell better in the South East of England and it is hoped that this will be the case with international markets. The company organised a short story competition for authors on its Web site for the winners and runners-up to have their first books published. There are also competitions for poetry and writing for children.

Web Site and E-Commerce Support

Networks are important to the business on a national level and to grow internationally. The power of the Web is also important and the company Web site has been set up to give creditability, publicise the competitions and people have been referred to the site for information. Since no one had heard of the company this was important. The Web site involves graphics and the competition had a good response. Another Web site is being constructed to complement the current site, which provides information about the company in order to sell books online. This will develop the current four pages into a 16-page site with online ordering. It is envisaged that this potential role of the Internet and the company's Web site will have a significant impact, on how the company will grow since founding, in terms of revenue, profit, numbers of staff and customers. The company is moving from step 3 to step 4 of the **e-commerce** ladder.

Mobile Phone Security

Profile and Background to the Company's Web Site and E-Commerce Development

The mobile phone security (MPS) company is a spinout of the university with limited public support through the spinout programme. It was formed in 2004 by the founder who as an undergraduate developed a unique patent pending software application, which overcomes password protection technology limitations. The application is different to existing mobile security software since it is undetectable. This provides high levels of data security since there is no evidence that data is hidden. Once the application is installed in a mobile phone it creates a second menu for users to store confidential contact information, office documents, pictures or video files. These are safe since there is no trace of the second menu, which is not visible in the event of unauthorised use, theft, or loss. Since the menu mirrors standard phone functionality it is easy for the user to navigate requiring little effort to learn.

Since the take up of 3G services has not been as strong as the industry forecast companies are looking for third party content to differentiate between their own and competitors' service and product offerings. This will result in third party software developers such as MPS to be in a strong position. It is envisaged that the primary route to the OEM market will be through regional licensing agreements with major network operators. Through the pre-installation of the software in phones this will enable users to experience the software application and will allow the encouragement of new potential users through direct marketing by the network operators. In order to encourage new users to adopt the service the try before you buy approach is a powerful tactic.

The ability to differentiate the network operators' product offering, for example the incorporation of e-mail facilities and second secure message

Table 4. Profile and background: Mobile phone security

Brief overview of the firm's activities, its mission and focus	
Industry	Data security industry
Technology	Mobile phone technology
Product/service	Application software
Market and targeted customers	Global
Company's current mission and focus	To develop the company in the data security industry over the next three years.

facilities for secure contacts, will relative to the downloadable version also allow a premium price. End user pricing of the network provider is expected to be in the range of £9 to £12 a year. As well as repeat business for the network operators each time a user upgrades a phone the software application will generate considerable new revenue streams. It is also anticipated that the software, with time phased licence agreements and enhanced product differentiation, will enable network operators to increase their market share through regional exclusivity rights and to further increase revenue. Table 4 summarises the profile and background of the company.

Development of the Web Site and E-Commerce

MPS is offering the application for sale globally to customers through main Internet download Web sites for compatible mobile phones. This was considered important in the firm's marketing and e-business strategy. The world wide market for mobile phones is over 800 million phone sales a year and the sequential licensing of software to phone providers and network operators will enable MPS to target markets with high growth rates. MPS has appointed legal experts to provide advice on patents since it recognises the importance of patent protection in all the major regional markets.

In countries not covered by the International Patent Cooperation Treaty network operators will be offered the software under licence to avoid delay that may result in infringements. The software source code has been encrypted to make piracy difficult. The trend to support real time sharing of information using mobile devices involves many sectors and the software application's ability to keep data secure will enable new public and private sector applications. On the basis of dual strategy and analysis of project payback, MPS can generate a payback fundamental of between ten times the project cost for Internet sales and a potential 57 times for a licensed agreement with a major network operator. The network operators, through the creation of new revenue streams, should be attracted to incorporate and invest in their mobile devices for the new technology.

Web Site and E-Commerce Support

The main target markets are the data security product/service markets. Although the launch of the Web site will provide information on the software application for global markets there is a need to be careful not to mislead competitors with how the software is being developed. It is planned for there to be a product comparison on the Web site, comparing the product with competitors, but this will have to wait for the patent to be approved. The University School of Computing developed the company Web site, which is considered to be exceptional and better than those of the competitors. The role played by the Internet and the Web site, in relation to competitors, will have particular importance in terms of revenue, profit, numbers of staff and customers. Again, the company is moving from step 3 to step 4 of the **e-commerce** ladder.

Pet Care

Profile and Background to the Company's Web Site and E-Commerce Development

The founder started-up as an incorporated company in May 2004, using Spinout programme public support, with a new product that needed development following considerable research into the market. When the company was at the early development stage, there was a need for a manufacturer. It was difficult to find early stage support since contacts were reluctant to provide backing and were cautious. The original idea arose from outside the University from a company formed by the founder in 1986. This produced waterbeds for pets and a cage system as a holding bay for animals before and after hospital. Collaborative work originally took place with another University. The bed, for use in animal hospitals, was new on the market and with this product, it was the first time the founder had started a company. From the experience of doing this the founder decided to start a company again.

With the present company, the first product is an outside cat cabin, which is being marketed on the company Web site. This has been developed following the founder's experience of housing cats while at work. There is a clear demand arising from owners not being able to have a cat flap in a wall, or where the cost to replace a door is prohibitive (@ £800 in some cases). From this the

idea for a cat cabin arose. Table 5 summarises the profile and background of the company.

Development of the Web Site and E-Commerce

In the first year, the company concentrated on the UK and Irish markets. Since this was a challenge, it was decided to concentrate on one product. In the second year the company sold into the European, United States, and Chinese markets. The Chinese market is a large window of opportunity since the majority of homes have a cat and therefore there is an immense market. Since the cat house is a unique shape representing the head of cat at the entrance it looks good. It is therefore functional since the cat head fits into the garden as a piece of furniture and appears as an attractive product to customers on the company Web site. This was taken into account in the overall marketing and e-business strategy.

Web Site and E-Commerce Support

For the first year, outlets were established including selling through the company Web site, pet stores, local shops, and large chain stores like Argos in the UK. The founder has also approached other outlets such as mail order catalogues. When a retailer sees a picture of the product they usually want to sell it. This has been the case with a large Irish retailer. There has been a good response and there appears to be a global market. Once the initial market has been established the company will consider other products in order to diversify and sell internationally. The role being played by the Internet and the company Web site is having a significant impact on revenue, profit and the numbers of customers. Since the company is selling its products through the Web site it is at step 6 of the **e-commerce** ladder.

Under Grad

Profile and Background to the Company's Web Site and E-Commerce Development

Under Grad is a company, which provides a scheme that encourages companies to employ the best engineering and technology students through the company's Web site. The co-founders started the company about four years ago in January 2003 with public support through the Spinout programme. The idea for the company arose due to the national decline in the number of students gaining employment in the areas of engineering and technology. Following this being recognised as an opportunity in 2002, a limited company was formed in January 2003. Office space was provided at the University spin-off premises with the help of the Head of the University Commercial Services. The ambition of the founders is to help the University and other universities (like minded organisations and departments) to find industrial employment for their engineering and technology students. The two founders are both employed by the University in the School of Technology and when they formed the company they were the two directors. Office space, support staff and

Table 5. Profile and background: Pet care

Brief overview of the firm's activities, its mission and focus	
Industry	Pet products
Technology	Pet care technologies
Product/service	Specialised pet care products—cat house, pet bed, and animal warm mattress.
Market and targeted customers	UK (in the first year)—pet super stores, multiple retailers, pet shops, privately owned high street outlets, veterinary surgeries. Europe (second year). North American market (third year).
Company's current mission and focus	Through the development and sale of pet products, the company will establish itself in the UK market and progress to the European and United States markets.

Table 6. Profile and background: Under Grad

Brief overview of the firm's activities, its mission and focus	
Industry	Employment
Technology	Student employment systems
Product/service	Employment service for companies to employ engineering and technology students.
Market and targeted customers	• Engineering and technology students • Companies • Universities
Company's current mission and focus	To maintain and consolidate company activities in the employment of engineering and technology students over the next five years.

facilities are provided in the School, as well as the office space at the University spin-off premises. Table 6 summarises the profile and background of the company.

Development of the Web Site and E-Commerce

The company was developed within the University's School of Technology. The firm places undergraduate students at a host company while studying part-time for a degree using the Web site. Two days are spent by trainees at the University and the rest of the week at work. Complex systems have been developed to support the scheme, by a franchise centre, through innovative support systems with the award of the ISO 9000:2000 accreditation of the work. Originally work was aimed at higher education institutions in Britain, but following modification overseas colleges and a private European training organisation have become involved. Franchise centres deliver key skills modules at level 1 through to five-year supported programmes. The company provides valuable work experience to students during their university course, with no fees and a bursary up to £9,000. Businesses benefit from motivated undergraduates studying at university, working with the businesses, and they become competent and experienced company members. Franchise centres are cost effective. These have been very successful and have helped to reverse trends in declining numbers and entry qualifications for engineering and technology students. There have also been follow-on efforts such as the retention of students. Through students being more aware of potential debt, and the incentive of a bursary and work experience they are attracted to the scheme.

Web Site and E-Commerce Support

Flexibility is a key factor and franchises are available for fees and maintenance fees with three levels of participation. Level 1, which is the placement class, is the entry level developed for overseas partners. The company provides the means to develop industrial contacts for customers through its Web site and many businesses are willing to have students on short placements. This was taken into account in the overall and e-business strategy. A matching section of the company Web site provides a means to do this. Level 2 involves an innovative student attendance monitoring system. An essential element of the programme is to develop a mature student attitude towards their work and studies. Level 3 is full membership and includes the two previous classes plus a full package providing the franchise centre with training and support to develop a network of companies and students. Documentation is provided to support the running of the programme with the required resources. On the technical side, the company has developed its own Web site. This is found to be a necessity when recruiting French students, since this is undertaken online on the Internet. The Web site is, therefore, seen as an important international tool in terms of revenue, profit and customers. The company is at step 3 of the **e-commerce** ladder.

FUTURE TRENDS

The key results, evidence, and experience from the empirical case study research highlight clear and precise reasons for the development of Web sites and e-commerce by the **global start-ups**. The limitations of the results are that in most of the cases they report early stage development of Web sites and e-commerce. Table 7 summarises the results of the global start-up case studies in terms of their step on the **e-commerce stairway**.

Table 7 illustrates that the vendors of goods (LBP, MPS, and pet care) are on a higher step of e-commerce than the vendors of services (CS, EMS, and UG) over the Internet. Indeed, pet care, founded in 2004, has reached stairway level

Table 7. Steps for the global start-up companies on the e-commerce stairway

Case	Company	Initials	Step
1.	Consultancy Services	CS	3
2.	Energy Management Systems	EMS	3
3.	Literary Book Publishing	LBP	3-4
4.	Mobile Phone Security	MPS	3-4
5.	Pet Care	PC	6
6	Under Grad	UG	3

6, while LBP and MPS, established contemporaneously or before, have only reached levels 3 or 4 due to Pet Care developing the sale of its products through its Web site further than LBP and MPS.

Since most of the global start-up companies are fairly young they have tended to report early stage development in terms of e-commerce. It is, therefore, planned to undertake follow-up interviews in future years to develop a longitudinal study to reveal e-commerce developments. In order to do this a coherent structure for both the data and the analysis will be essential.

CONCLUSION: THE E-COMMERCE STAIRWAY

In the future, more entrepreneurs will gain access to the Internet at lower cost, but if concerns such as security are not addressed e-commerce may be slow to grow. If more secure ways of business are developed on the Internet, consumers and businesses will not consider themselves vulnerable with personal information. The number of SMEs using computers in their operations will increase considerably in the future. In particular, the Internet is a quick and simple means of communication between SMEs and customers. Consequently, more companies in the future will be likely to use **e-commerce**. SMEs will be able to buy, sell, distribute, maintain products, and provide services over the Internet. This is shown by the **global start-up** case studies. By doing this, they will be able to achieve cost savings and have more customers with increased sales. Here, e-commerce will not replace traditional forms of shopping and business, but will provide a further option to the SME and the consumer. Business-to-consumer (b2c) development has been slower than business-to-business (b2b) e-commerce. For continued growth in online consumer sales there is a need for secure and cost effective mechanisms. Future consumers are likely to embrace e-commerce in greater numbers than at present and this will help the development of e-commerce for SMEs.

This chapter has revealed the important role of Web sites and e-commerce in the development of global start-ups. Although they are, in many cases, at an early stage of development the case studies show a critical need for e-commerce to develop international activities. In response to this the **e-commerce stairway** illustrates how a global start-up can progress up the steps of e-commerce activity.

It appears that global start-ups adopt a proactive approach to e-commerce in order to benefit from this medium. As they develop they need to keep pace with electronic developments as the international e-economy gathers momentum. There are therefore important implications of the e-commerce stairway for entrepreneurs, policy makers, practitioners, researchers and educators for the specific field of e-commerce developments for global start-ups. It is therefore apparent, from the findings of this chapter that because of the increasing importance of SMEs being able to sell their products and services over the internet, it is necessary for regional governments to develop an e-commerce policy, particularly as affects global start-ups, to ensure the future competitiveness of their regions.

REFERENCES

Arthur Andersen & National Small Business United (1998). *Survey of Small and Medium-sized Businesses*. Report, November. (pp.19-20).

Autio, E., & Sapienza, H. J. (2000). Comparing process and born global perspectives in the international growth of technology-based new firms. In W. D. Bygrave, C. G. Brush, P. Davidsson, J. O. Fiet, P. G. Greene, R. T. Harrison, M. Lerner, G. D. Meyer, J. Sohl & A. Zacharakis (Eds.), *Frontiers of Entrepreneurship Research*. (pp. 413-424). Babson College, Centre for Entrepreneurial Studies.

Autio, E., Sapienza, H. J., & Almeida, J. G. (2000). Effects of age at entry, knowledge intensity, and imitability on international growth. *Academy of Management Journal, 43*(5), 090-924.

Bell, J. (1995). The internationalisation of small computer software firms: A further challenge to "stage" theories. *European Journal of Marketing, 29*(8), 60-75.

Bolton Committee. (1971). *Report of the Committee of Enquiry on Small Firms* (Cmnd 4811) London: HMSO.

Brynjolfsson, E., & Smith, J. (2000). Frictionless commerce? A comparison of Internet and conventional retailers. *Management Science, 46*(4), 563-585.

Burgel, O., & Murray, G. C. (2000). The international market entry choices of start-yup companies in high-technology industries. *Journal of International Marketing, 8*(2), 33-62.

Coviello, N. E., & Munro, H. J. (1995). Growing the entrepreneurial firm: Networking for international market development. *European Journal of Marketing, 29*(7), 49-61.

De Boer, L., Harink, J., & Heijboer, G. (2002). A conceptual model for assessing the impact of electronic procurement. *European Journal of Purchasing and Supply Management, 8*(1), 25-33.

Forrester Research. (1998). *Growth spiral in online retail sales will generate $108 billion in revenues by 2003*. Retrieved November 19, 2006, from http://www.forrester.com

Harveston, P. D. (2000). *Synoptic versus incremental internationalisation: An examination of born global and gradual globalising firms*. Unpublished doctoral dissertation, The University of Memphis.

Inland Revenue. (1998). *Chapter 1—Encouraging the growth of e-commerce. Electronic Commerce: The UKs Taxation Agenda*. Retrieved November 19, 2006, from http://www.inlandrevenue.gov.uk/taxagenda/ecom1.htm

Jones, P., Muir, E., & Benyon-Davies, P. (2004). An evaluation of inhibitors to e-commerce and e-business growth. In G. Packham, C. Miller, & B. Thomas (Eds.), *The phenomenon of small business growth* (pp. 117-137) Monograph 5. Pontypridd: The Welsh Enterprise Institute, University of Glamorgan.

Jutla, D., Bodorik, P., & Dhaliqal, J. (2002). Supporting the e-business readiness of small and medium sized enterprises: Approaches and metrics. *Internet Research: Electronic Networking Applications and Policy, 12*(2), 139-164.

Kehoe, D. F., & Boughton, N. J. (2001). New paradigms in planning and control across manufacturing supply chains: The utilisation of Internet technologies. *International Journal of Operations and Production Management, 21*(5/6), 582-593.

Knight, G. A., & Cavusgil (1996). The born global firm: A challenge to traditional internationalisation theory. In S. T. Cavusgil & T. K. Madsen (Eds.), *Export internationalising research—enrichment and challenges. Advances in International Marketing* (Vol. 8, pp. 11-26). NY: JAI Press Inc.

Lambert, D. M., Cooper, M. C., & Pagh, J. D. (1998). Supply chain management: Implementation issues and research opportunities. *The International Journal of Logistics Management, 9*(2), 1-17.

Lewis, R., & Cockrill, A. (2002). Going global—remaining local: The impact of e-commerce on small retail firms in Wales. *International Journal of Information Management, June, 22,* 195-209.

Lumpkin, G. T. (1998). *Do new entrant firms have an entrepreneurial orientation?* Paper presented at the annual meeting of the Academy of Management, San Diego, CA.

Lumpkin, G. T., & Dess, G. G. (1996). Clarifying the entrepreneurial orientation construct and linking it to performance. *Academy of Management Review, 21*(1), 135-172.

Madsen, T. K., & Servais, P. (1997). The internationalisation of born globals: An evolutionary process? *International Business Review, 6*(6), 561-583.

Madsen, T. K., Rasmussen, E. S., & Servais, P. (2000). Differences and similarities between born globals and other types of exporters. In A. Yaprak & J. Tutek (Eds.), *Globalisation, the multinational form and emerging economies, Advances in International Marketing* (pp. 247-265). Amsterdam: JAI/Elsevier Inc.

Mamis, R. A. (1989). Global start-up. *Inc.*, Aug. 38-47.

McCue, S. (1999). Small firms and the Internet: Force or farce? In *Proceedings of the International Trade Forum* (pp. 27-29).Geneva.

McDougall, P. P., & Oviatt, B. M. (1996). New venture internationalisation, strategic change, and performance: A follow-up study. *Journal of Business Venturing, 11*(1), 23-40.

McGowan, P., Durkin, M., Allen, M., Dougan, C., & Nixon, S. (2001). Developing competencies in the entrepreneurial small firm for use of the Internet in the management of customer relationships. *Journal of European Industrial Training, 25*(2/3//4), 126-136.

Mehling, H. (1998). Survey says: E-commerce is crucial to success—Small businesses are eager to sell wares on the Web. *Computer Reseller News*, May 4, 787.

Ng, H. I., Pan, Y. G., & Wilson, T. D. (1998). Business use of the world wide Web: A report on further investigations. *International Journal of Information Management, 18*(5), 291-314.

Opportunity Wales. (2007). *On-line guides—the ecommerce ladder.* Retrieved March 6, 2007, from http://www.opportunitywales.co.uk

Oviatt, B. M., & McDougall, P. P. (1997). Challenges for internationalisation process theory: the case of international new ventures. *Management International Review, 37*(2) (Special Issue), 85-99.

Oviatt, B. M., & McDougall, P. (1995). Global start-ups: Entrepreneurs on a worldwide stage. *Academy of Management Executive, 9*(2), 30-43.

Oviatt, B. M., & McDougall, P. (1994). Toward a theory of international new ventures. *Journal of International Business Studies, 25*(1), 45-64.

Pflughoeft, K. A., Ramamurthy, K., Soofi, E. S., Yasai-Ardekani, M., & Fatemah, M. (2003). Multiple conceptualizations of small business Web use and benefit. *Decision Sciences*, *34*(3), 467-513.

Quayle, M. (2001, May). *E-commerce: The challenge for Welsh small and medium size enterprises.* Paper presented at Business Week in Wales Lecture (pp. 1-14) Cardiff: Cardiff International Arena.

Quinton, S., & Harridge-March, S. (2003). Strategic interactive marketing of wine—a case of evolution. *Marketing Intelligence and Planning*, *21*(6), 357-363.

Rasmussen, E. S., & Madsen, T. K. (2002). *The born global concept.* Paper presented in the 28th EIBA Conference, Athens, Greece.

Ray, D. M. (1989). Strategic *implications of entrepreneurial ventures "born international": Four case studies.* Paper presented at the Frontiers in Entrepreneurship Research, Babson-Kauffman Entrepreneurial Research Conference (BKERC).

Raymond, L. (2001). Determinants of Web site implementation in small businesses. *Internet Research*, *11*(5), 411-423.

Rennie, M. (1993). Global competitiveness: Born global. *McKinsey Quarterly*, *4*, 45-52.

Rialp-Criado, A., Rialp-Criado, J., & Knight, G. A. (2002). *The phenomenon of international new ventures, global start-ups, and born-globals: What do we know after a decade (1993-2002) of exhaustive scientific inquiry?* Working Paper, Department d'Economia de l'Empresa, Universitat Autònoma de Barcelon, Barcelona.

Roberts, E. B., & Senturia, T. A. (1996). Globalising the emerging high-technology company. *Industrial Marketing Management*, *25*(6), 491-506.

Saarenketo, S. (2002). *Born globals—internationalisation of small and medium-sized knowledge-intensive firms.* Unpublished doctoral dissertation, Lappeenranta University of Technology, Finland.

Sadowski, B. M., Maitland, C., & van Douyer, J. (2002). Strategic use of the Internet by small- and medium-sized companies: An exploratory study. *Information Economics and Policy*, *14*(1), 75-93.

Sellitto, C., Wenn, A., & Burgess, S (2003). A review of the websites of small Australian wineries: Motivations, goals, and success. *Information Technology and Management*, *4*(2-3), 215-232.

Servais, P., & Rasmussen, E. S. (2000, November). *Different types of international new ventures.* Paper presented at the Academy of International Business (AIB) Annual Meeting (pp. 1-27). Phoenix, AZ, USA.

Simons, J. (1999). States chafe as Web shopper ignore sales taxes. *The Wall Street Journal*, January 26, p.B1.

Smith, J., & Webster, L. (2000). The knowledge economy and SMEs: A survey of skills requirements. *Business Information Review*, *17*(3), September, 138-146.

Smyth, M., & Ibbotson, P. (2001). *Internet connectivity in Ireland.* Joint report by the Bank of Ireland and the University of Ulster. Retrieved March 6, 2007, from www.bankofireland.co.uk/whats_new/item.php?whatsnew_id=8

Sparkes, A., & Thomas, B. (2001). The use of the Internet as a critical success factor for the marketing of Welsh agri-food SMEs in the twenty-first century. *British Food Journal*, *103*(5), 331-337.

Standing, C., Vasudavan, T., & Borbely, S. (1998). Re-engineering travel agencies with the world wide web. *Electronic Markets*, *8*(4), 40-43.

Stockdale, R., & Standing, C. (2004). Benefits and barriers of electronic marketplace participation: An SME perspective. *The Journal of Enterprise Information Management, 17*(4), 301-311.

United States Department of Commerce (US-DoC). (1998). *The emerging digital economy.* Washington, DC.

Van Ketel, M., & Nelson, T.D. (1998). *E-commerce.* Retrieved May 18, 2006, from http://www. whatis.com/

von Goeler, K. (1998). *Internet commerce by degrees: Small business early adopters.* Retrieved November 8, 2006, from http://instat.com

Wakkee, I., van der Sijde, P., & Kirwan, P. (2003). *An empirical exploration of the global startup concept in an entrepreneurship context.* Working Paper. Holland: GS Leuven.

Williams, V., & Phillips B. D. (1999). *E-commerce: Small businesses venture online.* Report, Office of Advocacy, US Small Business Administration, Washington, DC. Retrieved July 1, 2006, from http://www.sba.gov/advo/stats/e_comm.pdf

Yankee Group (YG). (1998). Yankee Group finds small and business market missing the Internet commerce opportunity: Market Unsatisfied with current Internet solution provider offerings, *YG Communication,* November 17. Retrieved from http://www.yankeegroup.com

Zahira, S. A., Ireland, R. D., & Hitt, M. A. (2000). International expansion by new firms: International diversity, mode of entry, technological learning and performance. *Academy of Management Journal, 43*(5), 925-950.

KEY TERMS

E-Commerce: Buying and selling of goods and services over the Internet.

E-Commerce Stairway: The step of e-commerce an SME is on from a state of no e-commerce activity to a situation of advanced e-commerce trading.

Entrepreneurial Orientation (EO): The extent to which enterprises are willing to take risks, compete with other enterprises and engage in innovation and change.

Global Start-Ups: Enterprises which from their creation seek to exploit markets in other countries.

High Tech Businesses: Businesses which develop new technologies.

International Entrepreneurship (IE): Taking business opportunities in other countries involving innovation and risk taking.

Online Entrepreneurs: Entrepreneurs who run their business over the Internet through a Web site.

Technological Innovativeness: The extent to which significant technologies are created by an enterprise.

Chapter VII
E–Commerce Innovation in SMEs:
A Motivation–Ability Perspective

Alemayehu Molla
RMIT University, Australia

Richard Duncombe
The University of Manchester, UK

ABSTRACT

Small- and medium-size enterprises (SMEs) innovativeness to use e-commerce has received significant research attention. This chapter continues with this tradition and offers a theoretically grounded and deeper insight into the e-commerce innovation process in SMEs. This is achieved by proposing a motivation ability-based four-state developmental framework. Each of the four states is then described in terms of organisational readiness, organisational capability, e-commerce capability, e-commerce motivational factors, and commodity chain position. SME mangers can use the framework as a decision making tool to critically stock-take their innate state and to set realistic goals and expectations with regards to future e-commerce investments. The utility of the framework is demonstrated through case studies of 14 small-scale enterprises located in the Indian state of Karnataka. The result suggests that rather than static models of e-commerce adoption, temporal models that are dynamic in nature and that recognise e-commerce as an ongoing innovation process have more explanatory power to understand innovation in SMEs in such an environment.

INTRODUCTION

Small- and medium-size enterprises (SMEs) typically represent a significant proportion of any nation's economy in terms of their contribution to employment and gross domestic production. Governments and policy-makers throughout the world recognise these pivotal roles of SMEs and have been keen to identify strategies to boost their growth and competitiveness. One such strategy has been the promotion of innovative use of information and communications technologies (ICTs) in general and e-commerce in particular. The result of these policies plus entrepreneurial actions has been mixed. On the one hand, there are growing rates of e-commerce adoption among small businesses worldwide. On the other hand, the majority of such firms (especially those in the non-ICT sectors in transitional and developing economies) have yet to adopt e-commerce or have not moved beyond entry-level adoption (Molla, Heeks, & Balcells, 2006).

SMEs' innovativeness to use e-commerce has received significant research attention. Some work has focused on general categorisation of e-commerce in small enterprise (Chen, Haney, Pandzik, Spigarelli, & Jesseman, 2003). Others sought to understand the potential benefits of e-commerce to these firms' efficiency and competitiveness (Ibbotson & Fahy, 2004). The limited nature, or variability, of e-commerce adoption in SMEs has also been investigated through research studying factors that facilitate or inhibit adoption.

These works have made valuable contributions to our understanding of e-commerce innovation in SMEs but we perceived some limitations of past research that motivated our own work. These include (1) the tendency to "black box" the process of e-commerce innovation using a dichotomous scale that only differentiates e-commerce adopters (or those with an intention to adopt) from non-adopters, (2) lack of attention to what SMEs seek to achieve out of e-commerce innovation (3) the inherent assumption that the efficiency and competitiveness rationale drives e-commerce in SMEs, and (4) the focus on "factor-shopping" with little recourse to conceptual and theoretical models. This chapter, therefore, intends to address some of the above gaps and offer a theoretically grounded and deeper insight into the e-commerce innovation process in SMEs.

The aim is to advance the understanding of e-commerce in SMEs by using the motivation-ability theory. Using the theoretical lens of the motivation-ability theory, we propose a framework to understand e-commerce in SMEs. To demonstrate the utility of the framework, the paper uses evidence drawn from case studies of small-scale industries (SSIs) in traditional manufacturing sub-sectors in the State of Karnataka in India.

The remaining part of the chapter is organised in five sections. Section two provides the theoretical background, which is followed by the main thrust of the chapter in section three covering our four state developmental framework, its verification process and main findings. The last two sections discuss some of the themes and trends that emerged from the study and outline preliminary conclusions respectively.

THEORETICAL BACKGROUND

Understanding E-Commerce as an Innovation

Wigand (1997) identified innovation theory as one of the theoretical approaches through which one may view e-commerce. Innovation can be defined as ideas or objects that are new or are perceived as new (Rogers, 1995). Inevitably, different researchers promote different connotations of innovation. One of the differences emanates from the perturbations caused by the concept of newness vis-à-vis what was before or the precursor. Some reserve the concept of innovation for something that is radically different from its precursor (Davenport, 1993; Greve and Taylor, 2000). Others submit as innovation even if what is "new" is incrementally different from the precursor (Coopey, Keegan, & Emler, 1998; Straub, 1997). Overall though, it can be surmised that the newness in the innovation should be treated with respect to the context (organizational, social

Figure 1. A classificatory tree of innovation taxonomies

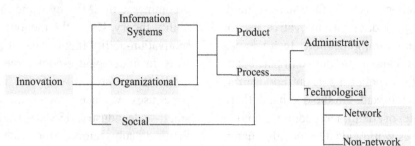

or individual) within which the innovation is to be discussed. This understanding is particularly relevant in the context of SMEs, which in most cases are not first adopters of innovations.

Organisational innovation is argued to represent a number of processes. Thompson (1965) proposed a three-stage model of the innovation process: initiation, adoption, and implementation. Zaltman, Duncan, and Holbek (1973) also suggested an organisation-oriented innovation process model that combined Thompson's last two stages into one and that consists of initiation and implementation. Rogers (1995) extended the two stages and conceptualised five stages of the innovation process as agenda-setting, matching, redefining/restructuring, clarifying, and routinising. Several taxonomies of innovation are documented in the literature. The most common classifications are administrative vs. technical (Rogers, 1995) and product vs. process (Davenport, 1993). Institutional and sociological theorists also describe innovation as a network phenomenon and further distinguish between innovations that are network technologies and that are not (King et al., 1994). A distinction also exists between organisational and information systems innovations (Swanson, 1994).

The different categorisations of innovation are not mutually exclusive and can be seen as forming structure (at least classificatory if not conceptual). Innovations could be classified as social, organisational or informational. Information systems innovations could be of product or process nature whereas social innovations reflect process innovations. A process innovation on the other hand could be administrative or technological and technological innovations would be either network based or non–network based. Figure 1 captures this structure.

E-commerce can be considered as a technological innovation. In this sense, it shares the features of all technological innovations. The basic technology in e-commerce is network based. The network is platform independent and interconnects not only organisations in a limited geographical area but also the entire globe to the extent of dismantling physical boundaries. A myriad of applications (information systems) operate over the network and are used to enable, change and drive business processes and create new forms of products, thus e-commerce is also a process and product innovation. E-commerce is also about enhancing, building and maintaining interactive relationships (mainly electronic in nature) within an organisation among different units and employees and outside an organisation with customers, government, suppliers, and the general public. Therefore, it can also be considered to represent an administrative innovation. E-commerce can also be argued to represent a social innovation as it precipitates potential changes, perhaps of a morphogenic nature, in the way society communicates, creates wealth, entertains, works and shops.

The innovativeness of SMEs to adopt and implement e-commerce has been widely researched. Most literature solicits factors that are responsible for the successful adoption and implementation of e-commerce (see Molla et al., 2006). A number of studies have identified distinct phases of e-commerce adoption emphasising the need for temporal consideration. On the basis of the innovation literature previously discussed, the e-commerce innovation in SMEs can pass through four phases: initiation, adoption, implementation, and assimilation (see Molla et al., 2006). The initiation phase involves forging effective communication links with clients or prospective clients. At this stage, perception and awareness of market opportunities is paramount and is derived largely from existing commercial relationships (De Berranger, Tucker, & Jones, 2001). The adoption phase involves key decision-making processes—whether to adopt or not adopt—involving choice of technology and business strategy. Implementation involves more complex processes that require higher levels of specialist knowledge and know-how. E-commerce implementation tends to be experimental, with real examples often characterised by "learning by doing," a process often beset by errors, setbacks and additional or unplanned costs. Finally, assimilation comes, which has been defined as the extent to which the use of e-commerce technologies become diffused across organisational work processes and routinised within the activities associated with those processes.

It is clear from these approaches that different organisational abilities are likely to be associated with each temporal phase. Here we would like to approach the e-commerce innovation as one indicator of SMEs' performance and use a relevant theory to explicate how such performance can be understood and enhanced.

The Motivation-Ability Theory

Performance has long been defined as a function of ability and motivation (Bird, 1989). Motivation-ability theory—attributed to Merton (1957)—postulates that a combination of organisational ability and motivation shapes the nature and intensity of actions and outcomes. For decision makers, this implies that both retrospective evaluation of innovation and prospective strategies to improvise it should address key capability and motivational issues.

Organisational Ability

Organisational ability has been defined in a variety of ways. Hostager, Neil, Decker, and Lorentz (1998) identify awareness, knowledge, skill, creative thinking, and experience as critical abilities that help SME managers to recognise opportunities in the environment. Grewal, Comer, and Metha (2001) define ability more simply as a two-dimensional construct of learning and capability. In the SME literature, various authors have recognised the impact of the ability of SMEs in the innovation process. For instance, Atherton and Hannon (2000) argue that SMEs' effectiveness in managing innovation requires the development of internal capabilities related to technical know-how. Much research into SMEs and adoption of e-commerce technologies has taken a resource-based view, stressing the meshing of internal—human, technological, and financial resources—leading to the creation of core competencies and competitive advantage in the market place (Caldeira & Ward, 2003; Cobbenhagen, 2000; Yap, Soh, & Raman, 1992). For the purposes of this chapter, organisational ability can be considered in three main categories:

- **Organisational readiness:** We define organisational readiness as the stock of human, technological and financial resources that an SME possesses. These resources shape the input based competencies required to create and deliver products and services to customers or clients. Iacovou, Benbasat, and Dexter (1995) uses financial (availability of finance to pay for e-commerce solutions) and technological resources (level of sophistication of ICT usage and ICT management) as two key indicators of organisational readiness affecting use of e-commerce. Organisational readiness can also be expanded to include intangible factors (such as managerial awareness and commitment) that are particularly relevant to the uptake of e-commerce in developing country environments (Molla & Licker, 2005).

- **Organisational capability:** This refers to the relationship between the tangible resources previously described and other intangible resources that give rise to know-how (how to do something). Capability emphasises invisible assets such as organisational reputation built up over time and embedded in SME routines. Coyne (1986) in Hall (1993) highlight: (a) regulatory capability, which arises from the possession of specific knowledge resources—primarily intellectual property rights (IPR), contracts (formal or informal) and trade secrets; (b) positional capability, which refers to the unique positions and reputation developed within commodity chains; (c) functional capability, which relates to the know-how, skills, and experience of mangers and other employees of the SME or SME network (such as clients and suppliers) to do specific tasks.

- **E-commerce capability:** Theories of take up of e-commerce technologies tend to make use of staged models (Daniel, Wilson, & Myers, 2002; Knol & Stroeken, 2001; Shiels, McIvor, & O'Reilly, 2003). Staged models of e-commerce evolution emphasise a move from less to more sophisticated applications, as well as from an emphasis on external communication functionality to back-to-back business process integration functionality.

A further aspect of organisational ability relates to the capabilities required for market access. E-commerce is widely believed to offer SMEs potential to access and link to commodity chains. Previous SME research indicates that in cases where SMEs belong to established market networks, competitive, and industry pressure through trading partners act as drivers of innovation (Kuan & Chau 2001; Iacovou et al., 1995). Capturing the relative commodity chain position of SMEs can help managers to assess to what extent such forces are influencing their e-commerce uptake and use. For example, when SMEs engage in import and export trade, they come under the influence of their stronger trading partners. This is particularly so when stronger clients (occupying a downstream commodity chain position) exercise their value chain power to specify the design, quantity, and quality of the products of SMEs. SMEs can be relatively weak players in such relationships. For instance, in the horticulture industry, supermarkets directly control the process and standards of how suppliers produce, package and distribute fresh horticultural produce (Dolan & Humphrey, 2001). Many SMEs and especially those in developing countries are not linked to established commodity chains and tend to operate outside—or peripheral—to such networks.

Motivational Factors

Organisational behaviour literature also emphasises the criticality of motivation. At present such factors are under-researched in the SME literature. However, the literature concerning e-commerce adoption suggests that the factors that propel change forward arise from either "market push" or "SME pull" forces. SME-pull refers to e-commerce adoption driven by a combination of managerially perceived benefits and commitment to change (Daniel, 2003; Mirchandani & Motwani, 2001; Poon & Swatman, 1999). In the SME pull context, SMEs managers' control their own choices, are knowledgeable enough to understand the potential of e-commerce and have developed a need for specific e-commerce solutions as a route to realising market opportunities. E-commerce market-push, on the other hand, refers to e-commerce adoption mainly driven by external forces (Elsammani, Hackney, & Scown, 2004). Here, SME managers lack the impetus for internally-driven change and are rather subject to market and change agent forces over which they have little control. In this sense, e-commerce based innovation requires not only awareness raising and the building of internal knowledge resources, but also changes in managerial attitudes and perceptions that guide decision making processes for SMEs (Jones, Hecker, & Holland, 2003). Overall though, three possible types of SME motivation for e-commerce can be highlighted:

- **Efficiency:** Mangers' need for greater efficiency is often identified as a driving motivational force behind innovation and innovativeness (Grewal et al., 2001). Specifically, research has considered the implications of the dynamics of market forces and the need to achieve competitiveness through cost leadership and differentiation strategies (Slater & Narver, 1995). Such an approach requires managers to make judicious use of scarce resources to build capabilities, pre-empt competition, and improve customer service.

- **Legitimacy:** The pursuit of legitimacy within the wider social context can be one of the motivating factors affecting SME e-commerce innovation (DiMaggio & Powell, 1983). The emphasis here is on managerial actions that are induced because of the need to meet certain regulatory (market or otherwise) demands. Agents acting at various levels (including governments and industry regulators) use coercive power to enforce certain behaviour or offer inducements (such as through financial incentives or compliance with quality standards) that

encourages or discourages certain behaviour or actions on behalf of SMEs (Grewal et al., 2001; Meyer & Scott, 1992).

- **Mimicking:** Another dimension of motivation that is well researched in marketing literature is the mimicking motive (Dickson, 1992). Central to this thesis is the notion that SMEs tend to copy the behaviours and actions of their successful competitors irrespective of efficiency or legitimacy considerations, thus mitigating the risk of innovation and increasing the likelihood of success. For instance, the mimicking motive dominated early adoption of Web sites and the development of the Dotcom boom.

To summarise, organisational ability can be looked at from two distinct dimensions. On the one hand, there is ability related to the stock of human, financial, and technological resources, and on the other hand, there is ability related to the technical and managerial know-how required to use those resources and get maximum returns out of them. In this sense, whilst SMEs might have more or less the same level of resources, they might differ in their ability to deploy and exploit those resources. The literature also suggests that motivations of efficiency, legitimacy and mimicking may have some influence in shaping the innovativeness of SMEs and their decision-making processes that lead to how e-commerce adoption is going to take place. It is clear that the characteristics of SMEs and their managers vary considerably according to their motivation and ability to influence the development of e-commerce initiatives.

MANAGING E-COMMERCE INNOVATION IN SMEs

A Four State Framework

In order to assist managerial decision-making and understand the differences among enterprises and their temporal e-commerce state, we propose a four-developmental state categorisation starting from the foundation state, through the exploratory state, to the graduation state, and finally the expert state. The foundation state captures those SMEs that have computers and or other ICTs but make no significant use of them (although some may use them for administrative purposes) and have no online capabilities. Exploratory state SMEs represents those SMEs that have access to e-mail and online information. Graduation state SMEs reflects those that have developed a Web site but with no advanced capabilities, whilst expert state SMEs refers to those with more advanced Web

sites with interactive, transactive and integrative capabilities.

Further, on the basis of our analysis of the literature and previous experience with SMEs (Duncombe & Molla, 2006; Molla et al., 2006), we propose five dimensions that can influence the e-commerce innovation process within SMEs. The dimensions are organisational readiness (OR), organisational capability (OC), e-commerce capability (EC), e-commerce motivational factors (MF), and commodity chain position (CCP). The five dimensions are further sub-divided according to the key factors that influence e-commerce innovation. Further, we have developed descriptors

Table 1. E-commerce four-states classification

Dimension	Factor	Foundation state	Exploratory state	Graduation state	Expert state
Organisational Readiness	Awareness:	No functional awareness of opportunities, threats, perceived benefits or risks of e-commerce	Some functional awareness of opportunities, threats, perceived benefits, risks of e-commerce	Growing functional awareness of opportunities, threats, actual benefits, risks of e-commerce	High awareness of opportunities, threats, actual benefits, risks of e-commerce
	Human resources:	Little ICT literacy and no access to computers for some employees	Some ICT literacy with restricted access to computers for most employees	Most employees ICT literate but with restricted access to computers	Most employees ICT literate with unrestricted access to computers
	Technological resources:	Mostly use non-digital technologies. Basic use of computers for administrative work. No direct access to digital networks	Access to the Internet for external communication purposes (e-mail)	Connected to the Internet with a Web presence	A Web presence with some back office applications. Might have a local area network
	Financial resources:	Severe financial resource constraints. (High-perceived costs of ICT and low perceived benefits)	High financial resource constraints. (High-perceived costs of ICT and some perceived benefits)	Some financial resource constraints. (Lower perceived costs of ICT and some perceived benefits)	Sufficient financial resources. (Lower perceived costs outweighed by high-perceived benefits)
	Commitment:	No vision and commitment to e-commerce	Some (unclear) vision on e-commerce but no demonstrable commitment	Clear vision on e-commerce and some demonstrable commitment	Strategic vision and demonstrable commitment to e-commerce
Organisational Capability	Regulatory capability:	SME does not possess IPR, contracts, and trade secrets	SME does not possess IPR and trade secrets but have some contracts	SME does not possess IPR, might have some trade secrets and contracts	SME possesses some IPR, might have some trade secrets and quite a lot of contracts
	Positional capability:	Stand-alone initiatives, and do not belong to established commodity chains	Some partnering with traders, but no reputation within commodity chain	Belong to established commodity chains and developed some reputation	Well established in commodity chain with good reputation
	Functional capability:	Very-low "know-how" of business planning, network, information and technology management	Some "know-how" of business planning, network, information and technology management	Adequate "know-how" of business planning, network, information and technology management	Good "know-how" of business planning, network, information and technology management.
E-Commerce Capability		Very limited, use mostly non-digital and some digital ICTs (e.g., telephones, fax, mobile phones)	Starting out with e-mail and some access to online information	Web presence with or without interactive and transacting capability	Web presence possibly with transacting capability and some business process integration
Motivation	Motivational Factors (1) (efficiency/ mimicking/ legitimacy)	No defined motivation for e-commerce	Mostly undefined, when defined, predominantly driven by mimicking	Some efficiency and legitimacy drivers but still shows mimicking tendency	Predominantly efficiency and legitimacy driven.
	Motivational Factors (2) (resource push/ market pull)	Predominantly (resource) push driven	Push driven with limited demonstration of pull (market drivers)	Pull driven but still exposed to push forces	Predominantly pull (market) driven
Commodity Chain Position		SMEs located outside core commodity chains	SMEs tend to be located up-stream and their proximity to core commodity chains is peripheral	SMEs are located up-stream but are well integrated into core commodity chains	SMEs are located down-stream and are well integrated into core commodity chains.

for each of the cells (an intersection of developmental state and motivation-ability factors). Table 1 summarises the framework. It is worth noting that SMEs might demonstrate different profiles of developmental states for each of the five motivation-ability dimensions and their corresponding factors. For instance, an SME which fits the description of a graduation state in awareness might be at the foundation state in terms of financial resources. This shows the dynamic nature of the proposed framework and how it might assist managers to locate vulnerabilities that need targeted attention and development.

Framework Enrichment and Verification

In order to enrich the previous framework we have conducted case studies of SMEs from India. The purpose of the case studies is to provide field evidence to inform the theoretical arguments.

Because of the limited number of cases and the inherent limitations of case study research, this should be considered as an attempt towards a preliminary verification of the proposed framework and a way of demonstrating its explanatory utility rather than a complete validation.

Research Methods

The fieldwork conducted in India during 2003 was based on the use of contextual case studies (Yin, 1994) which served as an appropriate method to assist in building an evidence-based theoretical framework. The State of Karnataka (see Figure 2) was chosen as a suitable region because it has an emerging ICT policy framework that is aiming to promote technology upgrading via e-commerce amongst SSIs. Karnataka also has an evolving technical, human, and regulatory infrastructure that is at least partly facilitative of e-commerce development within Small Scale Industries (SSIs).

Figure 2. Map of Karnataka

A total of 14 SSI cases were constructed based on semi-structured interviews carried out with owner/managers. The cases were chosen, firstly, on the basis that they were able to reflect the position of SSIs at different states of e-commerce evolution, and secondly, in order to provide a profile that reflected a range of sub-sectors and locations within Karnataka. Evidence was based on a relatively small number of case studies, and cases were chosen to be indicative and not representative of current developments in e-commerce for SSIs in India.

Specific data was collected from SSIs that measured and compared various aspects of their readiness and capability including an assessment of their financial, technical and human resources, as well as an assessment of the status of their e-commerce capability according to the level and effectiveness of e-commerce resources deployed. Additional qualitative data from interviews was used to build up a picture of e-commerce evolution within each enterprise according to the dimensions and factors outlined in the framework.

The Indian SME Sector

Since the time of Indian independence in 1947, a significant feature of the Indian economy has been the rapid growth of the SSI sector. The SSI sector is considered to have a major role in the Indian economy due to its 40% share of national industrial output along with an 80% share in industrial employment and nearly 35% share in exports. SSIs are distinguished from the large- and medium-scale industries on the basis of capital resources and labour force in the units. In 2003, there were more than 3.5 million SSI units trading throughout India, with a fixed investment of Rs.90.5 billion (US$1.8 billion). The SSI sector employed about 20 million people and produced Rs.7420 billion (US$148 billion) of output—Rs.860 billion (US$17 billion) of which went for export. These figures highlight the importance of the SSI sector (Duncombe & Heeks, 2005).

The SSI sector has been assigned an important role in the industrialisation of the country by the government of India. It is recognised that in an increasingly competitive and globalised world, SSIs need to compete more effectively in order to further boost domestic economic activity and contribute toward increasing export earnings. Thus, policy towards the SSI sector is now focused on how India's comparative advantage in ICT (predominantly software) can be spread to traditional manufacturing sectors (Verma, 2005). Detailed research, carried out in the Indian context, has also demonstrated the importance of innovation through ICT for increased performance and productivity of SSIs – particularly those seeking to penetrate international markets (Lal, 2003).

Findings

Data from the case studies illustrate a broad range of e-commerce experiences for SSIs, ranging from those that made no use of e-commerce, to the small number that were fully enabled to conduct transactions online. Individual profiles for four of the fourteen case study SSIs are outlined in the following section providing some detail of each enterprise according to the 4 levels and the 5 dimensions suggested in the framework. A summary of all the case studies and their assessed levels is contained in Table 2.

Case Study 3

Overall Rating: Foundation State

Located in the industrial area of Ilkal, Bagalkot, the enterprise produces granite slab and tiles, and carries out polishing and styling. There are eight employees and the business was established in 1992-93. The main customers are located in India, and the turnover in 2003 was 35 Lakhs (US$70,000).

Organisational readiness: The enterprise operates two landline phones, two mobile phones,

Table 2. E-commerce four-states classification—Case study summary analysis

Case Study Number (cases are ranked according to turnover)	Sub-sector (main products)	Location (see map)	No of FTE	% of goods for	E-Commerce Awareness	OR — Human Resources	OR — Technological Resources	OR — Financial Resources	OR — Commitment	OC — Regulatory Capability	OC — Positional Capability	OC — Functional Capability	EC — E-commerce Capability	MF — Motivational Factors (1)	MF — Motivational Factors (2)	CCP — Commodity Chain Position
8.	Food processing (spices)	Chitradurga	20		*	*	*	**	*	**	**	*	*	*	**	**
2.	Metal fabrication	Betgeri-Gadag	6		**	*	*	**	*	**	**	*	*	*	*	*
10.	Food processing (coconut)	Chamrajnaga	40		***	**	**	***	**	***	***	**	**	**	***	***
4.	Automotive (gaskets)	Bangalore	8	20%	****	**	**	**	***	****	***	***	***	***	***	***
6.	Agricultural machinery	Bellary	15		**	**	**	**	**	*	****	*	*	**	*	**
3.	Minerals (granite/marble)	Bagalkot	8		*	*	**	**	*	*	**	*	*	*	*	**
1.	Crafts (terracotta)	Kuvempunagar	6		***	**	**	***	**	**	***	**	**	**	**	**
13.	Office furniture	Bangalore	60		****	***	**	****	***	***	**	***	**	***	**	**
12.	Machine components	Bangalore	40		****	***	**	*****	***	***	****	***	**	**	**	***
11.	Electrical wire products	Tumkur	40		****	*****	**	*****	***	***	***	***	**	***	***	***
7.	Horticulture (tamarind)	Bijapur	19	10%	**	**	**	****	*	***	****	**	**	*	**	***
14.	Software	Udipi	95	100%	****	****	****	***	***	****	***	***	****	****	****	****
5.	Footwear	Malleswaram	8	95%	****	***	****	**	****	****	****	**	****	****	****	****
9.	Food processing (dried foods)	Malleswaram	20	50%	***	***	**	**	**	***	***	**	**	**	***	***

* Foundation State ** Exploratory State *** Graduation State **** Expert State

50 Rupees = US$1

FTE: full-time equivalent employee

and one Samsung PC with Windows 98. The enterprise is using software up to a basic level principally for document creating. Awareness of ICT is very low, with insufficient functional knowledge about computers or software. Local Internet connections are extremely slow, and phone lines often go dead. To make a complaint, a local telephone exchange must be contacted. They in turn have to be pestered continuously to repair the phone. For this enterprise there is a need to overcome a broad range of such infrastructure and institutional constraints. For example, rising costs related to electricity charges, kerosene, materials, and taxes levied on the industry, and ensuring product quality. The entrepreneur feels that more importance should be paid to these issues and eCommerce isn't really needed yet for his business.

Organisational capability: As the market is open, the enterprise possesses no regulatory capability, and caters to individual customers rather than belonging to established commodity chains. However, functional capability has been enhanced through use of mobile communications. The entrepreneur states that when potential raw material suppliers are contacted directly on the phone, rather than through e-mail or via other means, the rates charged are much less. Thus the integrity of cost related information of products that is formalized (possibly displayed and exchanged via eCommerce) is questionable.

E-commerce capability: The entrepreneur uses mobile phones primarily to interact with clients and dealers of raw materials. Use of phones gets an immediate response as it is a more direct means of communication. From an Internet cafe, the entrepreneur tried contacting clients while browsing on the net on a few sites. But these so-called potential clients did not respond when an e-mail was sent to them. Also the entrepreneur feels that the unit's finished products cannot be displayed on a Web site, as the rates of the product are highly variable and have to be discussed verbally.

Motivational factors: The market for the enterprise products is crowded and competition places downward pressure on costs. Thus there is an efficiency driver, but for enhanced speed and lower cost of communication, rather than internal functional improvements. The mobile provider has been most supportive through providing a cheap and convenient service. As the entrepreneur states: "Before when clients used to call and we are not present in the office, we used to miss them. But now when they call and if we are not in the office, the person in the office gives our mobile number to them, and we are contacted. Thus we do not have to stick around in the office but can also do other work alongside."

Commodity chain position: SME located outside core commodity chains.

Case Study 12

Overall Rating: Exploratory State

Located at Rajajinagar, Bangalore, the enterprise has 40 employees and was established in 1983. They manufacture machine components and pressed metal components. Their customers are 100% home market, but some customers' export products that contain their components. Their main customers are large motor engineering companies, and turnover in 2003 was almost 2 Crores (US$400,000).

Organisational readiness: The enterprise is well-informed about the opportunities of e-commerce due to their location in Bangalore. They have two landline phones; two mobile phones, and three PCs as well as a broadband Internet connection. They use Tally for accounting, and a customised software package is used for billing/and formatting invoices (obtained from a software supplier based in Bangalore). Organisational constraints are primarily high electricity costs, and lack of training in specialist software such as Unigraphics Modelling and AutoCad.

Organisational capability: Internet access has allowed them to register with a site called export India.com. Through this site they have received a lot of information from various similar units and clients from all over the world. They are currently enhancing their functional capability by integrating basic business processes such as inventory and product lists into Web-based tools. Awareness of the need for continuous upgrading of technology is apparent. However, the human element is retained in the unit, like the business owner says "each employee in my unit is treated like a family member, and we discuss implementation problems together"

E-commerce capability: Mobile communications are still the technology that has created the greatest efficiency gains. The CEO is always on the move. E-mail has also made communication much faster and easier. They cite an example where an entire transaction was done on the Web. "We received an order by e-mail from HAL in Bangalore. There was an application form on the net, which we filled in, and all further correspondence was followed up through e-mail, thus the entire transaction was completed through the net."

Motivational factors: There is some evidence in this case of motivational factors linked to both greater efficiency and market requirements. These are linked primarily to the need for upgraded communications with larger customers and suppliers. The enterprise is also making some progress in using ICT to automate business functions, and achieving some integration of functions.

Commodity chain position: The enterprise is located upstream but has received support in the use of e-mail from a customer who has already created their own Web site.

Case Study 4

Overall Rating: Graduation State

Located at the Peenya Industrial Estate, Bangalore, the business manufactures metal gaskets for spark plugs used in automobiles. Parallel to this activity is another development with use of computer-centred technology creating Computer Aided Design (CAD) of Gas Turbines and delivering them via e-mail to overseas customers. The business was established in 1987, there are 8 employees, and the turnover in 2003 was approx 25 Lakh (US$50,000).

Organisational readiness: Being an exporter, the enterprise has higher awareness of product, process, and market changes at the global level. Technological resources include three landlines, a mobile phone for personal use, and a Compaq PC purchased in 1998. They have an Internet connection via Touchtel, and make use of AutoCad and MS Office 2000. The enterprise is constrained financially resulting in the inability to procure new software and hardware. They complain about the high cost of proprietary licensed software, particularly high-end systems to support (for example) Pro E software.

Organisational capability: The enterprise achieved the ISO 9001 certification in the year 2000. The entrepreneurs have registered with TradeInfo.com, and have obtained a number of successful leads from this site, including a new client from Canada. They use e-mail and the Web to make contact with specialist organisations, such as in France, which are concerned with the development of industries encompassing various interests for the small-scale engineering sector. Hardware and software vendors are from the same city and if there is any problem, the entrepreneur calls the vendor onto site. There is no annual maintenance contract necessary.

E-commerce capability: They have a fast and efficient connection to the Internet due to their urban location. They have used e-mail/Internet to enhance the marketing and use of their own technologies. Recently, they started creating designs of Gas Turbines using CAD and sending them via e-mail to international business clients. Designs of Gas Turbine parts are rendered in 3-D using the Pro E software. These designs are sent via e-mail to clients outside India. In the beginning the entrepreneur asked another company (a CAD Centre based in Bangalore which specialized in this field) to make these Computer Aided Designs. Now the designs are created by the entrepreneur himself. However, use of e-mail/Internet does not remove the need for personal contact.

Motivational factors: Enhanced global networking capability through the Internet has created stronger market drivers for product and process innovations. This has created greater legitimacy with customers and the market in general. However, there is less evidence of internal efficiency improvements through ICT.

Commodity chain position: The business serves 100% home market for manufactured gaskets—supplying Motor India for example. The enterprise is well integrated into domestic automotive commodity chains, but retains an upstream position for global markets. Hence, there was a need to develop new product areas in order to directly enter international markets.

Case Study 5

Overall Rating: Expert State

Located at Malleswaram, Bangalore, the enterprise manufactures and markets traditional leather sandals. These are manufactured by artisans of a marginalised community in the Belgaum Region of Karnataka. There are four full-time employees in the field and four in the office. Established in 1999, it is run on a cooperative basis. Customers are mainly shoe stores, designer houses, and boutiques in Australia, Japan, Italy, and other countries.

Organisational readiness: Awareness of e-commerce is high due to the international outlook of the enterprise, and particularly that of the entrepreneur who travels widely. Donor agencies have provided funding for purchase of ICT equipment, software and training at subsidized costs. The enterprise has three computers at its head office and one in the manufacturing centre. However, Internet connectivity is limited in rural areas and finding trained staff is also difficult. Power supply remains erratic in the villages. Upstream communications to the producer groups are facilitated through mobile communications. The enterprise has also trained staff members in the use of computer software and they can now manage most communication via e-mail. The artisans come from a poorer section of society and their literacy levels are low. This has so far prevented them from being part of the process. The enterprise is trying to bring their levels to a basic standard so they may take a more substantial role in using ICTs.

Organisational capability: The enterprise retains the intellectual property rights to its original designs. However, showcasing their designs on the Web means they could be easily copied by others and passed off as their own. This is a key issue for the enterprise in the global market.

E-commerce capability: Orders are received via e-mail and company representatives follow up with a quotation. Clients also use e-mail to send in suggestions, alterations and photographic evidence of damages/faults in products that might need replacement. This helps improve the quality of their product design. A management information system keeps track of customers and predicts their buying patterns. This helps them to optimize their leather and accessories purchases and keep inventory levels low. Workers in the villages are able to speak to their head offices via mobile telephone. Decisions get taken faster and get communicated down the line cheaper. Hence, the time taken to develop a new product for a customer is reduced and delivery and production schedules are easier to monitor. The enterprise Web site contains a catalogue of its products and customers are able to browse and purchase its products via the integrated shopping cart application. The enterprise would like to make the Web site more sophisticated in terms of buyers being able to build their own footwear and mix and match colors. A digital camera is useful as images of new products or test designs can be edited and uploaded quickly.

Motivational factors: Implementation of ICT has been driven almost exclusively by customers' needs, and through this the enterprise had achieved legitimacy and reputation with clients who are purchasing a high value-added design-driven product. A local ISP assisted in software development and offered a free template based shopping cart application. With only limited computer know-how initially, the entrepreneur was able to put together an effective Web site and display their products to a worldwide audience.

Commodity chain position: The enterprise retains effective control over its commodity chain from product source to international buyer. They are able to sell a traditional product with enhanced design content directly to retailers of similar high value added products.

DISCUSSION AND TRENDS

The motivational ability-based framework proposed in this chapter was useful to profile the case enterprises and get a deeper understanding of the specific challenges they face in their endeavour to implement e-commerce innovation. The framework can also be used as a decision tool to locate, evaluate and manage some of the potential risks that are likely to affect e-commerce innovation. It can also assist those institutions that are involved in the promotion of e-commerce among enterprises to stock-take the profile of their clients and deliver a customised solution package that is relevant and appropriate for the specific needs of an enterprise.

SSIs identified at a foundation state (measured in terms of their e-commerce capability) severely lacked organisational readiness. They were heavily constrained by deficiencies in human, technological and financial resources, and lacked core business capabilities. ICT use, if any, tended to be rudimentary without automation of basic business processes. They tended to be unaware of opportunities related to e-commerce innovation. They tended to operate outside established value chains and did not come under the pressure of external clients. Here, survival in the domestic market remained the main motive (case studies 2, 3, 6, & 8). For managers of such enterprises, developing e-commerce, if they desire to do so, requires a multi-faceted approach that includes the development of their business, accumulation of assets and organisational capability. Unless e-commerce is used as a catalyst to bring such fundamental business transformation, investing in e-commerce might lead to draining important resources without much return.

Those at an exploratory state (case studies 1, 7, 9, 10, 11, 12, & 13) still knew very little about the requirements to conduct operations in an electronic market effectively, and exhibited only marginally higher e-commerce capability. However, for many of the factors surveyed, their organisational capability to learn the particulars of doing business in the marketplace was at a higher "graduation" level. On the other hand, their organisational readiness varied considerably. For some, lack of financial resources was the limiting factor (case studies 9 & 13), but for most of this group, it was their inability to develop adequate human and technological resources that was preventing them from graduating to a higher level. It was interesting to observe, therefore, that most of this group exhibited greater potential for innovativeness in terms of their organisational capability where a range of positive examples (regulatory, functional and positional) were observed. This implies that managerial action and external intervention should be directed towards leveraging existing strengths for e-commerce. However, a clear business case has to be made to ensure that e-commerce investments are not misdirecting resources that are essential for addressing core business challenges.

Only three enterprises were gauged to be moving through the graduation state to the expert state. The two expert level SSIs (case studies 5 & 14) exported nearly 100% of their goods and/or services, and they exhibited a high degree of maturity and development across all the factors surveyed. The single SSI identified at the graduation level (case study 4), although without a functioning Web site, was using e-mail in an interactive and creative manner. This SSI demonstrated growing (and sometimes high) organisational readiness and capability. We would expect this from other graduation level SMEs – although we failed to identify others from the cases observed. Managers of enterprises with such a profile should aim to develop strategies that are directed at e-enabling their key business processes so that the use of e-commerce forms part of their business routine.

Although the developmental state of the SSIs surveyed could be approximated as foundation, exploratory, graduation or expert, individual case studies indicated that SSIs tend to exhibit differing states of development across the five dimensions of the framework. For example, an SSI may have a growing awareness of, and commitment to, developing an e-commerce capability, but lack the resources (either human, technical or financial) to initiate change. An SSI may command the necessary resources, but lack the positional capability to participate in key commodity chains. This demonstrates that rather than linear models that treat SMEs at a certain stage of e-commerce or development, dynamic frameworks that open up the complexity and interaction of the various factors are useful to assist managerial decision making. Generally speaking, however, SSIs that had low organisational readiness and capability were also likely to have no clearly identifiable motivation for e-commerce. Those SSIs with greater organisational readiness and capability may approach e-commerce because of mimicking motives. It may be only SSIs with adequate resources and some core capabilities that pursue e-commerce on the basis of efficiency and/or legitimacy grounds.

Another observation concerns the interplay between the push and pull forces that are driving e-commerce adoption. For the majority of SSIs surveyed, organisational capability tended to be in advance of their e-commerce capability and their organisational readiness. Their motivation for e-commerce (where it was present) was still influenced by mimicking behaviour and resource-based factors. Conversely, it is highly apparent that SSIs at the expert level had been strongly motivated by market pull factors, and were increasingly able to take on a strategic approach to e-commerce, driven by the need for greater internal efficiency.

It is also apparent that both internal and external motivational factors are at play. Indian SSIs vary considerably according to their ability to drive e-commerce development from within. Internal change is not common without commensurate change driven by external forces. External agents are required in the first instance to raise awareness, to build internal knowledge resources, to change attitudes and influence the decision-making processes that can initiate e-commerce (Duncombe & Molla, 2006). The two case examples of successful e-commerce adoption were both driven by primary value chain customers. However, it was also apparent that other locally-based secondary external agents had also been instrumental—such as material suppliers, local ISPs, software suppliers and donor agencies. Entrepreneurs who were early adopters also exerted a great deal of influence over organisational capability and readiness, and in some cases were instrumental in initiating and sustaining contact with external agents. Hence, the motivational factors that impinge on the interaction between owner/managers and external change agents are likely to be paramount.

CONCLUSION

The indicative nature of the sample and the small number of cases make conclusions uncertain. The intention of this paper was to provide a theoretically grounded framework to understand SMEs progress in e-commerce and assist managerial decision making. The developed framework, which is further enriched with the case evidence from India, relates to SME's ability and motivation to engage in the process of e-commerce innovation. This implies that SME mangers should recognise e-commerce as an ongoing innovation process and stock-take their ability and motivation to successfully undertake this process on a continuous basis. In addition, this emphasises that those agencies that are involved in supporting SMEs need to consider the SMEs temporal state of e-commerce adoption in order to sequence, time and combine their interventions effectively. In terms of research, this paper suggests that competency should be defined according to the developmental state of the SMEs. It also implies that rather than static models of e-commerce adoption, temporal models that are dynamic in nature have more explanatory power to understand e-commerce innovation in SMEs.

A couple of final points can be made related to the approach taken in this paper—issues that will need to be addressed as the research continues. First, the focus of this research has been to consider e-commerce as an innovation to improve SMEs performance. The use of e-commerce, however, constitutes only one ingredient for improved business performance, and needs to be considered alongside a range of other intervention strategies that relate to other business development services. The framework suggested in this paper—which is representative of an integrated business development model–may provide a suitable vehicle for analysing broader business and sector development objectives.

Second, linear models of e-commerce innovation have been criticised for being too mechanistic and technology driven, rather than focusing on the human resource and knowledge-based factors that guide business growth and development. Linear models also fail to reflect the true complexity of the innovation process and the diverse needs of enterprises according to their market, their sector orientation and their access to resources. The framework approach suggested in this paper reinforces this critique and represents a more holistic, differentiated and adaptable approach that departs from simplistic step-by-step models of e-commerce evolution.

Third, the evidence presented in this model is based on a limited set of case studies. Future studies that are longitudinal in nature would be ideal to monitor how SMEs either progress, or abandon e-commerce and which of the motivational and ability factors are crucial in such decisions. It is hoped that this paper can be used to suggest improvements and modifications to existing theories of innovation adoption involving ICT for SMEs in general and which are applicable to SMEs located in transitional and developing economies in particular.

REFERENCES

Atherton, A.., & Hannon, P. D. (2000). Innovation processes and the small business: A conceptual analysis. *International Journal of Business Performance Management, 2*(4), 276-292.

Bird, B. (1989). *Entrepreneurial behaviour.* Glenview, IL: Scott Foresman & Company.

Caldeira, M. M., & Ward, J. M. (2003). Using resource-based theory to interpret the successful adoption and use of information systems and technology in manufacturing small and medium-sized enterprises. *European Journal of Information Systems, 12*(2), 127-141.

Chen, L., Haney S., Pandzik, A., Spigarelli, J., & Jesseman, C. (2003). Small business Internet commerce: A case study. *Information Resources Management Journal, 16*(3), 17-42.

Cobbenhagen, J. (2000). Successful innovation—towards a new theory for the management of small and medium-sized enterprises. Cheltenham, UK: Edward Elgar.

Coopey, J., Keegan, O., & Emler, N. (1998). Managers' innovations and the structuration of organizations. *Journal of Management Studies, 35*(3), 263-284.

Coyne, K. P. (1986). Sustainable competitive advantage—What it is and what it isn't. *Business Horizons, 29*(January-February), 54-61.

Daniel, E. (2003). An exploration of the inside-out model: E-commerce integration in UK SMEs. *Journal of Small Business and Enterprise Development, 10*(3), 233-249.

Daniel, E., Wilson, H., & Myers, A. (2002). Adoption of e-commerce by SMEs in the UK: Toward a stage model. *International Small Business Journal, 20*(3), 253-270.

Davenport, T. H. (1993). *Process innovation: Reengineering work through information technology.* Boston: Harvard Business School Press.

De Berranger, P., Tucker, D., & Jones, L. (2001). Internet diffusion in creative micro-businesses: Identifying change-agent characteristics as critical success factors. *Journal of Organizational Computing and Electronic Commerce, 11*(3), 197-214.

Dickson, P. R. (1992). Toward a general theory of competitive rationality. *Journal of Marketing, 56*(January), 69-83.

DiMaggio, P. J., & Powell, W. (1983). The iron cage revisited: Institutional isomorphism and collective rationality in organizational behavior. *American Sociological Review, 48*(April), 147-160.

Dolan, C., & Humphrey, J. (2001). Governance and trade in fresh vegetables: The impact of UK supermarkets on the African horticultural industry. *Journal of Development Studies 37*(2), 147-76.

Duncombe, R. A., & Molla, A. (2006). E-commerce development in developing countries: Profiling change agents for SMEs. *International Journal for Entrepreneurship and Innovation, 7*(3), 185-196.

Duncombe, R. A., Heeks, R. B. Abraham, S., & Lal, N. (2005). *E-commerce for small enterprise development: A handbook for enterprise support agencies in India.* Retrieved December 12, 2006, from http://www.ecomm4dev.org

Elsammani, Z. A., Hackney, R., & Scown, P. (2004). SMEs adoption and implementation process of Websites in the presence of change agents. In N. A. Y. Al-Qirim (Ed.), *Electronic commerce in small to medium-sized enterprises: Frameworks, issues, and implications.* London: Idea Group Publishing.

Greve, H. R., & Taylor, A. (2000). Innovations as catalysts for organizational change: Shifts in organizational cognition and search. *Administrative Science Quarterly, 45*(March), 54-80.

Grewal, R., Comer, J. M., & Metha, R. (2001). An investigation into the antecedents of organisational participation in business-business electronic markets. *Journal of Marketing, 65*(3), 17-34.

Hall, R. (1993). A Framework linking intangible resources and capabilities to sustainable competitive advantage. *Strategic Management Journal, 14*(8), 607-618.

Hostager, T. J., Neil, T. C., Decker, R. L., & Lorentz, R. D. (1998). Seeing environmental opportunities: Effects of intrapreneurial ability, efficacy, motivation, and desirability. *Journal of Organisational Change Management, 11*(1), 11-26.

Iacovou, C. L., Benbasat, I., & Dexter, A. A. (1995). Electronic data interchange and small organisations: Adoption and impact of technology. *MIS Quarterly, 19*(4), 465-485.

Ibbotson, F., & Fahy, M. (2004). The impact of e-commerce on small Irish firms. *International Journal of Services Technology and Management, 5*(4), 317-332.

Jones, C., Hecker, R., & Holland, P. (2003). Small firm Internet adoption: Opportunities forgone, a journey not begun. *Journal of Small Business and Enterprise Development, 10*(3), 287-297.

King, J. L., Gurbaxani, V., Kraemer, K. L., Mac-Farlan, F. W., Raman, K. S., & Yap, C. S. (1994). Institutional factors in information technology innovation. *Information Systems Research, 5*(2), 139-169.

Knol, W. H. C., & Stroken, J. H. M. (2001). The diffusion and adoption of information technology in small- and medium-sized enterprises through IT scenarios. *Technology Analysis & Strategic Management, 13*(2), 227-245.

Kuan, K. K. Y., & Chau, P. Y. K. (2001). A perception-based model for EDI adoption in small businesses using a technology-organization-environment framework. *Information & Management, 38*(8), 507-521.

Lal, K. (2003). E-business and export behaviour: Evidence from Indian firms. *World Development, 32*(3), 505-517.

Merton, R. K. (1957). *Social theory and social structure.* Glencoe, IL: The Free Press.

Meyer, J. W., & Scott, W. R. (1992). *Organizational environment: Ritual and rationality.* Newbury Park: Sage Publications.

Mirchandani, D. A., & Motwani, J. (2001). Understanding small business electronic commerce adoption: An empirical analysis. *Journal of Computer Information Systems, 41*(3), 70-74.

Molla, A., & Licker, P. (2005). Perceived e-readiness factors in e-commerce adoption: An empirical investigation in a developing country. *International Journal of Electronic Commerce, 10*(1), 83-110.

Molla, A., Heeks, R., & Balcells, I. (2006). Adding clicks to bricks: A case study of e-commerce adoption by a Catalan small retailer. *European Journal of Information Systems, 15*(4), 424-438.

Poon, S., & Swatman, P. M. C. (1999). An exploratory study of small business Internet commerce issues. *Information and Management, 35*(1), 9-18.

Rogers, E. M. (1995). *Diffusion of innovation* (4th ed.). New York: The Free Press.

Shiels, H., McIvor, R., & O'Reilly, D. (2003). Understanding the implications of ICT adoption: Insights from SMEs. *Logistics Information Management, 16*(5), 312-326.

Slater, S. F., & Narver, J. C. (1995). Market orientation and the learning organization. *Journal of Marketing, 59*(July), 63-74.

Straub, D. (1997). The effect of culture on IT diffusion: E-mail and fax in Japan and the US. *Information Systems Research, 5*(1), 23-47.

Swanson, E. B. (1994). Information systems innovation among organizations. *Management Science, 40*(9), 1069-1092.

Thompson, V. A. (1965). Bureaucracy and innovation. *Administrative Science Quarterly, 10*(1), 1-20.

Verma, H. (2005). Enhancing export competitiveness of Indian SMEs through ICT. *Technology Exports, 11*(3), Jan-Mar 2005.

Yap, C. S., Soh, C. P. P., & Raman, K. S. (1992). Information systems success factors in small business. *Omega—International Journal of Management Science, 20*(5/6), 597-609.

Yin, R. K. (1994). *Case study research: Design and methods* (2nd ed.). London: Sage.

Zaltman, G., Duncan, R., & Holbek, J. (1973). *Innovations and organizations.* New York: John Wiley.

Chapter VIII
E–Entrepreneurship:
The Principles of Founding Electronic Ventures

Tobias Kollmann
University of Duisburg-Essen, Germany

ABSTRACT

The fundamental advantages of information technology in regard to efficiency and effectiveness assure that its diffusion in society and in most industries will continue. The constant and rapid development of Internet-related technologies in the accompanying net economy has inevitably had a significant influence on various possibilities for developing innovative online business concepts and realizing these by establishing entrepreneurial ventures. The term "e-entrepreneurship" respectively describes the act of founding new companies that generate revenue and profits independent from a physical value chain. With this in mind, this article focuses on the process of creating electronic customer value within the net economy as well as the success factors and development phases of electronic ventures. Elaborating on these points should help to clearly define the area of e-entrepreneurship and provide evidence that the establishment of electronic ventures is worthy of special consideration in the context of research on information technology entrepreneurship.

INTRODUCTION

With the dawn of the Internet in the last decade of the twentieth century, a structural change in both social and economic spheres was induced. Information technology has become an integral part of daily life and its influence on the transfer of information has become ubiquitous. The fundamental advantages of Internet-related technologies, especially in regard to their efficiency and effectiveness, assure that its diffusion in society and in most industries will continue. Above all, Internet-related technologies have produced new possibilities with respect to how enterprises create value for their customers. By offering physical and digital products and services via the World Wide Web, customer value may no longer be created on a physical level only, but also on an electronic level (Amit & Zott, 2001; Lumpkin & Dess, 2004; Weiber & Kollmann, 1998). In fact, an entirely new business dimension, which may be referred to as the net economy has emerged (Kollmann, 2006; Matlay, 2004). This has inevitably had a significant influence on various possibilities for developing innovative business concepts and realizing these by establishing entrepreneurial ventures that generate revenue and profits independent from a physical value chain. In this context, the term "e-entrepreneurship" describes the act of founding new companies specifically in the net economy. The expansion of the classical use of the term "entrepreneurship," however, raises several questions that will be answered in this chapter. In particular, the chapter will give answers to the following questions:

1. Which possibilities for innovative entrepreneurial activities does the net economy offer to create an electronic customer value?
2. What are the success factors for founding a company in the net economy?
3. What are the typical development phases that an electronic venture will undergo during its initial years of business?

This chapter will elaborate on these points in order to clearly define the area of e-entrepreneurship. Moreover, proof should be provided that the establishment of electronic ventures is worthy of special consideration in the context of research on information technology entrepreneurship.

BACKGROUND: THE NET ECONOMY

From a historical perspective, only the product characteristics (quality) and corresponding product conditions (e.g., price, discount) determined the success of a product (Kirzner, 1973; Porter, 1985). At that time, it was important to either offer products or services to the customer that were cheaper (cost leadership) or qualitatively superior (quality leadership) to the competitor's

product. Later in history, speed and flexibility as two additional competitive factors joined the scene (Meyer, 2001; Stalk, 1988). On the one hand, it became increasingly important to offer products or services at a certain point in time at a certain place (availability leadership), while on the other hand, it became crucial to allow for customer-oriented product differentiation of important product characteristics (demand leadership).

Though these traditional competitive factors and the resulting strategies are still valid, one of the central characteristics of the post-industrial computer society is the systematic use of information technology as well as the acquisition and application of information that complements work-life and capital as an exclusive source of value, production, and profit. Consequently, the source of a competitive advantage will be rather determined by achieving knowledge and information superiority over competitors (information leadership). Those who possess better information about the market, potential customers, and customer expectations will be more successful than others. Whereas information previously held merely a supporting function for physical production processes, it has now become an independent factor for production and competitiveness in many industries (Porter & Millar, 1985; Weiber et al., 1998).

The growing relevance of electronic data networks such as the Internet has created a new business dimension. It is especially influenced by the area of electronic business processes that are concluded over digital data pathways (King, Lee, Warkentin, & Chung, 2002; Kollmann, 2001; Taylor & Murphy, 2004; Zwass, 2003). Due to the importance of information as a supporting and independent competitive factor, as well as the increase in digital data networks, it must be assumed that there will be two relevant trade levels on which the world will do business in the future. In addition to the level of real, physical products and services (real economy), an electronic trade level for digital products and services (net economy) is evolving. "The net economy refers to the commercial use of electronic data networks, that is to say, a digital network economy, which, via various electronic platforms, allows the conclusion of information, communication, and transaction processes" (Kollmann, 2006, p. 326).

The value chain of the real economy (Porter, 1985) divides a company into strategically relevant activities and identifies value activities that can be differentiated physically and technologically. The customer is prepared to pay for a valuable product that is based on these value activities. This product can then form the basis for establishing an enterprise in the real economy. In this model, the individual steps of a sequence of value generating or value increasing activities are analyzed in order to efficiently and effectively develop primary processes (for instance, in the areas of incoming logistics, operations, and outgoing logistics) and supporting processes (for instance, in the areas of technology development and procurement). Even here, information is extremely important when striving to be more successful than the competi-

tion. Information can be used to improve analysis and monitoring of existing processes. The crucial point is that information has previously been regarded as a supporting element only, but not as an independent source of customer value.

With the establishment of the net economy and the newly created dimension of information as an independent source of competitive advantage, value can be created through electronic business activities in digital data networks independent from a physical value chain as they are predominantly performed by the underlying information systems and do not include physical production machinery or personnel (Amit et al., 2001; Lumpkin et al., 2004; Weiber et al., 1998). These electronic value added activities are thus not comparable to the physical value creation activities presented by Porter (1985), as they are rather characterized by the way information is used. Such value activities might include, for example, the collection, systemization, selection, combination, and distribution of information. Through these specific activities of creating value

Figure 1. Value chain of the real economy vs. value chain of the net economy (Kollmann, 2006, p. 327)

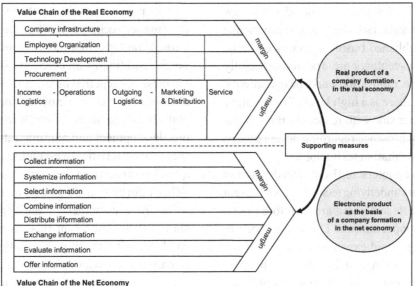

within digital data networks, an electronic value chain manifests itself (Figure 1). Based on this new value creation level, innovative business ideas evolve through the use of the various platforms and new digital products and Internet-based services are created. As customers are willing to pay for the value created by such an electronic product, it can form the basis for founding an electronic venture (e-venture) in the net economy (Kollmann, 2006).

FOUNDING ELECTRONIC VENTURES

In addition to having an electronic product when establishing an e-venture, it is also necessary to have a team of founders who have specific knowledge about the particularities of the net economy. Therefore, special emphasis needs to be placed on the combination of management and informatics to establish the company and guarantee the necessary technical processes. This is particularly important considering that information can change very quickly and with it the company's basis for the value creation activities in digital data networks. There is a further special characteristic trait of the net economy in addition to the electronic value chain – namely that this is a considerably new area of business and lacks the years of experience on which established business sectors can rely. Accordingly, e-ventures are oriented especially towards future innovations and developments. Furthermore, there is a high level of uncertainty on the customer side with respect to the amount and the timely presence regarding acceptance of innovative information technologies.

This risk is counteracted by the fact that the net economy and its underlying technologies represent a central growth sector and are therefore linked to numerous opportunities. This can be seen in the continuing, rapid expansion, and use of the Internet in the USA and Europe. Further, the level of investments in information technologies are still increasing, whereby, two aspects that are particularly pertinent for new companies become very clear. First, Internet-based platforms require a certain amount of capital or funding for the initial development and/or company, and, second, Internet-based technologies are subject to continuous change and constant development thus requiring subsequent investments. In addition to the need for capital to develop the technological platform, additional investments for the establishment of the new company in the net economy are necessary (such as personnel, organization, establishing a brand, sales, production, etc.).

This concludes the description of the basic conditions and requirements for establishing a company in the net economy. In particular, four central characteristic traits can be identified that clearly distinguish the process of establishing a business in the net economy from the "classical" company establishment in the real economy. First, an e-venture is often an independent, original, and innovative company. Second, an e-venture is characterized by enormous growth potential and, yet, is also marked by uncertainty of its future development concerning the true success of its technological platform (that, as a general rule, requires significant investments). Third, an e-venture is based on a business idea that can only be put into practice by the innovative use of information technologies. The idea itself focuses strongly on "information" as a competitive factor. Fourth and finally, an e-venture is based upon a business concept that involves the electronic creation of customer value offered on an electronic platform of the net economy. It requires continuous development and administration. In view of these characteristics of e-ventures, the following questions arise from the founder's point of view: What information do I need in order to create value for a customer? What type of platform should I use to present this information? How can I guarantee that my information product will remain attractive for the customer in future? How can my new firm grow independently? As a result of these questions, companies established in the net economy tend to be heterogeneous and more complex. They differ from companies established in the real economy in many aspects. This justifies an isolated and separate approach to researching how companies (i.e., e-ventures) are established in the net economy. In this context, e-entrepreneurship "refers to establishing a new company with an innovative business idea within the net economy, which, using an electronic platform in data networks, offers its products and/or services based upon a purely electronic creation of value. Essential is the fact that this value offer was only made possible through the development of information technology" (Kollmann, 2006, p. 333).

The Electronic Creation of Customer Value

Building upon the concept of creating information-based value in the net economy previously described, it must also be determined what kind of value is created in the eyes of the customer for which he would be prepared to pay (i.e., what makes an online offer attractive from the customer's point of view in the first place). In general, this might include the following six aspects:

- **Overview:** The aspect that an online offer provides an overview of a large amount of information that would otherwise involve the arduous gathering of information. The e-venture creates value through automatically structuring the information flood available.
- **Selection:** By submitting database queries, consumers can locate exactly the desired information/products/services more quickly with an online offer and, thus, more efficiently.
- **Mediation:** In this case, an online offer creates the possibility to bring together requests of suppliers and demanders more efficiently and effectively. By doing so, the e-venture creates a matching value.
- **Transaction:** This aspect refers to the possibility created by an online offer to design

and structure business activities more efficiently and effectively (e.g., with regard to cost aspects or payment possibilities).
- **Cooperation:** This aspect deals with using an online offer to enable various vendors or companies to more efficiently and effectively interlink their service or product offers with each other.
- **Exchange:** In this case, an online offer allows different consumers to communicate more efficiently and effectively with each other. The e-venture creates a communication value.

Considering these aspects of customer value, it is certainly possible that an e-venture can create several different types of value and that both structuring value as well as selection and matching value are created. After the identification of the creation of value, the perspective changes to the entrepreneur's point of view. The question to be asked here is how the customer value can be created. To answer this question, the electronic value chain can once again be applied. The electronic value chain separates an e-venture into strategically relevant activities in order to better understand cost behavior and recognize present and potential sources of differentiation. Thus, the electronic value chain represents respectively those value activities, which, for example, involve collecting, systemizing, and distributing information. Through specific value activities within the Internet, an electronic information product is created that represents value for which the customer is hopefully willing to pay. The electronic value chain therefore embodies the total value that is generated by the individual electronic value activities plus the profit margin. In the following paragraph, the most important value activities within the electronic value chain will be identified. It is these value activities that form the basis of an electronic value creation process within a company (Figure 2).

Figure 2. The electronic creation of customer value

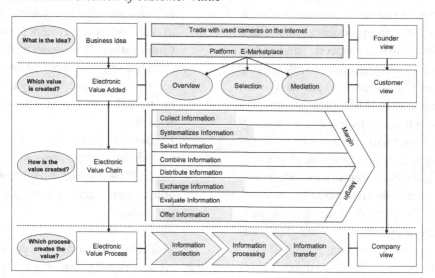

Should an idea be based upon, for example, dealing in used photo cameras in an e-marketplace in the Internet (founder's point of view), there is a typical way in which value can be electronically created. This value creation is directly reflected in the resulting added value for the user (customer view) and refers mainly to, in the example presented here, the overview, selection, and mediation functions. For instance, a supplier would be prepared to pay especially for the matching function, whereas a customer would be eventually willing to pay a fee for the overview function. In order to realize this creation of value, companies use the value chain to identify particularly those value activities that form the core of value creation. In order to do so, firstly, information on the object must be collected. Secondly, the location and the seller of the used camera must be determined, and, in a third step, systematically stored in a database. Using this database, information is then offered to the potential buyers who can formulate a query using appropriate search mechanisms. If a match is found through the query process, then the accompanying information pertinent to the request is exchanged. If all of this occurs, the final product is a transaction. The electronic value creation process from the company's point of view describes especially those information activities and/or the sequence of information activities, which in total create added value for the customer. This involves both the core and service processes. Core processes hold a true function in the creation of value, whereas service processes support the business processes along the value chain. As a general rule, the electronic value chain process begins with the input of information for the e-venture. In order to provide the targeted added value (e.g., overview function), the required information must first be gathered (e.g., who demands what at which level of quality and who offers it?). In the next step, the information is processed internally such that it can then be transferred on to the customer in the desired form as information output and in a way that specifically adds value for that customer. This process can be called the electronic value creation process and describes thus the core processes of most e-ventures. When considering e-ventures, it is then possible to formulate a representatively typical electronic value creation process (Kollmann, 1998):

Figure 3. Examples for electronic value creation processes

	Information collection	Information processing	Information transfer	Value added
google.com	Information about web sites and search queries (=Input)	Matching of search strings and web content	List of appropriate web sites (=Output)	Overview Selection
webmiles.de	Information about products, customer and web offers (=Input)	Allocation of incentive points for the usage of web content	Information about points, options for exchange, customer information (=Output)	Transaction Cooperation
delticom.de	Information about tires and customer requests (=Input)	Matching of demand and supply	List of adequate offers and their possibility for online ordering (=Output)	Overview Selection Transaction
guenstiger.de	Information about product prices and customer requests (=Input)	Structuring of product prices, matching of demand and supply	Product information, price information, customer information (=Output)	Overview Selection Mediation
travelchannel.de	Facts about destinations, online booking and travel reports (=Input)	Matching of demands and supply, structuring of travel offers and travel reports	Travel offers, destination information, travel reports (=Output)	Overview Selection Transaction Exchange

- The first step is the acquisition of information, which involves gathering relevant data that serves as an input for the additional creation of value. This results in the collection of useful data. This step in the value creation process can also be called *information collection*.
- The second step involves the conversion of the collected data into an information product for the customer. This step of the value creation process can be called *information processing*.
- The third step involves implementing the newly acquired or confirmed knowledge obtained from collected, saved, processed and evaluated data for the benefit of the customer. The result is an output of information, which creates value. This step can be called *information transfer*.

It is important to recognize that it is not sufficient to go through the sequence of this electronic value creation process (which is here presented in its most ideal form) just once. Rather, a continual process of acquiring, processing, and transferring information is necessary. This is essential, as in many cases, the information underlying the process of electronic value creation is coming from many different sources (such as customers, partner firms, third-party Web sites and databases) and thus constantly subject to change. Some examples of electronic value creation processes in the net economy are presented in Figure 3.

Success Factors of Electronic Ventures

If one takes a closer look at the new companies in the net economy equipped with electronic value chains and electronic processes of value creation (such as *google.com* or *YouTube.com*), there are a number of noticeable, common traits with regard to the way the e-venture was established. Mostly, it is a so-called original company founding, meaning that a completely new company is established without relying on any previously existing or available company structures. Additionally, one observes that these cases were most often independently established companies initiated by company founders seeking full-time self-employment to secure their independent entrepreneurial existence. Finally, it can be seen that established e-ventures were most often innovative companies (i.e., not established to imitate an existing company). An innovative start-up presents a situation in which the initiating factors, in the classical sense proposed by Schumpeter (1911), are combined in a new way. This new combination can involve both tangible and intangible factors. The increasing importance of information as a significant factor in competitive advantage has recently increased the significance of the intangible factors, in particular knowledge and know-how. Due to this, a number of newly formed companies in the net economy are established consistently upon new knowledge-based and conceptually creative factors (the way in which information is dealt with and processed in the context of electronic value creation to form an electronic product).

At first view, success factors for establishing a company in the net economy do not particularly differ from those in the real economy. Nevertheless, one does find specific differences in the realization of and development of these success factors that are directly dependent upon the particular conditions in the net economy. In particular, these differences cover the areas of management, product, market access, process, and finance (Figure 4) that will be discussed in the following paragraphs.

The *management* building block places emphasis on the founders, who, through their personality, motivation, and creativity, strongly determine the activities of an e-venture. Studies on the influence of technical, social, and methodical skills and capabilities of business founders determined that these have a positive influence on the successful realization of the activities involved with establishing a company (Walter, Auer, & Gemünden, 2002). This also holds true with respect to the motivation of the founder or the team of founders. High stress limit, pressure to succeed, self-confidence, and awareness of risk characterize the actions during the sustain-

Figure 4. Success factors of electronic ventures

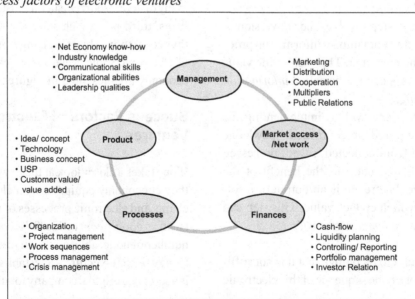

able phase of conception and thereafter in the realization phase. Whereas creativity on the one hand and analytical and conceptual thinking on the other dominate the first development phases of a new company, experience in the net industry, knowledge of the interrelated aspects of the net economy and real experience in operative management are significant points that matter when establishing an e-venture. In view of this, establishing a company in the net economy is very complex and the knowledge required to achieve this must be drawn similarly from the areas of informatics, information systems, and business administration. Accordingly, the founders must possess competence and know-how in all of these areas to a certain extent. However, an e-venture is often established by a team of founders due to the fact that seldom a single person possesses all of the following skills:

- **Informatics:** The technological aspect of the net economy makes it necessary to have a substantial understanding and knowledge of Internet-related standards and technologies, Internet architectures, databases, and software development.
- **Information systems:** The technological basis must be assessable with respect to its content and relevance for business issues. For this reason, it is important to have knowledge in areas such as IT security, data warehousing and data mining, e-business standards and electronic payment. It is just as important to understand the fundamental principles of the net economy, as it is to have sound overview of current existing business models and possibilities of creating electronic customer value.
- **Business administration:** At the business administration level, it is essential to have solid business knowledge. Topics, which should be especially emphasized here include marketing, business organization, management, as well as accounting and finance.

The *product* building block refers to the configuration of the services and offers of an e-venture. In this respect, the electronic product and/or service offer must be specified and communicated based upon its electronic added value. Thus, the essential question is, whether or not the customer needs the electronic offer/service provided by the e-ventures based on Information Technology and, if so, is the customer willing to pay for it? Further, it is the aim of the company to achieve added value for the customer through the realized output with electronically created value. Nevertheless, it is also the company's aim to assure its offer possesses a unique characteristic, which differentiates it from the other competitors. Furthermore, most e-ventures are dealing in new forms of business ideas and/or business models. From the customer side, initially it takes some time to get acquainted or acknowledge the effect provided as value added that results from such new ideas and models. For this reason, a regular reconnection with customers and users must take place, because in the end it is customer acceptance that determines if the electronic business idea is a success or not (Kollmann, 2006). Besides that, establishing a business in the net economy is singled out by the fact that an e-venture and its electronic business idea must not only satisfy a need, but also be superior compared to existing solutions in the real economy. For example, the need for books is already fulfilled through real bookshops. However, by offering overview, selection and transaction functions, Amazon.com creates an additional electronic value and was thus able to become one of the most successful players in the net economy.

The *processes* building block refers particularly to the need for a newly established company to quickly overcome that critical stage where its activities are informal and uncontrolled. This applies especially to work, finance, and organizational processes, which form a solid operative foundation in a newly established company. This essentially means that core processes must be firmly established and must also harmonize with the evolving company organization. Further, in this context it is also important that not too many activities are initiated simultaneously, because otherwise, there is an ensuing danger that some of these activities may not receive the full attention they require. Therefore, it is necessary to have a logical and effective project and process management. When dealing with an e-venture, sophisticated development and presentation of concrete workflows should be based on a model example of the value creation process that was previously determined. The company's business processes can then be conceptualized in parallel to the electronic process of value creation. These business processes should be understood as activity bundles necessary for realizing the value offer. They can be described as those targeted activities which are performed in a timely and logical sequence and their aim is directly determined by the company strategy (Hammer & Champy, 1993). Business processes thus describe the realization of the electronic process of creating value with the help of electronic resources within an e-venture. Particularly in the net economy, which is characterized by a high degree of virtualization, the knowledge of precise process flows is extremely important. Many business models in the net economy are based upon taking advantage of the effects of economies of scale. This is possible only when a large number of users can be serviced by either very few or with just one basic process (e.g., at online auction houses). The complexity of value creation, especially if the creation of this value involves the participation of multiple companies, requires a reduction of the process to the most essential steps. Weaknesses in core processes can then be more easily recognized. Especially with respect to electronic and thus automated process steps, mistakes can significantly impact

the success of a company. Moreover, the process is externally visible to customers. Therefore, the quality of process flows has a direct influence on the customer's usage behavior. Supported by the virtual quality of information products, process flows become representatives of the quality image. The customer rates a company based upon the usability, functionality, and security of its processes.

The *market access* building block does not only mean to assure market entrance and establishing a product and/or brand, but also means reaching the customer via an electronic communication channel. The focus here is the question: How do I reach the customer with my information product? Hereby, it is possible to achieve market access through company-initiated marketing and sales activities. However this seems to pose a signification problem considering the lack of resources of start-up companies. Market entry in the net economy is, in most cases, characterized by the fact that most e-ventures are unknown, have limited capital, lack of range of resources, and do not have an established network. Particularly the lack of financial means often leads to deficits for a newly established company in the area of service or product performance, communication/sales and market positioning. In order to eliminate these deficits, especially when dealing with e-ventures, cooperation strategies play an elementary role in supporting the market entrance and positively steering the company's further development (Kollmann & Häsel, 2006). In view of the existing resource limitations, traditional marketing campaigns based on buyer-seller relationships are too cost-intensive and thus not feasible for many e-ventures. Affiliate programs, on the contrary, are predominantly understood as marketing and sales concepts that are directly based upon a partnership-like relationship and profit-scheme compensation. The e-venture (merchant) concludes an advertisement and/or sales agreement with a cooperation partner (affiliate), who in turn integrates the merchant's service/product offer on their internet presence or Web site. If this results in a successful transaction, the affiliate receives a commission on sales (Rayport & Jaworski, 2002). In this way, a newly established company can reach, from the very beginning, a wide range of customer segments and establish a comprehensive sales network.

The *finance* building block is tasked with guaranteeing the establishment and evolution of the firm from a liquidity point of view. There are two essential aspects, which are of importance here: On the one hand, there is a significant need for investing in technology and in establishing the company in the starting phase, whereby, on the other hand, the free-cash-flow cannot be too negatively influenced. The financing and cash planning is often a significant weak point for companies in the net economy. In particular, there often is a lack of realism, resulting in euphoric turnover forecasts or underestimated financial requirements. Hence, there should be a continually updated finance planning that can provide a realistic estimate of the financial situation of the company at any given point in time and also present the actual financing requirement. The financing of a company in this case becomes increasingly a mixture of equity (own capital) and various forms of participations. In situations such as these, risk capital should be strategically used for investments (e.g., sales), for example, for generating cash flow. The financing of the company furthermore requires a secure controlling, especially on the cost-side of the business. A further aspect concerns the communication with investors who want to be informed on a regular basis about the development of the company (Kollmann & Kuckertz, 2006).

Development Phases of Electronic Ventures

The future development of a company in the net economy can be outlined by just one simple question: What will happen to the idea in the course of time? At the very core, when a new company is to be founded, an idea for a possible business concept exists. This idea must first be discerned and then assessed for its potential for success (phase of idea finding). In a subsequent step, the idea must be transferred to a plausible and sustainable foundation, and a corresponding business plan for the idea must be prepared (phase of idea formulation). This must be done in order to actually realize the idea in the next step (phase of idea realization). Success of the e-venture is, however, not only dependent upon the initial realization of the business model, but also depends on the continual development and appropriate adjustment to market demands (phase of idea intensification). Finally, the idea must be capable of continually growing with the market and developing into a long-term business (phase of idea continuation). In each of these phases, it is essential that certain tasks along with the previously outlined building blocks for establishing a company are fulfilled. The individual phases (Ruhnka & Young, 1987) and specific questions which are of significant importance throughout the development of a company in the net economy are illustrated in Figure 5 and will be further discussed in the following paragraphs.

In the context of the financing of a new company or start-up, the phases of finding, formulating and realizing the idea are considered to be the *early stage*. Generally, this stage is divided into the pre-seed, seed and a start-up phase. In the pre-seed and seed-phase, the company has not been founded yet. These phases reflect more specifically the time in which the future founders of a company are searching for the idea and planning the realization of their business model. Even if no company and no marketable product exists in these phases, there is nevertheless a need for capital as, for instance, market studies or acceptance and feasibility studies must be performed (costs for preparation). If the company is to be established based upon a business plan (idea formulation), the start-up phase begins, in which production capacities are established, personnel is sought and the market entry is prepared. For an e-venture, this most often means the programming of the internet platform and its functionalities (development costs). When a successful online start can take place and the product or service offer is introduced into the market, the start-up phase ends. Especially during this early stage, the product and management building blocks play an essential role as there will definitely be no further progress without them.

The early stage is followed by the *expansion stage*, featuring the launch of the product or service and its introduction to the market. Beginning here, one of the central, strategic targets of the company is to expand the presence of its product/service on the market and achieve constant turnover growth. The newly formed company then enters the expansion stage and the first stable income is earned. In this phase, it is absolutely necessary to

expand production and sales capacities. In order to achieve this, it is possible to form partnerships. As a general rule, the further expansion of the company cannot be solely financed through its cash-flow. The company is confronted with additional capital requirements. At this stage, potential investors can be offered far more security for their investment as compared to the early phase of the business development. Considering this, the management is nevertheless challenged by an entirely new problem of properly steering the growth of the company. This is the point where internal processes must be established. Within the expansion stage, the market access and processes building blocks are particularly important as, without them, further growth can most certainly not be achieved.

As soon as a company can rely upon an ever-increasing growth rate and guaranteed business income, the *later stage* of the company's de-

Figure 5. Development phases of electronic ventures

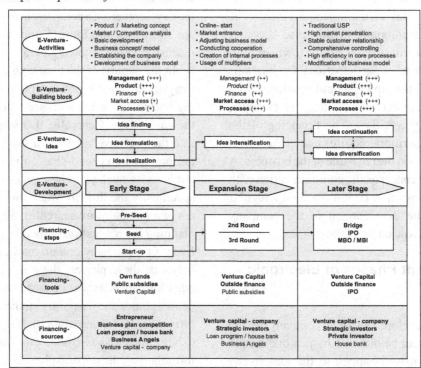

velopment has been achieved. From a turnover perspective, the company is stable in its business development and there is eventually the opportunity to consider a diversification of the original idea. The company has established unique selling aspects for its product or service that separate it from the competitors and has achieved a significant market penetration. This means that even the future growth of the e-venture can be calculated and risks can be better defined than in the previous phases of the business development. When there is a significantly high level of growth potential, the break-even point can be achieved by bridge financing or the preparation of an initial public offering. Investors from the previous financing rounds also have the option of a trade sale to a strategic investor as well as selling their shares back to the founders or the management in a management buy-out, or respectively a management buy-in. During the later stage, all of the building blocks play a significant role due to the fact that, generally, growth can only be obtained when all of these elements are functioning seamlessly.

FUTURE TRENDS

The creation of new ventures plays a decisive role for the social and economic development of every country. This is due to the fact that with each new venture created, a market participant comes into existence, which potentially stimulates the competition and drives the economy further. The founding of electronic ventures within the net economy is therefore a key topic for every national industry. As the significance of Internet-based technologies has triggered a technological and societal development that is irresistible, e-entrepreneurship can be expected to gain further importance in the future. With the proliferation of digital television and third generation mobile technologies, novel and innovative ways of delivering electronic value can be expected to emerge. The boundaries between

mobile services and the "stationary" Internet will increasingly become blurred. This will enable e-ventures to span multiple electronic channels and become a pervasive part of daily life. Moreover, the pervasiveness of digital technologies and changes in customer behavior are increasingly blurring the borders between electronic and physical trade levels. real economy and net economy are merging. Particularly in this context, the need for a complementary utilization of physical and electronic value creation activities can be expected, as customers will increasingly use online and off-line channels contemporaneously (Kollmann et al., 2006). Will customers in the future browse Web-based catalogs in order to create digital shopping lists that are then used in connection with a mobile phone to guide the customer through the physical retail store? Similarly, television has begun to turn into an interactive online channel incorporating distribution and service potentials going much beyond spot advertisements. For the combined management of physical and electronic value creation activities, a strategic cooperation between e-ventures and real economy firms can be expected to hold an outstanding potential, as this enables the partners to serve both online and off-line channels without extending themselves beyond their own means and competencies (Kollmann et al., 2006). Researchers will have to further elaborate the concepts presented in this chapter in order to explain the full range of commercial activities that future technologies will allow and future customers will ask for.

CONCLUSION

As this chapter has shown, the competent processing of information has to be the foundation of entrepreneurial attempts in the net economy. The chapter provided insight into how founders may conceptualize electronic value creation processes that create customer value, independent of a physical value chain. Thereby, the electronic value chain and the value-oriented collection, processing and transfer of information serve as a starting point for every e-venture. Once the business concept is in place, the general success factors for establishing a company in the net economy do not particularly differ from those in the real economy. However, studying the five building blocks of management, product, market access, processes and finance, the chapter suggests a range of specifics that must be borne in mind in order to succeed in the early, later, and expansion stage of an e-venture's life cycle. In addition, the importance of each of these building blocks has been found to be varying in the respective phases of development. The framework presented in this chapter may thus guide founders in setting priorities and assist them in adopting an analytical perspective on their current business activities. It should have become apparent that the net economy offers a wide range of opportunities to found electronic ventures. To fully exploit the potentials of Internet-related technologies, however, founders need to approach e-entrepreneurship in a systematic and precautious way that is backed by sound strategy, and never as an end in itself.

REFERENCES

Amit, R., & Zott, C. (2001). Value creation in e-business. *Strategic Management Journal, 22*(6/7), 493-520.

Hammer, M., & Champy, J. (1993). *Reengineering the corporation: A manifesto for business revolution*. New York: HarperBusiness.

King, D., Lee, J., Warkentin, M., & Chung, H. (2002). *Electronic commerce: A managerial perspective*. Upper Saddle River, NJ: Pearson Education International.

Kirzner, I. M. (1973). *Competition and entrepreneurship*. Chicago, IL: University of Chicago Press.

Kollmann, T. (2006). What is e-entrepreneurship?—fundamentals of company founding in the net economy. *International Journal of Technology Management, 33*(4), 322-340.

Kollmann, T. (2004). Attitude, adoption, or acceptance?—measuring the market success of telecommunication and multimedia technology. *International Journal of Business Performance Management, 6*(2), 133-52.

Kollmann, T. (2001). Measuring the acceptance of electronic marketplaces. *Journal of Computer Mediated Communication, 6*(2).

Kollmann, T. (1998). The information triple jump as the measure of success in electronic commerce. *Electronic Markets, 8*(4), 44-49.

Kollmann, T., & Häsel, M. (2006). *Cross-channel cooperation: The bundling of online and offline business models*. Wiesbaden: DUV.

Kollmann, T., & Kuckertz, A. (2006). Investor relations for start-ups: An analysis of venture capital investors' communicative needs. *International Journal of Technology Management, 34*(1/2), 47-62.

Lumpkin, G. T., & Dess, G. G. (2004). E-business strategies and internet business models: How the Internet adds value. *Organizational Dynamics, 33*(2), 161-173.

Matlay, H. (2004). E-entrepreneurship and small e-business development: Towards a comparative research agenda. *Journal of Small Business and Enterprise Development, 11*(3), 408-414.

Meyer, C. (2001). The second generation of speed. *Harvard Business Review, 79*(4), 24-26.

Porter, M. E. (1985). *Competitive Advantage*. New York: Free Press.

Porter, M. E., & Millar, V. E. (1985). How information gives you competitive advantage. *Harvard Business Review, 63*(4), 149-160.

Rayport, J. F., & Jaworski, B. J. (2002). *Introduction to e-commerce.* Boston: McGraw-Hill.

Ruhnka, J. C., & Young, J. E. (1987). A venture capital model of the development process for new ventures. *Journal of Business Venturing 2*(2), 167-184.

Schumpeter, J. A. (1911). *The theory of economic development: An inquiry into profits, capital, credit, interest and the business cycle.* 1934 translation. Cambridge, MA: Harvard University Press.

Stalk Jr., G. (1988). Time—The next source of competitive advantage. *Harvard Business Review, 66*(4), 28-60.

Taylor, M., & Murphy, A. (2004). SMEs and e-business. *Journal of Small Business and Enterprise Development, 11*(3), 280-289.

Walter, A., Auer, M., & Gemünden, H. G. (2002). The impact of personality, competence, and activities of academic entrepreneurs on technology transfer success. *International Journal of Entrepreneurship and Innovation Management, 2*(2/3), 268-289.

Weiber, R., & Kollmann, T. (1998). Competitive advantages in virtual markets—perspectives of "information-based-marketing" in cyberspace. *European Journal of Marketing, 32*(7/8), 603-615.

Zwass, V. (2003). Electronic commerce and organizational innovation: Aspects and opportunities. *International Journal of Electronic Commerce, 7*(3), 7-37.

KEY TERMS

Affiliate Program: Marketing and sales concept that is directly based upon a partnership-like relationship and profit-scheme compensation. The so-called merchant concludes an advertisement and/or sales agreement with a cooperation partner (affiliate), who in turn integrates the merchant's service/product offer on their Web site.

E-Entrepreneurship: Establishing a new company with an innovative business idea within the net economy, which, using an electronic platform in data networks, offers its products and/or services based upon a purely electronic creation of value.

Electronic Trade Level: A business dimension resulting from the proliferation of digital data networks and thus a new possibility of doing business in the so-called net economy, apart from the existing economy of physical products and services (real economy).

Electronic Value Creation: Refers to the creation of an added value by the means of a digital information product in the framework of the net economy. Electronic value is commonly created through value-adding activities such as the collection, processing, and transfer of information.

Electronic Venture (E-Venture): A recently founded and thus young e-business (startup). An e-venture results from a company foundation in the net economy.

Net Economy: Refers to the economically utilized part of digital data networks (such as the Internet) that allow carrying out information, communication and transaction processes, (and thus an electronic value creation) via different electronic platforms.

Real Economy: Refers to the real trade level of physical products and services (in contrast to the net economy, which refers to the electronic trade level of digital products and services).

Chapter IX
The Relationship Between Internet Entrepreneurs, Idea Generation, and Porter's Generic Strategies

John Sanders
Heriot-Watt University, UK

Laura Galloway
Heriot-Watt University, UK

William Keogh
Heriot-Watt University, UK

ABSTRACT

The chapter discusses the use of business strategies for pure Internet firms. It separates the strategic choices and directions used for idea generation, during start-up, and beyond business or brand establishment. Corroborating much of the literature, it argues that traditional notions of strategy might be inappropriate for some dotcom firms due to the high level of complexity, speed of change and competitiveness characteristic of the Internet environment. As has been observed by research, idea generation on the Internet can involve prospecting and reacting quickly to markets to a greater extent than amongst traditional businesses. Likewise, start-up strategies often appear to involve flexibility and an openness to strategic change in response to the fast dynamic nature of the online market. The chapter suggests alternative strategy models that might be useful in our understanding of Internet business creation and development.

INTRODUCTION

The current chapter explores idea generation, start-up (i.e., the first three years), and ongoing operational strategies for the establishment, sustainability, and growth within Internet-based firms, as opposed to off-line, traditional businesses. Specifically, the chapter refers to those firms that exist entirely on the Internet, and that are innovation driven—in terms of products/services or processes. Courtney, Kirkland, and Viguerie (1997) identify three strategic postures that firms can adopt in the **Internet environment**: shaping the future, adapting to the future, and reserving the right to play. For the current chapter, **Internet entrepreneurship** is associated most often with the first of these categories, but as will be shown, also can involve those firms that would be associated with the second.

A SUMMARY OF SMALL BUSINESS STRATEGY RESEARCH

By and large, studies investigating **business strategy** and planning processes have centred on the activities of large firms (O'Gorman, 2000; Wheelen & Hunger, 1999). These studies have resulted in the development of a large body of theory, frameworks, techniques and concepts for understanding and designing suitable strategic postures for large, not small firms (Beaver & Prince, 2004). Indeed, a number of writers (e.g., Covin & Slevin, 1989; Shrader, Mulford, & Blackburn, 1989) have argued that strategic management techniques are unsuitable for small firms. Further, where research has attempted to identify the use and impact of various strategies in small firms, results have varied. For example, there are many empirical studies that have identified a positive correlation between strategy and planning, and small business performance and growth (e.g., Beaver & Ross, 2000; Griggs, 2002; Masurel & Smit, 2000; Perry, 2001). Conversely though, other

studies have found a negative or no correlation between the use of planning by small business owners and performance (e.g., French, Kelly, & Harrison, 2004; Gibson & Cassar, 2005). A likely explanation for these inconclusive findings is the use of different **business strategy** and planning definitions by the studies examined. Within the extant literature the concepts "strategy," "strategic planning," "business planning," and "strategic management" are often used interchangeably. However, these expressions can and do represent very different things to owners, managers and scholars (Beaver et al., 2004). In the same way, research results are going to be influenced by how the planning construct is operationalised. For instance, in several studies, researchers have placed tremendous weight on the existence of a formal written plan that includes goals and objectives as symbolising a high degree of planning sophistication or formality. In the case of small businesses, various researchers argue that informal planning is just as valid as formal planning if owners or managers demonstrate **strategic awareness** (Lyles, Baird, Orris, & Kuratko, 1993; Robinson & Pearce, 1984). **Strategic awareness** is a much more desirable and important ability to possess than a formal business plan (e.g., Beaver et al., 2000; Georgellis, Joyce, & Woods, 2000). **Strategic awareness** is described as management's ability to calculate the effects of environmental changes, and then to re-position their firm's activities to take advantage of them (Gibb & Scott, 1985).

The **orthodox** perspective of **strategy formulation** holds that to preserve performance organisations make purposeful, logical and rational changes to their structures that cause them to be better aligned over time with their environment (i.e., they move from low to high performing structures). However, controversy surrounds the **orthodox** outlook because many authors believe strategy formulation cannot be described as a logical and rational process (Alvesson & Willmott, 1996). Brown and Blackmon (2005) state that the assumptions behind **business strategy** and planning were developed at a time when competitive environments were far more stable and predictable—making it possible to be rational and deliberate. A major critic of strategy formulation being a deliberate or planned organisational phenomenon is Mintzberg (1994). He argues that strategy is better described as an **emergent** process involving considerable learning, negotiation, and adaptation. This **emergent** process, he asserts, will provide better results in a complex and dynamic environment, whilst a deliberate approach in the same situation is unsustainable (Mintzberg, 1990).

A number of commentators believe that contemporary environmental changes are so rapid and unanticipated that planning is an ineffective activity and instead organisations need to be agile and flexible (e.g., Eisenhardt & Brown, 1999; Hamel, 2002). Intensifying competition demands that firms must be capable of rapid change to survive (D'Aveni, 1994). In particular, over recent years, the impact of the Internet on firm competitiveness has been much debated. Authors such as Evans and Wurster (1999) suggest that the Internet requires the development of new strategies, because traditional organisational value chains are being dissembled, creating new competitive rules. The notion that the Internet has created new competitive rules is echoed by many authors (e.g., Afuha & Tucci, 2001; Amit & Zott, 2001). The Internet is certainly a major business innovation (Scott & Walter, 2003), which has created uncertainty about whether existing management practices such as strategy and planning are still applicable.

Mintzberg, Quinn, and Ghoshal (1998a) discuss that the strategic direction of the entrepreneurial organisation lies with the entrepreneur and that the actual process of strategy formation is "semiconscious." The strategy comes from the mind of the "leader" from their experience(s) and intuition, and he or she promotes the **vision** in a single minded manner. The description also relates to other entrepreneurial characteristics identi-

fied by McClelland (1961) such as the need for achievement and a high internal locus of control. The ambiguity tolerance characteristic may also help to explain the approach of the entrepreneur as Mintzberg, Ahlstrand, and Lampel (1998b, p. 143) also see the entrepreneurial strategic **vision** as malleable, and that it "tends to be both deliberate and **emergent** (i.e., deliberate in overall **vision**, **emergent** in how details of **vision** unfold"). However, there is a great deal of complexity in the characteristics of the entrepreneur that make up this entrepreneurial approach, echoed by Cassia, Fattore, and Paleari (2006, p. 44): "the wide range of traits and characteristics attributed to entrepreneurship are so complexly interrelated that it seems difficult to ascribe them all to one single person or role." In a pragmatic sense, the entrepreneur would tend to be somewhat flexible in their approach as they seize an idea and seek to make it a reality. The general market focus of the entrepreneur tends towards identifying and occupying a niche within the market. Their skills and knowledge, coupled with being first to market may protect them as barriers to entry from competition, but only in the initial phases.

THE INTERNET ENVIROMENT

The **Internet environment** is defined as all presence and activity on the world-wide-Web and the various Internet technologies that support Web activity (such as secure payment facilities). This includes business activity but not exclusively. Social, entertainment, political and research activities and information are some examples of that which can be found in this evolving medium. Essentially, nowadays the Internet is used for virtually (sic) everything, and in time, as technology develops and creativity is applied, it will be used for things, and in ways, that we have not yet anticipated. The **Internet environment** is highly complex, and that complexity will increase further as volume of users and identification of uses for it increase. In the context of business specifically, the Internet entrepreneur is faced with attempting to trade and profit in a highly competitive environment in which markets are unstable and fast-moving, firms are highly interconnected, and uncertainty prevails (Chen, 2005, p. 213). Change is continual and often substantial whereupon "market needs and the technology required to meet those needs can change even while a product or service is still under development" (Kickul & Walters, 2002). Thus, as Morino (1999) points out, Internet entrepreneurs need to embrace this speed of change, and find ways to respond to transformation in business issues such as technology, market conditions and competition. For business, change and predictability predominate as concerns, as it is these elements contribute to the risks associated with the introduction of innovation to markets. However, Venkataraman and Sarasvathy (2001, p. 6-7) note that entrepreneurs themselves contribute to unpredictability and change in the business environment in that "entrepreneurial opportunities…do not necessarily lie about waiting to be discovered…or even to

be 'divined' by entrepreneurial geniuses…instead entrepreneurial opportunities are often residuals of human activities," and they note that these opportunities can come from any sphere of life: "it is an empirical fact that profits for the individual and the firm, and welfare for the economy come as much from Jerry Seinfeld's jokes and Michael Jordan's baskets, as from great technological inventions and the tearing down of the Berlin Wall" (ibid, p.7).

The **Internet environment** can thus be described as change-based and fast in terms of opportunity creation and market change. The current authors describe this state as characterised by continuous **Turmoil** including, for example, the effects of ongoing and increasing participation amongst users of all demographics and geographical backgrounds, new businesses and new **business models**, new online ways of generating income, new social activities, political activities and the emergence of new groups of users brought together by common interests. As these multiple participatory items occur, change, evolve, and adapt, they each have the

Diagram 1. Turmoil and market opportunities

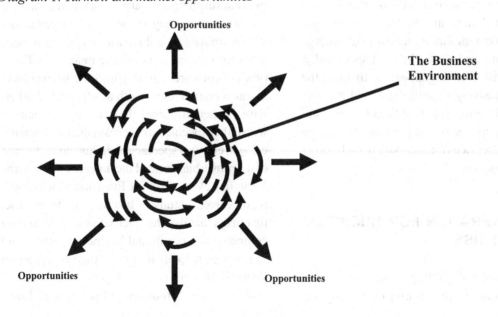

potential to cause a ripple effect in that they have the potential to change the behaviour of users, competitive strategies for businesses, consumer behaviour, etc. **Turmoil** can be seen as similar to chaos (i.e., a complex system characterised by "unstable aperiodic behaviour") (Kellert, 1993, p. 2) that "never repeats and continues to manifest the effects of any small perturbation" (Anelli, 2005). Authors such as Bouchikhi (1993), Kippenberger (1999), and Fitzgerald (2002) have applied the concept of chaos to business, but the current authors prefer the term "**turmoil**" as the level and nature of the complexity observed in the business environment is restricted by human intention, limitation, and activity. That said, it can be argued that from social and business points of view, exploitable zeitgeists and even creative destruction (Schumpeter, 1934), are created by non-repeating circumstances brought about by irregular and timely events. These circumstances may be comprised of compounding variables that may contribute to entrepreneurial opportunity and propensity (Bouchikhi, 1993). Furthermore, any entrepreneurship or innovation will further contribute to complexity and become a new variable in the **Turmoil** in that it "will inevitably change everything surrounding it" (Chen, 2005, p.262).

In Diagram 1, **turmoil** in the market appears to be a normal state and the business environment is in constant flux. Opportunities emerge in many areas, and on the Internet specifically, these can arise from organisations that use the Internet exclusively, organisations and markets that use the Internet as part of their business activity, or organisations that position themselves as providing service from outputs from Internet based organisations.

IDEA GENERATION FOR BUSINESS INTERNET USE

Venkataraman et al. (2001, p.7) state that "entrepreneurship consists in matching up the products

of human imagination with human aspirations to create markets for goods and services that did not exist before the entrepreneurial act." In short, this definition necessitates the element of innovation most often associated with entrepreneurship (e.g., Schumpeter, 1947; Stevenson & Gumpert, 1985). Entrepreneurship on the Internet is regarded as a specific type of technology entrepreneurship, but unlike general technology entrepreneurship Colombo and Delmastro (2001) found that Internet entrepreneurs tended to be younger, inexperienced in business, "less educated especially in technical domains" and highly market oriented. Chen (2003) found also that amongst Internet entrepreneurs there is a "high importance of the "fun" and excitement that the Internet offers and the chance to try out new ideas" (in Chen 2005, p. 237). Carrier, Raymond, and Eltaief (2004) refer to the "cyberentrepreneur" and define this as an entrepreneur who "creates a firm that is essentially founded upon electronic commerce, and whose main activities are based on exploiting networks using Internet technologies, intranets and extranets." Moreover, "cyberentrepreneurs introduce change into a commercially organised economic system" and thus represents "entrepreneurship in its most noble sense." **Internet entrepreneurship** (certainly at present), therefore, often comprises an entirely online business incarnation, where innovation and creation of new products, often for new markets are the main foci. These types of entrepreneurial firms have been subject to much commentary, both academic and otherwise, particularly since they are often associated with either spectacular success (such as Amazon, easyjet, eBay) or spectacular failure (as in the case of the proverbial burst of the dotcom bubble in the 1990s (e.g., Wolff, 1999)). Even now, Chen (2003) reports from a study of business on the Internet that firms that use the Internet as a value-adding component of traditional business practice "are 11 times more likely to survive than pure Internet [firms]." Despite this, new pure-Internet firms proffering new products and services and new ways of profiting continually emerge on the Internet, and it is now perceived as an environment where entrepreneurs are "radically redefining existing products/services" (Chen, 2005, p. 22) and true innovation in product and business method can be created (Small, 2000, p.1).

Early Internet business activity followed traditional business rules and models. It is likely that this contributes disproportionately to Internet business failure even now. Generating ideas and business success on the Internet, with its inherent complexity, speed of change and potentials often requires a specific application of creativity and opportunity exploitation. In a world where "the future is not merely unknown, but essentially unknowable" (Venkataraman et al., 2001, p. 10) new and different strategies may be required, both in terms of business operations, and also for generating a successful idea.

Carrier et al. (2004) found that idea generation amongst Internet entrepreneurs varies from traditional idea generation. Rather than create a new product or service and then test its market feasibility, Internet entrepreneurs are more likely to search the market for opportunities. Thus market opportunity or need is analysed first, and ideas or solutions generated in response. Galloway (2005) notes in a case study that for the Internet entrepreneur, idea generation involved the generation of several ideas at the same time, in response to perceived market opportunities. Additionally, this can be an ongoing process. Kickul et al. (2002) note that "internet firms that emphasise innovation and rapid response to change may be best positioned for recognising and identifying new opportunities." Again, this is not unique to Internet business: Miles and Snow in a 1978 paper identified prospector strategy, whereupon entrepreneurial firms continually search the market for new opportunities. Kickul et al. (2002) claim that this is a highly applicable Internet **business strategy**, and find a "relationship between [it] and e-commerce innovation."

Diagram 2. The entrepreneur and the right idea

The Entrepreneur
- Experience
- Enthusiasm
- Building on success
- Dreams
- Drive

- Etc.

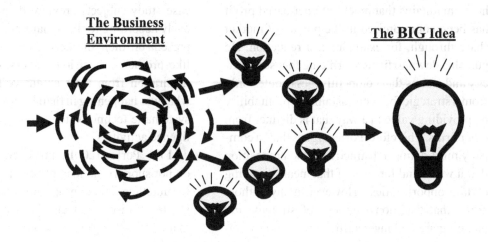

Diagram 2 illustrates that the entrepreneur dips into the **Turmoil** that is the Internet business environment and brings to the marketplace his or her experience and enthusiasm for developing something new. They may even be building on previous successes and the characteristics of determination and drive enable them to identify opportunities in a market in **turmoil**. In this way of working, innovation and identifying opportunities for potential niche markets are paramount and this diagram illustrates the potential for emergence of ideas. It is likely that an Internet entrepreneur would identify and present online a few ideas, and then focus on the idea to which the market responds best to take it forward as an opportunity in the marketplace.

INTERNET START-UP STRATEGIES

Beyond establishing the Internet firm, in terms of ongoing operations, Chen (2005, p.22) notes that traditional **business strategy** generally involves several stages: defining objectives, assessment of the external environment, assessment of the internal environment, identification of gaps, development of a strategic plan, and implementation of the plan. He claims that in the **Internet environment** this type of strategy poses difficulties in that Internet businesses have to "contend with other issues." Porter (2001), on the other hand, maintains that much Internet-based profit has been compromised in the pursuit of market share through, for example, cost reduction. He puts this down to firms sacrificing focused strategy and claims that competitiveness comes only from a strategic focus on sustainable profitability by providing value in a way that is distinct from other firms. Therefore, Porter argues that "a company must define a distinctive value proposition that it will stand for, even if that means forgoing certain opportunities." However, many authors argue that traditional notions of strategy and planning are no longer sufficient when the com-

petitive environment is volatile as the notion of strategic formulation is too static in nature (e.g., Rajagopalan & Spreitzer, 1997; Venkatraman, 1989). Other commentators agree with Porter's idea that the focus on the value proposition must be maintained, but argue that the value proposition to customers can be harder to identify in the **Internet environment**, therefore, a flexibility of approach is necessary (e.g., Chen, 2005).

Sanchez (1995, p.138) describes flexibility as "a firm's abilities to respond to various demands from dynamic competitive environments." Teece, Pisano, and Shuen (1997, p. 520) describe flexible organisations as those with the ability to "scan the environment, evaluate markets and competitors, and to quickly accomplish reconfiguration and transformation ahead of competition." Writers such as Mintzberg (1990) claim that often strategy has to be adapted in response to unforeseen circumstances. Therefore, firms may operate "strategies that were intended as well as those that were realised despite intentions" (Venkataraman et al., 2001, p. 13). Kickul et al. (2002) relate this idea directly to Internet firms in that they "must be continually prepared to make changes within the infrastructure of their business to meet and prepare for future opportunities." Thus, a responsive, flexible strategic approach is cited by these writers as being most appropriate within the **Internet environment**. Carrier et al. (2004) find empirical evidence to support this in that their case study subjects "reviewed [plans] continuously according to the dynamics and turbulence present on their markets...They behaved more like pro-active decision makers, drawing their inspiration from their extensive knowledge of what was happening in their sector, gleaned from systematic techno-watch and competitive intelligence activities."

Like Porter (2001), however, other writers do not support the idea of reaction and flexibility untethered as appropriate Internet **business strategy**. Eisenhardt and Brown (1998) found that in fast-changing environments, such as the

Internet, the most successful strategy involved operating with strict schedules for goals. Chen (2005, p.227) notes that "transitions are especially critical in fast-changing markets, where it is difficult to catch up after failure." Similarly, Gans and Stern (2003) note that for innovative firms in all environments "the challenge of any return on innovation often results in ad hoc strategy development and execution" and that "firms opportunistically take advantage of potential revenue opportunities as they present themselves, rather that choosing a strategy that…is most likely to yield the highest long-term return." Porter (2001), referring specifically to Internet firms, claims that, rather than concentrating on strategic profitability, firms have taken indirect revenues from things like click-throughs and advertising, and this has resulted in unsustainability as a result of lack of strategic focus. The debate, thus, goes on. Essentially, for some firms lack of focus jeopardises long-term sustainability where unsustainable income generation activities have distracted focus from the original value proposition to the extent that it is rendered a lost opportunity. Others, however, have been found empirically to have been able to achieve sustainability by being flexible to environmental flux and market reorientation.

It is most likely that these firms have, however, continued to maintain a primary general focus on sustainable profitability when responding to **emergent** opportunities and prospecting. The question is then, how do Internet firms avoid damage and improve success in their pursuit of competitive advantage and sustainability via flexible, responsive strategies.

STRATEGIC POSTURES FOR INTERNET FIRMS

Conceptualisation of the strategic decision-making and planning approaches used by Internet entrepreneurs can be demonstrated via Porter's (1980, 1985) generic strategies framework (see Diagram 3). This framework puts forward the notion that an enterprise gains competitive advantage by positioning its products or services within a market place via either cost leadership or product differentiation. Underlying Porter's framework is that long-term success is more likely to occur if an enterprise concentrates on only one of these positions; a combination of the two (i.e., "stuck in the middle") will lead to a lack of organisational coherence, which will compromise internal

Diagram 3. Porter's Generic Strategies (source: Porter, 1985, p.12)

		COMPETITIVE ADVANTAGE	
		Lower Cost	Differentiation
COMPETITIVE SCOPE	Broad Target	1. Cost Leadership	2. Differentiation
	Narrow Target	3A. Cost Focus	3B. Differentiation Focus

Diagram 4. "E-business competitive strategy as a continuum" (From Kim et al., 2004)

Competitive Advantage

Low Cost	*Combination of Both*	*Uniqueness*
Cost Leadership	Integrated Strategy	Differentiation

practices and damage the customer and employee experience. However, Kim, Nam, and Stimpert (2004) discovered in contradiction to **Porter's generic strategies** framework that successful Internet enterprises used a **hybrid strategy** that integrated elements of both cost leadership and differentiation. Indeed companies employing a **hybrid or integrated strategy** outperformed those pursuing "pure" positions (i.e., either a cost leadership or differentiation strategy).

Therefore, it is hypothesised that an Internet entrepreneur is more likely to develop a strategy for competitive advantage based on an **integrated strategy** where elements of cost leadership and differentiation are treated as part of a continuum (Kim et al., 2004). This is illustrated in Diagram 4 where the combination of low cost elements and uniqueness can lead to competitive advantage.

Kim et al. (2004) research findings fit well with the authors preceding discussion about how Internet entrepreneurs formulate their strategic plans (i.e., they use an **emergent** process). As illustrated in Diagram 5, these ideas can be successfully summarised via **Porter's generic strategies** framework. Specifically, Diagram 5 shows that an Internet entrepreneur typically identifies and selects, and then brings together elements of cost leadership and differentiation together in an integrated manner. It may not be clear to the entrepreneur exactly what they require as the **emergent** nature of their activities means that they will learn as they go along. However, the elements of customer focus are wide ranging in

this marketplace, where two-way communication is achieved from the first contact through the Web and this can be either automatic, in many cases, or person to person. The use of information is vitally important as a customer profile is automatically developed leading to potentially unique offerings for each individual customer but at the same time providing this service for a larger audience than would be possible in other **business models**. As time progresses, customer needs and service aspects can be tailored to meet the key needs of the customer, even anticipating them, through the use of this interactive medium. According to Kim et al. (2004), this use of technology and relationship with the customer goes beyond market segmentation and into market fragmentation. The process offers the benefits of reduced costs and automatic communications.

In sum, an Internet entrepreneur is typically much more experimental in how she or he develops their venture's strategy, they learn by doing. In this way, the entrepreneur identifies relevant activities directly from his or her experiences, and this process often lends itself to unique organisational arrangements which often blend conflicting positioning attributes according to Porter's framework. Whilst Porter considers being "stuck in the middle"as being problematic, a large number of enterprises within the United Kingdom that dominate their industries have successfully blended the two distinct strategies and gained a competitive advantage (Dobson and Starkey, 1993). In contrast, to Porter's generic approach,

Diagram 5. Proposed model

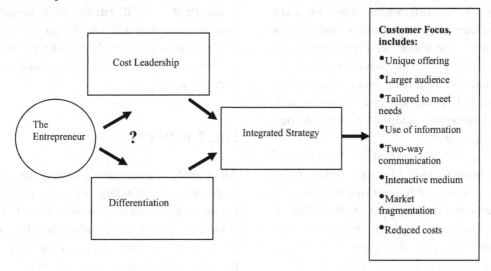

Miles and Snow's (1978) typology argues that a **hybrid or integrated strategy** is certainly a viable business entity over the long-term. Miles et al. (1978) describe companies following a **hybrid strategy** as analyzers. According to their classification scheme, companies that are analyzers exhibit characteristics of both defender- and prospector- type strategies.

DISRUPTIVE TECHNOLOGIES

Hybrid or integrated strategies can be compared to Christensen's (1997) notion of **disruptive innovations** or technologies. Christensen (1997) divides new technology into two classes: sustaining and disruptive. **Sustaining technologies** depend on incremental improvements to an already established technology. On the other hand, **disruptive technologies** are fundamentally new products, processes, and technologies that unexpectedly displace a dominant technology or product in the market place. The adoption of a unique business model by an enterprise is classified as being a disruptive technology as well. However,

no new technology is fundamentally sustaining or disruptive.

The disruptiveness of a new technology can only be judged by a company's business model. For example, the Internet was a sustaining technology for low cost airlines easyJet and Ryanair, because they were used to taking bookings directly from customers by phone. In other words the idea of setting-up an online booking operation that allowed customers to directly transact with the airline was not radical or disruptive; it was a sustaining technology for easyJet and Ryanair. The Internet helped easyJet and Ryanair to make money in the way their business activities were already designed to make money. In contrast, the Internet was very disruptive to British Airways, because it relied on travel agents to transact with their customers. Therefore, initially British Airways struggled to create an online booking operation as it tried to directly transact with its customers.

Furthermore, according to Christensen (1997), it is not unusual for a disruptive technology to at first lack the refinement of an established technology and it may even have performance problems. Due to these inferior attributes a disruptive technology will most likely not immediately satisfy the requirements of mainstream customers. Even so a disruptive technology's performance dimensions can still appeal to a new set of customers who have previously ignored the dominant technology, possibly because it has been too expensive or too complicated. Existing low-end customers may also be encouraged to adopt the new technology for the same reasons.

Drawing on the idea that the formation of a unique business model is analogous to a disruptive innovation, it is clear that a number of Internet entrepreneurs have put together different **business models** to target customers who often find contemporary products and services too expensive or too complicated. In forming these unique configurations Internet entrepreneurs are deliberately trading-off pure performance in favor of simplicity, convenience, and affordability. They offer products that are "acceptable" solutions to customers at a reduced price.

Offering an innovative performance dimension to either a low-end market or new customers, alongside technological improvements over time, means **disruptive technologies** often start to catch the attention of mainstream consumers as their maturity affords improvements on the original performance element (e.g., cost). The outcome of a disruptive process such as a successful new business model is to simultaneously cause the value chains of rival company into **Turmoil** and to create a new dominant design.

Christensen's (1997) argues that established companies find it difficult to oppose or embrace **disruptive innovations** because they are designed to work with sustaining technologies. Specifically, established companies are good at knowing their market, staying close to their customers, and having procedures in place to develop existing or known technologies. On the contrary, they often have trouble capitalising on **disruptive technologies** because they are at odds with company goals, assumptions and practices (i.e., managers build-up a mind-set and a way of doing things,

which is based on what they already know how to do). Predictably **disruptive technologies** are usually associated with small start-ups or independent spin-offs from large corporations that are not afflicted with these institutional barriers to creativity.

SPOT RUNNER

An example of a company's business model that is expected to transform its industry is **Spot Runner** (http://www.spotrunner.com/), which is located in the United States. **Spot Runner** is a pure Internet-based advertising agency, which targets small companies that generally cannot afford advertising on television. Historically television advertising has for the most part only been employed by large companies. However, for as little as $US500, **Spot Runner** can put into action a comprehensive advertising campaign for a client in under a week.

Founded by Nick Grouf and David Waxman Web-based **Spot Runner** offers its clients the use of an extensive library of pre-produced, high-quality television advertisements. Once clients have selected their footage, they can them customise it with their own logos, messages and images. These activities, along with the inherent overhead cost reducing aspects of an online operation, allow **Spot Runner** to minimise costs for small business clients. In contrast, other activities provided by the company add considerable value (i.e., once a client has provided details that personalise the footage selected); **Spot Runner** will apply its proprietary software to create a unique media plan for the client. The media plan will outline for the client which television networks will most effectively target their desired customers. After a client has approved the commercial and media plan, **Spot Runner** will then buy advertising space from local and/or national television networks and channels. Once the advertising has occurred, **Spot Runner** provides clients with easy to follow reports that explain where and when it happened, and details of the viewers who saw them. This type of service is similar to those offered by major advertising agencies to their clients!

The completed adverts are not visually eye-catching, humorous or creative masterpieces, instead they are economical and straightforward in their delivery. Top advertising agencies, such as Ogilvy and Mather, BBDO, McCann Erickson, Leo Burnett, or Saatchi and Saatchi have not responded to this threat, because they are not structured to serve the needs of such small customers. Moreover, the activities of **Spot Runner** are not yet perceived as a threat, because they are attracting customers that they would not have normally targeted. Nevertheless, the danger for the major advertising agencies is that large corporate clients will be enticed into using the services of companies like **Spot Runner** in the future, because the impact and reach of national television advertising is declining as consumers are increasingly choosing other sources of news and entertainment, particularly young adults. For instance, free commuter papers, magazines, multi-channel television and radio, mobile phones, online news sites, and the spread of blogs. Therefore, corporations may determine that investing more of their funds into cheaper local television advertising that is more likely to reach fragmented target customers such as young adults and teenagers is a more attractive option. Certainly advertising experts predict that Internet-based advertising agencies such as **Spot Runner** will attract the business of large corporations over time, not only because of their low cost and ability to reach difficult customers, but the services offered can only get better via further developments in technology.

GLASSESDIRECT.CO.UK

Another example of a company utilising a **hybrid strategy** business model that illustrates the characteristics of being a disruptive technology is **GlassesDirect** (i.e., http://www.**GlassesDirect**.co.uk). James Murray Wells has revolutionised the United Kingdom's optical industry by selling glasses at around 90% less than those charged by the major high street opticians. In spite of charging less than his competitors he still makes on average a respectable sixty percent gross margin on each pair of glasses sold. The business idea for this entrepreneurial venture began when James had to purchase a pair of prescription glasses from a high street retailer. When the shop's optician told him that the price of a new pair of glasses would cost him £150 he was horrified. As a financially struggling university student he was astonished that some "wire and glass" should cost so much. Inquisitive about the logic behind the high price of retail street glasses he decided to research the market.

He discovered that the suppliers used by the major retail outlets (i.e., eyeglass manufacturing laboratories which make to order prescription eyeglass lenses and then fit the lenses to a selected frame) can fabricate a standard pair of glasses for as little as £7. Based on his research James concluded there was a business opportunity in the cost differential between the £150 charged by the high street retailer and the suppliers manufacturing cost of £7. After much negotiation with various eyeglass manufacturing laboratories several agreed to make prescription orders for James' new venture, **GlassesDirect**. To make the most of the cost differential he utilised Internet technology and a telephone call centre to transact with customers.

To order glasses from **GlassesDirect** a customer must have their eyes tested by an optician, who is then obliged by United Kingdom law to provide her or him with a prescription (i.e., the amount of lens correction required to focus at either distance or for reading at close distances). The prescription must be not be less than two years old or less than one year old in the case of a customer who is over 70 years of age. Once a prescription as been obtained a customer can simply telephone or enter the details online at the company's Website. With the customers prescription details the company is then able to construct suitable lenses. Customers also select online the type of frames they wish to buy. To assist this selection process the company's Web site allows customers an opportunity to see what they would look like wearing any of its portfolio of spectacles. Specifically, **GlassesDirect** pioneered an Internet software system called "Customeyes," which allows customers whilst online to "try on" a pair of spectacles. Customers can do this by downloading a digital image of their face onto the company's Web site. Once the image is downloaded customers can then position the spectacles of their choice via their computer's mouse.

James' business model contrasts starkly with that of the incumbent eyeglass retailers', like Spec-Savers, Dolland and Aitchson, Vision Express and Boots, which all own an extensive retail branch network. This branch network is proving to be a costly asset for these retailers, because James via his online business model is able to sell top-quality spectacles, including designer frames, for a fraction of the price charged by the main incumbents. In keeping with a **hybrid strategy**, **GlassesDirect**'s business activities demonstrate a mix of cost reducing and differentiating (i.e., value-adding) factors. For instance, the company's infrastructure costs are negligible i.e., low staff numbers, free of costly eye testing equipment, do not offer advice about optical issues, reasonably priced computer technology, relatively inexpensive physical infrastructure and property location. At the same time other aspects focus on performing its activities in similar ways to its competitors (i.e., the lenses are made to the customers prescription and come with a scratch resistant coating, selection of designer frames, free spectacle case and cloth, reasonably priced spectacle trial service, glasses conform to industry standards, and it offers a money back guarantee).

The foremost drawback that customers may perceive regarding **GlassesDirect**'s business model is the lack of personal support. Many customers may find the personal consultation offered by a trained staff member at a physical retail outlet is a reassuring aspect of the purchase process, particularly when it comes to the selection of an appropriate style of spectacle frame. Moreover, if the spectacles the customers have bought from **GlassesDirect** require minor adjustments for fit, they need to approach an optical store for this service to be done at the cost of a small fee. For the most part high street retailers will offer this service for free if the glasses were purchased from their premises.

Since the business was established in 2004, the company as gone on to sell over 70,000 pairs of glasses. Presently the company sells between 200 and 300 pairs of glasses per day and sales are expected to reach £3.5 million by the end of 2007. The company predicts that sales will be around £10 million by 2008. The company has already branched out into contact lenses and plans to expand into the United States and a number of other countries as well. Venture capitalists have helped fund **GlassesDirect** growth by injecting £500,000. Part of the additional capital supplied by venture capitalists was used to launch an aggressive national advertising campaign, which involved sending out 1.5 million catalogues via national newspapers.

Certainly the two examples provided are not unique because other Internet companies have features that are consistent with a **hybrid or integrated strategy** (i.e., easyJet, Charles Schwab, E*Trade, Ameritrade, Amazon.com, Dell, and e-Bay). The Internets ability to significantly alter the economics and way of doing business means the absolutist position of Porter's cost/differentiation trade-off is weakening. Nowadays for the most part strategy specialists view the concept of generic strategies as only a general guideline for assessing value creation and market positions (Dess & Picken, 1999). Therefore, the "stuck in the middle" belief is no longer a clear-cut issue since the Internet is providing plenty of examples

Diagram 6. Adding value

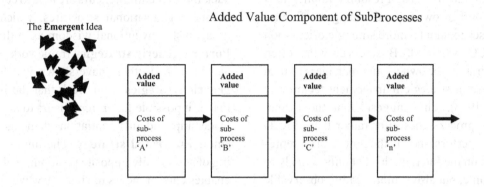

Added Value Component of SubProcesses

The **Emergent** Idea

of "trade-ons" (i.e., ventures that successfully combine supposedly conflicting concepts such as quality and cost). Moreover, some researchers (Fjeldstad & Haanaes, 2001; Parnell & Wright, 1993) state that a fundamental economic relationship exists between low cost and differentiation strategies. For example, increasing demand for an enterprise's high quality differentiated products may cause a decrease in the average fixed cost of each unit produced. Therefore the Internet can cultivate the potential for operating both low costs and differentiation for the ambitious entrepreneur.

The Internet's development has also fundamentally changed the traditional cost structures for many industries. Specifically, entrepreneurial Internet firms have placed less prominence on performing all of the required activities themselves such as raw material sourcing, manufacturing, personnel practices, sales, and so on, and have developed alliances with outside firms to manage many of these functions that were once done internally. This allows firms to concentrate on what they do "best," and these actions can improve product and service quality, delivery speed, and flexibility, while lowering costs at the same time. These issues are illustrated in Diagram 6.

Diagram 6 illustrates that strategy emerges within the control of the Internet entrepreneur who

creates an organisation of some sort to develop the opportunity further. Whether the Internet entrepreneur is using the Internet to conduct business, or providing an Internet service, or proving services to Internet companies, whatever type of organisation is created the process will have stages no matter what, and these stages should add value as each sub process leads to another (see Porter, 1985). However, there are also costs associated with these sub processes, which can be direct or indirect, and the skill of the entrepreneur and his or her team should add value to each stage provided quality and timing meet the required standards and objectives. The following diagram illustrates the emergence of the idea and the subprocesses. Added value will vary according to the knowledge, skill and expertise added at each stage. This holds good whether the organisation is based on clicks or bricks.

CONCLUSION

Within the literature on strategies in small firms generally, there is evidence that strategies vary by the stage of development reached by a firm. Strategy and planning evolve in a company and become more formal and sophisticated over the life cycle of the business (e.g., Churchill & Lewis,

1983; Scott & Bruce, 1987). Certainly, rapid growth and its associated resource implications will encourage owners and managers of small enterprises to adopt a more strategic orientation (Aram & Cowan, 1990). Business growth is often the inspiration for owners and managers to take up the use of strategic management techniques (Berry, 1998). This suggests that the formal planning process goes after rather than directs improved performance. In the context of entrepreneurship on the Internet, this not only is likely to be the same, but also is more readily observable due to the rate of change, including business successes, failures and growth. It appears that many Internet entrepreneurs generate ideas differently from off-line entrepreneurs, more often adopting a prospector-type means of identifying sustainable opportunities. Upon selecting an apparently promising idea to develop, initial strategic options can often involve adopting reactive, flexible strategies in order to become an established Internet players. Thereafter, if successful, an Internet firm may focus on the fixed value proposition via a (semi) formal strategic approach, for example, Amazon, as an established Internet success, no longer pursue eclectic revenues, nor do they aim to provide extraneous products and services (outside their expanding—through strategic growth—product range). Amazon now, along with the various strategic alliances they have made, pursue growth through a focused strategy on maintaining and increasing market share via their well-established value proposition of selling the widest range of media in the world, conveniently and at low cost, and supporting those sales with their now proven value adding services.

In terms of strategy, there are two camps amongst commentators—one that advocates adherence to strategy to increase the chance of long-term sustainability, and one that advocates a dynamic approach to strategy in order to respond to the environment. It is hypothesised that Internet entrepreneurs use an **emergent** or dynamic process to formulate enterprise strategy. Via adaptation, experimentation and customer feedback Internet entrepreneurs are able to configure unique organisational structures, which often go against conventional wisdom as outlined by **Porter's generic strategies** framework. Kim et al. (2004) and others have shown via **Porter's generic strategies** framework that the Internet makes it possible for entrepreneurs to blend cost leadership and differentiation elements into a single **integrated strategy**. The unique blending of supposedly opposite positioning elements enables entrepreneurs to create new ways of doing things or unique **business models**. Porter's "pure" strategies provide only a starting point for entrepreneurs, and then according to circumstances, they will be swapped, combined or doggedly pursued. As Dess et al. (1999) argue it is important to appreciate that the notion of **Porter's generic strategies** can be taken too literally. Even Porter (1980) cautions that "quality, service, and other areas cannot be ignored" (p. 35) when undertaking a cost leadership strategy or when organisations pursue a differentiation strategy they cannot "ignore costs" (p. 37). In general the logic behind Porter's classification is sound because most companies that attempt to straddle contradictory strategic positions struggle. Consequently, **Porter's generic strategies** notion as a standard piece of business advice has inherent merit. However, part of the success achieved by Internet entrepreneurs is that they question the assumptions behind the standard ways of doing things. As the chapter has illustrated the implementation of hybrid strategies by Internet entrepreneurs usually involves the creation of a unique business model, which can be conceptualised as being a disruptive technology. A disruptive technology brings to the market, a very different configuration of activities and frame of mind for the creation of business growth.

The Internet has made possible new types of **business models** that were previously difficult, or unfeasible, to put into practice. It is apparent that the **business models** being developed by Internet entrepreneurs are challenging established opinion in strategic management. The practical implication of this challenge is that "pure" strategies of low cost leadership or differentiation may not lead to a competitive advantage and superior performance. In its place an intermingling of these strategies may lead to a sustainable competitive advantage. A **hybrid or integrated strategy** does not mean having a lack of strategic focus or purpose; on the contrary, it results in a business model that is neither rigid in its planning nor opportunistic, but is likely to be based on a learning orientation. As a result this discussion lends support to the idea that pure generic strategies may not be the most beneficial, and that future Internet entrepreneurs should consider deliberately adopting hybrid generic strategies. A hybrid generic strategy better matches the characteristics of an Internet entrepreneur as it balances a commitment to a strategic **vision** with the flexibility to sense and seize opportunities as they happen.

The final implication is that the successful efforts of Internet entrepreneurs who use hybrid strategies are inspiring others to become entrepreneurs and to question conventional **business models**. For instance, the achievements of Stelios Haji-Ioannou, easyJet founder, serial entrepreneur and Chairman of easyGroup, provide a steady source of motivation and impetus to would-be Internet entrepreneurs in the United Kingdom. Stelios Haji-Ioannou and easyGroup continue to introduce a pipeline of disruptive Internet-based **business models** across unrelated industries; for example, they have established easyJet (i.e., a low cost no-frills airline), easyInternetcafe (i.e., a chain of the Internet cafes and a low cost method for getting online), easyCar (i.e., an online car rental service), easyMoney (i.e., online financial services), easy.com (i.e., a free Web-based email service), easyValue (i.e., an independent price comparison service for online shopping), easyWatch (i.e., a Web site for purchasing low cost watches), easyVan (i.e., an online Van Rental service), easyCruise (i.e., a no-frills cruise-line

service), easyHotel (i.e., a low cost online accommodation service), and easyCinema (i.e., inexpensive cinema viewing). Commentators and e-commerce experts state that Stelios activities in the United Kingdom have exponentially increased entrepreneurial activity related to the Internet, because he has stimulated interest in deconstructing existing **business models** across various industries and replacing them with online alternatives.

In summary, if a judicious and open entrepreneur allows his or her original notions about a "pure" strategy to be transformed according to market reactions, they are much more likely to gain insights about discovering exciting opportunities for delivering business operations in unique ways. The fundamental issue for the entrepreneur is that they allow learning to take place, and this opens the possibility of devising an **integrated strategy**.

Chen (2005, p. 240) reports that "as many as 29 e-**business models** currently in use have been described," and it is likely that there will be many more. The Internet continues to evolve both technologically and from a social point of view, and there are many challenges for Internet entrepreneurs as a result of the ongoing **turmoil**. Time and further research will suggest whether the authors' ideas about the way Internet entrepreneur formulate strategy is correct.

REFERENCES

Afuha, A., & Tucci, C. L. (2001). *Internet business models and strategies, text, and cases*. New York: McGraw-Hill.

Alvesson, M., & Willmott, H. (1996). *Making sense of management: A critical approach*. London: Sage Publications.

Amit, R., & Zott, C. (2001). Value creation in e-business. *Strategic Management Journal, 22*(6-7), 493-520.

Anelli, M. (2005). *What is chaos theory?* Ufdbparam (online) Retrieved August 6, 2005, from http://www.ufdbparam.info/spip/article.php3?id_article=2

Aram, J. D., & Cowan, S. S. (1990). Strategic planning for increased profit in the small business. *Long Range Planning, 23*(6), 63-70.

Beaver, G., & Ross, E.C. (2000). Enterprise in recession: The role and context of strategy. *International Journal of Entrepreneurship and Innovation, 1*(1), 23-31.

Beaver, G., & Prince, C. (2004). Management, strategy, and policy in the UK small business sector: a critical review. *Journal of Small Business and Enterprise Development, 11*(1), 34-49.

Berry, M. (1998). Strategic planning in small high tech companies. *Long Range Planning, 31*(3), 455-466.

Bouchikhi, H. (1993). A constructive framework for understanding entrepreneurship performance. *Organisational Studies, 14*(4), 549-570.

Brown, S., & Blackmon, K. (2005). Aligning manufacturing strategy and business-level competitive strategy in new competitive environments: the case for strategic resonance. *Journal of Management Studies, 42*(4), 793-815.

Carrier, C., Raymond, L., & Eltaief, A. (2004). Cyberentrepreneurship: A multiple case study. *International Journal of Entrepreneurial Behaviour and Research, 10*(5), 349-363.

Cassia, L., Fattore, M., & Paleari, S. (2006). *Entrepreneurial strategy.* Cheltenham: Edward Elgar.

Chen, S. (2003). Strategic decision-making by e-commerce entrepreneurs. *International Journal of Management and Decision Making, 4*(2/3), 133-142.

Chen, S. (2005). *Strategic management of e-business* (2nd ed.). Chichester: John Wiley and Sons.

Christensen, C. M. (1997). *The innovator's dilemma: When new technologies cause great firms to fail.* Boston: Harvard Business School Press.

Churchill, N. C., & Lewis, V. L. (1983). The five stages of small business growth. *Harvard Business Review, 61*(3), 2-11.

Colombo, M. S., & Delmastro, M. (2001). Technology-based entrepreneurs: Does the internet make a difference. *Small Business Economics, 16*(3), 177-190.

Courtney, H., Kirkland, J., & Viguerie, P. (1997). Strategy under uncertainty. *Harvard Business Review, 75*(6), 66-79.

Covin, J. G., & Slevin, D. P. (1989). Strategic management of small firms in hostile and benign environments. *Strategic Management Journal, 10*(1), 75–87.

Dobson, P., & Starkey, K. (1993). *The strategic management blueprint.* Oxford: Blackwells.

D'Aveni, R. A. (1994). *Hyper-competition: Managing the dynamics of strategic Maneuvering.* New York: Free Press.

Dess, G. G., & Picken, J. C. (1999). Creating competitive (dis)advantage: Learning from Food Lion's freefall. *Academy of management Executive, 13*(3), 97-111.

Eisenhardt, K. M., & Brown, S. L. (1998). Time pacing: Competing in markets that won't stand still. *Harvard Business Review, 76*(2), 59-69.

Eisenhardt, K. M., & Brown, S. L. (1999). Patching—restitching business portfolios in dynamic markets. *Harvard Business Review, 77*(3), 72-82.

Evans, P., & Wurster, T. S. (1999). *Blown to bits: How the new economics of information transforms strategy.* Boston: Harvard Business School Publishing.

Fitzgerald, L. A. (2002). Chaos—the lens that transcends. *Journal of Organisational Change Management, 15*(4), 339-358.

French, S. J., Kelly, S. J., & Harrison, J. L. (2004). The role of strategic planning in the performance of small, professional service firms—a research note. *Journal of Management Development, 23*(9), 765-776.

Fjeldstad, O. D., & Haanaes, K. (2001). Strategy tradeoffs in the knowledge and network economy. *Business Strategy Review, 12*(1), 1-10.

Galloway, L. (2005). Internet business and e-commerce. In D. Deakins & M. Freel (Eds.), *Entrepreneurship and small firms*, (pp.139-156). Maidenhead: McGraw-Hill.

Gans, J. S., & Stern, S. (2003). The product market and the market for "ideas": Commercialisation strategies for technology entrepreneurs. *Research Policy, 32*(2), 333-350.

Georgellis, Y., Joyce, P., & Woods, A. (2000). Entrepreneurial action, innovation, and business performance. *Journal of Small Business Development, 1*(1), 7-17.

Gibb, A., & Scott, M. (1985). Strategic awareness, personal commitment, and the process of planning in the small business. *Journal of Management Studies, 22*(6), 597-624.

Gibson, B., & Cassar, G. (2005). Longitudinal analysis of relationships between planning and performance in small firms. *Small Business Economics, 25*(3), 207-222.

Griggs, H. E. (2002). Strategic planning system characteristics and organisational effectiveness in Australian small-scale firms. *Irish Journal of Management, 23*(1), 23-53.

Hamel, G. (2002). *Leading the revolution.* Boston: Harvard Business School Press.

Kellert, S. H. (1993). *In the wake of chaos: Unpredictable order in dynamical systems.* Chicago: University of Chicago Press.

Kickul, J., & Walters, J. (2002). Recognising new opportunities and innovations: The role of strategic orientation and proactivity in internet firms. *International Journal of Entrepreneurial Behaviour and Research, 8*(6), 292-308.

Kim, E., Nam, D., & Stimpert, J. L. (2004). The applicability of Porter's generic strategies in the digital age: Assumptions, conjectures, and suggestions. *Journal of Management, 30*(5), 569-589.

Kippenberger, T. (1999). Is this chaos, at least in theory? *The Antidote, 4*(2), 64-66.

Lyles, M. A., Baird, I. S., Orris, J. B., & Kuratko, D. F. (1993). Formalised planning in small business: increasing strategic choices. *Journal of Small Business Management, 31*(2), 38-50.

Masurel, E., & Smit, H. P. (2000). Planning behavior of small firms in Central Vietnam. *Journal of Small Business Management, 38*(2), 95-102.

McClelland, D. C. (1961). *The achieving society.* NJ: D.Van Nostrand.

Miles, R. E., & Snow, C.C. (1978). *Organizational strategy, structure, and process.* New York: McGraw-Hill.

Mintzberg, H. (1994). *The rise and fall of strategic planning.* New York: Free Press.

Mintzberg, H. (1990). The design school: Reconsidering the basic premises of strategic management. *Strategic Management Journal, 11*(3), 171-195.

Mintzberg, H., Quinn, J. B., & Ghoshal, S. (1998a). *The strategy process* (Revised European Edition). London: Prentice Hall.

Mintzberg, H., Ahlstrand, B., & Lampel, J. (1998b). *Strategy Safari: A guided tour through the wilds of strategic management.* Hemel Hempstead: Prentice Hall Europe.

Morino, M. (1999). *Netpreneurs: A new breed of entrepreneur.* Ewing Marion Kauffman Foundation [online]. Retrieved from http://eventuring.kauffman.org/Resources/Resources.aspx?id=33588

O'Gorman, C. (2000). Strategy and the small firm. In S. Carter & D. Jones-Evans (Eds.), *Enterprise and small business: Principles, practice, and policy* (Vol. 16, pp. 179-208). London: Macmillan.

Parnell, J. A., & Wright, P. (1993). Generic strategy and performance: An empirical test of the Miles and Snow typology. *British Journal of Management, 4*(1), 29-36.

Perry, S. C. (2001). The relationship between written business plans and the failure of small businesses in the US. *Journal of Small Business Management, 39*(3), 201-208.

Porter, M.E. (2001). Strategy and the Internet. *Harvard Business Review, 79*(3), 63-78.

Porter, M. E. (1985). *Competitive advantage: Creating and sustaining superior performance.* New York: The Free Press.

Porter, M. E. (1980). *Competitive strategy.* New York: The Free Press.

Rajagopalan, N., & Spreitzer, G. M. (1997). Toward a theory of strategic change: A multi-lens perspective and integrative framework. *Academy of Management Review, 22*(1), 48-79.

Robinson, R. B., & Pearce, J. A. (1984). Research thrusts in small firm strategic-planning. *Academy of Management Review, 9*(1), 128-137.

Sanchez, R. (1995). Strategic flexibility and product competition. *Strategic Management Journal, 16*(Special Issue), 135-159.

Schumpeter, J. A. (1934). *The theory of economic development: An inquiry into profits, capital, credit interest, and the business cycle* (trans. R. Opie). Cambridge, MA: Harvard University Press.

Schumpeter, J. A. (1947). The creative response in economic history. *Journal of Economic History, 7*(2), 149-159.

Scott, M., & Bruce, R. (1987). Five stages of growth in small business. *Long Range Planning, 20*(3), 45-52.

Scott, G., & Walter, Z. (2003). DELPHI findings about Internet systems problems, with implications for other technologies. *Technology Analysis and Strategic Management, 15*(1), 103-115.

Shrader, C. B., Mulford, C. L., & Blackburn, V. L. (1989). Strategic and operational planning, uncertainty, and performance in small firms. *Journal of Small Business Management, 27*(4), 45-60.

Small, P. (2000). *The entrepreneurial Web: E-commerce tools for the new breed of Internet trader.* London: FT.com.

Stevenson, H. H., & Gumpert, D. E. (1985). The heart of entrepreneurship. *Harvard Business Review, 63*(2), 85-94.

Teece, D., Pisano, G., & Shuen, A. (1997). Dynamic capabilities and strategic management. *Strategic Management Journal, 18*(7), 509-533.

Venkataraman, N. (1989). The concept of fit in strategy research: Toward verbal and statistical correspondence. *Academy of Management Review, 14*(3), 423-444.

Venkataraman, S., & Sarasvathy, S. D. (2001). Strategy and entrepreneurship: Outlines of an untold story. In M. A. Hitt, R. E. Freeman & J. S. Harrison (Eds.), *Handbook of Strategic Management,* (pp. 650-668). Oxford: Blackwell Publishers.

Wheelen, T. L., & Hunger, J. D. (1999). *Strategic management and business policy* (6th ed.). New York: Addison-Wesley.

Wolff, M. (1999). *Burn rate: How i survived the gold rush years on the Internet.* London: Orion.

KEY TERMS

Disruptive Technology or Innovation: Are fundamentally new products, processes, technologies, or a unique business model that unexpectedly displaces a dominant technology, conventional business model or product in the market place.

Entrepreneurial Strategy: Business strategy involving risk, usually including innovation, and most often for the purposes of high growth.

Internet Entrepreneurship: The creation, establishment and growth of businesses that exist entirely online.

Prospecter Strategy: Continual scanning of the market for new opportunities and ideas

Strategic Flexibility: Where business strategy has the ability to react to opportunity emergence and respond to market dynamics.

Strategies of Emergence: Strategies that are created via an organic process, based on experience of the market and environment

Traditional Strategies: Business strategies that are commonly used and commonly observed, most often in the off-line environment, but including dotcom firms also, though usually post start-up phase.

Turmoil (chaos): Describing a business environment where change is multi-faceted (e.g., users, technology, expectations, competition), frequent, and fast and the cumulative effects include increasing levels of complexity within the environment.

Section IV
Networks and Partnerships

Chapter X
Integrating E–Supply Networks:
The Need to Manage Information Flows and Develop E–Platforms

Rana Tassabehji
University of Bradford, UK

James Wallace
University of Bradford, UK

Anastasios Tsoularis
Massey University, New Zealand

ABSTRACT

The Internet has reached a stage of maturity where its innovative adoption and implementation can be a source of competitive advantage. Supply chains are one of the areas that has reportedly benefited greatly, achieving optimisation through low cost, high efficiency use of the Internet, almost seamlessly linking global supply chains into e-supply networks. This field is still in its academic and practical infancy, and there is a need for more empirical research to build a robust theoretical foundation, which advances our knowledge and understanding. Here, the main aims and objectives are to highlight the importance of information flows in e-supply chains/networks, and the need for their standardisation to facilitate integration, legality, security, and efficiency of operations. This chapter contributes to the field by recommending a three-stage framework enabling this process through the development of standardised Internet technology platforms (e-platforms), integration requirements and classification of information flows.

INTRODUCTION

The advent of the Internet and its commercial explosion over the past decade has had widespread implications for business and society. The Internet has already had a huge impact on business all over the globe as it has enabled more and more organisations to become networked and share resources. Supply chain management is one of the areas that has reportedly benefited greatly with lean manufacturing and just-in-time being optimised by the low cost, high efficiency of the Internet to link global supply chains almost seamlessly. Supply chains have been transformed into "integrated value systems" where competitive advantage in the new e-economy can only be achieved through the effective implementation and use of new technologies and strategic integration of these systems (Handfield & Nichols, 2003). This field is still in its academic and practical infancy, and while there has been some research done in the area, it is mainly focused on individual case studies, which tends to be myopic and leads to the production of specific solutions that cannot be easily replicated. There are however many well established software packages that have been implemented in business and are publicised in the annual AMR Research list of 25 major global companies led by DELL, Nokia, and Procter and Gamble (Friscia, O'Marah, & Souza, 2004). From a review of the literature in the field, we argue that there is a need for more empirical research to be gathered to develop a core theoretical foundation and advance the practical application of e-business in supply chain management. By consolidating the major themes emerging from the literature, the importance of information flows in e-supply chains/networks, and the need for their standardisation to facilitate integration, legality, security, and efficiency of operations, is highlighted. This chapter contributes to the field by recommending a three-stage framework enabling this process through the development of standardised Internet technology platforms (e-platforms), integration requirements, and classification of information flows.

BACKGROUND

The rapid evolution and adoption of the Internet over the past decade has had serious implications on businesses. It has, for example, hastened the shortening of product lifecycles; facilitated mass customisation and globalisation of markets; increased further the pressure to reduce costs and increase revenues. At the turn of the century, technology and e-business were identified as being critical areas impacting on the future of supply chains and networks as a result of environmental factors in the 21st century (Monczka & Morgan, 2000). Technology and e-business have been widely predicted to: (a) develop "network" management as the most effective way of managing the changes and increasing complexity of supply chain activities); (b) enable activities of different firms in the supply network to be coordinated); and (c) integrate and consolidate information and systems to deal with globalisation (Gadde & Hakkansson 2001; Monczka et al., 2000). Each of these areas will be dealt with in more detail and aspects of these, will form the fundamental part of the 3 stage framework for standardisation of information flows in supply chains or networks.

E-Business and Supply Chains

There still remains a dearth of research into the role the Internet has across the manufacturing supply chain and its impact on the planning and control operation (Kehoe & Broughton, 1998; Kehoe et al., 2001b). An added complexity is that there is still no consensus on what e-business is specifically and technically (Tassabehji, 2003). In a study of supply chain management in the e-business era, CEO's of organisations identified the urgency of becoming an e-business, but the research could not identify any consensus in what an e-business actually is (Croom, 2001, 2005). This causes problems in terms of standardisation: without a common understanding or definition there can be no standardisation. From the academic literature and reports by practitioners in the field, we can identify three principal categories of e-business applications specifically related to the supply chain. These are electronic marketplaces, inter and intra organisational systems facilitating the flow of goods and services, information communication and collaboration, and customer services (Blascovich & Goffre, 2003; Donovan n.d; Phan, 2003).

These "e-business" applications are already being introduced into supply chain management–primarily as a collaborative use of Internet technology to enable integration of value and supply chains with key partners, by supporting business processes to improve speed, agility, real-time control, and customer satisfaction (Jelassi & Leenen, 2003). This is done largely through the use of computer and communication networks to transfer information electronically. Porter (2001) argues that the main advantages to an organisation is how e-business is deployed to benefit from the advantages of Internet technology, rather than whether it is deployed. There is consensus amongst academics and practitioners that the success of an e-business enabled supply chain depends on two major factors:

- Collaboration between partners (Norris, Hurley, Hartley, Dunleavy, & Balls, 2000) and integration of supply chains through linking information systems (Cigolini, Cozzi, & Perona, 2004; Zank & Vokurka (2003), which is also seen as a major source of competitive advantage;
- Information visibility (Garcia-Dastugue & Lambert 2003; Kehoe et al., 1998) including the ability to share accurate data and information from a wide range of operating areas across the supply network (Lancioni, Smith, & Oliva, 2000).

Supply chains are currently in a state of flux where they must be able to manage the complexity of stakeholders and flows of information and materials throughout, while still maintain their "leagile" optimised designs (Naylor, Naim, & Berry, 1999). Croom (2001, 2005) has suggested the existence of a staged evolutionary process in the adoption of supply chain strategies in relation to e-business systems, beginning with customer facing processes, followed by internal (operations) processes, supplier-facing processes, and finally total chain integration. This vision is supported by other academics and practitioners (Handfield et al., 2002; Poirer, n.d.) who see the supply chain of the near future as a synchronised flow of materials and information through a fully networked virtual business. This incorporates all the companies in the supply chain where not only are internal processes linked with customers and suppliers, but the whole value chain would be networked end-to-end, managed through creating value, and all stakeholders are in a win-win position. Modularisation is another trend that supply chains are experiencing where there is "value shifting" as systems are being integrated into smaller subsystems that can function alone or as a part of the network (Doran, 2003). Kehoe et al. (2001b) suggest the need for a supply chain resource planning approach where Internet technologies will enable supply chain partners to dynamically view and manage both demand and capacity data to create supply Webs. There is however little empirical research into the type and degree of integration that is taking place and how this can be measured in order to evaluate the impact on information flows and relationships between and within supply network partners.

The Importance of Information Flows

One of the critical foundations of supply networks is information flows. This is even more critical in integrated networks where physical material supply chains are being replaced by a network of information servers distributed across organisations. Gadde et al. (2001) see the exchange of information playing a significant role in creating network efficiencies, where efficient information flows are pre-requisites for co-ordination of activities in a network and for the exchange of information needed for resource development. Not only efficient flows of information, but also "information enriched" supply chains where the information systems are carefully engineered to match the specific supply chain requirements. For example, in an information enriched supply chain, all stakeholders receive marketplace data directly increasing transparency, reducing distortion, and avoiding double guessing. "Whereas information enriched concept is highly desirable in lean supply, it is obligatory in the achievement of agile supply. It is only when effective marketplace feedback is available that the next deliveries can be pulled from the supplier" (Mason-Jones & Towill, 2000, p. 55). The more accurate and timely the information flow, the more responsive companies are to changes in demand (Wallace et al., 2006). Also direct knowledge of end demand through the supply chain is a way to reduce both inventory levels and the bullwhip effect (Cigolini et al., 2004; Wallace et al., 2006)

However an exploration of the information flows that link all the supply chain members–Tier 1,2, 3 suppliers as well as the manufacturer, customer, and consumer/end-consumer–have not been fully researched and needs further investigation (Garcia-Dastugue et al., 2003).

Integration, Technology Infrastructures, and Supply Chains

Many current organisational supply chains are entrenched with manual processes and disconnected enterprise systems. Both Forrester Research and Aberdeen Group found no significant integrations between manufacturers and their suppliers' and customers' enterprise systems with the majority being driven by manual, spreadsheet-intensive,

only partially automated processes largely dependent upon different software systems within their own companies (Wailgum, 2006). Integrated IT infrastructures enable firms to develop a higher-order capability of supply chain process integration. This capability "enables firms to unbundle information flows from physical flows, and to share information with their supply chain partners to create information-based approaches for superior demand planning, for the staging and movement of physical products, and for streamlining voluminous and complex financial work processes" (Rai, Patnayakuni, & Patnayakuni, 2006, p. 227). Currently there is no universally accepted and widely implemented standardisation of technological architecture and applications across supply networks: for example the use of XML, middleware, Internet technology, the role of e-marketplaces and electronic auctions (Tassabehji et al., 2006a,b; Wallace et al., 2006). If the technology is to be fully exploited, there is a need for standardisation and developing Internet enabled "common systems infrastructure" (Kehoe et al., 2001a) to remove the problem of systems integration.

DISCUSSION

From the literature review, it can be ascertained that the main gaps in the research are a typology of e-business as it relates to supply networks, a deeper understanding of what integration is, its linkage with e-business, and its impact on supply networks, and a wider examination of information flows through the supply network in order to classify information according to a set of criteria, which will make it better support the needs and requirements of all the members in the supply network.

An ideal test bed for this kind of research is the process industry. The process industry sector is extremely important and one that is estimated to grow at an average of around 4% per annum until

2010 (staff 2003) based on the projections of demand from process industry products and services worldwide. Pharmaceuticals is estimated to be the fasted growing process industry with the trend in highly industrialised countries towards more productive, more efficient, more flexible plants which increase availability and environmental sustainability but are less resource intensive. As such, supply chain management and the Internet based tools that facilitate this management is a critical part of these strategies.

Towards a Standardised Approach to Integrated Supply Chains: Recommendations

The issues previously identified can be divided into three major parts. These are not mutually exclusive and there is a strong degree of conceptual overlap where information for all three stages can be sought at one interaction with stakeholders.

Stage 1: Develop a Typology of E-Business Technology and Applications Infrastructure in Support of Information Flow in Supply Chains

The internet has improved inter-organisational information systems' capability and is being adopted as a routine platform for information systems development, with Web services, wireless applications, and advanced software applications all being used to facilitate supply chain collaboration (Ho & Lin, 2004; Kehoe et al., 2001a; Mondragon, Lyons, Michaelides, & Kehoe, 2006). However, there is no exact definition of Internet based commerce (Soliman & Youssef 2003).

Thus there is a need to identify "e-business" technology and how it is used in the organisation's business supply and value processes including the use of electronic marketplaces and electronic auctions. The information will then be analysed to develop a typology of "e-business" according to the technology and applications used within the supply chain. This can eventually be used as a benchmarking tool and bring standardisation to the area. Figure 1 presents a taxonomy of relevant hardware and software, and their application in an e-supply network that we posit should be standardised.

E-commerce is currently seen as a technology fit rather than a relationship tool but this will change (Ruppel, 2006). In the future, collaborative product commerce (CPC), a set of tools that allows companies to manage product information and share it with suppliers and partners through the Web, is expected to co-ordinate and control virtually all supply, manufacturing and customer-relationship processes supported by an e-based infrastructure backbone (Mondragon et al., 2006).

Thus, there is a need to establish this common e-based infrastructure backbone to ensure interoperability and standardisation to support information flows (Soliman et al., 2003; Mondragon et al. 2006). There are already attempts to develop standardised Web-based platforms. For instance, the Web Services Interoperability Organisation (WS-I) which is a consortium of the top companies in the industry such as HP, Microsoft, IBM, ORACLE, and Intel, aims to promote interoperability among Web services based on providing Web services developers with common, industry-accepted definitions, and related extendible mark-up language standards support. This however is voluntary and is still in the early stages of development. Other industry standards like operating frequencies for RFIDs or UDDI (universal description, discovery, and integration) platform independent business registries for Web services are needed to ensure the widespread utilisation of these technologies (Mondragon et al., 2006).

In the standardisation process, there is also a need to incorporate other business related factors in the application. Mondragon et al. (2006), looking specifically at the automotive manufacturing sector, highlight the importance and reliance of sophisticated business models, such as supplier parks and full-service-vehicle supply, on the use of Web-based information systems to fulfil the build-to-order strategy.

Sharifi et al. (2006) believe that classification of e-marketplaces, which are sales and purchasing operations conducted over a common e-enabled platform, are critical to the management of their application and adoption. They use criteria such as ownership/structure, product/market type and required functionality for e-marketplace classification.

In a study of three supply chain management technologies (group decision support systems, EDI, and the Internet for electronic marketing (e-commerce)), each was found to improve information flows along the supply chain, the major criteria for success was the perceived needs of the users with respect to the implementation of the respective technology (Ruppel, 2006). Thus managers cannot expect to be able to implement all SCM technologies/tools in the same manner,

as different factors affect the adoption and use of different technologies.

From this, the typology and infrastructure we recommend needs to incorporate factors related to user needs such as degree of trust, cost, security, business strategies, objectives and business models. In the e-platform that is recommended in Figure 1, we have incorporated the already rapid growth of demand of online purchasing software from suppliers, and included the software that is and will be required to move beyond e-commerce and achieve e-supply networks. The importance of tools enabling sales and operational planning, lean operations, and VMI and CPFR has already been identified as being critical to the success of e-supply networks and need to be a part of the technological infrastructure (Friscia et al., 2004). It is the tools plus the connectivity that is of critical importance and these have been incorporated in our e-platform.

Figure 1. Standardising hardware and software in an E-supply network

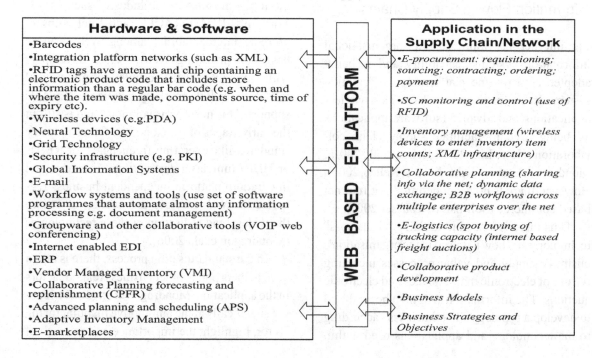

Stage 2: Determine the Degree of Integration Between Supply Network Partners

Although e-supply chain management is in its academic infancy, there are many well established software packages that have been implemented in business. AMR Research list 25 major global companies led by DELL, Nokia, and Procter and Gamble (Friscia et al., 2004) that have achieved success with supply chains, not only by enhancing process flows, but also by creating a platform on which suppliers, producers, distributors, and retailers can coordinate a response to the demand signal from customers. These SCM tools require a high level of integration and organisations must match the operational needs of these tools to the goals of the business. From the first stage, we can see that the technology has advanced extensively, but there is still much greater potential for its growth, development and maturity (Ruppel, 2006). With standardisation will come more and easier integration with the right partners.

Soliman et al. (2003) present a model of Internet based e-commerce in manufacturing where they emphasise the need for integration with internal and external processes already in place in the organisation. This is a challenging process involving a major re-engineering exercise accompanied by resistance to change.

There is a need to determine the strategic level of integration of systems and information flows and how effective they are in terms of achieving supply chain objectives. Evaluation of integration would also be made at an operational level examining systems and network diagrams as well as access; control; and permissions listings. One of the ways in which the degree of integration between supply network partners is to be determined, is to assess the importance of each respective partner in the process. There are already tools for sorecarding supplier portfolios that help manufacturers determine whether their suppliers are performing well on an individual basis (Hoch-

man, 2007). This could be extended to include an assessment of the level of critical importance each supplier in the value chain/network.

Developing such supply chain integration strategies for competitive advantage however requires a new organisational mindset. It will be a real challenge for successful supply chain players to understand the dynamics of power of their own position and other players in their industry enough, to be able to develop an open culture that will enable integration and close interaction with other supply chain partners. This kind of partnering, if achieved, can bring about mutual benefits and introduce performance measures, which reinforce collaboration and find novel ways of integrating information systems with other supply partners.

Stage 3: Examine Information Nodes Across the Supply Network and Identify Criteria for Classifying Information Flows

It is widely acknowledged that managing the flow of information within and between organisations will lead to efficiencies in organisational processes (Krovi, Chandra, & Rajagopalan, 2003). The methodological approach to this part of the research is based on systems thinking, with a process flow analysis of information passing though the e-business enabled supply chain using flow charts. Within these charts will be the identification of information nodes where the value of the node (i.e., "the entity or group of entities capable of altering the properties of information flow" (Krovi et al., 2003, p. 78)) is determined by the information content, the importance to decision making and the e-business infrastructure or technology infrastructure on which it relies. Tsaih and Lin (2006) identify two kinds of information processing infrastructures in a value chain: *contact points* where information is processed and the corresponding business task is carried out and *information channels* which carry the information flow. The information nodes thus can be divided into these two functional criteria. The role of the contact points and information channels also change dynamically where the information recipient could be both a decider and a communicator of information (Titus & Brochner, 2005).

The bi-directional information flows need to be analysed with the partner's capacity to handle the requirement and cause the fulfilment flow. The quality, timeliness, and cost effectiveness of the information determine the information flow efficiency (Titus et al., 2005). Cai, Jun, and Yang (2006) found that norms of Internet information sharing are positively associated with three key dimensions of Internet communication: formality (formal rules to effectively manage and control their Internet communication flows), frequency, and diversity of information. Other suggested information flow parameters (Krovi et al., 2003) include:

- **Velocity:** The speed of information arriving at a node.
- **Viscosity:** The degree of conflict at the node where there might be contradictory information components (this can potentially cause the bullwhip effect in supply chains).
- **Volatility:** Uncertainty about the content, format, or timing of information.
- **Density:** The number of intermediate nodes involved in the information processing channel.

Each of the participants in the supply network has a large number of needs to a) request b) aggregate c) filter information from different and multiple sources. All these factors will be a starting point in the classification of information flows.

Supply chains are no longer internal, but are multi-tiered, multi-echeloned with different configurations at each level with multiple players and multiple supply chains—internal or external. Three specific tiers of supply chains can be

identified (Van der Velde & Meijer 2003) namely internal supply chains, external supply chains, and total supply chains. Information can similarly be structured into three major categories:

- Firstly macro-environmental information—factors that impact on the macro-environment of the whole supply network—for example, political, legal, social, economic, and technological factors.
- Secondly meso-environmental information—industry specific factors—for example, new technological/or innovative developments in the industry, new competitors, or industry or sector specific information.
- Thirdly micro-environmental factors—factors that impact on the firm itself for example, internal systems, credit control policies, and training and skills development.

Part of the information classification process would also need to include identifying the type of information each supply network partner feels is necessary to supply chain management and then to classify that information according to its importance in achieving organisational objectives, decision making, progressing processes within the e-business enabled supply chain.

It is clear from current research in the literature that there are serious issues of trust and power in the use of e-business, particularly in the use of e-auctions and references therein and so issues of trust must also be included in the classification of information which will likely impact information flows. Partners in the supply network must also classify information according to the level of trust with partners they are prepared to share information.

The information gathered at this stage would be analysed to develop an information flow chart that clearly marks the source of the information, the type of information (internally generated/external report), its criticality, its speed of accumulation, relevance, and importance to supply networks

Table 1. Classification criteria for information flows

Information Node	Status	Information Flow Parameters	Information Type
Contact point • *Decider* • *Communicator* Information Flow	• Requirement • Fulfilment	• Viscosity • Velocity • Volatility • Density • Formality • Diversity • Frequency	• Macro-environmental • Meso-environmental • Micro-environmental

members, potential for conflicting sources of information, format and timing, sensitivity and willingness to share the information. The criteria for classification have been summarised in Table 1.

From this, a framework or series of frameworks can be developed to support the management of information flows across supply networks. This approach would be consistent with the "supply chain resource planning" suggested by Kehoe et al. (2001a,b).

CONCLUSION

The literature review conducted here revealed a dearth of theory building based on empirical research. The majority of the research was mainly descriptive and highlighted the importance of information flows in developing e-supply chains and networks. This is consistent with the findings of Gimenez and Laurenco (2004) who found that information flows was one of the main e-supply chain topics being dealt with in the Operations Management literature. They also found that the most used methodology by these researchers was descriptive. More empirical research needs to be conducted to study the impact of the Internet on several e-supply chain management processes.

From this literature review, we argued the necessity of standardising information flow in supply chains to facilitate integration, legality, security, and efficiency of operations. A three-stage framework that can achieve this standardisation was developed, and incorporates:

a. Consolidating the different constituents of e-business and developing a typology of technology and applications infrastructure to enable supply network partners to benchmark themselves against each other according to an explicit set of e-business criteria. This will enable closer standardisation and integration of systems throughout the supply network, which will facilitate further operational efficiencies.

b. Determining the degree of integration between and across supply network partners in order to evaluate the impact on information flows and efficiencies in the supply chain as a whole according to the degree and type of integration. By being able to classify integration of supply network partners, it will be easier to highlight bottlenecks and potential problems throughout the network.

c. Identifying information nodes across the supply network in order to examine and classify information flows that pass through them according to a number of criteria that will improve efficiency, leanness, and agility of the network as a whole and reduce problems such as the bullwhip effect.

The information resulting from this approach can then be used in future research to model e-business enabled supply chains and optimise the impact of Internet technology and types of information flows to create robust, reliable, agile and lean value networks.

REFERENCES

Blascovich, J., & Goffre, J. (2003). *Unlocking value from e-supply management*. A. T. Kearney Technology Watch. Executive Agenda. Third Quarter, 2003. Retrieved January 8, 2007, from http://www.atkearney.com/shared_res/pdf/EA63_unlocking_S.pdf

Cai, S., Jun, M., & Yang, Z. (2006). The impact of interorganizational Internet communication on purchasing performance: A study of Chinese manufacturing firms. *The Journal of Supply chain Management, 42*(3), 16-29

Cigolini, R., Cozzi, M., & Perona, M. (2004). A new framework for supply chain management. *International Journal of Operations and Production Management, 24*(1), 27-41

Croom, S. (2005). The impact of e-business on supply chain management: An empirical study of key developments. *International Journal of Operations & Production Management, 25*(1), 55-73.

Croom, S. (2001). *Supply chain management in the e-business era—An investigations into supply chain strategies, practices, and progress in e-business adoption.* BT/Warwick Business School, SC Associates, Coventry.

Donovan, M. R. (n.d.). *Supply chain management: Transforming with an e-strategy.* Supply chain management (pp. 176-180). Touch Briefings. Retrieved February, 5, 2007, from http://www.touchbriefings.com/pdf/977/supplychain4.pdf

Doran, D. (2003). Supply chain implications of modularisation. *International Journal of Operations and Production Management, 23*(3), 316-326.

Friscia, T., O'Marah, K., & Souza, J. (2004). *The AMR research supply chain top 25 and the new trillion dollar opportunity.* Retrieved January 8, 2007, from http://www.i2cis.ru/pdf/The_AMR_Research_Supply_Chain_Top_25.pdf

Gadde, L., & Hakkansson, H. (2001). *Supply network strategies.* John Wiley & Sons.

Garcia-Dastugue, S. J., & Lambert, D. M. (2003). Internet-enabled coordination in the supply chain. *Industrial Marketing Management, 32*(3), 251-263.

Giménez, C., & Lourenço, H. R. (2004). *e-supply chain management: Review, implications, and directions for future research.* IET Working Paper # 17 October 2004. Retrieved January 8, 2007, from http://www.ietcat.org/htmls04/cat/publicacions/wpaper/IET%20working%20paper%20017.pdf

Handfield, R. B., & Nichols, E. L. (2003). *Supply chain redesign: Transforming supply chains into integrated supply systems.* NJ: Financial Times Prentice Hall.

Ho, L., & Lin, G. (2004). Critical success factor framework for the implementation of integrated-enterprise systems in the manufacturing environment. *International Journal of Production Research, 42*(17), 3731-42.

Jelassi, T., & Leenen, S. (2003). An e-commerce sales model for manufacturing companies: A conceptual framework and a European example. *European Management Journal, 2*(1), 38-47.

Hochman, S., (2007). *Value chain complexity, Part 1: What is it, why it matters.* AMR Research. Retrieved February 8, from http://www.amrresearch.com/Content/View.asp?pmillid=20248

Kehoe, D. F., & Boughton, N. J. (2001a). New paradigms in planning and control across manufacturing supply chains—The utilisation of Internet technologies. *International Journal of Operations & Productions Management 21*(5/6), 582-593.

Kehoe, D. F., & Boughton, N. J. (2001b). Internet based supply chain management—A classification of approaches to manufacturing planning and control. *International Journal of Operations& Production Management, 21*(4), 516-524.

Kehoe, D. F., & Boughton, N. J. (1998). DOMAIN: Dynamic operations management across the Internet. *Proceedings of the International Federation for Information Processing Working Group 5.7 (IFIPWG5.7,)* (pp. 421-30). Kluwer Academic Publishers, Dordrecht .

Krovi, R., Chandra, A., & Rajagopalan, B. (2003). Information flow parameters for managing organisational processes. *Communications of the ACM, 46*(2) ,77-82.

Lancioni, R. A., Smith, M. F., & Oliva, T. A. (2000. The role of the Internet in supply chain management. *Industrial Marketing Management, 29*(1),45-56.

Mason-Jones, R., & Towill, D. R. (1997). Information enrichment: Designing the supply chain for competitive advantage. *Supply chain Management, 2*(4), 137-48.

Mason-Jones, R., Naylor, B., & Towill, D. R. (2000). Engineering the leagile supply chain. *International Journal of Agile Management Systems, 2*(1), 54-67.

Monczka, R., & Morgan, J. (2000, January 13). Competitive supply strategies for the 21st Century *Purchasing* , 48-59.

Mondragon, A. E. C., Lyons, A. C., Michaelides, Z., & Kehoe, D. F. (2006). Automotive supply chain models and technologies: A review of some latest developments. *Journal of Enterprise Information Management, 19*(5), 551-562.

Naylor, J. B., Naim, M. M., & Berry, D. (1999). Leagality: Integrating the lean and agile manufacturing paradigm in the total supply chain. *International Journal of Production Economics, 63*(1-2), 107-118.

Norris, G., Hurley, J., Hartley, K., Dunleavy, J., & Balls, J. (2000). *E-business and ERP–transforming the enterprise.* PriceWaterhouseCoopers John Wiley & Sons Inc.

Phan, D. D. (2003). E-business development for competitive advantages: a case study. *Information and Management, 40*(6), 581-590

Poirier, C. (n.d.). *Beyond supply chain to the networked enterprise.* From CSC Research Services. Retrieved September 20, 2006, from http://uk.country.csc.com/en/kl/uploads/196_1.pdf

Porter, M. E. (2001, March). Strategy and the Internet. *Harvard Business Review* pp. 63-78

Rai, A, Patnayakuni, R., & Patnayakuni, N. (2006). Firm performance impacts of digitally enabled supply chain integration capabilities. *MIS Quarterly, 30*(2), 225-240.

Ruppel, C. (2006). An information systems perspective of supply chain tool compatibility: The roles of technology fit and relationships. *Business Process Management Journal, 10*(3), 311-324.

Sharifi, H., Kehoe D.F., Hopkins J. (2006). A classification and selection model of e-marketplaces for better alignment of supply chains. *Journal of Enterprise Information Management 19*(5), 483-503.

Soliman, F., & Youssef, M. A. (2003). Internet-based e-commerce and its impact on manufacturing and business operations. *Industrial Management and Data Systems, 103*(8), 546-552.

Staff. (2003, July 1). *Process industry products, services to reach $786 billion by 2010*. Control Engineering. Retrieved September 20, 2006, from http://www.manufacturing.net/ctl/article/ CA307757.html?text=process+industry+produc ts%2C+services+to+reach+%24786+billion+by +2010&spacedesc=news

Tassabehji, R. (2003). *Applying e-commerce in business*. London: Sage Publications.

Tassabehji, R., Taylor, W. A., Beach, R., & Wood, A. (2006a). Reverse e-auctions: An exploratory study. *International Journal of Operations and Production Management, 26*(2), 166-184.

Tassabehji, R., Wallace, J., & Tsoularis, T. (2006b). Reverse e-auctions: Introducing agility to organisations. *International Journal of Agile Systems and Management 1*(4), 407-421.

Titus, S., & Brochner, J. (2005). Managing information flows in construction supply chains. *Construction Innovation. 5,* 71-82.

Tsaih, R., & Lin, W. (2006). The process-wide information organism approach for the business process analysis. *Industrial Management and Data Systems, 106*(4), 509-522.

Van der Velde, L. N. J., & Meijer, B. R. (2003). A system approach to supply chain design with a multinational for colorant and coatings. Retrieved September 20, 2006, from http://www.ifm.eng. cam.ac.uk/mcn/pdf_files/part6_5.pdf

Wallace, J., Tsoularis, T., & Tassabehji, R., (2006). Internet technology and stochastic automata to improve supply chain agility. *International Journal of Agile Systems and Management, 1*(4), 346-359.

Wailgum, T. (2006). *Integration liberation*. CIO Magazine. October 15, 2006. Retrieved January 15, 2007, from http://www.cio.com/archive/101506/integration.html

Zank, G. M., & Vokurka, R. J. (2003). The Internet: Motivations, deterrents, and impact on supply chain relationships. *S.A.M. Advanced Management Journal, 68*(2), 33-40.

Chapter XI
Virtual Teams in Health Care:
Maximising Team Effectiveness

Mary DeGori
Broadmeadows Health Service, Australia

Fang Zhao
RMIT University, Australia

ABSTRACT

This chapter describes an in-depth analysis of the methods to increase the effectiveness of virtual teams in health care using the Northern Alliance Hospital Admission Risk Program (HARP) Chronic Disease Management (CDM) Program as the test case. A conceptual framework of the specific components required for virtual team effectiveness and a survey tool to examine a team's performance (based on virtual team member perception) with each of these components is presented. The proposed conceptual framework of virtual team effectiveness categorises the determinants influencing the effectiveness of virtual teams into four key frames of leadership, team components, organisational culture, and technology. An empirical survey of 38 virtual team members within the Northern Alliance HARP CDM Program demonstrates high levels of agreement with leadership and some team components, however, limited agreement with the organisational culture and technology components.

INTRODUCTION

In today's turbulent health care environment, characterised at one extreme by economic slowdown, and at the other, by actively involved and informed health care consumers, hospitals are confronting the fundamental business challenges of survival

and success (Yavas & Romanova, 2005). Leaders in health-care organisations are developing and implementing a variety of initiatives aimed at demonstrating enhanced value as they struggle to compete in a volatile market (Richardson & Gurtner, 1999). Teamwork is one of the most common proposals for managing increasing organisational complexity and as a lever for change (Drew & Coulson-Thomas, 1997).

Several authors have documented the potential contributions of teams for health-care organisations in enhancing continuous improvement of quality, innovation, and customer satisfaction; in improving employee satisfaction; reducing operating costs and in improving response to technological change (Chan, Pearson, & Entrekin, 2003). Other reported benefits of teamwork include breaking down the boundaries to effective communication and collaboration, increasing the speed of action and raising the level of commitment, creating a more customer-focussed culture and increasing organisational adaptability and flexibility (Drew et al., 1997). Moreover, Holton (2001) suggests that the productivity of a group of individuals is greater than the sum of the outputs of each individual.

The use of teams offers two major advantages to an organisation. Firstly, teamwork has the capacity to empower people to utilise their abilities. This has relevance for both motivation and group cohesiveness. Secondly, the use of teams allows managers to focus their attention on strategic issues rather than supervising individuals (Chan et al., 2003). The nature of teams has changed significantly as a result of changes in organisations and the nature of the work that they do. Organisations have become dispersed across geography and across industries (Kimball, 1997). Equally, the convergence of IT and communication and the advent of the Internet have impacted dramatically on almost every aspect of our life. Indeed, the Internet and WWW have been seen as the catalyst for radical change in organisation activities and processes. The digital world offers a borderless and virtual village where individuals, teams, and organisations are interconnected and interdependent through a network of partnerships and relationships (Zhao, 2006). This has seen the recent emergence and proliferation of virtual teams.

The primary objective of this study is to conduct an in-depth analysis of the methods to increase the effectiveness of virtual teams in health care using the Northern Hospital Admission Risk Program Chronic Disease Management (HARP CDM) Alliance as a case study.

Based on an extensive review of the extant literature, the research develops and proposes a conceptual framework of the specific components required to maximise virtual team effectiveness, which can be used as a tool to examine a team's performance with each of these components (based on virtual team member perception). The major research question that this study proposes to answer is:

- How to maximise effectiveness of virtual teams in health care?

With ongoing changes in the health care environment terrain, characterised by a depleting workforce, funding constraints, rapid technological advancement, and increasingly, by actively involved and informed health care consumers, the evolution and proliferation of virtual teams has been recognised as an important issue affecting health care both at a local level and internationally. In order for hospitals and health care providers to provide a sustainable, responsive service, high quality, best practice, and patient centred-care, and to maintain a workforce of highly qualified and skilled staff, many health care organisations have adopted the model of virtual teams.

Therefore, this research is important with significant pragmatic value. The project offers a new solution or means of consideration of a globally relevant and increasingly common issue. It advances the current knowledge base about the specific factors influencing the effectiveness of virtual teams in health care. The project consolidates understanding of these factors and proposes a conceptual model. The conceptual model (derived from local and global research) that identifies and categorises the components influencing the effectiveness of virtual teams offers both operational and strategic benefit for both the Northern Alliance HARP CDM Program, the case program specifically, and the health care industry in general.

LITERATURE REVIEW

This section reviews principal literature on virtual teams and the effects of information and communication technologies on virtual teams. It also addresses the key elements of virtual team success and the qualities of the leader required for a successful virtual team in health care.

Virtual Teams

Virtual teams are teams of people who are physically separated (by time and or space), who primarily interact electronically and who may meet face-to-face occasionally (Gould, 2006). In order to classify all of the different possible conditions in which virtual teams exist, Kimble, Li, and Barlow (2000) propose the following scheme

(Figure 1). They describe eight possible scenarios, four in which team members work for the same organisation, and four where team members are from different organisations.

Gould (2006) described the characteristics of virtual teams:

- Virtual teams get the job done—they achieve the goals set for them.
- People can be trusted—work is completed despite the lack of physical presence of the leader.
- Few virtual teams are 100 percent virtual—virtual teams tend to have face-to-face meetings.
- Virtual teams take on the same basic structure as natural work teams.

Furthermore, virtual teams are like project or natural work teams with three added components:

- Different geography or locations of team members.
- Team members are from different organisations or parts of the organisation.

Figure 1. A classification of virtual team working (Adapted from Kimble et al., 2000)

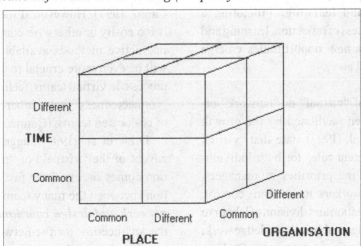

- Different durations or lengths of time that members work together as a team (Cantu, 1997).

Studies show that virtual teams offer many opportunities to organisations and team members. Virtual teams maximise productivity and lower costs; people can work from anywhere at any time and members can be recruited for their competencies, not just physical location (Connaughton & Daly, 2004; Gould, 2006).

Drew et al. (1997) have identified the competencies required by virtual teams:

- **Trust building:** Developing and nurturing effective business cooperation for projects.
- **Negotiation:** Agreeing mutually acceptable terms of business.
- **Information brokerage:** Trading information and knowledge about markets, customers, contacts, resources and partnerships.
- **Information transmission and amplification:** Ensuring information is available any place, any time and to anyone who needs it within the network.
- **Translation:** Promoting understanding and trust by translating different corporate cultures, languages and systems to partner organisations.
- **Adaptivity and learning:** Promoting a continual process of reflection, learning and reinvention as new opportunities emerge and others fall away.

The evolution of "virtual" or "network" organisations has been facilitated by the growth of teams. Drew et al. (1997) state that "virtual teams require different roles for both individuals and groups as the priorities of managers, professionals and workers move from control, delegation, specialisation and division of labour to coaching, supporting, enabling, knowledge work, and integration of business processes" (p. 173).

Moreover, a change in the attitude and approach of all virtual team members is essential for the full potential of the virtual team to be achieved (Kimble et al., 2000).

Team learning is an important determinant of an organisation's competitiveness. Team learning has been shown to be positively related to team performance and hence, team learning is gaining importance as a strategy for gaining greater competitive advantage (Chan et al., 2003).

According to Conner and Finnemore (2003), the characteristics of successful teams using virtual workplaces are not unlike those of other successful teams. Everyone on the team is committed, roles are clearly understood, norms of behaviour are established and members discuss and agree upon how they will work together in the virtual workplace.

ICT and Virtual Teams

"Electronic communication technologies are providing a historically unprecedented ability to work together at a distance" (Cantu, 1997, p. 4). Virtual teams benefit significantly from face-to-face meetings and these are particularly important in the early stages of team development (Lipnack, 1997 as cited by Cantu, 1997). Some experts suggest that 25% of team interaction should be spent in face-to-face meetings (George, 1996 as cited by Cantu, 1997). However, if meeting face-to-face is too costly or otherwise constrained, the many interactive methods available to virtual teams will be even more crucial to the communication process. In virtual teams, technology replaces the "connectedness" that is inherent in the functions of co-located teams. (Conner et al., 2003).

Drew et al. (1997) suggested that with the advent of the "virtual" or "network" organisation comes the need for fast and fluid connections between the many team members through *network and design coordination* (establishing the architecture for the network, protocols and coordinating mechanisms) and *knowledge man-*

agement (ensuring systems and technology are available and used to capture data, information and knowledge).

Therefore, virtual teams must be supported by a technology that is adapted to the way they function, and members must have a minimum level of hardware and software and skill in using the supporting technology (Conner et al., 2003). Virtual teams are unlikely to capitalize on their members' collective experiences or complete their work goal without the use of appropriate technology tools (George, 1996 as cited by Cantu, 1997). Kimble et al. (2000) state that "to be effective, virtual teams have to develop new ways of sharing knowledge and understanding in the electronic space" (p. 12).

Several kinds of technology can assist in making coordination for virtual teams relatively simple and highly effective:

- **Teleconferencing**
- **Video-conferencing and desktop video-conferencing:** A camera is mounted to the computer monitor and team members are able to see and hear one another as though meeting in an office (Lipnack, 1997 cited in Cantu, 1997).
- **Group software:** Enables multiple people to work on the same document at different times. Group software allows team members to work together on projects by sharing ideas and information, and by taking part in discussions with all team members. Group software offers security capabilities so that important or confidential information is not compromised when working together with individuals outside of the organisation (Lotus, 1997 as cited by Cantu, 1997).
- **Newsgroups, bulletin boards and electronic mail:** Internet based.
- **Intranets:** Intranets increase the potential for collaborative work. Intranets provide team members with the ability to view each others' progress and assist each other

in trouble shooting (Lake, 1997 as cited by Cantu, 1997).

- **Web-based conferencing:** An asynchronous tool that may facilitate the considered reflection and dialogue that is often difficult to achieve through e-mail alone (Holton, 2001).

Kimble et al. (2000) describe unreliable systems, incompatible networks, "slow" computers, and traffic congestion during certain times of the day as technological barriers to the success of virtual teams. Real-time multimedia communications integrating voice, data, text, and video are essential to operations of virtual teams. However, providing adequate technological support to virtual teams has been very difficult, integrated broadband telecommunications infrastructure is often not available in certain areas and costs associated with using, maintaining and upgrading advanced telecommunications services can be considerable (Kimble et al., 2000).

In an examination of the demands of emerging electronic and mobile technologies on expansive leadership, Diamante and London (2002) suggest that information technology has produced "a new context for leadership such that technology and social systems are integrally linked, with one affecting the other" (p. 405). According to Diamante et al. (2002), successful e-leaders are those who use the technology in a constructive way such that the technology and organisational systems adapt together. "Leaders need to understand the technology and its tie to social interactions. This requires continuous learning as both the technology and the organisation/social systems evolve" (Diamante et al., 2002, p. 406).

Without appropriate coordination of work through technology, losing regular contact with the team members' host organisation is possible. An absence of regular contact can be problematic to the team member, the team, and the organisation. For the team member, a loss of contact can mean that a direct supervisor will be unaware of contributions to the virtual team. As a result, the team member's performance in the virtual team is unknown. For the team, losing contact can mean not working towards the collaborative team vision or objective and losing valuable project development time (George, 1996 cited in Cantu, 1997). For the organisation, distance from and a lack of awareness of the progress of the virtual team can mean that greater knowledge or key learning about how the team coordinates its work are not maximised. Furthermore, other employees may be less prepared to participate in a virtual team if the organisation is perceived as being disinterested when it comes to virtual teams (George, 1996 cited in Cantu, 1997).

Team Norms

A focus on common purpose and work processes has a significant impact on a team's effectiveness as well as efficiency and keeps the team's work moving forward. As virtual team members are self-directed, much of the time, success of the team depends on how well they understand and agree upon their common purpose, goals and processes (Conner et al., 2003). Successful teams establish norms in the areas of goal setting, decision-making, alignment with a vision and mission, clarification of team roles and codes of conduct. A virtual teaming model proposed by Conner et al. (2003) describes the requirement for a combination of training and technology to produce consistent and defined group norms and processes. According to this model, "the overall goal is to improve team processes by teaching team members to collaborate in a new context, using technology, while working remote from one another" (Conner et al., 2003, p. 81).

Group Climate

Team climate has been defined as the shared perceptions of the "proximal work group" (Anderson & West, 1998 as cited by Gil, Rico, Alcover, & Barrasa, 2005). A proximal work group is considered as the team to which individuals are assigned, whom they identify with, and whom they interact with regularly in order to perform work-related tasks. According to an explanatory study by Gil et al. (2005) on the impact of change-oriented leaders on group outcomes in 78 health care teams, there are four factors that are related to team climate—vision, participation, task orientation, and support for innovation.

Group Potency

Potency has been defined in the literature as "the collective belief in a group that it can be effective" (Guzzo et al., 1993 as cited by Gil et al., 2005). Teams differ from each other based on the beliefs of all their members in the potential effectiveness of the team. This collective belief about current levels of effectiveness is influenced by the contexts within which groups act (Gil et al., 2005). Campion et al. (1993, 1996 cited in Gil et al., 2005) found that "group potency is a significant predictor not only of productivity, but also of the satisfaction of team members and management assessments of its performance" (p. 316).

Leadership in Virtual Teams

Leadership plays a key role in virtual teams. The purpose of leadership is "to create direction and the unified will to pursue it through the development of peoples' thinking and valuing" (Kent, 2005, p. 57). Success in virtual teams requires a change for the entire team, commitment from each member and strong leader direction. Without strong leadership and role modelling, virtual teams will "flounder or fail" (Conner et al., 2003; Kent, 2005; Mannion, Davies & Marshall, 2005).

Conner et al. (2003) identified four categories of leadership behaviours that encourage virtual team performance:

- Communications
- Establishing expectations
- Allocating resources
- Modelling desired behaviours

Leaders attempt to create a shared vision that enables people to focus their efforts and to prioritise their activities. The vision motivates individuals and creates a collective sense of value and significance (Kent, 2005). The ability of the leaders to support individuals to be effective within their work structure is significantly important if team members are to feel satisfied that they are part of something meaningful and rewarding (Conner et al., 2003).

In a study of 500 virtual managers, 90% perceived managing from afar to be more challenging than managing people on-site (Hymowitz, 1999 cited in Connaughton et al., 2004). Several authors have investigated and described these "challenges." A leader's "social presence" may be more difficult to achieve over time and space; trust among leaders and team members may be fragile; and the member's identification with the team, the organisation, and the leader him/herself may be challenged over distance (Connaughton et al., 2004).

Identification Between Team Members

Identification is critical for both proximate and distanced work relationships. Connaughton et al. (2004) define identification as "the process in which an individual comes to see an object as being definitive of oneself and forms a psychological connection with that object" (p. 90). Several researchers have found that organisational identification leads to a series of key outcomes:

- Individuals who are identified with the organisation are more committed to it.
- The more individuals identify with their organisation, the less likely they are to intend to leave or actually exit the organisation.

- Highly identified individuals are likely to behave in ways that are aligned with the organisation's identity, interests and beliefs.
- Identification and commitment affect organisational members' acceptance of influence attempts (Connaughton et al., 2004).

Trust in Virtual Teams

"The ability to work collaboratively is recognised as a core competency of a learning organisation" (Holton, 2001, p. 36). The creation of processes, methods, and opportunities for team members to participate in meaningful and deep dialogue necessary to create a shared future is a challenge for team building in a virtual environment. Trust develops through frequent and meaningful interaction, and trust symbolises the collaborative dynamic of a learning organisation (Holton, 2001). Collocation reinforces shared values and expectations, social similarity, and increases the threat of negative outcomes from failing to meet commitments (Paul & McDaniel, 2004). Hence, trust in virtual collaborative relationships is difficult to build.

The successful management of virtual teams demands trust and the development of new methods for management (Kimble et al., 2000). Establishing trust is fundamental to the successful formation and growth of any new work team (Glacel, 1997 cited in Holton, 2001). Trust reduces complexity in work teams by enabling individuals and groups with different knowledge bases and experiences to collaborate (Paul et al., 2004). Therefore, "How one creates trust within a team of individuals working across distance, time zones, cultures and professional disciplines is a challenge that an increasing number of organisational leaders will face" (Holton, 2001, p. 37).

A study by Jarvenpaa and Leidner (1998 cited in Kimble et al. 2000) about the creation and maintenance of trust in global virtual teams identified that teams that were not task focussed reported lower levels of trust and that trust was greater in teams that developed set patterns for communication with rapid response times to other team members.

Paul et al. (2004) identify the importance of trust in health care delivery where health care providers rely on collaboration as a primary means of complexity reduction. "Health care delivery is a collaborative activity whose quality, efficiency, and responsiveness is enhanced by the use of interdisciplinary teams" (Paul et al., 2004, p. 3).

As shown in this literature review, the effectiveness and success of virtual teams in general, and the virtual teams in health care in particular, is dependent upon a number of factors and contingencies. Empirical studies are needed to examine and advance the current knowledge base demonstrated in this literature review about the specific factors influencing the effectiveness of virtual teams in health care. To address the need, the authors of this chapter conducted the present study.

Organisational Culture

A study of the relationship between organisational culture and organisational outcomes by Platonova, Hernandez, Shewchuk, and Leddy (2006) found that in addition to influencing employee job satisfaction directly, organisational culture can also increase the impact of positive perceptions of job attributes on employee job satisfaction. Organisational culture can produce a competitive advantage and influence and improve business performance. Crucial to organisational success is a cohesive organisational culture (Platonova et al., 2006).

Several authors define organisational culture as a wide range of social phenomena including a collective sum of beliefs, values, symbols, meanings, behaviours, and assumptions held by organisational members or a social group (Platonova et al., 2006). Mannion et al.'s (2005) multiple case studies of the cultural characteristics of "high" and "low" performing hospitals in the

United Kingdom defined organisational culture as encompassing both "the way that things are done around here" (including patterns of behaviour, systems of patronage and reward, and process of accountability) as well as the shared beliefs, values and assumptions that underpin these visible manifestations. Schien (1990) as cited by Platonova et al. (2006), describes culture as a pattern of basic assumptions invented, discovered, or developed by a given group as it learns to cope with its problems of external adaptation and internal integration, and that has worked well enough to be considered valid, and therefore is to be taught to new members as the correct way to think, perceive and feel in relation to these problems. Hofstede (1998) as cited by Platonova et al. (2006), defines organisational culture as the "collective programming," which differentiates the members of one organisation from another.

Organisations possess distinct cultures that are related to organisational outcomes:

- Organisational culture appears to influence performance through the direct effect it has on worker attitudes.
- A complex interplay between organisational culture(s) and performance has been identified in acute hospitals (Mannion et al., 2005).
- Some studies have identified that participation in decision making has been found to result in a higher return on investment.
- Participation has also been found to be associated with perceived productiveness, satisfaction with the team and a desire to stay with the team.
- Organisations that foster a sense of involvement in decision-making appear to either make better decision because of broader employee input or gain greater commitment to executing the decisions that are made.
- Cultures that provide workers with a sense of empowerment within health care organisations have more successful outcomes.

- A focus on teamwork and supportive team values are other cultural contributors to performance. These values instil a sense of belonging to the organisation and its work.
- Cultures that stress willingness to change, innovation and competitive behaviour have been found to be better performers.
- Organisations with cultures that support methods for speedier decisions and multi-tasking behaviours outperform organisations without such cultures (Platonova et al., 2006)

In addition, research has identified other cultural characteristics that may be sources of sustained competitive advantage. These include open top-down and bottom-up communications, reliance on people as a source of competitive advantage, employee involvement, consistency, and adaptability (Platonova et al., 2006).

METHODOLOGY

The research design that this study follows is case study. As a research strategy, case study is used to explore and illustrate specific issues related to the effectiveness of virtual team in health care. Although a case study does not prelude a capacity for generalisation, it does offer analytic example and evidence for judgement (Yin, 2003). The case study contains several key steps and methods as follows.

Development of Survey Tool

An in-depth analysis and comparison of available published research and internet/electronic references relating to virtual teams and teams in health care was employed to derive key themes and factors for investigation through the virtual teams effectiveness survey.

Research articles from management, health care, and quality assurance publications were identified and included in the analysis.

Where available within the literature, survey questions were reproduced identically from the research papers analysed (Refer to the Appendix for the referenced Virtual Teams Effectiveness Survey).

The Virtual Teams Effectiveness Survey was developed using a standard 5-point Likert scale (which represents an interval measurement scale for data analysis purposes) and also includes open-ended questions for more descriptive (qualitative) responses. The questionnaire used for the Survey consists of 8 sections under the subheadings of:

1. Employee Satisfaction (Platonova et al. 2006, Gil et al. 2005).
2. Team Norms (Conner et al., 2003).
3. Leadership Behaviours (Connaughton et al., 2004).
4. Internal Team Learning (Chan et al. 2003).
5. External Team Learning (Chan et al. 2003).
6. Team Performance (Chan et al. 2003).
7. Culture (Platonava et al. 2000).
8. Technology (Conner et al., 2003, Connaughton et al., 2004).

The survey was developed based upon a literature review of several principal articles as shown above. The survey tool was pilot tested with a member of a virtual team (not within the health care industry) for testing of questionnaire wording, question sequencing, and questionnaire layout.

Prior to conduction of the Virtual Teams Effectiveness Survey, the survey tool was also pilot tested with two members of the Northern Alliance HARP CDM Program. Survey tool questions which were redundant due to language, meaning, or repetition were modified or deleted.

Virtual Team Effectiveness Survey

Conduction of a written survey was made with members of the Northern Alliance HARP CDM Program at various levels, including:

- Executive sponsors.
- Team Leaders.
- Team Members.
- Northern Alliance HARP CDM Program Manager.

All team leaders and team members of the Northern Alliance HARP CDM Program were invited to participate in the research project. The executive sponsors (or governance group) were selected according to their familiarity or interest with the Northern Alliance HARP CDM Program from an operational perspective. The sample size is 50 (including team members, team leaders, selected executive sponsors, and program manager).

All members of the Northern Alliance HARP CDM Program (as previously described) received an introductory letter and plain language statement by e-mail one week prior to the conduction of the survey to describe the purpose of the study and invite participation. The Northern Alliance HARP CDM Program email distribution list was utilised.

Briefing meetings were arranged with the various teams (within the virtual team) for the conduction of the written survey. Due to the nature of virtual teams, a face-to-face meeting with some teams was not possible. In these cases, the survey tool was e-mailed to the research subjects. The research subjects were instructed to return the survey by e-mail or post.

The professional role of the subject in the Alliance (team member, team leader, executive) was recorded and analysed in order to attempt to identify relationships between role and perceptual evaluations of performance and other measures

of effectiveness of virtual teams in health care. All other data was de-identified.

A computer survey software was used to record and collate the survey data.

Data Analysis

SPSS software was utilised to perform the basic descriptive statistical analyses such as:

- Frequencies
- Means
- Medians and standard deviations
- Cross tabulation

Qualitative research methods of coding and thematic analysis were implemented to identify key themes in responses to open-ended questions and "optional comments" which provided subjects with the opportunity to provide more information about their opinion regarding "what methods maximise effectiveness in virtual teams."

Development of Conceptual Model

A conceptual framework of positively influential factors identified through an in-depth review of published research and internet/electronic references has been proposed to categorise the specific components influencing the effectiveness of virtual teams. The results from the Virtual Team survey of the Northern Alliance HARP CDM Program will be examined within the frames of the conceptual model.

Methodological Limitations

Although great efforts were made to maintain a high quality standard in conducting this study, it should be noted that there are a few limitations during the conduction of the research and analysis of results.

The Case Study Team

The conduction of the survey was at an early stage in the virtual team development. Many of the team members are unaware of the Northern Alliance HARP CDM Program and some are new to the Alliance (employed less than 6 months).

The Research Design

The case study design investigates only one virtual team. This produced no ground for generalisation to the larger health care environment. Furthermore, the case study team is a metropolitan team with the greatest distance between organisational/worksites of 40km. Future study would investigate rural, national, and global teams with distances of space, time and culture.

In-depth interviews would have provided a deeper understanding of virtual team member perceptions of the specific components that influence virtual team effectiveness.

These limitations should be taken into account when reading this research report.

CASE STUDY: THE NORTHERN ALLIANCE ADMISSION RISK PROGRAM CHRONIC DISEASE MANAGEMENT PROGRAM

Background

In 2002, the Victorian (State) Government Department of Human Services (DHS) introduced the Hospital Admission Risk Program (HARP) funding initiatives aimed at reducing preventable hospital and emergency department presentations for complex and chronic diseases. The Department of Human Services (DHS) encouraged project submissions that fostered collaboration and partnership between health care sectors and with local government and community organisations. In 2006, the DHS is moving from project to program based funding for HARP initiatives. The formation of a program has resulted in the formation of virtual teams within the Northern Alliance HARP Chronic Disease Management (CDM) Program in two streams, a chronic disease stream and a complex needs stream. Thus all members of the Northern Alliance HARP CDM Program are members of virtual teams.

Figure 2. Relationships of an individual team member within the Northern Alliance HARP CDM Program

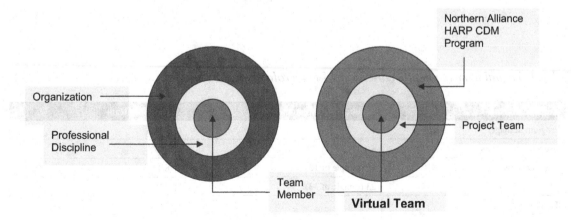

The Northern Alliance HARP CDM Program consists of the following organisations:

- Northern Health
- Plenty Valley Community Health
- Darebin Community Health
- Royal District Nursing Service
- Northern Division of General Practice
- University of Melbourne
- Hume City Council

Team members of the various projects in a state of evolution to program funding may be employees of an acute health organisation, community health organisation, local government, university or other health care organisation, however will also be members of virtual teams which comprise the project teams and the Northern Alliance HARP CDM Program itself.

Figure 2 is a diagrammatic representation of the relationships of an individual team member with various aspects of the different health care organisations.

How is Northern Alliance HARP CDM Program a Virtual Team?

The characteristics of the Northern Alliance HARP CDM Program include:

- Teams working at different physical locations

- Members of the same team working at different sites and employed by different organisations
- Team members communicate electronically and meet occasionally
- Team members working different days/hours (and hours of work may not ever coincide within the week)

Analysis of the Results of Virtual Teams Effectiveness Survey of Northern Alliance HARP CDM Program

Respondents and Response Rate

The response rate to the written survey on virtual teams of Northern Alliance HARP CDM Program was 76% (n = 38). Table 1 provides a description of the response rates based on respondent role within the Northern Alliance HARP CDM Program.

Ongoing workforce issues with chronic staffing shortages and team incumbent changes (at team member level) within the Northern Alliance HARP CDM Program resulted in a fluctuating sample size within the virtual team for the conduction of the case study. The sample size at the commencement of the research project was 50 individuals.

In all graphical and tabular representation of the results obtained, the following abbreviations apply:

Table 1. Virtual teams in health care survey—team role response rates

Respondent Role	Number of Respondents (n)	Response Rate
Program Manager	1	100%
Executive Sponsors	4	100%
Team Leaders	10 (sample of 12)	83%
Team Members	23 (sample of 33)	70%
Total	**38**	**76%**

Table 2. Employee satisfaction results

Question Number	Mean	SD	Mean	SD	Mean	SD
1.1	4.40	0.98	3.87	1.36	4.08	1.33
1.2	4.33	0.94	4.17	1.40	4.24	1.25
1.3	4	1.46	3.78	1.66	3.87	1.60
1.4	3.87	1.43	3.54	1.29	3.67	1.38

Table 3. Results for leadership components questions

	PM, ES, and TL	Team Members	All Respondents
	Mean		
3.1 Effective Leadership	4.13	3.64	3.84
3.3 Support	4	3.68	3.77
3.5 Behaviours	4.07	3.65	3.83
3.7 Identification	4.57	4.32	4.42
3.9 Trust	4.5	4.15	4.29
3.14 Isolation	2.47	2.67	2.58
3.15 Accessibility	4.07	3.5	3.74

- PM = Program Manager
- ES = Executive Sponsors
- TL = Team Leaders

Employee Satisfaction

The highest level of employee satisfaction was evident from the program manager, executive sponsors, and team leaders (particularly in response to Question 1.1—"Sense of accomplishment from work" and Question 1.2—"My work challenges me to use my knowledge and skills").

Leadership

The highest levels of agreement with Leadership related questions were in the program manager, executive sponsors, and team leaders group of respondents, particularly in those questions investigating trust and identification with leader (mean score of 4.5 and 4.57 respectively).

The team member respondents also reported high levels of agreement with the trust (Question 3.9) and identification with leader (Question 3.7) questions. However, team members tended to refer to their team leaders as the program manager in the leadership-related questions and this demonstrates a reduced awareness of the team members group of respondents about the existence of, and their membership of this virtual team.

The mean of all groups of respondents (PM, ES, and TL; team members and all respondents) indicated that they disagreed that "The physical distance between the Northern Alliance HARP CDM program manager and [the virtual team member] leaves me feeling isolated."

Question 3.7

92% of respondents strongly agree that they are willing to put a great deal of effort to help their manager and the Northern Alliance HARP CDM

Figure 3a. Leadership components

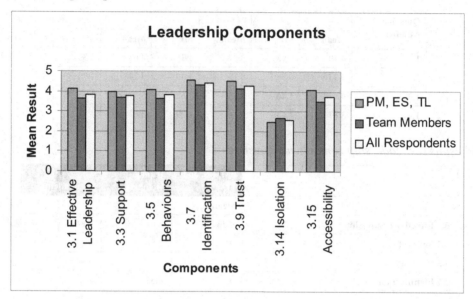

Figure 3b. Team components

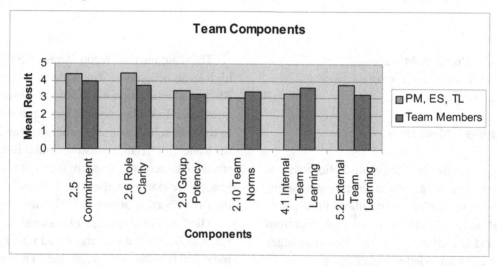

Program be successful. (92.9% = PM, TL, and ES; 90.9% team members)

Question 3.8

85.7% of respondents fully support the Northern Alliance HARP CDM program manager. (92.9% = PM, TL, and ES; 81% team members)

Question 3.9

85.3% of respondents strongly agree or agree that they can rely on the Northern Alliance HARP CDM program manager to do what she commits to. (100% = PM, TL, and ES; 75% team members)

Table 4. Northern Alliance HARP CDM Program vision and objectives

2.2 The Northern Alliance HARP CDM Program has a well-established vision and objectives.					
	Strongly Agree	Agree	Neutral	Disagree	Strongly Disagree
	5	4	3	2	1
PM, ES, and TL	0%	53.33%	33.33%	13.34%	0%
Team Members	23.81%	19.05%	47.62%	9.52%	0%
All Respondents	13.89%	33.33%	41.67%	11.11%	0%

Table 5. Results for team components questions

Question Number	PM, ES, and TL		Team Members		All Respondents	
	Mean	SD	Mean	SD	Mean	SD
2.5 Commitment	4.4	0.98	4	2.0	4.16	1.71
2.6 Role Clarity	4.43	1.25	3.74	2.06	4	1.92
2.9 Group Potency	3.4	1.42	3.19	1.70	3.28	1.61
2.10 Team Norms	3	1.57	3.38	2.0	3.24	1.88
4.1 Internal Team Learning	3.29	1.40	3.64	1.66	3.5	1.60
5.2 External Team Learning	3.8	1.08	3.2	1.96	3.46	1.75

Team

Works Effectively as a Team

The optional comments provided by the program manager, executive sponsors, and team leaders group demonstrate acknowledgement from this group of respondents that the Northern Alliance HARP CDM Program has only recently commenced to work together and consider itself a "team" and that while this is improving, considerable work is still required for the Alliance to work effectively as a team. While some services of the program continue to work relatively independently, others work together more effectively due to direct clinical links.

A number of team members indicated that they were unaware of the Northern Alliance HARP CDM Program.

Vision and Objectives

The Northern Alliance HARP CDM Program has not yet established its vision and objects.

Forty-seven percent of all respondents indicated that they agreed or strongly agreed that the Northern Alliance HARP CDM Program has a well-established vision and objectives. This indicates that they are in the Unconscious Incompetence stage of learning (conscious competence learning matrix) and were unaware that the virtual team's vision and objectives are yet to be developed. Forty-two percent of all respondents were neutral about the Northern Alliance HARP CDM Program vision and objectives.

It is probable that the virtual team members that responded positively consider the vision and objectives of the individual services (previously projects) within the Northern Alliance HARP CDM Program to be the vision and objectives of the alliance itself.

The mean result for both the PM, ES, and TL and the team members groups of respondents (4.4 and 4) indicates that members of the virtual team feel committed to the Northern Alliance HARP CDM Program.

The mean results for "I understand my role within the Northern Alliance HARP CDM Program" also reflects agreement about role clarity within of the different groups in the virtual team (mean and median results for all respondents were 4). While the mean result to this question for the team members group was 3.74.

The virtual team perceptions about group potency, established team norms, internal team learning, and external team learning were less positive. The responses indicated that respondents were Neutral about these elements of an effective virtual team (refer to Figure 3 and Table 5).

Organisational Culture

The results from the Organisational Culture Components series of questions indicate:

- Agreement with organisational culture questions about involvement in decision making and a willingness for change and innovation is higher in PM, ES, and TL group of respondents (mean of 4 and 4.2 respectively)
- A sense of empowerment is greatest in the team members group (mean = 3.77) though still within the neutral range
- Results for positive work environment and focus on teamwork were similar in each groups of respondents (Refer to Table 6 and Figure 4)

Electronic Communication Technologies

Fifty-six point eight percent of all respondents indicated agreement that the communication tools and resources within the Northern Alliance HARP CDM Program allowed them to be as productive as possible.

Table 6. Results for organisational culture components questions

	PM, ES, and TL	Team Members	All Respondents
7.1 Decision Making	4	3.3	3.58
7.2 Change and Innovation	4.2	3.59	3.84
7.3 Positive Work Environment	3.73	3.77	3.76
7.4 Empowerment	3.53	3.77	3.68
7.5 Focus on Teamwork	3.87	3.86	3.86

Figure 4. Organisational culture components

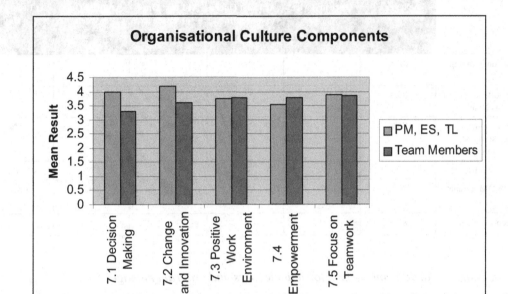

Table 7. Communication tools and resources

	8.1 The communication tools and resources we have allow me to be as productive as possible.				
	Strongly Agree	Agree	Neutral	Disagree	Strongly Disagree
	5	4	3	2	1
PM, ES, and TL	0%	42.9%	42.9%	7.1%	7.1%
Team Members	13.0%	52.2%	26.1%	8.7%	0%
All Respondents	8.1%	48.7%	32.4%	8.1%	2.7%

Table 8. Information about activities of the Northern Alliance HARP CDM Program

	8.2 I have access to information about activities of the Northern Alliance HARP CDM Program.				
	Strongly Agree	Agree	Neutral	Disagree	Strongly Disagree
	5	4	3	2	1
PM, ES, and TL	6.7%	66.6%	6.7%	20%	0%
Team Members	0%	47.8%	30.4%	13.0%	8.7%
All Respondents	2.6%	55.3%	21.1%	15.8%	5.3%

Table 9. Results for electronic communication technology questions

	Never	Once or Twice	At Least Once a Month	At Least Once or Twice a Month	At Least Once a Week	At Least Once a Day
Video conferencing	100%					
Group software (e.g., Lotus Notes)	85%				3%	12%
Electronic Newsgroups/ Bulletin Boards	76%	9%	3%	6%		6%
E-mail	3%	3%	3%	3%	17%	71%
HARP CDM intranet	76%	6%	3%	3%	9%	3%
Teleconferencing	85%	15%				

Table 10. Staff satisfaction comparison for team leaders and program manager

	Strongly Agree	Agree
2.5 Commitment	50%	50%
2.6 Role clarity	66.7%	33.3%
2.7 Everyone's view is listened to	16.7%	83.3%
3.1 Evidence of effective leadership	16.7%	83.3%
3.7 Identification with leader	100%	
3.8 Support for leader	100%	
3.9 Trust	60%	40%
3.15 Accessibility	40%	60%
6.4 Satisfactory quality of work	16.7%	83.3%
7.2 Innovation and change	50%	50%
7.3 Positive work environment	16.7%	66.7%
7.5 Focus on team work		83%

The greatest level of disagreement (14.2%) that the communication tools allowed individuals to be productive was in the PM, ES, and TL group of respondents.

Seventy-three point three percent of PM, ES, and TL agreed or strongly agreed that they have access to information about the activities of the Northern Alliance HARP CDM Program. This compares to only 47.8% of the team members respondents.

Ninety-seven percent of staff have used e-mail while working in the Northern Alliance HARP CDM Program (71% at least once a day).

Twenty-four percent of staff have used electronic newsgroups/bulletin boards while working in the Northern Alliance HARP CDM Program.

Table 11. Staff satisfaction comparison for team members

	Strongly Agree	Agree
2.5 Commitment	55.6%	44.4%
3.7 Identification with leader	75%	25%
3.9 Trust	71%	14%
4.2 Internal team learning	22.2%	77.8%
6.4 Satisfactory quality of work	37.5%	62.5%
7.2 Innovation and change	42.9%	42.9%
7.3 Positive work environment	25%	62.5%
7.4 Empowerment of members	50%	37.5%
7.5 Focus on team work	42.9%	51.1%

Fifteen percent of staff use group software in their work in the Northern Alliance HARP CDM Program.

FURTHER ANALYSIS AND DISCUSSION

Staff Satisfaction Comparison

The following analyses aimed to identify relationships between staff satisfaction and other components of virtual team effectiveness.

For each of the following staff satisfaction comparisons, respondents included in the analysis indicated agree or strongly agree for each of the four employee satisfaction questions (1.1, 1.2, 1.3, and 1.4).

Team Leaders and Program Manager

Executive sponsors were not included in this comparison, as their employee satisfaction would not be directly related to the functioning of the virtual team.

The total number of respondents (sample size) was 11. The number of respondents fulfilling criteria (n) was 6 (55%).

Results indicate that high employee satisfaction among the team leaders and program manager of this virtual team is related to high levels of commitment, role clarity, evidence of effective leadership, identification with leader, trust, accessibility of leader, high perception of team performance, a culture of innovation and change, a positive work environment and a focus on team work and support (Refer to Table 10).

Team Members

The total number of respondents (sample size) was 23. The number of respondents fulfilling criteria (n) was 9 (39%).

In addition to the components identified for the program manager and team leaders group of respondents, internal team learning, and empowerment of team members were further determinants of high employee satisfaction for the team members group (Refer to Table 11). For this group of respondents, however, accessibility of the program manager, role clarity, evidence of effective leadership and support for leader were not related to high employee satisfaction.

Perception of Effectiveness

The following analyses aimed to identify relationships between employee perception of team effectiveness and other components of virtual team effectiveness.

For each of the following perception of effectiveness comparisons, respondents included in the analysis indicated agree or strongly agree for Question 2.1 "The Northern Alliance HARP CDM Program works effectively as a team."

Team Leaders and Program Manager

The total number of respondents (sample size) was 11. The number of respondents fulfilling criteria (n) was 3 (27%).

The criteria in Table 12 appear to be related to a perception of virtual team effectiveness for the team leaders and program managers (as the respondents also rated agreement with these items).

In addition to the components determinant of high employee satisfaction, high team leader, and program manager perception of team effectiveness is also related to clear leadership behaviours, team discussion about ways to prevent and learn from mistakes and an involvement in decision making.

Team Members

The total number of respondents (sample size) was 23. The number of respondents fulfilling criteria (n) was 8 (35%).

The criteria in Table 13 appear to be determinants of a perception of virtual team effectiveness for these team members (as the respondents also rated agreement with these items):

Executive Sponsors

Fifty percent (n=2) of the Executive Sponsors Agreed or Strongly Agreed that "The Northern

Table 12. Perception of effectiveness comparison for team leaders and program manager

	Strongly Agree	Agree
2.5 Commitment	33.3%	66.7%
2.6 Role clarity	66.7%	33.3%
2.7 Everyone's view is listened to	33.3%	66.7%
3.1 Evidence of effective leadership	16.7%	83.3%
3.5 Leadership behaviours		100%
3.7 Identification with leader	100%	
3.8 Support for leader	100%	
3.9 Trust		100%
3.15 Accessibility	40%	60%
4.1 Internal team learning		100%
6.4 Satisfactory quality of work	16.7%	83.3%
7.1 Involvement in decision making	33.3%	66.7%
7.2 Innovation and change	50%	50%
7.5 Focus on team work		100%

Table 13. Perception of effectiveness comparison for team members

	Strongly Agree	Agree
3.7 Identification with leader	50%	50%
3.9 Trust	57.1%	42.9%
3.10 Accessibility	14.3%	71.4%
4.2 Internal team learning		87.5%
6.4 Satisfactory quality of work	25%	75%

Table 14. Perception of effectiveness comparison for team leaders and program manager—lack of effectiveness

Question		Response	
2.10	Team Norms	Disagree	66.7%
4.2	Internal Team Learning	Disagree	66.7%

Alliance HARP CDM Program works effectively as a team."

The determinants for a perception of an effective virtual team for these executive sponsor respondents were:

- Role clarity
- The Northern Alliance HARP CDM Program is open and responsive to change
- Clear leadership behaviours from the program manage
- Identification with the program manager
- Trust of the program manager
- Accessibility of the program manager
- External team learning
- Satisfactory quality of work
- Involvement in decision making
- The Northern Alliance HARP CDM Program willingness to change and innovation
- Access to information

Therefore, for all roles within the Northern Alliance HARP CDM Program, the most common determinants of a perception of effectiveness of the virtual team are:

- Trust
- Accessibility
- Identification with leader
- Satisfactory quality of work

Twenty-seven percent (n=3) of team leaders and program manager group of respondents disagreed or strongly disagreed with Question 2.1 "The Northern Alliance HARP CDM Program works effectively as a team."

The Table 14 components appear to be determinants of this perception.

Key Challenges of Working Within the Northern Alliance HARP CDM Program

Many of the responses to the question of challenges of working within the virtual team refer to the embryonic state of the Northern Alliance HARP CDM Program virtual team development. The fundamental challenges identified by the program manager, executive sponsors, and team leaders group were:

- The building of the team with common approaches, linkages and common processes. Streamlining and synchronising team processes and structures
- The merging of different agencies with different organisational cultures, priorities, and approaches
- Communication between all components/ services of the program
- Infrastructure and access to IT particularly for the community organisations
- Achieving a consistency in data collection and balancing the duality of local and virtual reporting

The responses of three team members clearly demonstrate the lack of knowledge of this group about the Northern Alliance HARP CDM Program:

- "Getting to meet them in the first place"
- "Involving each separate program so that they are aware of each other"

- "Not knowing much about the Northern Alliance HARP CDM Program

While several of the team member responses referred to the challenge of cross program communication, many of the reported challenges related to individual services and direct clinical/patient care provision issues.

Key Successes of the Northern Alliance HARP CDM Program

Respondents identified the following key successes of the Northern Alliance HARP CDM Program:

Virtual Team Successes

- The establishment of one program across funding boundaries with the sharing of ideas and expertise
- The development of cross sector partnerships at a governance level with shared commitment to a single set of goals

Exhibit 1.

Team Cultural Traits
Team cohesion
Respect for colleagues and diversity
Good communication
High staff knowledge and skill base
Hardworking

Leadership Cultural Traits
Support
Trust
Good communication

Organisational Cultural Traits
Empowerment
Flexibility
Positive work environment
Innovation
Focus on continuous improvement, evaluation and evidence-based practice

Care Delivery Successes

Achieving the greater HARP goals of reduced hospital admissions whilst contributing significantly to positive health outcomes and experiences for clients

Desirable Cultural Traits within the Northern Alliance HARP CDM Program

The traits shown in Exhibit 1 were reported as desirable cultural traits within the Northern Alliance HARP CDM Program.

A number of respondents described inclusiveness and cooperation as desirable cultural traits.

To feel like a valuable and informed team member involved in the development of the program" said a team member.

Undesirable Cultural Traits within the Northern Alliance HARP CDM Program

A persisting "single project mentality" related to the early stage of development of the Northern Alliance HARP CDM Program underpins the undesirable cultural traits identified by respondents. Staff currently identify themselves by their individual service, not as being part of the Northern Alliance HARP CDM Program. Respondents identified a tendency towards operating in silos and competition between some services within the Northern Alliance HARP CDM Program. Other related undesirable cultural traits include a lack of commitment to a common purpose and a segregation of services.

Figure 5. Conceptual framework of components required to maximise virtual team effectiveness

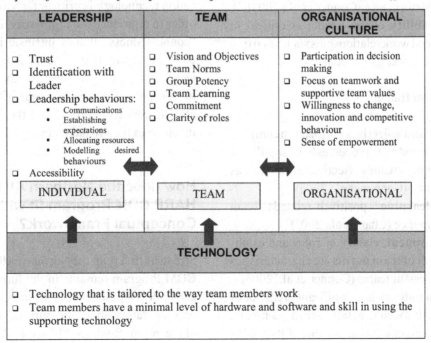

THE CONCEPTUAL FRAMEWORK OF VIRTUAL TEAM EFFECTIVENESS

The proposed conceptual framework of virtual team effectiveness (Refer to Figure 5) was constructed on the basis of a literature review of determinants influencing the effectiveness of virtual teams (for detail see the Literature Review section of this chapter).

The four key frames are leadership, team components, organisational culture, and technology.

In the leadership frame:

- **Trust** reduces complexity and is therefore important to the formation and development of any new work team (Glacel, 1997 cited in Holton, 2001; Paul et al., 2004)
- **Identification with leader** increases team member commitment and aligns individuals with organisational interests and beliefs (Connaughton et al., 2004)
- **Leadership behaviours** encourage virtual team performance (Conner et al., 2003)
- **Accessibility** of the Leader is critical in distanced work relationships such as virtual teams (Connaughton et al., 2004).

In the team frame:

- **Vision and objectives** is a focus on common purpose and work processes has a significant impact on a team's effectiveness as well as efficiency (Conner et al., 2003)
- **Team learning** is positively related to team performance (Chan et al., 2003)
- **Commitment, clarity of roles** and establishment of **team norms** are characteristics of successful teams (Conner et al., 2003)
- **Group potency** is a significant predictor of productivity, satisfaction of team members, and management assessments of its performance (Campion et al., 1993, 1996 cited in Gil et al., 2005).

In the organisational culture frame:

- **Participation in decision making** is associated with greater team member commitment to executing the decisions
- Cultures that provide workers with a **sense of empowerment** within health care organisations have more successful outcomes
- **A focus on teamwork and supportive team values** are contributors to performance.
- Cultures that stress **willingness to change and innovation** are better performers (Platonova et al., 2006).

These three frames do not exist or function in isolation. Organisational culture will influence both team and leader behaviour and performance, and there is also interdependency between leadership styles and competencies and the team performance and organisational culture.

In the technology frame, electronic communication technology is critical for virtual teams in order to reproduce the familiarity, intimacy, and "connectedness" that is intrinsic in traditional co-located teams (Conner et al., 2003). Therefore, technology (hardware, software, and applications) must support the specific needs of the individuals, the collective group, and the organisations involved in the virtual team.

How does the Northern Alliance HARP CDM Program fit within the Conceptual Framework?

Still in its first year, the Northern Alliance HARP CDM Program remains in the forming stage of group development. This stage is characterised by uncertainty about the purpose and structure of the group (Robbins, Millett, & Waters-Marsh,

Figure 6. The conceptual framework and the results of the Survey of Northern Alliance HARP CDM Program

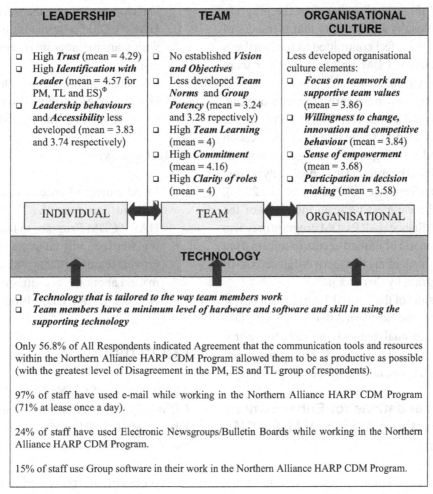

LEADERSHIP	TEAM	ORGANISATIONAL CULTURE
☐ High *Trust* (mean = 4.29) ☐ High *Identification with Leader* (mean = 4.57 for PM, TL and ES)ᵠ ☐ *Leadership behaviours* and *Accessibility* less developed (mean = 3.83 and 3.74 respectively)	☐ No established *Vision and Objectives* ☐ Less developed *Team Norms* and *Group Potency* (mean = 3.24 and 3.28 repectively) ☐ High *Team Learning* (mean = 4) ☐ High *Commitment* (mean = 4.16) ☐ High *Clarity of roles* (mean = 4)	Less developed organisational culture elements: ☐ *Focus on teamwork and supportive team values* (mean = 3.86) ☐ *Willingness to change, innovation and competitive behaviour* (mean = 3.84) ☐ *Sense of empowerment* (mean = 3.68) ☐ *Participation in decision making* (mean = 3.58)

INDIVIDUAL ⟷ TEAM ⟷ ORGANISATIONAL

TECHNOLOGY

☐ *Technology that is tailored to the way team members work*
☐ *Team members have a minimum level of hardware and software and skill in using the supporting technology*

Only 56.8% of All Respondents indicated Agreement that the communication tools and resources within the Northern Alliance HARP CDM Program allowed them to be as productive as possible (with the greatest level of Disagreement in the PM, ES and TL group of respondents).

97% of staff have used e-mail while working in the Northern Alliance HARP CDM Program (71% at lease once a day).

24% of staff have used Electronic Newsgroups/Bulletin Boards while working in the Northern Alliance HARP CDM Program.

15% of staff use Group software in their work in the Northern Alliance HARP CDM Program.

ᵠTeam Members tended to refer to Team Leaders as the Program Manager therefore, the All Respondents mean was not included

2004). The forming stage is complete when team members have begun to consider themselves as part of a group. While the team leaders, executive sponsors, and program manager are beginning to move into the next stage of storming represented by intra-group conflict against the control the group imposes on individuality (of the individual projects), the team members are just entering the forming stage (with many unaware of the Northern Alliance HARP CDM Program and the program manager and some only recently employed within the alliance).

The vision and objectives of the Northern Alliance HARP CDM Program are yet to be established, and although responses indicate that there are high levels of support and trust for the leader, many of the team member participants who responded positively identified their team leader as "the leader" rather than the program manager. Results also indicate that members of the virtual team feel committed to the Northern Alliance HARP CDM Program (or their team within this virtual team).

However, even in the early stage of storming, the Northern Alliance HARP CDM Program is fostering a culture of involvement in decision making and a willingness for change and innovation, which has been found to be positively related to team performance (Platonova et al., 2006). A reduced awareness by team members of the Northern Alliance HARP CDM Program may also be symptomatic of limited access to information about activities of the Northern Alliance HARP CDM Program by this group.

The results of the Virtual Team Effectiveness Survey from the Northern Alliance HARP CDM Program were analysed and compared to the proposed Conceptual Framework. Figure 6 is a diagrammatic representation of the comparison.

Recommendations for Enhancement of the Northern Alliance HARP CDM Program

Based on the literature review, results of the Virtual Teams Effectiveness Survey and analysis against the proposed conceptual framework of virtual team effectiveness, the following are recommendations to enhance the functions of the Northern Alliance HARP CDM Program.

Leadership:

- Biannual meeting with the teams (within the virtual team).
- Forum to meet other members of the Northern Alliance HARP CDM Program.
- Web-based forum for interaction between team members on specific topical issues.

Team:

- Development of specific Northern Alliance HARP CDM Program vision and objectives with team member involvement (at all levels).
- Communication of Northern Alliance HARP CDM Program vision and objectives to all members of the virtual team.

Technology:

- Development of an electronic newsgroup/bulletin board for the Northern Alliance HARP CDM Program to facilitate interaction between virtual team members and to provide team members with access to information about the activities of the Northern Alliance HARP CDM Program.

CONCLUSION

The formation of the Northern Alliance HARP CDM Program in 2006 from the union of several DHS funded HARP projects has meant that all members of the Alliance are members of a virtual team.

A conceptual framework of the specific components required to maximise virtual team effectiveness has been developed and proposed based on an extensive review and categorisation of literature relating to virtual teams. This conceptual framework can be used as a tool to examine a team's performance with each of these components (based on virtual team member perception).

The four key frames of the conceptual framework of virtual team effectiveness are leadership, team components, organisational culture, and technology.

The Northern Alliance HARP CDM Program has highly developed Leadership components as reported the team leaders and executive sponsors group. The team members group of respondents also reported agreement with leadership components, however, this group tended to refer to the team leaders (managers of the various services within the alliance) as "the leader" as many team members were unaware of the Northern Alliance HARP CDM Program.

The Northern Alliance HARP CDM Program has yet to establish a vision and objectives. However, the team component results of the virtual team effectiveness survey indicate a perception by all respondents of a focus on team learning, high levels of commitment and clear role distinction.

The results of the Virtual Teams Effectiveness Survey demonstrated less developed organisational culture elements within this virtual team and low levels of agreement that the communication tools and resources within the Northern Alliance HARP CDM Program allowed respondents to be as productive as possible.

For all roles within the Northern Alliance HARP CDM Program, the most common determinants of a perception of effectiveness of the virtual team were trust, accessibility, identification with leader, and satisfactory quality of work.

The implications of this study are significant for virtual team development and enhancement in order to facilitate health care organisation innovation. Additional research is required to establish the relative importance of each of the components in the conceptual framework and to examine the conceptual framework against other measures of effectiveness including financial measures, customer satisfaction, and patient outcomes.

Future Research Directions

The following areas are identified for future research to investigate mechanisms to maximise the effectiveness of virtual teams both for the research into virtual teams in health care as well as for the Northern Alliance HARP CDM Program.

Virtual Team in Health Care Research:

- Examine the relative importance of each of the components in the conceptual framework
- Examine the conceptual framework against other measures of effectiveness including financial measures, customer satisfaction and patient outcomes (Platonova et al., 2006; Richardson et al., 1999)

The Case Study Team:

- Utilise the recommendations of the current research report to inform the virtual team development
- Resurvey the Northern Alliance HARP CDM Program members in 12 months to assess change against the conceptual framework

REFERENCES

Cantu, C. (1997). *Virtual teams*. Retrieved July 26, 2006, from www.workteams.unt.edu/literature/paper-ccantu.html

Chan, C., Pearson, C., & Entrekin, L. (2003). Examining the effects of internal and external team learning on team performance. *Team Performance Management: An International Journal*, *9*(7/8), 174-181.

Connaughton, S. L., & Daly, J. A. (2004). Identification with leader. A comparison of perceptions of identification among geographically dispersed and co-located teams. *Corporate Communications: An International Journal*, *9*(2), 89-103.

Conner, M., & Finnemore, P. (2003). Living in the new age: Using collaborative digital technology to deliver health care improvement. *International Journal of Health Care Quality Assurance, 16*(2), 77-86.

Diamante, T., & London, M. (2002). Expansive leadership in the age of digital technology. *Journal of Management Development, 21*(6), 404-416.

Drew, S., & Coulson-Thomas, C. (1997). Transformation through teamwork: The path to the new organisation? *Team Performance Management, 3*(3), 162-178.

Gil, F., Rico, R., Alcover, C. M., & Barrasa, A. (2005). Change-oriented leadership, satisfaction, and performance in work groups. Effects of team climate and group potency. *Journal of Managerial Psychology, 20*(3), 312-328.

Gould, D. (2006). *Virtual teams*. Retrieved July 26, 2006, from www.seanet.com/~daveg/vrteams.htm

Gould, D. (1997). *Virtual organisation*. Retrieved July 26, 2006, from www.seanet.com/~daveg/ltv.htm

Holton, J. (2001). Building trust and collaboration in a virtual team. *Team Performance Management, 7*(3/4), 36-47.

Kent, T. (2005). Leadership and emotions in health care organisations. *Journal of Health Organisation and Management, 20*(1), 49-66.

Kimball, L. (1997). *Managing virtual teams*. Text of speech given by Kimball, L for Team Strategies Conference, Toronto Canada, 1997. Retrieved July 26, 2006, from http://www.groupjazz.com/pdf/vteams-toronto.pdf

Kimble, C., Li, F., & Barlow, A. (2000). *Effective virtual teams through communities of practice. management science. Theory method & practice.* Strathclyde Business School. Research Paper No.

2000/9. Retrieved July 26, 2006, from http://dissertation.martinaspeli.net/papers/communities-of-practice/kimble-et-al-2000-effective-virtual-teams-through-communities-of-practice

Mannion, R., Davies, H., & Marshall, M. N. (2005). Cultural characteristics of "high" and "low" performing hospitals. *Journal of Health Organisation and Management, 19*(6), 431-439.

Paul, D. L., & McDaniel, R. R. (2004). A field study of the effect of interpersonal trust on virtual collaborative relationship performance. *MIS Quarterly, 28*(2), 183-228.

Platonova, E. A., Hernandez, S. R., Shewchuk, R. M., & Leddy, K. M. (2006). Study of the relationship between organisational culture and organisational outcomes using hierarchical linear modelling methodology. *Quality Management in Health Care, 15*(3), 200-210.

Richardson, M. L., & Gurtner, W. H. (1999). Contemporary organisational strategies for enhancing value in health care. *International Journal of Health Care Quality Assurance, 12*(5), 183-189.

Robbins, S. P., Millett, B., & Waters-Marsh, T. (2004). *Organisational behaviour* (4th ed.). Pearson, Prentice Hall, Frenchs Forest, NSW.

Yavas, U., & Romanova, N. (2005). Assessing performance of multi-hospital organisations: A measurement approach. *International Journal of Health Care Quality Assurance, 18*(3), 193-203.

Yin, K.R. (2008). *Case stydy research: Design and methods.* Sage, CA.

Zhao, F. (2006). *Maximize business profits through e-partnerships.* Hershey, PA: IRM Press.

APPENDIX: SAMPLE QUESTIONS OF THE VIRTUAL TEAMS EFFECTIVENESS SURVEY

1. EMPLOYEE SATISFACTION (Gil et al., 2005; Platonova et al., 2006)

1.1   I get a sense of accomplishment from my work in the Northern Alliance HARP CDM Program.

Strongly Agree	Agree	Neutral	Disagree	Strongly Disagree
5	4	3	2	1

Optional Comment: _____

2.2   My work in the Northern Alliance HARP CDM Program challenges me to use my knowledge and skills.

Strongly Agree	Agree	Neutral	Disagree	Strongly Disagree
5	4	3	2	1

Optional Comment: _____

2. TEAM NORMS (Conner et al., 2003)

1.1   The Northern Alliance HARP CDM Program works effectively as a team.

Strongly Agree	Agree	Neutral	Disagree	Strongly Disagree
5	4	3	2	1

Optional Comment: _____

2.2   The Northern Alliance HARP CDM Program has a well-established vision and objectives.

Strongly Agree	Agree	Neutral	Disagree	Strongly Disagree
5	4	3	2	1

Optional Comment: _____

continued on following page

APPENDIX CONTINUED

3. LEADERSHIP BEHAVIOURS (Conner et al., 2003)

1.1   I see strong evidence of effective leadership from the Northern Alliance HARP CDM Program management structure.

Strongly Agree	Agree	Neutral	Disagree	Strongly Disagree
5	4	3	2	1

Optional Comment: _____

2.2   I receive appropriate recognition (beyond my pay) for my contributions and accomplishments in the Northern Alliance HARP CDM Program.

Strongly Agree	Agree	Neutral	Disagree	Strongly Disagree
5	4	3	2	1

Optional Comment: _____

Identification with Leader (Connaughton et al., 2004)

4.4   I am willing to put a great deal of effort to help my manager and the Northern Alliance HARP CDM Program be successful.

Strongly Agree	Agree	Neutral	Disagree	Strongly Disagree
5	4	3	2	1

Optional Comment: _____

4.5   I fully support the Northern Alliance HARP CDM Program Manager

Strongly Agree	Agree	Neutral	Disagree	Strongly Disagree
5	4	3	2	1

Optional Comment: _____

Trust (Connaughton et al., 2004; Paul et al., 2004)

continued on following page

APPENDIX CONTINUED

4.6   I can rely on the Northern Alliance HARP CDM program manager to do what she commits to.

Strongly Agree	Agree	Neutral	Disagree	Strongly Disagree
5	4	3	2	1

Optional Comment: _____

4.7   The Northern Alliance HARP CDM Program Manager has my best interests at heart.

Strongly Agree	Agree	Neutral	Disagree	Strongly Disagree
5	4	3	2	1

Optional Comment: _____

Isolation (Connaughton et al., 2004)

4.8   I often feel disconnected from what is happening in the Northern Alliance HARP CDM Program.

Strongly Agree	Agree	Neutral	Disagree	Strongly Disagree
5	4	3	2	1

Optional Comment: _____

4.9   I often feel that I am not really part of the Northern Alliance HARP CDM Program because I am located so far away.

Strongly Agree	Agree	Neutral	Disagree	Strongly Disagree
5	4	3	2	1

Optional Comment: _____

4.10   I often feel disconnected from fellow members of the Northern Alliance HARP CDM Program located apart from me.

continued on following page

APPENDIX CONTINUED

Strongly Agree	Agree	Neutral	Disagree	Strongly Disagree
5	4	3	2	1

Optional Comment: _____

4.11   The physical distance between the Northern Alliance HARP CDM Program Manager and I leave me feeling isolated.

Strongly Agree	Agree	Neutral	Disagree	Strongly Disagree
5	4	3	2	1

Optional Comment: _____

Accessibility (Connaughton et al., 2004)

4.12 I can easily reach the Northern Alliance HARP CDM program manager when I need to communicate with her.

Strongly Agree	Agree	Neutral	Disagree	Strongly Disagree
5	4	3	2	1

Optional Comment: _____

4. INTERNAL TEAM LEARNING (Chan et al., 2003)

1.1   In the Northern Alliance HARP CDM Program, people discuss ways to prevent and learn from mistakes.

Strongly Agree	Agree	Neutral	Disagree	Strongly Disagree
5	4	3	2	1

Optional Comment: _____

1.2   We regularly take time to figure out ways to improve our work processes.

continued on following page

APPENDIX CONTINUED

Strongly Agree	Agree	Neutral	Disagree	Strongly Disagree
5	4	3	2	1

Optional Comment: _____

5. EXTERNAL TEAM LEARNING (Chan et al., 2003)

1.1   The Northern Alliance HARP CDM Program frequently coordinates with other groups to meet organisational objectives.

Strongly Agree	Agree	Neutral	Disagree	Strongly Disagree
5	4	3	2	1

Optional Comment: _____

2.2   The Northern Alliance HARP CDM Program keeps others in the organisation informed about what we plan and accomplish.

Strongly Agree	Agree	Neutral	Disagree	Strongly Disagree
5	4	3	2	1

Optional Comment: _____

6. TEAM PERFORMANCE (Chan et al., 2003)

1.1   Recently, the Northern Alliance HARP CDM Program seems to be "slipping" a bit in its level of performance and accomplishments.

Strongly Agree	Agree	Neutral	Disagree	Strongly Disagree
5	4	3	2	1

Optional Comment: _____

1.2   Others often complain about the Northern Alliance HARP CDM Program's work.

continued on following page

APPENDIX CONTINUED

Strongly Agree	Agree	Neutral	Disagree	Strongly Disagree
5	4	3	2	1

Optional Comment: _____

7. CULTURE (Platonova et al., 2006)

1.1   I am able to be involved in the decision making which occurs in the Northern Alliance HARP CDM Program.

Strongly Agree	Agree	Neutral	Disagree	Strongly Disagree
5	4	3	2	1

Optional Comment: _____

1.2   The Northern Alliance HARP CDM Program encourages a willingness to change and innovation.

Strongly Agree	Agree	Neutral	Disagree	Strongly Disagree
5	4	3	2	1

Optional Comment: _____

8. TECHNOLOGY

1.1   The communication tools and resources we have allow me to be as productive as possible. (Conner et al., 2003).

Strongly Agree	Agree	Neutral	Disagree	Strongly Disagree
5	4	3	2	1

Optional Comment: _____

1.2   I have access to information about activities of the Northern Alliance HARP CDM Program. (Connaughton et al., 2004)

continued on following page

Strongly Agree	Agree	Neutral	Disagree	Strongly Disagree
5	4	3	2	1

1.3   In the last 12 months, how often (while working in the Northern Alliance HARP CDM Program) have you used the following electronic communication technologies?
(Please fill in one circle for each question to indicate your response)
(Cantu, 1997)

	Never	Once or Twice	At Least Once a Month	At Least Once or Twice a Month	At Least Once a Week	At Least Once a Day
Video conferencing	O	O	O	O	O	O
Group software (e.g., Lotus Notes)	O	O	O	O	O	O
Electronic Newsgroups/ Bulletin Boards	O	O	O	O	O	O
E-mail	O	O	O	O	O	O
HARP CDM intranet	O	O	O	O	O	O
Teleconferencing	O	O	O	O	O	O

Chapter XII
Rhizomic Network Analysis:
Toward a Better Understanding of Knowledge Dynamics of Innovation in Business Networks

Alexandra Steinberg
Ecole de Management—Lyon, France

ABSTRACT

There is a general consensus that networks and community interaction provide a critical mechanism for innovation. Of recent years, we have seen a growth of interest in the role of social networks, partly fuelled by the fact that the contemporary business world has become more dynamic, complex, and global. Today an increasing number of people work in geographically dispersed networks and across organisational boundaries. With this comes the need to re-think the ways in which innovation emerges across locations, enterprises, and geographies and consequentially, how this can be analysed. However, methods for the analysis of social networks have yet to better understand knowledge dynamics of innovation. It is argued for the need to (1) switch the unit of analysis from individuals' ideas to social construction of knowledge and (2) use the Deleuzo-Guattarian rhizomic view on networks to reveal not only the dynamics of meaning creation, but also those of meaning disruption, both essential conditions for the emergence of new concepts. A new approach, rhizomic network analysis (RNA) is explored, which aims to move analysis beyond mere description of relationship structures towards enabling the differentiation of the type of knowledge dynamics emergent. An example of an entrepreneurial business network is used to illustrate this approach.

INTRODUCTION

In recent years, there has been a growth of online networking sites, and one area that is expanding in the use of these networks is the corporate environment. Businesses are beginning to use online networks as a means to connecting employees and helping them to build profiles. This makes them searchable and be connected to other business professionals. Specifically in **e-business**, since the dotcom crash[1] in 2000, new online business networks have attracted large numbers of entrepreneurs to sign up to their Web sites. These are networks that connect entrepreneurial businesses by industry, functions, geography, and/or areas of interest. Examples in the English speaking arena are Ecademy.com, Ryze.com, and LinkedIn.com.

There is a growing interdisciplinary theoretical and methodological debate about ways in which communities and community interaction via networks can be best explained as a critical mechanism for innovation and knowledge management. On the one hand, there is general consensus that networks have gained a new significance due to the modern challenges of an increasingly complex and global world (e.g., Castells, 1996, Wittel, 2001). Yet, on the other hand, opinions are divided as to how social networks can be best captured analytically and understood in terms of the dynamics they engender for knowledge creation (e.g., Duguid, 2005; Snowden, 2005).

One of the central controversies revolves around social network analysis as perhaps one of the most influential research streams in modern sociology, information science, and organisational studies on the study of social communities in and across organisations (Carley & Hill, 2001; Cross & Parker, 2004). It has brought forward an industry of methods, software, and measurement tools and has provided various business applications of network analysis to describe and compare the structural characteristics of business networks across functional and geographical boundaries of

organisations (Caldwell, 2006a; Caldwell 2006b; Chung, Hossain, & Davis, 2005; Krebbs, 2005). It mainly stems from network theories that study structural representations of relations between objects (Borgatti & Everett, 1999). Social network analysis enables analysis of relation characteristics in networks, which, in turn, can provide insights into communication and information exchange structures and/or into the extent to which different functional organisational areas are integrated in terms of their information exchange processes.

Nonetheless, social network analysis has been widely criticised for its one-sided structural and individualist perspective on **knowledge**, creating a very atomistic view on networks as aggregation of individuals and on **knowledge** creation as a series of interaction processes between people as "knowledge unit holders." These drawbacks have been well summarised by Weissman (2000) in respect of organisation and society and by Snowden (2005) in terms of methods of analysis.

However, despite notable exceptions (Snowden, 2005), there have only been few attempts to forward alternative methods allowing us to generate insights into the social and dynamic characteristics of **knowledge** creation in networks. Despite strong arguments for the urgent need to better conceptualise the informal, social **knowledge** processes, and critiques of the economic underpinning view on **knowledge** (Duguid, 2005), actual alternatives that tackle the dynamic nature of **knowledge** in **innovation** are rare.

Perhaps the most prominent contribution in this arena has been made by social theorists concerned with organisational learning and **knowledge** creation in communities (e.g., Brown & Duguid, 2001; Lave & Wenger, 1991; Nonaka & Nishiguchi, 2001; Senge, 1990; Weick, 2002). Authors oppose individualist economic accounts of **knowledge** creation and argue that **knowledge** is created in inter-subjective, local interpretation processes in work practice (Weick, 2002). In a similar vein, with regard to networks, scholars argue that social **knowledge** creation processes need be located in the social practice of "networks of interest" and "communities of practice" (Duguid, 2005; Weick & Sutcliffe, 2001).

However, as this chapter argues, by leaving core meta-theoretical assumptions unquestioned, theorists have begun to lock themselves into a logical impasse about the ways in which we can think **"knowledge dynamics"** of **innovation**. The argument is that a more fundamental shift in perspective is needed in order to capture the **dynamics** of **knowledge** in networks. If we are to provide explanations as to how **social networks** enable **innovation**, we need to switch from seeing **knowledge dynamics** as mainly driven by social interaction to the dynamic interplay between meaning creation and meaning **disruption**.

This chapter attempts a rebalancing in respect of the use of **social networks** in arguments of **knowledge** creation and **innovation**. **Rhizomic network analysis** (RNA) is introduced as an approach to the qualitative analysis of **knowledge dynamics** in **social networks**. In what follows, I outline the theoretical grounding as well as the analytical approach of RNA. I then illustrate the approach of RNA with the case of the business network ecademy.

BACKGROUND

The approach of RNA is based on a study (Steinberg, 2005, 2006) that explored **knowledge dynamics** of **innovation** in **e-business entrepreneurship** networks. With regards to its theoretical claims, the following has been established:

1. Meta-theoretical assumptions with regard to the nature of **knowledge** are often taken for granted and thereby implicitly hamper research endeavours to better understand **innovation**. By meta-theoretical assumptions, we mean epistemological and ontological assumptions that inform and structure critical enquiry and that shape theorising.

Specifically, in order to better understand **innovation**, the very meta-theoretical assumptions of the nature of **knowledge dynamics**, deeply engrained into contemporary theorising, need to be examined. By **dynamics,** we mean social, intellectual, and/or physical forces that produce activity, movement, and change.

2. The current paradigm of social theorising concerned with alternatives to the dominant individualist, static and structural views on **knowledge** creation has become somewhat trapped in a relativist, anti-realist paradigm of explaining **knowledge** creation through processes of social influence relations between subjects or between subjects and their social context. By and large, social theorists reject essentialist realism, that is, above all the assumption is that **knowledge** exists in pre-existent units in human minds (De-Landa, 1998). However, the turn to context-driven, relational, and cultural concepts has brought with it, in an unquestioned fashion, only one alternative: this is the assumption that dynamic **knowledge** creation is patterned in dialectic influence relations. And this has created a closed and one-sided paradigm in its own right: any natural dynamic that is not patterned dialogically is thereby automatically excluded from analysis.

3. While it is ac**knowledge**d that the human dynamic of knowing is influenced to a considerable extent by physical forces of our embodied existence and the material world, this influence has rarely been examined beyond dialectic influence relations with the social environment. What is overlooked here is that **dynamics** in the physical realm might be patterned in different ways that may have a disruptive and creative effect on our **knowledge**.

Far from claiming that RNA will solve these meta-theoretocal issues in their entirety, this chapter provides a humble first step towards better understanding **knowledge dynamics** of **innovation** by looking at the Deleuzian ontology of becoming to open up our explanatory repertoire towards the more irregular and discontinuous patterns in **knowledge dynamics**. The Deleuzian perspective provides us with a new way of thinking about the ways in which our very nature as biological beings, part and parcel of a material world, continually impinges on the social **dynamics** that bring forth new **knowledge**. The case of **innovation** serves to specifically scrutinise the notion of **disruption**. **Innovation** is not only a social dynamic of **knowledge** creation of new concepts but also the result of the **disruption** of social meaning in sense experience.

THE APPROACH OF RHIZOMIC NETWORK ANALYSIS: CENTRAL ASSUMPTIONS

RNA is an approach to analysing the **knowledge dynamics** of **innovation** in **social networks**. The method is based on **post-structuralist** and **social constructionist** assumptions with regard to the nature of new **knowledge** creation; specifically it looks at **innovation** as a dynamic of the creation of new concepts: it examines the dynamic conditions for the emergence of new concepts in a **social network**. RNA is based on (1) the notion of **social construction** of **knowledge** in processes of social representation (Moscovici 1967/1976, 1984) and (2) the rhizomic view on networks by **Deleuze** and **Guattari** (1987b), which adopts

particularly patterns of **disruption** as essential pre-conditions for **dynamics** of creation.

RNA holds that it is an essential condition for the emergence of **innovation** is that both **social constructionist** and rhizomic **dynamics** are present and well intertwined. It focuses analysis on encounters between the **dynamics** of meaning creation and those of meaning **disruption**. RNA examines these encounters in two steps. Step 1 considers whether **dynamics** of **social construction** and rhizomic **dynamics** are emergent. Specifically, it looks at (1) the extent to which a social reference system is formed and (2) the extent to which a **social network** emerges as rhizomic. These two conditions are summarised in Table 1. Both are based on two central assumptions about the nature of **innovation** as a phenomenon of dynamic **knowledge** creation. Step 2 then looks at the extent to which these two conditions, if present, encounter each other (see Figure 1).

In what follows, these two steps will be outlined in terms of their theoretical and meta-theoretical grounding as well as their positioning in relation to dominant theorising on **knowledge** and **knowledge** creation. This is followed by an illustration of RNA using the example of Ecademy.

STEP 1: Conditions for the Emergence of New (Socially Shared) Concepts

Condition 1: Dynamics of Social Knowledge Construction

The first condition for the emergence of new concepts is the extent to which networks emerge

Table 1. Conditions for the emergence of new concepts

	Condition 1	Condition 2
Network	Extent to which a social reference system is formed	Extent to which network is rhizomic
Focus of analysis	Dynamics of social construction	Dynamics of assemblages and disruptions

as social reference systems. By social reference system, we mean a **community** in which meaning is shared and continually re-created. With this, RNA recognises that **innovation** is partly a phenomenon of social **knowledge** creation and switches the unit of analysis from individuals' ideas in isolation to the **social construction** of **knowledge**. For novelty to emerge as an **innovation** - as an innovative new concept - in the social realm, people need to experience it by collectively making sense of it in communicative interaction.

What does it take to generate an innovation? The desire to seek something new, the satisfaction of finding something, is inextricably linked to sharing, debating, and co-constructing the meaning of these findings with others who also recognize them as new. This is what RNA hones into: the process of socially constructing meaning about a novelty is a key ingredient for **innovation**. If a novel phenomenon does not become socially accepted as an **innovation**, it remains unknown and unacknowledged. But not only entirely novel phenomena can become **innovations**; **social construction** is even more central in cases of **innovation** where it was not an entirely novel phenomena that triggered it, rather a new ways of sense-making of an existent phenomenon.

Think, for instance, of the new-ness that the World Wide Web has introduced. Its innovative character is not merely constituted by the technological invention of the Internet; this has existed long before the actual rise of the concept of online communication. The innovative character of the World Wide Web was rather inherent to what Castells (1996/97) described as the emergence of a new logic of time, space and interaction around the Internet; the novel ways in which actors, information, commodities and capital travel along new routes and connect in novel patterns. Hence, the innovative character of the World Wide Web can be better understood by looking at the ways in which the new world of concepts and ways of sense-making around the Internet emerged; the

way in which worldwide technological connectivity was taken up and made sense of by people collectively.

With this focus on **social construction**, RNA counters classic individual-centred assumptions on the nature of **innovation**, widespread in contemporary theorising. A critical look at contemporary perspectives of **innovation**, both in economic and psychological literatures, highlights a view that assumes **knowledge** to originate primarily in units in individuals' minds. New **knowledge** creation is often causally attributed to new ideas conceived by individual entrepreneurs.

Mainstream economic theorising centrally features the individual entrepreneur as the main unit of analysis with regard to **knowledge** creation in **innovation**. Both Keynesian and neo-classic economic theory portray the entrepreneur as an agent of change whose special abilities drive **innovation** in the economy (Holcombe, 1999). In this literature, the entrepreneur is portrayed as an individual with special qualities that are beneficial for economic growth and **innovation** (Bassetti, 2003; Bolton, 1971; Brockhaus & Horwitz, 1986; Storey, 1982): **knowledge** creation is implied in concepts of traits and qualities of entrepreneurs.

An example of a model that is often drawn on in this context is the knowledge-attitude-belief (KAB) model based on the theory of reasoned action (Ajzen, 1985; Ajzen & Fishbein, 1980). This is still today one of the most widely adopted psychological models in business and policy research on **knowledge** creation[2], postulating a linear relationship between people's individually held **knowledge**, attitudes and behaviour; with mental constructs such as attitudes seen to be the triggers of action. Economic theories drawing on psychological models such as these suggests that better individual **knowledge** will lead to new ideas and thus **innovation**.

More recent conceptualisations of **knowledge** creation take a more social approach, looking at how **innovation** is created in communities and networks. Authors turned away from studying the individual as main unit of analysis, arguing that the emphasis placed on the qualities of the individual has been exaggerated (Filion, 2003). Some have adopted an ecological approach, looking at communities and clusters of organisations and their patterns of interaction when innovating (Aldrich, 1999; Aldrich & Zimmer, 1986; Mezias & Kuperman, 2001). Similarly, situated cognition theorists argue that **knowledge** creation is "situated" in social context, that doing and thinking are intertwined and affect one another (e.g., Brown, Collins, & Duguid, 1989; Clancey, 1994; Lave et al., 1991).

Others look at the impact of modern changes in the nature of social relationships on **innovation**. The core notion is **knowledge** dissemination and the argument is that in today's digitised, globally networked and knowledge-centred economy (Chell, 2000; Quah, 2003; Shane, 2000) it is paramount for successful **innovation** that ideas can diffuse more rapidly and more widely (Agre, 1999; Castells, 1996; Wittel, 2001;). The aim is to better understand the contemporary nature of social relationships in order to explain the extent to which an idea can disperse widely throughout society (Bjornenak, 1997; Chell, 2000; Quah, 2003).

Despite this timely shift in perspective towards a social perspective, in a similarly unquestioned fashion as in economic orthodoxy, **knowledge** is taken to exist in "items" (e.g., Quah, 2003) that are equated with economic commodities such as money, labour, and land (Stacey, 2000). **Knowledge** is typically spoken of as though it were all of a piece; a stable entity-like item that people possess; pre-given, as if it had been in this piece forever; and unified, that is, as though essentially **knowledge** comes in only one kind. A rational and functionalist view on **knowledge** is taken (Smircich, 1983), which portrays **knowledge** as a pre-existent economic resource that can be controlled by humans. It is also a view that is similarly to classic economic theories

locating these **knowledge** units into the minds of individuals.

Opposing this exclusive focus on the individual, RNA draws on the theory of social representations (Moscovici, 1961/1976, 1984) to argue for **knowledge dynamics** as driven by **social construction**. Developed by Serge Moscovici in the 1960s as a theory for "the study of social knowledge" (Moscovici, 2001, p. 9), **social representations theory** locates **knowledge** creation at the interface between the individual and the social. The theory rejects the Cartesian tradition of assuming the individual mind as the location of **knowledge** creation by adopting a Hegelian dialectic approach of creation in order to introduce "a new synthesis between the individual and the social" (Deaux & Philogène, 2001, p. 5).

At the centre of social representation as a dynamic dialectic process of social influence stands the creative force of the unfamiliar. Duveen (2000) called this the power of new ideas. Moscovici suggests that when people are presented with the unfamiliar, as for instance in "competing versions of reality" (Rose et al., 1995), or in different "stocks of **knowledge**" (Flick, 1998), this is perceived by people as a threat (de-Graft Aikins, 2004) and therefore people are "under the compulsion" (Moscovici, 2000, p. 50) of anchoring and objectifying[3] the unfamiliar in the familiar. In other words, the theory argues that in response to the challenge of the unfamiliar, people familiarise the unfamiliar and thus create new **knowledge** by socially re-negotiating (re-presenting) it in a new way (Moscovici, 1984).

The study of social representations offers a framework for studying **knowledge** "in the making," directing attention to the continual reconstruction and adaptation of shared concepts in response to the novel (Moscovici, 2001). From this perspective, the driving force of social **knowledge dynamics** can be understood as the evolution of new meanings in everyday communicative interaction (Flick, 1998), triggered by the need to re-negotiate familiar concepts against unfamiliar, challenging ones in social interaction (Moscovici, 1984).

This perspective provides us with a handle on examining how a **community** reacts to novelty. This is why RNA looks as a first condition of **innovation** at the extent to which a social reference system is emergent in a network. Crucially, this will allow us to diagnose how a **community** is likely to deal with a novelty. If a **community** handles novelty well in that it can be integrated flexibly into the existing set of core meanings then there will be a higher likelihood for new concepts to emerge.

Analytically, RNA establishes this by (1) identifying the core meaning system by means of thematic analysis of data from communicative interaction. Analysing themata means identifying the central shared concepts, the central, most stable and familiar meanings shared by a social **community** (Moscovici & Vignaux, 2000). They are the main evaluative dimensions of sense-making used by a **community** of people as they are well-known, highly familiar social references, perceived as universally justifiable[4]; (2) RNA then looks at the extent to which this system of themata is open or less open to change, looking at the "why?" and "how?" of recent or sudden changes in these themata, seeking to identify challenging or novel phenomena that change was in response to. I will illustrate this procedure methodologically at a later point by using the example of Ecademy. But first, let us consider the second condition of RNA in terms of **innovation**.

Condition 2: Rhizomic Dynamics of Assemblages and Disruptions

The second central condition for new concepts is the extent to which a network is "rhizomic." The term rhizomic refers to **Deleuze et al's** (1987b) notion of the rhizome as an approach to thinking about networks as discontinuous becomings[5]. **Deleuze** et al. assume that what is given to us in experience is not a world of pre-defined beings (es-

sences) but intensive processes of spatio-temporal **dynamics** (becomings) (DeLanda, 1998). This directs attention to the potentialities of becoming: to novel, spontaneously emergent, unexpected connections between seemingly disparate events or phenomena.

Deleuze developed the notion of the rhizome together with his co-author **Guattari** in his later work; it is especially featured in their seminal work "*A Thousand Plateaus*"[6] (Deleuze et al., 1987b). The rhizome is an analogy, looking at networks as phenomena of creation—as phenomena that create multiplicity and expanding complexity in discontinuously overlapping connections (Deleuze et al., 1987b). Based on the image of the underground "hidden" wanderings in plants' roots (Wood & Ferlie, 2003), **Deleuze** et al. see creative **dynamics** in networks emergent from the growth and movement of rhizomes; in their view, creative "becoming" is patterned like the wanderings of a rhizome[7]. From this perspective, creation emerges from unusual assemblages—combinations, mergers, incorporations, and associations, which are only to a little extent tied to existing cultural meanings or relations (Deleuze & Parnet, 1987).

By looking at networks as rhizomic phenomena of becoming, RNA counters that **knowledge dynamics** are exclusively patterned in a predictable way by social influence relations. As has been shown elsewhere (Steinberg, 2005), it is not sufficient to assume the driving force for **innovation** lies exclusively in the social realm of epistemological creation. Rather, the **dynamics** of **social construction** need to be seen in relation to the continuous movement and creation in the embodied and physical world.

While a focus on social **knowledge** construction clearly takes a dynamic perspective on the emergent character of knowledge, and while social representations theory views knowledge creation predicated on the emergence of a novel phenomenon; this novelty, however, is mainly seen as stemming from dialectic differences and tensions, that is, dialectic relations between different types of knowledge held by different communities (Flick, 1998).

Similarly, in the wider social literature on **knowledge** creation and social interaction, a novel idea is widely assumed to be triggered by some form of challenge to our sense making through dialectic influence relations with others or with what we experience. For instance, research on **knowledge** management and organisational learning (e.g., Brown et al., 1991; Hoshmand & Polkinghorne, 1992) focuses in a similar fashion as **social representations theory** on explanations of **knowledge** creation through dialectic influence relations in social practice. Scholars argue that new **knowledge** creation is rooted in and triggered by "knowing" in interaction in organisational practice (Blackler, 1995; Varela, Thompson, & Rosch, 1991).

However, this is a view on **knowledge** as exclusively emergent from existent concepts or entities—notions that at the time they challenge our understanding of something are themselves already "understood" and socially mediated notions. However, this ignores challenges or triggers from "non-concepts," from phenomena that, at the time we experience them, do not make sense or we perhaps experience intuitively or "merely" feel them but they nonetheless impact on our way of sense-making.

Why is this important? To be able to explain how novelty emerges, we need to be able to also account for those "irrational" moments of **disruption** of our sense-making and reflection; those instances when current meaning is disrupted. This might be a feeling, a sudden sense experience or event that does not make sense in terms of a given social reference system of meaningful concepts. Generally, novel phenomena, are usually phenomena that we refer to as original, unheard-of or unexampled, as they do not have any meaning attributed to them (yet). When we experience them we refer to them as intuition, feelings, something that we know without being able to describe.

This is what RNA describes here as **disruption**: a **disruption** of our "normal" everyday way of sense making by something that does not make sense—that does not relate to any pre-existent concept. This is why RNA hones into rhizomic becoming as an important dynamic of **innovation** as this brings knowing closer to the **dynamics** in the material world, which we are crucially part of as biological beings. In this way, we acknowledge that **knowledge** creation is not exclusively a dynamic taking place in the disembodied minds of individuals or in a separate ontological[8] sphere to embodied experience. Rather, it is assumed that new **knowledge** originates primarily in the intersection of the sphere of thought and interaction with the experienced biophysical world.

RNA draws on **Deleuze** et al.'s (1987b) argument for experience of the physical world and its spatio-temporal **dynamics** as the main site to explore conditions for creation (DeLanda, 1998). **Deleuze** et al. challenge the classic meta-physical assumption that thought and understanding rule over human perception in sense experience (Bogue, 1989; Bryant, 2000). The argument is that different human faculties such as thought (faculty of understanding) or sensibility (faculty of sense experience) are all essential in generating creation – creation through continuous **disruption** of each other. In this sense, our sense experience of the material, embodied world may in a similar way determine what we come to construct or make sense of a particular phenomenon, not merely our (disembodied) thought about a phenomenon.

Specifically, for RNA this means that the force of creation and movement in the physical realm needs to be recognised in a particular effect on **social construction**: this is the effect of de-familiarisation. De-familiarisation occurs when a dominant way of sense making in a **community** is disrupted by events. Events, in a Deleuzo-Guattarian sense, are a potential site of the conception of ideas (Deleuze, 1968). And crucially, the Deleuzo-Guattarian notion of events does not refer to the human reflection of experience in

Table 2. Summary of social constructionist and rhizomic dynamics and their effect on knowledge

	Social constructionist dynamics	**Rhizomic dynamics**
Condition	Evolution of shared meanings (themata) of concepts	Rhizomic movement, discontinuous, multiple, divergent flow of events
Knowledge creation	Shared social references and meanings evolving from communicative interaction	New connections arising from crossings and disruptions of different rhizomic patterns
Effect on knowledge	Collective adjustment of knowledge (familiarisation)	Experience disrupting and inspiring knowledge construction (de-familiarisation)

sense-making, rather a condition of possibility, the "inventive potential" (Massumi, 1992, p. 140) of creation that comes with a spatio-temporal dynamic such as physical pressure, tension, differences in intensity.

Looking at networks in such a way, shifts the analytical focus from an exclusive focus on networks as an aggregation of connections between pre-existent human knowledge-nodes in the social world to networks as an intensity of processes of becoming that potentially impact on our sense experience and impact on the way we make sense. We avoid thinking about novelty as being conceived first in the mind, and then later implemented in the experiential realm of action in terms of an "outside" environment. Rather, forces in the "environment" become part and parcel of knowledge dynamics in that it potentially affects and disrupts sense making.

Analysing networks with RNA, then, means (1) conceiving of them as rhizomes, as phenomena of processes of becoming rather than exclusively networks of influence relations between knowledge nodes and (2) exploring the extent to which novel assemblages disrupt social construction; in other words, the extent to which a social network is not only a context of meaning familiarisation but also one of meaning disruption.

Before we move to the second step of RNA, Table 2 provides a summary of social constructionist and rhizomic dynamics as well as of their effect on knowledge.

STEP 2: Three Types of Encounters

As for the second analytical step, RNA looks at the extent to which both conditions of the creation of new concepts, social constructionist and rhizomic dynamics, encounter each other. This is for the reason that social construction without disruptions would mean that there is little amount of change in a social context and vice versa, a high degree of rhizomic dynamics without any presence of social construction would mean that even though there is a lot of movement and creation, there is no human reference system that this movement and creation can cut into; hence, novelty would not even enter the social realm of sense-making. Figure 1 illustrates the three types of encounters that RNA concentrates on, mapping continua of social constructionist and rhizomic dynamics onto each other.

To diagnose innovative knowledge dynamics, then, RNA focuses on the following three forms of encounters.

Type 1 Encounter

This type of encounter describes a social context in which **dynamics** of social **knowledge** construction dominate social sense making. This means people's sense making is revolving around central and socially objectified themata that are rarely challenged. Rather, people frequently reiterate them in discourse and if there is a novel

Figure 1. Knowledge dynamics: Types of encounters

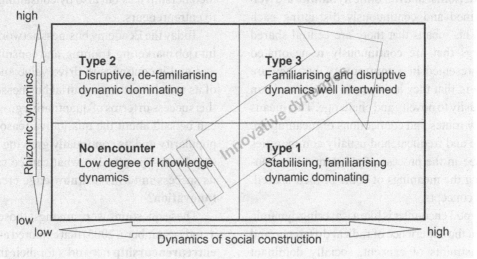

theme presented, people would react with a lot of resistance. This would also mean that overall the dominating dynamic is a familiarising and stabilising effect of certain themata in sense making; people would feel a strong sense of belonging to a certain way of sense-making; hence, a strong and highly familiarised social reference system. By contrast, **disruptions** of such a social reference system would be rare, novelty would usually be rejected or ignored. A highly institutionalised organisation is an example of such a **knowledge dynamic**; it is usually social systems with a strong sense of coherence and ordering, highly static in a sense that meanings and events are often pre-categorised and anticipated. Under such conditions, it is unlikely that novelty is going to surface other than in what might be a temporary **disruption** (perceived negatively) of meaning of a strongly socially accepted and shared concept.

Type 2 Encounter

This type of encounter describes a context in which de-familiarising **dynamics** dominate.

This means that people do not share a sense of belonging to a social reference system, the degree to which themes are shared and continuously re-negotiated is low. Rather, what we would find is a variety of disjointed and dispersed meaning elements that are not integrated or related to any pattern of socially shared and anchored meaning. For instance, we can think of an agglomeration of individuals or groups that are inspired by many new ideas and are very open to change and novelty, yet, who share no reference system to bring these new ideas into relation to. This type of dynamic would usually result in a highly unstable social system, de-centred and multi-facetted but with no social coherence or stability. In a similar vein as in the Type 1 encounter, in such a scenario it is unlikely that novelty is going to evolve socially into shared concepts.

Type 3 Encounter

RNA holds that Type 3 encounters point toward a social context in which new concepts (and thus innovation) are likely to emerge. A Type

3 encounter describes a context in which **social constructionist** and rhizomic **dynamics** are well intertwined and continuously disrupting each other. This means that there are central shared meanings that are continuously re-negotiated and represented in a **community**, but they are flexible in that they are open to change and can adapt easily to novelty and challenge. This means that new routes and connections of meaning are possible and frequent, and usually communities would be in the process of substantially reconstructing the meanings of some of their shared, central concepts.

A Type 3 encounter is like a wavering dynamic between the experience of radical difference and the constraints of existent, socially dominant meanings. Together, this creates a discontinuous rhythm of opening up and closing down, which produces a spiralling dynamic of **disruption** and adaptation of meanings, an alternation between increasing complexity and inspiration by sense experience and the constitution of concepts. This movement, in its new combinations and crossings, allows novelty to be unleashed and while overall, it moves a meaning system forward, at the same time, it hinders it from becoming a chaos.

To illustrate how this diagnostic on **knowledge dynamics** can help the analysis of business networks we now consider the example of Ecademy (Steinberg, 2005).

The Case of Ecademy

In 1998, two entrepreneurs in London's (UK) outskirts launched a **social network** for **e-business** entrepreneurs called Ecademy.com, which involved a Web-based networking service offering online introductions to entrepreneurs, as well as regular networking events in London. They expected initial membership of a dozen additional members per month; they achieved hundreds shortly after launch. Today, they have catapulted their network start-up into a global business network with more than 80,000 members worldwide. In fact, Ecademy has transformed

into a growth engine that is driven not just by membership fees but also by consulting services to entrepreneurs.

Today the Ecademy business network extends into job marketing, training, and consulting services and it continues to drive value and growth of its member entrepreneurial businesses. Given this success in terms of quantitative growth, what can be said about the qualitative reasons for its popularity and its continually growing membership base? Specifically, what can be said about its success in terms of **knowledge** creation and **innovation**?

These questions were amongst those asked in a study (Steinberg, 2005) that explored **e-business entrepreneurship** networks for their innovative **dynamics**. As for the research design used, a novel combination of methods of analysis was used to address the challenge of operationalising the notion of rhizomic **dynamics**; an area that has been virtually unexplored from a methodological angle. The methodological design of this study is outlined in detail elsewhere (Steinberg, 2005); in what follows I briefly outline the main points.

1. RNA necessitates some form of thematic analysis of the content of people's discourse. This is important as the **dynamics** of **social construction** are mainly to be captured by tracing changes in themata in communicative interaction. In this study, this was realised by analysing the content of 25 semi-structured interviews and a focus group with **e-business** entrepreneurs.

2. RNA requires explorative sampling of respondents; a pre-defined population with socio-demographic boundaries would contradict the aim of better understanding networks in its character as social reference systems, which span across organisational or other **community** boundaries. The study adopted an approach of data corpus construction which is functionally identical to purposive sampling (Bauer & Aarts, 2000; Gillespie, 2004; Gaskell & Bauer, 2000), yet

samples contents, such as shared meanings and novel phenomena. There were minimal candidate criteria for potential respondents: (1) respondents had to be actively involved in creating a nascent small or medium-sized businesses since or since shortly before the dotcom crash; (2) respondents' entrepreneurial business had to be in Internet-enabled business (Small Business Service, 2004; Whinston, Barua, Shutter, Wilson, & Pinnell, 2001) and (3) the location of the business had to be London[9].

3. The focus on RNA on rhizomic **dynamics** demands a novel approach to data analysis, one which integrates Deleuzo-Guattarian ideas into social psychological analysis. While the importance of Deleuzo-Guattarian logic is claimed by many scholars, convincing empirical investigations of their ideas are rare. However, as Brown and Lunt (2002) have argued, Deleuzo-Guattarian ideas offer the possibility of a novel re-interpretation of classic procedures of research. They invite us to re-think the variety of methods that researchers have at their disposal in the context of a new understanding of a theory. What matters, they argue, is not the research instruments per se, but,

the way we approach [research methods], the phenomena we choose to attend to ..., and the way in which we understand the relationship between the [research method] and the theoretical ... (Brown et al., 2002, p. 20)

With this in mind, the study cited here proves an example of how the Deleuzo-Guattarian notion of **disruptions** and assemblages was operationalised by triangulating (Flick, 1992) the data from the interviews and the focus group with a Deleuzo-Guattarian interpretation of participant observation (Steinberg, 2005).

Participant observation was chosen as it was important to "think becoming" along Deleuzo-

Guattarian lines, allowing the researcher to escape "the process of question and answer [which] is made to nourish dualisms" (Deleuze et al., 1987, p. 19). This is important as we are interested in **disruption**, in events of de-familiarisation rather than the familiarising dynamic of social dialogue re-iterating central themata. Participant observation enabled to turn to a "rhizomic mode of analysis" that leaves behind the "grille" (Deleuze et al., 1987, p. 19) of invested concepts—in this case, the invested dialectic concepts about networking. It offers the opportunity to concentrate on what was presented rather than re-represented (Deleuze, 1983) and thus to highlight particularly those phenomena in my experience of networking that did not "make sense" either in relation to the "grille" of concepts in an a list of questions for an interview or focus group (researcher's expectations).

In parallel to the interviews and the focus group, I "observed-as-participant" in entrepreneurs' firms when interviewing, in coffee houses, a business fair and at networking events. Networking events took place in restaurants, bars, a media club, and a theatre. I participated in online networking as well as in eight face-to-face events. In experiencing what entrepreneurs experienced I concentrated on phenomena that were ambivalent to dialectic patterns from either my own expectations (such as in the interview topic guide) or from interview discourse. I focused on startling phenomena I experienced, events which did not translate into any pre-existent concepts (in my own or respondents' discourse) and new connections that would seem counter-intuitive to be working together (according to pre-existent concepts) yet, nonetheless, worked extremely well together.

Ecademy: A New Concept of Trusted Business Networking

The case of Ecademy was an example of a network where there were several indicators for Type 3 encounters in **knowledge dynamics**. At first sight, Ecademy's success seemed to be due to the fact that first, it grew considerably in terms of membership numbers and second, successfully launched new services that could be offered to the network members. One could conclude from this that the success of this network was mainly a case of revenue through consulting services. This would, however, leave unexplained as to why it became so popular and why it grew so rapidly in terms of membership numbers.

The analysis with RNA showed that the success of Ecademy was not exclusively a case of sales of consulting services, but also an innovative new form of business network that enabled trusted business relationships. Specifically, RNA surfaced an emergent **knowledge** dynamic that showed how a dominant shared theme about trust was becoming disrupted by a novel emergent process of generating trust via online networking. This contributed, at the time of the study, considerable value in fostering a thriving business **community**.

The new concept of trust in Ecademy unfolded in encounters between (1) the **dynamics** of **social construction** of a new social reference system around the **community** of **e-business** entrepreneurs, mediated by the historical challenge of being publicly associated with a negative image of dotcom **entrepreneurship** and (2) rhizomic **dynamics** emergent from new combinations between affect and technology in online networking, which became significant in the everyday experience of networking.

As for the **social constructionist dynamics**, the thematic analysis of the data from semi-structured interviews and the focus group yielded a meaning system that showed that the main meaning at stake was the question of a sense of identity of the modern, post dotcom crash business **community** of **e-business** entrepreneurs. An adaptive dynamic of social representation was found that served respondents to familiarise modern elements of **e-business** with traditional aspects of entrepreneurial business. Three central themata structured entrepreneurs' discourse as evaluative dimensions when sense making of their business **community**: (1) collective versus individual, (2) long-term versus short-term and (3) modern versus traditional.

The question as to whether **e-business entrepreneurship** was associated with the dotcom boom was the main challenge for entrepreneurs and in response, a new social representation of **e-business entrepreneurship** as collective, strategic and long-term business approach had emerged that contrasted dotcom business approaches. Entrepreneurs were in the process of creating a new sense of identity as a business **community** by debating the extent to which **e-business entrepreneurship** has evolved as a modern and new business sector, which is different to dotcom **entrepreneurship**. There was a strong concern for collective-ness as well as for generating strategic, long-term client value. At the same time, entrepreneurs were keen to emphasise that they valued traditional business rules. Together this created a new social reference system, via which respondents evaluated **e-business entrepreneurship** positively as a new era of business against the notion of "dotcom **entrepreneurship**" that was attributed negatively.

As a subset of these central themata found, the theme of "trust vs. distrust" played a prominent role. It served entrepreneurs to oppose the negative dotcom image: respondents constructed a morally "better" version of networking by contrasting them to the "arrogant" and self-interested style of informal networking in the dotcom era. Mainly, the debate framed by the trust-distrust theme can be grouped into two themes: "informal networking events" and "online networking." Face-to-face networking was strongly contrasted to online networking as well as to networking events in the pre-dotcom crash era and more traditional face-to-face events in the realm of business referral networking. Informal networking events were represented as more trustworthy than online networking as they were face-to-face.

As for the rhizomic **dynamics**, the experience of networking via Ecademy had begun to disrupt the dominant way of sense-making of online networking as distrustful. This was mainly due to the fact that trust had begun to emerge from new assemblages[10] of friendship and online networking technologies. Lines of affect and lines of technology[11] crossed each other in new ways, which individuated in a new force that empowered online networking to be trusted. The main phenomenon in which this new assemblage individuated[12] and disrupted sense-making was in the online visibility of one's contacts via the personal profile page.

The personal profile page was at the centre of this dynamic. It was in and around the personal profile pages of members of Ecademy that a buzzing universe of interaction amongst entrepreneurs was found; it was here that the creation of a new social reference system of e-business entrepreneurship took place. The personal profile page was a personal Web-space that Ecademy members were assigned to upon registration. Via one's personal profile page one could publish all types of information about oneself and one's business. Essentially, the personal profile page allowed members to create a profile of oneself and then seek out for connections with "friends" and "friends of friends" online.

The tool of the personal profile page opened up one's personal network to an unlimited array of contacts. Once registered with Ecademy, one was immediately connected to the online universe of personal profile pages and could browse the pages of other entrepreneurs in related business fields or sub-networks. Members could communicate with each other either by leaving a message in their guestbook, or through a "private message" system. One could also directly contact "friends of friends." Equally, one's own page could be accessed by all other members of a network; it was also searchable via a search tool.

However, the sheer limitless potential of expansion of one's personal network was variously disrupted by several tools that make one's contacts publicly visible. A central one was the list of friends. It was a tool featured on each personal profile page, embedded into an automatic process of the online system that tracked one's online interactions. More precisely, the list of friends was a dedicated space on the personal profile page that was automatically generated: whenever two network members requested and confirmed their contact online, it added the names of one's contact to a list on both personal profile pages.

A common way of interacting, therefore, was to contact other entrepreneurs by browsing their personal profile pages, and subsequently sending a guestbook note or personal message. Once a first contact was established, the online system automatically offered the option to "request or confirm friendship" with new contacts. Such confirmation would then result in the name of the contact being displayed on the list of friends, generating a link to that contact's personal profile page from one's own page.

Contacts that network members made in this way were called "friends." There were a variety of "contact management tools" such as private messaging, guestbook features, special interest sub-groups, Weblogs and message boards—all of which could be used to generate new contacts.

This way of interacting online let friendship become an online tool for entrepreneurs: a technology of making business contacts that integrated the personal profile page into the daily socialising apparatus of entrepreneurs. The ways in which lines of technology and lines of affect became enmeshed in Ecademy created new conditions for rearrangements in trust that would otherwise depend primarily on face-to-face interaction. Online interaction became a viable medium to establish trusted relationships amongst entrepreneurs.

Gathering contacts via tools such as the list of friends on Ecademy became a major business activity that was deemed as contributing to entrepreneurs' trustworthiness and credibility for future business. The more a network member could "prove" via the quantity and quality of "friends" on the list of friends and via the amount of guest-book sign-ins that he or she "had" friends, the more this person was deemed trustable and successful. The technology of visualisation of one's contacts thus also became an affect-becoming of technology in that the visualisation of one's network of friends was the central "organ" of the network—a large and "busy" list of friends online emerged as a quality criterion for trustworthiness as a business.

What emerged was that networking online became part of the entrepreneurs' technology to establish reputation and to be considered a trustworthy business partner. A mechanism of "vetting each other online" arose that functioned much like a quality filter for establishing trust to other potential contacts. The technology of the network became part of one's "real" personal reputation.

This new sense of establishing trusted business connections online variously disrupted the dominant themata of online networking as anonymous and distrustful. The experience of networking provided by Ecademy opened this milieu up to create a new sense of e-business entrepreneurship ready to compete against other types of business, not merely against its own history.

This is what made Ecademy innovative: a new dynamic had emerged that empowered entrepreneurs to understand and tackle e-business entrepreneurship in novel ways as a community. A new concept of business networking was shaping that worked for entrepreneurs without being rooted in concepts of trust via proximity or shared history. It was an emergent new concept of trusted business networking that created change in sense making: new potentialities emerged for discourse to be "freed up" from the dominant theme of the shared history of the dotcom boom and the notion of online interaction as distrustful.

But Ecademy had gone one step further. It not only scrutinised the absence of a basis for trust in digitised interaction, but it also connected it in new ways with face-to-face networking. As part of the new concept of trusted business networking, there was a new emergent discourse of "network management": at the time of the study, a new debate of effective network management had begun to emerge amongst some of the Ecademy members. Network management had begun to be discussed as a new factor in generating competitive advantage for e-business entrepreneurship against larger multi-national businesses.

Network management was a notion that built strongly on the concept of trusted business networking and structured networking activities around it. It was, for instance, manifested in that Ecademy had begun to frequently host face-to-face networking events that initially took place in London either biweekly or monthly, at different venues, but also increasingly nation-wide and internationally. These face-to-face meetings were closely intertwined with the trusted online networking via the list of friends. They functioned like an extension of the list of friends that intensified this new form of networking; they extended the list of friends into entrepreneurs' private life as well as their everyday life "outside" the online network - the friendship-technology "became entangled" with the "real" everyday life of entrepreneurs.

Overall, therefore, the intersection of the dominant dialectic meaning-system with the new concept of trusted business networking had the effect of (1) discontinuing the salience of representations of trusted networking in **e-business entrepreneurship** as mainly determined by face-to-face contacts, and of (2) generating a starting point for a new perspective on networking as a type of managed business based on trusted online networking. Together, this enabled **e-business** entrepreneurs to break away from their shared past and move into a new direction of competitive and innovative network management based on a new sense of what it meant to be part of the e-entrepreneurial business **community**.

FUTURE TRENDS

What Ecademy had tackled was the inability of traditional business networks to manage the quantity of contacts and connectivity beyond a certain threshold of size and complexity, but crucially, by, at the same time, addressing issues of anonymity and the risk of false identities in online communication. This supports scholars (e.g., Lash, 2000; Rheingold, 1994; Tucker & Jones, 2000) who argue that there is a new form of trust emergent not only in online interaction, but also generally as a social phenomenon: a new type of network sociality (Wittel, 2001), that, at its very centre, features an emotional attachment to an apparently bodiless and physically disparate way of engaging with others via computer-mediated social **community** (Rheingold, 1994).

In Ecademy, business interaction in the real and virtual worlds have become combined in such a way that it allows entrepreneurs to establish flexible and ephemeral conditions for new business contacts and future partnerships independently of face-to-face contact. Thus, via this type of network, people, places and ideas could be linked into new combinations, generating a new sense of what Castells (1996) called "real virtuality." It was the distinct way in which Ecademy emerged as a **community** held together in real virtuality that was innovative and empowering: friendship and trust acquired a new technological character at the same time as technologies such as the list of friends became gradually part of the "real world" of social interaction of entrepreneurs.

Ecademy's success in terms of its new concept of trusted business networking provides an example that is promising in terms of UK policy for entrepreneurial business support. Since the dotcom crash, there is a growing number of initiatives in UK policy on small business and **entrepreneurship**[13] to enhance entrepreneurs' capabilities and skills (Gibb, 1993). Amongst these are efforts through educational establishments and governmental institutions, such as support agencies (Byers, 2000; DTI, 2000), to equip individual businesses and entrepreneurs with appropriate skills for Internet-enabled business (Small Business Service, 2004).

The case of Ecademy presents an example of what type of business support and **community** entrepreneurs might be seeking. Specifically, given that there is increasingly evidence that policy measures such as the above address entrepreneurs' needs only to a small extent (e.g., Harding, 2002, 2003), the new concept of trusted business networking as illustrated by the case of Ecademy, suggests an approach to **entrepreneurship** policy and intervention that focuses to a greater extent on establishing trusted business networks rather than concentrating exclusively educational measures for individuals.

CONCLUSION

The purpose of this chapter has been to introduce RNA as an approach to diagnose business networks in terms of their **knowledge dynamics** of **innovation**. The main benefits for analysis are (1) that RNA shifts the focus of analysis from structural and relational characteristics of **social networks** to emergent **dynamics** of meaning change in relation to meaning **disruption**, and (2) that thereby RNA allows analysis to assess qualitatively whether there are conditions emergent that would favour the creation of new concepts. This overcomes some of the issues identified with implicit assumptions about the nature of **knowledge** in conventional approaches to analyse **knowledge** creation and **innovation**.

To explore these new diagnostic opportunities further, however, further research is necessary to develop our methodological repertoire to operationalise Deleuzo-**Guattarian** thought on rhizomic **dynamics**. As we have seen in this chapter, RNA was operationalised by means of thematic analysis of discourse and a new approach to data analysis informed by Deleuzo-Guattarian philosophy of "thinking rhizome." While this proved an invaluable first step, nonetheless, specifically the notion of **disruption** needs to be tackled in a more fundamental conceptual way in terms of sense experience. While with the current approach sense experience of networking could be described as "affecting" new assemblages and disrupting sense-making of networking, it would be of great benefit to be able to apply a conceptual construct of affect **dynamics** (based on Deleuzian logic) to guide the analysis.

A promising inroad here is the study of affect and intuition as biopsychological phenomena. Drawing from neuropsychology and cognitive psychology, it is well established in biopsycho-social studies that individual novelty-seeking behaviour can only be examined and understood in relation to the neuro-physical states (emotion, movement, sense and biological rhythms) we are in (e.g., Amabile, 1996, Amabile, Barsade, Mueller, & Staw, 2005; Simonton, 1981). For instance, researchers in this arena look at how real-world complications such as personal interruptions, stress, power conflicts, scheduling constraints, private agendas, and so forth impact on our sense making. These are generally ignored in research, even though they impact on a daily basis on the course of our activities and sense making.

However, the challenge that remains is to find ways in which conceptions such as affect can be moved onto a meta-theoretical platform that recognises rhizomic becoming as patterns of **dynamics**. Rather than assuming dialogic influence relations between neuo-physical states and sense-making, theorising needs to become more realist taking into consideration dynamic patterns of creation in the material world in their own right. It is time to open a new chapter in the study of **knowledge dynamics**: that of the inter-relation between embodied sense experience and social sense making—yet, not in a essentialist or dialectic sense—in a rhizomic sense.

REFERENCES

Agre, P. E. (1999). *Rethinking networks and communities in wired societies.* University of California. Retrieved 2002, from http://dlis.gseis.ucla.edu/people/pagre/asis.html

Ajzen, I. (1985). From intentions to actions: A theory of planned behaviour. In J. Kuhl & J. Beckmann (Eds.), *Action-control: From cognition to behaviour.* Heidelberg: Springer Verlag.

Ajzen, I., & Fishbein, M. (1980). *Understanding attitudes and predicting social behavior.* Englewood Cliffs, NJ: Prentice-Hall.

Aldrich, H. E. (1999). *Organizations evolving.* London: Sage.

Aldrich, H., & Zimmer, C. (1986). Entrepreneurship through social networks. In D. Sexton & R. Smilor (Eds.), *The art and science of entrepreneurship.* New York: Ballinger.

Amabile, T. M. (1996). *Creativity in context.* Boulder, CO: Westview Press.

Amabile, T. M., Barsade, S. G., Mueller, J. S., & Staw, B. M. (2005). Affect and creativity at work. *Administrative Science Quarterly, 50*(3), 367-403.

Bassetti, P. (2003). *Innovation, social risk, and political responsibility.* London: Public Lecture at the London School of Economics, 14.5.2003.

Bauer, M., & Aarts, B. (2000). Corpus construction: A principle for qualitative data collection. In M. Bauer & G. Gaskell (Eds.), *Qualitative researching with text, image and sound: A practical handbook.* London: Sage Publications.

Berger, P. L., & Luckmann, T. (1966). *The social construction of reality: A treatise in the sociology of knowledge.* Harmondsworth: Penguin, 1967

Bergson, H. (1911/1983). *Creative evolution* (A. Mitchell, Trans.). Lanham, MD: University Press of America.

Bjornenak, T. (1997). Diffusion and accounting: The case of ABC in Norway. *Management Accounting Research, 8*(1), 3-17.

Blackler, F. (1995). Knowledge, knowledge work and organizations: An overview and interpretation. *Organization Science, 16*(6), 1021-1046.

Bogue, R. (1989). *Deleuze and Guattari.* London: Routledge.

Bolton, J. E. (1971). *Small firms: Report of the committee of inquiry on small firms.* London: Her Majesty's Stationery Office.

Borgatti, S., & Everett, M. (2000). Models of core/periphery structures. *Social Networks, 21*(4), 375-395.

Brockhaus, R. H., & Horwitz, P. S. (1986). The psychology of the entrepreneur. In D. Sexton & R. Smilor (Eds.), *The art and science of entrepreneurship.* New York: Ballinger.

Brown, J. S., Collins, A., & Duguid, S. (1989). Situated cognition and the culture of learning. *Educational Researcher, 18*(1), 32-42.

Brown, J. S., & Duguid, P. (1991). Organizational learning and communities-of-practice: Toward a unified view of working, learning, and innovation. *Organization Science, 2*(1), 40-57.

Brown, J. S., & Duguid, P. (2001). Knowledge and organization: A social-practice perspective. *Organization Science, 12*(2), 198-213.

Brown, S. D., & Lunt, P. (2002). A genealogy of the social identity tradition: Deleuze and Guattari and social psychology. *British Journal of Social Psychology, 41*(1), 1-23.

Bryant, L. R. (2000). *The Transcendental Empiricism of Gilles Deleuze* (unpublished manuscript). Chicago: Loyola University of Chicago.

Byers, S. (2000). *"Knowledge 2000"—Conference on the Knowledge Driven Economy.* Department of Trade and Industry. Retrieved February 12, 2002, from http://www.dti.gov.uk/knowledge2000/byers.htm

Caldwell, T. (2006a). Social networking technologies. *Information World Review, 230,* 26.

Caldwell, T. (2006b). Who shares, wins. *Information World Review, 230,* 26.

Carley, K. M., & Hill, V. (2001). Structural change and learning within organization. In A. Lomi & E. R. Larsen (Eds.), *Dynamics of organizations: Computational modeling and organizational thoeries* (pp. 63-92). Live Oak: MIT Press/AAAI Press.

Castells, M. (1996). *The rise of the network society.* Malden, MA: Blackwell.

Castells, M. (1996/97). *The information age: Economy, society, and culture.* Oxford: Blackwell.

Chell, E. (2000). Towards researching the "opportunistic entrepreneur": A social constructionist approach and research agenda. *European Journal of Work and Organizational Psychology, 1 March 2000*(1), 63-80.

Chung, K. S., Hossain, L., & Davis, J. (2005). *Social networks and ICT correlates to individual performance.* Paper presented at the Applications of Social Network Analysis Conference, University of Zurich

Clancey, W. J. (1994). Situated cognition: How representations are created and given meaning. In R. Lewis & P. Mendelsohn (Eds.), *Lessons from learning* (pp. 231-242). Amsterdam: North Holland.

Colebrook, C. (2002). *Understanding Deleuze.* Crows Nest, Australia: Allen & Unwin.

Cross, R., & Parker, A. (2004). *The hidden power of social networks.* Boston, MA: Harvard Business School Press.

Curran, J., & Blackburn, R. (2001). *Researching the small enterprise*. London: Sage.

Deaux, K., & Philogène, G. (2001). *Representations of the social*. Oxford: Blackwells Publishers Inc.

De-Graft Aikins, A. (2004). *Social representations of diabetes in Ghana: Reconstructing self, society, and culture*. Unpublished Thesis, London School of Economics and Political Science, London.

DeLanda, M. (1998). *Deleuze and the open-ended becoming of the World*. Paper presented at the Chaos/ Control: Complexity Conference, Bielefeld, Germany.

Deleuze, G. (1995). *Negotiations*. New York: Columbia University Press.

Deleuze, G. (1983). *Kant's critical philosophy: The doctrine of the faculties*. London: The Athlone Press.

Deleuze, G. (1968). *Différence et répétition*. Paris: Presses Universitaires de France.

Deleuze, G., & Guattari, F. (1987a). *Anti-Oedipus: Capitalism and schizophrenia* (translation). New York: Viking Press.

Deleuze, G., & Guattari, F. (1987b). *A thousand plateaus: Capitalism and schizophrenia*. London: Athlone Press.

Deleuze, G., & Parnet, C. (1987). *Dialogues* (H. Tomlinson & B. Habberjam, Trans.). London: The Athlone Press.

Dodd, S. D., & Anderson, A. R. (2001). Understanding the enterprise culture: paradigm, paradox and policy. *International Journal of Entrepreneurship and Innovation, 2*(1), 13-27.

DTI. (2002). *DTI Data Internet Scoping Study— Section One (the Outsider's View)*. London: Department of Trade and Industry.

DTI. (2000). *A new future for communications—Summary of proposals*. Department of Trade and Industry. Retrieved November 15, 2001, from www.communicationswhitepaper.gov.uk

Duguid, P. (2005). The art of knowing: social and tacit dimensions of knowledge and the limitations of the community of practice. *The Information Society, 21*(2), 109-118.

Duveen, G. (2000). Introduction: The power of ideas. In G. Duveen & S. Moscovici (Eds.), *Social representations: Explorations in social psychology*. Cambridge: Polity Press.

Farr, R. M. (1996). *The roots of modern social psychology, 1872-1954*. Oxford: Blackwell Publishers.

Filion, L. J. (2003). *From entrepreneurship to entreprenology*. HEC, The University of Montreal Business School. Retrieved 2003, from http://www.sbaer.uca.edu/Research/1997/ICSB/97ics006.htm

Flick, U. (1992). Triangulation revisited: Strategy of validation or alternative? *Journal for the theory of Social Behaviour, 22*(2), 175 -197.

Flick, U. (1998). Everyday knowledge in social psychology. In U. Flick (Ed.), *The psychology of the social*. Cambridge, UK, New York, NY: Cambridge University Press.

Gaskell, G., & Bauer, M. (2000). Towards public accountability: Beyond sampling, reliability and validity. In M. Bauer & G. Gaskell (Eds.), *Qualitative researching with text, image and sound: A practical handbook*. London: Sage Publications.

Gibb, A. (1993). The enterprise culture and education. *Entrepreneurship Theory & Practice, 11*(3), 11-34.

Gillespie, A. (2004). *Returning surplus: Constructing the architecture of intersubjectivity*. Unpublished Thesis, University of Cambridge, Cambridge.

Gray, C. (1998). *Entreprise and culture*. London: Routledge.

Harding, R. (2003). *Global entrepreneurship monitor (GEM)—United Kingdom 2003*. London: London Business School.

Harding, R. (2002). *Global entrepreneurship monitor (GEM)—United Kingdom 2002*. London: London Business School.

Hegel, G. W. F. (1830). The encyclopedia of the philosophical sciences (Part 1). The science of logic. In W. Wallace (Ed.), *The logic of Hegel*. London: Oxford University Press (1873).

Hegel, G. W. F. (1807). *Phenomenology of spirit* (A. V. Miller, Trans.). Oxford: Clarendon Press (1977).

Holcombe, R. G. (1999). Equilibrium versus the invisible hand. *Review of Austrian Economics, 12*(2), 227-243.

Holton, G. (1978). *The scientific imagination: Case studies*. Cambridge: Cambridge University Press.

Hoshmand, L. T., & Polkinghorne, D. E. (1992). Redefining the science-practice relationship and professional training. *American Psychologist, January*, 55-66.

Krebbs, V. (2005). Social network analysis software and services for organizations and their consultants. Retrieved June 20 2005, from http://www.orgnet.com

Lash, S. (2000). *Silicon alleys: Networks of virtual objects*. Paper presented at the Virtual Society? Get Real! Conference, 4-5th May, Said Business School, University of Oxford, Hertfordshire, UK.

Lave, J., & Wenger, E. (1991). *Situated learning: Legitimate peripheral participation*. Cambridge: Cambridge University Press.

Marková, I. (2003). *Dialogicality and social representations—The dynamics of mind*. Cambridge: Cambridge University Press.

Marková, I. (2000). The individual and society in psychological theory. *Theory & Psychology, 10*(1), 107-116.

Massumi, B. (1992). *A user guide to capitalism and schizophrenia: Deviations from Deleuze and Guattari*. Cambridge: The MIT Press.

Mezias, S. J., & Kuperman, J. (2001). The community dynamics of entrepreneurship: The birth of the American film industry, 1895-1929. *Journal of Business Venturing, 16*(3), 209-233.

Moore, C. F. (1986). Understanding entrepreneurial behaviour. In J. A. Pearce & R. B. J. Robinson (Eds.), *Academy of management best papers proceedings*. Chicago: Forty-sixth Annual Meeting of the Academy of Management.

Moscovici, S. (2001). Why a theory of social representations? In K. Deaux & G. Philogène (Eds.), *Representations of the social*. Oxford: Blackwells Publishers Inc.

Moscovici, S. (2000). *Social representations: Explorations in social psychology*. Cambridge: Polity Press.

Moscovici, S. (1988). Notes towards a description of social representations. *European Journal of Social Psychology, 18*(3), 211-250.

Moscovici, S. (1984). Introduction: le domaine de la psychologie sociale. In S. Moscovici (Ed.), *Psychologie Sociale*. Paris: Presses Universitaires de France.

Moscovici, S. (1984). The phenomenon of social representations. In R. Farr & S. Moscovici (Eds.), *Social representations*. Cambridge: Cambridge University Press.

Moscovici, S. (1961/1976). *La psychanalyse, Son Image et son Public*. Paris: Presses Universitaires de France.

Moscovici, S., & Marková, I. (2000). Ideas and their development: A dialogue between Serge Moscovici and Ivana Marková. In S. Moscovici (Ed.), *Social representations: Explorations in social psychology*. Cambridge: Polity Press.

Moscovici, S., & Vignaux, G. (2000). The concept of themata. In G. Duveen (Ed.), *Social representations: Explorations in social psychology*. Cambridge: Polity Press.

Nonaka, I., & Nishiguchi, T. (2001). Conclusion: Social, technical, and evolutionary dimensions of knowledge creation. In I. Nonaka & T. Nishiguchi (Eds.), *Knowledge emergence: Social, technical, and evolutionary dimensions of knowledge creation*. Oxford: Oxford University Press.

Quah, D. (2003). *Creativity and knowledge: Managing and respecting intellectual assets in the 21st Century - Clifford Barclay Memorial Lecture*. London School of Economics. Retrieved from http://econ.lse.ac.uk/staff/dquah

Rheingold, H. (1994). *The virtual community—Finding connection in a computerized world*. London: Secker & Warburg.

Rose, D., Efram, D., Gervais, M. C., Joffe, H., Jovchelovitch, S., & Morant, N. J. (1995). Questioning consensus in social representations theory. *Papers on Social Representations, 4*(2), 1-6.

Senge, P. (1990). *The fifth discipline: The art and practice of the learning organization*. New York: Doubleday.

Shane, S. (2000). Prior knowledge and the discovery of entrepreneurial opportunities. *Organization Science, 11*(4), 448-469.

Simonton, D. K. (1981). Creativity in western civilization: Intrinsic and extrinsic causes *American Anthropologist, New Series, 83*(3), 628-630.

Small Business Service. (2004). *A government action plan for small business: Making the UK the best place in the world to start and grow a small business—The evidence base*. London: Department of Trade and Industry.

Smircich, L. (1983). Concepts of culture and organizational analysis. *Adminstrative Science Quarterly, 28*(3), 339-358.

Snowden, D. (2002). Just in time knowledge management. *KM Review, 5*(5), 14-17.

Snowden, D. (2005). From atomism to networks in social systems. *The Learning Organization, Special Issue "Knowledge Sharing," 12*(6), 552-562.

Stacey, R. D. (2000). *Strategic management & organisational dynamics—the challenge of complexity* (3rd ed.). London: Financial Times/ Prentice Hall.

Steinberg, A. (2005). *Emergent knowledge dynamics in innovation: Exploring e-business entrepreneurship after the dotcom crash*. Unpublished thesis, London School of Economics and Political Science, University of London.

Steinberg, A. (2006). Exploring Rhizomic becomings in post dotcom-crash networks: A Deleuzian approach to emergent knowledge dynamics. In F. Zhao (Ed.), *Entrepreneurship and innovation in e-business: An integrative perspective*. Hershey, PA: Idea Group Inc.

Storey, D. (1982). *Entrepreneurship and the new firm*. New York: Praeger.

Swayne, C., & Tucker, W. (1973). *The effective entrepreneur*. Morristown, NJ: General Learning Press.

Tucker, D., & Jones, L. D. (2000). Virtual organisation: The new competitive arena of the global entrepreneur. *Management Case Quarterly, 3*(2), 29-33.

Valsiner, J. (1998). *The guided mind*. Cambridge, MA: Harvard University Press.

Varela, F., Thompson, E., & Rosch, E. (1991). *The embodied mind: Cognitive science and human experience*. Cambridge, MA: MIT Press.

Wagner, W. (1994). Fields of research and sociogenesis of social representation: A discussion of criteria and diagostics. *Social Science Information, 33*(2), 199-228.

Weick, K. E. (2002). Puzzles in organizational learning: An exercise in disciplined imagination. *British Journal of Management, 13*(S2), S7-S15.

Weick, K. E., & Sutcliffe, K. M. (2001). *Managing the unexpected*. New York: Jossey-Bass.

Weissman, D. (2000). *A social ontology*. New Haven, CT: Yale University Press.

Whinston, A., Barua, A., Shutter, J., Wilson, B., & Pinnell, J. (2001). *Measuring the Internet economy*. Cisco Systems & University of Texas. Retrieved July 18, 2001, from www.internetindicators.com

Wittel, A. (2001). Toward network sociality. *Theory, Culture & Society, 18*(6), 51-76.

Wood, M., & Ferlie, E. (2003). Journeying from Hippocrates with Bergson and Deleuze. *Organization Studies, 24*(1), 47-68.

KEY TERMS

Entrepreneurial Business Networks are social organisations offering different types of resources to entrepreneurs to start or improve entrepreneurial projects. The goal of most entrepreneurial networks is to bring together a broad selection of professionals and resources that compliment each other's endeavours. Initially a key priority is to aid successful business launches. Subsequently provide motivation, direction, and increase access to opportunities and other skill sets. Promotion of each members talents and services both within the network and out in the broader market increases opportunities for all participants.

Gilles Deleuze and Félix Guattari are known as classic writers in the development of critical theory in the late twentieth century. **Gilles Deleuze** (January 18, 1925-November 4, 1995) was a French philosopher of the late 20th century. From the early 1960s until his death, Deleuze wrote many influential works on philosophy, literature, film, and fine art. His most popular books were the two volumes of Capitalism and Schizophrenia: Anti-Oedipus (1987a) and A Thousand Plateaus (1987b), both co-written with Félix Guattari. **Pierre-Félix Guattari** (April 30, 1930-August 29, 1992) was a French pioneer of institutional psychotherapy, as well as the founder of both Schizoanalysis and Ecosophy. Critics often loosely describe the Deleuzo-Guattarian approach to philosophy as "artistic" and indeed, at a first glance, the work of Deleuze and Guattari may appear rather complex and "different." Their writings teem with new terminology such as lines of flight, assemblage, intensity, rhizome, becoming, machinism to name but a few. However, a thorough reading of Difference and Repetition (Deleuze, 1968) and A Thousand Plateaus (Deleuze & Guattari, 1987b) unveils a rather different picture: what we find is a carefully crafted philosophy that is fundamentally concerned with the dynamics of emergence. Deleuze and Guattari's work is a paradigm of thinking about the social dynamics of innovation. It is a logic that is fundamentally concerned with dynamics of experience aiming to discover conditions under which new concepts (Deleuze, 1995, p. 103) might be produced. Deleuze and Guattari fundamentally reject Hegelian dialectics as a dynamic that generates movement.

Hegelian Dialectics: In classical philosophy, dialectic refers to an exchange of propositions (theses) and counter-propositions (antitheses) resulting in a synthesis of the opposing assertions, or at least a qualitative transformation in the direction of the dialogue. Over the years, it has been refined and interpreted in various ways, ranging from mathematical algorithms to political manifestos such as in Marxism. In social representations theory, it is particularly Hegel's dialectic method which informed theorising (Marková, 2003). Specifically, Moscovici used the Hegelian dialectic to develop a dynamic and inter-subjective notion of shared representation for social psychology (Marková, 2003). Moscovici's main theoretical achievement in establishing this was to overcome the Cartesian subject-object dichotomy by demonstrating how knowledge evolves from an inter-subjective meaning construction process. It was here where his theorising was particularly inspired by the Hegelian dialectic model of movement (Hegel, 1807, 1830). In social representations theory, Hegel's (1830) dialectic model is mainly featured as a triadic dynamic that continually evolves in "being," in essences, concepts and identities (Colebrook, 2002) and that passes on through the difference between such beings. This is the notion that one begins with a clearly delineated concept (thesis), then moves to its opposite (antithesis), which represents any contradictions derived from a consideration of the defined thesis. Thesis and antithesis are contrasted and synthesised to form a new thesis (Marková, 2003).

Innovation is defined here a particular type of social knowledge dynamics; it is one which revolves around the emergence of entirely new, socially shared concepts – new meanings, ways of interacting and experiencing – that, at the time they emerge, do not have a place in a given social reference system of meaningful concepts. They are usually phenomena that we refer to as original, unheard-of or unexampled as they do not relate to our existing repertoire of concepts. The construction of these new concepts happens in a dynamic process of de-familiarisation of existing meaning (through some sort of disruption that we experience) and, in turn, through the familiarisation of novelty (see also knowledge dynamics and RNA).

Knowledge Dynamics is defined in this chapter as the movement emerging from the cross-fertilisation of the social dynamics of communicative interaction with the continuous dynamics of creation in the material world. This causes all sorts of disruptions and discontinuous flows that, in our everyday experience, play an important role in the way in which we come to make sense of novelty.

Post-Structuralism is a broad historical description of intellectual developments in continental philosophy and critical theory originating in France in the 1960s. The prefix "post" refers to the fact that many contributors such as Jacques Derrida, Michel Foucault, Gilles Deleuze and Félix Guattari (the latter two are cited in this chapter) were highly critical of structuralism. In direct contrast to structuralism's claims of culturally independent meaning, post-structuralists typically view culture as integral to meaning. Post-structuralism is difficult to define or to sum up. There are two main reasons for this. Firstly, by its very nature, poststructuralism rejects definitions that claim to have discovered "truths" or facts about the world. Secondly, very few people have willingly taken the label "post-structuralist." Rather, they have been labeled so by others. This means that no one has ever felt compelled to construct a "manifesto" of poststructuralism. Thus its exact nature and whether it can be considered a single philosophical movement is debated.

Rhizomic Network Analysis (RNA) is an approach of analysing and diagnosing social networks for their type of knowledge dynamics of innovation. The method is based both post-structuralist and social constructionist assumptions of creation and emergence. By combining theories by Deleuze & Guattari on the analogy of the rhizome to better understand the logic of discontinuity and disruption of movement and creation with social representations theory in terms of its dialectic logic of social knowledge construction, it takes a novel analytical view on knowledge dynamics. It offers a new paradigm of understanding the potential of new un-precedented connections, of disruptions and of experience in the emergence of novel concepts. This counters research shaped by a logic of thought that attributes innovation causally to individuals or to the diffusion or transfer of knowledge units between different, artifically separated spheres. This is important, as economic theories based on this view of knowledge often devise educational measures focused on individuals' knowledge or measures that reinforce the bridging of theory and practice, cognition and interaction. RNA argues, by contrast, that if we are to better understand innovation, we need to look at knowledge creation in social construction and shared experience in communities, in its interplay with disruption by dynamics in the physical world.

Social Constructionism is a sociological theory of knowledge developed by Peter L. Berger and Thomas Luckmann (1966). The main social constructionist theory cited in this chapter, Moscovici's (1961/1976, 1984) theory of social representations, developed this theory further for social psychology. The focus of social constructionism is to uncover the ways in which individuals and groups participate in the creation of their perceived reality. It involves looking at the ways social phenomena are created, institutionalised, and made into tradition by humans. Socially constructed reality is seen as an ongoing, dynamic process; reality is re-produced by people acting on their interpretations and their knowledge of it. Social constructionists argue that all knowledge, including the most basic, taken-for-granted common sense knowledge of everyday reality, is derived from and maintained by social interactions. When people interact, they do so with the understanding that their respective perceptions of reality are related, and as they act upon this understanding their common knowledge of reality becomes reinforced. Since this common sense knowledge is negotiated by people, human

typifications, significations and institutions come to be presented as part of an objective reality. It is in this sense that it can be said that reality is socially constructed.

Social Networks operate on many levels, from families up to the level of nations, and play a critical role in determining the way problems are solved, organisations are run, and the degree to which individuals or communities succeed in achieving their goals. In this chapter, social networks are defined here as the social communities and reference systems that emerge from the flexible connectivity of individuals or organisations through various forms of technology, enabling them to construct and create new knowledge together.

Social Representation Theory is a body of theory within social psychology originally coined by Serge Moscovici (1961/76, 1984). It is inter-related with both discourse analysis and discursive psychology. Social representation theory is popular among European social psychologists, especially those on the continent. The theory of social representations was developed by Serge Moscovici in the 1960s as part of a broader intellectual goal for a social psychology of knowledge. Social representations theory aimed to serve as a conceptual interface between psychology and sociology (Deaux et al., 2001) in the explanation of how knowledge dynamics play a role in processes of social change (Moscovici & Marková, 2000). Starting from the Hegelian principle of dialectics, Moscovici opposed the Cartesian notion of knowledge as "located" either within the individual or the social, critically emphasising that knowledge is not statically located in either the individual or the social but is rather continually brought forth in the constructive force of communicative interaction (Farr, 1996). It is difficult to provide a singular definition of social representations as many see the actual phenomena as too elaborate to capture its entirety (Marková, 2000) and the history of the concept too rich to be easily compressed into a single definition (Moscovici, 1988). Others see this as a precondition for further development and elaboration (Valsiner, 1998; Wagner, 1994). However, in relation to the particular phenomenon of knowledge dynamics discussed in this chapter, it can be said that Moscovici's conceptualisation of social knowledge offers a perspective of how new knowledge arises from social construction, embedded in a dialectic meta-theory. Social construction is seen as an inter-subjective process driven by the creative force of the tension between the unfamiliar and the familiar.

ENDNOTES

1   Worldwide stockmarket collapse of high-tech firms' values. In the UK alone, hundreds of dotcom firms experienced bankruptcy. The dotcom crash not only meant a major change for the whole sector of e-business entrepreneurship, but it also created a "start-from-scratch" scenario for many entrepreneurs and raised new questions as to how knowledge management in entrepreneurial business can be approached.

2   Theories have been forwarded, for instance, that explain the economic effectiveness of the creation of new ideas as a function of specific entrepreneurial motivational states (e.g., Swayne & Tucker (1973), Moore's (1986)).

3   Anchoring means classifying and naming something new or strange. Moscovici (1984) writes people strive "to anchor strange ideas, to reduce them to ordinary categories and images, to set them in a familiar context" (p.29). Objectification describes the process of when something anchored leaves the world of the abstract and takes shape in artefacts or physical practices. Objectification, like anchoring, serves to familiarise the unfamiliar.

4   As Marková (2000) emphasized, themata are the meaning currency that gives communication and interaction their sense in a social group. They take the form of dyadic oppositions or contrasts, such as "Generic/specific", "individualism/sociality" or "simplicity/complexity" (Holton, 1978).

5   Becoming is a Deleuzian term with which Deleuze took up Nietzsche's idea that being is becoming: there is an internal self-differing within the different itself, the different differs from itself in each case. Everything that exists only becomes and never is.

6   A Thousand Plateaus is itself designed as a rhizome; it is written as a stream of events, alliances, connections (rather than a discussion of concepts), refusing to follow a single chain of signification. Their writing is a rhizomic becoming itself as it ceaselessly achieves multiplicity by establishing unusual connections.

7   Deleuze and Guattari draw on Bergson's (1911/1983) notion of creative evolution, specifically on Bergson's point that "real" movement always involves a living interpenetration rather than a derived relationship between discrete points or positions in space. What Deleuze and Guattari envision is a pattern of dynamics as the multiplication of connections in a rhizomic system, which cannot be reduced to any sort of fixed pattern or constellation of unities. For them, this is a condition under which new concepts might be produced. This creates a perspective on networks as phenomena of discontinuous movement, multiplicity, and disruption, underscoring the importance of unpredictable and divergent patterns of combination.

8   Ontology is a word that is used in many different ways. It is often considered to be identical with metaphysics, or as the branch of metaphysics dealing with the nature of being or reality. Here it is used in a more

literal sense reflecting its Greek word-stem "ontos" (to be) as the science of how a thing (object or concept) comes into being.

9 London was selected as the context to conduct the exploration due to the fact that it is probably the most vibrant setting of e-business entrepreneurship in the UK and thus was likely to provide a rich source of diversity in terms of e-entrepreneurial businesses from which to recruit respondents for the study.

10 Please note that in the account on Ecademy, Deleuzian terms such as "becoming," "lines," and "assemblages" are used. This follows the Deleuzo-Guattarian approach to "think rhizomic" writing an analysis pointed to the possibility of escaping from "the process of question and answer [which] is made to nourish dualisms" (Deleuze & Parnet, 1987, p. 19). It enabled the analysis to turn to a rhizomic mode of analysis that would leave behind the "grille" (Deleuze & Parnet, 1987, p. 19) of invested concepts—in this case, preconceived concepts about networking. Rather than merely reiterating these, it offered the opportunity to concentrate on what was presented rather than re-represented (Deleuze, 1983) and thus to highlight particularly novel phenomena from the study.

11 Lines are Deleuzian terms referring to the fact that rhizomes are ambivalent to fixed points or the dyads in an oppositions - they make a rhizome what it is: de-rooted. A line can be an event, an affect, a nonsense, a percept, a something, a movement. Lines can connect to anything; yet can be broken at any instant, only to take off again in any direction. In comparison to dialectic lines of progression, lines do not function in terms of lines with a beginning and an end (Deleuze & Guattari, 1987b). In the analysis of this study, therefore, lines were thus about attempting not to look for origins or destinations, but to focus thinking and writing on what was "in-between", that is, on those aspects that were ambivalent to existing evaluative dimensions, and second, on future-directedness of things instead of historical anchors.

12 Individuation is a Deleuzian term, which refers to a process of seamless and endless differentiation.

13 The UK has been investing a large amount of funds into enhancing entrepreneurial innovation since the late 1970s (Curran & Blackburn, 2000) due to its central importance for the UK economy. Small and medium-sized businesses accounted for over 99% of the UK's 3.8 million businesses at the start of 2002. In addition, since 1995 entrepreneurship is reported to have contributed to a steady increase in job creation and productivity growth in the UK (Harding, 2002, 2003). Today, the UK government spends around £2.5 billion a year on services targeted at small businesses (Small Business Service, 2004). The vision is to "make the UK the best place in the world to start and grow a business" (Small Business Service, 2004, p.4).

Chapter XIII
Toward the Conceptual Model of Continuous Improvement Teamworking:
A Participant Observation Study

Suryadeo Vinay KISSOON
RMIT University, Australia

ABSTRACT

This chapter develops and underlines the concept of continuous improvement teamworking approach in a major banking organization. It is not a complete explanation of the continuous improvement teamworking approach but rather an illustration of the emergence of a new form and type of teamwork approach especially with banking organization becoming virtual organization and more competitive. With virtual meetings and interactive electronic communication, people at work above their normal face-to-face teamworking activities are having meetings, communication and sharing of information through a modernized continuous improvement teamwork approach with or without necessarily being in the immediate place of work but physically apart working across space, time, and organizational offices linked with Webs of digital collaborative communication technologies. The continuous improvement teamworking model is developed by the researcher using a deductive reasoning approach with 15 years of practical experience working with teams in a continuous improvement and change environment coupled with phenomenological methodology of ethnography (moderate participant observation as the method of collecting data) in the retail banking sector. This study has been done for nearly nine months, which represents about 190 hours spent in the major Australian retail bank. The model is a virtuous CTIO circle, which reflects the concern (issue)—task (action)—interaction (involvement and connection)—outcome (result) phases. It illustrates the new evolving consultative, participative, and interactive virtuous teamworking approach. The finding from the participant observation study has shown that synchronous conferencing, internet online functional services, continuous improvement, and team meetings form the essential four core elements of the CTIO model. The adoption of a continuous improvement teamworking approach is assisting in better running of retail banking operational activities and in achieving better performance. This chapter is important to senior managers and managers in improving the operational activities of their businesses to be more competitive.

INTRODUCTION

Purpose of Research

The purpose of this research has been to examine the central concept of continuous improvement teamwork approach in the retail banking sector with team members using the method of phenomenological design resulting from moderate participant observation. At this stage, continuous improvement teamwork is defined generally as continually working toward resolving a concern through team face-to-face interaction and/or virtually relating to a common goal set to achieve organizational objectives.

Rationale for Research

Unlocking organization, connecting people, technology, and gaining productive quality performance through continuous improvement teamworking approach in the retail banking sector.

Background of Study

Banks within the industry and from outside are experiencing competition (Gandy & Chapman, 1997). Under the new **financial reforms** brought about by the Australian government through the Financial Services Reform Act (FSRA) in 1998, there has been an increase in competitiveness of the Australian Banking institutions. Deregulation is **redefining a new form of competitive and sophisticated banking sector** (Battellino, 2002; Hutley & Russel, 2005). Over the last decade, the impact of regulation on the banking and financial services industry in Australia has many implica-

tions for banking top management teams and future policy makers. With this **specialization of the financial system** and strong growth of the financial markets, Australian major banking organizations are striving to become number one. The banking and financial services industry has been moving toward continuous improvement to **improve customer service**, **continually improving processes**, and enhance performance and profitability (Battellino, 2002; Duncan & Elliot, 2002; Hutley et al., 2005; West, Tjosvold, & Smith, 2005).

The banking and financial organizations are shifting from customer satisfaction to quality customer service (Duncan et al., 2002). Australian banking organizations are adopting total quality management (TQM) concepts through teamwork and **continuous improvement.** Similarly, Six-Sigma (Dawson & Patrickson, 1991), the interactive electronic communication approach (Haskins, 2002), and online Web functional services have been adopted in the banking sector to benchmark performance. The TQM concepts, which started in the manufacturing sector in the United States are now being shifted to the service sector (Cohen & Brand, 1993; Greenwood, 1992). Since, the teamwork notion is central to TQM (Shapiro, 1997), the best TQM program is likely to fail without employee commitment, engagement, involvement, consultation, and participation. As the banking and financial sector is moving toward virtual organizations, the new form of ongoing virtual and **interactive group work** (Igbaria & Tan, 1998) and electronic communication are also being adopted. This is being **continually improved upon in line with the process** of continuous improvement. Team convergence through e-teamwork (Haskins, 2002) is also another issue coming to foster better **quality customer service** where information technology also does matter when aligned with banking and financial organization competencies to achieve competitive advantage.

To tackle this challenge of **competitiveness**, retail banking organizations are putting more emphasis on employees working well as a team by also using digital electronic communication to deliver a quality customer service. Employees working for the bank are being directed toward working together as a team to deliver **quality customer service** (Arvan, 1988; Bernstel, 2002; Lampe and Sutton, 1992 as cited by Goh, 2000; Margerison, 2002; Tagliaferri, 1982). Banking employees are using virtual teamworking linked with Webs of digital collaborative communication technologies and use of continuous improvement concepts to **perform better and gain competitive edge**.

THE EMERGENCE OF CONTINUOUS IMPROVEMENT TEAMWORKING APPROACH

From Deregulation to E-Teaming Leading to Continuous Improvement Teamworking

The numbers 1 to 4 and arrows direction showing in Figure 1 indicates the contribution of authors, situations, and sequences leading to the continuous improvement teamworking approach. This approach has been developed following work done by the various authors from literature reviews, what has been observed through the participant observation studies and the researcher's personal experience working with teams to show the classificatory framework leading to the emergence of the CTIO model in the Australian retail banking sector. But with the start of deregulation in early

Figure 1. A classificatory framework illustrating continuous improvement, teamwork and e-teamwork leading to the emergence of the continuous improvement teamwork model

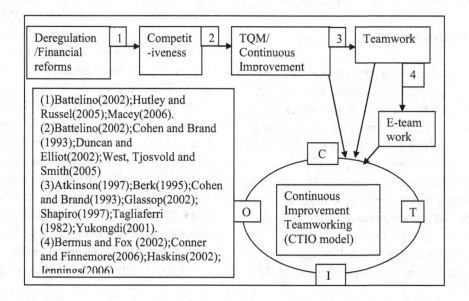

1980's and advanced technology, the Australian banking sector has constantly been changing to a new form of continuous improvement teamworking approach to efficiently run the organization in **gaining competitive advantage for quality customer service**. To summarise, the research reported here illustrates, as shown in Figure 1, that **deregulation** through Financial Services Reform Act in 1988 has led the Australian Banking sector to stronger competition. With competition, there has been the adoption of TQM through continuous improvement to improve quality of service. Teamworking has been initiated to improve performance of banking organization as teamwork is the heart of TQM. With advanced technology, automation of the banking sector through intranet, internet, telephone banking, service online, voicemail, distributed operating systems, computer supported cooperative work systems, groupware, other electronic communication and the crucial leadership role of the manager to make the staff working as team, e-teaming encapsulated in the process of continuous improvement is being used in the banking sector. These have been making the Australian banking institutions to operate more effectively using the continuous improvement teamworking approach.

CONTINUOUS IMPROVEMENT AND TEAMWORKING

The Continuous Improvement Approach: A TQM Foundation

Total quality management (TQM) is a discipline started in the manufacturing sector in the United States in the 1920's (Berk & Berk, 1995). After more successful implementation in Japan, the TQM philosophy came back to succeed in the manufacturing sector firstly in the United States and in other industrialized nations to become a worldwide concept (Berk et al., 1995). TQM

has taken a revolutionary approach to continually improve quality of goods, performance and workplace productivity. As described by Cohen et al. (1993), companies that have adopted TQM strategies have learned to work better and gain **competitive advantage** allowing employees to make use of their knowledge and available experiences. Nowadays, TQM is being implemented in the banking sector through continuous improvement, teamworking approach, six sigma's, change management, just-in-time, and quality customer service. Continuous improvement suggestions were primarily mentioned by Steve Michael who was an assembly supervisor in Parsons-Elliason (Berk et al., 1995). **Continuous quality improvement** requires a new way of managing work where employees are not only ordered but asked to think and participate in the process of organizing work (Cohen et al., 1993). Continuous improvement is an **initiating TQM journey** and consists of measuring key quality and other process indices such as customer satisfaction in the service sector.

The Value and Versatility Role of Teamwork in Modern TQM

Teamwork, after being successfully used in the manufacturing sector, has shifted into service sector companies. The quality circles and teamwork approach has shown positive impact on the quality of work life, productivity, and absenteeism in the banking sector (Lampe et al., 1992) as cited by Goh (2000). According to Tagliaferri (1982), as "quality circles" fade, a $371-million-asset bank (Depositors Trust Company) in Augusta Maire tried "top down" teamwork. The bank operated a team employees program by successfully involving managers and employees from different places of work, which was supported by the top management team. A team can be defined as a group of people working together to achieve a goal (Conti & Kleiner, 1997) or as **collaborative**

activity of individuals (Shapiro, 1997). Teams became more popular in the 1980s (Snee, Kelleher, & Reynard, 1997). Teamworking has been improving organizational health (Woodcock, 1989) as cited by Ingram et al. (1997) and driving quality forward (Peterson, 1991) as cited by Ingram et al. (1997). The quest to reduce the gaps between poor quality to good quality and low profitability to that of high profitability can be facilitated by the implementation of teamwork. Creating teams with an edge involved the complete skill set to build powerful teamwork (Harvard Business School, 2004). Without teamwork, there is an absence of TQM, which changes employees to do right thing, right first time and every time (Quality Systems, 1996).

VIRTUAL TEAMWORKING

Virtual Teamworking Approach

As stipulated by Stamatis (2003), team management is important for the implementation of quality management in financial organization. According to Edwards and Wilson (2004), virtual teamworking has been researched with networked teams, parallel teams, project development teams, production teams, service teams, management teams, and action teams. However, no work seems to have been done relating to virtual teamworking in the retail-team banking sector in Australia. As cited by Goggin (2004), "the marriage of computing and communications in Australia was dominated by telecommunication with the transmission of voice and data transmission used connections designed for voice which had data carrying capability grafted onto them until about 1990." Virtual teamworking came afterwards with improvement in network operating systems where employees can be electronically connected. The benefit that technology brought to the creative process networked virtual teamworking is the ability to link individuals who could not otherwise be included. Electronic links have widened the creativity pool of human resources peripheral for team members, individual teams and external teams through **being electronically connected** when needed (Nemiro, 2004).

Organizational Electronic Teamwork and Cooperative Working (E-Teaming)

With e-business involving changes in five interwoven factors, namely people, process, organization, business models, and technology, e-teaming is a new sociotechnical issue involved in the new form of teamworking approach. E-teaming's methodology is built upon the model of **effective virtual teaming**. As explored by Conner and Finnemore (2003), a study has provided valuable results showing benefit for individuals with efficient, rich interaction between team members, for the group, to the team climate and leadership. Dependence on **face-to-face interaction** has been reduced. The potential of virtual teaming to be improved continuously is being explored and is part of this study. Virtual teamworking is also more focused as everyone on the team is committed, their roles are clearly defined, norms of behaviour are fully set in advance and team members agree on how they will work together in the **virtual workplace**.

"Virtual environments(VEs) offer a unique medium for human-computer interaction (HCI)" (Jacko & Sears, 2003, p. 622). The theory of **human-computer interaction** was originally developed by David Kiaras from the University of Michigan and Peter Polson of the University of Colorado for the usability parameters like training time and productivity (Carroll, 1989). The human-computer interaction is becoming an important issue for organization with sophistication and technology advancement of **electronic communication systems** for better e-teaming as described by Bermus and Fox (2005).The introduction of communication technology into a UK service sector organization, led to a virtual team of development staff providing support to over 100 organizations (Conner et al., 2003). This has illustrated the **e-teaming's approach** to principles of adult learning and change management. The focus of e-teaming methodology is on team processes (Conner et al., 2003). This shows the emergence of the concept of e-teaming in the service sector, which is primarily focused on the interoperability of teams, tasks and technology. By the convergence of teams, tasks and technology in the concept of e-teaming, there is improved productivity leading to better performance and results. The importance of HCI and productivity is important in a **competitive environment**. "One way of demonstrating the importance of HCI is by showing tangible benefits that can be talked of in cash terms" (Preece et al., 1994, p. 19). The UK-based service sector company's experience is relevant to this literature review, as the **interconnectivity of teams**, tasks and technology has also been introduced in the banking sector. This has been observed during the participant observation study. The continuous improvement teamworking approach is different to e-teaming as illustrated by Conner et al. (2003) as it involves virtual teams and conventional teams, tasks and technology in a continuous improvement environment.

Online Virtual Group Interoperability Revolution

Futurists predicted the increasing use of virtual corporations (Davidow & Malone, 1992), Igbaria et al. (1998), **virtual teams** (O'Hara-Devereaux & Johansen, 1994), Igbaria et al. (1998), virtual desks (Patterson, 1994), Igbaria et al. (1998), and virtual employees (Fortune, 1994)" as cited by Igbaria et al. (1998). As described by Hallberg (2005), the term networking relationships refers to two different concepts about how one computer makes use of another computer. Teleworking is about working from a distance with employers, colleagues or customers using information and communication technologies (Denbigh, 2003). This type of **digital working** enables team members' **group conversations to be captured electronically**. The "online training revolution" (Mitrione as cited by Jenning, 2006) has gained momentum in the last five years. It also provides more knowledge and greater flexibility especially where employees are time-poor. The same is presently occurring in the financial and banking sector where financial institutions are moving their **business to employees (B2E)** by providing everything through their **online services**, internet and intranet online space. As stipulated by Hallberg (2003), the open system interconnection (OSI) which is a reference model that conceptually describes how networks work and the International Standards Organization (ISO) body that defines many quality standards, including network standards are also being related to the **online virtual networking**.

Use of Technology in a Collaborative Team Environment

As described by Edwards et al. (2004), the term "virtual" was originally called virtual reality (VR) and used to describe a set of technologies that gave people a sense of being present and interacting in a space other than where they are physically situated. Within VR, a virtual environment is a computer-generated three-dimensional representation of objects, which the participant experiences visually, through a range of display devices from a desktop computer. Alternatively, staff in banking organizations, though co-located as observed in the participant observation study, are interacting as a team through **electronic working meeting**, **computer-supported cooperative work** (CSCW) system(e.g., teleconferencing, group calendars and schedules, e-mail and bulletin boards, voicemail) and other virtual working support tools.

Group Decision Support Systems, E-Collaboration, and Groupware

As mentioned by Nemiro (2004), various works on **collaborative work systems** have been done relating to the integration of Six-Sigma and high performance organizations for sustainable improvement, strategic design for **collaborative** work systems, building collaborative organization, creativity in virtual working arrangements, the creative process of virtual teams, profile of virtual teams and collaboration. Edwards et al. (2004) have written on the move toward **virtual working**, technology for virtual teams, virtual team complexities, managing **virtual workers** (caring-daring and sharing), success strategies, communication strategies, change management aspects, and supporting systems for virtual team. Kock (2005) studied on the use of e-collaboration for business process improvement. His work over recent years has led him to the definition of the term "e-collaboration" as a fast emerging area where information and communication technologies support distributed teams. The use of **e-collaboration tools**, when properly done, can improve the speed and reduce the cost of implementing Six-Sigma, ISO 9000 quality management systems, and capability maturity model (CMM) certifications (Kock, 2005). As described by Mandviwalla (1993), a significant number of collaborative systems have been developed, documented, and researchers refer to these systems with a variety of terms such as group decision support systems (GDSS), **computer mediated communication systems** (CMC), group support systems (GSS), computer supported cooperative work systems (CSCW), and groupware. Groupware is generically used to describe information systems that support collaborative work groups and typically has a multiple-user component (Mandviwalla, 1993). **Collaborative computing** is changing how information moves and is managed in business. Emerging groupware environments enable workers to collaborate through **internetworked**

computers and interact freely to achieve common purpose (Khoshafian & Buckiewicz, 1995). For instance, in the banking sector, the collaborative group tool and computer-mediated interpersonal communication being used, allow the superior in designing a meeting group support system where the chairperson gives instructions to staff on what tasks and main focus need to be done on a weekly basis to achieve set organizational objectives.

CONTINUOUS IMPROVEMENT TEAMWORKING APPROACH

The Continuous Improvement Teamwork Concept

Teamwork in the context of TQM, is an important aspect of quality management and results in continuous improvement (Shapiro, 1997). It has been noted that there is a gap in literature regarding the continuous improvement teamworking approach. A continuous improvement model was designed illustrating the voices of the customer and the process. However, in this model nothing was mentioned about the voice of the people as a team interacting face-to-face with digital electronic communication for running the business, which could be reflected in terms of the **continuous improvement teamwork approach**. The effect of employee interaction, together with virtual teamworking through the consultative and participative approach of continuous improvement teamworking led to the CTIO model as illustrated in Figures 1, 2, and 3. In a model of teamwork as developed by Shapiro (1997), seven main factors were hypothesized for effecting teamwork. Also in another model proposed by Schermerhorn et al. (1995) as cited by Ingram et al. (1997), teamwork can be studied in a three-stage sequence, which identifies those inputs and throughputs leading to successful outputs. Nothing is mentioned about the **continuous improvement activity of teamwork** showing the gap in literature. The CTIO

Figure 2. Showing the CTIO model and virtual teams new knowledge contribution to the total teamwork way

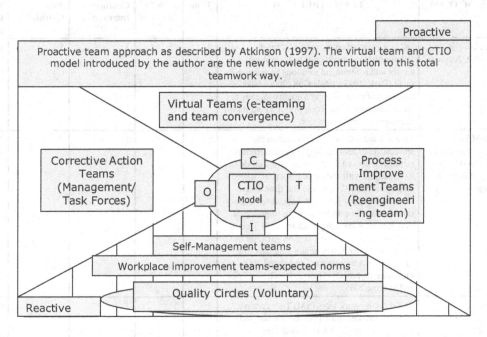

model is different as it involves team member interaction through the process of consultative, participative and **interactive electronic communication networking**. There has been a shift from quality circles to virtual teams through a proactive team approach as shown in Table 1 and Figure 2. The different teams in Table 1, are differentiated using a severity score of 1 to 5 related to five main selection criteria. The **virtual team** and the CTIO model in Figures 2 and 3, are incorporated as the new knowledge contribution to this total teamwork way as previously described by Atkinson (1997).

Continuous Improvement Teamwork in the Australian Retail Banking Sector

As described by Bernstel (2002), one Southeastern Pennsylvania bank learned the power of teams in

1999. The quest for competitive advantage among banking organizations is likely to lead banks to go toward teamwork to perform more productively (Bernstel, 2002). To have the continual support and engagement of banking staff, all major Australian banking institutions have been focusing on the internal role of consultation and participation through people management and technology to work as a team. Nevertheless, with banking organizations becoming virtual organizations, team work is not only the solution as was the case ten years ago. The incorporation of quality management, continuous improvement of operations, and processes together with the use of modern technology, teamwork, and **e-collaboration tools** in the form of **e-teamwork** is the new issue for improving productivity and performance in the banking sector. Table 1 illustrates the classification of various teams using a set of five major selection criteria namely: time, **face-to-face**, **continuous**

Table 1. Describing the types and differentiation of team with each team structure description

TYPES OF TEAM	TEAM STRUCTURE	Time	Face To face	Continuous Interaction	Task Oriented	Virtual Commu-nication
QualityCircle-(QC) (Deming PDCA cycle)	QC is a group of employees who meet voluntarily to identify on-the-job problem causes and recommend solutions to management (Berk, 1995), while Goh (2000) talks of meetings of minds during a quality journey to attain customer satisfaction through continuous improvement and teamwork.	4	5	3	5	0
Kaizen-DMAIC Define-Measure-Ana-lyze-Improve-Control. A structured Problem solving methodology.	Kaizen team (DMAIC) is evolved in the application of lean method in manufacturing settings. It is used for any intensive well-de-fined project with dedicated resources, where employees work 3 to 5 days full time away from their regular jobs with basic data collec-tion already done and immediate implementa-tion of typical team approach to cover desired work. Participant treated as if on vacation from regular responsibilities minimising handling of emails, voicemails etc…and spend 100% of their time on project (George, Rowlands, Price and Maxey, 2005).	5	5	2	5	2
Self-directed work team or Self Managed Team (SMT)	Self-directed work team (SMT) are creative, problem solving and empowered teams work-ing on a day-to-day basis, setting their own goals and decide on the problem to be tackled (Conti & Kleiner, 1997).	3	5	3	5	0
Corrective Action Team (CAT)	CAT is referred to as "task forces" where management define the problem and select team members from appropriate work teams. Team is efficiently operational as members are practised problem solvers (Atkinson, 1997).	4	5	3	5	0
Process Improvement Team (PIT)	PIT is a proactive team appointed by manage-ment with defined tasks for the part of the business to be examined. The team challenge is to seek improvement, working on the philoso-phy that there is always a better way of doing things considering time, knowledge gaining and improved technology. Members are re-engineering team, selected from appropriate workplace teams and include technology expert (Atkinson, 1997).	5	5	1	5	3
Workplace Improve-ment Team (WIT) (Expected Norms)	WIT is supported actively by enlightened management. There is a growing degree of involvement by the workplace members. A critical involvement mass is reached when participation in improvement activities be-comes as a norm. Common characteristics of team working involves induction processes, new staff selection relates to team working and enhancement of workplace team building activities (Atkinson, 1997).	3	5	5	5	0

continued on following page

Table 1. Continued

Virtual Team (VT)/ e-Teaming	Virtual teams (VT) are groups of people who find themselves separated by distance and/or time, yet have common tasks to perform. The interactions of virtual team members will rely on electronic communications media such as e-mail, audio and video conferencing and web-based tools (Edwards and Wilson, 2004). Similarly as described by Conner and Finnemore (2003), virtual Teams unlike conventional teams, though physically apart, works across space, time, and organisational boundaries with links improved by webs of digital collaborative and electronic communication technologies. There is a reduction in dependency on face-to-face meetings through the use of phone and video conferencing and intranet as an important aspect of e-management. e-Teaming`s methodology is build upon the model of effective virtual teaming.	3	0	4	4	5
Continuous Improvement Team (CIT) (New definition)	CIT is a team that are continually working towards resolving a concern through team face-to-face interaction and/or virtually relating to common goals set to achieve organizational objectives.	5	5	5	5	5

Figure 3. The continuous improvement teamworking model

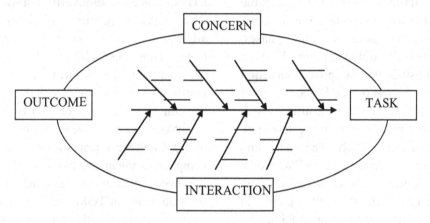

interaction, task-orientation, and **virtual communication** factors. These differentiation factors are selected from literature, what was physically observed in practical settings and the experience of the author working with teams by using a paired comparison analysis (PCA) chart (Quality Systems, 1996).

THE PROPOSED CONTINUOUS IMPROVEMENT TEAMWORK MODEL

The proposed CTIO model has been the interest of the researcher for more than a decade by working with the different types of teams as illustrated in Table 1. The author had also won several Industry-Based Excellence Awards with some of the types team put into practical application for improving productivity and performance.

The continuous improvement teamwork model is proposed based on the following: (1) author's previous practical experience working in teams for nearly 15 years, (2) a gap in literature on continuous improvement team working aligned with **virtual teams practice**, (3) observing what is really occurring in the workplace after working in a major leading retail Australian Bank for nearly one and a half years, (4) the deductive reasoning approach, and (5) the participant observation study conducted over 9 months. The following model is presented according to up-to-date understanding and observations made in the retail banking sector. The focus is mainly in the banking sector as there are various interactions between team members especially when there is a concern. Thus, the model is a **virtuous circle** which reflects the concern (issue)-task (action)-interaction (involvement and connection)-outcome (result) phases. The CTIO cycle is illustrated in Figure 3. At the beginning of the study 39 descriptive observation domains as represented by the fishbone arrows inside the CTIO model were identified which has been further investigated in the moderate participant observation study. The cause and effect diagram as shown inside the CTIO model depicts the 39 domains to be investigated where some are described at the start of the project in the descriptive observation section of Figure 5.

Unique Features and Challenges of the Continuous Improvement Teamworking Model

Promoting a culture of employee involvement as found by Dawson et al. (1991) to cope with competition was one of the main variables for better service quality in the Australian banking industry. The retail banking sector is becoming

a central point for major banks as the "moment of truth" between front line workers and the customers. All issues relating to customer service are becoming a serious concern for local banks. Everything is being monitored with a view to totally satisfy consumers and meet their needs and wants. The concept of teamwork, **e-teamwork**, **virtual communication,** and TQM/continuous improvement are becoming crucial parameters to address customer concerns effectively. The emergence of the continuous improvement teamworking approach addresses all of these issues for smooth operational activities of the bank as it is the customers who run the bank.

As mentioned by Yeh, Smith, Jennings, and Castro (2006), a three-dimensional teamwork model was adapted from the Belbin team role model, Andia's team pyramid model, Thompson et al.'s team process evolution model, and original works of the authors as a doctoral learning with the University of Phoenix. The originality of the work has introduced an **innovative teamwork** model, which provides organization direction to continually evaluate the development and processes of teams. Thus, the CTIO model is different as it involves the notion of virtual teamworking and **continuous improvement** to the basic teamworking concept. The work of Escriba-Moreno and Canet-Giner (2006) have shown the combined use of TQM and work teams for companies to gain competitive advantage. However, the continuous improvement teamworking approach model shows the association of TQM, work teams and virtual teams combined together for organization to gain **competitive edge**. The addition of the virtual teams to the concepts of TQM and teamwork is the knowledge contribution to the existence of the CTIO model.

The **continuous improvement teamworking approach** is presently being used in a major Australian banking institution where the concepts of teamworking, virtual teamworking and continuous improvement as mentioned before are amalgamated to foster **better productive per-**

formance and improve customer service. Record profits and increase in share price were announced by the media and achieved for the first time by the financial institution, which employs about 32,000 employees. By using a blend of both **face-to-face interaction** and **virtual communication networks** together with Continuous Improvement, there is better productivity and improved performance as observed in the major financial organization. The routine face-to-face meetings are held from daily to twice per week ,with the use of teleconferencing, voicemails, faxes, memos, notice boards, emails with attachments, audio and video conferencing, electronic meeting systems, group calendars and other **collaborative virtual environments tools**. By the adoption of the CTIO model on any relevant situational basis, it becomes much easier for the senior managers and managers to properly run the technological, operational and people management sides of the business.

The retail banking sector has been chosen for the purpose of this research as it is the engine of the banking sector especially in an environment of **severe competition** as explained before. However, there are various other issues and challenges such as the reduction of process, operational and social awareness with virtual teams, data storage, and security aspects, **communicating digitally**, reduced nonverbal feedback mechanism, emotions, and feelings during virtual networking, leadership characteristics, change management for resistance to change, employees job rotation, induction of new employees, environment and future office set-up, confidentiality, ethical and compliance issues, future regulations related to online services, cultural and **connectivity** issues, convergence of technology, future technology change, individual differences in e-teaming, **human-groupware operating support systems,** and some other concerns, which may crop up later but need to be further observed. These are issues for further research. The good things noted from this research is that by the combination of consultative, **participative, and interactive** ways

of communicating results in better outcomes whereby senior managers and managers are continually seeking improved teamworking activities. In fact, with the usefulness, up-to-date, peripheral, reliability, flexibility, suitability, practicality, and perennial effects of the continuous improvement teamworking approach, improved performance, and profitability has been achieved in the major Australian bank.

METHODOLOGY

The essential core element of ethnography in qualitative research is the concern with the meaning of actions and events we seek to understand (Spradley, 1980).The researcher for the purpose of this study has used ethnography as an approach as described by Spradley (1980) to socially acquire and share knowledge for understanding the observed pattern of **human-computer interaction**, telecommunication technologies, and other objects used in a major retail bank by team members in their daily work activities **interacting together** face-to-face and virtually as a team. The main method of this phenomenological methodology of collecting data has been participant observation. Team members who were managers, business customer service representatives, team leaders, and customer service staff in a major Australian banking organization have been used as the unit of analysis. The aim of the methodology was to interpret how team members communicate together synchronously and asynchronously with their immediate superior or other team members to report and share operational, technical, employee issues, sales, customer service objectives and targets. Though there are a number of different styles of ethnography, the researcher has used a medium degree of involvement with a moderate participation type according to his skills and training to provide insights and offer an opportunity to see the happening in reality of the continuous improvement teamworking activities.

As summarized by Boydan and Taylor (1975) as cited by Collis and Hussey (2003), and Patterson (1990) as cited by Collis and Hussey (2003), the researcher has adopted the following approach in performing the participant observation methodology by building trust with participants, involved with the phenomena, gathered data and views from team members as far as possible including the researcher's own experiences, captured team member experiences in their own words, thoughts and feelings, writing and synthesizing of all field notes recorded.

Moderate Participant Observation Type

As described by Spradley (1980), moderate participation occurs when the ethnographer seeks to maintain a balance between being an insider and an outsider, between participation and observation. As the author has been working part-time in the banking institution and also been a researcher doing the participant observation study, he has chosen the moderate level of involvement. Being a moderate insider to the major banking organization has been the best approach to identify and design the CTIO model by observing its practical occurrence in real life work situations.

Triangulation of Data

Triangulation can overcome potential bias and data triangulation is collected at different times or from different sources in the study of a phenomenon (Collis & Hussey, 2003). To overcome any bias in the participant observation study, the data triangulation methodology has been used. The descriptive, focused, and selective observations have been done at different times and in nine different places in the major Australian banking organization. By observing at different times and locations, it was becoming clear and precise to the author about the major domains of the Continuous improvement teamworking approach model. The

domains are illustrated in Figure 5. Each time and in different places where team members and their superiors were **interacting** regarding a task to meet the **concern** of a customer, the CTIO model was emerging. In this participant observation study, the author as the moderate participant observer used introspection by using himself as a research instrument. Triangulation was also used by the author for the ethnography questions asked and observations simultaneously done progressively from the descriptive observations to the selective observations process to come to the right observation pattern and conclusion.

The Ethnographic Research Cycle Used

An earlier version of the ethnographic research cycle qualitative methodology was presented at the international conference 2007 of the Association of Qualitative Research and manuscript publication in the Journal of Qualitative Research. The paper won the best refereed paper in the award presented by the author as a Ph.D candidate. This book chapter has pursued further indepth research about the theoretical framework of the Continuous Improvement Teamworking Approach.

In contrast to the linear sequence research process, the ethnographic research cycle was used for conducting the participant observation. Though there are many other factors affecting teamwork, this study was confined mainly to the Continuous improvement teamworking approach, which also relates to the **e-teamwork** evolving as a **virtual process workgroup** aligned with the desired groupware structure. The research scope can be classified between the micro-ethnography and macro-ethnography (Spradley, 1980) as team members were observed from one major Australian banking organization. The mode of ethnographic inquiry used was mostly a topic-oriented ethnography on continuous improvement teamworking, which narrows the focus to the selective observation process of participant observation regarding the adoption of virtual teamworking in the retail banking sector. The narrowing process was done by asking ethnographic questions. Throughout the observational process of nine months, several questions as shown in Figure 4 were asked and tried to look for possible answers by the researcher for coming to a reliable and valid conclusion about the **continuous improvement teamworking approach.**

Descriptive observations were done where the general overview of **team members interaction** were observed including leadership, communication, team meetings ,**e-teamwork**, conferencing, use of **intranet and online functional services**, engagement , consultation and participation, relationship building , delegation, and so on. The narrowing process was done by the author by using the 5W-1H (when, what, who, whom, and how) questioning skills technique as described by Berk

(1995). After more analysis and repeated observations in the field, the researcher still narrowed further the investigational process to make selective observation, which related to team meetings, synchronous conferencing, **teleconferencing**, using of intranet, organizational Web site, **online functional, and portal services.**

The Developmental Research Sequence Using 5W-1H Technique

Step One: Locating the Continuous Improvement Teamwork Activities as a Social Situation

The three elements, which were firstly identified, were the retail branches of the major bank in Australia as the places, the team members as the actors and the use of computers, telecommuni-

Figure 4. The ethnographic research cycle as described by Spradley (1980) used for this observational study; the 5W-1H questioning skills technique has been introduced by the researcher to better focus on the selective observational aspects

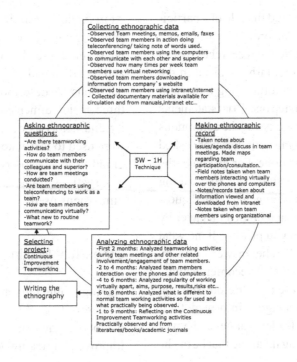

cation technologies, faxes, newsletters, memos, downloaded information to team from company's Web site and intranet, team meetings, conferencing, video play, quiz, role play, training, etc…as activities. Questions were developed throughout the observational process and assessed by the undermentioned selection criteria. The questions depicted had addressed the concern related for the phenomena contributing for the continuous improvement teamwork approach. The 5W-1H questioning skills technique as introduced by the author was used to fully understand and situate the relevant questions as shown on the ethnographic research cycle. The most appropriate questions were then selected. The selection of the most suitable questions to be analysed under the participant observational study were further determined using the Solution Matrix with selection criteria giving a weighted index using the paired comparison analysis chart (PCA) as illustrated by Quality Systems (1996).

Step Two: Doing the Participation Observation

The researcher has also used the role of a participant observer rather than an ordinary participant. Introspection was used by the researcher by being more engaged and regularly involved in the observational process by not missing important activities as described in step one. Brief statements relating to questions for assessing the continuous improvement teamworking activities were asked with specific tasks to be done. For example, the researcher had to draw a statement after asking each manager the teleconferencing related question. Question asked to each branch manager by the researcher was "Can you please tell me what are you actually doing?" The answer given by all branch managers were "teleconferencing!" The statement was written as "Before starting teleconferencing all managers informed their subordinates and team leader that he or she will be doing teleconferencing meaning that he or she

will be busy and not to be disturbed." Normally it was observed that the teleconferencing can last from one hour to two hours.

Step Three: Making an Ethnographic Record

A field notebook was set up by the researcher relating to the study. The language used was mostly English language except French and Indian languages used by the observer to a number of employees in the bank. The other language used was an ice breaking exercise to easily interact and communicate with some bank employees. The researcher needed to have clarification from the appropriate person working in the major banking organization relating to some technical words and operational activities. Statements were written as condensed notes for each task done relating to questions posed by the researcher as the research observational cycle progressed.

Step Four: Making Descriptive Observations

At first, the descriptive observation was used by approaching the activities without any particular specific question in mind. Each thing seen and recorded had an influence on the observer's questions. A descriptive questions matrix with three major dimensions (namely object, activity and actor) as described by Spradley (1980) were used to facilitate the formulation of 'initial grand tour' questions and making the relevant observations. Table 2 illustrates the three major dimensions used.

Step Five: Making a Domain Analysis

Having collected and recorded many pages of descriptive observations in the researcher notebook, patterns relating to the continuous improvement teamwork approach were system-

Table 2: Showing the three dimensions in a descriptive question matrix

ACTOR	ACTOR	OBJECT	ACTIVITY
	Team members were the actors.	Team members use computers and telecommunication technologies through teleconferencing.	Team members communicate to superior and other colleagues through conferencing, faxes etc
OBJECT	While doing teleconferencing, branch managers use online computer software, telephones and intranet.	All the objects includes telephones, faxes, computers, memos,emails,voice-mails, newsletters, courier, manuals, floppy disc, computer manage learning etc.	Computers are used by branch managers to input sales figures achieved to target, objectives to meet for week, listen to teleconferencing , takes notes, print etc…
ACTIVITY	Team members need to listen, take notes, type to give feedback and communicate to everyone doing teleconferencing. Also refer to manuals, webpage menu, weekly planner etc…	Computers provide information to access webpage, weekly planner, Manuals to refer to operational activities and telephones for listening, Sales forecast and achieved targeted actions etc…	Teleconferencing, e-learning,virtual networking,team meetings,Faxes, ATMs, emails,Intranet, manuals,Planners,Operation alactivities,,Memos,Newsletters,Documentsdownloaded, Video conferencing,Online functional services etc.

atically examined. It was noted that during team meetings, team members were sitting around a rectangular table or in a triangular or circular setting facing each other. The branch manager or the team leader was always the one to chair the team meetings. Brainstorming sessions were used where each team member's views in general or about a specific issue (e.g., such time-out and log-in problems, filings, security issues, sales, referrals etc…) were asked individually by the branch manager or team leader. During synchronous conferencing, the branch managers were always in their offices in front of their computers and telephones. Only branch managers, team leaders and business service officers were seen to be doing teleconferencing.

DESCRIPTIVE OBSERVATIONS FOCUSED OBSERVATIONS SELECTIVE OBSERVATIONS

The manager or team leader was a kind of leader, coach, mentor, guide, support member, and ready to provide information and advice to team members throughout the sessions. Continuous supervision and monitoring were regularly seen to be done by superiors to address any concern or issues raised by staff or customers where their concerns were beyond the capacity of the customer service staff to be addressed. When the concern was not within the capacity of the branch to handle, intranet/online services, telephones, faxes, groupware operating support systems, and so on were used to contact other staff in other offices for assistance through the available network support system. Override facilities were seen to be given by superiors for better monitoring of transactions being done. Authorizations for approval of cash advances were done by the interactions of the customer service representatives with an automated voice telephone system and using the computers. Intranet online functional services which resemble the B2E activities were also used.

As illustrated in Figure 5 and 6, at the beginning of the study, 39 descriptive observation domains were done by physically and visually observing what was really happening in the major Australian retail bank. Progressively, selective observations were done using interviews with a

Figure 5. Participant observation starting from wide descriptive to focused and selective observations as designed by Spradley (1980)

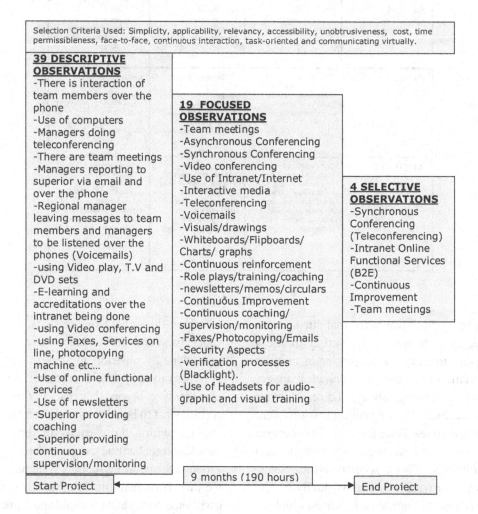

set of selection criteria as illustrated in Figure 5 and 6. After a systematic review and fine tuning as explained throughout the methodology in this study, 19 focused observations were done. With more practical experience over time and greater understanding of what was really occurring in the retail banking organization, the researcher has made selective observations where only 4

core elements of the continuous improvement teamworking approach were discovered and summarised. The four elements of the CTIO model are further explained in details in the taxonomic analysis of the four major domains (Figures 7, 8, 9, and 10). Steps involving cultural themes and cultural inventory have not been used for the purpose and scope of this study.

Figure 6. The CTIO model development and refinement in the process through the participant observation study

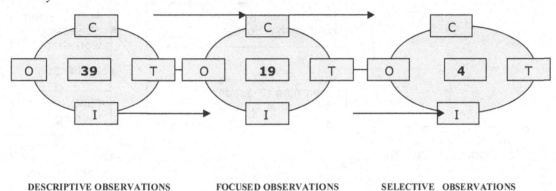

DESCRIPTIVE OBSERVATIONS   FOCUSED OBSERVATIONS   SELECTIVE OBSERVATIONS

Figure 7. A taxonomic analysis of the conferencing domain

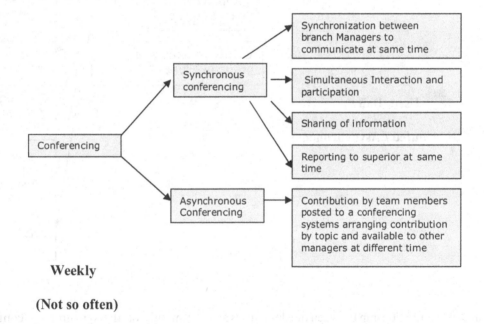

Weekly

(Not so often)

Step 6: Making Focused Observations

After spending around two months doing surface investigation by doing descriptive observations, the researcher used the in-depth investigation to decide on what questions to focus on. Kinds of objects such as computers, telecommunication technologies and devices, manuals, faxes, newsletters being used by team members, and so on,

began to be more frequently observed from the second to the fourth months. Similarly, kind of activities such as synchronous and asynchronous conferencing, teleconferencing, video conferencing, team meetings, and so on, more focused observations were done. The same was done for kind of acts, kind of relationships, kind of actors, kind of goals, kind of time, kind of places to further narrow the observational process. Any cause

267

Figure 8. A taxonomic analysis of the intranet online functional services

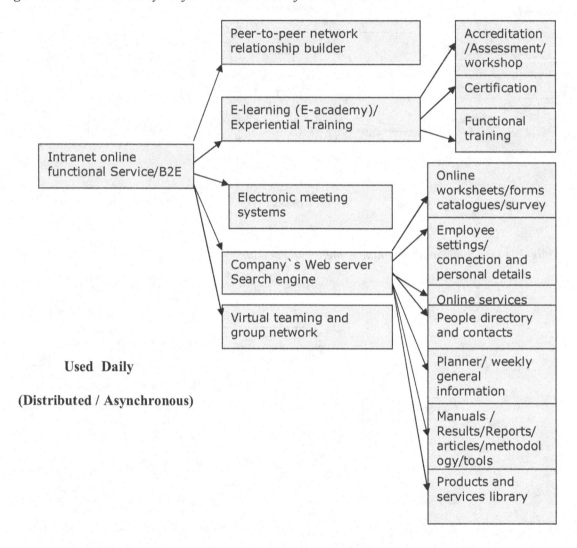

and effect relationship between the domains was individually analysed by the investigator.

Step 7: Making a Taxonomic Analysis

To illustrate this step, the taxonomic analysis of the major domains are shown in Figures 7, 8, 9, and 10.

Step 8: Making Selected Observations

As from the fourth month, onward selected observations were done. The researcher focused mainly on the synchronous conferencing, team meeting, teleconferencing, and intranet domains for depicting the right ingredients for the new issues relating to the emergence of Continuous improvement teamworking approach. During the first two to four months more descriptive questions were ask such as " Can you describe how do you work as a team?." In the following four months, more structured questions were asked. For example, branch managers were asked in-depth questions specific to a particular domain such as: "What do you do during teleconferencing?" The ethnographic interviewing process did assist

Figure 9. A taxonomic analysis of the continuous improvement domain

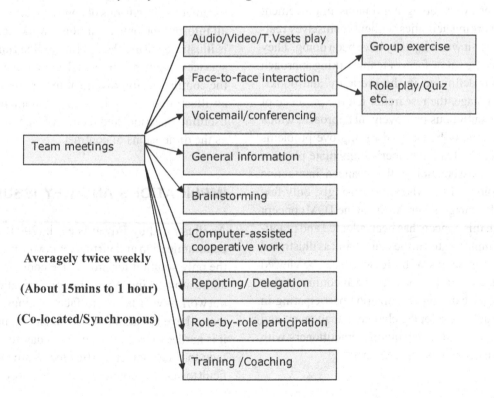

Figure 10. A taxonomic analysis of the team meetings domain

Table 3. Paradigm chart illustrating the componential analysis of intranet online functional services, team meetings, teleconferencing and continuous improvement domains

DOMAIN	Dimensions of Contrast		
	Usefulness	Action	Feeling
Intranet online functional services	Very good	Business/Personal	Taken seriously
Team meetings	good	Minutes of meetings	Good
Teleconferencing	good	Business	delight
Continuous Improvement	Brings quality	Delegation to staff	Interesting

the investigator in shaping and better positioning the CTIO model in the continuous improvement teamwork approach adopted and being used by team members in the retail banking sector. Selective observations were done with the structured questions asked to team members. In fact, team members were doing continuous improvement teamworking activities without themselves realizing that it was what they have been doing. They were doing a new form of teamworking approach with no definition in the literature and books. At that stage, the researcher felt the presence of TQM/continuous improvement approach, which is continually being used to improve problems or issues in team member's immediate place of work in association with advanced interactive technological knowhow. Surprisingly, only few branch managers were aware of the TQM concept though this concept has been adopted and practically implemented in the major bank as illustrated on the company's Web site, which can be viewed online at any time. However, it was confirmed that the major banking organization participating in this study has adopted change management and Six-Sigma with a few quality practitioners with black belts and many green belts.

Step 9: Making a Componential Analysis

A componential analysis as described by Spradley (1980) includes the entire process of searching for contrasts, sorting them out, grouping some together as dimensions of contrasts, and entering all information onto a paradigm worksheet. This is illustrated using the internet online functional services, team meetings, teleconferencing, and the continuous improvement major components as illustrated in Table 3 as the domains with usefulness, action, and feeling of team members as the dimensions of contrast.

IMPLICATIONS AND KEY ISSUES

As illustrated by Edwards et al. (2004), virtual communication and virtual teamworking are not the only solution for productive communication and teamworking. Virtual communication does not work as well as face-to-face meetings. Virtual teams have the additional difficulty namely that it is harder to build trust without day-to-day and face-to-face contact. Virtual teams are more difficult to manage, communication is more complex, and it is time-consuming. There is little osmosis or sharing of ideas, team shared objectives are harder to commit, being co-located does not mean that the team talk to each other and that it takes much longer to get to know people really well. There are also other difficulties such that large numbers of people become free at the same time, limited knowledge of problem space, restriction on travel and difficulty in contacting team members when need to discuss a matter. Moreover, it is not easy to have an informal discussion, there is a lack of regular contact between team members, need to keep talking as on the phone, need to constantly informed superior what you are doing, virtual team would be more difficult the bigger it got (e.g., more than ten is very difficult) and so on. Considering the negative aspects of virtual teamworking, financial organizations are still maintaining the use of face-to-face teamworking on top of virtual teamworking. This is why through the continuous improvement teamworking model, organizations are practically making use of both face-to-face contact to build trust and virtual teamworking for better, efficient and smooth running of operational activities. In the major Australian banking organization, it has been observed that there is mostly daily to twice face-to-face interaction every week in form of team meetings, huddles, coaching, training, and induction programmes. Subsequent meetings also use the intranet, e-mails, memos, faxes, audio, video/TV sets, voicemails, teleconferencing, newsletters, weekly planner, online services, e-academy Web sites, and some others for better communication.

Nowadays, employees need not be solely in one immediate place to work as a team. With the advent of modernized technological knowhow in computer science, communication networks, online functional services, virtual enterprises and virtual communications, employees can still work as a team though co-located or virtually apart. Virtual teaming has got many advantages as stipulated by Edwards et al. (2004) such as convenience in working time, less time spent in travelling, ability to select on skills not on geography, the interchange and sharing of experiences and little time wasted on the non-productive things that stable teams amuse themselves with. It was also mentioned that it provides personal flexibility, ability to bring people into the team as necessary for short-term bit of work, there is cooperation, and there is better relationship. It was also found that there is best use of individual skills as focused on what really needs to be done, team size is suited to the task, there is team goal setting, better speed of response, ability to run a thin organization, more time to do the work, variety in work type, suitable location and many others. Nevertheless, organizations considering the positive aspects of virtual teamworking are also maintaining and using together the face-to-face people interaction to effectively run the organization. A mixture of teamwork and e-teamwork was seen to be the right ingredient for organization to perform better.

Continuous improvement as is a concept, which has proved itself in the manufacturing and services sector. Today, continuous improvement has been initiated in the four major Australian banking organizations for superior customer service. As repeated before, recently these banking institutions have been adopting Continuous Improvement in the form of six-sigma, change management, process improvement, continuous reinforcement, and one-to-one coaching. Problem solving activities (Six-Sigma/DMAIC), change management, teamworking, green belt and black belt accreditation modules and many others are available for training via the company's online intranet functional services. In the process of continuous improvement, many operational manuals, surveys, catalogues, quality management methodologies and tools, e-learning and e-academy for accreditations, online certifications, people directory, products and services library, employee settings, results, performance indicators, and many others have been individualized to each employee on their computer screen and virtual desk through the company's online functional services. The online functional service emerging with business to employee (B2E) is an area of further research.

OBSERVATIONS AND CONCLUSION

Researchers, practitioners, and managers have seen the evolution of virtual communication, virtual teams, virtual desks, virtual offices, and virtual companies. Total quality management, after proving itself in the manufacturing sector, has shifted to the financial service sector. Banking organizations are adopting continuous improvement and Six-Sigma as change management programs since the banking sector is becoming more competitive. Without teamwork, there is no continuous improvement and Six-Sigma. Major organizations seem to have well implanted the concepts of teamwork. However, to gain more competitive edge banking organizations are enhancing the concept of teamwork further by combining the continuous improvement concept and standard teamworking practices coupled with virtual teamworking activities to be more competitive and perform better. This research has focused on the adherence of the virtual interactive communication process to the normal teamworking and continuous improvement activities in a major Australian retail banking organization. This has illustrated the emergence of a new form of consultative, participative, and interactive virtual teamworking approach continually working as a team to further improve performance and be competitive according to organizational goals, values, and objectives. Team members adopting the continuous improvement teamwork approach are defined as a continuous improvement team.

This chapter's main goal was to illustrate the new form of continuous improvement teamworking approach where the concepts of teamworking, virtual teamworking, and continuous improvement are adopted together. Through a systematic participant observation study, the findings of this study reveals that there is a close relationship between the four major domains of the CTIO model which relates to teleconferencing, online functional services, continuous improvement and team meetings. As a result of the findings, better use of people at work, teamworking, communication technology, operational and functional systems can be used through the continuous improvement teamworking approach model to efficiently and productively run organizations. It is better for an organization to employ people with up-to-date technological know-how, with a good understanding of continuous improvement teamworking while working face-to-face and/or virtually to constitute a dynamic and hybrid team to be competitive and achieve better performance. This book chapter is relevant to senior managers and managers who are attempting to use continuous improvement teamworking through the CTIO model as an effective asset for obtaining productive performance and achieving competitive advantage for their firms.

REFERENCES

Adam, E. E. (1992). Quality improvement as an operations strategy. *Journal of Industrial Management and Data Systems, 92*(4), 3-12.

Asif, S., & Sargeant, A. (2000). Modelling internal communications in the financial services sector. *European Journal of marketing, 3*(4), 299-318.

Arvan, A. (1988). Those fabulous Japanese banks. *Bankers Monthly, 105*(1), 29-35.

Atkinson. C. (1997). The total team way. *National Society for Quality through Teamwork (NSQT), 7*(3),32-34, Salisbury, England.

Australian Bankers' Association. (2004). *Code of banking practice.* Sydney NSW, Australia.

Avkiran, N. (1997). Models of retail performance for bank branches: Predicting the level of key business drivers, *International Journal of Bank Marketing, 15*(6), 224.

Badiru, A., Chen. J., & Jen. J. (1992). IEs help transform industrial productivity and quality in Taiwan. *Industrial Engineering, 24*(6), 53-55.

Barad, M., & Kayis, B. (1994). Quality teams as improvement support systems (ISS): An Australian perspective. *Management Decision, 32*(6), 49-57.

Battellino, R. (2000). *Deregulation.* Paper presented at the Australian Finance and Capital Markets Conference, The Westin Hotel, Sydney, Australia.

Belbin, M. (1981). *Management teams: Why they succeed or fail.* London: Butterworth-Heinemann.

Berge, Z. L. (1998). Differences in teamwork between post-secondary classrooms and the workplace. *Education and Training, 40*(1), 194-201.

Berk, J., & Berk, S. (1995). *Total quality management, implementing continuous improvement.* Kuala Lumpur, Malaysia: S. Abdul Majeed & Co. in Association with Sterling Publishing Company,Inc.

Bermus, P., & Fox. M. (2005). *Knowledge sharing in the integrated enterprise, interoperability strategies for enterprise architect.* New York: Springer.

Bernstel, J. B. (2002). Teaming with possibilities. *ABA Bank Marketing, Washington, 34*(3), 14-12.

Carroll, J. M. (1989). *Interfacing thought: Cognitive aspects of human-computer interaction.* MA: The MIT Press.

Cohen, S., & Brand, R. (1993). *Total quality management in government (USA).* A practical guide for real world. The Jossey-Brass Publication administration series.

Collis, J., & Hussey, R. (2003). *Business research: A practical guide for undergraduates and post-graduate students* (2ⁿᵈ ed.). Palgrave Macmillan: Creative Print and Design.

Conner, M., & Finnemore, P. (2003). Living in the new age: Using collaborative digital technology to deliver health care improvement. *International Journal of Health care Quality Assurance, 16*(2), 77-86.

Conti, B., & Kleiner, B .H. (1997). How to increase teamwork in organizations. *Training for Quality, 5*(1), 26-29.

Coppola, N. W., Hiltz, S. R., & Rotter, N. G. (2004). Building trust in virtual teams. *IEEE Transactions on Professional Communication, 47*(2).

Covey, R. S. (1989). *The 7 habits of highly effective people: Powerful lessons in personal change.* New York: Free Press—A division of Simon and Schuster, Inc.

Cowan, R. A. (1984). *Teleconferencing: Maximising human potential.* Preston Publication.

Creswell, J. W. (1998). *Qualitative inquiry and research design: Choosing among five traditions.* California: SAGE Publications, Inc.

Denbigh, A. (2003). The *Teleworking handbook, the essential guide to working from where you want* (4ᵗʰ ed.). London, UK: A & C Black.

Dawson, P., & Patrickson (1991). Total quality management in the Australian Banking sector. *International Journal of Quality and Reliability Management, 8*(5), 66-76.

Duncan, E., & Elliot, G. (2002). Customer service quality and financial performance among Australian retail financial institutions. *Journal of Financial Services Marketing, 7*(1)25-38.

Edwards, A., & Wilson, J. R. (2004). *Implementing virtual teams: A guide to organizational and human factors.* Aldershot/Hants: Gower Publishing Limited.

Escriba-Moreno, M. A., & Canet-Giner, M. T. (2006). The combined use of quality management programs and work teams. A comparative analysis of its impact in the organizational structure. *Team Performance Management, 12*(5/6), 162-181.

Gandy, A., & Chapman C. S. (1997). *Information technology and financial services, the new partnership.* The Chartered Institute of Bankers. Chicago: Glenlake Publishing Company Ltd.

George, M. L., Rowlands, D., Price, M., & Maxley, J. (2005). *The Lean Six Sigma Pocket. 60 Toolbook. A quick reference guide to nearly 100 tools for improving process, quality, speed and complexity.* Mc Graw-Hill.

Glassop, L. I. (2002). The organization benefits of teams. *Human Relations, 55*(2), 225-249.

Goggin, G. (2004). *Virtual nation: The Internet in Australia.* Sydney: UNSW Press.

Goh, M. (2000). Quality circles: Journey of an Asian enterprise. *The International Journal of Quality & Reliability Management, 17*(7), 784-793.

Greenwood, F. (1992). Continuous improvements to meet customer expectations. *Journal of Systems Management, 43*(2), 13-15.

Hallberg, B. A. (2003). *Networking: A beginner's guide* (3rd ed.). McGraw-Hill/Osborne.

Harvard Business School. (2004). *Creating teams with an edge: The complete skill set to build powerful and influential teams.* Boston: Harvard Business School Press.

Haskins, J. S. (2002). e-teamwork: Using an intranet to your advantage. *AFP exchange*, Bethesda, *22*(1), 62-67.

Hallberg, B. (2005). *Networking: A beginner's guide* (4th ed.). Emeryville, CA: The McGraw-Hill Companies, Inc.

Hensley, R. L., & Dobie, K. (2005). *Assessing readiness for six sigma in a service setting.* Managing Service Quality, Vol.15. No.1. Greensboro, USA: North Carolina A & T state University, Department of Business Administration.

Hooper, N. (2005). The Australian Financial Review newspaper, pp.1 & 17.

Hutley, P. S. B., & Russell, P. A. (2005). *An introduction to the Financial Services Reform Act, 2001* (3rd ed). Australia: LexisNexis Butterworths.

Igbaria, M., & Tan, M. (2002). *The virtual workplace.* Hershey, PA: IDEA Group Publishing.

Ingram, H., Richard, T., Scheuing, E., & Armistead. (1997). A systems model of effective teamwork. *The TQM magazine, 9*(2), 118-127.

Institute of Quality Assurance (IQA-bulletin). (March 2005-April 2006). *Quality world.* Grosvenor Crescent, London: Friary Press.

Jacko, J. A., & Sears, A. (2003). *The human-computer interaction handbook: Fundamentals, evolving technologies, and emerging applications.* Mahwah, NJ: Lawrence Erlbaum Associates Publishers.

Jenning, J. (May 6, 2006). Accountancy toes the online approach. Accounting and Finance.

James, R. (1991). Quality service in banking: how to turn good intentions into reality. *Hoosier Banker*, Indianapolis, *74*(11), 43.

Khoshafian, S., & Buckiewicz, M. (1995). *Introduction to groupware, workflow, and workgroup computing.* John Wiley and Sons, Inc.

Kissoon, V. S. (2007). The research ethnographic research cycle as a substantial qualitative methodology to illustrate the continuous improvement teamworking model. In *Proceedings of the Biennial International Conference* (Professionally Speaking: Qualitative Research and the Professions), Association of Qualitative Research, Melbourne, Australia.

Kissoon, V. S. (2007). Continuous improvement teamwork approach in the banking sector. In *Proceedings of the 5th ANZAM and 1st Asian Pacific Operations Management Symposium* (Future Challenges of the Asian Pacific Region), Melbourne, Australia.

Kissoon, V. S. (2007). A process management improvement practical application through the teamworking approach. In *Proceedings of the 21st ANZAM International Conference* (Managing our Intellectual and Social Capital), Sydney, Australia.

Kock, N. (2005). *Business process improvement through e-collaboration: Knowledge sharing through the use of virtual groups*. Hershey, PA: Idea Group Publishing.

Landesberg, P. (1999). In the beginning, there were Deming and Duran. *The Journal for Quality and Participation*, Cincinnati, 22(6), 59-60.

Macey, J. R. (2006). Commercial banking and democracy: The illusive quest for deregulation. *Yale Journal on Regulation, 23*(1).New Haven: Yale University, School of Law.

Mandviwalla, M. (1993). *The world of collaborative tools*. Paper presented at the People and Computers VIII Conference (HCI'93), Computer and Information Sciences, Temple University, Philadelphia, USA.

Margerison, C. J. (2002). *Team leadership, A guide to success with team management systems*. UK: Thomson.

McCracken, S. (2001). *Banking and financial institutional law*. Published in association with the Australasian Institute of banking and Finance. Sydney: Thomson legal and Regulatory Limited trading as Lawbook Co.

Mink, G., Mink, P., & Owen, K. (1987). *Groups at work, Techniques in training and performance development series*. Englewood Cliffs, NJ: Educational technology Publications.

Mitchell, R. (1999). Quality circles in the U.S: Rediscovering our roots. *The Journal for Quality and Participation, 22*(6), 24-28.

Moncrief, M. (April 12, 2006). Banking reporter, The Age business newspaper.

Moutinho, L., & Phillips, P. A. (2002). The impact of strategic planning on the competitiveness performance and effectiveness of bank branches: A neural network analysis. *International Journal of Marketing, 20*(3), 102-110.

Nemiro, J. (2004). *Creativity in virtual teams: Key components for success*. San Francisco: John Wiley & Son, Inc.

Nurmi, R. (1996). Teamwork and team leadership. *Team performance management: An International Journal, 2*(1), 9-13, MCB University Press.

Preece, J., Rogers, Y., Sharp, H., Benyon, D., Holland, S., & Carey, T. (1994). *Human-computer interaction*. Essex, London: Pearson Education Limited.

Quality Systems. (1996). Quality Control Circle hand Book, Singapore.

Ramona, N. C., & Fjermestad. (2006). *Collaborative project management: Challenges and opportunities for virtual teams and projects in e-collaboration*. USA: Oklama State University and New Jersey Institute of technology.

Ricchiuto, J. (2005). *Appreciative leadership, building sustainable organizations*. Cleveland: Designing life books.

Shapiro, J. C. (1997). The impact of a TQM intervention on teamwork: A longitudinal assessment. *Team performance management, University of Oxford, 3*(3), 150-161.

Silverman, D. (2001). *Interpreting qualitative data: Methods for analysing talk, text, and images*. London, UK: SAGE Publications Ltd.

Simon, S., & Schuster. (2004). *The seven and eight habits of highly effective people.* Covey-Principle Centered Leadership Programme.

Singapore Technologies Automobile. (1996). *Business improvement handbook* (5th ed.). Singapore: Singapore Technologies.

Singh, M. (2005, November 23-25). *Business to employee (B2E) e-management.* Proceedings of the 6th International We-B (Working for E-Business) Conference, Melbourne, Australia.

Silverman, D. (2001). *Interpreting qualitative data, methods for analysing talk, text, and interaction.* USA: Sage Publication.

Sommer, S. S. (2002). *A practical guide to behavioural research: Tools and techniques* (5th ed). New York: University of California.

Snee, R. D., Kelleher, K. H., & Reynard, S. (1997). *Improving team effectiveness* (Report No. 156). New York: CQPI, University of Wisconsin.

Spradley, J. P. (1980). *Participant observation.* USA: Thomson Learning Academic Resource Centre.

Stamatis, D. H. (2003). *Six-Sigma for financial professionals.* NJ: John Wiley and sons, Inc

Tagliaferri, L. E. (1982). As quality circles fade, a bank tries top-down teamwork. *American Bankers Association, ABA Banking Journal, 74*(7), 98.

Terziovski, M., Sohal, A., & Moss, S. (1999). Longitudinal analysis of quality management practices in Australian organizations. *Total Quality Management, 10*(6), 915-926.

The Weekend Australian Financial Review. (2006). *CBA ushers in the people era.* 2006. pp.13. Retrieved April 1-2, 2006, from http://www.afr.com

Timm, P. R., & Jones, C. G. (2005). *Technology and customer service: Profitable relationship building.* NJ: Pearson Education, Inc, Pearson Prentice Hall.

Thompson, L., Arlanda, E., & Robbins, S. (2000). *Tools for teams: Building effective teams in the workplace.* Needham Heights, Pearson Education, Inc.

Tranfield, D., Parry, I., Wilson, S., Smith, S., & Foster, M. (1998). Teamworked organizational engineering: Getting the most out of teamworking. *Management decision, 36*(6), MCB University Press.

Tyree, A. (2005). *Banking law in Australia* (5th ed.). NSW: Centrum Printing. LexisNexis Butterworths

Turvey, N. K., & Neal, A. (2001). *High performance work practices and business success. Evidence from Australian Enterprises. Results of the 2001 National Survey.* Queensland, Australia.

West, M., Tjosvold, D., & Smith, K. (2005). *The essential of Teamworking, International Perspectives.* West Sussex: John Wiley and Sons Ltd.

Yeh, E., Smith, C., Jennings, C., & Castro, N. (2006). Team building: A 3-dimensional teamwork model. *Team Performance Management, 12*(5/6), 192-197.

Yukongdi, V. (2001). Teams and total quality management. A comparison between Australia and Thailand. *The International Journal of Quality and Reliability Management, 18*(4), 387.

Zetie, S. (2002). The quality circle approach to knowledge management. *Managerial Auditing Journal, 17*(6), 317-321.

Chapter XIV
Cooperation Between Universities and ICT Enterprises

Juha Kettunen
Turku University of Applied Sciences, Finland

Lauri Luoto
Turku University of Applied Sciences, Finland

ABSTRACT

This study presents the regional development of universities aiming to increase their external impact on their environment. The purpose is to show that the activities of regional development and quality assurance at universities are important means of promoting the development of ICT in the region. Regional development is analysed in this study using the approach of quality assurance, which provides a general framework to analyse the cooperation between universities and enterprises operating in information and communication technology. The approach provides practical concepts, examples, and tools for universities to increase their external impact on their respective regions. The analysis of regional development strengthens the ability of the university to design its external engagement in its activities, report on the result achieved and prepare itself for external evaluations. The study contributes to the knowledge and practice of regional development in higher education and presents how educational institutions can support their regional engagement and incorporate the regional development in its activities. Regional cooperation between a higher education institution and ICT enterprises is illustrated with examples. Conclusions and recommendations are drawn based on the findings.

INTRODUCTION

Regional development and quality assurance emphasise different aspects of universities. These approaches have been developed independently of each other, but they can be integrated in the action plans and everyday work of educational institutions. These approaches promote the high-quality interaction of the university with its environment. The promotion of the information and communication technology (ICT) is especially important in the regions where the ICT has potential to increase the economic growth, employment, and welfare.

The strategic plans of regional development describe the direction and scope of the region in the future. The strategic plans adapt the financial and human resources of an organisation to the changing environment, markets, and customers to meet the expectation of stakeholders (Johnson & Scholes, 2002; Steiss, 2003). Universities are moving from the traditional public orientation towards a market orientation, which emphasises the engagement and outreach in its environment (Kettunen, 2004a, b, 2006a, b). The management of universities has also moved in an entrepreneurial direction (Kettunen & Kantola, 2006).

Quality assurance is a widely accepted holistic approach providing a framework for organisational development. Quality assurance is rather a philosophical approach to management than a technical quality standard. This interpretation of quality emphasises the autonomous role of universities. The development towards autonomy has increased the responsibility and accountability of the institutions. They have to report to their stakeholders on the external regional impact. Cooperation with enterprises using appropriate ICT has an increasing role in higher education.

The empirical part of this article describes the case of the Turku University of Applied Sciences (TUAS). ICT is one of the focal areas in the institution's overall strategic plan. The institution has a strategic theme of focusing its activities to meet the needs of the region. The institution also has a specific strategic plan for ICT. The strategic plans are implemented using the Balanced Scorecard approach and the management information system tailored to the institution (Kettunen & Kantola, 2005). The external impact of the institution is described in the societal and customer perspectives of the balanced scorecard. Measures with target values are annually set to promote the external impact.

The institution has cooperation with many outstanding global and local ICT enterprises. The article presents some typical cases of strategic alliances. The TUAS has a joint Education Support Centre with Microsoft Corporation. The institution also has close cooperation with the global Cisco Systems Inc. In addition, cooperation with the local enterprises such as GoodMood Ltd., MasterPlanet Ltd. and ICT Turku Ltd. is active. The TUAS built up a wireless local area network (WLAN) with the help of the local enterprises, the City of Turku and other universities.

The experience of this study shows that many ICT enterprises are willing to establish strategic alliances with educational institutions. Many of these enterprises have development projects related to education and recruit personnel among the graduates. The cooperating enterprises are in the front-line of technology transfer and are able to make offers of computers, software, and services at a reasonable price and make contracts for research projects with the institution.

This study is organised as follows: The study first introduces the main concepts used in this study and presents the quality assurance of universities in the context of regional development.

Then the contribution of the TUAS in regional development is presented. Thereafter the article describes empirical cases of cooperation between TUAS and ICT enterprises to promote economic growth, employment and welfare in the region. Finally, the results of the study are summarised and discussed in the concluding section.

BACKGROUND

Concepts of Regional Development

Higher education institutions (HEI) include traditional universities and universities of applied sciences or polytechnics. The traditional universities are science-oriented institutions, whereas the universities of applied sciences are new universities with a professional orientation. Polytechnic is an old term, which is used only rarely instead of the university of applied sciences. The terms "higher education institution" and "university" are used here interchangeably.

Universities have traditionally been serving international and national academic communities with low levels of local territorial embeddedness (Chatterton & Goddard, 2000). Due to the expansion of higher education, however, there has been a trend from the 1990s onwards in all Western countries to expect universities to benefit the community more directly in return for public funding (Schutte & van der Sijde, 2000). The role of universities in contributing to the social, cultural, and economic development of their environments is often known as a third mission or role of institutions. The name refers to the fact that the two other roles are research and education (Etzkowitz & Leydesdorff, 2000; Gunasekara, 2004).

According to Chatterton et al. (2000), a regionally-engaged university can become a key asset and powerhouse for economic development, since regional availability of knowledge and skills is as important as the physical infrastructure. Universities can contribute to the achievement of regional development goals in all their activities by establishing new institutional management structures to meet the demands of various regional stakeholders more effectively. The regional engagement of an institution does not only mean responding to the regional demands for skilled employees and research but also establishing an ongoing dialogue with the local community.

Clark (2001) states, based on his empirical study in five countries, that there is a growing imbalance between demands made upon universities and the capacity of traditional universities to respond it. Thus, there is a need for entrepreneurship at universities to cope with the new requirements. The concept of entrepreneurial university is based on an idea that it is possible for a university to shape its environment and have

a diversified funding base and, at the same time, strengthen university collegiality, autonomy, and educational achievement. What is needed for this kind of combination is to have a management system that both gives power to departments to liberate their energies and provides sufficient university-level leadership.

Church, Zimmerman, Bargerstock, and Kenney (2003) identify the activity of having interaction with the external non-academic community as "outreach," but use the term interchangeably with the term "engagement." The term outreach is defined by Michigan State University (1993) as follows: "Outreach is a form of scholarship that cuts across teaching, research and service. It involves generating, transmitting, applying, and preserving knowledge for the direct benefit of external audiences in ways that are consistent with university and unit missions."

The definitions of the third role of universities differ in the way the region is described. Should the interaction between the university and its environment take place in a particular geographical area to meet the needs of that area, or is it important as such, no matter where it takes a place. The Finnish Act on Universities of Applied Sciences states that institutions should "work in cooperation with business and working life as well as other institutions, especially in the region where they are located." The traditional universities have defined their mission to serve the whole of society.

In the United States of America, the third mission has been defined as outreach or engagement (Church et al., 2003). The Finnish universities of applied sciences aim to support the regional development, which reflects the intended aim of the institutions to focus their activities to meet the needs of the region where they operate. It is therefore appropriate to use the term "regional development" instead of outreach and engagement. The selected term is widely used in the European Higher Education Area.

The success in the fulfilment of the regional development of a university can also be evaluated by results. The criteria may include the presence of a regional development strategy, HEI's contribution to the development of regional strategies, the proportion of graduates employed in the region, the university's role in the creation of new enterprises, the provision of continuing education and contributions to cultural development (Kinnunen, 2001).

Figure 1 describes the concept of regional development and the interdependence of the main roles. The concepts have been adopted from Bringle, Games, and Malloy (1999) and applied in this study to the Finnish universities of applied sciences. The third role or mission of a university may actually be quite a misleading concept for regional engagement, because regional development is rather an aspect in other missions than a mission in its own right.

The education category of regional development includes supervising and guiding students to participate in community service. This category includes traditional course-based project and service learning, profession-related career training and students volunteering in the community if their degree programme is involved. Volunteer students may serve the community as part of a class and learn more for their careers. In this category, it is difficult to make a clear distinction to the service.

The service category of regional development includes activities, which are typically based on the productisation of the results of research and development. The products are typically presented in the service catalogues on the Web or in brochures. The service includes many activities that are not outreach, such as the internal support service for the institution and community service activities in which the personnel member participates as a citizen but not as a scholarly expert.

The research and development category of regional development includes evaluation studies, policy analyses, technical assistance, and technology transfer. Such activities are regional development when they are conducted in collaboration with businesses, non-profit organisations, schools, healthcare organisations or other external constituents. This category includes the projects in which the university uses its expertise to interact with external groups in a reciprocal relationship.

The support unit for regional development provides outreach instruction for the different administrative units of the institution. The support unit also documents the external impact of

Figure 1. Regional development and other tasks of the universities in the local community

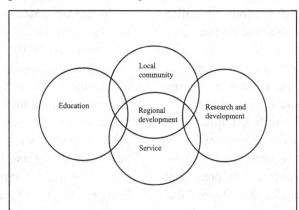

the institution. The documentation is useful in several ways. The institution is accountable to its stakeholders on its external impact. The information provided by the support groups helps management to plan the external engagement for ensuring that the units contribute appropriately to the institution's regional commitment.

The support unit for regional development helps the institution's management, the Finnish Higher Education Evaluation Council, and other stakeholders to evaluate the institution's engagement and outreach. The quality assurance systems of universities are regularly evaluated in the European Higher Education Area. The evaluation of the regional development or the external engagement is an important part of quality assurance, because it ensures that the education, services, and research and development appropriately meet the needs of the region and society.

Quality Assurance in Higher Education

In recent decades, universities in Finland, as in other western countries, have gained more financial and operational autonomy from the government. This shift has caused a need for effective governmental steering mechanisms. The concept of autonomy corresponds to the concept of accountability in higher education. The more autonomous the institution is the greater is the need to report to the stakeholders on the strategic objectives achieved.

Kivistö (2005) argues that the relationship between central government and publicly funded universities can be described using principal-agent theory. The principal engages the agent to perform some service on behalf of the principal. The agent usually receives payment or other benefit in return for the efforts. The main issue in theory is how is it possible for a principal to establish such incentive and information structures that cause the desired agents to behave according to interests and objects of the principal. Recent developments in nation-wide quality assurance systems for universities can be understood as principals' attempts to strengthen their information and incentive structures.

The European ministers responsible for higher education from 40 European countries have decided to establish a European Higher Education Area with a mechanism for quality assurance by 2010. The autonomous universities are responsible for their quality assurance systems. Therefore there is no single approach to quality assurance in higher education. The procedures for the quality audit may also vary between countries. In Finland, the aim is to combine external evaluation with internal development processes of universities. The evaluations are development-focused rather than accountability-focused.

The universities have had the process ownerships of evaluations (Liuhanen, 2005). For example, university evaluations conducted in Finland in 1990s were required by the Ministry of Education, but the universities were allowed to decide the theme and timing of the evaluation and nominate members to the peer review groups. Giving the process ownership to the universities has, to some extent, encouraged them to utilise the evaluations. The idea of ownership is not far from the idea of empowerment. Empowerment means giving means to achieve something. Empowerment as a paradigm of evaluations emphasises the role of an evaluation as a tool for internal improvements rather than external accountability.

Regional Development in Quality Assurance

Regional development is related the concept of the "fitness of purpose" of quality assurance. According to Woodhouse (1999), it is the most commonly accepted definition of quality among higher education. The concept focuses on the defined mission and strategic objectives of the institution with no check of the fitness of the processes with regard to any external objectives or expectations.

At the institutional level, this quality concept is incorporated in the strategic plan. On the lower organisational levels, the tasks and development steps needed for quality assurance are defined in the annual action plans.

It is common to make a distinction between the concepts of "fitness of purpose" and "fitness for purpose" (Saari, 2006). Fitness of purpose is related to environment of an institution including the regional expectations and customer satisfaction. The institution's external impact on the region also belongs to this category. Fitness for purpose is based on the ability of an institution to fulfil its mission and strategic objectives (Harvey & Green, 1993). The external evaluators may assess whether the resources, methods and other organisational arrangements are adequate to achieve the desired outcomes in regional development.

The godfather of quality management, W. Edwards Deming, has pointed out that the first step in quality assurance is the identification of customer needs through market research (Kogure, 1998). How can universities carry out market research and who should be questioned? The customers of the universities are clearly different from the customers of enterprises. The institutions should clearly define their geographical region and plan the degree programmes, which are important for the region. The role of central government is to supervise universities and provide them with financial resources.

Local economic outlooks, regional strategies and other information are used to plan changes to the education and other activities. Students have their own views, which are not necessarily consonant with the needs of working life. The demand for labour is the fact that defines how graduates gain employment in the region. Universities try to reach a consensus by open discussion, using the knowledge of technological and societal change and all the relevant information available.

The quality of education needs to be considered from the point of view of customers, because the contents and objectives of education are planned to satisfy their needs. An important aspect of education is that the subjective expectation of the student may be different from the needs of employers in the region. The image of the educational institution affects the values students attach to their expectations of education. Applicants make up their minds regarding the education before they can be certain about its quality and employment prospect. The institution's responsibility for students is associated with the planning of education and takes place before the students have even applied to the institution.

The Contribution of the TUAS in Regional Development

The TUAS has emphasised its accountability and reported on its contribution to society and especially to its local community by a social responsibility scheme. The institution has published a corporate social responsibility report since 2003. This is a report where the approach of Global Reporting Initiative (2006) is used to analyse the external impact of the institution on its region.

The report is partly based on a survey made among the personnel at the institution. In 2005, a survey was made to ascertain the commissions of trust and working group memberships with regional impact of the personnel of the TUAS. Such memberships are, for instance, expert tasks in various working groups, municipal commissions of trust or memberships on the boards of enterprises or organisations. The Web survey was completed by 156 persons, accounting for 21% of the full-time personnel of the TUAS.

Table 1 describes the extramural commissions of trust and memberships of the working groups at the TUAS. The positions and memberships of the personnel are related to the regional, professional, or working life organs. The regional organs include municipal or other regional or sub-regional organs. The professional organs include professional associations, trade unions,

Table 1. Extramural commissions of trust and memberships of the working groups of the personnel at the TUAS

	Share, %	Frequency
Regional organs:		
Municipal organs	14	55
Regional or sub-regional organs	7	26
Professional organs:		
Professional associations	16	63
Trade unions	15	57
Other associations and societies	23	89
Working life organs:		
Enterprises	8	31
Business organisations	4	14
Other	13	48
Total	100	383

or other associations and societies. The working life organs include private enterprises, business organisations, and others.

The number of memberships and commissions of trust reported at the TUAS was 383 at the TUAS. In these the share of regional organs is 21%, professional organs is 54% and working life organs 25%. More than 80% of the organs were operating in Southwest Finland. Almost half (46%) of the tasks were connected with employment at the institution. The personnel of the TUAS has an important effect on the region in the educational fields of technology, social services, and health care and fine arts.

The TUAS has systematically documented and recorded its links with working life since 2003. Each administrative unit of the institution reports at the beginning of each year on the concrete working life contacts of the previous year. Forms of cooperation include practical training, commissioned Bachelor's theses, diverse projects, research and development ventures, and the service operations of the institution. The reporting of the links

with working life helps management to promote regional development and provide services such as software to help customer relationships.

Table 2 describes the shares of the various forms of collaboration with the working life at the TUAS 2003-2005. The practical training of students clearly constitutes the largest share of collaboration. The reason is that the degree programme includes compulsory practical training, which is usually 30-45 ECTS credits and takes more than half a year of the typical study period of four yeas. The theses have a share of 10 %. The aim is that all the theses should be commissioned. They are written for enterprises or other organisations in order to help the students to obtain the development skills needed in working life and gain employment. The share of service activities and other collaboration has been increasing.

Figure 2 depicts the working life collaboration contacts of the TUAS in South and Middle Finland. The sparsely inhabited North Finland has been left out, because there are only relatively few contacts. In 2005, Finland had 432 municipalities,

Table 2. Shares of the various forms of collaboration with the working life at the TUAS 2003-2005

	2003	2004	2005
Practical training, %	68	63	53
Bachelor's theses, %	12	9	10
Service activities, %	8	7	11
R&D projects, %	3	4	5
Delegations, %	0	2	4
Commissions of trust, %	2	1	1
Other collaboration, %	7	14	16
Total, %	100	100	100

Figure 2. Working life collaboration contacts of the TUAS in 2005

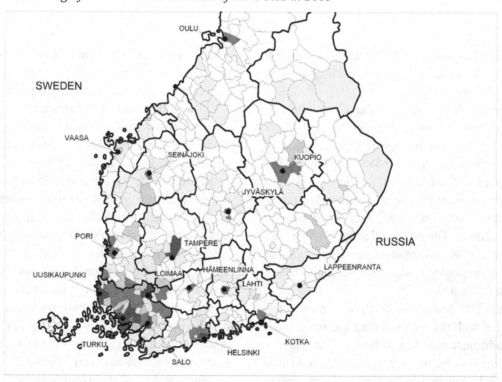

Table 3. Shares of working life partners located in and TUAS graduates employed in Southwest Finland

	2003	2004	2005
Collaboration partners, %	75	77	72
Employed graduates, %	75	74	74

Table 4. Number of working life partners and contacts of the TUAS

	2003	2004	2005
Collaboration partners	1725	2490	2340
Collaboration contacts	6511	7838	7492

which form 19 regions having regional councils. Turku is the capital city of Southwest Finland, which is the region located in the South-West of Finland by the Finnish Archipelago. Southwest Finland has 54 municipalities.

The strategy of the TUAS has focused the activities of the institution to meet the needs of Southwest Finland. The contents of the degree programmes and research projects are planned to serve Southwest Finland. The map shows that most of the working life contacts are in Southwest Finland. The strategic plans have been effectively implemented and the activities of the TUAS are regionally concentrated. The TUAS also has a few nationally important degree programmes such as those in fisheries, library and information service and beauty and cosmetics. Therefore, the TUAS has working life contacts all over the country.

Table 3 shows the shares of working life partners and TUAS graduates employed in Southwest Finland. It can be seen that the TUAS is a highly focused regional institution. The share of col-

laboration partners was 72-77 % in Southwest Finland. In addition, 74-75% of the graduates gained employment in Southwest Finland. The education and other activities are targeted mainly at enterprises and other organisations in the private sector. In 2005, the share of the private sector was 59%.

Table 4 shows the number of working life partners and contacts of the TUAS in 2003-2005. The number of partners has varied from 1725 to 2490, depending on the activities of the institution. The number of contacts has varied from 6511 to 7838. The institution aims to increase the number of partners, which will open up new possibilities for practical training, theses, and projects during studies. In order to increase cooperation the institution has made general agreements with the enterprises and public sector organisations to promote cooperation. The agreements include many ICT enterprises.

Regions are typically described and developed using the concept of clusters introduced by Porter (1990, 1998). They are geographical concentrations of interconnected universities, enterprises and other organisations. They may compete but also cooperate with each other. The main clusters of Southwest Finland include the ICT, biotechnology, and maritime industries. All the universities in the region are committed to the promotion of ICT, where economic growth and employment is expected.

MAIN FOCUS OF THE CHAPTER: EXAMPLES OF COOPERATION

Microsoft ESC: A Learning Environment and a National Support Centre

The education support centre (ESC) is a learning environment developed by Microsoft Corporation. ESCs are student-led centres providing support services for users of personal computers in educational institutions and other public sector organisations. The centres operate in close cooperation and typically within the partner universities. The ESC concept has spread to many European countries so that there is typically one centre in each country.

ESC Finland has operated in association with the TUAS since spring 2005. The centre provides its services to various customer organisations through service agreements. The ESC concept has brought to Finland a new innovative way of training ICT professionals at the tertiary level. By cooperating with Microsoft Corporation, the TUAS has an opportunity to build a learning environment that would not otherwise be possible.

The students working in ESC Finland first take Microsoft certification courses and examinations, which constitute the quality control of the services provided for customers. By utilising the courses planned by Microsoft Corporation and its partners, the TUAS conserves its own resources and, at the same time, can make sure that the

students receive the most recent knowledge of Microsoft products.

In the centre there are both engineering and business students working in an enterprise-like environment. Students acquire both study credits and working experience when solving problems of their customers. They also learn at the grassroots level how to run a service business and in that way the ESC concept also enhances students' entrepreneurial skills.

For the public sector, organisations operating in South-West Finland, ESC Finland provides an affordable support service for Microsoft products. This kind of service was not previously available on the market. ESC Finland also provides its services to the TUAS itself. Thanks to cooperation with the producer, the ICT students and teachers of the TUAS have the latest releases of Microsoft software products, which support high-quality learning.

The TUAS also has other kinds of cooperation with Microsoft Corporation. Recently the TUAS organised a competitive bidding for Microsoft Office software on behalf of all the 31 Finnish universities of applied sciences. Joint purchase is a cost-effective way to obtain software. Without the joint bidding all the institutions would have prepared their own respective purchases, which would have increased the workload and also the price of the software.

Cisco Network Academy: Building Regional Networks

The Cisco Network Academy is a higher education partnership scheme of the network device manufacturer Cisco Systems Inc. Through the programme, the institution and the students may use Cisco-made online material and examinations. The students also have access to the material off-campus on a 24/7 basis and can pursue their studies whenever and wherever they prefer. The institution saves resources and improves quality as the teachers do not need to plan and teach courses by themselves. Another advantage is that the study materials are always up to date. The Cisco Network Academy courses are utilised at the TUAS both in compulsory and optional study modules.

The students are able to take Cisco certification examinations at authorised testing centres. The courses taken at the TUAS have the same content as the Cisco certification courses elsewhere. The certificates of the Cisco Network Academy are recognised and accepted all over the world. Passing the examination improves students' employability and makes their professional skills more transferable. Exchange students visiting the TUAS can take courses, easily transfer credits to their home institutions and continue their studies there.

The TUAS has also promoted lifelong learning in local ICT enterprises by tailoring the Cisco Network Academy courses to their adult students. Continuing education helps to transfer the international technology to meet local needs. Up-to-date ICT is especially important for Finland, because it is a small, open economy, where international communication and trade are crucial.

The Cisco Network Academy is organised on a hierarchical basis. The TUAS is the leader of the Cisco network of educational institutions in Southwest Finland. It facilitates network training at other educational institutions by providing them with teacher training and online materials. Thus the TUAS is building regional networks and has a major impact in the quality of network technology training in the region.

GoodMood: Improving Accessibility

GoodMood is an example of an innovative and relatively young ICT enterprise founded in Turku. The enterprise is developing Webcasting technologies and offers both software products and complementary services for communication needs utilising streaming media. The use of Webcasting technologies improves the cost-efficiency of the

activities and offers benefits especially for organisations and networks where the units or partners of the network are distant from each other.

The TUAS utilises GoodMood's WIP solution, which enables live interactive meetings and on-demand presentations distributed through the internet. The TUAS has campuses in five towns in Southwest Finland, which means significant challenges in organising the internal communications. Using GoodMood WIP the institution has delivered lectures to different places and arranged briefings of the management simultaneously on all campuses. The Webcasting offers benefits especially for the smallest campuses, where the number of courses provided would otherwise be limited.

GoodMood WIP can be used not only in international communication, but also provides useful services for local enterprises. The Webcasting system encourages small and medium-sized enterprises especially to improve their productivity by applying new technologies in a cost-efficient way in marketing communication, negotiating with customers, and training personnel.

SparkNet: A Wireless Network for Innovations

SparkNet is the largest and most extensive wireless network solution in Finland with about 100,000 users. The SparkNet coalition was established in 2003 by local universities, the City of Turku, MasterPlanet Ltd. and ICT Turku Ltd., which is a development company coordinating the cooperation in the ICT field in Turku Region. Today there are also other partners, both in Turku, Southwest Finland, and elsewhere in the country.

SparkNet is based on the idea of exploiting existing network resources wirelessly. The members of the SparkNet coalition build pieces of a public wireless fidelity (WiFi) network instead of building their own WiFi network. Each partner of the SparkNet cooperation has invested in their own relatively inexpensive equipment. The cooperation is an innovative example of fruitful cooperation between the universities, municipalities and development enterprises.

Using SparkNet the students and employees of the TUAS have access to the wireless network via their mobile devices from all local university campuses, students' halls of residence and various public places. SparkNet makes it easy and affordable for students to pursue their studies wherever they want using video conferencing, voice over internet protocol (VoIP), online courses, and other systems. Having plenty of users, SparkNet is also a great platform for innovations and new business opportunities.

A representative of ICT Turku Ltd. is a member of the employers' advisory board in ICT at the TUAS. The TUAS has 26 advisory boards to help the institution to cooperate with the local enterprises and to develop education, research, and services to meet the needs of the local community. It is essential that the main clusters of the region are strongly represented in the advisory boards. The ICT advisory board has accomplished valuable work to promote regional development.

A Summary of the Cooperation with the ICT Enterprises

The TUAS has emphasised its regional engagement with the ICT clusters in various ways. The purpose is to improve the quality of learning, learning environments and to strengthen the external impact of the institution. The examples of cooperation describe various kinds of cooperation. Cooperation may be international, national, and local. Local cooperation is not limited to ICT enterprises; there are also examples of the cooperation with the municipalities and other universities.

Table 5 presents a summary of the activities, networks, and external impacts of the cooperation between the TUAS and ICT enterprises. The cooperation with ICT enterprises provides, for example, better learning environments and materials and provides students with transferable qualifications. The activities of the university are extended to international, regional, and local networks, where the university can help small and medium-sized enterprises especially and municipalities in networking on a win-win

Table 5. Activities, networks, and external impacts of cooperation with ICT enterprises

	Activities	Networks	External impact
Microsoft ESC	• New enterprise-like learning • Provision of transferable qualifications	• International cooperation with other ESC centres	• Affordable support services to public organisations • Internationalisation
Cisco Network Academy	• Provision of high-quality online materials • Provision of transferable qualifications	• Regional network of educational institutions	• Skilled labour force • Tailored courses for enterprises
GoodMood WIP	• Better access to courses	• Webcasting services offered to SMEs	• Cost-effective network communication
SparkNet	• Studying irrespective of place • Research on wireless networks	• Sharing resources with municipalities and universities on a win-win basis	• Opportunity to join the largest WiFi network in Finland • Cost efficiency

basis. The cooperation with ICT enterprises has numerous positive external impacts. It provides services to the public and private organisations and cost-efficient communication in the domestic and international environments.

As concluded in the background section, regional development should not be seen as a separate mission of universities, but rather as an aspect in universities' education, research and development and service activities. All the four cases previously described are serving several basic missions of universities. Education is a major activity of universities and, in Finland as well as in many other countries, public funding in mainly based on the results of education. Consequently, all the activities performed by the universities, whether aiming at network building or service operations, should also have a positive impact on credit accumulation. Two first cases (Microsoft ESC and Cisco Network Academy) are combining service functions and enhanced learning. All the cases but Microsoft ESC are also promoting online learning that is a powerful tool for avoiding unnecessary prolongation of study periods, especially with students who are working part time or who have small children.

FUTURE TRENDS: EDUCATION POLICY

The European Ministers responsible for higher education made a major contribution to the Bologna Process in the Sorbonne Declaration in 1998. The process aims to create the European Higher Education Area by the year 2010 (Bologna declaration, 1999). Initially the main focus of the process was the adoption of a Europe-wide system of easily comparable degrees based on two main cycles, undergraduate and graduate. In 2003, the European Ministers decided to approve the agreed set of standards, procedures and guidelines on quality assurance (Berlin Communiqué, 2003).

Based on these decisions, the European countries have set up national programmes for the enhancement of quality assurance in higher education. In Finland, all the HEIs are expected to establish quality assurance systems and will be externally audited by 2010 (FINHEEC, 2006). Many HEIs already have quality assurance systems, but they do not necessarily cover all their operations, as they are expected to do. HEIs' contribution to regional development is traditionally not at the core of universities' mission statements. Therefore many universities do not yet have quality assurance systems for regional development. In this respect, there is a need for developing new methods in the near future.

CONCLUSION

Education policy has guided universities to regional development and emphasised their external impact on the local community and society. The TUAS is a regionally-oriented institution, whose strategic plan outlines focusing its activities to meet the needs of its region. The institution has defined its region as Southwest Finland, where most cooperating partners are located. About 75 % of graduates find employment in this region.

The ICT cluster is important for Southwest Finland. The role of ICT has been recognised in many regional strategies. It is also important in the strategy of the City of Turku and the TUAS. The future economic growth of the ICT cluster is expected to be rapid compared to many other clusters. Therefore attention and resources have been targeted on the ICT cluster. The TUAS has declared its mission to take responsibility for the highest professionally-oriented education in Southwest Finland.

In keeping with their autonomous position, universities are responsible for quality assurance in all their activities. The concept of "fitness of purpose" is used to describe quality assurance in regional development. The concept focuses on how well the institution has defined its mission and strategic objectives to meet the needs of the region. On the other hand the concept of "fitness for purpose" emphasises how well the institution is able fulfil its mission by steering its internal processes and allocating financial resources to achieve external impacts on its region.

The practical examples described in this study show that the cooperation between the universities and ICT enterprises takes many forms. Cooperation provides better learning opportunities for students. It provides better learning environments and materials and produces transferable qualifications, which can be recognised in international environments. The cooperation with the ICT enterprises strengthens the networks of universities and customer organisation. The increased cooperation and networks provide cost-efficient means to develop the region and society.

Earlier in the chapter it was pointed out that the first step in quality assurance is the identification of customer needs. In the case of a regionally engaged university, the institution should define its geographical region, identify the needs of the region, and establish mechanisms to follow up the success in satisfying them. The four practical examples described in this chapter, illustrate the ways how a university can gain information of working life needs through close cooperation with ICT enterprises. This is a precondition for quality teaching and learning. In the case of the TUAS the results of the regional development are reported and communicated to the stakeholders using annual corporate social responsibility reports. The reports include the indicators of the external impact of the institution and the thematic maps of the coverage of the cooperation with the local community. Examples of the contents are also quoted in this chapter. The reporting is important for any HEI who desires to develop a quality assurance system that also covers the regional operations of the institution.

REFERENCES

Berlin Communiqué. (2003). *Realising the European higher education area.* Communiqué of the Conference of Ministers responsible for Higher Education in Berlin on 19 September 2003. Retrieved February 10, 2007, from http://www.dfes.gov.uk/bologna/uploads/documents/Berlin_Communique1.pdf

Bologna Declaration. (1999). *Joint declaration of the European Ministers of Education.* Retrieved February 10, 2007, from http://www.dfes.gov.uk/bologna/uploads/documents/BOLOGNA_DEC-LARATION1.pdf

Bringle, R. G., Games, R., & Malloy, E. A. (1999). *Colleges and universities as citizens.* Boston: Allyn & Bacon.

Chatterton, P., & Goddard, J. (2000). The response of higher education institutions to regional needs. *European Journal of Education, 35*(4), 475-496.

Church, R. L., Zimmerman, D. L., Bargerstock, B. A., & Kenney, P. A. (2003). Measuring scholarly outreach at Michigan State University: Definition, challenges, tools. *Journal of Higher Education Outreach and Engagement, 8*(1), 141-152.

Clark, B. (2001). The entrepreneurial university: New foundations of collegiality, autonomy, and achievement. *Higher Education Management, 13*(2), 9-24.

Etzkowitz, H., & Leydesdorff, L. (2000). The dynamics of innovation: From national systems and "mode 2" to a Triple Helix of university-industry-government relations. *Research Policy, 29* (2), 109-123.

FINHEEC. (2006). *Audits of quality assurance systems of Finnish higher education institutions.* Audit Manual for 2005-2007. Publications of the Finnish Higher Education Evaluation Council

4:2006. Retrieved February 10, 2007, from http://www.kka.fi/pdf/julkaisut/KKA_406.pdf

Global Reporting Initiative. (2006). *A common framework for sustainability reporting.* Retrieved November 14, 2006, from http://www.globalreporting.org/Home

Gunasekara, C. (2004). The third role of Australian universities in human capital formation. *Journal of Higher Education Policy and Management, 26*(3), 329-343.

Harvey, L., & Green, D. (1993). Defining quality. *Assessment and Evaluation in Higher Education, 18*(1), 9-34.

Johnson, G., & Scholes, K. (2002). *Exploring corporate strategy: Text and cases.* Cambridge: Prentice Hall.

Kettunen, J. (2006a). Strategic planning of regional development in higher education. *Baltic Journal of Management, 1*(3), 259-269.

Kettunen, J. (2006b). Strategies for the cooperation of educational institutions and companies in mechanical engineering. *International Journal of Educational Management, 20*(1), 19-28.

Kettunen, J. (2004a). Bridge building to the future of Finnish polytechnics. *Journal of Higher Education Outreach and Engagement, 9*(2), 43-57.

Kettunen, J. (2004b). The strategic evaluation of regional development in higher education. *Assessment & Evaluation in Higher Education, 29*(3), 357-368.

Kettunen, J., & Kantola, I. (2005). Management information system based on the balanced scorecard. *Campus-Wide Information Systems, 22*(5), 263-274.

Kettunen, J., & Kantola, M. (2006). Strategies for virtual learning and e-entrepreneurship. In F. Zhao (Ed.), *Entrepreneurship and innovations in e-business: An integrative perspective* (pp. 107-123). Hershey, PA: Idea Group Publishing.

Kinnunen, J. (2001). Korkeakoulujen alueellisen vaikuttavuuden arviointi (Evaluation of the regional impact of higher education institutions). Finnish Higher Education Evaluation Council Publications 5:2001. Helsinki: Edita.

Kivistö, J. (2005). The government-higher education institution relationship: Theoretical considerations from the perspective of agent theory. *Tertiary Education and Management, 11*(1), 1-17.

Kogure, M. (1998). *TQC in Japanese corporations-its review and a new way of development.* Tokyo: Nikkagiren.

Liuhanen, A. M. (2005). University evaluations and different evaluation approaches: A Finnish perspective. *Tertiary Education and Management, 11*(3), 259-268.

Michigan State University. (1993). *The defining dimension of university outreach.* Report of the provost's committee on university outreach. Retrieved October 11, 2006, from http://www.msu.edu/unit/outreach/missiondefinition.html

Porter, M. (1990). *The competitive advantage of nations.* London: MacMillan.

Porter, M. (1998). *On competition.* Boston: Harvard Business School Press.

Saari, S. (2006). Mistä korkeakoulujen laatukäsite ja laatu määrittyy? *Hallinnon tutkimus, 2,* 54-62.

Schutte, F., & van der Sijde, P. (2000). *The university and its region.* Enschede: Twente University Press.

Steiss, A. W. (2003). *Strategic management for public and nonprofit organisations.* New York: Marcel Dekker.

Woodhouse, D. (1999). Quality and quality assurance. In J. Knight & H. de Wit (Eds.), *Quality and internationalisation in higher education* (pp. 29-44). Paris: OECD.

KEY TERMS

Cluster: Clusters are geographic concentrations of interconnected enterprises, specialised suppliers, service providers, firms in related industries, and associated institutions in particular fields that compete but also cooperate.

Fitness for Purpose: The term describes how well the organisation is able to fulfil its mission by steering its internal processes and allocating financial resources to achieve the desired objectives.

Fitness of Purpose: The term describes how well the organisation has defined its mission and strategic objectives to meet the needs of the customer or region.

Higher Education Institution: Higher education institutions include traditional universities and profession-oriented institutions, in Finland called universities of applied sciences or polytechnics.

Quality Assurance: Some authorities make a distinction between quality assurance and quality control. Quality assurance rests on prevention, management systems, effective audit and review, while quality control includes monitoring, finding and eliminating causes of quality problems.

Strategic Planning: Strategic planning involves taking a view of the whole organisation and planning for the long term with clearly articulated values, mission, vision and strategic choices. The process of strategic planning helps management to lead the organisation towards the achievement of strategic objectives.

WiFi: Wireless fidelity describes the underlying technology of wireless local area networks. It was developed for use in mobile computing devices, such as laptops, in local area networks.

Chapter XV
Trust in Organizations:
An Islamic Perspective

Muhammad Mohtsham Saeed
University of Innsbruck, Austria

ABSTRACT

Recent changes in the overall global business atmosphere, for example, opening of economies, increase in exchange relations, volatility of the business environment, innovative products and services, rapidly changing markets, and knowledge-based firms and information-based systems all demand quick sharing of quite sensitive information. This swift sharing of sensitive information is a major source of competitive advantage in today's age and is not possible without trustworthy relationships of top management with external as well as internal customers (employees) of a business. Islam is the second biggest religion in the world with over 1/4th of the world's population as its followers. Where traditional literature believes that long-term relationships result in trust development, Islam considers that trust development results in building and maintaining long-term relationships. This chapter is specifically meant to highlight the role of trust from an Islamic perspective in a leader-followers relationship as well as a leader-customers relationship.

INTRODUCTION

Recent changes in the global business atmosphere have tremendously increased the requirements, which a business has to fulfil to remain competitive. The latest developments such as fast changing technologies, increase in exchange relations, interdependence of businesses, complex and knowledge based firms with their innovative ways to survive and thrive, customer care complexities, and swift relationship building requirements, etc., can only be handled with trust based relationships both within and outside an organization. In the world of far reaching technological advances and information based productions systems, which require a frequent sharing of sensitive information, trust becomes an even more important element (Bachmann & Lane, 1998).

As an important mechanism for coordination (Bradach & Eccles, 1989), trust has truly become a major source of competitive advantage in today's world. Especially due to shifting of organizations from formal/traditional organizational structures to a more flexible and group oriented atmosphere mostly on short-term basis, organizations need to build up methods for development of a swift trust. (Meyerson, Weick, & Kramer, 1996)

Religion on the other hand, has a major impact on human behavior, social interactions, and relationships (Abuznaid, 2006). Islam, which is the second biggest and fastest growing religion in the world (Armstrong, 2000) is often thought to be a misunderstood religion (Qutb, 1997). It is a complete code of conduct, which provides guidelines about every aspect of life including business. However, if we look into the literature, although there has been a lot of work in the western literature on "trust" but Islamic viewpoint on "trust" or "trust based leadership" has always remained a secret. This work is specifically meant to bridge the gap by eradicating such misconceptions, unveiling Islamic viewpoint on trust, highlighting the role of trust in leader-followers and leader-customers relationships and providing some clear guidelines to the business managers and leaders of Islamic world in their own religious/cultural context as to how trust can be made helpful for their business growth.

For this purpose, a trust based Islamic leadership model has been developed which highlights various trust based relationships within and outside an organization. Although all the relationships included in the model are important but we, in this article, after giving a brief introduction of the model as a whole, will be more focusing on role of trust in relationship of a leader with his followers and customers.

In context of leader-followers relationship, the renowned leadership model from Hersey and Blanchard (2006) has been amended/adapted according to Islamic teachings to assist Islamic leaders/managers in delegation of power process keeping in view the capabilities and willingness of their team members. For this purpose, four different levels of trust (T1, T2, T3, T4) have been identified which a leader can afford to exhibit for four different types of followers (R1, R2, R3, R4). Two case studies from Motorola and Bank Alfalah have also been included in this context. Whereas two other case studies (1) Grameen Bank (Bangladesh) and (2) Kashf Foundation (Pakistan) have been used to highlight the role of a leader's trust on customers in enhancement and expansion of a business.

BACKGROUND

Literature Review

Trust has got reasonable attention by different literatures of social sciences, for example Lewicki and Bunker (1996), Gambetta (1988), Saparito, Chen, and Sapienza (2004), and Langfred (2004) etc., and every literature has touched the issue from its own perspective. For example "Trust in Organization" written by American authors Kramer and Tyler (1996) is focused on American organizations, which might not be suitable for Islamic organizations. Although the relationship between societal trust and superior performance of overall economies has so far received some attention (Fukuyama, 1995) however the key role that trust plays in a leaders relationship with his followers or customers, has not got its due weight age so far. Especially, if we look at the issue from Islamic point of view, no or a very little attempt seems to have been made to derive the lessons from the Holy Seerah when we study it from power perspective (Siddique, 1998).

The available literature mostly covers the cultural or religious issues of Islamic countries and in some instances also talks about Islamic leadership/management in general. For example,

Hofstede (2003) in his renowned book "Culture's Consequences" is more concentrating on comparison of values, behaviors, institutions, and organizations between different nations which included some Islamic countries as well. Azmi (2002) has given a brief overview of the nature of Islamic state and leadership. On the other hand Beekun and Badawi (2004) have thrashed out leadership roles, the moral bases of Islamic leadership, exploring the leader follower relationship, and a couple of leadership models in general. There is another good piece of work by Ali (2005) who has tried to highlight Islamic school of thought from a business point of view by linking the human nature and motivation to Islam. Recently, Farid (2006), the CEO of "Alchemy Technologies" has written a wonderful account of his entrepreneurial exploits "Blue Screen of Death." No doubt, it is a wonderful attempt by a young Pakistani entrepreneur to tell his stories of three failed ventures followed by a tremendous success and is no doubt a good book on entrepreneurial failures and success but unfortunately all these pieces of work have failed to highlight the key role that trust plays in a leader-followers and leader-customers relationship in an Islamic context.

Trust in Islam

And if one of you deposits a thing on trust with another let the trustee (faithfully) discharge his trust, and let him Fear his Lord conceal not evidence; and whoever conceals it,—his heart is spoiled with sin. And Allah knows all that you do. (Holy Quran, 02-283)

Islam asks for creation of a trustworthy relationship, at the same time Islam also considers breaking of ones trust as highly undesirable and sinful. One who breaks the trust has been described as one with a sinful heart by Islam. Islam considers trust as a basic element in every type of relationship including the leader-followers and leader-customers relationships off course.

The true relationship between a leader and his followers or customers can survive only where an element of trust exists between the two. This will eradicate the suspicions in minds of both and they will help each other in the bad times too as much as they do in good times (Beekun et al., 2004).

For a leader-followers relationship Islam asks for an open and transparent delegation of powers process, based on capabilities and willingness level of the team members. Whereas for a leader-Customers relationship Islam encourages for a relationship based on goodwill and mutual trust and discourages the one based on selfishness or own profit maximization.

O you who believe! Eat not up your property among yourselves in vanity: but let there be amongst you traffic and trade by mutual goodwill. (Holy Quran, 04-29)

Leadership in Islam

Every one of you is a shepherd and every one is answerable with regard to his Flock. (Sahih Muslim, 20-4496).

The concept of leadership in Islam is a bit different from the traditional approaches to leadership. In Islam leadership is more than just an assignment; it is an exhibition of trust in all types of circumstances in both one's religious as well as worldly life. Prophet PBUH said that every one amongst you is a shepherd and is answerable with respect to his flock. He elaborated it further by saying that a caliph is shepherd over the people and shall be questioned about his subjects (as to what he did for the physical and moral well being of the people). Similarly a servant is a guardian over the property of his master and shall be questioned about as to how he safeguarded his trust. "Beware every one of you is a guardian and will be questioned with respect to his trust."

In fact, leadership in Islam is nothing but exhibition of a trust. It represents a psychological contract between a leader and his followers that he will try his best to guide them, to protect them and to treat them fairly and with justice (Beekun et al., 2004). When a leader will not break trust placed on him, the followers will also try their level best to meet the expectations of their leader and the trust exhibited on them. With respect to their morals, people resemble their rulers more than they resemble their fathers (Ali-The 4th Caliph).

In short, an Islamic organization always keeps trust in the centre of its core corporate values. Where the level of responsibilities assigned to an employee or the position given to a leader represent in fact the level of trust placed on his or her skills.

Trust-Based Islamic Leadership Model

Earlier, we discussed basic concepts of trust and leadership independently and their related significance in the organization from an Islamic perspective. Here we will try to interlink the both concepts to see the role that trust plays in Islamic leadership.

As shown in Figure 1, in every Islamic country, religion plays a fundamental role in shaping the cultural norms of the society. Religion has been an important source of all these shared values, common beliefs, normal behaviors, general perceptions, and overall understanding of the Muslims. Individuals make family and families when get together make a society. Being units of the society, all three, the leader, the followers and the customers' influence and are influenced by the cultural values of the society. So it is a reciprocal impact. Due to this impact of culture, which itself is an outcome of a big force (i.e., religion), a relationship of mutual trust develops between the leader and the followers.

In Islamic leadership, in addition to the trust of the followers, a leader is also equally trustworthy for his customers. This cycle of trust-based relationships doesn't complete unless the most important aspect, trust on Allah is included into it. All the Muslims know that nothing can happen to them except what Allah has ordained for them. He is Master. It is in Allah that the believers should put their trust (Holy Quran, 09-51)

Figure 1. Trust-based Islamic leadership model

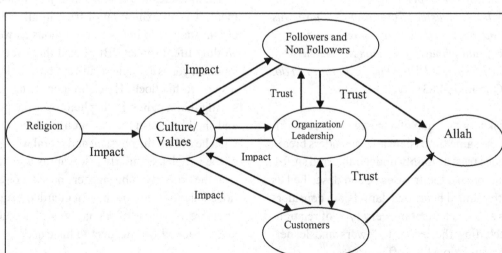

Though all the Muslims believe firmly in struggling hard to achieve the desired goals but eventually they put their trust on Allah for the outcome knowing that If Allah helps them, none can overcome them: If He forsakes them, who else is there to help them (Holy Quran, 03-160).

Although, to have a better understanding of a trust based Islamic approach to leadership and to see how this trust based Islamic mechanism works in the organizations, one needs to go into detail for each of the above relationships separately. But we in this article will be concentrating on the two most important relationships: (1)leader-followers relationship, and (2) leader-customers relationship.

LEADER-FOLLOWERS RELATIONSHIP

The jewel is valuable but your order is more valuable (Ayyaz).

These are the words of Ayyaz, when famous King Mahmood called all his ministers (who used to complain about king's blind trust on his own released slave Ayyaz and giving him control on all state funds) to show them the reason behind his great level of trust on his true follower. The king gave the most precious jewel in the treasury to all his ministers one by one and asked them to break it. All the ministers refused to do so thinking that it was the most favorite jewel of the king but when it came to Ayyaz, he without waiting a moment, hit it hard with a hammer and shattered it into pieces. Seeing this, the king asked Ayyaz "Why have u broken the jewel while all others have simply denied to do so because it was so valuable" Ayyaz replied beautifully, "the jewel is valuable but your order is more valuable."

The previous incident in Islamic history is a brilliant example of a leader's trust on his follower's skills and in return the follower's ability to fulfil his trust accordingly. On the other hand,

it also shows that not every employee is equally trustable. Although Islam stresses the need for a trust-based relationship between leader and his followers but at the same time Islam also requires leader to be vigilant and watchful. Islam doesn't ask for a blind trust at all. Since all the people are not the same. In every organization, there are some people who try to take undue advantage of their positions instead of working with zeal and zest for the accomplishment of the common objective. Allah warned Prophet to remain careful about these people. " *On their lips they have obedience but when they are not with you, a portion of them keep discussing all the night something very different from what you have told them but Allah records their nightly things. So keep clear of those, and put your trust on Allah, He is enough as disposer of affairs*" (Holy Quran, 04-81).

This makes it even more important for the leaders to differentiate between followers with respect to their trustworthiness but the real question is how to do that? The model below will help us answering the question.

4/4-An Islamic Model of Trust

Hersey et al. (2006) in their renowned leadership model have described four different leadership styles relating them to four different types of employees on the basis of their Capabilities and Willingness for a proposed task. Although the model is widely accepted and is quite helpful for managers/leaders to choose the most appropriate leadership style for their followers/team members, it ignores the element of trust which is very crucial for a successful leader-follower's relationship.

Following the same four broad categories of employees, we hereby will try to bridge the gap by identifying four different levels of trust in the light of Islamic teachings, which a leader can afford to exhibit for each of the above categories of employees. In figure 2 below, four levels of employee's trustworthiness have been identified as T1, T2, T3, and T4 for each category of em-

Box 1.

Types of Employees	Levels of Trust
R1 (Unable but Willing)	T-1 (Not trustable at all)
R2 (Unable and Unwilling)	T-2 (Trustable to a little extent)
R3 (Able and Willing)	T-3 (Trustable to very much extent)
R4 (Able but Unwilling)	T-4 (Fully Trustable)

Figure 2. Different categories of employees and relative levels of trust(Adapted from Hersey et al., 2006)

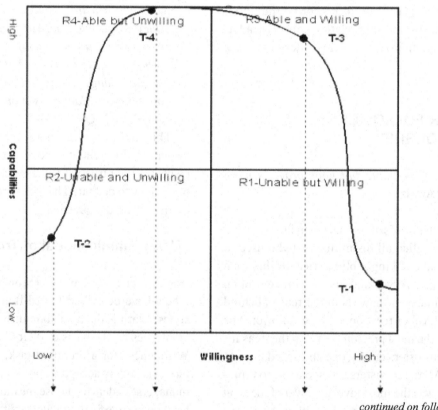

continued on following page

ployees (R1, R2, R3, R4) respectively depending upon their level of capabilities and willingness for a proposed task (see Box 1).

To have a better understanding of the division of employees together with their corresponding levels of trust and Islamic philosophy behind all these categorizations, every category has been discussed in detail hereunder.

Fully Trustable (R4-Able but Unwilling)

In Islam, knowledge, expertise/capabilities, are highly appreciated whereas willingness and covetousness for a post are highly discouraged. So the employees with highest level of capabilities and lowest desire for a higher post have been

Figure 2. continued

Trust Level-2	Trust Level -4	Trust Level-3	Trust Level-1
Unable and Unwilling (R2)	Able but Unwilling (R4)	Able and Willing (R3)	Unable but Willing (R1)
1-Trustable to a little extent (just to explore the talent)	1-Fully Trustable	1- Trustable up to very much extent	1-Not trustable at all
2-Requires full time monitoring to ensure the smooth running of operations.	2-Monitoring required very rarely.	2-Initially Requires quite Frequent Monitoring but then can be reduced gradually to the level-4	2-Requires a full time supervision and a close monitoring system to ensure the smooth running of operations.
3-Requires training/ Refresher courses and motivations to bring a positive change in their capabilities and attitude towards work.	3-Does not require any further Trainings; Employees of this category know their job very well and keep themselves updated about the latest developments in their field.	3-Doesn't usually require any further training but it may be useful to offer them sometimes refresher courses just to polish their capabilities.	3-Before assigning any task, all necessary training/Refresher courses are required to enhance their capabilities to a level required for the proposed task.
4-Requires regular encouragement and recognition of performance (Incentives, Rewards, Performance bonuses, etc)to make them active and useful members of the organization.	4- Once a task is assigned, employees of this category are usually self triggered, enthusiastic and motivated for their targeted goals. But occasionally a leader's pat on their shoulders can be even more helpful.	4-This level also doesn't necessarily require Recognitions for smooth running of operations Appreciations are however necessary to get extra ordinary results.	4-Requires Encouragement & recognition of performance for every tiny achievement to raise their productivity
5 –A centralized system is the most suitable one. Allowing freedom of expression to the members, all the important decisions are to be taken by the leader himself till the time they reach Level 3.	5- Maximum decentralization of authority is possible. This level of trust allows full liberty to the members to take the decisions on their own. The role of leader in such cases is only of a facilitator.	5-Although Powers can be decentralized to very much extent allowing a greater control to the followers, leader is still involved in all important decisions taken.	5 - A fully centralized system is the most appropriate one.

categorized as the most trustable ones mainly because:

- They have all required capabilities, knowledge, and expertise to carry out the proposed task efficiently without inviting any trouble or threat to the business, and
- Secondly they are not covetous for any higher post. They do not struggle for it as such. They are dedicated hardworking people focusing whole-heartedly on their work. There can be no possibility of any misappropriation of authority or funds in such a case.

If we look at the leadership paradigm of life of the Prophet PBUH, these were the two most significant factors that he used to determine trustworthiness of his followers for a task. Who can forget "Fatah Khaiber"? When he declared to give the flag next morning to a man who will be granted a magnificent victory by Allah. Next morning when every body present had a strong desire to be the one who gets the flag, Prophet PBUH called for "Ali" who was not even there due to his eye trouble. He spat in his eyes (which made him all right as he was never ill) and gave him the flag. Ali being so happy for this honor went to the war and won the battle elegantly. (Sahih Muslim, 31-5917)

Prophet knew that Ali had no desire for the flag but had the excellent fighting capabilities so he preferred him to all others present there having a strong desire in their hearts to get the flag. And its not just Ali the fourth caliph, if we look into the history, selection of all four caliphs of Islam was made by the people. None of them ran after the leadership position or came forward as a candidate for caliphate. In Islamic leadership the basic ideology is the trust of others over somebody due to his distinctive and unique qualities and not the self interest or desire to become a leader.

Employees of this category are usually self-triggered and just need an opportunity to prove their abilities. Bolman and Deal (1997) provide us a beautiful example from the modern world in this regard.

Case Study 1: Hosain Rasoli

A brilliant case study from "Motorola" demonstrates how it impacts when a leader entrusts his highly capable employees with the tasks, which are beyond their imagination. Hosain Rasoli (A Muslim working for the company as a technician) was involved with power transformers. He often used to think about how these perform in the field. He was assigned to improve the quality of the transformers. After collection of information from various sources about the transformer, he finally convinced the development engineering team to re-design the parts and this eventually resulted in a 400% better product reliability. Rasoli is now Mr. Power Amplifier in Motorola.

An Islamic leader needs first to identify those members of his team who never ask for a higher position but who are dedicated focused and determined individuals and should then assign them important tasks, this will create a sense of responsibility, confidence, and ownership of the task in their mind and they will work with even greater passion and commitment, which ultimately will result in extra ordinary outcomes far beyond expectations of the leader. This is probably why that Sam Walton (the owner of Walmart stores) had to say that:

Extraordinary results can come from empowering ordinary people.

Trustable up to Very Much Extent (R3-Able and Willing)

Although Islam discourages covetousness in employees for some post, but since it cannot be generalized that every employee willing to get some higher post does have some mild intentions behind it, highly capable employees, willing to take charge of a higher post are also considered to be trustworthy to a greater extent by Islam. However, they require a little monitoring and supervision by leader in order to differentiate between those who have their hidden motives and those who really want to do something in their life and are determined to strive for harder goals. If we recall Quranic story of Prophet Yousuf when drought resulted in severe shortage of edibles i.e. wheat etc and he wanted to be appointed as In charge of Granaries and storehouses, the king of the time, appointed him to his desired post irrespective of the fact that he himself had asked the king to put him in charge. The king knew that he wanted to do real service to the people and couldn't have any hidden motives and he was the only one who could successfully manage the storehouses during such a long drought period (Yousaf, 1989).

Similarly, Umar the second caliph of Islam too followed the same rule and selected Utbah ibn Ghazwan as commander of the army squad to capture the city of Ubullaha, which was considered to be a huge arms depot of the Persian forces. Although there were many candidates and Utbah was also one of them having a desire to get leadership of such a challenging task. He was selected only because of Umar's trust on his fighting and commanding skills. He knew that Utbah (RA) was a brave soldier who had fought all-important wars including Uhud, Khandaq and Badar etc. He had also fought a terrible battle of

Yammammah and returned unscathed. He was known for his exceptional skills in the use of spears and arrows the basic weapons used in the wars those days (Hamid, 1995) and his integrity and devotion to his religion was unquestionable.

So this shows that an Islamic leader can still trust a follower even if he asks for a position himself but that is only if (1) the follower is the most capable of all and (2) The leader has no doubt (based on his past experience) about the follower's integrity and candor.

Trustable to a Little Extent (R2-Unable and Unwilling)

Training and refresher courses help in motivation and subsequent conversion of the idle part of an organization's human resource into a productive one. The employees who are neither capable nor covetous for any higher post fall in this category. Islam is a religion of optimism discouraging strongly disappointments (Holy Quran, 39-53). Islam doesn't totally discard them. After giving necessary training to refine their talent and reinstate their motivation and passion for work such employees are also considered trustable to a little extent by Islam. And depending upon their performance, afterwards this level of trust can gradually be increased, allowing the employees more freedom with lesser monitoring and supervision by leadership.

Case Study 2: Ijaz Farooq

Realizing the significance of training/refresher courses, top management of Bank Alfalah (a fastest growing bank with a big network of Islamic banking in Pakistan) believes in developing the potential of the bank's employees to the fullest extent. Its "training and development centre" is responsible for organizing multi-level high quality training programmes for all the staff members in

all possible areas of banking. This is obligatory for each staff member of the bank to attend at least one training program in a year. Where TDC is unable to provide specialized training for certain group of staff members, services of well reputed external trainers are hired to fill the gap. Ijaz farooq presently working as executive in charge (chairman) Islamic banking started his career with bank as a dispatcher of bank's correspondence but with the passage of time, bank provided him the learning/training opportunities at bank and encouraged him through motivation to ornament himself with related qualifications.

Initially he was entrusted to work as a cashier and later on with the passage of time seeing his honesty, dedication, and talent flourishing day by day, top management of the bank kept on increasing the level of trust on his skills and capabilities and decreasing the supervision/monitoring level by the bank leadership. Today he is country head of Islamic Banking and is all in all in his area of operations.

Not Trustable at All (R1-Unable but Willing)

The real spirit of Islamic leadership lies not in winning positions or occupation of higher seats, it lies in winning and occupying hearts of the people (Iqbal, 2006). In the last category we refer to that particular group of employees who are at the lowest level of knowledge/skills but have strongest desire for a higher post. Since Islam strongly discourages covetousness for a higher post especially where it is not coupled with required capabilities, this type of employees is not considered to be trustworthy at all.

Prophet PBUH himself refused to such people who asked for a position and Prophet PBUH did not find them competent and capable for any task. For example, Abu Musa entered the apartment of Prophet PBUH with his two cousins. One of them addressing the Prophet PBUH said "please appoint us as rulers of some lands that Allah has entrusted to you. The other also seconded his opinion and requested for the same." Prophet PBUH refused them straightaway saying:

We do not appoint to any position one who asks for it nor anyone who is covetous for the same (Sahih Muslim, 20-4489)

Similarly, Abu Dharr when requested Prophet PBUH for his appointment to a public office, Prophet PBUH stroked his shoulders with his hand and said:

Abu Dharr, you are weak and authority is a trust and on the Day of Judgment it is a cause of disgrace and repentance except for those who fulfilled their obligations properly (Sahih Muslim, 20-4491)

Sometimes it also happens that employees are enthusiastic and a little impatient to go for harder targets but due to lack of experience cannot realize the future problems associated with that task. They think themselves to be capable but in reality they are not. Here it is the responsibility of an Islamic leader to foresee the future and decide if interested member is fully prepared to carry out a task or not. A man from the Ansar took the Messenger of Allah (May peace be upon him) aside and said to him Will you not appoint me governor as you have appointed so and so." He (the Messenger of Allah) said "you will surely come across preferential treatment after me, so you should be patient." (Sahih Muslim, 20-4549).

In a nutshell, an Islamic leader does not appoint any person to any position who is incapable but covetous for a higher post because if given a position, such a person will concentrate more on his personal ambitions rather than working for common goal of the organization. Even if he doesn't, his appointment can not be beneficial for the business from any angle.

Role of Followers in Making the Relationship Successful

Due to reciprocal nature of trust based relationship between a leader and his followers. In Islam followers too have some responsibilities for developing a trustworthy, open and friendly atmosphere in the organization. Without their trust on leader's abilities or obedience to his instructions, such a trust-based mechanism cannot work. It is obligatory on them to listen to the orders of the leader and obey him in adversity and prosperity, in pleasure and displeasure and even if someone else is given preference over them as a leader (Sahih Muslim, 20-4524) and to avoid dispute on delegation of powers to any such person who is deemed to be a fit recipient thereof in the eyes of the leader. (Sahih Muslim, 20-4538). Obedience should be accorded to him in all circumstances without questioning his compatibility to the position except when they find some clear signs of his disobedience to God which can be the only justified reason for non compliance of a leader's orders (Sahih Muslim, 20-4541).

This way, when leader and followers both fulfil their responsibilities in the light of golden teachings of their religion, a relation of mutual trust develops between the two automatically which is inevitable for any business to reach the heights of excellence.

LEADER-CUSTOMERS RELATIONSHIP

Parallel to a leader's trust on his followers, Islamic leadership also needs to develop and maintain a trustworthy relationship with business clients. Where traditional literature believes that long-term relationships result in trust development, Islam considers that trust development results in building and maintaining long-term relationships.

Thinking from a materialistic perspective, it looks very impractical to put one's business at risk and to build business relationships 100% based on trust without protection of one's own interests, but if we take it from Islamic perspective, neither it is something related to an imaginary dream world nor it is impractical or unbelievable in a real business world of today. Muhammad Younas of Grameen bank has turned it into an on-ground reality by basing whole of bank's business on a single characteristic i.e., trust on customers and in return experiencing an unbelievable growth of his business.

Case Study 3: Grameen Bank

For less privileged class of the society, getting a business loan through traditional banking is nearly impossible. These banks usually demand collateral, mortgage etc before entering into any sort of lending agreement. Since the poor people don't have any assets to offer as collateral, they are not considered to be trustworthy and reliable by traditional banking system.

But Younas, a Muslim economist in Bangladesh has made it possible for them. Grameen Bank (GB) has reversed conventional banking practice by removing the need for collateral and creating a banking system fully based on mutual trust.

In 1976, he started his business by lending less than a dollar's amount to each of the needy artisans in Jobra, a small village in Bangladesh. The idea was to trust such people who had nothing to offer as collateral and enable them to earn their livelihood respectfully. At that time; he didn't realize that he was giving a new trend to the banking industry of his country.

When we initiated disbursing tiny loans, we could never imagine that one day we alone would be reaching the figure of four million borrowers two and a half decade later (Muhammad Younas)

A sum of less than a dollar was off course a very tiny amount itself but it helped remarkably the artisans in earning their livelihood. On the other hand, this trust based approach proved to be equally beneficial for his business as well which experienced a rapid growth and was turned into a formal bank in 1983.

Now the Bank has emerged as a big giant on the map of banking world and as of May 2006, it has 6.61 million borrowers, 2226 branches, and 18795 staff members who provide services in 71,371 villages of Bangladesh covering 100% of the rural area in the country.

The tremendous performance of Grameen bank is by no means less than a miracle for traditional bankers who cannot even think about giving out loans merely on the basis of trust unless they are satisfied with the amount of securities offered against proposed loans. To safeguard the interest of the bank they trust on securities and still they face (sometimes very severe) bad debts problems. Whereas Grameen bank on the other hand trusts the people and enjoys a rapid expansion, with an overall 99% recovery rate and quite reasonable profitability.

It follows the principle of total trust i.e. no collateral, no legal Instrument, no group guarantee or joint liability and no restriction on utilization of the loan amount. Borrowers are at liberty to use their funds wherever they want.

Due to one golden principle of trusting the customers, Grameen Bank today is the best known micro credit bank of the world. Where such a trust-based mechanism has made the bank an exemplary institution, it has also played a quite significant role in reduction of poverty and enabling a large number of people to earn their livelihood respectably. The positive impact of the bank's business on its poor and formerly poor borrowers has been documented in many independent studies carried out by external agencies including World Bank, IFRPI etc. Further admitting the bank's contributions towards poverty reduction and bringing a positive change in the life of the mankind, Muhammad Younas of Grameen Bank has recently been awarded the Noble Prize for Peace.

Case Study 4: Kashf Foundation

Seeing remarkable success of Grameen Bank, Kashf foundation in Pakistan started its operations in 1996 with a client base of 15, consisting of poor women residing in Lahore, the second biggest city in Pakistan. Following the same guidelines of Grameen Bank, Kashf too targeted the low income women (mostly from the poor areas) who can't otherwise qualify for a loan through conventional banking system of the country. Kashf trusted the poor women and offered them the loans on easy terms and conditions. Kashf keeps its Loan approval process very simple. There is no requirement of collateral or a personal guarantee. Further paying back the loan's instalments on time entitles the borrower for even greater amount of credit and at lesser rates of interest.

Provision of micro credit to the poor women on such borrower friendly terms and conditions brought a pleasant change in their daily lives and they started earning their livelihood respectably. On the other hand Kashf's business too experienced a rapid growth. Kashf today is a leader in the Pakistan Microfinance Network and is the only microfinance institution in Pakistan with a specific focus on women.

Main reason behind such a rapid expansion was the complete trust in its clients allowing them an easy access to a greater amount of capital on revolving basis. Kashf now operates in all the major districts of Punjab Province in Pakistan and is considered one of the most efficient microfinance providers in South Asia, with a perfect recovery rate of 100%.

FUTURE TREND/RESEARCH POSSIBILITIES

The attention of the business world is now diverting from traditional approaches to Islamic ethical and moral standards. For example, many Islamic products of financing are now being introduced by various western financial institutions in order to capture the big market of Muslim inhabitants. There needs to be a lot more research on different aspects of business from an Islamic perspective. Specifically for trust development purposes, the role of trust in relationships of followers with each other and its subsequent impact on an organizations performance is yet to be explored. Another possibility could be to examine the reciprocal trustworthy relationship between followers and customers from an Islamic point of view. A cross cultural comparison afterwards can also be a good idea.

CONCLUSION/SUMMARY

The basic ideology behind Islamic leadership is the trust of the people over somebody whom they chose for their leadership (due to his distinctive and unique qualities) and not the self interest or desire of someone to be a leader. Similarly, the level of responsibilities assigned to an employee represents in fact the level of trust placed on him by the leader.

Islamic leadership involves various relationships and every relationship is based on a single characteristic i.e. Trust. That is why an Islamic organization always keeps trust in the centre of its core corporate values and considers exhibition of trust indispensable for all types of relationships especially leader-Followers and leader-customers relationships.

For an ideal working environment in an organization, Islam stresses a lot for creation and maintenance of trustworthy relationship between a leader and followers. Since Islam is a complete code of conduct. It doesn't only stress, it gives clear guidelines to make it work. Where it requires followers to trust their leader's knowledge, expertise and wisdom and refrain from disputing delegation of power decisions made by him, it also gives leader a full mechanism to determine the trustworthiness of the followers and provides 4 different levels of trust which a leader can afford to exhibit for 4 different types of followers, depending upon their capabilities and willingness level for a post or task.

In Islam, Knowledge, expertise/capabilities are highly appreciated whereas willingness and covetousness for a post are highly discouraged. So the employees with highest level of capabilities and lowest desire for a higher post have been categorized as the most trustable ones whereas the followers with lowest level of capabilities and highest covetousness for a post are not found trustable at all.

Although Islam discourages willingness/covetousness in employees for some post, but since it cannot be generalized that every employee willing to get some higher post is not trustworthy at all, highly capable employees, willing to take charge of a higher post are also considered to be trustworthy to a greater extent by Islam. Even if an employee asks for a position himself, an Islamic leader can still trust a follower to a greater extent provided:

1. The follower is the most capable of all.
2. The leader is internally satisfied about his integrity and candour.

Islam is a religion of optimism. It acknowledges the fact that training and refresher courses help in motivation and subsequent conversion of the idle part of an organization's human resource into a productive one. That is why, the employees who are neither capable nor covetous for any higher post are also considered trustable to a little extent after giving them necessary training/refresher courses.

In short, the trust based relationship between a leader and his follower is reciprocal in nature in Islam. If a leader trusts the members and assigns them some tasks, members too are supposed to deploy all their efforts to fulfil the trust exhibited on them in order to ensure smooth and efficient running of the trust mechanism. This Islamic mechanism of trust based leadership works like a bicycle with two wheels (i.e., leader and the followers). The wheel ahead (the leader) leads the bicycle (the organization) to its desired destination with a trust that wheel behind (the followers) will provide a full support to get ahead. And wheel behind provides its full assistance with complete trust that the wheel ahead has the ability to take the bicycle to the desired destination in the shortest possible time and through best possible ways, without inviting any threats/accidents to the bicycle (the organization).

Parallel to a leader's trust on his followers, Islamic leadership also needs to develop and maintain a trustworthy relationship with business clients. In this context Islam advocates the idea of trusting the people not objects. Trust on customer works as an accelerator for the business growth and expansion as we have seen its impact in case of Grameen Bank and Kashaf Foundation.

The reciprocal trustworthy relationship of a leader with his followers and customers and a collective trust of all three on Allah create an atmosphere where open, quick, and smooth flow of information becomes possible thus enabling the top management to take well-timed and accurate decisions and remain competitive in today's rapidly changing market.

On one hand, where the study will help Muslim world to have a better understanding of leadership notions in their own religious context, thus enabling the managers and leaders of the companies operating in any Islamic country, to exploit their true potential by encouraging an active participation/an open communication based on trust within and outside the organization. This will be equally helpful for the non-Muslims to understand leadership paradigm of Muslim world and to interact with more than one billion Muslims throughout the world in a better way. Especially for the multinational/foreign companies having their operations in the Muslim countries with an altogether different values/culture, this work will be very useful.

REFERENCES

Abuznaid, S. (2006). Islam & management—what can be learned. T*hunderbird International Business Review, 48*(1), 125-140.

Ali, A. J. (2005). *Islamic perspectives on management & organizations.* Glos: Edward Elgar Publishing Limited.

Alsharif, M. M. (2005). *Sahih Muslim: The Authentic Hadiths of Muslim* (Imam Muslim Bin Hajaj Bin Naysaburi). Garden Grove, CA: Dar Al Kotob & Jarir Bookstore.

Armstrong, K. (2000). *Islam: A short history.* New York: Random House.

Azmi, S. (2002). Islamic economics. New Delhi: Good word Books Pvt Ltd.

Bachman, R., & Lane, C. (1998). T*rust within & between organizations: Conceptual issues & empirical applications.* Oxford: Oxford University Press.

Beekun, R. I., & Badawi, J. (2004). *Leadership- An Islamic perspective.* Beltsville, Maryland: Amana Publications.

Behzadnia, A. A., & Denny, S. (1981). *To the commander in chief from Imam Ali to Malik-e-Ashter.* Houston, TX: Free Islamic Literature.

Bolman, L. G., & Deal, T. E. (1997). *Reframing organizations: Artistry, choice & leadership.* San Francisco: Jossey-Bass.

Book, L. Y. (2001). Strategic management. In *Management in Malaysia.* Kuala Lumpur: Malaysian Institute of Management.

Bradach, J. L., & Eccles, R. G. (1989). Price, authority & trust: From ideal types to plural forms. *Annual Review of Sociology, 15*(1), 97-118.

Davis, K. (2002). *Organizational behaviour-human behaviour at work.* New York: McGraw-Hill.

Deresky, H. (2004). *International management-managing across borders & cultures.* NJ: Prentice Hall.

Dirks, K., & Ferrin, D. (2002). The role of trust in organizational settings. *Organization Science, 12*(4), 450-467.

Dirks, K., & Ferrin, D. (2002). Trust in leadership: Meta-analytic findings & implications for research & practice. *Journal of Applied Psychology, 87*(4), 611-628.

Farid, J. A. (2006). *Blue screen of death: A Desi, s misadventure in the land of opportunity.* Karachi: Alchemy Technologies.

Fukuyama, F. (1995). *Trust-the social virtues & the creation of prosperity.* London: Hamish Hamilton.

Gambetta, D. (1988). Can we trust. In D. Gambetta (Ed.), *Trust-making & breaking of cooperative relations.* Oxford: Blackwell.

Garfinkel, H. (1967). *Studies in ethno methodology.* Englewood Cliffs, NJ: Prentice-Hall.

Hamid, W. A. (1995). *Companions of the Prophet.* Leicester: Kitaboon.

Heisig, U., & Littek, W. (1995). Trust as a basis of work organization. In W. Littek, & T. Charles (Ed.), *The new division of work,* (pp.17-56). Berlin: De Gruyter.

Hersey, P., Blanchard, K. H., & Johnson, D. E. (2006). *Management of organizational behaviour:*

Leading human resource. New Jersey: Prentice Hall.

Hofstede, G. (2003). *Culture's consequences: Comparing values behaviors institutions & organizations across nations.* California: Sage Publications Inc.

Hosmer, L. T. (1995). Trust-the connecting link between organizational theory & philosphical ethics. *Academy of Management Review, 20*(2), 379-403.

Iqbal, M. (2006). Bang e Dara. Lahore: Iqbal Academy.

Knox, S., & Maklan, S. (2005). Case study-guarenttee trust bank of Nigeria: Building a trusted brand in financial services. *Thunderbird International Business Review, 47*(6), 737-756

Kramer, R. M., & Tyler, T. R. (1996). *Trust in organizations.* London: Sage Publications.

Langfred, C. W. (2004). Too much of a good thing: The negative effects of high trust & autonomy in self-managing teams. *Academy of Management Journal, 47*(3), 385-399.

Lewicki, R. J., & Bunker, B. B. (1996). Developing & maintaining trust in working relationships. In R. M. Kramer, & T. R. Tyler (Ed.), *Trust in organizations: Frontiers of theory & research* ,(pp. 114-139). Thousand Oaks, CA: Sage Publications.

Limerick, D., & Cunnington, B. (1993). *Managing the new organisation.* Chatswood: Business & Professional Publishing.

Lorenz, E. H. (1988). Neither friends nor strangers: informal networks of subcontracting in French industry. In D. Gambetta, D. (Ed), *Trust making & breaking of cooperative relations,* (pp. 194-210). Oxford: Blackwell.

Meyerson, D., Weick, K. E., & Kramer, R. M. (1996). Swift trust & temporary groups. In R. M.

Kramer, & T. R. Tyler (Ed.), *Trust in organizations: Frontiers of theory & research* (pp. 166-195). Thousand Oaks, CA: Sage Publications.

Mishra, A. (1996). Organizational response to crises—The centrality of trust. In R. M. Kramer & T. R. Tyler (Ed.), *Trust in organizations: Frontiers of theory & research,* (pp. 261-287). Thousand Oaks, CA: Sage Publications.

Qutb, M. (1997). *Bhrantir Berazale Islam.* (Translated by Razzaq, A.A. Islam-The Misunderstood Religion). Dhaka: Dhunik Prokashani.

Ring, P. S., & Van De Ven, A. H. (1992). Structuring cooperative relationships between organizations. *Strategic Management Journal, 13*(7), 483-498.

Sabel, C. (1992). Studied trust-building new forms of cooperation in a volatile economy. In F. Pyke, & W. Segenberger (Ed.), *Industrial districts & local economic regeneration,* (pp. 215-250). Geneva: IILS.

Sako, M. (1992). *Prices quality & trust-interfirm relations in Britain & Japan.* Cambridge: Cambridge University Press.

Saparito, P. A., Chen, C. C., & Sapienza, H. J. (2004). The role of relational trust in bank-small firm relationships. *Academy of Management Journal, 47*(3), 400-410.

Siddique, K. (1998). *Political dimensions of Seerah.* London & Toronto: ICIT.

Thompson, J., & Martin, F. (2005). *Strategic management, awareness, & change.* London: Thomson Learning.

Williamson, O. E. (1993). Calculativeness, trust, & economic organization. *Journal of Law & Economics, 34*(1), 453-502.

Yousaf, A. A. (1989). *Holy Quran: Text, translation & commentary.* Beltville, MD: Amana Corporation.

Zaheer, A., & Venkatraman, N. (1995). Relational governance as an interorganizational strategy: An empirical test of the role of trust in economic exchange. *Strategic Management Journal, 16*(5), 373-392.

Zucker, L. G. (1986). Production of trust – International source of economic structure 1840-1920. *Research in Organizational Behaviour, 8*(1), 53-111.

Section V
Innovation and Knowledge Management

Chapter XVI
Supporting Innovation Through Knowledge Management in the Extended Enterprise

Mikel Sorli
Fundación LABEIN, Derio, Spain

Dragan Stokic
ATB, Bremen, Germany

ABSTRACT

Managing of knowledge for innovation in an extended enterprise (EE) environment is a key issue. This in turn requires effective utilization of information and communication technologies (ICT). This chapter addresses the application of ICT for knowledge management (KM) needed for innovation in industry. An ICT-based KM system to support innovation process in EE environment (i.e., to support mastering of the innovation process) is presented. The main objective of the new AIM system is to provide the means of stimulating the creation of innovative ideas in general, and specifically on potential product/process improvements and on problem solving. The AIM system supports collection of such ideas throughout EE from people involved with the products and processes, as well as a development of the collected ideas into innovations.

INTRODUCTION

In current global markets, **innovation** is generally one of the most critical factors for success in industrial firms. Former advantages based on aspects such as costs reduction, natural resources, and geographical situation are no more valuable since globalization is flattening these issues and furthermore, needed natural resources are usually coming from outside. One must always be meaningful of the need of fostering innovation fighting against usual themes as: "cut your costs," "get focused." Nowadays the motto should be "innovate or lose." This new situation imposes changes in the way the companies work. One of these changes has to be accomplished in the field of new product development that is the basis of the success of manufacturing companies (Sawaguchi, 2001; Sorli, 1999).

New ways of working move ineluctably toward the **extended enterprise**. The extended enterprise (EE) concept in parallel with the concurrent enterprising looks for how to add value to the product by incorporating to it knowledge and expertise coming from all participants on the product value chain. Manufacturers need to benefit from "extended enterprise" techniques (Dyer, 2000) by involving all people from throughout the product life cycle (suppliers, customers, design, production, and servicing) to provide their product knowledge to enhance product development and support. This new paradigm implies a quite new scenario: knowledge capturing and sharing, new forms of interrelationship between companies and persons.

Innovation is important for all companies, and just as important is the need to get innovative products to the market place quickly. Therefore, it is important to talk about "Management of **product development time and process improvement/innovation time within EE**." Under this new paradigm, companies able of "mastering" the development time can launch the product/service into the market or improve their processes (e.g., shop-floor process, maintenance processes etc.) just spending the planned time and resources and at the right moment, meaning at the exact date when the product achieves the higher and faster market penetration. This will give back to the company higher market share and better returns.

As it has been previously mentioned, knowledge useful to design engineers comes in many forms and it can come from many sources inside and outside the company. A common need among companies is to be able to acquire and process this knowledge so that a greater, richer, centralized source of knowledge and information is available to produce better designs, faster, with greater innovation, and with less re-inventing the wheel. Therefore, ICT based systems to support management of knowledge related to product/process innovation is of key importance.

This chapter presents one ICT based solution of effective management of knowledge for product/process innovation.

BACKGROUND

On this framework industry in the XXI century has to face these challenges by using techniques to deal with aspects as:

- **Extended enterprise (EE) (Davis & Spekman, 2003):** Enterprises are surpassing physical boundaries and establishing durable links with other companies: engineering, sub-contractor, providers, but are mostly at a loss on how to deal with customers in both ends of the chain. The customer is clearly a very relevant actor at the conceptual phase of the product life where the designer has to understand customer's needs and feelings as well as at the other end of it when the extended product has to live together with the user along its operating live.
- **Concurrent enterprising:** As the idea of EE refers to a longer time frame, concurrent enterprising focus more in the specific relationship among companies to set up new operations: new product development and launch, marketing activities covering a wider range than only the physical product by itself (extended product) and others.
- **Extended product:** Product is rapidly changing from physical tangible product to a plus of intangible assets related to fulfill-

ing requirements, fitting the right product to the right needs, servicing the product and maintaining it through its life, empowering the user to get the best from it and last but not lest facilitating the product retrieval and eventual replacement in a environmental friendly manner.

- **Support of ICTs (Levy, Rajaraman, & Ordille, 1996):** Besides some psychosocial changes, the technical challenge is related to the massive use and incorporation to industry of the new IT and Internet based technologies. There is a strong human implication in the users about getting used to the new technologies and changing the way the work has to be performed, especially related to knowledge management (KM) in an EE environment, leading to a number of problems which have to be considered when applying ICTs in industry.

- **E-working:** A newly issued term that implies working at a distance by using information and communication technologies (ICT). It covers not only the software/hardware tools but goes beyond physical aspects including social behavior and cultural change. The old ways of working change in a great amount since e-working allows workers such things as interacting on real time with people in distant locations or working on round-the-clock modus passing the token on from one to another through different time zones

From this basis, the new trends should be to extend the e-Working systems to the whole life cycle of the extended product. In such way, new working methods will be able of supporting the "extended enterprise" to monitor and capture knowledge from the "extended product" all through its life cycle. This will cover from the conception of the product/service to its disposal and back to "re-incarnation," that's to say: launching improved new extended products based on the knowledge collected from the existing ones.

PROBLEMS ADDRESSED

The new system described in this chapter—AIM system—supports the collection of innovative ideas and relevant knowledge (AIM, 2005) throughout the EE for new and existing process and product developments. These ideas and knowledge will later be developed in a collaborative way fostering industrial innovations as team work will be enhanced by cooperation between manufacturers, customers, and suppliers by means of the Internet facilities provided by the AIM system, "accelerating" innovation into the market.

As stated, one of the most important targets for the AIM tool is the collection of ideas throughout all the EE. For this, every worker is called to provide ideas and opinions on how improving the productive process and product quality. The problem to be solved here is the motivation for the workers to use a tool to which they are not familiar. A system of incentives could be tried, which must be decided by the companies, and the assumption that any initiative coming from each actor is always well considered must be acquired.

It must be assured, therefore, that all operators can introduce ideas easily. This poses the problem of structuring of user interface for introduction of ideas into the system in such a way that people not trained in using the tool are able to quickly do it. To achieve this, the distinction of the AIM users in three categories (administrator, process designer, and standard user) is done. For the standard user, the introduction of ideas must be friendly and easy, only needing to relate them to the product, unit, or process for which the idea could be useful.

The rational followed to support innovation process in EE is based on the following assumptions:

- The ideas for product/process innovations have to be collected throughout an EE in order to use all potentials for innovation available in an EE

- The ideas are proved either as possible solutions to identified problems in products/ processes or as potential improvements of products/processes

- The ideas generation and gathering can be stimulated by provision of knowledge on:
  - o Problems related to processes/ products
  - o "Similar" ideas on products/processes.
  - o All other available knowledge on (extended) products/processes

- Ideas have to be effectively assessed to select those, which are most likely to lead to innovative solutions (process or product innovations)

- Ideas may need to be combined to achieve innovations

AIM system has very much based on TRIZ concepts (Altshuller, 1988; Kohnhauser, 1999; Terninko, Zlotin, & Zusman, 1996), from which the general concepts and the methodology for innovation using the innovation algorithm (Altshuller, 1999) have been integrated.

The main objectives of using AIM solution are:

- To develop a means of stimulating the creation of innovative ideas for innovation in broad sense, and specifically on problems solving and on potential product/process improvements and collecting them from people involved with the products and processes.

- To provide aids to efficiently gather information/knowledge on problems and improvement potentials regarding products and processes as a base for required innovation.

- To provide an approach to combine (experience based) knowledge on products/processes and innovation ideas.

- To develop a way of processing these ideas and storing them into a structured knowledge repository. To ensure that all useful knowledge (innovative information) is saved and made available.

- To develop a means of analysing innovative ideas to determine which are useful, and which are not, that is, to enable the viability of ideas to be assessed.

- To develop the best means of delivering the innovative ideas to the product and process designers for maximum effect.

In order to meet above listed objectives and baseline scenarios the analysis of the state-of-the-art relevant for the addressed system has been carried out. The state-of-the art involves the following aspects:

- Methods which can be used to develop innovative ideas

- Extended enterprise

- Methods for ontologies building

- ICT Tools which support the innovations process

- ICT Tools for gathering knowledge on problems and product/processes

- Innovation assessment

Although the main technologies mentioned are available in the market, the results of the analysis of the state of the art revealed that:

1. Practical means for developing ideas into innovations in products and processes are still missing. This will involve taking what is currently available and producing methods of rapidly taking many creative ideas, and assisting people to work together in a structured manner to develop these ideas into innovations.

2. Methods and tools for capturing and structuring innovative ideas, over EE, in a way

that enables the best use for product/process innovation are still missing.

3. Providing means for team development of innovative ideas over EE is a high challenge and asks for a generic approach for development of ontologies applicable in the context of specific products/processes.

Methods Which Can Be Used to Develop Innovative Ideas

The only known and proved ways of generating innovative ideas are currently based on generic means helping human brains to open their focus, use the lateral thinking, and try to be creative. Some creative tools have been developed along the years: Brainstorming, lateral thinking, 6-3-5, think-tank, affinity diagrams, etc. based on the psychological sciences upon the works and ideas of known people as Osborne (creator of the brainstorming and the innovation checklist), De Bono (Six Thinking Hats, The Lateral Thinking) and others.

On the other hand, tools extensively used in design such as QFD, VM, FMEA, and others give a very valuable help in identifying where innovation is needed either by market pressure (QFD), high cost (VM) or potential failures (FMEA) but have few if any hint on how actually innovate.

The most important method for the new CAI system is TRIZ (theory of inventive problem solving). TRIZ is a recently developed methodology giving a more systematic and technological approach promoting not only idea generation, but also a consistent comprehensive method to convert ideas into feasible concepts.

Extended Enterprise

Extended enterprise (Duffy & Tod) concept in parallel with the concurrent enterprising looks for how to add value to the product by incorporating

to it knowledge and expertise coming from all participants on the product value chain.

The concept of EE has been defined in similar ways as can be seen in the following two samples:

- **Extended enterprise** (GlobePro Project. Helsinki University of Technology; Laboratory of Information Processing Science) is a set of real organizations. EE is the competence pool, resource pool, infrastructure and means for doing business. It is the base set from which organizations are tied in formation of functional consortia.
- **EE** (Anthony R. Sukdeo, TECHNOCORP. August 22, 2006 in Wikipedia) is a concept that is derived from the Enterprise terminology in application to both internal and external business relationships and associated services extended across multiple divisions (the holding, subsidiaries and branch offices) in one or more countries. With the evolution of networked technologies, efforts have been made to integrate and consolidate all business resources (humans and systems) for improved management and operations within a global competitive environment. This generalized effort is termed EE resources management.

As previously indicated, manufacturers need to benefit from "**extended enterprise**" (Burton & Shaw, 2005; Hagel & Singer, 1999; Short & Venkatraman, 1992) techniques by involving all people from throughout the product life cycle to provide their product knowledge. This knowledge needs to be saved and managed. Loss of this knowledge results in increased costs, longer time-to-market, reduced quality of products and services. By improving products and customer support manufacturing companies will be more competitive, and employment will increase.

Manufacturing companies have to shift towards the use of EE technologies and KM for customer/product support. This new paradigm implies a quite new scenario in which aspects as knowledge capturing and sharing and the new forms of interrelationship between companies and persons result of very high relevance.

The key idea behind the EE concept is to develop means supporting the collection of all useful knowledge throughout the EE for new and existing process and product developments, and to develop this knowledge into a means of fostering industrial innovations. Innovation by combining the ideas and feedback from all parts of the product life cycle, including customer interaction with existing products and new product ideas, and including customer service and field engineers, including suppliers, and including pooling of knowledge between multiple sites.

Companies need to be able to extend their own enterprises (by removing barriers of geographic location and human resource problems) to encompass the customer's operations where the supplied industrial products are being used. They need to provide the expertise to support the products in situ (including problem solving support, and diagnostic analysis of customer feedback) just as though the company expert was there with the customer solving the problems. This will involve EE model of the technical expertise of the companies in supporting their products at the customers' site.

This new paradigm addresses issues of significant importance to industry: the use of e-business technologies for EE product knowledge systems permitting ubiquitous human interaction, across and beyond industrial organizations, getting organizations to work better with each other. The novelty of the approach is to focus on product knowledge, which is not managed today, and which comes from suppliers, customers and employees (and tacit or informal knowledge generated by internal staff) involved in the development, support and use of products. It represents the next evolution of product information systems, taking standards and practices forward to support co-operative working and partnerships.

Methods for Ontologies Building

Methods for ontology building (Gruninger & Uschold, 1996) are of a special relevance for the AIM system, since they have to serve as a basis to put together and re-use innovative ideas from different actors within an extended enterprise. An overview of the ontologies building approaches and tools relevant for innovation management is provided in Kirchhoff, Kuczynski, and Stokic (2005). This overview indicates that ontologies attract high intention of RTD community. However, their application in practice is not still wide spread and additional RTD activities are needed to provide application oriented method for product and process innovation domain. Especially what is needed is a means for continuous update of ontologies enabling long life of knowledge systems.

ICT Tools Which Support the Innovations Process

There are two software tools based in the TRIZ methodology for inventive problem solving: IBW (Innovation Work Bench) and TECH OPTIMIZER (Both based in USA). Both software packages use schematic representation of problems and automated analysis of generated diagrams that guides the user to the abstract solution. Technical information and examples are included for helping the user in the particularization of the solution. However, these are both aimed at the scientist level of user, and not at the industrial manufacturing level.

Ideafisher, Inspiration professional edition, is another tool for helping to generate ideas. However, again this is aimed at the specialist level, and is not appropriate for industrial companies.

However, some tools exist to support application of other methodologies (QFDCapture from ITT for QFD, GAMDEC/GAMTREE from France for the FMEA, CDCF for Function Analysis according to French standard AFNOR X50-X51, DECIDOR and EXPERT CHOICE supporting decision-making for concept evaluation, etc).

ICT Tools for Gathering Knowledge on Problems and Product/Processes

There are many commercially available products providing means to capture knowledge on problems and product/processes, which are relevant for the development of certain AIM modules. The tools analyzed primarily address heuristic (case base reasoning and rule base reasoning) and model based reasoning approaches. Some examples are listed here:

- Good examples of CBR tools are KATE, Easy Reasoner, ReCall, Know How. They all are tool kits to develop case-based reasoning applications. For example, the KATE Software Suite is an Internet based tool-kit.
- TER includes a rule-based system, which supports forward and backward chaining.
- GRADE contains tools to assist in the diagnosis and repair process. It captures and automates the knowledge from the process. Diagnostics rely on model-based reasoning and case-based reasoning.
- RODON contains simulation and diagnosis software.
- Diagnostician provides a development tool and a run-time tool.

The main problems with these reasoning methods/tools is a re-use and sharing of knowledge among different experts and partners within distributed and extended industrial companies, since the most of the existing tools are missing capabilities to provide presentation of the cap-

tured knowledge in appropriate form to different actors.

Innovation Assessment

Some tools already exist to help assessing innovation capacity:

- Innovation styles for groups from the Innovation Group Consulting Inc. According to its description, the product is unique and focus on evaluating *how are you innovative* rather than *how innovative are you*. It is based on the fact that all people are unique individuals and while everyone has the capacity to be creative and innovative, each of us expresses this potential differently
- Innovation system architecture (ISA) from the same company. Assess your team's or organization's "infrastructure" to cultivate, support and sustain innovation. It incorporates the innovation group model for creating the framework or architecture for sustaining organizational innovation
- The innovation assessment program by United Inventors Association. It is an inventor/innovator assistance service that provides inventors, entrepreneurs, and product marketing/manufacturing enterprises with an honest and objective third-party analysis of the risks and potential of their ideas and inventions. This is why it focuses on invention evaluation

SOLUTIONS AND RECOMMENDATIONS

The approach for the development of the AIM system as a KM system to support innovation in EE is based on three business cases, used to ensure that the system concept and development is driven by industrial needs, and that these needs are met. The business cases use the AIM system in different ways enabling to develop and test AIM system for different scenarios, ensuring its general applicability.

Technological Solution Description

Based on the previous analysis of the state-of-the art and the end-users requirements it was decided to base the AIM system upon TRIZ concepts from which the general concepts and the methodology for innovation using the Innovation algorithm has been integrated. As indicated above, existing methods aim at the scientist level of user, and not at the industrial manufacturing level. AIM intends to provide methods and tools, which are applicable in the industrial environment.

A combination of TRIZ, RBR, and CBR as well as repositories of ideas and knowledge on product/processes (included in models) is applied, which is currently not available for innovations development domain. TRIZ methodology refers to the use of past knowledge to overcome problems

and both RBR and CBR use past information, gathered in rules or cases, to reach a result. The necessary knowledge to realise these reasoning methods will be provided in the AIM system, either as innovations, ideas, or product and process knowledge. The reasoning methods are very adequate to present a possible solution for problems (i.e. new ideas or previous solutions), because the system contains information on past experiences. All three reasoning approaches are used to combine the ideas into innovation concepts by providing set of ideas that may fit together, providing previous appropriate combinations.

The AIM system is thought as a process of innovation (Zlotin & Zusman, 1999), which means that an Idea will undergo a complete cycle, in order to be collected, documented, classified and used in the AIM system. Ultimately, ideas turn into innovations, which is one of the main objectives of the system. This section provides a rough overview of the life cycle of an idea. Figure 1 shows the complete path that an idea undergoes in the system.

Figure 1. AIM innovation life cycle

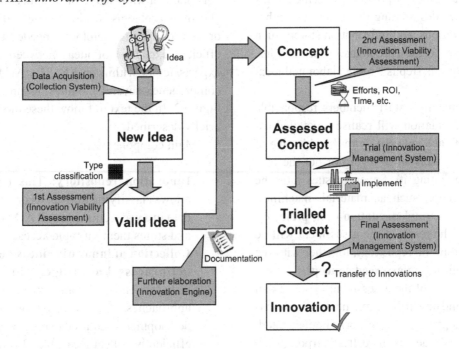

This life cycle is the basis of the innovation process, containing the activities to be realised to achieve innovations in the concurrent enterprise. The life cycle starts with data acquisition, where ideas are collected using an appropriate graphical user interface, accompanied by knowledge acquisition methods. The users of EE will use remotely the system to document their thoughts and viewpoints concerning the products and services of a company.

The AIM system performs a first assessment of the **new ideas**, with the purpose of making a rough classification. This classification will be an identification of the idea type, according to the information that it contains: improvement, potential cause, action, or new product/process. The main objective of this first classification is to attribute a type to each **new idea**, enabling its fast identification by the appropriate staff members of the company.

With all the ideas classified by type, a responsible staff member will develop **valid ideas** further, by first collecting any additional information that might be relevant for the **valid idea**, and further elaborate it. All the information can be useful to enable the best possible assessment. This step also includes relating the idea to any other ideas, innovations, and information stored, such as products, processes, problems, causes, actions. The result of this step is a more elaborated idea: **Concept**.

The company's staff members responsible for ideas' evaluation will realise a detailed assessment of each **concept**, with the objective of supporting a decision of trying or not the idea (i.e., implementing it). Several issues must be considered here, such as material, machines, staff members, implementation cost, profit, efforts, ROI. The result of the assessment will be documented in the repository, together with the concept, defining an **assessed concept**.

If the result of the assessment expresses an expensive and unworthy implementation, the **assessed concept** will probably not be implemented, and this has to be documented. It is then possible to keep the concept in the repository to reuse part of its information, or delete it. When the assessment provides positive results, the **positively assessed concept** is tried, and the complete development process is documented in the repository. The most important part of this documentation is the result obtained from the trial implementation, which expresses the success of the concept or not, and defines a **trialled concept**. The complete documentation of the concept (i.e., **trialled concept**), collected until this step, enables the final classification of the initial ideas. Based on the assessments and the trial implementation is possible to identify if the idea is successful, and therefore constitutes an **innovation**.

Developments

The AIM system follows a component-based architecture, enabling an easy extensibility, robustness and customization, and supporting the activities identified in the idea life cycle.

Main RTD challenges contemplated basically the combination of advanced methods for generating innovative ideas with "classical" methods for collection of knowledge on products/processes and their problems. It also includes the development of specific ontologies needed to enable efficient exchange of ideas between different experts/actors within an EE. The AIM system comprehends several modules, as presented in Figure 2. In the text to follow these modules are briefly described.

Main components are:

- **Innovation repository:** This repository allows classifying ideas and corresponding data in a way common to all AIM modules, and stores them for rapid access.
- **Collection of innovative ideas and product/process knowledge:** This module is based on a combination of 'classical' approaches/ commercial tools and new developments required to provide means to efficiently collect ideas, but also to collect

Figure 2. AIM system and relation to innovation life cycle

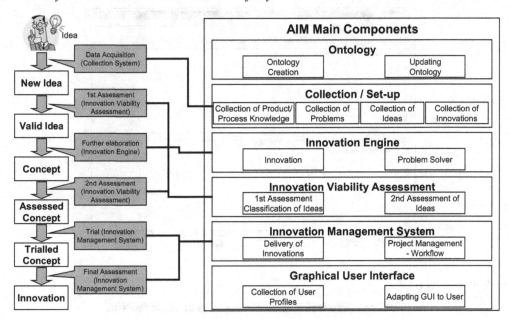

knowledge on product and process problems for which ideas are needed. In order to optimally support users in introducing their ideas different Graphical User Interfaces (GUIs) were implemented to add or edit ideas. Any user can choose the most appropriate GUI, and this choice can be modified at any moment. The simplest GUI implemented is the Easy GUI, which is represented in Figure 3 (Campos, da Silva, & Stokic, 2004).

The so-called advanced GUI contains more information on the idea, as can be seen from Figure 4. In this GUI, besides the information contained in the Easy GUI, it is also possible to see or edit documents, Internet links, and problems related to the idea.

- **Innovation engine:** This module provides a systematic methodology for the development of ideas into innovation concepts, by sharing and working on these ideas in a structured

framework. TRIZ methodology serves as a baseline approach (Kohnhauser, 1999) for this module, where the in-depth analysis of technical requirements and manufacturing failure situations is performed, structured knowledge is delivered, and graphical aids for team working and creation of concepts are provided.

- **Innovation viability assessment:** This module provides a structure (based on rapid consulting within the company of evaluation of developments and risks, combined with a multi-criteria decision support—DSS) to assist users in assessing the feasibility of new ideas at the collection stage, and innovation assessment facilities for design teams. It is important to focus on feasible, good innovative knowledge, and develop this.

- **Innovation management system:** This is a means of providing an efficient way for planning and monitoring the use of the innovation

Figure 3. Easy GUI

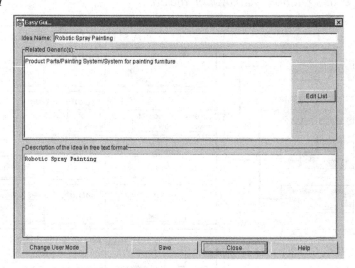

Figure 4. Advanced GUI

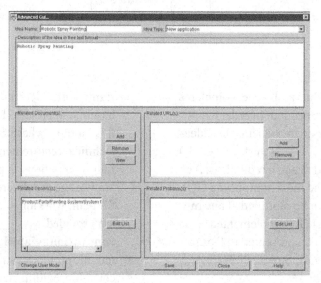

knowledge during design activities and a structured delivery of the innovations/ideas to the process and product design teams.

The **main features** of the AIM system are:

- AIM enables users along the EE to introduce ideas and report problems.
- AIM enables the complete modelling of the EE (i.e., the departments, staff, processes,

products, customers, innovations), in order to support an appropriate and efficient structure and classification of ideas and problems.

- AIM provides functionality to validate the ideas, classifying them by type.
- AIM includes an extensive search system for ideas, using all possible attributes as search parameters, in order to support definition, elaboration, and combination of ideas and further development of innovative concepts.

- AIM supports users in the technical development of ideas, following a TRIZ-based methodology, for in-depth analysis of technical contradictions.
- AIM supports users, following a TRIZ-based methodology, in depth-analysis and solving of problems and failure situations.
- AIM supports the assessment of the ideas developed in terms of technical viability, resources, costs, benefits.
- AIM comprehends innovation management functionality to determine and monitor the process of innovation.
- AIM enables functionality to maintain a common ontology used in several sites, by comparing local and global ontologies.
- AIM allows online monitoring and access to innovation processes through Web-services providing statistics on system's use and success (e.g., new ideas, status of innovation process, users, number of innovations, number of problems solved).

One of the key aspects of the AIM KM system is **ontology**, which enables sharing and reuse of knowledge and reasoning behavior across different users, domains, and tasks. Ontology can be seen as complementary reusable components to construct knowledge bases. The AIM system is going to be used by a wide spectrum of users with different technical backgrounds and sometimes with different languages. Therefore, it is highly important to have a common dictionary that makes evident to avoid misunderstandings. By adding and retrieving innovative ideas, it is essential to ensure that certain words or keywords really mean that the users are going to enter. Ontology is used in the AIM system to enable knowledge exchange among different subsidiaries of an EE (Davis et al., 2003). It can even help in the translation of words between different languages. The ontology supports searching for ideas and problems and other knowledge stored in the system. After analysing three ontology tools, it has been decided to use the tool Protégé-2000, which seems to be the most suitable one to satisfy the end user requirements (Kirchhoff et al., 2005).

Results

This section presents findings and achievements of the integrated system validation by the industrial end-users. In order to ensure reliable validation of the AIM methods and tools, metrics were defined to enable a quantitative assessment of the system development progress and the results achieved. These metrics include business metrics—benefits for the end-users and technical metrics—fulfilment of the requirements upon the tools.

Aiming to provide appropriate procedures for self-assessment throughout the system development, the system prototypes were installed in the industrial environment enabling the tools testing under real conditions. The prototypes tests carried aimed at a definition of new workflow flows to be realized using the AIM system and allowed the end-users to provide valuable feedback regarding the AIM system. This feedback was used to improve prototype of the modules.

Business Case 1: Innovation Process in SME

The business line selected for the scenario is the development of new products and cutting methods, and maintenance of cutting tools, which is the process where the most off-site involvement of personnel happens, and is the one where innovation is most needed. Therefore, the business case focuses on innovation generation, to achieve new products and processes, and also on solving problem occurred with cutting machines supplied to customers. The main business targets were to increase the number of ideas generated by the company for new products or cutting processes by 50-70%, to reduce the time for solving the product problems by 25%, and to use the improved innovation process, supported by the AIM system, as a marketing tool to show existing and new customers that this is a high-tech company.

The tests of the prototypes involved the managing director of the company, the works and sales manager, and one shop floor tool designer. In future tests, when the full prototype is installed, the entire shop floor will be involved. In addition, sales will also be involved in testing the AIM system. The works manager, supported by the managing director, defined the company model of the company, and introduced it in the AIM repository, using the set-up tool provided. The model included several tools designed by the company, and problems collected in the past, with respective solutions. Afterwards, problems reported by customer were introduced in the AIM repository, using the collection system, with the complete description. In several cases, ideas were collected to help solving these problems. The application of the AIM system to elaborate these ideas into innovation was tested as well.

Business Case 2: Innovation in Service and Engineering Medium Company

The business case area is the business of providing a complete air compressor system solution to customers, and then supporting this air compressor system (extended product). The selection of the air compressor business is because it involves (and needs to innovate and enhance this involvement) significant interactions with suppliers and customers. The main focus of the company business case is to collect information from customers about needed solutions. This information can be seen as problems, which need solutions to be provided by the company. The main objectives were to increase the number of innovative suggestions on products from customers and suppliers by 50% (specifically by 60% with large suppliers and customers), to increase the number of innovative ideas on products from employees by 50% and to increase the number of implemented innovation/new concepts of offers to customers by at least 30%.

The tests of AIM's prototype were realised by the managing director, one account manager, and one service manager. This group will be extended during the tests of the full prototype, to include sales engineers, service engineers, management, suppliers and customers. Customers and suppliers were indirectly involved, as they did not use the tool yet, but information provided by them was introduced in the repository by the company employees. The company model was defined by the three users involved in the tests, using the set-up tool provided by AIM. This model included several air compressor systems developed by the company and provided to several customers. In addition, the problems related to these systems were also introduced. With this basic information defined, it was possible to begin collecting problems regarding actual and future air compression systems, using AIM collection system. The process of solving these problems included also the collection of ideas and transformation of these ideas into solutions (innovations).

Business Case 3: Innovation in Multiple Site Manufacturing Process

The third company business case focuses upon innovation in multiple site manufacturing process based on the identified problems.

The selected business case area is the manufacturing process of cans in two plants. In one plant, the process selected to test AIM system is a bottleneck machine called "Necker." This machine in the production floor requires a generation/collection of innovative ideas in order to improve the process as well as the quality of the products. Since this bottleneck machine (Necker) creates a number of complex problem/failure causes asking for complex activities to remove these causes, the AIM tools should support a collection of ideas on this production step. To solve the problems, an innovation management system is needed which gives the staff members in the shop floor, as well as engineers, a consolidated overview on problems in production and proposals of causes/ actions to remove these problems. The similar process (with similar problems) is selected in the other plant. The testing process at this company was realized by the process engineers and plant managers and selected maintenance workers who defined the plant model, especially the necker machine, using the set-up tool provided. This information was the basis to collect problems and ideas. Afterwards, about 350 problems and solutions registered in paper forms in both plants were introduced in the AIM system. In addition, ideas to solve these problems and improve the manufacturing processes were collected. The solving of new problems, with special emphasis on re-use of knowledge between two plants, was considerably improved, with an increased number of ideas collected from the employees on how to solve these problems (by 25%—see Table 1).

The AIM tools provide information on problems identified, in different forms, depending on the expertise of actors, and gather ideas from shop-floor workers as well as process design experts and support collaborative work on evaluation of these ideas. The tools provide 'similar' ideas in order to support ideas gathering and evaluation. The challenging task is how to motivate shop floor workers to provide their ideas and collaborate on innovative solutions for process improvements. The objective is to support cross regional teams building within different subsidiaries including international teams (cooperation between subsidiary in Germany and subsidiary in Poland), where one of the key problem is appropriate (multilanguage) ontology. Once fully introduced in the first two plants, it is expected to bring improvement in productivity and reduction in waste due to effective process improvements by about 5-7% but once introduced in at least eight plants world wide, the benefits (due to exchange of ideas on common problems) may bring improvements of over 12%.

Table 1 presents validation results obtained, where the current measures are compared against the objectives defined in the system development start. Each company measured different values depending on its own specificity (e.g., number of ideas collected, number of problems solved in a time period, number of innovations implemented in the products or processes, costs reduction arising from AIM innovations) after the introduction of the AIM system and compared with the records before the introduction of the system. Some of the requirements are not measurable (n.m.) or were not at the point of starting using the system (n° 12) and some measures were not available (n.a.) for several reasons. Basically two types of indicators can be found: those that can be measured with real figures (1, 2, 5, 6 , 7, 8, & 11) and those that are not measurable but give a feeling of real advantage for users (3, 4, 9, 10, & 12).

The results of tests led to the conclusion that the modules developed are satisfactory from functionality point of view. The functionality implemented was working without major problems, and in a robust and reliable way. The results presented in the Table clearly indicate that the main expected improvements were successfully achieved.

FUTURE TRENDS

Innovation is a serious job that cannot rely only on software tools as sophisticated as they could be; there is a real need of methodologies helping people to innovate. Creativity and innovation do not arise directly from any tool itself. In fact, creativity steams only from the human's brain and becomes an innovation only when applied to solve specific technical problems that will increase the added value to the final consumer. One should remind that only combination of the three factors (new idea, implementation on product and market success) is the real way of achieving innovation.

Table 1. Validation results of the prototype (n.a.—not applicable, n.m.—not measured)

Requirement	Objective	Assessment of prototype		
		BC1	BC2	BC3
Increase the number of innovative suggestions on products from customers and suppliers by a structured Web link.	50%	50%	50%	n.a.
Increase the number of innovative ideas on products from employees, by means of easy to use facilities.	70%-100%	60%	50%	n.a.
Collect the corporate knowledge from the company.	n.m.	OK	OK	OK
Establish a classification scheme for product/process knowledge to be used for further development.	n.m.	Yes	OK	OK
Increase the number of implemented innovation/ new concepts of offers to customers.	at least 30%	30%	30%+	-
Increase the number of innovative ideas on processes from employees within an EE, making easy the introduction of information.	50%	50%	50%	25%
Increase number of innovative solutions of the identified problems within processes.	at least 30%	30%	30%	10%
Reduce time and efforts to solve product/process problems.	at least 25%	25%	25%	20%
Have a managed way of developing ideas into new practical concepts.	n.m.	Yes	OK	-
Have a structure to record and classify ideas.	n.m.	Yes	OK	OK
Reduce wastes and costs associated with problems, and supporting customers.	12 %	12%+	25%+	Ca. 10%
Shorten the time needed to collect and implement new ideas in the manufacturing process.	n.m.	Yes	OK	OK

Besides that, innovation means team working which means sharing information. People are in general very reluctant to share information unless they will obtain something in change.In that sense, the most important actual drawback is related to the reluctance of human beings to share experience, expertise, information, etc. that's to say: "Knowledge." Then a very important line of research is starting in the psycho-social fields providing mechanisms helping to override this barrier. The most convincing arguments will come by showing the unquestionable benefits and the enormous possibilities for the employees in sharing and inter-changing knowledge with their peers in order to achieve a "win-win" environment.

Within this scope, new products design, and development is a key area on which these new approaches will provide to industrial companies new methodologies enabling them to develop products including differentiating performances at very low prices. The problem of the management of distributed innovation knowledge in complex manufacturing systems, often spreading over many countries should be addressed. This problem is of a general nature, widely applicable and of essential significance in the worldwide manufacturing industry, both in large and small companies. These new EE and KM approaches are expected to be a good help to push manufacturing companies moving towards increasing innovation rates throughout these new paradigms.

Very promising research lines in the near future should be:

- Combination of methodologies to promote innovation, techniques for team working, creativity, and fostering information sharing by creating "win-win" situations will be really a must in the short term in order to enhance the possibilities of the emerging Web based collaborative working environments
- Integration of engineering tools and human sciences tools in the previously mentioned way
- Migration of tools to the Web based collaborative environments
- Development of new ICTs focusing on the new working paradigm and even shifting it in order to enhance and empower their possibilities
- Systems for comprehensive Product KM System enabling to manage the overall life-cycle of manufactured "Extended products"

On a general basis, the future research on the area of "product KM" will continue to explore the possibilities arising from ICT tools in order to capture implicit knowledge from the persons in a way enabling its storage and re-use. Since the modern approaches for products/processes innovation in industry require involvement of many different teams in EE context, it is of particular importance to provide ICT solutions, which support collaborative work on innovation. The increasing trend of globalised manufacturing environments and a radical increase in number of product variants in modern manufacturing industry (e.g., build-to-order) requires new forms of collaboration among teams involved along product/process innovation life cycle (e.g., design, planning, production scheduling, manufacturing, after sales services etc.), as well as seamless knowledge and experience sharing among these teams, often distributed geographically and in time. There is a clear need to efficiently support

different collaboration patterns (synchronous, asynchronous, multi-synchronous collaboration etc.). This is especially a challenge for manufacturing industry in many leading industrial countries facing massive migration of manufacturing facilities towards Eastern European and Asian countries.

There is a strong trend to provide advanced ICT solutions for collaborative work on innovation. So-called collaborative working environments (CWE) may support innovation processes in manufacturing industry. The objectives are to develop new collaborative working platform to support collaboration among teams in manufacturing industry (regarding different collaboration patterns, semantically enriched contents for collaborative work etc.) enabling more effective innovation processes (Stokic, 2006). The platforms are intended to support collaborative work on innovation within organised teams in industry in EE context, but there is a trend to provide platforms to support collaboration between teams in industry and ad-hoc groups and wider communities (e.g., RTD communities, customers etc).

In this subject field, there are some facts that have to be taken into consideration:

- Collaborative working among distributed teams is becoming a "must" due to globalization.
- ICT technologies (mainly Web based) are the key enablers of this new working paradigm.
- CWE have to focus in product knowledge captured from the whole value chain no matter how geographically dispersed they may be.
  - o **Manufacturing:** Designers, manufacturers, suppliers, customers, maintenance, etc.
  - o **Business:** Vendors, buyers, intermediaries, after-sales services, logistics, financials, etc.

CONCLUSION

Innovation is a critical factor in the success of industrial companies, and just as important is the need to get innovative products to the market quickly, as well as to innovate processes with minimum efforts and time. Such innovation must happen within an EE context. Managing of knowledge for innovation in an EE environment is a key issue. This in turn requires effective utilization of ICT.

This chapter presents an example of a successful ICT based system for effective management of knowledge needed within innovation processes in an EE context. The overall objective of the AIM system is twofold: (i) Increasing Innovation and (ii) accelerating their introduction to the Market. From the system validation through Industrial scenarios, it can be concluded that systematic approaches applied to incremental innovation lead to increased efficiency within innovation development process, confirming the basis and assumptions of the work. Specific achievements of the AIM system may be listed as:

- Developing means of stimulating the creation of innovative ideas and collecting them from people at EE level involved with the products and processes.
- Developing ways of processing these ideas and storing them into a structured knowledge repository. To ensure that all the useful knowledge (innovative information) is saved.
- Developing means of analysing innovative knowledge to determine which is useful, and which is not. That is, to enable the viability of ideas to be assessed.
- Developing means of delivering the innovative ideas to product and process designers for maximum effect.

The AIM system is targeted at industrial companies with complex products and processes, which have to provide significant product and process knowledge/information throughout the product life cycle, and which need to harness the product and process innovation with knowledge from their staff, suppliers and customers. The AIM system, thus, leads to important business benefits on the fields of:

- Reduction of process/product innovation cycle-time.
- Reduction of time and efforts for solving product/process problems.
- Improvement of process efficiency and reduction of wastes.

However, the solution presented has certain limitations: the AIM tools do not fully support collaborative work on innovations regarding e.g., different collaboration patterns (which is a strong trend as previously indicated), the reasoning methods used do not efficiently utilise semantics to support knowledge sharing. The current work on new, upgraded versions of the tools is, therefore, focused on solving several fundamental RTD problems, such as "cooperativity" of tools and semantic based KM.

ACKNOWLEDGMENT

The previously described work has been partly carried out in the project AIM (Acceleration of Innovative Ideas to Market) co-funded by the European Commission (EC) under contract (Ref. n° IST-2001-52222). The authors would like to acknowledge the EC for the support as well as all members of the consortium in the AIM Project for their contribution during the development of the various ideas and concepts presented in this work.

REFERENCES

AIM. (2005). IST-2001-52222: *Acceleration of innovative ideas to market*. Project public report, EC.

Altshuller, G. (1988). *Creativity as an exact science*. New York: Gordon and Breach Science Publishers.

Al'tshuller, G. S., Shulyak, L., & Rodman, S. (1999). *The innovation algorithm*. Worcester, MA: Technical Innovation Center.

Blake, A., & Mann, D. (2000). *Making knowledge tangible*. CMC and DuVersity, September 2000.

Brazil, K., Serdella, A. (2005). *Next generation extended enterprise*. Juniper Networks, USA.

Browne, J., Sackett, P. J., & Wortmann, J. C. (1995). Future manufacturing systems—Towards the Extended Enterprise. *Computers in Industry*.

Busby, J. S., & Fan, I. S. (1993). The extended manufacturing enterprise: Its nature and its needs. *International Journal of Technology Management*, Special Issue on Manufacturing Technology: Diffusion, Implementation and Management.

Burton, T. T., & Shaw, T. E. (2005). *Building the lean extended enterprise through adaptive supply chain networks*. LAI (Lean Aeronautics Imitative).

Campos, A. R., da Silva, R., & Stokic, D. (2004). Integrated approach for innovation and problem solving in dynamic virtual enterprises. *Proceedings of the INDIN 04*, Berlin.

Caskey, K. R. (1995). *Co-operative distributed simulation and optimization in extended enterprise*. IFIP WG5.7 Conference Proceedings.

Davis, E. W., & Spekman, R. E. (2003). The extended enterprise: Gaining competitive advantage through collaborative supply chains. *Financial Times Prentice Hall*.

Davis, G., Wilt, C., Dillon, P., & Fishbein, B. (1997). *Extended product responsibility: A new principle for product-oriented pollution prevention*. The University of Tennessee. The Gordon Institute, INFORM.

Dynes, S., Breschbühl, H., & Johnson, M. (2005). *Information security in the extended enterprise*.

Duffy, J., & Tod, M. (2004). *The extended enterprise: Eliminating the barriers*. CIO Magazine. Retrieved from http://www2.cio.com/analyst/report2118.html

Dyer, J. H. (2000). *Collaborative advantage: Winning through extended enterprise supplier networks*. Oxford University Press.

Gruninger, M., & Uschold (1996). Ontologies: Principles, methods, and applications. *Knowledge Engineering Review, 11*(2).

Hagel, J., & Singer, M. (1999). Unbundling the corporation. *Harvard Business Review, March-April 1999*.

Harrington, L. (1995). Taking Integration to the next level, *Transportation and Distribution*.

Haskell, D. (2005). *What is extended product responsibility?* NZ2000 Plastics, Otaki, New Zealand.

Hunt, I., Pereira Klen, A., & Zhang, J. (1997). Cross border enterprises: Virtual or extended! *ISIP'97 OE/IFIP/IEEE International Conference on Integrated and Sustainable Industrial Production*, Lisboa, Portugal.

Johanson M. *White Paper: Sharing Product Data Through Life in the Extended Enterprise –the share-A-space™ solution*. Eurostep Commercial Solutions AB, Sweden.

Kirchhoff, U., Kuczynski, A., & Stokic, D. (2005). *Set-up and maintenance of ontologies for innovation support in extended enterprises*.

Int J Adv Manuf Technol, Published online: 12 October 2005

Kohnhauser, V. (1999). Use of TRIZ in the Development Process. *Triz Journal, June 1999.*

Kühule H, Wagenhaus G (2005) *Extended Enterprise Architectures (E2A)-Towards a powerful Mode of Production.* Otto-von-Guericke-University Magdeburg.

Levy, A., Rajaraman, & Ordille, K. (1996). Querying heterogeneous information sources using source descriptions. *Proceedings of the 22ⁿᵈ VLDB Conference.*

O'Neill, H., & Sackett, P. J. (1994). *The extended manufacturing enterprise paradigm.* Management Decision.

Rabelo, R., & Camarinha-Matos, L. (1996). Towards agile scheduling in extended enterprise. In L. M. Camarinha-Matos, H. & Afsarmanesh (Eds.), *Proceedings of BASYS'96: Balanced Automation Systems II—Implementation Challenges for Anthropocentric Manufacturing.* Chapman & Hall.

Sawaguchi, M. (2001). Study of effective new product development activities through combination of patterns of evolution of technological systems and VE. *Triz Journal. March 2001.*

Schekkerman, J. (2004). *Another View at Extended Enterprise Architecture Viewpoints.* Institute For Enterprise Architecture Developemets.

Short, J., & Venkatraman, N. (1992). *Beyond business process redesign: Redefining Baxter's business network.* Sloan Management Review, *34*(1), Fall 1992

Sorli, M. (1999). Innovación en el Diseño de Productos. *Forum Calidad Journal.*

Sorli, M., Stokic, D., Gorostiza, A., & Campos., A. (2006). Fostering innovation in practice through TRIZ-based CAI tool. *International Journal of Computer Applications in Technology (IJCAT),* special issue on Computer Aided Innovation (CAI).

Sorli, M., Stokic, D., Gorostiza, A., & Campos, A. (2006). *Managing product/process knowledge in the concurrent/simultaneous enterprise environment.* Robotics and Computer Integrated Manufacturing. Elsevier (2006) p. 399–408. Volume 22, October-December 2006. ISSN 0736-5845.

Sorli, M., Mendikoa, I., Barbero, J. I., & Carrillo, A. (2006). *Distributed product design and manufacturing based on KBE. Computer Supported Cooperative Work in Design II;* Lecture Notes in Computer Science 3865. Springer-Verlag Berlin Heidelberg, 2006, ISSN 0302-9743.

Stokic, D. (2006). *A New Collaborative Working Environment for Concurrent Engineering in Manufacturing Industry.* Proc. CE 2006, 13th ISPE International Conference on Concurrent Engineering, Juan-les-Pins, France.

Szgeo, O., & Andersen, B. *Modeling the Extended Enterprise: A comparison of Different Modeling Approaches.*

Terninko J, Zlotin B. & Zusman A (1996). *Step by Step TRIZ. Creating Innovative Solution Concepts.* Responsible Management Inc.

Zlotin B. & Zusman A. (1999). Managing Innovation Knowledge. *Triz Journal.*

Chapter XVII
E–Learning and Knowledge Management in the Global Context

Andrew Creed
Deakin University, Australia

Ambika Zutshi
Deakin University, Australia

Jane Ross
University of Maryland – University College, USA

ABSTRACT

This chapter discusses how the independent nature of entrepreneurs, combined with the enabling features of digital information technology (IT), may lead to a situation where paper-based and campus-specific classroom education is at best uncomfortable and at worst almost meaningless. It describes how IT literacy preconditions the current generation of learners toward acceptance of e-learning technologies as they are currently emerging. The management of industry knowledge rests on an IT platform, which responds to individual needs in specialized roles in disparate parts of the world. The purpose of the chapter is to define and capture the latest thinking in applied education and relate this to the mindset of the emerging generation of entrepreneurs. To this end, industry and business education cases are drawn upon to illustrate key points, and a framework is provided for better understanding knowledge management in the emerging global context of e-learning technologies.

INTRODUCTION TO LEARNING AND KNOWLEDGE MANAGEMENT: THE LINK EXPLORED

This section looks at the inter-relationships between "learning" and "knowledge management" aspects and how their understanding and attributes have changed over the past few decades.

What is Learning?

How do we define and explain learning? There are a number of interpretations and definitions, all of which focus on awareness of new information or different way of doing things. All living creatures, regardless of their species, go though a learning curve as part of continuous environmental adaptation. Humans learn in a combination of ways, dependent on their learning preferences, backgrounds, experiences, and learning styles. Observation, reading, listening, training (in and out of classrooms, or jobs), and individual experiences, are some of the mediums of learning new information. A typical learning sequence for someone in an established economy involves going to a school to get an understanding of the basic concepts followed by an undergraduate degree in choice of field such as marketing, management, information technology, medicine, or law. In the past few decades, subsequent to globalization forces, having an undergraduate degree is not sufficient to remain competitive in the marketplace and accordingly entrepreneurs and intrapreneurs (or corporate managers) alike are furthering their knowledge by undertaking advanced university degrees and other types of training and vocational updating. Globalization and the rapid uptake of technology (including Internet), together, are transforming education as it has been known, with subsequent evolutions in the way learning occurs and the way in which knowledge is managed. E-learning and new forms

of knowledge management are hallmarks of the global technology era.

Definitions of learning that properly capture the nuances of the practice, and the art, of being a student or a teacher vary between commentators. There exist a number of standard descriptions of learning, but a valid question often pertains to the exact nature of learning. For example, is learning a process or a set of characteristics that become manifest in a person? Ramsden (2003, p. 6) asserts that learning is about altering the way one perceives phenomena related to a subject. This definition accedes to the fact that learning is, at least, not a noun. Stepping outside the formality of western languages, we find instances where the subject, rather than acting out the verb is recipient of the action, as in "learning is happening with Mary, or learning is going on with Mark."

Biggs (2003, p. 13) proposes that learning is about "conceptual change." This definition approaches the fact that context of a situation determines learning, almost as much as the individual learner's perception of the context. Laserna (1990), from her work in Columbia, indicates how ease of learning is associated with the environment in which learning occurs. Likewise, Nandwa (1990) reveals how learning in Kenya is embedded traditionally in the social community and occurs within the medium of the oral literature, which belongs to the community. Change to the Internet environment, therefore, requires management of the processes as well as the structure and context against which learning occurs. From the perspective of individuals and businesses in the global economy, positioning learning as a type of personal, social, and organizational change is a productive area that can enable a clearer perspective of what learning is, where it happens and how it occurs.

Loi and Dillon (2006) reassert the ecological view of learning as emerging from a system in which both stasis and change play their parts. In the ecological metaphor, information can flow through the landscape (the learning space) and become transformed. The emergence of a knowledge management field brings education and organizational management to a juncture. It represents the realization that learning is central to continuous improvement, and that appropriate organizing of information establishes an environment in which knowledge can be gained, stored, and transformed. While all members within a given social organization do not necessarily think alike, they will over time come to share knowledge as a body of common ideas (Olsen, 1968). Davenport and Prusak (1998) see knowledge as a combination of experiences, values, context, and expert insight. The continuing quest for improved organizational performance through creativity and innovation depends on continuous learning at individual and organizational levels. Through learning, information can become knowledge. With knowledge, a new cycle of information is generated, processed, and re-examined to refresh the learning process.

What is Knowledge Management?

Knowledge management is the framework of principles and procedures that drives the transformation of organizational information into knowledge. Extending this idea in the business and service domains, "knowledge management is essentially an organizing principle aimed at satisfying and where possible, exceeding customer expectations" (Hlupic, Pouloudi, & Rzevski, 2002, p. 92). The value-adding nature of knowledge management emerges in this latter definition. Day (2001) reminds that knowledge management has historical roots, citing Otlet's 1920 vision of a "global totality" of organized information, which could potentially promote rational thinking and foster better communication.

Knowledge derives from information, and information is provided increasingly in digital form. Arrangements of digital information begin to resemble places (Kolb, 2000), which is con-

sistent with the ecological concept of a learning landscape according to Loi and Dillon (2006). Web pages are referred to as "sites" precisely because the metaphor of space is appropriate, and "communities of practice" (Wenger, 1998) can emerge in some virtual spaces because people can congregate as they might in a town or village square, or in a classroom. With congregations come discussion, or information processing, and the development of knowledge. Turning plain information into meaningful knowledge is a kind of value generation, which is the realized benefit of knowledge management, and is becoming increasingly a digital experience. However, it is still clear that knowledge management is not exclusive of traditional forms of human interaction. In the same way that general management focuses on resources and ways to maximize efficiency and effectiveness in space and time, and within budget, so knowledge management in digital spaces deals in the currency of electrons and requires efficient, effective management. Resources under management include bandwidth, memory, and central processing units, as well as the creative input of people.

Communication technologies and emerging information technologies have established a platform for traditional fields of education to converge. The activities of entrepreneurs, when synchronized with effective knowledge management systems, can create, change, and sustain global opportunities in education and business alike. The context is one in which large amounts of information about what learning is must occur. This accentuates that the benefits are not assured until good management of technology is adopted. As interactive, social learning software becomes more prevalent across the next generation of broadband communication networks (Cochrane, 2006), the capabilities needed by people to learn and to manage in this environment of advancing complexity are different and significant. Due to convergence of technological applications and functions, the terms Internet and information technology are used interchangeably in this chapter.

GENERATION Y: A BACKGROUND

There is little doubt about the transformation in the way people interact, communicate, and operate in the digital era, with technological innovations such as the Internet playing a very significant role. Students at all levels are becoming today's and tomorrow's entrepreneurs and corporate managers. Educators and institutions alike are adapting to the increasing influence of technology in daily work and decision-making. Students (part of Generation Y, also known as Millennials; Buckingham, 2006; Eisner, 2005; Oblinger & Oblinger, 2005; Roberts, 2006) learning styles and preferences have changed as they were born in an environment filled with digital media. This group is also referred to as "digital natives" by Prensky (2001a, b) as compared to "digital immigrants," people from generation X and earlier, who were exposed to Internet and computers in their later years.

Increasing numbers of students as digital natives are challenging conventional teaching and learning methods. In fields of information, such learners now feel more of a need for connection than they identify the need to remember content. One could suggest that connection itself is becoming the major issue. By this we mean that knowledge about how to conduct information search, how to manipulate data, how to connect from one digital device to another, assumes dominance in the information needed for proficiency in a specialized field. In any given discipline, the answers to questions can be found in the sea of Internet-based information by knowing how to search for it (for example Google the word or phrase). This accessibility tends to usurp the need for grasp of content that was required before the era of interconnected information. What is important to digital natives is not content retention

or memory but rather knowing how to locate content quickly. To capitalize on this as way of enhancing the process of learning, governments worldwide are gathering and inter-connecting information. For example, in the UK government is pressing schools to implement and use technological mediums such as interactive whiteboard to augment understanding along with the use of information and communication technology" (Glover, Miller, Averis, & Door, 2005, p. 155; see also Pittard, 2004).

Use of cell phones, ipods, and other connecting technologies are now ubiquitous in countries worldwide. Students throughout Thailand, Hong Kong, Singapore, and other parts of Asia-Pacific countries are well connected. SCUP (2004) observed in United States that, amongst generation Y students, nearly every one of them has a cell phone and access to instant messaging/text messaging wherever they are, and social networking software is increasingly becoming part of the online experience. Similar findings were made by Frank N. Magid & Associates who reported that "more than half of all teens own a mobile phone, nine out of ten teens have a home computer with Internet access and a quarter of 18 to 24-year olds have Internet-enabled cell phones" (Miller, 2006, p. 14, see also Roberts, 2006).

The implication of the increased adoption of technology within the community is that learning should occur through dominant media. As digital devices transform to become e-learning technologies, there is a ready generation of learners eager to have their experience through such devices. The Australian situation with this technological and generational shift runs a close parallel with the U.S. with a number of Australian universities allocating millions of dollars for upgrading and installing new technologies to support e-learning initiatives (Alexander, 2001). In views of Macfarlane (2000, p. 38) if Australian universities "fail to bring their online learning systems to international standards," they face an inevitable threat from overseas institutions. Schacter and

Fagnano (1999, p. 339) while discussing the different approaches to learning, such as computer based instruction, socio-cultural learning theory, computer-supported collaborative learning, constructive theories, and cognitive science, emphasize that "computer technologies are most effective when they are designed according to different educational and psychological theories and principles." We contend that principles are a type of connection that adds context to the sea of information. This relationship between technology usage and pedagogy has also been emphasized by Glover et al. (2005). For instance, survey findings of 728 students, representing graduate and undergraduate levels across 20 courses found that the majority of the students viewed use of technology to enhance their learning positively (Shuell & Farber, 2001). "Eighty-eight percent of students said [that] the use of technology in the class helped them to learn the material and skills involved in the course and 86% indicated that the use of technology helped to illustrate concepts which facilitated their learning" (Shuell et al., 2001, p. 125). Such studies reflect the increased acceptance, understanding, and usage of digital media by Generation Y individuals (and other student groups) to gather, analyze, interpret, and generally learn new information and manage knowledge.

Every nation depends on continuous learning and knowledge management for development and sustained prosperity. Well educated people can deliver not only competitive advantages for companies based globally, but also comparative advantages for nations that generally foster their best people and encourage creativity and invocation. When smart people and advanced information management technologies are brought together, the results of this union magnify. Learning and knowledge management go hand in hand. It is the net generation, the digital natives, who appear poised to respond most diligently to some of the knowledge management developments linked with technology.

ENTREPRENEURSHIP: POTENTIAL TO MERGE WITH A NEW GENERATION

Entrepreneurs are individuals who work independently and commonly have attributes such as opportunity identification, vision, financial risk, leadership, and management skills (see, Kearins, Luke, & Corner, 2004; Waddell, Singh, & Musa, 2006; Zutshi, Zutshi, & Sohal, 2006). Massie (1987, p. 222-223) points out key traits psychologists have identified as entrepreneurial, including, the need for achievement, an internal locus of control, and a tolerance of ambiguity (see also McShane & Von Glinow, 2005). Russo (2001) looks more broadly at processes unique to entrepreneurship, including how the early phases of entrepreneurship involve transferring risk to others; that most entrepreneurs deal in incremental, often low-tech innovations, have limited experience in their fields, often do not systematically plan their strategies, and that venture capital rarely funds early entrepreneurs. Please note that for the rest of the chapter the terms entrepreneurs and intrapreneurs (or corporate managers, those who are employed by an organization and are required to work towards a target decided for them) are used interchangeably.

Watkins (2005, p. 1) describes generation Y as "the generation of high-speed Internet access, cell phones and instant messaging." A significant demographic shift has occurred in which it is common for members of the new generation to make their presence felt diversely in investment markets, such as real estate, where they engage with new technologies, expressing some of the networking and opportunity-seeking characteristics of entrepreneurs. Jayson (2007) explains that the need for achievement, especially financial achievement, is motivating high proportions of generation Y. In addition, the Millennials enjoy being noticed and recognized with awards and accolades. Van Eck (2006) joins Prensky (2001a, b) in affirming that virtual games have become part of the training that occurs in a young mind, at least in preparation for understanding how to coordinate ideas and resources in generative activity, and to have expectation of reward for effort. This early programming to engage, network, and achieve is consistent with behaviour of digital natives. Accordingly, there is potential for affinity between some characteristics of generation Y digital natives and the usual view of an entrepreneurial individual. For instance, Digital Natives are described by Prensky (2001a, b) as demonstrating parallel rather than sequential cognitive functions, a craving for interactivity, twitch-speed multitasking in favor of reflective thinking, and interest in games and associated rules. Multitasking in the current sea of digital information and engaging parallel thought processes are essential opportunity-seeking techniques (see also Martin, 2005; Jorgensen, 2003).

In addition, the general dearth of systematic planning by entrepreneurs is consistent with the cherry-picking approach of generation Y when faced with large quantities of information, their intellectual creations emerge spontaneously rather than develop linearly. The propensity for social interactivity is clearly expressed in digital natives who are found everywhere on the Internet and are enthusiastically embracing mobile technology as a way to stay in touch with their peers and maintain their networks. Social software is currently burgeoning as a tool that is realizing the intense need for human interactivity and offering emergent social connections in unprecedented configurations (Martin, 2005).

It is not surprising that entrepreneurial developments emerge from a generation that is more connected than ever before and is quick to process market concepts and opportunities. The fact that the preceding generation of baby boomers are gradually exiting from the centre of economic activity means generation Y is poised to replace them, suggesting that the increasing convergence of this generation with entrepreneurship and enterprise needs to be recognized and well

understood. It is this merging of the generations in the common pursuit of learning and enhanced knowledge management in the dynamic global environment that warrants further analysis and reflection.

Global Industry Reliance on Information Technology: The Learning Mindset of an Entrepreneur

An entrepreneur thinks creatively and uses recycled information to generate innovation. Diaz and Rodriguez (2003) discuss the heightened level of internal control exhibited by entrepreneurs. Technology represents a means for increased control over information, money, and physical resources (Chay, 1993). For long-term sustainability of their business, entrepreneurs tend to embrace opportunities for control over resources, and intuitively understand the transformational effect of the emerging technologies. Lynn (1969) identifies the link between creative transformation and entrepreneurship noting the similarities between entrepreneurs and other transformational personality types.

Global industry relies upon innovation for success, and the education of entrepreneurs needs to include ways by which knowledge can be captured and transformed to foster innovation. Entrepreneurs, when communicating in a face-to-face and/or a virtual world, play a role in either stimulating or dampening the learning process and attainment of new knowledge. Supportive environments that stimulate trust and the free, collegial exchange of ideas contribute to increasing the knowledge base. An egocentric, self-centered approach on the other hand can lead to misunderstandings and an emergence of biases and prejudices (Marlow, Stanley, and Connors, 2005). The unprecedented emergence and growth of technologies that enable the capture, processing, and dissemination of data to become information that feeds human knowledge has enabled global industries to prosper in short spaces of time. Finance, education, research, along with other industries that rely on information processing and society as a whole are obvious benefactors. Considering that the core function of communication is ubiquitous in most industries, and that internetworking has brought communication devices into such close connection globally, the convergence of knowledge management and global business is having spectacular consequences. In the context of global trade, it is now the grasp of information and its management that moves individuals and companies to leading positions. The ability to connect digitally with leaders worldwide and the emergence of the information economy, along with the central role of information technology (IT) as a medium, is transforming the way people trade, communicate, and learn.

Van Alstyne and Brynjolfsson (2005, p. 22) discuss how information technology affects the "capacity to select, search, screen, and connect," which in turn alters knowledge profiles, community membership, diversity and integration of the partnerships that we voluntarily form. Cross border business has experienced this kind of foundational shift in recent decades. For instance, Kristiansen and Ryen (2002) explain that amongst the social success factors of Asian entrepreneurs, including, kinship and social networks, comes modern communication technology, which enables faster transfer of knowledge and finance. The connections enabled by IT infrastructure have impacted on almost all aspects of business, including economics, accounting, and communications. Geographic border dissolution has been one effect, sometimes in a political sense, but mostly in the minds of entrepreneurs, who now tend, at least theoretically, to trade with ease between countries. In these settings, national boundaries are among the least of the logistical considerations.

There are knowledge management challenges requiring solutions if the global opportunities for entrepreneurs are to be fully realized. For instance, Faye, McArthur, Sachs, and Snow (2004) discuss the unevenness in economic growth rates of developing countries. In addition to the usual geopolitical and infrastructure factors, including human resources development (such as education), they emphasize, especially in relation to landlocked countries, a dependence on neighbors. This dependence extends, tellingly, to neighbors' administrative and technology systems. This refers to the information management processes of countries that adjoin landlocked developing nations and the information conduits between the neighbors. As nations learn and grow they appear to do so symbiotically and, where the relationship involves balanced flows of information data, economies are good, but where administrative linkages are strained, this leaves the poorer neighbor at a disadvantage in terms of access to the information and knowledge skills that underpin global markets.

Transition from Learning to E-Learning: Examples and Experiences

E-learning is an approach to facilitate and enhance learning through information and communications technology. The equipment and software that is used in this endeavor is collectively referred to as e-learning technology. Since learning has already been defined as a context and process resulting in transformation or change, we need to consider the extent that change can occur through traditional vs. new educational media. Postman (1985, p. 145) discusses the obvious intellectual revolutions that have occurred in the recorded history of humankind. Fifth century Athens changed from an oral culture to a written one and Plato's writings often acknowledge the issues involved. Sixteenth century Europe is noted for its introduction of the printing press, which exponentially expanded the quantity of writings emanated around the world. The digital era is currently burgeoning and thinkers as diverse as Marshall McLuhan, Aldous Huxley, George Orwell and Don Tapscott have attempted to capture the essence and direction of expected changes. Since revolution is the operative word, it may take a while yet to assess the impact of digitized electrons on human ways of communicating and learning.

Kolb (2000, p. 124) discusses experiences with digital information. He draws an analogy with physical space and asks the question, "Is there any there?" He further suggests that digital media (e-learning technologies) have destructive elements that must be consciously harnessed and controlled if they are to be turned into educational value. "Computers are meta-tools ... that can morph into different forms and different kinds of interactions" (Kolb, 2000, p. 132). This appears to suggest that good management education can occur online, despite some opinion in academic circles that the online experience is somehow inferior to traditional classroom opportunities to interact face-to-face. If Kolb's (2000) conception of online as space is relevant and, like any space, it can be designed well or poorly, then good virtual space arrangement by teachers would reasonably lead to good learning experiences. Just as furniture in a room maximize utility and aesthetics, so the virtual space may be improved by collaborative efforts to rearrange the objects within.

Dewey (1963) conducts a broad dissection of the art and practice of education in a number of seminal texts. Dewey (1963) observed that there is a brutal reality at work in education. The teacher has more knowledge than the student. The student's task is to do and learn, which, is often painful. This indicates that teachers may have equal access to knowledge through ICT but continue to be more "developed" than students in relation to application and experience. There remains a harsh aspect of education when a student realizes they still have to apply what they learned—to demonstrate a full and complete understanding, rather than just a rote memory. This in some way recognizes the students' own contribution to their learning outcomes. This is an integral aspect of education—students are themselves part of the product that emerges. Knowledge is not so much transferred as integrated and transformed.

On a broader front, Smith (2005) explains that Reeves and Nass (1996) studied individual reactions to the computer and found that the computer elicited feelings that are usually attributed amongst people in a face-to-face group. It appears that people may not make unconscious distinctions between the real and the mediated thereby taking what the media presents as the real thing. As a result, educators often need to intervene in online education to be sure critical thinking emerges as an accurate response. People can react quite emotionally to subtle variance in application of language. Post a discussion thread message with a word that can be interpreted ambiguously, and the flame begins. Alternately, leaving an online classroom unattended for long periods may result in students to feeling ignored.

As academics we have experienced, and found that there exists, a direct relationship between the extent of involvement and spontaneity of our responses in the learning management system, and the level of student satisfaction. Students, especially distant/off-campus ones, appreciate and publicly applaud the academic who is quick and responsive but not so the academic who fails to address the issues within 24-48 hours from the time of posting the query. Rightly or wrongly, these experiences are reflected in our student evaluations and hence academics are under immense pressure to have a quick turn around of student queries. The challenge, however, faced by academics is not that they do not wish to respond to the students, but rather time, as many universities do not incorporate the time required to respond to student queries as part of an academic's workload.

Dillon (2004) presents a focused critique of the most significant theories in relation to information and communication technologies (ICT) in education. He argues that an ecological metaphor is most relevant for understanding learning, knowledge and ideas and the interactions that occur through contemporary ICT. The concept of an adapting, sometimes evolving field of resources and connections fits comfortably with contemporary developments in e-learning and simultaneously supports views such as those of Dewey (1963) which keep human interaction at the heart. The gathering, processing, and transmitting of information is rapidly changing business models worldwide. For example, joint ventures along numerous axes are formed and dissolved to meet knowledge needs as they arise. Often it is individuals and small companies, which have the competitive advantage in this new global environment and its ever changing virtual spaces.

There exist some fascinating examples of e-learning technologies being used to effectively assist education (both in and out of classroom). For instance, consider one author's experience of changes in learning processes in the meat processing industry, an industry that one might intuitively expect is least likely to concern itself with e-learning. Killing and processing animals for food is a physical, organoleptic activity. Despite this perception, an Australian initiative to develop digital learning resources to assist the learning and development of meat safety skills for workers in this industry stands as a fascinating example of knowledge management and e-learning. Since meat processing is among Australia's largest export industries, and Australia is one of the worlds leading exporters of meat, there is a strong imperative to keep training resources updated. To maintain a competitive advantage and continue to grow, the industry needs competent workers who understand meat safety issues at every stage of the processing chain.

A meat safety toolbox was produced by Australian National Training Authority (2004). The brief was for an e-learning resource comprising a variety of digital learning objects. One of your authors was a writer and instructional designer for the educational design organization contracted to complete the toolbox. The product

has taken a unique position as a set of resources that certainly does not replace one-to-one and hands-on training of meat workers, but augments what industry trainers do. In fact, a number of specific resources, such as digital images of exotic diseases, are exceedingly valuable. A novice in the trade rarely has the opportunity to encounter such diseases. When learning what to look for and how to respond, the availability of a virtual representation of the problem is very powerful. This is similar to the value of flight simulators for pilots, or simulators for medical procedures for surgeons in training.

Another example of successfully deploying e-learning technologies is in University of Maryland University College's (UMUCs) online Master of Business Administration (MBA) program aimed at full-time working adults. The education of global business managers requires a flexible and relevant mode of delivery, however, not unlike that of food processing, it requires a significant applied emphasis (UMUC, 2004). Management is an applied art, especially as it emerges in the highly dynamic field of global business. Among the earliest entrants into the fully online MBA market, UMUC is today increasingly in a competitive environment where advantages can only be maintained by effectively balancing academic rigor with immediately deployable management skills. The institution has faced rapid growth in enrolments and the challenges associated with maintenance of educational standards. One innovative unit team in the MBA program, *AMBA606 Organizations and the External Environment*, aims to use its human and technological resources to focus on quality educational outcomes. As the team continues its teaching work within the proprietary learning management system, WebTycho, it simultaneously works on collaborative team building amongst the academics using a variety of communication technologies (Creed, Ross, Stewart, Bolesta, Hladik, & Backhaus, 2006). This requires careful and diligent facilitation, since the team is virtual with members scattered across various parts of the globe. This virtual teaching team with a reliance on information and communication technology is the platform for reflective research into online teaching practices with related publications, and the development of models of educational communication (see Backhaus, Bolesta, Creed, Ross, & Stewart, 2005).

E-Learning and Knowledge Management in Education

Internet searches provide access to myriad information sources but we need to remember that this information is available in a public domain and comes with limited or no evaluation of the content credibility. For example, Wikipedia is a website that can be edited without independent validation of content accuracy. Any one can post data on the public domain and it is up to the individual involved to filter for relevant and reliable knowledge. Another aspect of digital media is accompanied with concerns of security (Lightner, Yenisey, Ozok, & Salvendy, 2002), privacy (Brey, 2005), confidentiality (Bergum, 1998; FPC, 2001), anonymity (Bergum, 1998; FPC, 2001), and trust (Adam, 2005), whether being practiced in educational, industry or professional sectors. The obligations to address the above-mentioned issues remain, (for organizations as legal entities as well as for individual students and managers), and, in some cases, are magnified given the ability of technology to track and disseminate sensitive information. Whether engaged in business in one country or another, the responses occurring in education and business relationships set the tone or atmosphere in which a relational ethic must be defined and acted upon. Relational ethics involves "initiating and maintaining conversation, and it means that ethics is found in day-to-day obligations and responses to one another" (Bergum, 1998).

Trust and privacy (see Brey, 2005) between the individuals/parties involved is critical especially when communication is taking place in a technological, virtual environment. The net generation of entrepreneurs—the e-entrepreneurs, cannot act in an ethical vacuum. The business of improving business—and education—is one of learning and relearning in the midst of fast changing technologies. As businesses expand beyond geographical boundaries in search of new markets there is heightened emphasis and pressure on entrepreneurs involved to address potential areas of cultural clashes to ensure harmony within- and outside interactions with their stakeholders. Kearins et al. (2004, p. 51) when citing Hannafey (2003, p. 10) raise the question of potential gap in practice of ethical attributes by entrepreneurs possibly due to "harsh demands of entrepreneurial environments." Last but not the least, the issues of organizational memory and the positioning of intellectual capital become critical. An organization can lose this pivotal strategic information as intrapreneurs move around looking for new challenges, or even retire or become retrenched (Coffey & Hoffman, 2002). Knowledge management becomes entwined with human resources management in this context in the sense that people carry knowledge with them and it is in a company's interest to know where commercially valuable people and information reside.

In the debate between satisfying the needs of our current and future students we sometimes overlook the needs of the educators teaching these students. The only way academics can keep up and match the demands of the constant technological changes and the software used by their respective universities is if they regularly update their own skills. Does this really happen? Generally, academics are left up to themselves (and pressurized) to be motivated and implement various software in their subjects without receiving formal training in them as otherwise universities will be required to part with their resources (time and money). The difficulty then is how can universities and students alike expect responsiveness and accuracy of use of technology when the academics have not been "shown the way"? Another drawback is that excessive use of digital technology with our family, friends and stakeholders (including communication between students; with academics; with colleagues in organizations) has in some ways fundamentally altered the actual learning process of our students. Academics globally are observing that when posting messages on the electronic database within a subjects' site or when writing an e-mail, students are using acronyms and emoticons, not doing a spelling or grammar check, a habit they have formed following communicating via sms from an early age. When condemned by an academic on their writing, the students have difficulty in understanding the reasons behind it and that they will need to write full words and sentences when they enter the corporate world.

FULL CIRCLE: IMPROVING LEARNING KNOWLEDGE MANAGEMENT WITH IT: FUTURE TRENDS AND CONCLUSION

The global clash of cultures continues. Everywhere people must relate to each other for trade and commerce, for peace and goodwill. Domestic markets are limited and product cycles are often short. Growth opportunities can be found worldwide in what Mann and Gotz (2006) call "borderless business." The importance of appropriate protocol for dealing with customers with diverse backgrounds and different expectations about good business is often poorly understood or ignored. As perceptions about the world are continually challenged and such different people meet, relational ethics involving right and good relationships between people are vital (Bergum & Dossetor, 2005). Peck (1993) calls for a return to civility, which involves addressing aspects of trusts, ethics, and basic etiquette.

Something at the core of capitalism excites the entrepreneur. Perhaps, though, it is more fundamental than capitalism. The principles of trade are rooted in economics, in comparative advantage and that is part of the human survival mechanism. When the human desire for creativity is considered, we are more directly in the realm of the entrepreneur. Entrepreneurs are known for their "get-up-and-go" and challenging ways, as well as for their abilities to open new areas as intermediaries between existing and new business opportunities. So it should not be surprising that entrepreneurs—as students and learners—will make new demands on education and learning systems. The entrepreneurial learner comes with special considerations and needs, including demands for "just-in-time learning." Increasingly, students see themselves as buying their education rather than earning it. They commonly express their belief that they are entitled to their grade as well as customer satisfaction. At the same time, institutions of higher learning are positioning themselves as profit-based businesses with services to produce and sell (Weisser, 2005).

Trends to form business and knowledge relationships on a "just-in-time" basis have inherent traps. In the quest for acceleration of operations, the time for trust, relationship, content, and skill building can be drastically shortened with understandable consequences. At times business experience may be valued over the theoretical knowledge base that is necessary for sustainable business and sustainable business practice. When profit is the motive, even business schools are getting into the "business" with attendant possibilities for decline into mediocrity as institutions become growth oriented and students are fast tracked into programs that halve the time to earn a business degree (King, 2006). But we raise the question about the value and process of learning, if students are increasingly becoming our customers, buying subjects and courses, how do we ensure that they have actually gained new knowledge and not solely bought a piece of paper? Who has the onus for ensuring that our future entrepreneurs are knowledgeable and have learned from their predecessors mistakes, if they do not go though the learning cycle?

The educators of managers in the contemporary global environment encounter communication platforms for delivery and must negotiate ways to develop teaching and learning styles (pedagogies and/or andragogies) for adult learners. Understanding the philosophy and practice of education, interpretation and the linkages with communication is a critical feature of the modern situation. Kanuka and Anderson (1998) for example, remind us of the growth of constructivism and the view that, "knowledge is generated through social intercourse." This is an interesting statement that at once distinguishes communication from education and, yet, inextricably binds the two. It also puts self direction and interpretation at the centre of learning.

Depending on who we ask, all cohorts (generation Y students, mature age student, academics, universities, and industry practitioners) have different views, perceptions and expectations from IT as a medium of gaining, learning and transferring new information and knowledge. The challenge that we face as educators of future entrepreneurs is ensure that whilst dealing with different learning styles, they are equipped with skills to identify and adapt to the constant evolution of their customers and other stakeholder demands in the decades to come. There is no turning back from the potentially further increased use of IT and Internet as medium of communication and transaction in our personal and professional communication and transactions. In the short term, one of the major predicaments that academics need to answer is the complaint from our current mature age students when studying in the same class as generation Y students. How do we ensure that our two disparate groups of students, one with no work experience vs. another with decades of experience, can both learn something new from our teaching? A balance between teaching basic concepts to generation Y students and skills to resolve real life work issues for our mature age generation X or baby boomers students needs to be delicately established, and this is where expertise in the subject and experience of an academic can play a crucial role.

The e-learning technologies used by staff and students at various universities needs to be identified in future research and comparisons should be made with industry organizations so as to identify the best practice for implementing e-learning technologies that satisfy the learning styles of all stakeholder groups. Future studies also should identify the link, if any, between different learning styles of generation Y and generation X or baby boomers, and use of IT, whether the latter enhances or hinders this process.

REFERENCES

Adam, A. (2005). Delegating and distributing morality: Can we inscribe privacy protection in a machine? *Ethics and Information Technology, 7*(4), 233-242.

Alexander, S. (2001). E-learning developments and experiences. *Education + Training, 43*(4/5), 240-248.

Australian National Training Authority. (2004). *Meat safety toolbox*. Australian Flexible Learning Framework, Commonwealth of Australia. Retrieved November 17, 2006, from http://toolboxes. flexiblelearning.net.au/series4/414.htm#desc

Backhaus, W., Bolesta, M., Creed, A., Ross, J., & Stewart, J. (2005, July 9-12). Faculty collaboration in teaching global business. MBA Teaching Process: A Case Analysis of Collaborative Communication Applied as a Teaching Preparation Resource in a module of the Online MBA at University of Maryland University College. *Proceedings of the Academy of International Business*. Quebec: Canada.

Bergum, V. (1998). *Relational ethics*. What is it? In Touch. 1(2). Retrieved September 29, 2006, from http://www.phen.ab.ca/materials/intouch/vol1/intouch1-02.html

Bergum, V., & Dossetor, J. (2005). *Relational ethics, the full meaning of respect*. Hagerstown, MD: University Publishing Group.

Biggs, J. (2003). *Teaching for quality learning at university* (2ⁿᵈ ed.). Buckingham: Open University Press.

Brey, P. (2005). Freedom and privacy in ambient intelligence. *Ethics and Information Technology*, 7(3), 157-166.

Buckingham, M. (2006). Engaging generation Y: An interview with Marcus Buckingham. *ASTD*, August, 60(8), 27-30.

Chay, Y. (1993). Social support, individual differences, and wellbeing: A study of small business entrepreneurs and employees. *Journal of Occupational and Organizational Psychology*, 66(1), 285-302.

Coffey, J., & Hoffman, R. (2002). A knowledge modeling approach to institutional memory preservation. *The Journal of Knowledge Management*, 7(3), 38-49.

Cochrane, T. (2006, December 3-6). Learning with wireless mobile devices and social software. *Proceedings of the 23ʳᵈ Annual Conference of the Australasian Society for Computers in Learning in Tertiary Education. "Who's Learning? Whose Technology?"* Sydney: Australia.

Creed, A., Ross, J., Stewart, J., Bolesta, M., Hladik, M., & Backhaus, W. (2006, December 13-15). Tapping global human resources in an MBA teaching team: Insights with implications for management education worldwide. *Proceedings of Australian and New Zealand Academy of Management 2006 Conference*. Management: Pragmatism, Philosophy, Priorities. Rock Hampton: Australia.

Davenport, T. H., & Prusack, L. (1998). *Working knowledge: How organizations manage what they know*. Boston: Harvard Business School Press.

Day, R. (2001). Totality and representation: A history of knowledge management through Eu-ropean documentation, critical modernity, and post-fordism. *Journal of the American Society for Information Science and Technology*, 52(9), 725-735.

Dewey, J. (1963). *Experience and education*. London: Collier Books.

Diaz, F., & Rodriguez, A. (2003). Locus of control, nAch and values of community entrepreneurs. *Social Behavior & Personality: An International Journal*, 31(8), 739-748.

Dillon, P. (2004). Trajectories and tensions in the theory of information and communication technology in education. *British Journal of Educational Studies*, 52(2), 138-150.

Eisner, S. (2005). Managing generation Y. *SAM Advanced Management Journal*, 70(4), 4-15.

Faye, M., McArthur, J., Sachs, J., & Snow, T. (2004). The challenges facing landlocked developing countries. *Journal of Human Development*, 5(1), 31-68.

FPC. (2001). *Guidelines on privacy in the private health sector*. Australia: Office of the Federal Privacy Commissioner.

Glover, D., Miller, D., Averis, D., & Door, V. (2005). The interactive whiteboard: A literature survey technology. *Pedagogy and Education*, 14(2), 155-170.

Hannafey, F. T. (2003). Entrepreneurship and ethics: A literature review. *Journal of Business Ethics*, 46(2), 99-110.

Hlupic, V., Pouloudi, A., & Rzevski, G. (2002). Towards an integrated approach to knowledge management: "Hard," "soft" and "abstract' issues." *Knowledge and Process Management*, 9(2), 90-102.

Jayson, S. (2007). *Generation Y's goal? Wealth and fame*. USA Today. January 10, 2007. Retrieved February 7, 2007, from http://www.usatoday.com/news/nation/2007-01-09-gen-y-cover_x.htm

Jorgensen, B. (2003). Baby boomers, generation X and generation Y? *Foresight, 4*(5), 41-49.

Kanuka, H., & Anderson, T. (1998). Online social interchange, discord, and knowledge construction. *Journal of Distance Education.* ICAAP. Retrieved December 16, 2006, from http://cade.athabascau.ca/vol13.1/kanuka.html

King, M. (2006). MBAs decline into mediocrity. The Montreal Gazette. Friday, November 24.

Kearins, K., Luke, B., & Corner, P., (2004). What constitutes successful entrepreneurship? An analysis of recent Australian awards experiences. *Journal of Australian and New Zealand Academy of Management, 10*(1), 41-55.

Kolb, D. (2000). Learning places: Building dwelling thinking online. *Journal of Philosophy of Education, 34*(1), 121-133.

Kristiansen, S., & Ryen, A. (2002). Enacting their business environments: Asian entrepreneurs in East Africa. *African & Asian Studies, 1*(3), 165-186.

Laserna, C. (1990). Lessons in milking and math. In J. Ross & V. Bergum (Eds.), *Through the looking glass, children, and health promotion*. Ottawa: Canadian Pubic Health Association.

Lightner, N. J., Yenisey, M. M., Ozok, A. A., & Salvendy, G. (2002). Shopping behaviour and preferences in e-commerce of Turkish and American University Students: Implications from cross-cultural design. *Behaviour & Information Technology, 21*(6), 373-385.

Loi, D., & Dillon, P. (2006). Adaptive educational environments as creative spaces. *Cambridge Journal of Education, 36*(3), 363-381.

Lynn, R. (1969). Personality characteristics of a group of entrepreneurs. *Occupational Psychology, 43*(2), 151-152.

Macfarlane, D. (2000). Unis urged to join the e-revolution, *The Australian*, November 22, p.38.

Mann, C., & Gotz, K. (2006). *Borderless business: Managing the far-flung enterprise*. West Port, CT: Praeger.

Marlow, M., Stanley, K., & Connors, S. (2005). Collegiality, collaboration and Kuleana: Complexity in a professional development school. *Education, 25*(4), 557-568.

Martin, C. (2005). From high maintenance to high productivity: What managers need to know about generation Y. *Industrial and Commercial Training, 37*(1), 39-44.

Massie, J. (1987). *Essentials of management*. NJ: Prentice-Hall.

McShane, S., & Von Glinow, M. (2005). *Organizational behavior* (3rd ed.). New York: McGraw Hill.

Miller, J. (2006). Catching generation Y. *CMA Management*, April, 13-14.

Nandwa, J. (1990). Oral literature as a tool for children's education in Africa. In J. Ross & V. Bergum (Eds.), *Through the looking glass, children, and health promotion*. Ottawa: Canadian Pubic Health Association.

Olsen, M. (1968). *The process of social organization*. Holt, NY: Rinehart & Winston.

Oblinger, D., & Oblinger, J. (2005). Educating the net generation. A new EDUCAUSE e-book. Retrieved February 16, 2007, from http://www.educause.edu/content.asp?PAGE_ID=5989&bhcp=1

Peck, S. (1993). *A world waiting to be born: Civility rediscovered*. New York: Bantam Books.

Pittard, V. (2004). Evidence for e-learning policy. *Technology, Pedagogy, and Education, 13*(2), 181-194.

Prensky, M. (2001a). *Digital natives, digital immigrants*. On the Horizon, 9(5), 1-2. Retrieved February 7, 2007, from http://www.marcprensky.

com/writing/Prensky%20-%20Nati ves,%20Digital%20Immigrants%20-%20Part1. pdf

Prensky, M. (2001b). *Digital natives, digital immigrants, Part II: Do they really think differently?* On the Horizon, 9(6), 1-2. Retrieved December 16, 2006, from http://www.marcprensky.com/writing/Prensky%20%20Digital%20Natives,%20Digital%20Immigrants%20-%20Part2.pdf

Postman, N. (1985). *Amusing ourselves to death: public discourse in the age of show business.* New York: Viking.

Ramsden, P. (2003). *Learning to teach in higher education.* London: RoutledgeFalmer.

Reeves, B., & Nass, C. (1996). *The media equation: How people treat computers, television, and new media like real people and places.* Cambridge: Cambridge University Press.

Roberts, C. (2006). Retaining tomorrow's technician …. the generation Y worker is accustomed to instant gratification. *Fleet Equipment*, July, 32(7), 11.

Russo, A. (2001). *Five myths about entrepreneurs: Understanding how businesses start and grow.* Washington DC: National Commission on Entrepreneurship.

Schacter, J., & Fagnano, C. (1999). Does computer technology improve student learning and achievement? How, when, and under what condition? *Journal of Educational Computing Research*, 20(4), 329-343.

SCUP. (2004). *Trends in higher education: November Ed. Society for College and University Planning.* Ann Arbor, MI.

Shuell, T. J., & Farber, S. L. (2001). Students perceptions of technology use in college courses. *Journal of Educational Computing Research*, 24(2), 119-138.

Smith, R. (2005). Working with difference in online collaborative groups. *Adult Education Quarterly, 55*(3), 182-199.

UMUC. (2004). Graduate program information. University of Maryland University College. Retrieved February 14, 2007, from http://umuc. edu/grad/mba/mba_information.shtml

Van Alstyne, M., & Brynjolfsson, E. (2005). Global village or cyber-balkans? Modeling and measuring the integration of electronic communities. *Management Science, 51*(6), 851-868.

Van Eck, R. (2006). Digital game-based learning: It's not just the digital natives who are restless. *EDUCAUSE Review, 41*(2), 16-30.

Waddell, D., Singh, M., & Musa, A. (2006). Entrepreneurial opportunities on the Internet. In F. Zhao (Ed.), *Entrepreneurship and innovations in e-business: An integrative perspective* (pp. 179-199). Hershey, PA: Idea Group Publishing.

Watkins, J. (2005). *Gen Y knocking at the door of ownership.* The Washington Times. November 18, 2005. Retrieved February 7, 2007, from http://www.washtimes.com/fhg/20051117-083543-6983r.htm

Weisser, S. O. (2005). *Believing in yourself as classroom culture.* Retrieved November 25, 2006, from http://www.aaup.org/publications/ Academe/2005/05jf/05jfweis.htm

Wenger, E. (1998). *Communities of practice: Learning, meaning, and identity.* Cambridge: Cambridge University Press.

Zutshi, A., Zutshi, S., & Sohal, A (2006). How e-entrepreneurs operate in the context of open source software. In F. Zhao (Ed.), *Entrepreneurship and innovations in e-business: An integrative perspective* (pp. 62-88). Hershey, PA: Idea Group Publishing.

Chapter XVIII
E-Learning:
The Cornerstone to Transferring Entrepreneurship Knowledge

Cecilia Hegarty
University of Ulster, UK

ABSTRACT

*Entrepreneurial knowledge and innovation resonates with positive views, hence the need to tell everyone about entrepreneurship and give students the opportunity to learn more about it. By the same token, universities have long experimented with different learning environments to accommodate student needs (Hannay & Newvine, 2006). Internet-based education and distance learning are commonly known as e-learning. E-learning provides a method of reaching high volumes of students within a culturally rich virtual workspace. It is arguable that e-learning has become a cornerstone tool in entrepreneurship delivery. This chapter aims to stimulate debate among practitioners on the use of information technology in the process of **entrepreneurial learning**. Learning activity, pedagogical shifts within the wider disciplines of **entrepreneurship education,** and the spin-off effects for entrepreneur training programs are all considered. The application of information technology through entrepreneurship e-learning packages is shown to have magnified the entrepreneurship potential in wider society.*

INTRODUCTION

Education is on the brink of a major paradigm shift if we listen to Two Siew Chin and Williams (2006). Following the explosive growth in educational opportunities offered over the Internet, Campbell informs us: "new technologies are increasingly relied upon to support innovative approaches to business education" (2000, p. 351). The adoption of these technologies has become a vital source in sustaining traditional universities striving to cope with demanding changes in the education landscape. Students getting into debt by paying steep university fees expect to receive an education responsive to their individual needs. This leads to increased competition between universities and when coupled with the growing demand for entrepreneurship courses and increased pressure on resources, this has initiated educators within Business faculties to rethink delivery and turn their attention to e-learning methods. There is an overwhelming body of research to support this shift. Academic research on **online learning** has catapulted over the last six years. This is illustrated in Hiltz and Goldman's (2005) book while they highlight further improvements in approaches are necessary, overall they indicate that e-learning courses are as effective if not more effective when compared to "in-seats" courses at university level. Similarly, improving the way we teach entrepreneurship and train entrepreneurs has been an ongoing debate within management science and related disciplines in recent years.

Having accepted that there has been great expansion in the number of entrepreneurship courses offered in universities, it is important to outline what entrepreneurship and **entrepreneurial learning** means in the context of this research and why both phenomena are now demanding greater attention. Entrepreneurship has always existed in some form but as economies become more entrepreneurial driven and focused on creating an enterprise culture entrepreneurship can now be considered as a human and cultural behavioural concept rather than simply an economic one. Following Gartner's (1989) direction, research has moved on from studying the actual entrepreneur and towards a processual understanding of entrepreneurship. The entrepreneurial process is recognisably different from managerialism because something new is created. It can be viewed as holistic and a dynamic process, which is both an art and a science.

For instance, the growth in entrepreneurial activity within the creative industries shows how the entrepreneurial process accommodates art and science. Jack and Anderson (1999) inform us that as academics we cannot replicate the experiences of successful entrepreneurs probably because entrepreneurship does not take place in a vacuum. We can however use these experiences to develop theory and bridge the abyss between art and sci-

ence. In summary, the entrepreneurial process is treated through a positivist approach where logic and analysis are deployed to validate theory.

By comparison the process of **entrepreneurial learning** is more closely aligned to management education because it encompasses action learning a theory of management where learning incurs reflection upon actions being taken within real organisations (McLaughlin & Thorpe, 1993) and is similar to the Harvard business case online (Sensiper, 2000, p. 618) and also similar to project-based learning "...the theory and practice of utilising real-world work assignments..." (De-Fillipi, 2001, p. 9). Hanti and Kairisto-Mertanen (2006) provide more recent evidence of how learning entrepreneurship through real life company assignments can spread the entrepreneurship agenda into the wider university curriculum and simultaneously create networks between education, industry, and enterprise in the region. **Entrepreneurial learning** is about developing entrepreneurial capability since it can be argued that there is a learning experience from merely establishing a new enterprise. Another view is concerned with "learning by doing" that Kolb (1984) takes a step further in his cycle of experiential learning. Kolb believes that while you can learn by doing, the concepts learned are modified when you start to practice behaviours and reflect upon them, learning is thus modified by experience. Experiential learning has implications for knowledge transfer, since the outcomes of the process could be said to represent only historical record and not knowledge of the future. Both education and training in entrepreneurship has been carried out through many guises. For example improving core skills such as business planning or through personality attributes. In summary, in both education and training contexts, individuals are continually learning (changing, doing, experimenting, and sense making) throughout the development of their own lifecycle. On a point of clarification, it is generally accepted that during the **learning process** attitudes, habit, skills, and knowledge are acquired and behaviour is altered but this does not *necessarily* lead to behavioural changes as suggested by Huber (1991) and later support by Gibb (1995).

Aims

This chapter considers the role of e-learning in developing the keystones of entrepreneurial knowledge. This research focuses on the tertiary education sector in the UK and is undertaken within Northern Ireland, a currently underperforming region in terms of globally monitored levels of entrepreneurial activity. Entrepreneurs in Northern Ireland have high success rates hence the task for government and educators is to transfer knowledge at a wider level including non-business disciplines. As a result over the last five years, the UK has seen an increased emphasis on enterprise learning within disciplines such as science and technology and as part of a wider university curriculum. One of the most effective ways for Northern Ireland's universities to drive the entrepreneurship agenda is through e-learning. In the UK, government have pledged their support for the development of e-learning; Singh, O'Donoghue, and Betts (2002) report Department of Education and Employment (DEE) plans to invest £200 million to invest in pursuit of the e-university. This is part of a general bid to raise the standard of higher education.

The objectives of this chapter are related to four enquiries:

1. How we understand **entrepreneurial learning** from a student perspective and from the view of the practising entrepreneur?
2. What are the pros and cons of **online learning**?
3. How e-learning methods fit within the model of evolution of **entrepreneurship education**?

4. How to determine the added value of applying information technologies to entrepreneurial potential?

Context

The context for this study is framed under four main headings:

1. Learning process
2. Online learning
3. Entrepreneurship education
4. Entrepreneurial learning

Firstly by illustrating the process of learning for students and entrepreneurs we can gain better insights into how knowledge is developed. Secondly, developing an understanding of what constitutes **online learning** and its emergence highlights significant developments in university education and student demands and how **online learning** is suited to entrepreneurship teachings. Thirdly by exploring how **entrepreneurship education** has evolved and our current understanding of the subject, this gives us a better idea of the learning outcomes that should be achieved through entrepreneurship programmes in education. Finally, since higher education is a key part, but for many a first part, in continual learning it is important to (a) understand how educators should prepare nascent entrepreneurs and (b) how professional trainers should approach **entrepreneurial learning** for practising entrepreneurs. The literature evidence points to the value of learning by doing and reflection, and continually learning through the flexibility offered by e-learning.

Learning Process

Learning is a highly complex phenomenon that at a basic level describes the assimilation of factual information (i.e. ,tacit knowledge that has immediate utility but no real long-term implications).

Basic learning is sometimes termed single-loop learning (See Argyris & Schon, 1978). In contrast, higher forms of learning stimulate fundamental change for the learner because the learner reflects on current know-how and recognises the advantage of changing behaviours—this can be termed double-loop learning. Deeper learning involves all three learning domains cognitive, affective, and psychomotor and concerns knowing how to do something as well as knowing when to apply the knowledge. Schon (1983) describes learning as a process of reflection on action while examining messy complex problems. Learning can be said to be different for the student and entrepreneur in terms of the level of reflection. Entrepreneurs can reflect on daily operations and make strategic changes upon reflection of their actions so that the next time they face the same issue where the same principles apply they can repeat the corrective behaviour. In effect, this means reflection has long-term implications if they engage in higher-level learning and learn to proactively reflect. For students, reflection is not easily assessed and for this reason has pervaded timetabling schedules. **Online learning** environments, however, provide greater opportunities for students to present their views and reflect on the views of their online peers through a gradable online workspace.

Online Learning

Online learning tools enable reflection through public places of asynchronous (discussion boards) and synchronous chat rooms (multi-way) and personal spaces of Web logs or blogs, instant messaging and reflection journals. Learning logs are not new, but they have only more recently been applied through information technology to create online student learning logs. Here the student benefits from receiving feedback from a wider audience and not only the e-tutor and the reflective student can actively create knowledge. Hernández-Ramos (2004) provides an interesting account of how schoolteachers that regarded their

job as isolated used information technology to reflect on their performance and in turn improved their practice. From a student perspective there is evidence to suggest, "shy students" with less vibrant personas are better able to contribute to classroom discussions in the online environment (Ferdig & Roehler, 2004). Furthermore learner satisfaction with Web-based instruction has been linked to the level of interaction perceived by students (Perez-Prado & Thirunarayanan, 2002). The reflection part of the technology should be further developed, as there is a need to improve online discussion forums to promote higher order thinking.

"The success of the British Open University in the 1970s marked the beginning of technologically assisted open learning environments and the movement known as distance learning" (McIsaac, 2002). **Online learning** is a more recent adaptation of correspondence courses that uses Internet-based technology instead of traditional printed materials. Unlike first and second generations of distance learning, **online learning** is different in that it does more than simply distribute learning materials, it involves interactive learning, good communication with easy two-way flow of information and ideas between e-tutor and e-learner and between e-learners. The technological shifts in distance learning within university education are summarised in Table 1. As education delivery moves with the technology of the times they are distinct advantages for more learners hence making education more inclusive to all people in society.

Besides the benefits of e-learning as saving travel time (Wheatley & Greer, 1995), there are qualitative benefits of participating in an international classroom especially if studying an entrepreneurship course. A recent study showed that **online learning** allowed students the opportunity to use information technology in an autonomous way (Drennan, Kennedy, & Pisarksi, 2005). Such autonomy parallels the real-life entrepreneurial situation, which is thought an important element

Table 1. Technological shifts in distance learning

Mode of distance learning	Mode of communication	Type of student	Example
Correspondence course	Printed materials and telephone	Full-time employed, with dependents, affordability issues	Open University courses
Telecourses	Audio tapes, local radio and television stations	Convenience student requiring less travel	Alice Springs School, Central Australia
Internet-based courses – e-learning	WWW, WebCT, interactive simulations, video, and e-mail	More inclusive—Beginner-mature learner, with disabilities	Under- & post- graduate degree module in universities globally

of current **entrepreneurship education** (Kirby, 2003).

Perhaps universities still face quality issues where on-campus courses tend to be more valued than off-site, **online learning**? If this is the case all academics should be educated on the merits of e-learning and universities should seek to maximise the use of online technology on all courses. In summary whilst dilemmas remain for technical and scientifically oriented courses using WebCT environments says Baker (1986), e-learning is largely suited to **entrepreneurship education** and indeed to **entrepreneurial learning** as proven by practitioner use of virtual incubators. In the argument for online entrepreneurship courses, the cons are largely redundant. Since studying e-modules by itself does not create more entrepreneurs; caution must be exercised so that educators are not tempted to adopt a module-specific view, that is, a narrow view to **entrepreneurship education**.

Entrepreneurship Education

Entrepreneurship education needs to be embedded within the overall design of a 3-4 year programme according to Plaschkla and Welsch's (2005) "degree of integration" theory. This option allows for entrepreneurship teaching to be supported by a number of different actor groups, on a number of different and unexpected courses, and entrenched into the wider university curriculum (p. 329). Spyros and Christos (2006) cite that stu-

dents prefer compulsory entrepreneurship courses embodied in their conventional curriculum. It appears pedagogy needs to combine theoretical and conceptual approaches with integrated practice. In terms of how this has moved on from the earliest approach, which was characterised by general management education. It appears that while there was an initial focus on small business education, this has evolved to processual understandings (Boyd & Vozikis, 1994). This does not mean that curricula were complete during these transition periods, because they were largely market-driven. Gibb (2006) gives a recent illustration where the focus is on the sub-parts such as the business plan, corporate venturing, rational thought processes and so on that only serve to dampen the true entrepreneurial spirit. We need to move towards a wider societal concept of entrepreneurship activity embracing notions of being visionary, being strategically intuitive and using tacit knowledge to develop entrepreneurial ideas. This would seem a sensible idea because Hannon (2005, p. 13) reported that graduates are prevented from being entrepreneurial because of a lack of skills including: entrepreneurial opportunity spotting, general start-up skills, management, financial, sales/marketing skills, market knowledge, and research of sourcing gaps in the supply chain at local, national or international level. Gibb's opinion is well positioned since it places considerable emphasis on the entrepreneurship enigma and the uniqueness of individual entrepreneurial processes. Students of entrepreneurship should be aware that some entrepreneurs succeed but some fail and they should be made to feel comfortable with the concept of failure. Fiet (2001) blames both the descriptive nature of entrepreneurship teachings and the lack of integration between research findings and theory, for the lack of reality in the education experience. At the core of **online learning** is self-directed learning and this is important to the subject of entrepreneurship because it offers a means to mimic the entrepreneurial role and to ignite enthusiasm whilst requiring discipline within the learning environment. As an educator to adopt the heroic view of entrepreneurship surely has a negative impact upon developing capability? This would be better attributed to government. Educators and students are likely to find more use in promoting individuality within an entrepreneurship course, which ultimately means unique and flexible course design and assessment. "Flexible learning is an alternative to the fixed contact teaching model traditionally associated with higher education" (Campbell, 2000). If we accept Gartner's (1985) view that the difference between entrepreneurs is greater than that between entrepreneurs and non-entrepreneurs, **entrepreneurship education** must cater for a broad spectrum of learners.

More students are choosing to study entrepreneurship; they desire to be streetwise by having business sense. Now the challenge is to reduce the significant gap between finding entrepreneurship attractive and having the self-efficacy to carry it through to positive action. Research would suggest there is a huge pool of latent talent in Northern Ireland where the "right **entrepreneurship education**" could serve to inspire positive action.

Entrepreneurial Learning

Traditionally there have been two learning arenas for entrepreneurship programmes, the university, and the organisation (Leitch & Harrison, 1999,

p. 90). In the university context, there has been unprecedented growth in the number and type of programmes provided through third level education. Research however has largely been restricted to content, delivery and programme evaluations. Those educators in the business of changing mindsets and fostering positive attitudes towards entrepreneurial opportunities have steered clear of quantifying the number of graduates starting a new venture. This has instead been the focus of those funding education initiatives and those in government roles; perhaps this may change with the emergence of academic entrepreneurship. However, assessing the training scene for practising entrepreneurs would nevertheless be insightful to enterprise educators since their role is often to provide preparatory **entrepreneurship education**. The objective of enterprise training or **entrepreneurial learning** as it is defined in this chapter, by comparison is largely to provide continual **entrepreneurial learning** (Garavan & O' Cinneide, 1994), which requires better articulation and integration of universities, management schools and professional trainers. Evans and Volery (2001) suggest in the organisation context there are three elements central to course content:

1. Opportunity recognition
2. Marshalling of resources
3. Developing capability

In McHugh and O'Gorman's (2006) survey of entrepreneurs in informational technology, engineering, manufacturing and the business service sector in the southeast of Ireland, they revealed enterprise education assists entrepreneurs in better handling business operation issues. Like many earlier authors (for example Kirzner, 1973), they suggest that certain individuals stumble across opportunities but if they were educated in enterprise they might become an opportunity creator and better business survivors with more capability. For instance greater ability to plan, conduct market research and avoid daily operational issues. Their findings also evidence that **entrepreneurial learning** can be maximised through longer-term training programmes, which is contrary to earlier findings. Sullivan (2000) views much learning as experiential, which has implications for "mode and timing" and favours the "just-in-time" approach where specific assistance is offered in response to critical incidents. Sullivan does however state that effective learning is well served through a mentoring relationship, a view that has been supported by Northern Irish entrepreneurs. In the organisation context, clearly the arguments for adopting different approaches to **entrepreneurial learning** are hugely reliant upon stage in entrepreneurial lifecycle and hence how to consolidate earlier knowledge and training. Studying how entrepreneurs learn according to what they know already has been dubbed "practical theory" or "personal theory" and shifts the emphasis onto entrepreneurs to engage in meta-cognition (to make sense of their own learning experiences) and create individual learning maps because learning is both planned and emergent according to Megginson (1996).

Participants

The participants for this research have undertaken entrepreneurship e-learning modules devised by the Northern Ireland Centre for Entrepreneurship (NICENT). NICENT acts as an umbrella organisation for Northern Ireland's two universities and partner colleges in further and higher education and has out-performed its targets for students graduating with qualifications in entrepreneurial studies. The Centre has become the UK leader in education for the use of e-learning to create greater awareness of entrepreneurship. NICENT was established under the Science Enterprise Challenge Initiative and is one of thirteen centres of excellence across the UK. Others include Cambridge Enterprise; North East Centre for Scientific Enterprise; Oxford Science Enterprise Centre; Mercia Institute of Enterprise; University of Nottingham Institute for Enterprise and Innovation; Wessex Enterprise Centre; White Rose Centre for Enterprise; Manchester and Liverpool Science Enterprise Board; Centre for Scientific Enterprise Limited; The Entrepreneurship Centre, Imperial College; SIMFONEC and in Scotland the Scottish Institute of Enterprise which includes 20 Scottish Higher Education Institutes.

The participants for this study are taken from full-time undergraduate degree programmes within science and technology disciplines. Average student age is 20 years old, having some part-time work experience and peripheral knowledge of entrepreneurship largely attributed to Local Development Agency (Invest NI) promotional campaigns on television, radio and local media and "BIG" (Big-time entrepreneurs) success stories in national newspapers. Students have registered to study the NICENT learning outcomes through a combination of modules making up the overall degree programme. The mode of delivery for **entrepreneurship education** comprises e-learning, face-to-face workshops, site visits, work placements and project assignments. This research concentrates on the e-learning component that contains high interaction via computer simulations, videos, texts, workbooks, discussion forums and online reflection logs. E-learning involved 100% continuous assessment. Most students were provided with e-learning content through the WebCT environment although some have now moved onto WebCT vista. The lecturers underwent training before becoming e-tutors that enables them to maximise the potential of the technology and ensure appropriate usage and thus positive learning experiences for all.

Findings

First the structure of the course is documented to show the similarity in subject content to the traditional classroom based entrepreneurship course. The level of variance is related to the technology and online tools. The main issues associated with the course content are outlined. Educators and students had concerns about four broad factors. Secondly, the findings emphasise the importance of learner control. Finally, both the learner and educator experiences are compared.

Content

The online course structure generally looks like the following:

1. General information about teaching team, subject coordinator.
2. A detailed subject outline—rationale, outcomes, structure, aims, objectives, learning outcomes, teaching & learning methods, content, assessment, resources, and guidance notes.
3. Introductory workshop may involve speakers—entrepreneurs, RDAs etc.
4. Structured subject content—use of text and graphics, "lecture" notes (theory) and learning activities provide critical framework, complemented by discussion boards & a face-to-face workshop interspersed.
5. Other content—Frequently asked questions (FAQ), helpful hints, calendar, announcements area and e-mail system, non-assessed quizzes, questionnaires, and glossary.

The main content issues were related to four broad factors:

1. Digestibility factor—amount of new information presented in an environment that students were habituated to scanning on WWW.
2. Stimulation factor—The need for "stimulated reading"—balance of text and graphics and the usefulness of links where students were diverted in order to back-up content.
3. Navigation factor—How easy it was to navigate the content.

4. Knowledge factor—How to test and apply information to create new knowledge.

Note while students were aware and had thought about the knowledge factor lecturers were more concerned with this factor. The lecturer could be said to have "found new channels of learning." For instance, to relieve their concerns e-tutors tended to make ambiguous statements in the discussion forums to challenge student thinking. Student reflection logs gave an indication of knowledge download in real time but when reviewed over the entire duration of the course gave greater insights into their individual learning maps. There were connections to illustrate how **entrepreneurship education** models entrepreneurial practice. For example e-learner autonomy to entrepreneur's way of life, group work illustrating intrapreneurship, or research or project work establishing connections with key stakeholders in the region.

Learning Control

For many students facing the e-learning environment for the first time, there was evidence of a definite shift in the locus of control where the e-learner must take control of his or her own **learning process**; this transition proved challenging for some. Equally, the lecturer needs to have "more faith" in the students when becoming an e-tutor and succumb to a different teaching style to create a "comfortable" learning zone that often exposes e-learner and e-tutor to greater vulnerability. While part of the success of the courses was linked to "the new environment for learning," most of the success was attributed to the capabilities of the technology and lack of IT problems.

Educator Experience

Firstly, the research would be incomplete without mentioning that embedding entrepreneurship, enterprise and business aspects onto science, engineering, and technology courses were new for NICENT. The NICENT Teaching Fellows worked hard to convince their colleagues of its merits and in doing so created a number of enterprise champions. As a result e-learning was farmed out from NICENT and these results demonstrate the experiences of the "converted colleagues." The findings show that the electronic interface accommodates lectures of pure science subjects that wish to comfortably embrace the enterprise agenda. Also, the lecturer and learner are "learning together" because of the new information assimilated and each applying this information to what they know already promotes deeper knowledge and understanding of the subject. Educators can also work from home and thus were able to re-allocate their teaching hours from actual delivery into on-demand developmental and support tasks. Educators highly rated the experience judging from the quality of their individual experiences and by the quality of the student work produced.

Learner Experience

Despite initial teething problems, largely technical, students were able to "bond easily" online and "feel a sense of community." Since the majority were new to e-learning, some had used the technology before as an "information hot-spot," distinguishing the obligatory material from the optional proved difficult for some e-learners. Frequently cited were: "information overload" "so many useful links, which ones are best?" This finding indicates that learners were not habituated to flexible learning and thus did not maximise the true benefits of e-learning because of a fear that "big browser" was monitoring their progress. Perhaps this is a price that has to be paid considering how institutionalised students have become through traditional education delivery methods. However, the research shows that this gap can be narrowed by giving students clear instruction to the subject and continually repeating

the same instruction and by demonstrating how to use resources to be an autonomous learner. The sceptics' points must also be addressed at the outset. The following example illustrates a question posed during this research: "Is this not just a cheap way for the Uni. to delivery our course, we have no lecturer expertise and we have to print out own notes?!." It was outlined that while the overhead costs for the faculty can be reduced there are more student than educator advantages. It was critical to convince students they would not be left to "sink or swim." Overall, a few words were consistently used throughout by students in course evaluations:

1. Students were often "anxious" when faced with new content & new delivery at the same time.
2. Students could become temporally "disorientated" within WebCT environment by use of WWW links and in trying to get to grips with this new learning environment it "disoriented" them from the work in other modules.
3. The "flexibility" which the software provided was at first difficult to cope with as students devoted "too much" of their time to it but students grew to appreciate its "flexibility."

All three points above were influenced by the 100% continuous assessment; students usually completed an end of module exam thus finding e-learning assessment more difficult. Note also, the students in this study were mostly young, full-time students not requiring "flexibility" for job and family requirements.

To date the results are encouraging. Students have reported that they have learnt how to better plan, develop, and negotiate giving them increased confidence levels in taking on new projects. Students are taught for enterprise because they are developing an entrepreneurial skills set. The following citation refers to the main advantage of not teaching this particular subject in the traditional classroom: "This course was the most real-to-life experience I've had." Students clearly favour the learner-centred approach adopted.

DISCUSSION

A major discussion point on these findings has to be the level of emphasis on the technology-side of the subject when there are equally important issues remaining to be resolved in the subject content side. If our role as educators is to "enable students to be able to stand back and to knowledgeably scan the entrepreneurial landscape." E-learning must provide the means to learn from that distance. However some may hide behind their online existence as "cyber-anonymous peers." Campbell (2000) suggested "Web-based technology is all about sharing ideas and information between individuals," by allowing students to communicate effectively in the WebCT environment we allow for this multi-way flexible exchange.

It is interesting that when we compare e-learning to traditional lecturing the level of autonomy is frightfully high, whilst we were not able to make direct comparisons in this study, there is research to support this. Hannay et al. (2006) for instance, found that over 90% of students reported that they read the assigned textbook in their online courses compared to less than 60% on traditional courses. In the traditional classroom environment, students naturally rely more heavily upon the lecturer. This proves that **online learning** helps to create autonomous learners. The third point for discussion develops the first two on technology and content theory because it concerns the practical elements to learning entrepreneurship. Learning by doing is valued by students. In fact, Evans et al. (2001) state that students: "learn much more than those attending traditional classroom lectures (p. 339). Not only are e-learners having the chance to learn by doing but they are afforded the opportunity to reflect upon their learning. This in turn should

mean that **entrepreneurship education** creates reflective practitioners fit for an entrepreneurial career. On a final discussion point, we must consider the added value through e-learning delivery. In experimenting with the delivery of third level education there are a number of complimentary methods that could lead to a more blended learning approach. Whilet Hannay et al. (2006) believe there is merit in introducing hybrid courses into the learning curriculum (i.e., 50% online 50% traditional). Whatever the case, we need to have a real-life context thus entrepreneurship delivery through e-learning is challenging and requires the educator to have continuing enthusiasm and persistence in order to deliver the theory and at the same time provide elements of realism.

Lessons Learned

A number of lessons as to how to support e-learning delivery have been learned especially. From the student perspective e-learning requires:

1. 24-hour access – there can be issues with migration to new software.
2. Gentle reminders and prompts to encourage discussion and behind the scenes reading.
3. A printed course guide book known as the "bible" such as a textbook.
4. Supporting subject "e-material" (e.g., electronic packs relating to blocks of content).
5. Students require e-tutors to use the various tools within the online environment to vary and improve the learning experience.
6. Transparency in assessment procedures.
7. E-tutor feedback through a combination of public and private spaces.

Educators' need to:

1. Sort technical problems before the course commences and provide ongoing technical support.

2. Devote essential course time to introducing students to the online environment.

3. Allow students to conduct an informal exchange to begin with, for example, making introductions.

4. Outline the structure of the online course and e-tutor and student roles (e.g., netiquette, response times, advertise specific clinic times).

5. Encourage students to network online (i.e., respond to peer postings and monitor network activity from an appropriate e-tutor distance).

6. Provide regular feedback and summaries/ weaves as appropriate.

7. Check for "Web lurkers" privately (e-mail system) to ensure trust in the learning environment for all.

Educators of entrepreneurship would do well to remember that there will be teaching limitations because (a) many students are not "entrepreneur-ready," (b) entrepreneurship is a process not a stasis. Providing resource-rich teaching materials to stimulate innovative thinking and imaginative acquisition of knowledge is thought to be key to e-learning success in entrepreneurship. It is debatable whether students become more intrapreneurial or entrepreneurial as a result of undertaking these e-modules. From a staff point of view the success of online pedagogy will depend on the ability of teaching staff to develop an interactive environment. Campbell (2000) highlights some concern that the technological shift not only forces us to rethink teaching and learning but also the functioning and structure of universities. Perhaps this is an example of being driven by market demand but there is some tentative evidence that RDAs are involved in restructuring their departments and in particular their approach to professional training.

Future of E-Learning

How do we determine the added value of applying information technologies to entrepreneurial potential? Grouping together as educators to pool resources has been mentioned a few times throughout the course of this research for instance Singh et al. (2002, p. 224) indicates how several (79) UK universities proposed to team up together to deliver courses and Teo Siew Chin et al. (2006) report on the more globally-based Universitas 21 consortium (p. 13). Interestingly Evans et al. (2001) also mention the value of networking online for entrepreneurial survival and success and refer to good test cases, including Ernest & Young's Online Ernie for professional consultancy and First Tuesday a network of 18,000 members from entrepreneurs to investor stakeholders participating in online discussions and information sharing. The centre worked in close co-operation with experts in the different university departments including IT and e-learning, staff development and life-long learning as well as external Web design companies to alleviate misuse of the online environment and to avoid sending the wrong signal about what e-learning involves—it is more than a hot bed of information it is about developing ideas within an environment of like-minded individuals. By embedding entrepreneurship within overall degree programmes and not as a stand-alone module this does not detract from the core subject content but rather teaches the same subject within different boundaries.

E-learning environments provide a good example of embedding subject content at different levels so that individual learner needs are satisfied - deeper and higher order learning can occur. "It is well known that entrepreneurs exhibit individualistic tendencies and it appears to be validated with respect to education" (Evans et al., 2001, p. 343). There are some vulnerability issues for members of the higher education community in considering moving more towards online delivery methods because of the long-lasting "in-seats mentality." Trends show more people are working full-time and studying part-time, also ICT skills have increased so the future of e-learning is bright.

CONCLUSION

This chapter has sought to debate the practicalities of e-learning for the subject of entrepreneurship. There is a positive case of the value of online modules for both e-tutors and e-learners. E-learning allows for effective communication and collaborative working between students and academic staff within a rich shared virtual workspace. Multi-way interactions are taking place between individuals and technology. The key is in the quality of the online interaction.

Certain pitfalls include screening educator and student IT capabilities, appropriate usage of the technology to maximise the learning experience and providing teaching discipline within broader boundaries. Jack et al. (1999) summed, "...we need to loosen our academic apron strings to let our students' imagination soar." Using virtual environments where participants can interact is not only useful to students but would also be of benefit to practising entrepreneurs and those willing to partake in continual learning. Evans et al. (2001) suggest that the Internet is a powerful medium to provide the business development services much needed by entrepreneurs, since in the information age it is difficult to overestimate the strategic importance of information as a critical resource.

At institute level, traditional universities have been accused of being afraid of the huge paradigm shift in education however for economic reasons they have been forced to engage in accommodating students and thus to engage in newer modes of delivery. This chapter has described how NICENT has lead education delivery by online methods. It is recommended there are dedicated persons steering and piloting online programmes within different faculties within further and higher education institutes and if possible such persons would be distributed within different departments.

At European and national policy level, government programmes have paid good attention to the importance of e-commerce, business to business (B2B) and the importance of digital technologies. Yet while policies refer to life-long learning they have given little weight to the use of ICT for learning. The information age ought to accommodate **online learning** environments in order to raise education standards within wider society.

The findings of this research add to a small but growing body of research aimed at determining the achievement of students enrolled in entrepreneurship Web-based courses. Further advances in WebCT technologies make this an importance area for future researches into the effectiveness of e-learning delivery methods. Areas for future study include comparisons between traditionally taught modules versus online modules, the impact of e-learning on entrepreneurial potential, course design issues, and the technological developments associated with **online learning**.

REFERENCES

Argyris, C., & Schon, D. A. (1978). *Organisational learning: A theory of action perspective.* Reading, MA: Addison-Wesley.

Baker, K. (1986). Dilemmas at a distance. *Assessment & Evaluation in Higher Education, 11*(3), 219-230.

Boyd, N., & Vozikis, G. (1994). The influence of self-efficacy on the development of entrepreneurial intentions and actions. *Entrepreneurship Theory and Practice, 18*(4), 63-77.

Campbell, J. (2000). Using Internet technology to support flexible learning in business education. *Information Technology and Management, 1*(1), 351-362.

Drennan, J., Kennedy, J., & Pisarksi, A. (2005). Factors affecting student attitudes toward flexible online learning in management education. *Journal of Educational Research, 98*(6), 331-340.

Evans, D., & Volery, T. (2001). Online business development services for entrepreneurs: An exploratory study. *Entrepreneurship & Regional Development, 13*(1), 333-350.

Ferdig, R. E., & Roehler, L. R. (2004). Student uptake in electronic discussions: Examining online discourse in literacy preservice classrooms. *Journal of Research on Technology in Education, 36*(2), 119-136.

Fiet, J. O. (2001). The theoretical side of teaching entrepreneurship. *Journal of Business Venturing, 16*(1), 1-24.

Garavan, T. N., & O' Cinneide, B. (1994). Entrepreneurship education and training programmes: A review and evaluation—Part 1. *Journal of European Industrial Training, 18*(8), 3-12.

Gartner, W. (1985). A conceptual framework for describing the phenomenon of new venture creation. *Academy of Management Review, 10*(1), 696-706.

Gartner's (1989). Who is an entrepreneur? is the wrong question. *American Journal of Small Business, 12*(3), 11-32.

Gibb, A. A. (1995). Learning skills for all: The key to success in small business development. *International Council for Small Business (ICSB) 40th World Conference Proceedings*, Sydney.

Gibb, A. (2006). *[Internet] entrepreneurship: Unique solutions for unique environments is it possible to achieve this with the existing paradigm?* Background paper to the plenary presentation to the International Council for Small Business World Conference June 2006, Melbourne. Returned July 2006, from http://www.icsb2006.org/docs/Allan_Gibb-Plenary_Paper_ICSB2006.pdf

Hanti, S., & Kairisto-Mertanen, L. (2006). Making students learn about entrepreneurship through real life company assignments. *EFMD 36th EISB Conference Proceedings on Embedding Entrepreneurship Education in Europe: Evaluating Effective Policy and Practice at the Institutional, Regional and National Levels*, September 2006, Southampton.

Haavind, S. (2006). Book review of learning together online: Research on asynchronous learning networks. *Journal of Interactive Online Learning, 5*(2), 217-223.

Hannay, M., & Newvine, T. (2006). Perceptions of distance learning: A comparison of online and traditional learning. *Journal of Online Learning and Teaching, 2*(1), 1-11.

Hannon, P. (2005). The journey from student to entrepreneur: A review of existing research into graduate entrepreneurship. *Intent Conference July 2005*, School of Management, University of Surrey: London.

Hernández-Ramos, P. (2004). Web logs and online discussions as tools to promote reflective practice. *The Journal of Interactive Online Learning, 3*(1), 1-16.

Hiltz, S. R., & Goldman, R. (2005). *Learning together online: Research on asynchrous learning networks*. NJ: Lawrence Erlbaum Associates.

Huber, G. P. (1991). Organisational learning: The contributing processes and the literatures. *Organisation Science, 2*(1), 88-115.

Jack, S. & Anderson, A. (1999). Entrepreneurship education within the enterprise culture: Producing reflective practitioners. *International Journal of Entrepreneurial Behaviour and Research, 5*(3), 110-125.

Kirby, D. (2003). *Entrepreneurship*. London: McGraw-Hill Publishing.

Kirzner, I. M. (1973). *Competition and entrepreneurship*. Chicago: University of Chicago Press.

Kolb, D. (1984). Experiential learning: Experience as a source of learning and development. NJ: Prentice-Hall.

Leitch, C. & Harrison, R. (1999). A process model for entrepreneurship education and development. *International Journal of Entrepreneurial Behaviour and Research, 5*(3), 83-102.

McHugh, M., & O'Gorman, B., (2006). Enterprise education does make a difference. *EFMD 36th EISB Conference Proceedings on Embedding Entrepreneurship Education in Europe: Evaluating Effective Policy and Practice at the Institutional, Regional and National Levels*, September 2006, Southampton.

McIsaac, M. S. (2002). Online learning from an international perspective. *Journal of Education Media International, 39*(1), 17-21.

McLaughlin, H., & Thorpe, R. (1993). Action learning: A paradigm in emergence: The problems facing a challenge to traditional management education and development. *British Journal of Management, 4*(1), 19-27.

Meggginson, D. (1996). Planned and emergent learning—consequences for development. *Management Learning, 27*(4), 411-428.

Perez-Prado, A., & Thirunarayanan, M. O. (2002). A qualitative comparison of online and classroom-based sections of a course: Exploring student perspectives. *Journal of Education Media International, 39*(2), 195-202.

Plaschka, G. & Welsch, P. (2005). Emerging structures in entrepreneurship education: Curricular designs and strategies. In R. van der Hrost, D., S. ing-Kauannui, & S. Duffy (Eds.), *Keystones of entrepreneurship knowledge*, (pp. 322-338). Blackwell Publishing.

Sensiper, S. (2000). Making the case online Harvard business school multimedia. *Information, Communication, and Society, 3*(4), 616-621.

Singh, G., O'Donoghue, J., & Betts, C. (2002). A UK study into the potential effects of virtual education: Does online learning spell an end for on-campus learning? *Behaviour & Information Technology, 21*(3), 223-229.

Spyros, V., & Christos, C., (2006). Entrepreneurial education and training in the tertiary level institutions of Greece. *EFMD 36th EISB Conference Proceedings on Embedding Entrepreneurship Education in Europe: Evaluating Effective Policy and Practice at the Institutional, Regional and National Levels*, September 2006, Southampton.

Sullivan, R., (2000). Entrepreneurial learning and mentoring. *International Journal of Entrepreneurial Behaviour & Research, 6*(3), 160-172.

Teo Siew Chin, S., & Williams, J. B. (2006). A theoretical framework for effective online course design. *MERLOT Journal of Online Learning and Teaching, 2*(1), 12-21.

Wheatley, B., & Greer, E. (1995). Interactive television: A new delivery system for a traditional reading course. *Journal of Technology and Teacher Education, 3*(4), 343-351.

KEY TERMS

Entrepreneurship Education: Educational programmes that are holistic and dynamic in delivering core elements of entrepreneurship theory and practice.

Entrepreneurial Learning: The process undertaken by real-life entrepreneurs to continuously develop an entrepreneurial skills set and reflect on practice.

Learning Process: Process of assimilating factual information, which can occur at either a basic or higher level.

Online Learning: A method of learning enabled by the application of informational technology.

Section VI
Innovation Process

Chapter XIX
Innovations from Business Process Models

James Perotti
Rochester Institute of Technology, USA

ABSTRACT

This chapter asserts that process models are an excellent platform for a continuous stream of innovations. Such models can illuminate opportunities for new products and services and for new ways of distributing products and services. These dynamic models make it possible to coordinate the efforts of multiple business partners in order to better serve customers with quality, speed, and responsiveness to their needs. There is increasing evidence that businesses using these models to discover opportunities have achieved a sustainable advantage over their competitors.

INTRODUCTION

Business Week's annual feature section on innovation demonstrates the recognition of how important innovation is to business. Many of the articles describe how to motivate innovative behaviors, how to effectively move innovations from idea to the marketplace. This chapter will describe a larger context for innovating. It will show that software process models plus ancillary systems are already being used for discovering opportunities for innovating, for testing out innovations, and for bringing new products and services to market.

Innovation took on a new focus during the 1980s and 1990s, when thousands of new e-businesses came into existence and made millionaires of their owners. E-businesses demonstrated that there were hundreds of business models beyond the traditional ones (e.g., portals such as Amazon, auction sites such as eBay, business to business, business to government). Innovation literature exploded during this dot.com era, much of it trying to generalize about what these businesses were about—their business models—and how these new innovative businesses came into existence. Stakeholders forced the owners of the many start-up dot.com businesses to make explicit how their businesses were to operate in order to make money—or at least generate revenue. Many knowledgeable people doubted that Amazon.com or Google had a workable business model. Many of these start-ups were small, unique, and served a narrow market niche. Many failed because their success prompted larger firms to copy, even improve upon, the original business concept.

These were business-model innovations, and from this confusion came a standardized and accepted concept of a business model. Chesbrough and Rosenbloom (2004) present a basic framework describing the elements of a business model. They list the following six components:

1. **Value proposition:** A description of the customer problem, the product that addresses the problem, and the value of the product from the customer's perspective.
2. **Market segment:** The group of customers to target, recognizing that different market segments have different needs. Sometimes the potential of an innovation is unlocked only when a different market segment is targeted.
3. **Value chain structure:** The firm's position and activities in the value chain and how the firm will capture part of the value that it creates in the chain.
4. **Revenue generation and margins:** How revenue is generated (sales, leasing, subscription, support, etc.), the cost structure, and target profit margins.
5. **Position in value network:** Identification of competitors, complementors, and any network effects that can be utilized to deliver more value to the customer.
6. **Competitive strategy:** How the company will attempt to develop a sustainable competitive advantage, for example, by means of a cost, differentiation, or niche strategy.

This relatively recent definition of a business model puts the business into a larger context by recognizing its essential relationships with sup-

pliers, partners, wholesalers, distribution systems, and with customers. The requirement of specifying a business model draws attention to the larger competitive environment. The model's emphasis on how customers perceive value forces owners to specify how each business partner contributes part of the value. The business model, in other words, forces business people to take a process view of business. It forces managers to consider the importance of their relationships with partners, to think about how best to coordinate the whole supply chain process to maximize adding value to customers. Dell's competitive advantage is built on its excellent supply chain management, and its careful focus on every element of process to the degree that it routinely uses half the overhead of its leading rivals per unit of sales (Breen, 2004).

Howard Smith reiterates the idea that innovation is no longer just a concern for the R&D departments. Innovations are needed from every aspect of the business, from every business process:

In a 2003 Communication on Innovation Policy, Erkki Liikanen, EU Commissioner for enterprise and the information society, wrote: "Innovation is ... a multi-dimensional concept, which goes beyond technological innovation to encompass ... new means of distribution, marketing or design. Innovation is thus not only limited to high tech sectors of the economy, but is rather an omnipresent driver for growth." Companies that recognize this will not define innovation as owned by one part of the organization. Every aspect of how an organization operates is subject to innovation—administrative innovations, marketing innovations, financial innovations, design innovations, manufacturing innovations, service concept innovations, and human resource management innovations. These process innovations are echoes of the reengineering mantra of the early 90s (Smith, 2006).

Information technology has become an essential part of the business model's supply network. The network is the communications link for the process partners. At its best, supply chain software is also a visible model of the supply chain's operations. Supply chain innovations affect how offerings are created and distributed to customers—from suppliers to delivery, to distribution, to customer. Process technology innovations improve the customer satisfaction with better quality, faster and lower cost delivery. Enabling technologies provide the platform on which teams create new initiatives, collaborate on their design, and ultimately bring them to market. All are examples of how information technology supported processes add value to a business, value that the customers are easily able to perceive.

There are, of course, many e-businesses which are little more than automated processes (e.g., Ditech.com for loans, PriceQuote for insurance, Hertz Car Rental). These businesses represent the ultimate example of optimization. These businesses rely upon other businesses to complete their processes; thus the automated process extends across multiple business partners. While process automation seems to be the ideal, it is only workable when the process itself is well structured and, hence, programmable. The processes emphasized here require multiple human interventions because customer demands are unpredictable and sometimes novel. But clearly more process automation is desirable.

The University of Innsbruck hosts a major computer science initiative, "Semantic Web Enabled Web Services," which aims to standardize machine-to-machine processing and, in that way, open up the future development of ever more intelligent communications between partners. Web services and the semantic Web are software tools for integrating hardware platforms and software applications; Web Services provide the linkages between machines, the semantic Web provides the translations of the shared data. Such technologies underlie the process models, which span multiple businesses. They facilitate sharing information among multiple business partners' machines in an extended supply network. Without these

technologies, the coordination of large processes would be impossible.

This chapter will emphasize how the coordinative capabilities of the process models can focus the attention of multiple business partners on both satisfying customers and seizing opportunities for new products and services. Process models have facilitated the transition from the traditional hierarchical business structure to the more horizontal customer-facing process structure. Process models have facilitated larger and more complex processes involving multiple partners. And process models have facilitated a higher level of responsiveness to customers, including serving them with a steady stream of new products and services.

The process model's ability to mirror the process itself, including the reactions of the customers, illuminates possible opportunities for process improvements. The resultant visibility is a powerful foundation for learning and development. Often the modeling software can both mirror the process, it can also become a platform for experimentation or for simulating variants of the process. Simple innovations can result by experimentation with customers' needs and wants; more sophisticated innovations can result from extensive simulations.

BACKGROUND

Process models exploded in popularity as the successes of supply chain management became ever more apparent. All the computer journals have carried extensive coverage of supply chain management. The other successful process software is customer relationship management (CRM); it too had a large number of articles written about it in both the computer magazines and the marketing journals. Information systems and management literature about these process models came together under the name "Business Process Management" (BPM). Burlton published *Business Process Management* in 2001; that was followed in 2002 by Smith and Fingar's book, *Business Process Management: The Third Wave.* Many other BPM books have followed.

AMR research sets off in another direction with its publications about "Demand-Driven Supply Networks," unfortunately these publications are restricted to business partners, although AMR's Caruso, Cecere, and O'Marah shared an online Webcast (2004) entitled "Demand-Driven Supply Networks" (DDSN). BPM's notion is that supply chains are an excellent means to "push" goods from suppliers, to producers, to distributors, to retailers, to customers. DDSN's notion is the supply chains are an excellent means to discover customer opportunities; customer information is "pulled," analyzed, and acted upon. This is a post-BPM conception of process models. Very similar to DDSN is the "sense and respond" approach favored by the "adaptive" management authors.

One of the earliest mentions of *The Adaptive Corporation* occurs in 1984, when Toffler wrote this in his book *The Adaptive Corporation* (1984):

The corporate environment has grown increasingly unstable, accelerative, and revolutionary.... The adaptive corporation, therefore, needs a new kind of leadership. It needs managers of "adaptation" equipped with a whole set of new nonlinear skills (p. 2).

Toffler is among the first to apply systems theory to business. Brown and Eisenhardt published *Competing on the Edge* in 1998. Kelly and Allison published *The Complexity Advantage* in 1999. *Surfing The Edge of Chaos* was published in 2000 by Pascale, Millemann, and Gioja. These books characterized business organizations as complex adaptive systems seeking survival in a volatile and turbulent environment. These insights about the struggle of business organizations to survive in a fast changing environment come from biology. When plants, for example, receive more sunlight or more rain, they adapt to the new conditions;

the plant species evolves in order to take better advantage of the new conditions. An adaptive enterprise, by analogy, is one that continuously adapts itself to take better advantage of changing conditions in the business environment.

The central concept of this chapter is that innovations from process models arise when customer opportunities are routinely discovered and acted upon. This is the core insight of Haeckel's book, *The Adaptive Enterprise: Creating and Leading Sense-And-Respond Organizations*, published in 1999. Haeckel is the major source for "sense and respond" management or what he calls "adaptive management." His former employer, IBM's Advanced Business Institute, has employed a sense and respond approach in some of its business consulting units. Joe Artega from IBM Business Consulting Services shared a set of slides entitled: "Adaptive Management Systems Overview," which explain how to implement sense and respond management. Although Hewlett Packard heavily advertises its products as platforms for the adaptive enterprise, it is not really part of this approach. Mani Chandy founded Caltech's "Infospheres Project" for sense and respond computing systems and started the iSpheres Corporation, which sells "event servers" designed to augment the ability to "sense" and better capture customer information. As part of a co-presentation with Haeckel, He also shared a presentation entitled: "Event Servers for Sense and Respond Applications." Finally, Meyer and Davis describe future directions for adaptive management in their 2003 book, *It's Alive: The Coming Convergence of Information, Biology, and Business.* As Meyer and Davis reflect on ways in which an adaptive business can survive in a business environment that is complex and unpredictable, they suggest that businesses generalize the mathematical tools developed for biology, such as genetic algorithms, embed them in information technology such as the event server, and apply them to interpreting the business environment.

ORGANIZATIONAL COORDINATION

Alfred Sloan established the dominant organizational theory for General Motors in the early part of the last century. He structured General Motors into decentralized operations and centralized controls; budgets and quotas were set in Detroit, but each of the separate divisions had entirely separate operations. This is the classical "command and control" structure, which places operational controls at the top. Top management controls its dispersed operations "by the numbers." This approach worked well when General Motors dominated the U.S. market; it no longer works well in a highly competitive industry that requires consistent improvements and innovations. The management problem now facing General Motors is that of delivering a steady stream of innovative car designs when it is structured and managed to efficiently produce and sell moderately improved cars.

General Motors now realizes that managing 50 decentralized manufacturing plants, a dozen separate car and truck divisions—plus its parts plants—is no longer a competitive approach for the automotive industry. The new CEO, G. Richard Wagoner, Jr., has announced efforts to achieve cost savings by standardizing parts and by sharing components across car lines; he is attempting to achieve some synergy from his global operations (Terlep, 2007). But the recently announced layoff of 30,000 employees demonstrates the problem; cost cutting will not save GM. The company must design, manufacture, and sell more innovative cars.

Sloan's legacy can be found in many floundering large U.S. businesses. An organization with a many-layered hierarchical structure and separate functional departments cannot readily respond to changing customer demands. Sloan failed to consider the necessity of innovation, but the assumption was that top management would develop strategies to take advantage of market opportunities. But the strategic approach has not worked for General Motors or Ford. The cars resulting from a strategic approach tended to be too little, too late—they were not innovative enough, competitors' models had more features than GM or Ford's new models. The major barrier to customer responsiveness is a structural barrier; having decentralized functional departments and separate divisional units means that innovative ideas must be handed off from desk to desk, must move from layer to layer. Here is another example of this problem. When Carly Fiorina took over as CEO of Hewlett Packard in 1987:

She found a company with 87 business units each with its own top management team, sales organization and profit and loss accounts. Its founders believed that small, semi-autonomous business units fostered entrepreneurship and innovation. The HP "Way" became legendary but time passed it by. Overhead and internal competition ate up costs and time. HP's customers complained that the firm was very difficult to do business with; individual product units coordinated their own operations but there was no coordination of the overall customer relationship. There was constant duplication of resources and a growing lack of organizational identity (Keen & Sol, 2005, 5-6.).

Toyota is an example of a global business that is hugely competitive. Toyota's profits are greater than all the Detroit car makers' combined over the previous five years. While Toyota's "lean manufacturing" process model is the best known, it is one of many process models that help Toyota become ever more dominant in the automotive industry. But it is Toyota's internal sales and marketing bible, "The Toyota way in sales and marketing," which clearly states that fully satisfied customers is the source of its success (Hill, 2006).

These manufacturing and marketing processes are interconnected, the entire business is integrated. Toyota is globally integrated and coordinated; parts and interfaces are standardized as are the processes for manufacturing and design. Toyota is spending an estimated $1 billion to implement a massive information technology system that will model every aspect of the cars' designs, production sequences, just-in-time parts availability, and the distribution to the dealers. This shared process model platform is the foundation for the collaboration and coordination to which Toyota's managers attribute its success (Liker, 2004, p. 5).

The Toyota story is widely known. Liker's book, *"The Toyota Way,"* was an international best seller. The top management of Ford, Chrysler, and General Motors must know that they have to emulate Toyota. Why haven't they aggressively moved to better integration of their processes, better coordination of their operations?

The answer, too, is well known—it's about leadership. Top management has to change the structure and culture of the business; it has to move employees out of their comfort zones in well defined functional or divisional units and make them part of larger processes. There are "walls" around the specialized functions which give the people there a feeling of ownership and control of their jobs. Processes are large and vague; initially they offer little comfort to the team members. The point of process models is that they mirror the process, enabling employees to see themselves and their contributions in the model. They can also see their impact upon the customers and the customers' satisfaction with their efforts. Moving from departmental units to processes requires strong consistent leadership from top management. Hamel and Keen suggest that accomplishing this restructuring is the essential innovation of the early 21st century.

MANAGEMENT INNOVATION

Gary Hamel is now a major proponent of management innovation. His recent article in the Harvard Business Review has drawn lots of attention to that topic. Hamel (2006) asserts that, if one looks back over the last 100 years of industrial competition, it is management innovation, more than any other sort of innovation, that has produced big and enduring shifts in industry leadership. Hamel defines management innovation:

A management innovation can be defined as a marked departure from traditional management principles, processes, and practices or a departure from customary organizational forms that significantly alters the way the work of management is performed. Put simply, management innovation changes how managers do what they do (p. 2).

Hamel later becomes clearer about how managers need to innovate:

In a big organization, the only way to change how managers work is to reinvent the processes that govern that work. Management processes such as strategic planning, capital budgeting, project management, hiring and promotion, employee assessment, executive development, internal communications, and knowledge management are the gears that turn management principles into everyday practices. They establish the recipes and rituals that govern the work of managers. While operational innovation focuses on a company's business processes (procurement, logistics, customer support, and so on), management innovation targets a company's management processes (p. 4).

Keen et al. (2005) take management innovation to the next step by being very explicit about one type of management innovation. They feel that executive management's principle task to design the coordination for the business organization. Keen et al. explain the successes of Toyota, Wal-Mart, Southwest, FedEx, etc. in terms of their overall coordination. They praise the efforts of former CEOs like Carly Fiorina at HP, Lou Gerstner at IBM, Michael Dell at Dell for crafting formal designs to unify their businesses. Like many other business authors, they believe that harnessing and directing the efforts of all employees to a common purpose is an unbeatable "strategy." They reject the conventional strategic approach, however, in favor of an organizational design for coordination. They describe the failures of many organizations to execute strategy as failures of coordination—the organization built on specialized functions has become many separate "fiefdoms." The problem with many large businesses, they believe, is the lack of coordination: "miscoordination that is the historical product of a morass of procedures, parties, and tasks that have accumulated their own identity and power" (p. 3). They argue that top management must first plan and sell an enterprise-wide design to coordinate all aspects of the business, and then management must put into place a disciplined implementation of that coordination design. While Hamel would praise these same businesses for their strategic approach (i.e., a strategy of coordination), Keen et al. offer the better explanation that management's design and execution of an organizational structure is really what accomplishes the coordination that creates these successes (p. 10).

What is distinctive about some of the best businesses in the world is how well coordinated they are. Dell, for example, has excellent synchronization of its supply chain/demand chain resulting in the fastest possible inventory turns. Wal-Mart, too, has a tightly integrated supply chain/demand chain that extends from customers back to a multitude of suppliers. Southwest Airlines, competing in a horribly unprofitable industry, makes money by its standardization of operations and its highly choreographed processes. All three use information technology to coordinate their operations, culture, and knowledge base; all three are designed to focus every employee on the big coordinative strategy delivery. Finally, Keen (2004) emphasizes that all three "have an explicit enterprise coordination design owned at the top."

The management innovation for these excellent companies is that they are explicitly designed for

coordination. It requires executive management to transform the business organization from its decentralized and fragmented organizational structure to a process-focused business. That entails having every employee's work activities being defined as part of a larger whole, a larger customer-facing process with process outcomes specified in advance.

SUPPLY CHAIN MANAGEMENT EXEMPLIES THE PROCESS APPROACH

Supply chain management (SCM) systems represent a compelling argument for the use of process models. Keen et al. give these reasons why businesses feel it imperative to adopt a supply chain management system:

- The top 10% of SCM performers in any industry use half the working capital per unit of sales than their median competitors (Source: University of Maryland Supply Chain Management Center).
- The fraction of U.S. GDP tied up in inventory and SCM costs has dropped by 40%. The amount tied up in distribution and transportation has halved, from 19% to 9% of GDP (The Economist).
- "Supply chain excellence" companies use 15% less inventory, have 35% shorter cash-to-cash cycle times and 60% higher margins than the average large firm (AMR Research). Keen et al., 2005, p. 12)

The business process management (BPM) movement claims to be the theoretical context for understanding what supply chain management is all about. A survey by *Information Week* of 300 businesses concluded that BPM would be the top spending priority in 2006 (Whiting, 2006). Business process management can be described in these terms:

1. Creating an end-to-end software model of a core business process, including links to suppliers, partners, and customers.
2. Moving employees from functional departments into process teams focusing on results for the customers.
3. Using the technology to simulate, monitor, and analyze process performance.
4. Improving the performance of the process by a sequence of continuous process improvements.
5. There are now ten or more books with "business process management" in the title. BPM is a valuable step foreword because it describes how to deploy processes using process models. Again, the many successes of supply chain management validate this approach. But BPM does not go far enough; it is not intended to be an appropriate management approach for innovation. It is a major step in the right direction.

Keen is dismissive of business process management because it is the successor to business process reengineering, and much too like it. BPM is about process optimization and not about customer satisfaction, much less about innovation.

Chappel, writing at the BPMG.Org Web site offers this definition: "BPM commonly refers to viewing an organization as a set of processes that can be defined, managed, and optimized…To technical people, BPM typically refers to a group of technologies focused on defining, executing, and managing process logic."

Here is another definition from the BPMG.org Web site attributed to workpoint:

> In its simplest form, business process management (BPM) is the definition, modeling, execution, automation and management of business processes. Organizations worldwide use BPM to coordinate work between people and systems, with the ultimate goal of improving organizational efficiency, responsiveness and reliability.

Despite the claim that BPM differs from business process reengineering, the emphasis on improving processes in the above definitions belies that claim. Reengineering did not succeed as a management approach because it imposed a process structure on unwilling participants. The "management" side of business process management is heavily focused on the performance benefits that can be achieved by first going to a process approach and, second, optimizing the processes for performance. This type of management approach is not innovative, it repeats the goals of the reengineering craze. Adding BPM software which models the process certainly helps with the transition, but if the goal of relentless optimization of the process remains, and if reluctant employees are forced into a process orientation, there will undoubtedly be resistance and failures for the very same reasons that scuttled the reengineering movement.

ADAPTIVE MANAGEMENT & DEMAND-DRIVEN SUPPLY NETWORKS

AMR research created and now capitalizes on the idea of demand-driven supply networks. They analyzed a large number of successful supply chain networks and came up with a list of characteristics essential to that success. The first characteristic is that the emphasis is on the "pull" of customer information, rather than on the "push" of goods to those customers—feedback, rather than feed-forward. The goal is to influence and shape the demand, not just monitor it. Another emphasis is on the coordination of the business partners, by managing how the partners should react to customer demand. The most important characteristic is that the network's demand drives innovations. AMR also notes that its business leaders emphasize collaboration with their partners in the supply "network." Rather than thinking about the process as linear and sequential supply chain, they emphasize the coordination and collaboration necessary to meet non-linear customer demand. It is the effectiveness of the network, which allows these businesses to seize market opportunities (Caruso et al., 2004).

Conceptually, there is little difference between the demand-driven supply network approach (DDSN) and the sense and respond (S&R) approach. The sense and respond approach provides a broader and more complete context for understanding how to generate innovations. DDSN is more narrowly focused on businesses, which are part of a supply network (e.g., suppliers, producers, distributors, retailers). DDSN is validated by its amazing list of "Top 25" businesses; AMR suggests that their successes are in part due to DDSN But these companies could as easily be described as examples of sense and respond management. Here are the AMR's choices for the top ten DDSN companies for 2006: Dell, Procter and Gamble, IBM, Nokia, Toyota, Johnson and Johnson, Samsung, Wal-Mart, Tesco, and Johnson Controls (O'Marah, 2006).

Haeckel distinguishes between "make and sell" businesses and "sense and respond" businesses. The "make and sell" organization assumes an environment that permits predictability; management can then rely upon strategy and planning to achieve its goal of becoming efficient and profitable. The underlying assumption of the sense and respond approach is that the environment is too complex and unpredictable to rely upon planning or sales predictions. Taking a page from biology and systems theory, the appropriate approach in an uncertain environment is the adaptive approach, which requires a "sense and respond" approach. Whether the context is business or biology, survival requires adaptation, and adaptation requires innovative responses to the changing environment. Here is a summary about the business environment from Dr. Chandy's iSphere's presentation:

- **World:** Fluid & constantly changing; managing by adapting.

- **Information:** Scattered across applications & organizational boundaries; shared situational awareness.
- **Business/human behavior:** Asynchronous/non-linear.
- **Speed:** Faster response to environmental changes & critical events.
- **Adaptation:** Massively distributed rapid decision making; empowerment and local self-synchronization (Chandy, 2005).

To simplify a bit, the supply chain management and the business process management incorporate a "make and sell" approach. Managers direct the process, from start to end. Retail managers predict how many products will be sold and they negotiate with producers about how many should be made. The supply chain optimizes the "push" of goods down the chain toward the customers. But many businesses have firsthand experience with the instability and unpredictability of the market. To compensate for having been blind-sided by events, managers are proactively gathering and analyzing all available information from their customers. They are carefully monitoring events in the market and learning how to quickly respond to them. This is "sense and respond." It is mostly about information coming from the customers, not just about the goods sent to the customers. It is about taking advantage of opportunities, not efficiency.

Bradley and Nolan (1998) note that the business process approach, the sense and respond approach, is driving many businesses from vertical integration to strategic horizontal alliances. These alliances are able to seize larger market opportunities, to bring more capabilities and speed to the marketplace.

Driven by this revolutionary change in information technology, a paradigm shift is taking place in the way companies competed and are managed. Traditional "make and sell" strategies, tied to the annual budget cycle, are being replaced by radically faster, real-time, "sense and respond" strategies. Rather than competing by forecasting customers' needs and then planning the year's production using inventories to match supply and demand, firms are relying on real-time sensors to continuously discover what each customer needs, sometimes even anticipating unspecified needs, and then quickly fulfilling those needs with customized products and services delivered with heretofore unavailable capabilities and speed. The result is an almost immediate response to consumers' demand through dynamic resource allocation and execution (p. 4-5).

These businesses are not only gathering information, they are searching for innovative opportunities in the market. This, then, is how sense respond is the context for innovations. "Demand-driven" is another way of saying the same thing. Customer demand "pulls" goods down the supply chain, but the backward flow of information from the customers drives management's decision-making. Haeckel's *"Adaptive Management"* (1999) describes how effective sensing of customer requests results in a reduction in response cycle time, an improvement in response quality (as evaluated by customer), and an increase in the scope and number of requests successfully addressed.

SENSE, INTERPRET, DECIDE, ACT LOOP (SIDA)

"Adaptive management" is a phrase used by Haeckel to suggest the appropriate strategy for businesses to respond to a dynamic business environment. Based on systems theory, the adaptive organism actively exchanges information and resources with its environment, processes what it has learned and acquired, and then adapts to better take advantage of the environment. iSpheres' Professor Chandy presents adaptation in terms of a "Sense Interpret Decide Act" (SIDA) loop. The sensing and interpreting of environmental information is the most critical part of the organization's ability to adapt, to find new ways to grow in response to the environment.

Most businesses now seek information about their customers. Adaptive management makes the discovery of environmental information the essential ingredient for success. It requires augmenting the technology to capture information about customers, markets, competitors, weather alerts, anomalies, etc. The sheer quantity of available information is overwhelming. Chandy and other Stanford professors are working on programming an "event processor," popularly called a "BAM" (business activity monitor), to filter and categorize information gleaned from customers. Stanford University's Sense and Respond Web page describes how customers can be targeted:

In place of broadcasting uniform messages to a wide audience in an indiscriminate fashion, sense and respond (S&R) attempts to pinpoint the right individual with the right message—or, product or service. S&R, if properly implemented in the context of supply chain management, could reduce various costs and headaches such as stockouts, excess inventory, poor customer service, low yield of customer response to ad campaigns, and inaccurate delivery time quotes (Whang, 2005).

The "BAM" captures every imaginable kind of customer and market information, performs some preliminary categorization, and sends all of it to appropriate process team members for interpretation. Haeckel comments: "Successfully adapting systems have the property of translating noise into meaning at a faster rate that the arrival of apparent noise." (Haeckel, 2004) The "BAM" augments the sensing ability of the organization by improving what is sensed, and by sorting and filtering so that the business is not overwhelmed by the sheer quantity of noise.

Given that the success of the whole process of capturing information depends on the ability of the "sense" part, the "Top 25" spend a lot of time on sensing technology. Many companies now use programmable "event processors" or "business activity monitors" (BAM), which are specially designed servers to capture, filter, and categorize diverse kinds of information about customers. As the name suggests, the event server notes events and changing market conditions; it pulls data from a wide variety of sources and can capture many formats: email, database, Web services, signal, XML documents. Here is how iSphere's revised event server is described in the company's Web page:

iSpheres said the EPL Server 5.1 enables real-time intelligence—the ability to automatically synthesize and analyze massive amounts of real-time data to detect critical scenarios, from inside and outside the organization, from business applications to Web sites and news feeds so decisions can be made quickly and proactively (Gupta, 2005).

THE INTERPRETIVE ROLE

The ultimate goal of the interpretive role is to discover marketing opportunities, potential innovations, or new ways to add value. Quantities of already filtered information are sent to appropriate people in the supply network. These team members work with the information in an MIS supported decision support software tool, which subsequently tracks their decisions and follow up actions. This software provides a preliminary processing of the information through the business rules engine (BRE) and the boundaries established by top management. Here is Chandy's summary of interpretive activities:

- Filtering events according to monitoring rules; complex event processing.
- Correlating multiple isolated events as the environment changes to gain more meaningful awareness.

- Deciding worthiness of event correlations.
- Multiple methodologies: time-series analyses, parametric evaluation, text analysis.
- Anomaly (event) detection (Chandy, 2005).

The "decide" and "act" phases of the SIDA loop are directed at taking advantage of opportunities or responding to customer problems. Each role includes responsibilities for playing the appropriate role, fulfilling commitments, and completing the deliverables. New products or services for customers are the ultimate deliverables.

The many failures of re-engineering are reminders that an unthinking adoption of the process approach is a hazardous undertaking and will likely result in heavy employee resistance. The publication of Haeckel's book, *Adaptive Enterprise: Creating and Leading Sense-and-Respond Organizations*, spells out how to build collaborative teams and the relationships between them. His book describes how to motivate employees to participate in a process approach.

Joe Arteaga of IBM's Business Consulting Services has taken Haeckel's ideas and developed prototype software to implement teams responsive to customers (Arteaga, 2005). There are two major parts to this approach. The first requirement is that top management develops the context for the coordinated processes; the context describes the purpose and boundaries of the process. The second requirement is the design and implementation of the team structures; Haeckel calls this a commitment management system. It is a way to clarify roles, to clarify how each person is responsible to the customers.

The commitment management system is a human resource dream (or nightmare). It all begins with a database of employees' capabilities or competencies, gleaned either from the employees or from the needs of the customers. Then employees are identified with roles, which are bundles of competencies. Finally, employees are asked to commit to and be accountable for specific roles. Employees negotiate their assigned roles. As things change, roles are re-negotiated. That is why Haeckel calls this a commitment management system. Finally, there is a formal plan to develop teams responsible for satisfying specific types of customer demand. Every known kind of customer request is matched to a specific group of people. Since many large processes span multiple organizations, some team members could be in one organization and others in another.

THE FUTURE OF PROCESS MODELS IN BUSINESS

System theorists have applied the analogy of evolution and adaptation to business. Acceptance of the systems theory literature has been modest; it is difficult to understand and difficult to implement. Haeckel's success was bolstered by the huge acceptance of supply chain models, which became the platform for adaptive management. Business models and business simulations came into widespread use about the same time as biotechnology models and simulations. Modeling and simulations now dominate biotechnology research; outside of CRM and SCM, business has made little use of process models.

Future directions for sense and respond process models are described by Meyer and Davis (2003) in their book, *It's Alive: The Coming Convergence of Information, Biology, and Business*. Starting with the idea that the exponential growth in biotechnology makes it the next economic "wave;" add the enormous successes resulting from the use of process models in biotech research, the acceptance of biotechnology methods by business people is greatly helped. Meyer et al. assert that research in biotechnology, heavily dependent on information technology, yields many promising

techniques to help businesses make better sense of the turbulent business environment.

Meyer et al. are part of the growing list of business authors who make use of the concept of the adaptive enterprise. Plants evolve slowly; adaptation takes many generations and a large group of plants. The business environment changes quickly; each business has to adapt quickly, if it is to survive. Hence the more quickly it can sense and respond, the more likely its survival. Process models can help speed adaptation by formalizing scanning the environment for threats and opportunities and by taking advantage of the opportunities discovered. The major difficulty with seizing opportunities is that of making sense of the overwhelming amount of environmental information.

Here is how Meyer et al. describe the convergence:

Recently, computer scientists have found that they can simulate biological functions "in silico" to elucidate everything from population genetics to the functioning of heart cells. Biological systems can now be expressed in digital form, and analyzed using digital techniques. At the same time, computer scientists have been making the trip in the reverse direction, using the concepts of evolution in novel ways to solve real-world problems. "Genetic algorithms," for example, take the ideas of sexual recombination and selective pressure from biology, express them in simplified form in software, and apply these software tools to business problems, from factory scheduling to engine design to credit scoring Meyer et al., 2003, p. 25).

The authors cite a number of promising biotechnology modeling tools with applicability for business. The BAM is a good example. To sort through the huge amount of market data captured by a Business Activity Monitor, genetic algorithms and genetic programming turn out to be remarkably effective at filtering out noise and categorizing notable events. Biological recombination through breeding is the way in which nature achieves innovation. Researchers can direct the process of breeding by using computer selected best fits, by having the computer quickly ignore iterations which show little promise and by selectively including iterations that are likely to improve the process.

Genetic algorithms, for example, are software programs that search for optimal ways to combine parts of a production schedule, or parts of genes, into a best fit (Meyer et al., Davis, 2003, p. 82ff). Koza, a Stanford computer science professor, created genetic programming which combines elements of computer programs and functions; these are progressively evolved over a series of iterations. The worst results are discarded; the best are combined together and run again and again. The end result is an optimal solution. Genetic programming simulates recombination in a sped up evolutionary process (Koza, 2004). Agent-based simulations capture the behavior of individual agents as they interact within a defined context of rules. The behavior of a flock of birds was simulated by Reynolds by giving each "boid" three simple steering behaviors:

- Avoid crowding local flockmates.
- Fly toward the average heading of local flockmates.
- Move toward the average position of local flockmates (Meyer et al., 2003, p. 77).

Evolution operates through the interactions between organisms as they struggle to survive and markets operate through the decisions and interactions of self-interested parties. Agent-based simulations can model these behaviors. Examples of applications include modeling of consumer behavior, including word of mouth and social network effects, workforce management, traffic management, and portfolio management.

Meyer et al. conclude that these biotechnology techniques provide a laboratory in which business can run controlled experiments. They note that, since the market environment is unpredictable and discontinuous, the simulations must deal with nonlinear behavior.

Software agents, genetic algorithms, and agent-based simulations have in many instances applied the core ideas from evolution—self-organization, recombination, selective pressure, and co-evolution—to practical problems in business and other fields...Two examples are design problems with multiple conflicting constraints...and issues of behavior such as crowd control...Both classes of problem are marked by nonlinear behavior (that is, a small change in the rules can lead to a big change in the outcome) (Meyer et al., 2003, p. 92).

In universities across the world, faculty from physics, chemistry, material sciences, computer science, biology, and business are pooling their efforts and labs to do research in biotechnology and nanotechnology. The ability to see, simulate, and manipulate matter at the molecular level is precisely what a process model facilitates; it gives them the ability to monitor events, to run the code and execute the process, and to innovate by simulating, learning, and experimenting. This is what is happening in biotechnology, this is what might well happen in business.

The ability to better visualize the basic structures underlying biology yielded many new advances in biotechnology. But the fundamental source of the innovations in biotechnology was its ability to build models of these structures, to model how the pieces interacted, and to document the knowledge learned from these models, and then build ever larger, more encompassing biological models. Biotechnology is all about models.

Simulation is becoming a new scientific instrument, a "macroscope" allowing us to see the structure that determines the behavior of human-scale systems the way the microscope began to reveal the cell. Rigorous experimentation can now augment intuition, conventional wisdom, and observation (Meyer et al., 2003, p. 70).

The underlying assumption in building these models is that "code is code: researchers can "translate biology into information, and information into biology because both operate on the basis of coded instructions, and those codes are translatable. When you get down at the bottom of things, code is simply code" (Meyer et al., 2003, p. 27-34) A software program is made up of coded instructions; a program is a sequence of steps which the computer executes. In that sense, software is often a dynamic model, representing the activities of a process. By building the software to accurately mimic the process activities, the researcher learns how the process operates, how the process achieves its results. So, a researcher can learn about the process from the model or, by analysis of the process itself, the researcher can discover its sequence of activities and built a software model as an exact representation of those sequences.

Business organizations are human constructs. There might be thousands of business models which could be modeled, but there are 90 trillion cells in a human body. Each business might have hundreds of work processes, some of them unique, but, again, the total number is small in comparison to the diversity of biotechnology. Information technology and biotechnology converged as hundreds of startup companies began to sell databases of software models of DNA segments, of proteins, of enzymes, etc. Biological recombination could then occur in the computer, but much, much more quickly. Researchers can now purchase and combine models to produce innovative improvements in molecular structures. Meyer et al. (2003) quote Jay Short, CEO of Diversa, to describe nature's diversity: "We have a library of two million strains of microorganisms. For perspective, only 10,000

microbial species have been written up in the last century" (p. 59).

CONCLUSION

Some of the most successful businesses in the world, AMR's "Top 25," employ demand-driven processes. Their competitive edge results from their intimate knowledge of their customers. They work with their partners to continuously adapt to the business environment by using process software as a platform for "sense and respond" behavior. Using technology to augment their capturing of market information facilitates their learning and focuses their innovative efforts. The process itself becomes the platform for innovations which are responses to customers' needs and wants.

This chapter has described two ways in which process models can become platforms for innovation. A process model makes objects, events, and decisions visible and accessible to those who would learn from them. Technology companies employ process models in their research; the visibility provided by the models greatly helps learning; simulating with the models provides a platform for finding out how to improve the process or product. Many process models are platforms for simulations of new processes or simulations showing the impact of modifications to existing processes. Of course, these human artifacts are imperfect representations; they are always incomplete, omitting certain things and overemphasizing others. In biotechnology, the learning resulting from building the process models is itself a major innovation; from these models of DNA, RNA, etc. are flowing a growing wave of medical discoveries. The full employment of process models in business has allowed some less complex businesses to fully automate themselves.

Business process models can also support innovation by describing market opportunities and assisting with coordinating responses to those opportunities. A growing number of businesses have made the transition to a process orientation; this is a major achievement for them, and a major innovation. Moving employees from the security of their functional departments into a process environment produces huge resistance, often outright refusal. A great part of the reluctance comes from moving from the security of the department to the uncertainty of a process. That trauma is greatly mitigated by a process model which visibly mirrors the entire process, displaying both the activities of the participants in real time as well as the customer outcomes of the process. The process model, then, houses the process team, while encouraging team collaboration. Again, the process model facilitates; it gives business partners the ability to monitor events, to run the code and execute the process, and to innovate by simulating, learning, and experimenting This is a new and innovative way of working, of coordinating, of managing.

REFERENCES

Arteaga, J. (2005). *Adaptive management system overview.* Retrieved December 30, 2006, from http://senseandrespond.com/downloads/S_R_AMS_Overview_JArteaga_6-28-2005

Bradley, S., & Nolan, R. (1998). *Sense & respond: Capturing value in the network era.* Boston, MA: Harvard Business School Press.

Brain, M. (2001). *How cells work.* Retrieved December 30, 2006, from http://science.howstuffworks.com/cell7.htm

Breen, B. (2004). Living in Dell time. *Fast Company, 11*(88), 86, November 2004.

Brown, S., & Eisenhardt, K. M. (1998). *Competing on the edge.* Boston, MA: Harvard Business School Press.

Burlton, R. (2001). *Business process management: Profiting from process.* Indianapolis, IN: Sams Publishing.

Caruso, D., & Cecere, L., & O'Marah, K. (2004). *Demand-driven supply networks.* Retrieved December 30, 2006, from http://www.amrresearch.com/Content/View.asp?pmillid=17647

Chandy, M. (2005). *Event servers for sense and respond applications.* Retrieved December 30, 2006, from http://senseandrespond.com/downloads/iSPHERES_S_R_WEBCAST.ppt

Chesbrough, H., & Rosenbloom, R. S. (2004). The role of the business model in capturing value from innovation. *Industrial and Corporate Change, 11*(3), 529-555. Retrieved December 30, 2006, from icc.oxfordjournals.org/cgi/content/abstract/11/3/529

Collins, J. (2001). *Good to great.* New York: Harper Business.

Dodgson, M., Gann, D., & Salter, A. (2005). *Think, play, do: Technology, innovation, and organization.* New York: Oxford University Press.

Gardner, R. A. (2004). *The process-focused organization.* Milwaukee, WI: ASQ Quality Press.

Gross, M. (2001). *Travels to the Nanoworld.* Jackson, TN: Perseus Book Group.

Gupta, D. (2005). *EPL Server 5.1 Released by iSpheres.* Retrieved December 30, 2006, from http://www.ebizq.net/news/5826.html

Haeckel, S. (2005). Becoming a sense and respond organization. Retrieved December 30, 2006, from http://senseandrespond.com/downloads/iSPHERES_S_R_WEBCAST.ppt

Haeckel, S. (1999). *Adaptive enterprise: Creating and leading sense-and-respond organizations.* Boston, MA: Harvard Business School Press.

Hamel, G. (2006, November). *Continuous management innovations.* Speech presented at the Fortune Innovation Forum, NY.

Hamel, G. (2006). The why, what, and how of management innovation. *Harvard Business Review, Feb. 1, 2006*, 1-5.

Hamel, G. (2003). Innovation as a Deep Capability. *Leader to Leader, Winter*(27), 19-24.

Hammer, M. (2001). *The agenda*. New York: Crown Business.

Hill, G. (2006). *The Lean CRM-Toyota Story*. Retrieved December 30, 2006, from

http://chearie.wordpress.com/2006/06/14/the-lean-crm-toyota-story-you-can-have-a-strategy-that-works-in-manufacturing-and-marketing-environments-2/

Keen, P. (2005). *Organizational transformation through business models*. Retrieved December 30, 2006, from http://www.peterkeen.com/recent/articles/index.htm.

Keen, P. (2004). *Business process management is not workflow automation*. Retrieved December 30, 2006, from http://www.peterkeen.com/recent/articles/index.htm

Keen, P. (2004*). Knowledge mobilization*. Presentation at The Millennium Technology Conference. Helsinki, Finland.

Keen, P. (2004). *What exactly is a business process?* Retrieved December 30, 2006, from http://www.peterkeen.com/recent/articles/index.htm

Keen, P., & Sol, H. (2005). *Coordination by design: Chapter one*. Retrieved December 30, 2006, from http://www.peterkeen.com/forthcoming/publications.htm

Kelly, S., & Allison, M. A. (1998). *The complexity advantage*. New York: McGraw-Hill.

Koza, J. (2004). What is genetic programming? Retrieved December 30, 2006, from http://www.genetic-programming.com/

Liker, J. (2004). *The Toyota way*. New York: McGraw-Hill Corporation.

Meyer, C., & Davis, S. (2003). *It's alive: The coming convergence of information, biology, and business*. New York: Crown Publishing.

O'Marah, K. (2006). *AMR research releases second annual supply chain top 25*. Retrieved December 30, 2006, from http://www.amrresearch.com/Content/View.asp?pmillid=18895

Pascale, R., Millemann, M., & Gioja, L. (2000). *Surfing the edge of chaos*. New York: Crown Business.

Pisano, G. P. (2006). *Science business: The promise, the reality, and the future of biotech*. Boston, MA: Harvard Business Press.

Silverthorne, S. (2006). *Science Business: What Happened to Biotech? Q&A with Gary Pisano*. Harvard Business School Working Knowledge. Retrieved December 30, 2006 from http://hbswk.hbs.edu/item/5503.html

Smith, H., & Fingar, P. (2002). *Business process management: The third wave*. Tampa, FL: Meghan-Kiffer Press.

Smith, H. (2006). *Process innovation*. Retrieved December 30, 2006, from http://www.bptrends.com/publicationfiles02%2D06%20COL%20Proc%20Innovation%20P%2DTREZ%20Smith%2Epdf

Terlep, S. (2007). *Toyota overtakes GM*. Retrieved January 30, 2007, from http://www.toyotaweekly.com/index.php?categoryid=1&p2_articleid=5

Whang, S. (2005). *Sense and respond—The next generation business model*. Retrieved December 30, 2006, http://www.gsb.stanford.edu/news/research/supplychain_whang_senserespond.shtml

Whiting, R. (2006, November 6). BPM gets smarter with a little help from BI. *Information Week*, November 6, 2006.

KEY TERMS

Adaptive Enterprise/Corporation: One which guides its renewal and survival by successfully interacting with the business environment; adaptation is a biological concept that describes how plants survive environmental changes.

Business Process: Is an aggregation of operations performed by people and software systems containing the information used in the process, along with the applicable business rules (Savvion Web site).

Business Process Management (or **BPM**): Refers to activities performed by businesses to improve their processes. While such improvements are hardly new, software tools called business process management systems have made such activities faster and cheaper. BPM systems monitor the execution of the business processes so that managers can analyze and change processes in response to data, rather than just a hunch. BPM differs from business process reengineering, a technique popular in the 1990s, in that it deals not just with one-off changes to the organization, but long-term consequences (Wikipedia).

"Business reengineering: The process of fundamentally changing the way work is performed in order to achieve radical performance improvements in speed, cost, quality, market share, and return on investment." (Michael Hammer)

Biotechnology: Refers to recombinant DNA based and/or tissue culture based processes that have only been commercialized since the 1970s. Recombinant DNA biotechnology allows us to take virtually any gene and express it in any organism; we can take the genes that make crimson color in plants and put them into guinea pigs to make pink pets, or, we can take the genes that help arctic fish survive the freezing temperatures and put them into food to increase the amount of time it can grow before it freezes (Wikipedia).

Demand-Driven Supply Networks: Refer to supply chain partnerships that emphasize capturing information about customer demand, analyzing it for potential opportunities for innovation, and managing the entire network of partners to create innovations.

Event Server: A dedicated computer server with software designed to capture, filter, and categorize all available information about a particular marketing situation.

Model, as used in this chapter, displays or mirrors the events of a process as it executes; some models only monitor events, other models can simulate what occurs if rules or events are altered.

Recombination: The formation of new genetic sequences by piecing together segments of previously existing ones. Recombination often follows deoxyribonucleic acid (DNA) transfer in bacteria and, in higher organisms, is a regular feature of sexual reproduction (Science Encyclopedia).

Sense and Respond: A phrase made popular by Haeckel to describe how businesses should use adaptive behavior to respond to the business environment; the business would "sense" customer behavior and perceptions, and then respond to discovered needs and wants.

Simulation: A type of model which permits experimentation with the events or constraints of a real process; for that reason it is an excellent platform for learning.

Chapter XX
Performance Measurement in Innovation Processes

Jan Strickman
University of Oldenburg, Germany

Axel Hahn
University of Oldenburg, Germany

Stefan Häusler
OFFIS – Institute of Computer Science, Germany

Kevin Hausmann
OFFIS – Institute of Computer Science, Germany

ABSTRACT

This chapter introduces a new approach for performance measurement in product development and innovation processes. It shows that there is a great need in practice to increase the efficiency of product development processes because existing approaches are not sufficient to give enough information about a running project. These approaches both from science and industry are analysed and a new attempt is introduced that aims at the integration of concrete project data with information about the product by using Semantic Web technologies. Furthermore, the authors want to show that there is an emerging gap between productivity increase and the complexity of product development processes. This will be a challenge in the future and has high potential for research that has to be done in close cooperation with industry.

INTRODUCTION

"To measure is to know." This quote by Sir William Thomson (1824-1907, doyen of thermody-namics, better known as Lord Kelvin) describes a fundamental paradigm of science: the generation of knowledge by describing the properties of an object with impartial, physical measures. He went on saying that "If you cannot measure it, you cannot improve it," thus describing a primary goal of management: guiding an economic endeavour to success. Ultimately, success in the business context means a profitable market performance. But how is this performance rated? As a physicist, Lord Kelvin would have said that the best performance measure is power. It is defined as the rate at which work is performed and is measured in Watts (W, see Figure 1).

But this physical measure falls short of assessing the economic performance of a company, a project or a business process. Here other means of performance measurement such as shareholder value, time to market or customers served per hour have been devised as indicators of economic success.

Performance measurement techniques are an integral part of the management toolbox. The literature of economics describes a vast amount of performance measurement methods for almost all branches of business. While classical fields of business sciences such as manufacturing (Maskell, 1991), human resources (Fitz-Ens, 2001), marketing or finance, and accounting (Neely, 2002) are well understood and have generally accepted performance indicators, the understanding and management of R&D and innovation processes are a source of ongoing research and dispute. The reasons for this deficit can be found in the very special nature of innovation and R&D. Firstly, innovation activities can cover a wide range of activities from "applied projects to competency-building programs to basic research explorations" (Hauser & Zettelmayer, 1997). This calls for distinct, goal-oriented measures. Secondly, innovations are no longer the result of a single

ingenious inventor who single-handedly creates ground-breaking new products—if they ever were. New products and innovations brought to the market today are the result of many experts working together in a somewhat structured, however complex, dynamic, and sometimes chaotic course of action: a development process often carried out in a global engineering network (Gausemeier, Hahn, Kespohl, & Seifert, 2006). The third common trait of R&D and innovation processes is their intangibility caused more and more virtual development methods (CAx-technology, Crabb, 1997) or completely invisible products such as software, nowadays the driving force behind many innovations (e.g., in mechatronics (Cetinkunt, 2006) or consumer electronics) (Rooijmans, Aerts, & van Genuchten, 1996). Product development or engineering consists of conceptualization, construction, and computation, thus it is characterized as an information processing process even though it covers material processes such as prototyping and testing.

Despite all of these specific traits, performance measurement in innovation and product development is a challenging research area since its creativity, complexity and its intricate management demands call for new, integrated solutions. At the same time, it is of vital and growing importance to any company's success in today's fast paced and global markets. A fresh range of products and high R&D investments are prerequisites for market success (see Little, 2004). Despite their high priority and the immense governmental and industrial research investments, many innovative endeavours and product development programs are subject to uncertainty, risk, and ultimate failure. Depending on the sector and degree of innovation, many studies (GPM, 2004; Harmuth, 2003; Mandl & Stiegnitz/Lichter, 1999; Standish Group, 1994) show that a significant percentage of innovation projects fail or exceed economic limits. The reasons for this high failure rate can be found in the aforementioned traits of innovation processes that are conducted in a multidi-

Figure 1. Physical definition of power

$$P(W) = \frac{\partial E}{\partial t} = \frac{\partial W}{\partial t}$$

mensional construction space, making constant change between generalization and specialization, abstraction, and concentration and between different views necessary (Gausemeier et al., 2006). This complexity carries on into the supporting IT-systems. For almost any demand in engineering specialized computer aided engineering-systems (CAE) exist, however, these systems often lack integration and interoperability. Thus "information silos," representing only a small portion of the product, are built up. They prevent an overall estimation of performance because the many interdependencies between the partial models they represent cannot be evaluated. But the problem of inherent complexity in R&D is not the only one; it is the daily bread & butter business of engineers trained to handle just these questions. Apart from technical issues, R&D is often faced with organizational questions regarding the availability of resources, shortening production cycles or competing ideas. This leads to target conflicts that make a strategic and operative evaluation of performance aspects of innovations necessary (Horsch, 2003). A study of the German Project Management Institute (GPM, 2004) shows that project management and controlling have become key issues when dealing with innovations. Thus, two factors govern successful innovations and high performance: technology excellence and project management competence (Strickmann & Hahn, 2007).

In this chapter, we discuss issues and approaches to determine the performance of innovative endeavours such as R&D programs and new product development both from the technical and the commercial viewpoint. Meaningful performance figures on the commercial level can only be generated if we take technical aspects into consideration. To meet these requirements, the following course of action is proposed:

1. Describe and devise methods to analyze the performance of R&D and innovations *based on actual development results*.

2. Introduce a flexible model to formally represent development processes and data, based in existing IT-structures.

3. Show the feasibility of the proposed solution in a controlling oriented environment to assess innovation performance with key performance indicators (KPI).

To achieve these goals the rest of this chapter is structured in the following manner. At first, a broad definition of the terms innovation, product development and performance measurement is given. This is achieved with a through literature review and discussion of the current state of the art and challenges in measuring innovation performance. In the next subchapter, common issues and problems are examined in detail and methods to solve them are provided. The section titled future trends examines an approach to implement the solutions provided using ontologies and semantic Web technology. The chapter closes with a summary and a critical evaluation.

INNOVATION

To begin the discussion of performance measurement in innovation processes, a definition of innovation and its concretion in this chapter, product development, need to be given. A basic definition is given, for example, by the Merriam-Webster Online Dictionary (http://www.m-w.com/dictionary/Innovation) as:

1. The introduction of something new.
2. A new idea, method, or device: NOVELTY.

Economic innovations have been characterized by Schumpeter as either a new (quality of) a good, a new production method, a new market, a new supply source or a new organization which can be either of a gradual or a radical nature (Schumpeter, 1934). A fitting definition has been given by Drucker (2003) with "change that creates a new dimension of performance" since it directly links novelty and innovation to performance, our object of study. In a business context, innovation is defined as "the successful exploitation of new ideas"(Department of Trade and Industry, UK, http://www.dti.gov.uk/innovation/index.html). The management of innovation in businesses is investigated by a wide variety of research organizations, companies, and methods of which a broad selection is gathered at the "International Society for Professional Innovation Management" (http://www.ispim.org). There are two main sources of innovation: external, end-user innovations and internal manufacturer innovations created in formal R&D processes (von Hippel, 1988). The central issue of R&D is the creation, selection, and execution of new ideas to create real innovations (i.e., put them to a use meeting customer requirements). This process can be depicted using the innovation funnel in Figure 2, which is often used to describe the idea that product development the most common way of introducing and managing innovation in an industry setting.

PRODUCT DEVELOPMENT PROCESSES

Combining Schumpeter's and Drucker's definitions, we investigate the performance of (1) new goods or production methods created by (2) industrial product development processes. While research is focused to create new ideas and technologies, the development process starts with selecting the most promising ideas and combines them into marketable products (Kern, 1993). The product development process usually covers classic engineering tasks from conceptualization and design to simulation, prototype building, and testing. It is embedded in the value creation chain of a company, linking research activities and market requirements to production, distribution, service and recycling, thus a part of the product lifecycle. Due to the high degree of interaction, the number of persons, and the novelty involved, it is the most knowledge intensive and complex business process, which calls for special management and controlling methods (Hahn, Hausmann, Preis, & Strickmann, 2006).

New products and innovations brought to the market today are the result of many experts

Figure 2. The innovation funnel (see Gassmann, 2006)

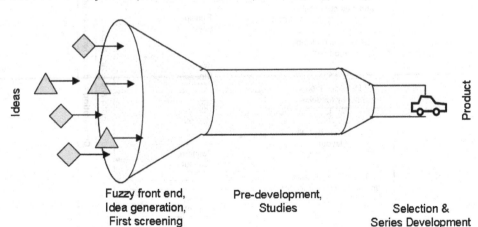

working together in a development process. Development processes run from idea selection ("the fuzzy front end") and first product definition (requirements specification) to the start of (series) production often going through a number of phases with specific goals. Each phase adds more detail and information to the product model (Ehrlenspiel, 2003; Kahn, 2004). The content and sequence of phases depends on the industry sector under consideration, most sectors have developed their own best practice approach, some of which will be presented here to illustrate the complexity and entropy to be dealt with when creating a development process model for performance measurement.

Due to the intangibility and complexity of its products, the software industry has a large supply of procedures to guide software development and software engineering has been a dominating field of research ever since the first computers were developed in the 1940s (Sommerville, 2004). Classic procedures of software engineering are the waterfall-model of Royce and the spiral model by Boehm (1988). The most commonly known modern, object-oriented approach to software engineering is the Rational Unified Process (RUP) by Jacobson, Booch, and Rumbaugh (1999) (aka "The three amigos"). Its success is largely due to its sound foundation on the unified modeling language (UML, www.uml.org, (Jacobson, Booch, & Rumbaugh, 2004)). Other well known development procedures are the V-Model (http://www.v-modell-xt.de), a tailorable solution devised by the German government or "eXtreme Programming" (XP, Beck, 2003), which is an agile, incremental and iterative approach with short cycles and few

Figure 3. Construction scheme according to VDI 2221 (1993)

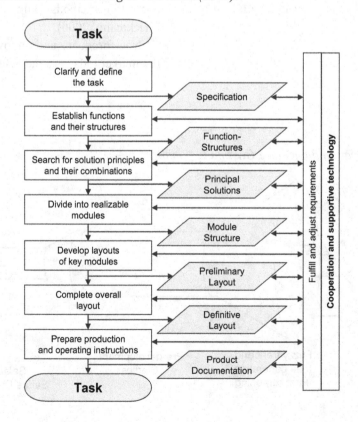

formal requirements. A through inspection of software development processes can be found in Sommerville (2004) and Balzert (2000).

Leaving pure software development and moving into more hardware-oriented industries such as mechanical engineering or electronics the level of interaction between different disciplines increases dramatically. Due to their innovative and unique nature, product development activities are usually carried out as a project, often involving diverse organizations across the globe. The challenges faced by global engineering networks and in integrated product development are described in detail by Gausemeier (2006). They are met by more structured approaches like design flows in chip design and mechatronics (www.vlsi.wpi. edu/Webcourse/flow/flow.html), process schemes (e.g., Figure 3) and control gates in the automotive industry (Cooper, 1990).

Development processes follow an iterative, incremental procedure, best explained with the TOTE-scheme (Miller, Galanter, & Pribram, 1986) shown in Figure 4.

All of them face identical challenges:

1. Dealing with technical complexity.
2. Understanding the interactions and dependencies between phases and partial models.
3. Determining the status of the project in terms of time, cost and quality (Evaluating performance in each "Test"-phase).

Performance Measurement and Controlling

While engineers love to address the first issue, which can be mastered well by CAx-Software, IDEs or product data management systems, the two later issues are less easy to tackle.

IT support and scientific exploration of individual domains is good, but hardly any research has been done on formally modelling and understanding development processes based on the actual observation of development activities and their (digital) results (= partial product models). Thus a sound, flexible and integrated model enabling automatic transformation of technical qualities into economic key figures is needed. This is especially true for each test-step where an evaluation of a product model (consisting of many elements from various domains) compared to requirements decides whether the results are "good enough" or if iteration is necessary. A promising application domain for such a system is project controlling—a crucial issue in development projects as previously shown.

Any project manager is faced with two key questions:

1. Does my product meet the requirements? (product performance).
2. If it doesn't, how do I make ends meet within the project's goals (process performance).

These questions are mostly answered by the "gut feeling" of an experienced project manager

Figure 4. The TOTE-Scheme of continuous improvement

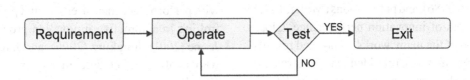

who bases his decisions often on informal reports ("No worries, I'm almost done.") or partial information ("We spent 300K$ on this task, but what's that worth?"). Apart from operative issues in a single project, strategic decisions also rely on sound controlling data. Applications are, for example, product portfolio optimization, investment decisions, or major reorganizations such as the introduction of virtual engineering or upgrading to a parametric CAD-environment. Here scientific methods for performance measurement shall be introduced and examined for both the operative and the strategic level.

State of Science...

Martino (1995) introduces methods for the fuzzy front end of innovation: selecting the best ideas with ranking methods, economic measures (net present value, cash flow analysis), simulation and cluster analysis. The factors to be considered at this early stage contrast technical data such as the stage of innovation with the projects environment in terms of market chances, and political trends. Martino stresses the necessity for objective data and the scaling of subjective information, which is prevalent at the early stages of innovation.

An excellent overview of R&D metrics and measurement systems is given by Hauser (1996). The bibliography covers 154 articles from R&D, marketing and economics literature dating from 1972 to 1996 concerned with the measurement of R&D performance. Many of these are based on market surveys and empirical data or are concerned with very specific measures such as the R&D effectiveness index (McGrath and Romeri, 1994), customer satisfaction (Ellis and Curtis, 1995), process time and cost analysis (Ellis, 1997), financial measures or patents (Griliches, 1990; Jaffe, 1986), and publications (Miller, 1992) as indicators of innovation performance. Close inspection of the many works mentioned reveals that many solutions provided on the strategic level have a heuristic or subjective approach (e.g.,

"strong alignment of technology strategy with the corporate and business strategy," "technology transfer, and communication are important," see Szakonyi (2003)) rather than objective algorithmic measures.

The algorithmic measures suggested are of limited applicability and mostly refer to financial effects rather than the innovation project itself. As Mechlin and Berg (1980) point out "there can be no shortcut, no easy formula, for assessing the value of corporate research," but the solution of "accepting the imprecision of R&D processes" by not measuring at all suggested by Galloway (1971) is not acceptable considering the paramount importance of innovation. Rather, a differentiated approach for the different stages of innovation (called "tiers" in by Zettelmeyer and Hauser (1995)) and the diverse questions such as project planning, monitoring or strategic evaluation needs to be proposed (European Industrial Research Management Association, 1995). This calls for an integrated approach, which (1) covers all aspects of engineering processes and products and (2) is flexible to answer different information needs (Griffin & Page, 1995).

Extensive research on the topic of innovation performance management has been done in Germany, most notably by Wildemann (2006). He shows strategies to increase innovation performance in case studies and is centred on innovation controlling. Central to his work are measurement of efficiency and effectiveness, two key drivers of performance that need careful differentiation. Effectiveness is "doing the right things" (e.g., choosing the right product or the best technical solution while efficiency means "doing things right" thus addressing the process). Both need to be considered and measured in order to achieve performance. Other German authors preoccupied with performance measurement and project controlling in automotive innovation processes are Jenne (2001), Jungkurz (2005), and Jania (2004) who apply product data management-systems (PDM) as source for project controlling (Jenne), process evaluation and process mining (Jungkurz), and change management (Jania). These approaches acknowledge the fact that isolated indicators are not suited to reflect a development project status and hence use product and process (meta-)data to arrive at improved development knowledge. The dominating data format for PDM-Systems used by the three authors is STEP, the standard for the exchange of product model data (PDM Implementor Forum (2002)). It is a powerful standard with diverse application protocols that offer an integrated model of a particular domain (e.g., AP 214 for the automotive industry or FUNSTEP in the furniture sector) but is of limited applicability in cross-domain applications.

Model based approaches have the advantage of highlighting key factors of the reality they represent, but since they are a limited excerpt from reality built for a specific cause, they cannot be expanded much beyond their original design and are hard to map to adjacent models. Other model based approaches for representing the content of innovation projects are metrics for conceptual software models as described by Genero, Piattini, and Calero (2005), models from operations research as suggested for managing complex projects (Williams, 2002) or as suggested in the ARIS framework by Scheer (1998).

... Administration and Industry

International organizations and standardization bodies have also acknowledged the need to measure and compare the performance of R&D activities. The Organization for Economic Cooperation and Development (OECD) has issued two important guidelines in this sector, which have found broad international acceptance. The Frascati Manual offers a conceptual framework to collect issue and compare R&D data (OECD, 1993). Its main pillars for measurement are financial investments to R&D, patents, bibliometrics and human resources, linked to innovation processes on a very abstract scale and the financial output dimension. The Oslo Manual focuses on better measures of innovation in order to assess the impact of knowledge generation on economic growth and well being on a national scale in order to provide policy makers with sound analysis tools (OECD, 2005). The Oslo Manual is concerned with the collection of innovation data at the level of the firm and is focused on capturing the dynamic innovation process and the driving factors behind them (for example, innovation activities, expenditures and internal/external linkages between sources of information, knowledge, technologies, practices and human and financial resources).

Apart from national economics taking a deep interest in the state of R&D, independent standardization bodies have developed metrics and frameworks to asses the maturity of development processes such as CMMI (Carnegie Mellon Software Engineering Institute, 2006) or SPICE (Automotive SIG, 2005). Both standards define qualitative guidelines to assess the capability and maturity levels of an organization's defined process groups such as organizational process performance (OPP) or CMMI project monitoring and control. Due to their generalized approach, they lack objective metrics and rely on subjective appraisals, or audits.

Different industries have come up with specific solutions to drive and assess performance. Good examples are the software industry and mechanical engineering, especially the automotive industry. Software engineering first came up with product metrics in order to assess the qualities of their intangible products. The automotive industry is characterized by global players manufacturing complex and highly variable products in a competitive market where lead times are ever shorter and process efficiency is of paramount importance. Here Clark and Fujimoto (1991) have written a through revision of factors that drive performance. However, they lack an approach to determine these factors with quantitative measures.

Summary of the Current State

All methods introduced above lack at least one of these properties, which we have identified as crucial for successful performance management:

1. **Broad, general scope:** Many of the metrics and methods devised for measuring innovation performance are of isolated nature, measuring only one property. This is not sufficient to represent the complexity inherent to innovative projects.

2. **Derivation from actual work results:** Most performance measurement solutions rely on indirect indicators of performance such as number of patents or investments made but not on the product/project model itself. This often leads to measuring insignificant properties, thus good decisions are made harder.

3. **Integration, flexibility and expandability:** Open frameworks that allow the interpretation of a certain property in the entire innovation context across domain boundaries and from operative to strategic level are rare. Model based approaches so far suffer from little flexibility and expandability.

NEW INNOVATION PROCESSES

In the previous paragraph, we have given an overview of performance measurement solutions for innovation processes. We have also argued why they are not satisfiable for today's innovation culture. Table 1 illustrates how innovation processes have changed and why new solutions are necessary.

Table 1 reveals the shortcomings of traditional performance measures such as patents, R&D investments or market share as they are either input- or output-oriented but do not capture the properties innovation process itself. They have a low correlation with the product under development, suffer from distortion due to accounting conventions and age distortion (e. g. monthly reports often are too late to identify a problem) and are generally focused on past performance instead of current data and future trends (Schaefer, 2002). Today's performance measurement strategies introduced before suffer from vertical and horizontal gaps as pictured in Figure 5. At the product level, different domains with heterogeneous data models and measures exist, making it hard even to formally model and understand the

Table 1. Traditional and modern innovation methods

	"Classic" Innovation Methods	"New" Innovation Methods
Effect	Short term, dramatic *Invention of the Automobile*	Long-term, durable, marginal *New fuel injection pump for better mileage*
Pace	Slow, big steps *Steam Engine*	Fast, small steps *Double complexity in integrated circuits every 18 months (Moore's law)*
Actors	Few, established companies *Ford, IBM*	Every employee, outsiders, start-ups *Google, Segway*
Information Exchange	Secret, internally *Patents*	Open, networked communities *Open Source*
Technological Enabler	New Inventions *Transistor*	Existing know-how, recombination, marketing *Cell phone with camera*
Procedures	Hierarchical, functional organization *over-the-wall-engineering*	Flat hierarchies, engineering networks *temporal, project oriented teams*

Figure 5. Gaps between innovation domains and levels

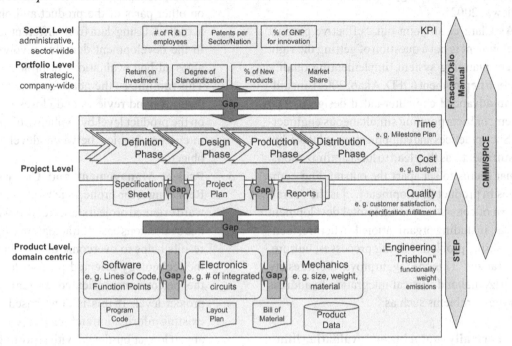

interdependencies that will eventually make the product work. This continues when considering the project or the portfolio level. Information exchange between these different granularities is mostly document-based (e. g. via reports or text files) and not integrated. The performance measurement frameworks we have introduced reflect this discontinuity as well.

Since business performance cannot be deducted from a few KPIs like ROI or investments alone, a change in performance measurement systems to track nonfinancial measures based on product and project data is necessary. According to Eccles (1991), "five activities are essential: developing an information architecture, putting the technology in place to support this architecture, aligning bonuses, and other incentives with the new system, drawing on outside resources, and designing an internal process to ensure the other four activities occur." These activities can be carried out "based on new technologies and

more sophisticated databases." In this chapter, we examine requirements and solutions to address the first two activities outlining measures to achieve the other three. An information architecture for innovation performance management must be a framework covering all levels and domains where innovation occurs. This horizontal and vertical integration must be based on IT-systems found at each level and in each domain (e.g., IDEs, PDM-Systems, CAx-Software, project management solutions, ERP). The metrics introduced later in this chapter must be well balanced and correlate to bonuses and incentives, since any single-factor or unbalanced performance measure can produce dysfunctional behaviour. The integration of external resources is part of the open framework definition. The last activity, the process of introducing the integrated performance measurement framework is of course company specific because there is no standard algorithm or template for performance measurement in innovation and technology" (Friedlob, Schleifer, & Plewa, 2002).

As Clark et al. point out, "effective product development is not a question of getting the right project planning system, implementing quality function deployment (QFD, Akao, 2004), installing an advanced computer-aided design (CAD) system, or incorporating simultaneous engineering. Such practices and equipment are valuable, but not sufficient," as they lead to local optimizations. "What seems to set apart the outstanding companies in product development [...] is the overall pattern of consistency in their total development system, including organizational structure, technical skills, problem-solving processes, culture, and strategy." This once again proves the necessity of horizontal and vertical integration to address everyday problems such as:

1. **Formally capturing and evaluating innovation processes:** Since a multitude of experts work together over a long period of time to bring a product idea to a manufacturable product definition, ways to model the product development process are necessary. Today this is done by project plans and templates, basic product configurations or reference models. They are suitable for their purpose, but fail to capture the dynamics and interdependencies of creative innovation processes. Thus to achieve, consistency between all steps of the development process and the product parts, a lot of management work, reports and review meetings are necessary. To avoid this non-value-adding overhead, a meta-model for innovation processes and products is necessary which is ideally based on existing models in the innovation process such a CAD-data, UML-models or virtual prototypes.

2. **Examination and comparison of innovation processes, methods, and tools:** Provided a reference meta-model for innovation processes exists, it can be used to protocol all development steps and evaluate their effects on other parts of the product and planned activities. Using data from different sources in the development domains involved enables ad-hoc evaluations of project status. This minimizes the need for time-wasting meetings and reviews and closes the gaps on the product level by explicitly modelling interdependencies between development objects.

3. **Project Management and Controlling:** Replacing error-prone, inaccurate and backward oriented project status reports with ad-hoc evaluations based on actual development results helps to overcome the gap between the technology-oriented product level and the performance-oriented, organizational project level. If this is done based on the existing information architecture, engineers are no longer burdened with reporting their status. The indirect status measurement via indicators is replaced by reliable data thus relieving project controllers from guess-work and relying on their "gut-feeling."

4. **Strategic Alignment of Innovations:** As soon as a number of projects has been conducted based on a general reference model for innovation processes, statistical evaluation of project and product properties can take place. It becomes possible to evaluate common pitfalls in engineering procedures or to compare different methods and tools in similar problem settings. Looking at cross-company engineering networks, different approaches can be aligned and organizational interoperability improved.

5. **Interoperability of IT-Systems:** Not only performance measurement and evaluation benefit from an integrated and flexible reference model of development data. The interoperability of IT-Systems and their supported workflows can be greatly improved if n:m interfaces can be replaced by a 1:n reference model.

The integrated reference meta model is the first step to implement the five benefits outlined above. The transformation of actual innovation data into the reference model is the second step, the third being the evaluation of the integrated data with existing and new performance measurement metrics. How these three steps can be implemented using semantic nets and ontologies is explained in the following paragraph.

UNDERSTANDING INNOVATIONS BY MODELS AND MEASUREMENTS

As stated before it needs more than financial data to measure the quality of a developed product or the current status of a product development project. An important source to determine such values are the characteristics of the product themselves. Only with attributes describing the product it is possible to make an exact statement about how a product matches the requirements defined at the beginning of a project and therefore about the product quality and project status.

The solution proposed in this chapter integrates data from operative source systems thus describing the product and its development process as one integrated model, which can be used as a basis for metric definition and execution.

As shown in Figure 6 the integrated product reference model consists of so called "partial product models." Each of these models gives a complete description of the product at a different level of abstraction. Which kinds of product partial models are needed depends on the domain and project. Ideally they are based on existing domain reference models (e.g., UML, STEP) and are the result of an ontology engineering process. The partial models picked in Figure 6 are requirement definition, functional design, conceptual design, implementation, test, and quality assurance.

To begin with, for each partial model a conceptual ontology (t-box) defines the artefacts

Figure 6. Vision—towards the integrated product model

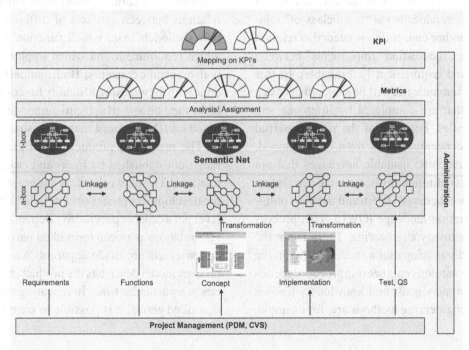

created in this particular stage of the development process. The figure displays them in the line labelled "t-box."

Ontologies initially came from philosophy and describe the part of meta physics that deals with the nature of being. In recent years, ontologies were adopted in computer science and can be understand as an explicit specification of a conceptualization (Gruber, 1993). Ontologies are an abstraction from technologies, data structures, architectures, or applications (Angele & Nierlich, 2003) and are well suited for the representation of semantics between elements and different views on the information modelled. Therefore ontologies are able to model more complex relationships than simple data models (e.g., database schemas), which gives only a representation of data, but not a semantic description of the relationships between different concepts.

Conceptual ontologies (t-boxes) consist of two main elements: concepts and relations. Concepts are a description of real elements occurring in the domain that should be modelled (e.g., requirements, functions, or implemented artefacts). Ontologies offer two ways of connecting these concepts to each other. It is possible to connect concepts hierarchically via "is-subclass-of" relations. If another connection is needed, a relation is used (e.g., the relation "implements" between function and requirement is thinkable). In this manner, a semantic net will be spanned between concepts that are completed by inference and integrity rules. For each of the needed partial models a conceptual t-box must be developed. Common machine readable languages that are used for this definition are the resource description framework schema (RDF(S)) and the Web ontology description language (OWL). This process is called ontology engineering. There is not the one and only ontology for a specific domain, the result of an ontology engineering process depends on the designers goals and knowledge. Known ontology engineering methods are, for example,

Noy and McGuinness (2001) or Methontology (Gomez-Perez, 1997).

In a specific project, the a-box then is filled with corresponding instances (e.g., a specific requirement for a product is modelled as an instance of the concept "requirement" as established by the t-box). This procedure is shown in the line labeled "a-box." For some partial models, this is done manually; in others an automatic transformation from operational data is possible. Requirements, for example, are normally recorded manually. In this case, the a-box model may replace the text file, allowing easy reuse in subsequent project phases, and is created and maintained using an ontology editor. Other a-boxes can be created by a transformation (indicated as arrows), for example an XSLT-conversion of UML-diagrams. However, these are examples only: If the requirements are already captured in a structured way, the manual maintenance can be replaced by a transformation easily.

With the transformation of data from different operational source systems into one single format the second step in creating an integrated product model is done. To get one step further, the proposed solution allows the establishment of relations between artifacts of different product partial models (e.g., which function stands for which requirement and which implementations realize specific concepts). Both manual linking as done with the widespread quality function deployment-method as well as (semi-) automatic linking based on ID or pattern matching is possible.

The result is a product partial model spanning net established by inter- and cross domain relations. The network offers a representation of the development process at a detailed integration level not available previously. Dependencies and interrelations between individual partial models and artefacts are made apparent. An integrated product model describes the product characteristics at a particular time. In repeating the process described above, it is possible to create multiple

Figure 7. The goal question metric approach for fault reduction

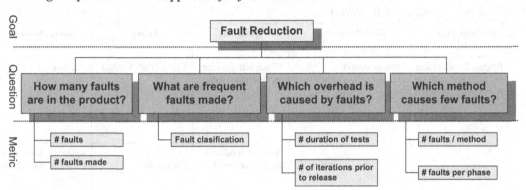

"snapshots" of the product's state. These snapshots enable the determination of the product's growth and maturity along the timeline.

Based on this integration performance evaluations can be conducted, whose results flow into higher KPIs, as indicated on the top of Figure 6. Thus, not only horizontal but also vertical integration is made possible.

The integrated reference model so far is no solution for performance measurement: To pour water into the wine, the vast amount of technical information clouds the economical information. It needs to be carefully extracted by well suited, valid, and carefully combined metrics. Because despite all measuring efforts, a great number of projects still fails or exceeds its planned limits. This is due to the complexity and interdependencies of the various partial models and often enough badly chosen metrics. Focusing on budget compliance in a time critical process will lead to its failure. A metric is defined to measure ONE process or product quality (IEEE Standard for Software Quality, 1998). A single metric gives little insight into the status of a project, thus methods for combination of metric values need to be derived. Well known methods for combining metrics in order to ease their interpretation are the earned value method which contrasts work done (= value achieved) with expenses occurred or trend diagrams for costs or milestones.

To avoid these problems and arrive at sound, crystal-clear metrics that are suited for a company's information needs, the goal question metric approach from the TAME-project (Basili & Rombach, 1988) is proposed. It helps to find fitting metrics for an information request by asking appropriate questions answered by a set of metrics as presented in Figure 7 for fault reduction metrics. In analogy to the example, it is possible to derive a high level KPI value from several "low-level" metrics. Although there are already a great number of metrics that have been defined in literature and applied in actual projects, a flexible approach for the creation and modification of metrics is needed. Metrics that proved to be useful in one project are possibly of much less use in other ones. Especially for projects in different domains, different metrics are needed.

Metrics can be classified by a number of dimensions such as object of study, research goal, quality characteristic, etc. (see Piattini, Genero, Poels, & Nelson, 2005), the most common one being the object of study. Usually, one differentiates between product and process metrics, combined models give insight into the overall status of the project.

To summarize the solution suggested Table 2 shows the application of measuring a business process covering different domains by integrating and interpreting partial information from various sources.

Table 2. Derivation of metrics for time-critical product development using information from PM- and PDM-Systems (Friedlob et al., 2002)

Business Process	Goals/Objectives	Questions	Metrics	Source System
Product Development	Time to Market	Which activities are on the critical path?	Critical Path Method	PM-System
		Will the product be finished on time?	Degree of Completion	Release Status of Parts in the PDM-System
			Earned Value Analysis	Combination of PM- and PDM-Data

Related Activities

There are just a few existing approaches that try to measure product development performance and productivity. Reasons for this lack of research activities are the secrecy of product development and the unavailability of industry data on the one hand, on the other hand the complexity of a long process involving many actors. A commercial product for the semiconductor industry is Numetrics (see Nummetrics, 2005). After the design process, data will manual be entered and analysed. Therefore only post project analysis comparing to other projects is possible with the calculated results. To increase the benefit of performance measurement, it is elementary to calculate the current performance and productivity during a project to react on the results. Even one step further would be to measure the influence of investment decisions on the project's performance. A research project dealing with these issues for the semiconductor industry in more detail is PRODUKTIV+, funded by the German Federal Ministry for Education and Research (http://www.bmbf.de). In this project, a semiconductor specific productivity model will be developed that aims at integrating the technical data occurring in a project with business data and KPI-systems. To create a better fundament for investment decisions, analysis and simulation methods measure their potential and real impact on KPIs. The project is still in progress, final results are therefore not yet available. Furthermore the project does not follow a common domain independent approach, so it is unlikely to be used in other domains.

FUTURE TRENDS: PERMETER—MEASUREMENT OF PRODUCTIVITY IN PRODUCT DEVELOPMENT

As illustrated throughout this chapter, product development is a complex and knowledge-intensive process. It is both vital and challenging: Vital since the value of successful, market-oriented innovations is paramount in times of globalization, allowing few companies to neglect it; Challenging for its intricate management demands and the frequent exceedance of cost targets. To address the requirements of successful product design various methods, such as process models, simultaneous engineering, integrated product development etc. have been proposed.

The approach taken by Permeter is to be seen vertical (i.e., supplementary), in respect to these methods. Without interfering the processes selected, it aims at the integration of the actual data and information created during the developing process, breaking the isolation of their individual digital formats. This integration is facilitated by the usage of modern semantic modelling technologies and results in a model of project and product where the artefacts represented are linked in a both semantic and machine-processable manner. Besides other usage scenarios, Permeter proposes the application of the integration's result as a basis for performance assessment based on reporting. In particular, it provides a "project cockpit" summing up all important information on the development's progress.

Permeter is applied in order to improve the efficiency and control of product development processes. It offers comprehensive product model integration facilities fostering performance assessment. On the semantically integrated models created, up-to-date metrics and report capabilities are supplied. They are bound to improve the project managers understanding, steering information and decision making.

Figure 8 illustrates the workflow of Permeter. Input for the Permeter framework comes from three sources. Firstly, project data (for example the project schedule as outlined by MS Project) is imported to establish the setting the analyzed innovation takes place in. Secondly, product meta information is added, opening buckets for the actual development artefacts to reside in. Lastly, the created grid is filled with raw data from the engineering process, such as CAD file data, source code or chip layout information. In order to allow link-up between the sources all input is transformed into a generic modelling paradigm, namely into OWL/RDF ontologies.

With inputs and connections in place the analysis can start. It is based on the integrated project-product-models—created by the previous steps—representing the development process at one distinct point in time. For the analysis multiple of such models from different point in time are loaded and looked into. The examination is driven by metrics and results into reports on the innovation and its performance.

Figure 8. The Permeter-Workflow

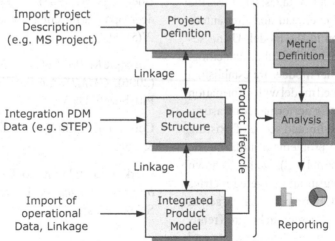

CONCLUSION

Performance measurement of innovation processes is a fascinating and highly relevant task, but has yet evaded full scientific coverage and suffers from many practical issues. Starting from a general introduction into the terms of innovation, development processes and discussing the dimensions of performance, we have introduced an overview of existing approaches. We have shown that the current state of research and industry is either focused on local, domain oriented solutions or on top level KPIs that are not related to the product and cover only past events. A promising approach lies in model-based solutions that are used to support innovation processes with IT-solutions, but still gaps between different domains persist. Another gap lies between the technological paradigm of engineers and the organizational, economical thinking of managers. In the future, innovation processes will face severe challenges. As the complexity of upcoming products increases, the number of potential issues will rise exponentially.

Nevertheless, help is under way. Expanding the model based approach with semantic Web technology and ontologies, we have shown how an open, flexible performance measurement framework can be build from a semantic reference meta model. The transformation from operative development system data has several advantages: It reduces the reporting and review overhead and guarantees up-to-date information in the model. Using semantic reasoning techniques or explicit modelling, relations between partial models are established creating a new, integrated model with information previously unavailable for performance measurement. To overcome the limited scope of existing metrics and evade the problems of unfit metric application ('metric gambling'), we have shown how to define meaningful and targeted metrics based on the integrated reference model and actual development results. In the section Future Trends we have outlined upcoming developments and

introduced Permeter, a software system able to "eavesdrop" on development results and process data from PM-Systems, PDM-solutions, software engineering IDEs, and chip design tools.

REFERENCES

Akao, Y. (2004). *QFD-Quality Function Deployment*. Productivity Press.

Angele, J., & Nierlich, A. (2003). *Semantic business integration—speed up your processes*. Ontoprise Whitepaper Series

Automotive SIG. (2005). *Automotive SPICE Process Reference Model*, release V4.3, http://www.automotivespice.com/AutomotiveSPICE_PRM

Balzert, H. (2000). *Lehrbuch der Softwaretechnik*. Spektrum. In R. G. Cooper (1990). Stage-gate systems: A new tool for managing new products. *Business Horizons, 33*(3), 44-54.

Basili, V. R. & Rombach, H. (1988). The TAME project: Towards improvement-oriented software environments. *IEEE Transactions on IEEE Transactions on Software Engineering, 14*(6), 758-773.

Beck, K. (2003). *Extreme programming*. Boston: Addison-Wesley.

Boehm, B. W. (1988). A spiral model of software development and enhancement. *IEEE Computers, 21*(5), 61-72.

Carnegie Mellon Software Engineering Institute. (2006). *CMMI® for Development, Version 1.2*. Pittsburgh, USA.

Cetinkunt, S. (2006). *Mechatronics*. John Wiley & Sons.

Clark, K. B., & Fujimoto, T. (1991). *Product development performance*. Boston: Harvard Business School Press.

Crabb, H. C. (1997). *The virtual engineer: 21st century product development.* Society of Manufacturing.

Drucker, P. F. (2003). *The essential Drucker: The best of sixty years of Peter Drucker's essential writings on management.* HarperCollins.

Eccles, R. G. (1991). The performance measurement manifesto. *Harvard Business Review, 69*(1), 131-137.

Ehrlenspiel, K. (2003). *Integrierte Produktentwicklung.* München, Germany: Hanser.

Ellis, L. (1997). *Evaluation of R&D processes: Effectiveness through measurements.* London: Artech House Publishers

Ellis, L. W., & Curtis, C. C. (1995). Measuring customer satisfaction. *Research Technology Management, 38*(5), 45-48.

European Industrial Research Management Association. (1995). *Evaluation of R&D Projects,* EIRMA Paris, Working group reports, Report No. 47.

Feldmüller, D., Frick, A., & Grau, N. (2006). *Welche Kompetenzen benötigt das IT-Projektmanagement?* Paper presented at interPM conference, Glashütten, Germany.

Fernandez, M., Gomez-Perez, A., & Juristo, N. (1997). METHONTOLOGY—From ontological art towards ontological engineering. *In Proceedings in the AAAI97 Spring Symposium Series on Ontology Engineering (pp. 33-40).* Stanford, USA

Fitz-Enz, J. (2001). *How to measure human resource management.* McGraw-Hill.

Friedlob, G. T., Schleifer, L. L. F., & Plewa, F. J. J. (2002). *Essentials of corporate performance measurement.* New York: John Wiley & Sons.

Galloway, E. C. (1971). Evaluating R&D performance—Keep it simple. *Research Management, 14*(2), 50-58.

Gassmann, O. (2006). Innovation und Risiko - zwei Seiten einer Medaille. In O. Gassmann & C. Kobe (Ed.), *Management von Innovation und Risiko.* Berlin, Germany: Springer.

Gausemeier, J., Hahn, A., Kespohl, H. D., & Seifert, L. (2006). *Vernetzte Produktentwicklung.* München, Germany: Hanser.

Genero, M., Piattini, M., & Calero, C. (2005). *Metrics for software conceptual models.* Imperial College Press.

Gómez-Pérez, A., Fernández, M. & Juristo, N. (1997). METHONTOLOGY: From ontological art towards ontological engineering. In Proceedings from AAAI Spring Symp. Series, (pp. 33-40). Menlo Park, CA. AAAI Press.

GPM Deutsche Gesellschaft für Projektmanagement e.V., P. C. G. D. (2004). *Studie zur Effizienz von Projekten in Unternehmen.*

Griffin, A., &. Page, A. L. (1995). The PDMA success measurement project: Recommended measures for product development success and failure. *Journal of Product Innovation Management, 13*(6), 478-496.

Griliches, Z. (1990). Patent statistics as economic indicators: A survey. *Journal of Economic Literature, 28*(4), 1661-1707.

Gruber, T. R. (1993). A translation approach to portable ontologies. *Knowledge Acquisition. 5*(2), 199-220.

Hahn, A., Hausmann, K., Preis, S., & Strickmann, J. (2006). Ein Konzept für das Entwicklungscontrolling auf PLM-Basis. *HMD Praxis der Wirtschaftsinformatik 249.*

Harmuth, U. (2003). *Erfolgsfaktoren für Projekte.* Unpublished master thesis, University of Wuppertal, Germany.

Hauser, J. R. (1996). *Metrics to value R&D: An annotated bibliography.* Cambridge, MA: Marketing Science Institute Working Paper.

Hauser, J. R., & Zettelmayer, F. (1997). Metrics to evaluate R,D&E. *Research Technology Management, 40*(4), 32-38.

Horsch, J. (2003). *Innovations- und Projektmanagement.* Wiesbaden, Germany: Gabler.

IEEE. (1998). *IEEE Standard for a Software Quality Metrics Methodolog Institute of Electrical and Electronics Engineers.*

Jacobson, I., Booch, G., & Rumbaugh, J. (2004). *The unified modeling language reference manual.* Boston: Addison-Wesley.

Jacobson, I., Booch, G., & Rumbaugh, J. (1999). *The unified software development process.* Boston: Addison-Wesley.

Jaffe, A. B. (1986). Technological opportunity and spillovers of R&D: Evidence for firms patents, profits, and market value. *American Economic Review, 76*(5), 984-1001.

Jania, T. (2004). *Änderungsmanagement auf Basis eines integrierten Prozess- und Produktdatenmodells mit dem Ziel einer durchgängigen Komplexitätsbewertung.* Doctoral Dissertation, University of Padeborn, Germany.

Jenne, F. (2001). *PDM-basiertes Entwicklungsmonitoring.* Doctoral Dissertation, University of Karlsuhe, Gemany.

Jungkurz, R. M. (2005). *PDM-basierte Überwachung komplexer Entwicklungsprojekte.* Doctoral Disseration, Technical University of München, Germany.

Kahn, K. B. (2004). *PDMA handbook of new product development.* New York: John Wiley & Sons.

Kern, W. (1993). Forschung und Entwicklung. In U. Arentzen & E. Winter (Ed.), *Gabler Wirtschaftslexikon,* Wiesbaden, Germany: Gabler.

Little, A. D. (2004). *Innovation Excellence Studie 2004.*

Mandl-Striegnitz, P., & Lichter, H. (1999). Defizite im Software-Projektmanagement – Erfahrungen aus einer industriellen Studie. *Informatik / Informatique 5,* 4-9.

Martino, J. P. (1995). *R&D project selection.* New York: John Wiley & Sons.

Maskell, B. H. (1991). *Performance measurement for world class manufacturing: A model for American companies (corporate leadership).* Productivity Press.

McGrath, M. E., & Romeri, M. N. (1994). The R&D effectiveness index: A metric for product development performance. *Insight, 5*(3), 1-12.

Mechlin, G. F., & Berg, D. (1980). Evaluating research—ROI is not enough. *Harvard Business Review, 58*(5), 93-99.

Miller, G. A., Galanter, E., & Pribram, K. A. (1986). *Plans and the structure of behavior.* Adams Bannister Cox Pubs.

Miller, R. (1992). The Influence of primary task on R&D laboratory evaluation: A comparative bibliometric analysis. *R&D Management, 22*(1), 3-15.

Neely, A. (2002). *Business performance measurement.* Cambridge University Press.

Noy, N., & McGuiness, D. (2001). *Ontology development 101—A guide to creating your first ontology.* Stanford University.

Numetrics Management Systems. (2000). *Measuring IC and ASIC design productivity.* White Paper submitted to the Fabless Semiconductor Association (FAB), Santa Clara,CA.

OECD. (2005). *Oslo manual.* OECD Publishing.

OECD. (1993). *The measurement of scientific and technical activities.* OECD Publishing.

PDM Implementor Forum. (2002). *Usage guide for the STEP PDM Schema V1.2.* Retrieved from http://www.prostep.org

Piattini, M., Genero, M., Poels, G., & Nelson, J. (2005). Towards a framework for conceptual modelling quality. In C. Genero/Piattini (Ed.), *Metrics for software conceptual models.* London, UK: Imperial College Press.

Rooijmans, J., Aerts, H., & van Genuchten, M. (1996). Software quality in consumer electronics products. *Software, IEEE, 13*(1), 55-6455-6455-64.

Scheer, A. (1998). *Wirtschaftsinformatik.* Berlin, Germany: Springer.

Schumpeter, J. (1934). *The theory of economic development.* Cambridge, MA: Harvard University Press.

Sommerville, I. (2004). *Software engineering (international computer science series).* Addison Wesley.

The Standish Group (1994). *The CHAOS Report.* West Yarmouth.

Schaefer, O. M. (2002). *Performance measures in value management.* Berlin, Germany: Erich Schmidt Verlag.

Strickmann, J., & Hahn, A. (2007). *Integrierte Wissensbasis für Projektcontrolling und Änderungsmanagement.* Paper presented at the 4th Conference on Professional Knowledge Management – Experiences and Visions, Potsdam, Germany

Szakonyi, R. (1990). 101 tips for managing R&D more effectively - I. *Research Technology Management, 33*(4), 31-36.

VDI. (1993). *VDI-Richtlinie 2221: Methodik zum Entwickeln und Konstruieren technischer Systeme und Produkte.* Düsseldorf, Germany: VDI.

von Hippel, E. (1988). *The sources of innovation.* Oxford University Press.

Wildemann, H. (2006). *Innovationen.* München: TCW.

Wildemann, H. (2006). *Innovationscontrolling, Leitfaden zur Selektion, Planung, Steuerung und Erfolgsmessung von F&E-Projekten.* München, Germany: TCW.

Williams, T. (2002). *Modeling complex projects.* Chichester, UK: John Wiley & Sons.

Zettelmeyer, F., & Hauser, J. R. (1995). *Metrics to evaluate R&D groups: Phase I, qualitative interviews," Working Paper #125-95.* Cambridge, MA.

Chapter XXI
Finding and Growing Innovators:
Keeping Ahead of the Competition

Debbie Richards
Macquarie University, Australia

Peter Busch
Macquarie University, Australia

ABSTRACT

Innovation is seen by many organizations as the next frontier to be managed in order to gain a competitive advantage and remain sustainable. Innovation management shares much in common with knowledge management, both being recognized as involving a resource, which resides in individuals, can be value-added and transferred via (teams of) people, is difficult to capture, is highly contextual, and continually evolving. We believe that innovation is even harder to define, represent, and transfer due to its intrinsic relationship with creativity and novelty generation. Nevertheless, we seek to determine if patterns of behavior do exist which can be used to predict likely future innovative behavior. Current psychometric tests used to test for innovation or creativity often do little more than identify various personality traits or characteristics which can be used to suggest an individual who might be suitable to fill a recognized gap in the organization. We offer an approach, building on our work along psychological lines with tacit knowledge measurement in the ICT domain that seeks to capture responses to real scenarios experienced by recognized innovators and entrepreneurs. These scenarios and responses are used to evaluate the degree to which the respondent can be considered an innovator so that areas of personal or professional development may be identified.

INTRODUCTION

There is a close link between knowledge management (KM), competitiveness, and innovation.

Innovation is often defined as the turning of knowledge into "new products, processes, and services to improve competitive advantage and meet customers' changing needs" (Gloet & Terziovski,

2004, p. 404). Also, since innovation is closely tied to an organizations culture (Cottrill, 1998), strategies for knowledge management, which affect the attitudes and beliefs of individuals will play a vital role within the organization to nurture creativity and innovation type knowledge (Gloet et al., 2004). Swan and Newell (2000) state: "the assumptions underlying the interest in KM are that innovation, not just efficiency or quality, will be the primary source of competitive advantage and that knowledge is central to a firm's capacity to innovate" (p. 591).

Innovation intrinsically involves change (Roffe, 1999), resulting in a difference in any or all of the following: product, material, process, market, problem/need addressed. This can be seen as doing something new with new things in new ways with new people to solve new problems. Moving along this "innovation highway depends on the knowledge evolution" as knowledge is used and adapted within each phase and as part of the creativity required to move between each phase (Carneiro, 2000, p. 87). Peters (1997) notes that constant innovation is essential for our individual and organizational survival. One-off innovation may bring a period of success, but since competitive-advantage exists only as long as it takes the competitors to match or better your strategy and thus tend to be short-term (Hamel and Prahalad, 1989), innovation must be ongoing and tightly aligned to an organization's strategic policies down to its operational activities. Due to ongoing competition and change, companies seek to "reduce costs, improve quality, increase productivity, or effect innovation. However, the changes introduced by most companies commonly address the first three of these factors and less often, the last." (Roffe, 1999, p. 224). This orientation can be seen in the type of knowledge management schemes and tools and training and development programs being implemented. Our research seeks to take a different line of attack, which is focused on identifying and developing innovative individuals. While the approach we offer is not

specific to ICT innovators and entrepreneurs, the study involved scenarios and participants from the ICT domain. Further, innovation is often associated with advances in ICT and the researchers' background and past studies have been in ICT fields of study and organizations.

BACKGROUND

In this chapter we do not take a "managerial perspective" of innovation (Andrianopoulos, 2001) in which the focus is on tools and management strategies for identifying good ideas and nurturing them all the way to the market, possibly via either a *mechanistic* or *organic* organizational approach to innovation (Burns & Stalker, 1994). Instead we take a socially situated (Clancey, 1997) view of innovation, in which innovation can be seen to be context dependent and always evolving. This aligns to our view of knowledge and cognition as socially situated.

A process-oriented view, sees innovation as comprising a number of phases such as idea creation, initial application, feasibility determination and final application (Roberts, 1988) or more informally as a "complex design and decision process involving the diffusion, implementation and utilization of new ideas" (Swan et al., 2000, p. 592). Viewing innovation as a process is a key aspect of our approach. As Thomas, Watts Sussman, and Henderson (2001) state, these processes include making sense of our environment, particularly ambiguous new events, in a way that allows new connections to be made to familiar situations. However, innovation is not simply a process of trial-and-error rooted in experience. Innovation needs to produce timely and ongoing results "involving a complex mix of tacit knowledge, implicit learning processes, and intuition" (Fenwick, 2003, p. 124).

There is clearly a connection between tacit knowledge and innovation knowledge (Leonard & Sensiper, 1998). Both have been recognized to support competitive advantage, are highly experience based, and difficult to articulate. We have thus adapted our research using work-place scenarios to capture tacit knowledge to workplace scenarios to capture innovation knowledge. Unlike psychometric approaches such as the Kirton adaption-innovation (KAI) (Kirton, 2001) inventory or the Myers-Briggs type indicator (MBTI) creativity index (Gough, 1981), which seek to identify personality types, we focus on the behavior (response to a situation) of individuals who have had results rather than on character or personality traits (such as self-confident, independent or risk-taker). As innovation is a process, different characteristics are needed at different times. Even to define someone as creative does not qualify them as an innovator. Let us consider in more depth the connection between creativity and innovation.

CREATIVITY AND INNOVATION: ISSUES, CONTROVERSIES, AND PROBLEMS

Creativity is transforming the 21st century in much the same way as the plough transformed the 18th century (Florida, 2002). Creativity is typically seen as the starting point for innovation (Zampetakis & Moustakis, 2006). Both of which are closely linked to entrepreneurship, which normally involves innovation (Baumol, 1993), and ongoing creativity to overcome obstacles (Amabile, 1996).

Zampetakis et al. (2006) conducted a study which linked a student's self-perception of creativity with their family environment and eventually their intention to go out to establish a new business (i.e., become an entrepreneur). If the family environment provided a culture of self-employment and being creative there was greater entrepreneurial intent. In contrast, university was not found to affect entrepreneurial intent and in some cases, such as numerous years of studying

business, intent was decreased. The significance of intent was based on the view that attitude (from family background) led to intention resulting in entrepreneurial behavior.

Identifying or classifying individuals as creative leads us into the psychology literature. Prior to the empirical social psychology research into creativity of Simonton (1981) and Amabile (1983, 1996), the huge body of creativity research was primarily focused on individual differences in creative abilities or the characterization of the personality traits of a creative individual. Amabile (1996) recognized that creativity was not simply an innate feature of one's personality, but that creative performance relied on task motivation; domain-relevant skills and creativity relevant skills, which could be enhanced by intrinsic motivators and inhibited by extrinsic motivators. Such a view has enormous ramifications for innovation and knowledge management and training and development programs. For example, offering people shares in the company or a pay rise is a form of extrinsic motivator that may in effect place pressure that restricts freedom of thought and encourage people to come up with "innovations" that seem to fit with what management are looking for. True innovation will find solutions, often to invented problems, that may be contrary to what management expected and, as history reveals, has been opposed repeatedly by management. The 3M post-it note is a classic example of an individual's persistence, which paid off, despite ongoing rejection of the ideas (McLeod & Winsor, 2003).

Creativity without skill will not be sufficient to deliver an innovation. Skill without the intrinsic motivation to pursue creative strategies will also not deliver innovation. However, we can not expect an individual to be skilled and motivated in all areas requiring creativity and some phases require greater degrees of one or the other. Multidisciplinary teams and even different individuals and teams at different phases of the innovation cycle are needed. Roffe (1999) sums this up nicely: "organizations need people with different kinds of skills to succeed in all steps of the innovation process; idea generators who create new insights, information gatekeepers linked with knowledge sources, product champions who advocate adoption of new practices, project managers who undertake the technical functions needed to maintain an innovative project on track; and leaders who actively encourage, sponsor and coach others to pursue innovation" (p. 234).

While teams, rather than individuals, are often responsible for innovation (Van de Ven, Angle, & Poole, 2000) putting a group of creative and enthusiastic people together will not guarantee successful innovation if people come from different cultural backgrounds. Culture itself can be defined as "the learned ideas, values, knowledge, rules, and customs shared by members of a collectivity (such as those based on ethnicity, gender, sexuality, indigeneity, age, disability (Holmes, Hughes, & Julian, 2003, p. 157). Different knowledge management strategies may be needed to handle innovation knowledge. For instance, sharing knowledge with others in your ingroup is relatively easy, but innovation requires bringing in new ideas and perspectives from outside existing groups. Being asked to share knowledge with people from outgroups may result in resistance. Knowledge will need to be continuously negotiated (Swan et al., 2000). Knowledge strategies to break down these barriers include: team building games, or the use of champions or mediators that are accepted by both groups as knowledge links. We take up some of these ideas again in the final discussion.

THE SOLUTION

Our methodology combines a number of techniques, one of them being the use of narrative (Polkinghorne, 1988). The real-life stories of recognized innovators are used to create scenarios, which can be viewed as cases grounded in the real world and based on experience, thus spanning both codified (explicit) and practical (tacit) knowledge (Richards & Busch, 2003). The scenarios were developed from case studies in the literature and interviews with recognized innovators. Using an approach adapted from Sternberg, Wagner, Williams, and Horvath (1995), we capture knowledge-in-action via the responses of our participants to the scenarios.

The complete research instrument is a four-part questionnaire including:

- Biographical details (Part A) (e.g., name, age, education, and employment; see Table 2)
- Self-assessment (Part B); see Figure 2
- A set of four/five randomly assigned scenarios and responses (Part C); see Table 1
- Request to suggest new scenarios and possible responses (Part D)

We have developed an inventory of 12 ICT-related innovation scenarios, which have been taken from case studies in the literature, such as Bell and McNamara (1991) and later reality checked by an ICT innovator/entrepreneur. Figure 1 shows scenario 4, which was created from a case reported in the media and similar to other situations that have arisen in the games industry. Overall, the 12 scenarios cover a range of situations faced by entrepreneurs. The example given is one of the more sensational situations, most of the scenarios are less emotionally or ethically charged. A number of responses to the scenario are offered. Table 1 provides the possible responses to scenario 4 in Figure 1. For each possible scenario response, survey participants are asked to indicate their choice using two 7-point likert scales, one to indicate their realistic and another to indicate their ethical choice, which range from very bad to very good.

For each scenario participants were also asked to identify which of the following innovation stage/s the scenario belonged to: "Idea generation—Typically a technical insight into a product or process or thought about a service"; "Opportunity recognition: An opportunity is identified for developing an idea into a new product, process or service"; "Development: Usually involving prototype development and marketing testing"; or "Realization: Typically realising how to market the product and introduce it to the customer." Respondents were able to choose more than one stage.

To enable identification of cohorts within the second sample population, we included a self-assessment section within the survey (see Figure 2). In addition in the final section (Part D) we invited participants to: add new answer options and rate them and add new scenarios, answer options, and ratings. Suggesting alternative answer options was seen to be particularly important to identifying people who are able to come up with alternative ideas.

Our approach bears some resemblance to the work of Rae (2004) in that we endeavor to capture the "story" of the innovator's career and "significant learning experiences" in their career. Like Rae, we also used interviews to capture stories from entrepreneurs, innovators, investment angels, and venture capitalists but we did not become involved in their actions and environments or for such an extended period of time (two-years). From Rae's research, a model of entrepreneurial learning has been developed comprising a set of questions for each of the model dimensions: personal and social emergence; negotiated enterprise and contextual learning. While the research technique, model, and outcomes differ to our work, we are similarly motivated to provide some practical solution to teaching and learning of innovators and entrepreneurs. As Rae notes, currently most educational programs teach about innovation and entrepreneurship, rather than offering students

Figure 1. Scenario 4, answer option Created from http://www.cnn.com/2004/WORLD/europe/07/29/uk.manhunt/index.html, http://news.bbc.co.uk/1/hi/england/leicestershire/3535268.stm

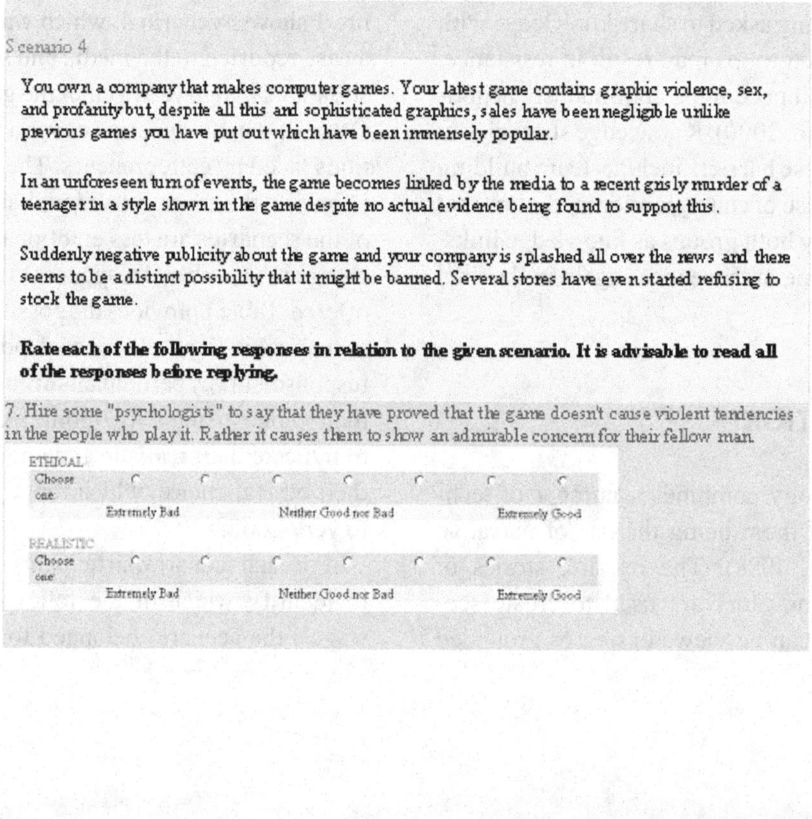
Scenario 4

You own a company that makes computer games. Your latest game contains graphic violence, sex, and profanity but, despite all this and sophisticated graphics, sales have been negligible unlike previous games you have put out which have been immensely popular.

In an unforeseen turn of events, the game becomes linked by the media to a recent grisly murder of a teenager in a style shown in the game despite no actual evidence being found to support this.

Suddenly negative publicity about the game and your company is splashed all over the news and there seems to be a distinct possibility that it might be banned. Several stores have even started refusing to stock the game.

Rate each of the following responses in relation to the given scenario. It is advisable to read all of the responses before replying.

7. Hire some "psychologists" to say that they have proved that the game doesn't cause violent tendencies in the people who play it. Rather it causes them to show an admirable concern for their fellow man.

ETHICAL

Choose one

Extremely Bad — Neither Good nor Bad — Extremely Good

REALISTIC

Choose one

Extremely Bad — Neither Good nor Bad — Extremely Good

Table 1. Answer options for scenario 4

#	Answer Option
1	Pull the game off the shelves immediately. Send an open letter to various widely read newspapers apologising for any negative effects the game causes.
2	Do nothing, rationalising that all the negative press will cause an increase in demand for the game as many of your target market will want to buy it to find out what the fuss is all about. If a particular store refuses to stock your game, so what? There are plenty of other stores around that will.
3	Put out a new version of the game with toned down content and a new name as a second product. You don't want to cause any trouble, but you still want to sell the game.
4	Pull the game off the shelves and be done with it. It isn't a particularly good seller anyway, so there's no point getting into a lawsuit over it. If you spare yourself all that trouble you can focus on your other more popular games. There's no point publicly announcing your innocence since nobody would believe you anyway.
5	Sue someone for defamation.
6	Put out a bunch of family-friendly G rated games to take the attention off the game in question.
7	Hire some "psychologists" to say that they have proved that the game doesn't cause violent tendencies in the people who play it. Rather it causes them to show an admirable concern for their fellow man.

Figure 2. Part B of the questionnaire: Self Analysis

Innovation Inventory Part B: Self Analysis

Which of the following do you consider yourself to be?

Not an innovator / Budding innovator / Innovator but not yet widely recognised / Recognised innovator

How many years of experience have you had as an innovator?

How many patents (provisional or final) have you submitted?

How many innovation awards have you won?

Have you received other recognition as an innovator?

Do you have your own start-up company?

Are you involved with a team of innovators? No / I am a team member / I am a team leader

What role does innovation play in your worklife? None / Minor / Major

the opportunity to learn to become innovators or entrepreneurs.

SAMPLE POPULATIONS AND DATA ANALYSIS

Our study identified four cohorts of participants from two sample populations. The first population involved 73 3rd year undergraduate students who were finishing a group-based management unit in which they were required to identify a market opportunity and product, build a business case for the product culminating in presentation of their business plan to a panel of experienced and successful innovators, venture capitalists, and entrepreneurs. The cohort were aged 20-27, predominantly male, highest educational qualification being high school, and overwhelmingly ethnic (which means non Anglo-Celtic in the Australian environment) specifically concentrated in the Chinese and to a lesser extent subcontinental ethnic groups. This group are referred to as the "undergraduate" cohort.

Our second sample population were involved in a comparable activity, known as the New South Wales (NSW) Enterprise Workshop (EW). This program has run for around 20 years and is sponsored by the Australian NSW State Government to assist inventors, innovators, and budding entrepreneurs to develop their ideas into a sound business plan that can be presented to a distinguished panel of venture capitalists, entrepreneurs, innovators, and business people. Both the undergraduate and Enterprise Workshop courses run over a half-year period and involve working in teams to develop the business plan. The EW includes about three weeks of face-to-face sessions on accounting, IP protection, marketing, and market research, personnel management, raising capital, business and strategic planning and project management. The participants in our study included workshop attendees, presenters, mentors, and judging panellists. Some participants were in innovation supporting roles such as investment angels, patent attorneys, accountants, and venture capitalists. Participants were recruited face-to-face and/or via email and telephone. Approximately 45 individuals were contacted.

Almost all participants provided their name and thus it was also possible to validate the most appropriate category based on biographies of the presenters, mentors, and panellists, which had been made available to participants. Additionally, the first author was an attendee of the EW and thus also had personal knowledge of each individual.

Based on the self analysis (Part B) and our previous validation process, we identified three cohorts within our second population: recognized innovators; intermediate innovators some of whom may have already achieved some success together with individuals with many years experience in supporting innovators; and novices, which included individuals who had achieved no success, did not aspire to be innovators or who had lesser experience in supporting innovators.

From the first population, 71 out of 73 chose to participate to form the *undergraduate* cohort. Each participant randomly received four scenarios. This provided around 23 responses to each scenario. From our second population we received 27 responses (a response rate of over 50%), however eight of these declined as they did not consider themselves as innovators or able to comment on scenarios within the ICT context. The biographical data of the 19 who completed the questionnaire are given in Table 2. It can be seen that the population is much older, predominantly only English speakers (one Chinese speaker and three of European heritage). Of these 19, 9 were identified as innovators, six as intermediate, and four as novices. Each participant randomly received five of the 12 scenarios. Thus we received a total of 6-9 responses from all three cohorts for any one scenario. With such small numbers for each individual scenario, qualitative analysis would not yield statistically significant results. To determine if differences and patterns of responses could be found between our cohorts we manually compared each scenario-answer option combination using diagrams such as the ones shown in Figure 3. To assist with interpretation of the patterns and position our findings within the current literature on creativity and innovation, we refer back to some of the characteristics of innovators mentioned in an earlier section.

FINDINGS

In this section we will demonstrate the analysis technique introduced above and describe the patterns that emerged by working through one scenario in detail, scenario 4. This will lead into a characterization of the responses of the four cohorts in general.

Scenario 4 (see Figure 1), obviously raises some ethical issues ranging from individual conscience to business and professional ethics.

Figure 3. Scenario 4, answer option 7: "Hire some 'psychologists' to say that they have proved that the game doesn't cause violent tendencies in the people who play it. Rather it causes them to show an admirable concern for their fellow man."

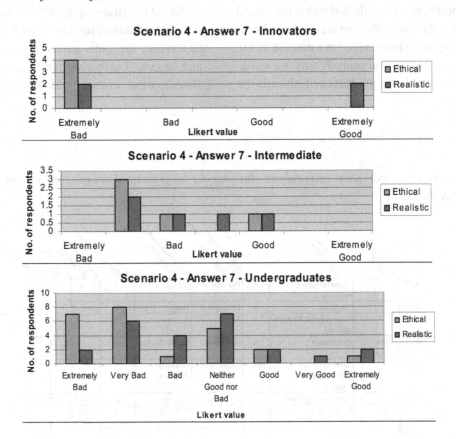

As a real case from an innovator's experience, we have not created it to push any buttons or test any preconceptions. As noted previously, most of our scenarios were not so sensational but the example reveals a pattern we found in other less emotive scenarios. We will work through each of the answer options for scenario four, discussing the preferences of each cohort toward each response from an ethical and realistic point of view. For this scenario, only three of the four cohorts are represented: innovators (4), intermediate (6) and undergraduate (24). In general, what is uncovered is a tendency for the innovators to be decisive

and extreme in their decision-making, the intermediates to be polarised more centrally and the undergraduates to be spread across the options. The answer options are given in Table 1.

As can be seen in Table 3 for scenario 4, all responses, except for answer options 3 and 4, showed the same tendency overall towards being positive (good) or negative (bad) towards an answer option regardless of the cohort. The mean and median response for each cohort is shown to reveal the strength of the response. Split is used to express an (almost) equal mix of good and bad responses. In some cases, even though the mean/median may be 4.0 (the neutral position), we have identified the trend for the non-neutral responses. For example, in Figure 4 we see that the undergraduate group show a preference towards bad rather than good (ethically and realistically), but the large number of neutral responses has resulted in a median of 4.0. If we relied on statistical analysis only, we would conclude that the undergraduate and ethically the intermediate cohorts showed no preferences in either direction.

We see that option 2 is the most strongly preferred realistic option of the innovators. This is in fact what the producers of the game did and as a result, the game gained a lot of popularity and success. Further we note that option 2 was also the most strongly ethically rejected option

Table 2. Enterprise workshop respondents showing the biographical details for three of the cohorts involved in the study

Age	LOTE	Current Occ.	# Subordinates	Emp. type	Highest Qual.	Yrs. Innov. Exp.	# Patents	# Awards	Startup Co.
25-29		Manufacturing engineer	1	Permanent	B.Eng.	0			
30-34		Engineer	0	Permanent	Hons.	0			
30-34		Demand and Business Analyst	0	Permanent	B.Comm.	0			
30-34	Swiss-German	Researcher	0	contract	Dr. Sc. Techn.	6			N
35-39		State Manager (Construction company)	16-20	Permanent	Graduate Diploma	0			N
35-39		Venture Capitalist	0	Permanent	Masters	3 to 5	1 to 2		Y
35-39	Dutch	Researcher	0	Contract	PhD Comp. Sc.	6	1		N
40-44		None			B.Sc.(Hons) B.Ec.(Hons)	0			Y
40-44		Training Facilitator	0	Permanent	Bachelors	0			N
40-44		Solicitor	3 to 5	Permanent	Hons.	0			N
40-44		Business Advisor	0	Contract	Masters	6 to 10			N
40-44		Engineer	3	Pemanent	Ph.D.	7	2	2	Y
40-44		Farmer/Grazier	0-2	Permanent	H.S.C.	20	2	1	
45-49		Principal and Consultant	0	Contract	Masters	0			Y
45-49		R&D Manager	>20	Permanent	Masters	6 to 10		>10	N
55-59		Professor	0	Permanent	Doctorate	11 to 20			N
60-64	Hungarian	Senior Reearch Director, Market Research Company	0	Permanent	Doctorate	a lot			N
60-64		Business Development Executive	0	Permanent	Doctorate	a lot	a lot		N
65-69	Chinese	Consultant	0	Permanent	Doctorate	a lot			Y
70+		Venture Capitalist	6 to 10	Permanent	Masters	a lot			Y

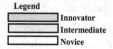

Legend
Innovator
Intermediate
Novice

Table 3. Mean, median and differences between the responses for each cohort for Scenario 4

Mean Median	Innovator			Intermediate			Undergraduate			Difference Innovator vs. Intermediate		Difference Innovator vs. Undergraduate	
	Ethical	Realistic	Diff	Ethical	Realistic	Diff	Ethical	Realistic	Diff	Ethical	Realistic	Ethical	Realistic
Scenario 4 – 1st Option	Good	Bad		Split	Bad		XGood	Bad		-1.3	-0.7	-0.5	-0.5
	5.5	3.5	-2.0	4.2	2.8	-1.4	6.0	3.0	-3.0	-2.5	0	+0.5	0
	6.5	3.0	-3.5	4.0	3.0	-1.0	7.0	3.0	-4.0				
Scenario 4 – 2nd Option	Bad	Good 5.25		Bad	Good		Bad	Good		+1.35	-0.25	+0.75	-0.25
	2.25	6.5	3.0	3.6	5.0	1.4	3.0	5.0	2.0	+3	-1.5	+1.0	-2.5
	1.0		5.5	4.00	5.0	1.0	2.0	4.0	2.0				
Scenario 4 – 3rd Option	Split	Good 4.75		Good	Good		Split	Good		+0.75	-0.35	0	-0.35
	4.0	5.0	.75	4.6	4.4	-0.2	4.0	4.4	0.4	0	-1.0	0	-1.0
	5.0		0.	5.0	4.0	-1.0	5.0	4.0	-1.0				
Scenario 4 – 4th Option	Xgood	Xgood		Good	Bad		Good	Bad		-1.9	-1.45	-2.5	-1.25
	6.5	5.25	-1.2	4.6	3.8	-0.8	4.0	4.0	0	-2	-1.0	-3.0	-1.0
	7.0	5.0	-2.0	5.0	4.0	-1.0	4.0	4.0	0				
Scenario 4 – 5th Option	Xbad	Bad		Bad	Bad		Bad	Split		+1.25	-0.4	+0.25	0
	2.75	4.0	1.2	3.4	3.6	0.2	3.0	4.0	1.0	+1.5	0	-0.5	0
	2.5	4.0	1.5	4.0	4.0	0	2.0	4.0	2.0				
Scenario 4 - 6th Option	bad	bad		Split	Bad		Bad	Bad		+0.5	-0.3	+0.5	+0.5
	3.5	3.5	0.5	4.0	3.2	-0.8	4.0	4.0	0	+1	0	+1.0	+1.0
	3.0	3.0	0	4.0	3.0	-1.0	4.0	4.0	0				
Scenario 4 - 7th Option	Xbad	Split		Bad	Bad		Bad	Bad		+1.8	-0.8	+1.6	-0.5
	1.0	4.0	3.0	2.8	3.2	0.4	2.6	3.5	0.9	+1	-1.0	+1.0	-0.5
	1.0	4.0	3.0	2.0	3.0	1.0	2.0	3.5	1.5				

by the innovators, with a mean difference of 3.0 and a median difference of 5.5 between the ethical and realistic responses. Overall, the innovators appear more willing to do the opposite to what they believe is right, though in other cases they seem to treat the two options as indistinguishable, as in answer options 3 and 6.

On our 7-point Likert scale, one indicates all participants selected extremely bad and seven indicates all participants thought the response was extremely good. Each row shows the results for each option for scenario 4 separated into columns by cohort. The ethical and realistic columns within each cohort first show the overall response (e.g., good or bad) followed below by the mean and the median response below that. The diff column for each cohort shows the difference between the ethical and realistic result to reveal the extent of disagreement within each cohort between their ethical and realistic responses. The final two columns reveal the differences between the mean and median responses by innovators compared to the other two cohorts for each option for scenario 4.

From the 7 answer options three main patterns of responses have occurred:

1. Extreme responses by the innovators (30/56[1] responses either extremely good or extremely bad, only 9/56 responses were neutral), reserved responses of intermediates (only 1 of the 70 responses was extremely bad or good, 22/70 responses were neutral) and a mix and spread responses of novices (80/336 extreme, 65/336 neutral). Such a pattern can be seen in Figure 3 and was evidenced in answer options 1, 2, 5, 7 and to some degree in answer option 4.

2. Across all scenarios, differences between ethical and realistic responses were larger for innovators; followed by undergraduates, intermediate, and novices. For example, see Table 3.

3. Some answer options elicited an identical response to the answer option from an ethical and realistic perspective for our innovators. This pattern can be seen in Figure 4 and was evidenced in answer options 6 and 3 to a lesser extent.

When asked, "What stage(s) of the Innovation process do you think the solution to this scenario would fall under," all of our four innovators chose the *realization* stage of innovation. Our intermediates or budding innovators were more divided in their opinions, varying from *realization* (3 intermediates), *opportunity recognition* (1 intermediate) and *idea generation* (1 intermediate). Of the 26 in the undergraduate cohort who answered scenario 4 (remembering they were randomly assigned), 24 provided an opinion on the stage of innovation development they felt the scenario was at. Overwhelmingly, *realization* was most commonly chosen (by 16 of the undergraduates). *Opportunity recognition* was next most popular

(but only by 5 of the undergraduates). *Idea generation* and *development* were each chosen by only four of the undergraduates. What is interesting is that the undergraduates have behaved somewhat similarly to the recognized innovators, with the intermediates the least decisive in their opinions as to the stage of innovation development.

Our recognized innovators provided no further suggestions for dealing with scenario 4. While we had hoped for their suggestions given that we are dealing with the final phase of realization and the fact that the innovators tended to be the more senior people and thus time poor, this is not so surprising. However, one of our intermediates was enthusiastic, providing a number of extra

Figure 4. Scenario 4, answer option 6—"Put out a bunch of family-friendly G rated games to take the attention off the game in question."

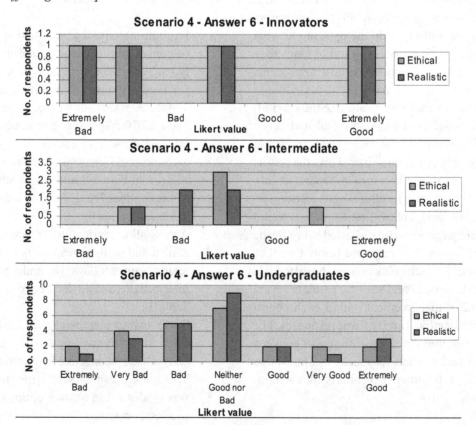

responses. The first of these was "Go for it! The bad publicity may spike demand for the game. If retailers do not stock it[,] sell it over the Web. Maybe put out a bit of viral marketing to drive sales." To which this 40-44 year old male, felt ethically extremely bad, but realistically quite good about it. Another suggestion by this individual was to "Take the game of[f] the shelves and recall existing ones, offering people their money back or [a] credit voucher for other games from the company. Take out ad[vertisement]s in the press and send out press releases." To which he ethically felt extremely positive about, but realistically only just positive about. And finally, the closely related but extended suggestion of "Sack[ing] the people responsible for the decision to go ahead with this game. Take the game of[f] the shelves and recall existing ones, offering people their money back or [a] credit voucher for other games from the company. Take out ad[vertisement]s in the press and send out press releases." To which he felt both ethically and realistically only just positive about such a suggestion. Our undergraduate cohort was less vocal in their suggestions, but one 21 year old Farsi speaking female suggested "Apologiz[ing] publicly. Pull [the] item off shelf and bring out a modified version, abusing the advertising that is already coming your way for free." To which the undergraduate concerned felt the idea was ethically a very good and realistically an extremely good idea.

We actually found that the intermediate cohort as a whole were more dissimilar to the innovators than individuals within the undergraduate or novice cohort. This may indicate that some of the undergraduates and novices are likely to become successful innovators further along in their careers and that the intermediates primarily represent people who have already had the opportunity in terms of number of years in the work force to become innovators if they had had the ability and/or inclination to do so. In fact, many of the participants in this category were in related but support type roles such as patent attorneys and venture capitalists. It is interesting to note that years of experience, dealing with innovations does not qualify someone as an innovator and that intrinsic motivation and innate skills are also necessary.

RECOMMENDATIONS FOR IDENTIFYING INNOVATORS

Due to the small sample size and the single study, we are cautious in claiming that our findings extrapolate to other populations and across knowledge domains. Also, since we are dealing with knowledge usage related to innovation and knowledge is contextual, we selected case studies and chose to interview innovators from the ICT domain, however few of the respondents from the second population had a background in ICT. We had originally planned to separate our dataset into ICT and non-ICT people, but decided against this as it would have reduced the numbers even further and made the dataset unusable. However, it does not appear that the innovators or intermediates with an ICT background behaved differently to those not in ICT. This is in keeping with studies which have shown that people who are street smart in one domain tend to be savvy in other domains of endeavor (Sternberg et al., 1995; Wagner & Sternberg, 1985) and is also consistent with the view below of innovators as having general (Adair, 1990) and broad interests (Amabile, 1996). With these caveats in mind let us consider the potential of the instrument for identifying and developing innovators and how our findings compare to the characterizations of innovators in the literature.

According to Kanter (1997), innovators exhibit: comfort with change, clarity of direction, thoroughness, participative management style, persuasiveness, persistence, and discretion. Roffe (1999) based on the findings of Quinn (1985) and Adair (1990) compiled the following set of attributes of innovators: need orientation (a combination of feeling a need to achieve together with a lack of resources to do so); ambivert (balance of extrovert tending more towards introvert); generalist (wide range of interests); experts and fanatics; higher intelligence; independence; independent judgment; vivid representation (can draw out what others have not recognized or observed); achievement (take interest in problems in which they feel they have a competitive advantage); curiosity (sustained); intuitive and imaginative; conscientiousness; creative tension (can hold conflicting ideas without premature resolution); long time horizons; low early costs (seek to decrease early risk); multiple approaches; flexibility and quickness; incentives (they can see the tangible benefits and personal rewards); availability of capital (persistent in seeking capital considering multiple sources).

Similar to Roffe, Amabile (1996) identifies the following personality traits: broad interests, independence of judgment, autonomy, set of creativity relevant skills such as divergent thinking and judgment suspension. For entrepreneurs defined as innovators who start their own business, McClelland (1987) identifies: desire to solve problems and the satisfaction that they were able to set and achieve their own goals; moderate risk takers based on assessment of alternatives; need for recognition and feedback on their success; and tolerance for ambiguity, similar to Adair's (1990) "creative tension." Mintzberg and Waters (1982) talk about "controlled boldness" where the entrepreneur carefully researches the options and then takes a decision.

We find the characteristics offered in Schweizer's (2004) novelty-generation model (NGM) particularly useful as they recognize that different characteristics are needed at different phases of the innovation cycle. Schweizer's (2004) *novelty-seeking* phase requires curiosity, excitability, impulsiveness, easily bored, disinhibition, and proactivity. The next phase, *creativity*, has two subphases, novelty finding, and novelty producing. Personal traits required in novelty finding

include divergence, self-confidence, openness, memory/low LI, attention, and egocentricism. Novelty producing requires: self-confidence, perseverance, assertiveness, memories/skills, egocentrism, and risk-taking. The final phase is *innovative performance*, which requires: self-confidence, perseverance/assertiveness, proactivity, extroversion, and competitiveness.

The purpose of the study reported was not to test whether these various attributes were held by our innovators. If this had been our goal we would have employed the various psychometric tests available and would have created scenarios, which embody these personality traits. Instead we seek to use these characterizations as a means of interpretation, validation and exploration of the responses. Many of the characteristics were not or could not be tested through our scenarios, for example thoroughness, higher intelligence, ambivert, experts and fanatics, vivid representation, low early costs and creative tension. However, a number of the characteristics were evident in our innovators. For example, the extreme responses of the innovators is consistent with innovators possessing clarity of direction, self-confidence, assertiveness, risk-taking, and possibly independent judgment. Other elements evidenced by the innovators' responses include: comfort with change, thoroughness, participative management style, persuasiveness, persistence, discretion, need orientation, independent judgment; achievement; curiosity; conscientiousness; creative tension; long time horizons; incentives, availability of capital. While not the case for scenario 4, the ability of our innovators to offer alternative responses to other scenarios and new scenarios indicates their ability to be imaginative; consider multiple approaches and respond to situations in a flexible and quick manner and was not evidenced to the same extent by the other cohort.

The patterns of behavior that we found in our data showing differences between the innovators and other cohorts encourages us to believe that the scenario-based approach can be used to identify innovators. Further, our intended implementation of the instrument would be for scenarios to be developed within an organization and completed by the identified innovators, and possibly by others to allow the contrast to emerge. The instrument would be used during the recruitment phase to identify whether the applicant responded similarly to the other innovators. Responses may not necessarily be the same; they may in fact take the alternate extreme point of view or suggest completely opposite or original solutions. What is expected is that similar patterns of behavior would be demonstrated, for example, taking an extreme view, suggesting alternatives or responding the same or differently from an ethical or realistic point of view. As we discuss in future work, it is our goal to develop algorithms that will detect the innovators patterns and then determine the distance between applicants' responses and the innovators patterns.

RECOMMENDATIONS FOR DEVELOPING INNOVATORS

We see that the approach may also have a role in identifying and developing innovators that are already working for an organization. As companies increasingly realize that their personnel are their most valuable asset, the desire to grow employees is becoming a greater priority. Methods for developing innovative employees, includes mentoring programs, job rotation, performance systems and organized training events. Within these training programs, the following core activities need to be included: "needs identification; setting objectives; designing and delivering content, getting feedback and evaluation" (Roffe, 1999, p. 235).

We propose that the scenario approach can be used as a technique that identifies areas in which employees are performing like innovators and where there are shortcomings. By having scenarios that relate to each of the innovation phases and identifying which characteristics of

innovators are related to a particular scenario, we can build up a picture of what strengths can be exploited and rewarded and what weaknesses should be minimized. If we view the weakness as a risk, then risk management strategies can be employed. For example, the risk can be avoided by bringing in others with the skill or characteristic. Alternatively, the risk perhaps can be mitigated via some form of training or mentoring.

Getting the ideas of innovators accepted usually involves a champion. In a study involving 72 innovations in 39 companies, Howell (2005) found that organizations can be proactive in identifying and developing champions of innovation. Just as innovators themselves have been characterized, champions of innovation can use their personal internal and external networks to hunt out ideas and opportunities, tie the innovation to the organization goals, convey confidence, enlist support of key stakeholders, and be persistent in the face of opposition (Howell, 2005). While it is conjecture at this stage, we would like to explore whether our approach could be used to identify an intermediate cohort of innovation supporters who could be assisted in their important roles as potential mentors and champions.

FUTURE TRENDS

Taking our socially situated view of innovation, innovative individuals will only exist and flourish if the organizational climate permits. We are increasingly seeing restructuring of organizations to foster an innovation culture (Mintzberg, 1991) (e.g., 3M and Tenix), in which employees are given the freedom, encouragement and support to think of new ways of innovating and improving all and any aspect of the organization. "Reduced—or a lack of—controls can free employees and give them a sense of empowerment. For example, the biggest motivator of the younger generations is a lack of control on them. This lack of control frees their minds, which allows them to engage in activities that bring about innovation" (Amar, 2004, p. 97). Knowledge sharing is also facilitated in open environments (Amar, 2004).

The link between knowledge management and innovation strategies is strong, with many approaches seemingly treating innovation as a particular type of knowledge to be nurtured. Knowledge management techniques that have and can be applied to the management of "ideas" and "innovation-type" knowledge include communities of practice (Lave & Wenger, 1991), storytelling (Snowden, 2002), intranets, video-conferencing, company encyclopaedias, LotusNotes™ databases, and e-mail sifting tools such as Tacitmail™ (Bennett & Gabriel, 1999) and the use of social software such as e-mail, WebLogs, and Wikis.

Factors affecting innovation within organizations may not be the same as factors affecting interorganizational innovation. Within an organization, particularly within a coherent group, innovation is often driven by functionality and efficiency concerns and requires less organizational support. In contrast, interorganizational and between group innovation requires greater management and control and appears to be more strongly affected by contextual and environmental factors such as economic influence and critical mass theories (Prescott & Conger 1995), thus requiring different strategies for innovation transfer. Fenwick (2003) found that innovative learning processes "involve multiple strategies and demand conditions of freedom, patience, support, and recognition" (p. 123). Similarly, Tatnall and Davey (2003) stress the importance of socio-technical factors, and have developed an ecological model of sustained innovation particularly focused on encouraging the adoption of innovation involving the introduction of ICT. These views tie in with the increasing emphasis on a more networked business world, the promotion and use of social networks and supporting approaches such as social network analysis (SNA) (Scott, 1991) and increased interest in social software as previously mentioned.

Innovation and, to a lesser extent, entrepreneurship is currently a hot topic. Every company wanting to remain competitive would at least claim to have innovation high on its agenda. When the hype and popularity of the concept wane in future years, to be replaced by a new hot topic, it will be easier to distinguish solid research and practice in this area though funding and organizational support may be less forthcoming.

CONCLUSION AND FUTURE WORK

The use of a survey-based instrument for identifying innovators provides a relatively simple means of capturing data about the individual, their past successes, experiences and current responses to scenarios related to innovation. Using the results of innovators as a measure against which to compare other respondents is also relatively straightforward by calculating various statistics using the responses to the Likert Scale questions. However, although the survey method typically lends itself to quantitative analysis, in the study reported we did not have sufficient numbers for each cohort and scenario to find statistically significant differences. Such a situation is likely to occur when we are capturing data from real innovators. We trade off small numbers with greater ecological validity. In this work we have taken an interpretivist rather than a positivist approach (Schwandt, 1988) as we do not seek to test a set of hypotheses or begin with any preconceived notions of expected behavior of entrepreneurs. Instead we qualitatively explored the data to see whether noticeable differences existed in the responses between the cohorts which emerged based on their biographical details, their responses to the self-assessment section and our validation of their achievements where their identity was known.

The end product is intended to be a straightforward instrument which is given to (potential) employees to see whether they are likely to be innovators and in which areas they may need further development. As this work is currently ongoing research, the goal of this chapter had been to describe patterns of behavior, and how they were found, which differentiate an innovator from others. This detailed analysis process would not be required when the validated instrument and approach is finalized but is included for scientific examination.

What we have not explored in this chapter is why a certain (type of) response may be preferred by an innovator and not by a non-innovator. To a large extent, trying to understand why a response has been preferred can raise more questions than they answer. This is because the scenarios tend to be rich and multi-faceted. While we have interest in understanding innovators better and what makes them different, the main goal of the approach is to identify who behaves like an innovator and thus has the potential to become one.

We briefly introduced Schweizer's (2004) novelty-generation-model. We have chosen to adopt the NGM as our framework for structuring the capture and application of the innovation knowledge inventory. In a future study, we will seek to capture scenarios from interviews with innovators that address each of the personality/cognitive traits and skills, individual behaviors, individual motivations, and the behavior of others. We have selected this model as it is well grounded in the theory and previous work on creativity and innovation and provides definitions and concepts which we believe can be applied to the development of an innovation knowledge inventory. The NGM is a biopsychosocial approach. The approach recognizes that at a genetic level some people are, for instance, more inclined to look for new problems and are able to come up with novel solutions. We will be working with clinical psychologist Schweizer on developing our framework.

Further, we intend to compare our approach to the key psychometric approaches offered for innovation testing. Following the NGM,

through personality testing of innovators we will be identifying the individual's personality type, degree of novelty seeking, creativity and innovative type behavior. This further involves determining whether different combinations of traits (e.g., "conscientiousness," "agreeableness," etc.) map onto various phases of the creativity process (the innovation cycle). A pilot study, followed by a full study, will be conducted in 2007 using established personality measures to identify "natural innovators," as measured by "objective" creativity outcomes. The personality measures will also be compared with the scenario outcomes to see whether the personality measures contribute any predictive validity here. This, in itself, is something novel. The general aim would be to identify which measures (or subsets thereof) are most appropriate at the various phases of innovation and be the basis of providing tools for industry in terms of predicting potential innovative candidates. In 2008/2009, to provide a complete *innovator model*, which incorporates the biological side of creativity and innovation, we will be conducting neuroimaging. A selection of approximately 20 participants identified as high and low creative individuals will undertake fMRI imaging whilst doing creativity measures designed for use in fMRI scanners.

Once we have developed and validated our revised innovation inventory of scenarios and personality/creativity tests, we intend to adapt and extend the tool to allow the scenarios to be randomly assigned to potential and existing employees so that it can be used to identify individuals, and to what extent, they behave similarly to the identified innovators. We will need to devise various algorithms to determine acceptable ranges of behavior and incorporate the use of weightings to allow some scenarios to be more or less important in generating a score. A similar approach will be needed to handle scores to the personality tests. For personnel selection, the goal would be to provide an innovation index/score ranking applicants to assist with the selection process. The tool may be extended to allow other details regarding other selection criteria to be included to make the process more streamlined. For training purposes, algorithms will be developed which will provide scores indicating what knowledge is currently lacking in the individual and to propose a training programme for the individual. The ultimate goal is a comprehensive technique for profiling and identifying innovators. As in the study reported in this chapter, we intend to conduct a new study primarily with innovators from the ICT domain, however as part of our study we will include some participants from outside ICT to determine the general applicability of the approach to innovators and entrepreneurs in general.

ACKNOWLEDGMENT

Thanks to Meredith Taylor our hard-working research assistant, Prof. Gordon Bell and all of our research participants. This work is partially funded via a Macquarie University Safety Net Grant.

REFERENCES

Adair, J. (1990). *The challenge of innovation.* London: Kogan Page.

Amabile, T. M. (1983). *The social psychology of creativity.* Berlin, Heidelberg, New York: Springer.

Amabile, T. M. (1996). *Creativity in context.* Boulder, CO: Westview Press.

Amar, D. A. (2004). Motivating knowledge workers to innovate: A model integrating motivation dynamics and antecedents. *European Journal of Innovation Management, 7*(2), 89-101.

Andrianopoulos, C. (2001). Determinants of organizational creativity: A literature review. *Management Decision, 39*(10), 834-840.

Baumol, W. J. (1993). *Entrepreneurship, management and the structure of payoffs.* Cambridge MA: MIT.

Bell, G., & McNamara, J. F. (1991). *McHigh-Tech ventures: The guide for entrepreneurial success.* New York: Perseus Books Publishing L.L.C.

Bennett, R., & Gabriel, H. (1999). Organizational factors and knowledge management within large marketing departments: An empirical study. *Journal of knowledge management, 3*(3), 212-225.

Burns, T., & Stalker, G. M. (1994). *The management of innovation,* Tavistock, 1961, 3rd Ed, Oxford University Press, Oxford.

Carneiro, A. (2000). How does knowledge management influence innovation and competitiveness? *Journal of Knowledge Management, 4*(2), 87-98.

Cottrill, K. (1998). Reinventing innovation. *Journal of Business Strategy, 19*(2), 47-51.

Fenwick. (2003). Innovation: Examining workplace learning in new enterprises. *Journal of Workplace Learning, 15*(3), 123-132.

Florida, R. (2002). *The rise of the creative class: And how it's transforming work, leisure, community, and everyday life.* New York: Basic.

Gergen, K. (1999). *An invitation to social construction.* Beverly Hills, CA: Sage.

Gibb, A. A. (1996). Entrepreneurship and small business management: Can we afford to neglect them in the twenty-first century business school? *British Journal of Management, 7*(4), 309-321.

Giunipero, L., Dawley, D., & Anthony, W. (1999). The impact of tacit knowledge on purchasing decisions. *Journal of Supply Chain Management.* Tempe; Winter (electronic).

Gloet, M., & Terziovski, M. (2004). Exploring the relationship between knowledge management practices and innovation performance. *Journal of*

Manufacturing Technology Management, 15(5), 402-409.

Gough, H. (1981). Studies of the Myers-Briggs type indicator in a personality assessment research institute. The *4th National Conference on the Myers-Briggs Type Indicator,* Stanford University, July 1981, CA.

Hamel, G., & Prahalad, C. K. (1989). Strategic intent. *Harvard Business Review, 67,* 63-76.

Holmes, D., Hughes, K., & Julian, R. (2003). *Australian sociology: A changing society.* Sydney: Pearson.

Howell, J. M. (2005). The right stuff: Identifying and developing effective champions of innovation. *The Academy of Management Executive, 19*(2), 108-119.

Ibrahim, A. B., & Soufani, K. (2002). Entrepreneurship education and training in Canada: A critical assessment. *Education + Training,* 44(8/9): 421-430.

Kanter, R. M. (1997). *Rosabeth Moss Kanter on the frontiers of management.* Boston: Harvard Business Press.

Kirton, M. (2001). Adaptors and innovators: Why new initiatives get blocked. In J. Henry (Ed.), *Creative management* (2nd ed, pp. 169-180). London: Cromwell Press Ltd.

Lave, J., & Wenger E. (1991). *Situated learning: Legitimate peripheral participation.* Cambridge UK: Cambridge University Press.

Leonard, D., & Sensiper, S. (1998). The role of tacit knowledge in group innovation. *California Management Review, 40*(3) (electronic).

McClelland, D. (1987). Characteristics of successful entrepreneur. *The Journal of Creative Behavior, 21*(3), 219-233.

McLeod, R., & Winsor, B. (2003). *Entrepreneurship case studies: 3M.* Scottish Institute for Enterprise and Napier University Edinburgh. Retrieved from http://www.sie.ac.uk/UserFiles/File/3m.pdf

Mintzberg, H. (1991). The innovative organization. *The Strategy Process: Concepts, Contexts, Cases.* 2nd Edn, Prentice Hall, Englewood Cliffs, NJ, pp. 731-746.

Mintzberg, H., & Waters, J. (1982). Tracking strategies in an entrepreneurial firm. *Academy of Management Journal, 25*(3), 465-499.

Quinn, J. B. (1985). Managing innovation: Controlled chaos. *Harvard Business Review, 63*(3), 73-84.

Peters, T. J. (1997). *The circle of innovation.* London: Hodder and Stoughton.

Polkinghorne, D. (1988). *Narrative knowing and the human sciences.* New York: SUNY Press.

Prescott, M. B., & Conger, S. A. (1995). Information technology innovations: A classification by it locus of impact and research approach. *Data Base Advances, 26*(2-3), 20-41.

Rae, D. (2004). Entrepreneurial learning: A practical model from the creative industries. *Education + Training, 46*(8/9), 492-500.

Richards, D., & Busch, P. (2003). Acquiring and applying contextualised tacit knowledge. *Journal of Information and Knowledge Management, 2*(2), 179-190.

Roberts, B. (1988). Managing invention and innovation. *Research Technology Management, 31*(1), 1-19.

Roffe, I. (1999). Innovation and creativity in organizations: A review of the implications for training and development. *Journal of European Industrial Training, 23*(4/5), 224-237.

Schwandt, T. (1998). Constructivist, interpretivist approaches to human inquiry. In N. Denzin & Y. Lincoln (Eds.), *The landscape of qualitative research.* Beverly Hills, CA: Sage.

Schweizer, T. S. (2004). *An individual psychology of novelty seeking, creativity, and innovation.* RIM Ph.D. Series, 48.

Simonton, D. K. (1981). Creativity in western civilization: Intrinsic and extrinsic causes. *American Anthropologist, 83*(3), 628-630.

Snowden, D. (2002). Narrative patterns: Uses of story in the third age of knowledge management *Journal of Information and Knowledge Management, 00,* 1-5.

Sternberg, R., Wagner, R., Williams, W., & Horvath, J. (1995). Testing common sense. *American psychologist, 50*(11), 912-927.

Swan, J., & Newell, S. (2000). *Linking knowledge management and innovation.* Paper presented at the European Conference on Information Systems (pp. 591-598). ECIS, Vienna.

Tatnall, A., & Davey, B. (2003). ICT and training: A proposal for an ecological model of innovation. *Education Technology and Society, 6*(1), 14-17.

Thomas, J. B., Watts Sussman, S., & Henderson, J. C. (2001). Understanding "strategic learning": Linking organizational learning, knowledge management, and sensemaking. *Organization Science, 12*(3), 331-45.

Van de Ven, A. H., Angle, H., & Poole, M. S. (2000). *Research on the management of innovation: The Minnesota studies.* New York: Oxford University Press, August, 2000 (paperback) Originally printed 1989.

Van Yperen, N. W. (2003). Task interest and actual performance: The moderating effects of assigned and adopted purpose goals. *Journal of Personality and Social Psychology, 85*(6), 1006-1015.

Wagner, R., & Sternberg, R. (1985). Practical intelligence in real world pursuits: The role of tacit knowledge. *Journal of personality and social psychology, 49*(2), 436-458.

Zampetakis, L. A., & Moustakis, V. (2006). Linking creativity with entrepreneurial intentions: A structural approach. *The International Entrepreneurship and Management Journal, 2*(3), 413-428.

ENDNOTE

[1] 4 innovators x 7 answer options x 2 responses (ethical and realistic).

Chapter XXII
International Dimensions of Innovation in Technology

Valerie S. Perotti
Rochester Institute of Technology, USA

ABSTRACT

This chapter develops a set of seven dimensions, which may be applied to each sovereign nation as a guide to allow for systematic consideration and comparison of opportunities and challenges across borders. Under the assumption that innovation itself requires a unique set of skills or opportunistic settings, the chapter then explores each dimension's applicability to situations particularly associated with innovation in technology. Using current research and examples from world business, the chapter moves to a brief discussion of projected future developments in the field and related research needs.

INTRODUCTION

"There is no reason anyone would want a computer in their home." (Ken Olson, president of Digital Equipment Corp. 1977, speaking to the World Future Society and quoted in TIME magazine.)

World businesses may have been slow to recognize the potential for global impact through information technology, and, while the arrival of the microchip and the earliest desktop computers was derided by some and heralded by others, few today would deny the significance of technology in the hands of the masses.

The lifeblood of technology is innovation, and the greatest growth in research and development spending today is taking place not in the United States or Europe but in China and India (Jareszelski, Dehoff, & Bordia, 2006). While, admittedly, that spending may be coming from developed nations' purses, the decision-making as to where, how, and why to innovate is leading the world to the east.

Peering into the chaotic maelstrom where the vortices of technology, innovation, and globalization brew the future is vital. Even the smallest entrepreneurial organization must learn its elements. At the same time, the work of understanding it is challenging, frightening, and hopeful. The microchip—itself an innovation of as-yet-unknown proportion—powers the world wide engine and enables the interaction of societies and peoples known to one another only through myth and legend before its invention. The three notions—globalization, innovation, technology— are inextricably intertwined. This chapter aims to explore the contextual elements that enhance or inhibit fruitful interaction among the three.

BACKGROUND

Innovation. Simply put, one might define innovation by its Latin derivation: *in novare*—to make new. Its simplicity belies the potential uses and distortions of the term, however. As an example, Lotte Tarso, in her book, *Innovation in the Making* (2001) identifies and distinguishes among four types of innovation:

1. **Incremental:** Innovations are improvements of processes, products, and methods, often found by technicians or employees during their daily work.
2. **Radical:** Novel, surprising, and different approach or composition.
3. **Social:** Spring from social needs, rather than from technology, and are related to new ways of interaction.
4. **Quantum**: Refers to the emergence of qualitatively new system states brought by small incremental changes.

For purposes of this chapter, innovation is defined as the process of creating something new which has a significant result—whether within or outside of some prior context. This definition would include both process and product innovations, but would exclude small modifications of process or product. The "innovation" here specified must be genuinely "new." As such, the definition appreciates the remarks of Alan Greenspan (2004), former Chairman of the U.S. Federal Reserve Board to the Federal Reserve Bank in Chicago: "Innovation, by its very nature, is not forecastable."

Technology. Somehow, it seems fitting to turn to the internet and its ubiquitous "Wikipedia" for a definition of technology, which is at once comprehensive and well suited to the goals of this chapter:

(Gr. technologia (τεχνολογία) < techne (τέχνη) "craft" + logos (λόγος); "reason") Technology predates both science and engineering. It may be defined as: "Solutions for real human problems by the development and application of tools, machines, materials, goods, or information in the form of skills, knowledge, processes, blueprints, plans, diagrams, models, formulae, tables, engineering designs, specifications, manuals, or instructions."

This definition provides the opportunity to stress that technology is not a derivative of the 20th and 21st centuries. Quite the contrary, as pointed out by Michael Bordo, international business itself began when trade across distances was facilitated by ships—a form of technology that required no microchips!

The definition is adopted here also because it omits the usual emphasis upon commercial needs and applications of innovation, thus recognizing the possibility for innovative enhancement of the quality of life as well as economic success. And, although many would infer that technology speaks specifically to information or communication-related developments, this definition would clearly include all forms of human solutions such as biotechnology, energy technology and, yes, those technologies yet to come.

National Environments. With recent weather-related catastrophes such as global warming, the Indonesian *tsunami* and the earthquake in Sumatra, public attention has shifted to the earth's environment and ecology as a matter of grave concern. Hence, the word "environment" carries contemporary implications that it might not otherwise have had. This study does not deal with this definition of "environment."

Rather, in this study, the word has a very different and specific application. Here it is used to indicate that complex of factors, which surround and impact the organization in a given time and place. An organization's environment impacts its ability to locate the resources it needs to survive, the capacity it has to produce its product or service, and the rewards it is able to retrieve for its stakeholders. If one considers one organization, located in one place, at a given time, the environmental factors affecting its processes are relatively easy to identify.

One extreme example (http://www.st-mike.org/medicine/bs.html) that might prove fruitful is the work of the surgeon. In the late 15th century, following the devastation of the plague in Europe, peripatetic barbers routinely practiced the healing arts including surgery. There were no major "hospitals," and the primary mode of care was the setting on of leeches and blood-letting, premised upon the belief that destructive elements or "humors" in the blood could be removed through such practice. Thus, a man could have his hair cut, beard trimmed, and fever cured at one visit from the barber. Since such practitioners traveled to ply their trade, the availability of "patients" or "customers" would be exhausted in one town and the barber would move on to the next. The barbering profession was formalized through guilds and royal recognition, with a special barber-surgeon serving each European royal household.

It took some 200 years for pressure to end the endorsement of such practice to come from the emerging group of physicians who believed that education in the physical arts was needed for an individual to truly "cure" the sick. Subsequently, royal households disenfranchised their barber-surgeons and "accreditations" and endorsements were withdrawn. With the establishment of The Royal College of Surgeons in London, the era of the barber-surgeon had effectively ended.

Little imagination is required to see the barber-surgeon as a product of the environment. Plague—customers—royal endorsement—"technology" (leeching)—politics—education. Without these factors, the "profession" could not have emerged and then been eliminated. Today's environment for surgical professionals bares the marks of many of the same environmental factors—politics, education, technology, and more.

The Maelstrom: Innovation and Technology Vortices. As noted above, international business itself is attributable to technology—whether through primitive ships that facilitated trade across rivers or through photons that today drive millions of cell phone conversations around the world. But technology is attributable to innovation. Without "making something new," the tools enabling technological advance would not exist, And, finally, of course, innovation springs from the challenges of internationalization. Italy may claim pasta for its own, but Marco Polo would admit that he brought it home from the Middle Kingdom.

As Charles M. Vest, (1999) former president of Massachusetts Institute of Technology, described the challenges facing policy makers in this regard, innovation is no longer an isolated practice inside an isolated company. Rather,

We must think of it in terms of a global innovation system. The system is a chain of events that runs from the generation of new knowledge to the education of young men and women to do things with that knowledge, and ultimately, to the creation of new products, processes and services in the commercial workplace (p. 96).

Perhaps this intimate mutuality is best expressed by Narula (2003) when describing the dynamic interactions between technology and globalization. He makes the point that the two phenomena are continually evolving, both independently and mutually (he uses the term "co-evolving"). "The word 'concatenation' describes this well," he says. "It implies that technology and globalization are inextricably linked together, yet are not the same object" (p. 13). This chapter adopts Narula's insight with one exception: as demonstrated above, innovation, too, is co-evolving and concatenated with technology and globalization as it evolves.

With these observations in mind, this chapter aims to identify the forces at work in the waters circling the *maelstrom*—namely the unique characteristics of individual nations that support or inhibit innovation in technology. The hope, here, is that all manner of organizations—commercial or beneficent—may come to understand better the opportunities and challenges each nation brings and, in so understanding, make more known what is now unknown. With a set of concepts within which to frame the unknown, organizational visionaries may be able to find unique and opportunistic settings for enabling the innovation, which must characterize the evolving organization.

The environment. To continue and expand on the analogy, the forces in the turbulent waters surrounding the *maelstrom,* in fact, create the frenzy within, just as the various elements of the environment create the pressures on organizations and individuals to innovate in technology. Putting it naively, without demand for ever newer, faster, cheaper, smaller products, workers today would still be using four bit mainframes. Without infrastructure improvement, cell phones could not be the ubiquitous tools they have become.

The *maelstrom* is a system of interactions among elements in its environment, and "Comprehension of a system cannot be achieved without a constant study of the forces that impinge upon it" (Katz & Kahn, 1966).

Systems theorists like Katz et al. (1966) and Laurence and Lorsch (1967) have well established the fact that no successful organization stands in isolation, but rather must exchange information and resources with its environment to survive. "To the extent that an organization's ability to adapt to its outside environment is dependent on knowing and interpreting the external changes that are taking place, environmental scanning constitutes a primary mode of organizational learning" (Chun, 2001, p. 1).

Most recently, researchers have begun to study the synergistic interactions between organizations and their environments. Albers and Brewer (2003) explore the ecology of organizations with respect to innovation:

The evolution of the business environment to the business ecosystem results from companies working cooperatively with other organizations to support new products, satisfy customers, and create new market innovations. It is clear that organizations are becoming more aware of the benefits in their surrounding environment (p. 1).

The dimensions. Similarly, organizational theorists since the mid 1960's have broadly accepted that there are definable elements in the environments of organizations. While the lists may vary slightly, it is generally accepted that the following represent common dimensions of an organization's environment: competitive, economic, technological, political, legal, demographic, and socio-cultural (Hahm, 1993).

Since the development of the concept of "organizational environment," researchers have further refined and applied the notion to various business problems. Chesbrough (1999), for example, reported finding three specific environmental factors, which affect organizational ability to pursue innovation opportunities in the hard disk industry: technology, regulation, and markets.

While numerous studies have addressed such specific factors in international innovation, this study has uncovered no recent work that specifically and systematically addresses the environmental factors that would affect innovation in technology from an international point of view. The study, therefore, aims to suggest a rubric for exploring the unique characteristics which would enable or inhibit technological innovation across borders. The intention is to raise managerial awareness of a potential new source of information to facilitate choices and thus optimize innovative efforts by capitalizing on such assets that emerge primarily from the differences in national environments.

Business Models Have No Passports

To those who lack experience, crossing national boundaries to accomplish goals may seem relatively easy. Find a spot. Get a passport. Set up shop. But observing those major corporations who have failed or, at least, faltered at ventures overseas, one can begin to understand the complexity of such an effort.

General Electric in Hungary. When the opportunity presented itself in 1989, General Electric made a quick strategic decision to acquire Tungsram, a privatized Hungarian firm, hoping to improve sales in Europe where, in 1985, its market share was just about a third of Tungsram's 5 to 6%. Things did not go well. In the first two years after the purchase, Tungsram's sales plummeted.

eBay. On December 19, 2006, The *Wall Street Journal* announced that U.S.-based online auction house, eBay, would be departing China. Three reasons are cited. First, eBay lost significant market share to local, free rival *Taobao*. eBay's market share is dropping despite eliminating transaction fees in China. Finally, China is preparing new regulations limiting foreign ownership of companies operating online payment systems such as PayPal. Without a cooperative local partner, eBay was forced to withdraw.

These companies illustrate the outcomes incurred by organizations attempting to function successfully abroad. Success, in these cases,

means survival and profitability. Failure means not only the loss of potential market revenue but also the loss of "sunk costs" invested in the original move. In each case errors of judgment, miscalculation or lapses in research and preparation might be blamed.

In the following section, the seven dimensions identified by organizational theorists as described above are applied to national environments and applied, specifically, to innovation in technology. Subsequently the examples of Tungsram and eBay are used to explain and exemplify how the dimensions might be applied to an analysis of the national environment.

THE SEVEN DIMENSIONS

While a geographic border may present the tangible limits of a country's boundaries, less tangible dimensions differentiate it from its neighbors—whether those neighbors be "next door" or continents apart. Some of those dimensions are discernible. Good international attorneys can, often, learn the facilitating and inhibiting laws of a nation, which pertain to an organization.

More often, such dimensions are subtle and pervasive, perhaps not overtly acknowledged by the members of the nation. Indeed, the citizens may be entirely unaware of the uniqueness of these characteristics. As an example, Nigeria routinely appears at the bottom of indices gauging internal corruption (researched and published annually by "Transparency International"). While the process of paying or receiving bribes seems perfectly natural there, people outside Nigeria perceive it as "corrupt."

An Underlying Assumption. When multi-national organizations (MNCs) do business away from their home countries, the "foreign" company is a guest in the host country. Rights and privileges pertaining to nationals do not pertain to guests, while, at the same time, responsibilities of guests may be even greater than those of nationals.

Understanding and appreciating this notion may be facilitated by an understanding of these seven dimensions of national environments:

1. The political dimension
2. The socio-cultural dimension
3. The economic dimension
4. The competitive dimension
5. The legal and regulatory dimension
6. The communication dimension
7. The technological dimension

The reader will note that this study varies from the Hahm dimensions cited earlier. Hahn includes a dimension referred to as "demographic" which is excluded in this list. Meanwhile, this compilation adds a "communication" dimension. The rationale for these adjustments lies in the assumption that socio-cultural dimensions include demographics, while communication is so powerful an environmental force that it requires unique attention.

The political dimension. Components of the political context in a nation would include such matters as existing political structures and operations, locally differentiated structures and operations, stability or volatility in the national political scene and political risk.

Looking back to the General Electric situation in Hungary, one realizes that national politics has a role to play in GE's dilemma. The moment in time at which G.E. chose to purchase Tungsram was a cataclysmic one. Hungary was just emerging from a centralized communist government. While, admittedly, the purchase of the company was a bargain, the lack of preparation for this new environment created a naïve approach, which belied GE,'s other experience abroad.

"No nation on earth has an effective system for taking into account the profound effects that technologies exert on social and political structures" (Sclove, 1999). Many political leaders fear that globalization, facilitated and empowered by technology, "…undermines that national state" (Berger, 2000). While most would welcome the

transformative technologies that bring freedom from disease or hunger, the openness and speed of access that communication-related technologies offer threaten limits to power that could conceivably topple some political structures. Hence, political stratagems such as censorship, regulatory hurdles, or moralistic tirades by religious leaders may present obstacles that even the most persistent organization may grow tired of fighting.

The socio-cultural dimension. Why, one wonders, would the Chinese consumer choose *Taobao* instead of eBay for his or her auction transactions? Taobao is an upstart company, untested in the Chinese (or any) market compared to eBay. One answer might lie in the socio-cultural context.

A culture is that pattern of thought, speech, action, and artifacts which distinguishes one group or clan from another. Cultures emerge from deeply held values, which, in turn, are based on assumptions about the meaning of life, nature, and humanity. Cultures are learned and evolved over generations and permeate the society they characterize to such a level that it may be completely unaware that there are other ways of thinking.

Three important international business researchers characterize culture in this way:

- "The collective programming of the mind which distinguishes the members of one group or category of people from another" (Hofstede, 1991).

- "Culture is the way in which a group of people solves problems" (Trompenaars & Hampden-Turner, 1998).

The researchers have studied businesses in different national settings to try to establish the cultural parameters that differentiate one nation from another. While occasionally criticized, their results have been widely published and used in countless confirming research projects. Indeed, business decision-makers have turned to these thinkers to assist in business decision-making. Hofstede (pp. 251-420).

While an elucidation of the studies and the emergent variables far exceeds the scope of this chapter, it may be helpful to know that Hofstede identified four scales which he believes successfully differentiate one culture from another:

- **Individualism-collectivism:** The tendency of people to express concern for themselves and immediate family only as opposed to expressing concern or taking action on behalf of the group or clan. Collectivists tend to prefer working in groups or teams with reward and responsibility shared, while Individualists prefer individual work, reward, and responsibility.

- **Power distance:** "The extent to which less powerful members of institutions and organizations accept that power is distributed unequally"

- **Masculinity-femininity:** The extent to which a society seems to prefer "success, money and things," or "caring for others and the quality of life"

- **Uncertainty avoidance:** "The extent to which people feel threatened by ambiguous situations and have created beliefs and institutions that try to avoid these."

At the risk of great oversimplification, one might apply these characteristics to the problem of eBay in China. As a collectivist culture, the Chinese would naturally choose clan over outsider. Despite the obvious benefits of a tried and tested provider, the loyal Chinese would likely prefer a provider with a Chinese name and affiliation.

The Uncertainty Avoidance variable is, however, more relevant to the issue of innovation in technology. Where peoples "feel threatened" by the ambiguous or unknown, the "new" is not to be trusted.

In *An Exploratory Examination of the Influence of National Culture on Cross-National Product Diffusion*, authors explore how techno-logical innovation spreads throughout national cultures, and they identify cultural characteristics that affect countries' receptiveness to innovation (Dwyer, Mesak, & Hsu, 2005). The study suggests that innovations should be introduced first in countries that are high in collectivism (e.g., South Korea), short-term oriented (e.g., the United States), high in masculinity (e.g., Japan), and/or high in power distance (e.g., France). This would enhance the product's diffusion rate relative to that which would be found in individualist, long-term-oriented, low-masculinity, or low-power-distance cultures. Additional studies in this field are emerging and well warranted.

The socio-cultural context includes numerous other variables relevant to innovation. What, for example, is the penetration of education in the population? Is that education strong in relevant areas of technology? What are the population demographics? Is the population largely too young to be of immediate assistance? Too old to master new ways of doing things?

The economic context. Perhaps the best documented of the dimensions explored here, national economic profiles are available from numerous sources: *The Economist*, The World Bank, The United Nations—these are but a few of the sources which publish at least annually the economic statistics of most of the sovereign nations of the world. However, certain specific national characteristics seem to support or inhibit technological innovation.

Again, the Tungsram example looms large. A communist governmentally owned company would have promised lifetime employment to its employees and would have held company performance information closely. Employees would have seen the role of the employer as providing a livelihood (not making a profit). Employee-related costs would have been seen as serving the public good. Cutting such costs would have been deemed inimical to the people.

Transition from any strong, dominant economic approach to another is a complex and lengthy process. Even now, decades after the disruption of the socialist economies of the former Soviet Union, vestiges of those practices influence the conduct of business in its former members, despite their movement toward market economies. Melo, Denizer, and Gelb (1996) identified three stages in such transition through their research. Development of technology and innovation in such societies must consider the level of economic progress toward a market approach. If, for example, a corporation expected its management to understand and lead a profit-centered organization, it would need to assure itself that local managers clearly understood the relationship between costs and profits, as well as understanding the role of management in striving toward profitability.

Other economic issues requiring consideration include currency—how readily does the home country currency flow into the host country? How readily does the local currency transition to the host country? The strength of the local currency will determine how costly a product would ultimately become if manufactured there, for example.

More recently (2002-03), a study conducted by the Czech Statistical Office of Czech companies engaging in technological innovation of process or product, respondents were asked to indicate factors which inhibited innovation. Economic factors ranked first among the many that were identified. Both innovators and non-innovators indicated the following economic factors as the biggest barriers to innovation: lack of appropriate source of finance (33% of innovators, 38% of non-innovators), innovation costs too high (31% of innovators, 38% of non-innovators) and connected excessive perceived economic risks (20% of innovators, 25% of non-innovators). From the point of view of enterprises, economic factors were the main barrier to innovation

Other economic concerns that might be considered:

- **Currency stability.** Will this currency behave consistently enough to sustain technological development? Will it travel? How is it valued?

- **Discretionary spending.** If the product or service innovated is to be sold in the host country, are there enough consumers able to purchase?

- **Cost and quality of labor.** The dilemma here is: relatively uneducated workforces ease costs, but highly educated workforces are, by and large, a requirement for technological innovation in fields such as biotechnology or information technology.

The Competitive Dimension. Few would disagree that it is competition that drives the engine of business forward, and, thus, that technological innovation is a direct result of competition. However, competition, in this context, may foster or discourage technological innovation.

For example, competition at the macro level—that is, among nations—for technologically advanced business investment can differentiate between a fertile or sterile environment for innovation. As indicated earlier, some countries compete aggressively for such investment by offering regulatory support or financial incentives.

At the micro level, the organization must consider what, exactly, competes with the proposed product or service. In other words, if the innovation leads to the desired result—will anyone buy it? The proper question to ask, then, is what can/will consumers substitute for this product or service? An example might be super or "big box" markets.

In a nation where the average consumer has easy access to personal transportation, the idea of a one-stop location where everything from appliances to fresh carrots may be purchased seems reasonable. Self checkouts make the independent consumer's visit speedy and self-reliant. In a country where few super markets exist, it may be tempting to believe that developing a self-service big box market is an idea whose time has come. But it is possible that the competition is actually the local village with its small independent fishmonger and greengrocer. Consumers may prefer daily walks to small local shops for fresh food and socialization. Self-checking items may be abhorrent when that process would normally be handled by a grocer or butcher with whom one is personally acquainted or who maintains a day-to-day ledger to be reconciled once per month in cash.

The point here is that the enterprise must be open to the possibility of competitors who are not even in the same business. Who is a major competitor of local television in the U.K.? The local, family pub. What competes with MacDonald's in China? Street noodle hawkers.

The Legal-Regulatory Context. eBay's experience with China's changing regulations directly impacts profitability and, ultimately, the will to persist in the host country. While a company's attorneys (both at home and in the host country) may well understand an existing legal tenet, it is virtually impossible to anticipate a new one. Much depends on the relative ease with which one may come to know and understand the laws and regulations related to technological innovation. "Intellectual property, licensing, antitrust, trade, securities, privacy, and employment—these are some of the new laws of the competitive jungle. Today, you cannot innovate without understanding patent, copyright, and trade-secret law" (Downes, 2004).

A case in point is the fairly recent refusal (Broersma, 2005) of the European Union to adopt software patent regulations. After a series of iterated and reiterated versions of proposed legislation, EU legislators succumbed to pressure from EU software developers and open source enthusiasts to eliminate patent laws that would conform more to those in the U.S. or China. Hence, EU locals developing new software are essentially free of paying royalties for adaptations of the major corporate software that is protected in the U.S. Clearly, EU sites would be hospitable to innovation in software development that is built on or "borrows from" existing platforms (assuming no special profit to be made from the work), but not hospitable to truly new, blank page, innovative information technology development created for profit by non-European corporations.

To illustrate further, a sovereign nation may be a good example. Malaysia, a Southeast Asian country of complex history, determined in the early 1970s to enfranchise its people through economic development. The intent was communicated by then Prime Minister Mahathir in the form of "Vision 2020," a plan for the orderly and dramatic economic transformation of a people. Among the many steps proposed and implemented from that time to this is a legal and regulatory environment that is as accessible as the internet. By clicking on http://www.cmc.gov.my/ the potential investor anywhere in the world can reach the Malaysian Communication and Multimedia Commission where licensing, regulatory and much other relevant information can be found. Because the legal system is based on British Code Law, transacting business is relatively predictable for western nations. Indeed, the site emphasizes the interest of Malaysia's government in creating a regulatory environment where technological innovation can thrive.

This "open" approach to clearly stating and making accessible the internal legal and regulatory structure of a nation is considered "transparent." The transparent legal environment is accessible and navigable and, in Malaysia's case, consciously designed to attract and sustain the involvement of external investment. The opposite approach is referred to as "opaque." Investors interested in doing business in North Korea, for example, have incredible difficulty obtaining copies of or access to current laws and regulations. Faced with an "opaque" curtain, it would take a passionate and highly motivated investor to persist long enough to learn what needs to be done.

The Communication Dimension. While acknowledging the significance of language as a barrier to human and commercial interaction, it is equally important to note that, at a certain level of competence, innovators speak the same "language." The word "biotechnology" is "*biotekno-logia*" in Finnish, "*biotecnologia*" in Portugese and "*bioteknologi*" in Bahasa Indonesia. When innovation is being explored at the highly advanced level of "R&D" where only the most sophisticated and most educated interact, the enterprise may expect a certain level of mutual understanding no matter what the nations involved.

However, when such innovation is created or implemented through the hands of the layperson or the non-technical manager, communication (even in a common language) may become complicated by such issues as non-verbal proprieties. An example: in Islamic countries it is highly insulting to show the bottom of the shoe. In many other countries, the bottom of the shoe has no significance. In the U.S. resting one's feet on a desk or table suggest comfort, ease, and control of a situation. The bottom of the shoe is revealed inevitably. In Japan, it is incredibly rude to say, "no." It is much more likely that a refusal of a proposition would be greeted with a statement like, "we will see." Many a salesperson has spent useless hours awaiting a decision in a foreign country when he had already received one that went unrecognized.

Looking back at the cultural variables identified by Hofstede, power distance is relevant here. Where superiors and subordinates interact in high power distance cultures, communication is more likely to be top-down, command and control messaging. In low power distance cultures, where superiors and subordinates are essentially equal, communications will be free flowing. Suggestions for process or product innovation are much likelier to come from the low power distance employee (Hofstede, 1991).

Hall, (1976) one of the first to explore human factors in international business, identified two types of communication: high context and low context. Context is information surrounding a communication that supports and endorses a mes-

sage. In high context countries, messages may be implicit and augmented by the manner or setting in which the message is delivered. In low context cultures, messages are taken literally. Meaning is invested in the word or phrase, and little attention is paid to the context. Japan is considered by Hall to be a high context culture. The subtlety of a raised eyebrow may change the entire meaning of a message. The United States is considered a low context culture.

In a multi-country study of ERP systems: Von Eringen and Waarts (2003) report that low context cultures have a significantly higher innovation adoption rate than do high context cultures. They explain the readier penetration of business by technological innovation on the belief that low context managers rely more on rational, economic arguments. The content of message about the innovation seems more important than the manner or context of the communication.

The Technological Context. In most cases, innovation away from the home country must rely upon the readiness and hospitability of the host country technologically. Implicit here are several key issues: (1) The host country's technical infrastructure; (2) The penetration of technology in the population of the country; (3) The technical competence of the labor pool.

Technical infrastructure refers to reliable access to world networks at a reasonable rate of speed and cost. Penetration of technology refers to the number of general or institutional users of technology. Technical competence of the labor pool refers to the education about and experience with the various tools of technology. The Center for International Development at Harvard University publishes an annual Global Information Technology Report dealing with the technologically related characteristics of some 100 countries. Among characteristics identified are ratios of internet service providers, users per service provider, cell phone users compared to the general population statistics.

Once again, Malaysia serves as a positive example of a country, which has positioned its technological assets to support innovation in technology. In 1996, Prime Minister Mahathir launched the Multimedia Super Corridor.

15 kilometers wide and 50 kilometers long, the MSC is an infrastructure of high speed fiber backbone available to business and industry. At least 205 companies, including 29 MNCs such as Motorola Multimedia, Microsoft, Sun Microsystems, Reuters, and Oracle have joined the MSC. With a young, well-educated population of 20 million of which 42% are between the ages of 15 and 39, the talent is readily available. And perhaps one of the most important factors is that "the government is willing to be a guinea pig to test technology," says Govinathan Pillai, managing director of Sun Microsystems. Other initiatives include the establishment of the MSC Central Incubator, the introduction of venture capital funding and the provision of management support structure to nurture start-up IT and multimedia companies. Both initiatives are part of a program comprising research & development grants, marketing support and human resource development to catalyze the growth of a critical mass of local technopreneurs and small and medium-scale enterprises (Special Report, The Washington Times, April 28, 1999).

By grave contrast, in an article called "The Trouble with India," Hamm (2007) connects a profound deficit in physical infrastructure with India's comparatively small share of world wealth. He maintains that the advances made in information technology will not continue in a country where employees cannot get to their high tech jobs because of impassable roads and undrinkable water. He cites the case of Intel Corporation, which chose Vietnam over India as a chip assembly site. The reason given was the lack of a constant and reliable source of electricity. "The infrastructure deficit is so critical that it could prevent India from achieving the prosperity that finally seems within its grasp" (p. 50).

FUTURE TRENDS

To reiterate, Alan Greenspan remarked : "Innovation, by its very nature, is not forecastable." However, it is exciting to anticipate the potential when the world's researchers turn fuller attention to the issues raised in this chapter. When one considers that Hofstede's work in documenting cultural differences in business was first published in 1990, it is clear that investigations in this field are accelerating almost as rapidly as the rate of innovation.

Relatively recent in the process is the term, "open innovation"—companies seeking ideas, knowledge and technology outside themselves, often outside their core businesses in order create or implement new things. Examples include pharmaceutical company, Novartis, which brings in approximately 50% of its new molecules from universities and start-up alliances; in its aerospace division, Rolls-Royce has established strategic technology innovation relationships with more than 25 universities around the world (Innovare, 2007). Researchers will begin exploring the circumstances under which such open innovation may be harnessed, controlled and made to work for a given company without surrendering competitiveness. Further, researchers will begin to explore unique national assets which make one or another country an especially valuable source for open innovation.

"Creation Nets" are networks where hundreds or thousands of people from diverse settings collaborate to create new knowledge and to build on one another's work. Here one can visualize a boundless world where political boundaries are no longer discernible and differences among participants are only cultural or linguistic. Research in this area will yield insight as to how to optimize the dynamic interplay of structure and freedom to yield the best results.

As research becomes more sophisticated, it is to be expected that ever-finer points of difference will emerge that distinguish bio-innovation from info-innovation from nano-innovation and so on. One might envision matrices being developed whereby national uniqueness could be intersected with innovation uniqueness to help companies determine optimal locations for highly specialized work.

It is likely that the international innovation competitions which have begun to see fruition recently will continue to bring widely diverse minds to bear on common human problems. The $10 million X Prize competition will lead, eventually, to commercially viable manned space travel. As this approach to innovation begins to gather headway, data may be collected on the processes by which breakthroughs are attained. The very role of the competition itself needs to be examined as it suggests incentives for innovative achievement in different national cultures.

An important investigation must take place soon into the assets that the various countries bring to technological innovation. Those characteristics, which today may seem counterproductive to technological innovation may, with astute analysis, be seen to be facilitative and fruitful in some unique way. For example, a nation where "Uncertainty Avoidance" is high might be perceived as resistant to innovation, but may, in fact, be an ideal location for the profoundly repetitive production of chips or motherboards.

Clearly, numerous thinkers are asserting that the future of the world's economic growth is in the hands of India and China (for example, Deloitte Research, 2006). Concomitantly, technological innovation is likely to be more emerging in Asia. Formerly developing nations, aided by the foreign direct investment, and uninhibited by aging infrastructure and capital investment, are strategically positioned to lead the way in the near term. The challenge to western corporations lies in learning to collaborate across wide cultural barriers.

In an optimistic and extraordinarily well developed volume, *The Fortune at the Bottom of the Pyramid,* Prahalad (2005) asserts that social and economic transformation will occur for the genuinely poor (Bottom of the Pyramid) once they are seen as potential consumers. His contention is that, once we accept such people as consumers, "the only way to serve that market is to innovate" (p. 100) The concomitant challenge of the future for technological innovation across the world is to raise up the poorest while achieving good business results by keeping costs and prices low enough while making quality products accessible enough.

CONCLUSION

The Ford assembly line transformed a society, yet today the US auto industry skirts bankruptcy. Some would argue that over-confidence in early success of its technology led, ultimately, to its current state. Digital Equipment Corporation, having derided the possibility of selling computers worldwide, exists no more. While there are heavy challenges associated with innovating internationally, the penalties for companies not learning to evolve through innovation can be severe.

It seems reasonable that "large firms have real difficulty creating radical innovations outside the core areas of business to which they are committed" (Understanding Private-Sector Decision Making for Early-Stage Technology Development, http://www.atp.nist.gov/eao/gcr02-841a/execsum. htm). Corporations build upon known successes. Perhaps similarly, this study argues that organizations tend to resist the unknown, in the form of unfamiliar nations, as settings for innovation.

As an example, the *Journal of the American Medical Association* recently published an article titled, "Overdose: How Excessive Government Regulation Stifles Pharmaceutical Innovation" (2007). The article details the regulatory burden that US pharmaceuticals shoulder when they attempt to try new things. Yet any number of other sovereign nations could, potentially, be development sites for new products, services, or delivery systems if the corporations were willing to access and engage them. In fact, the rapid growth and economic improvement of some nations has opened entirely new potential markets for such innovation. Yet some are loathe to move into such unfamiliar arenas, preferring to devote resources to attempting to change the directions of current domestic legislation.

Like the vortices of the *maelstrom,* impactful forces can be identified and defined so as to reveal the hidden center where this study began—a mysterious and astounding synergy of environmental forces creating a natural phenomenon of huge proportion. The future of innovation in technology may rest upon the capacity of the business community to identify and utilize the dynamic forces at work in different countries to maximize innovative development. Like any dynamic force, the environmental elements, exposed to each other and to the outside world, are constantly changing, modifying and building. Future researchers will find, in the *maelstrom,* a fruitful and rewarding challenge for many years to come.

The environmental dimensions discussed here are a way of suggesting that the management literature does provide the means for reducing the levels of "organizational discomfort" with unknowns. Specifically, the seven dimensions provide a framework for enterprise to explore and profit from the potential offered in new geographies.

REFERENCES

Albers, J. A., & Brewer, S. (2003). Knowledge management and the innovation process: The eco-innovation model. *Journal of Knowledge Management Practice*, June. Retrieved January, 2007, from http://www.tlainc.com/articl52.htm

Berger, S. (2000). Globalization and politics. *Annual Review of Political Science 3,* 43-62.

Bordo, M. D. (2002) Globalization in historical perspective, *Business Economics, 11*(January), 20-30.

Broersma, M. (2005). *EU rejects controversial software patents proposal.* Enterprise Apps. Retrieved from http://www.eweek.com/article2/0,1895,1834392,00.asp

Chun, C. W. (2001). *Environmental scanning as information seeking and organizational learning.* Information Research, 7. October. Retrieved December, 2006, from http://informationr.net/ir/7-1/infres71.html

Chesbrough, H. (1999). *The role of the institutional environment on the organizational impact of innovation.* Harvard Business School. Retrieved December, 2006, from http://smealsearch2.psu.edu/cache/papers/Business/1419/http:zSzzSzemlab.berkeley.eduzSzuserszSzbhhallzSzchesbrough.pdf/the-role-of-the.pdf/

Czech Statistical Department Report #9605-04. (2004) Retrieved December 16, 2006 from http://www.liberec.czso.cz/eng/edicniplan.nsf/publ/9605-04-2002_2003.

Deloitte Research. (2006). *China and India: The reality beyond the hype.* May. Retrieved January 5, 2007, from http://www.deloitte.com/dtt/research/0,1015,sid=2318&cid=117814,00.html

Downes, L. (2004). First empower all the lawyers. *Harvard Business Review, 82*(12), 19.

Dwyer, S., Mesak, H., & Hsu, M. (2005). An exploratory examination of the influence of national culture on cross-national product diffusion. *Journal of International Marketing, 13*(2), 48-69.

Greenspan, A. (2004). *"Globalization and innovation" Speech to the Federal Reserve Bank.* Chicago. Retrieved December 15, 2006, from http://www.techlawjournal.com/home/newsbriefs/2004/05b.asp

Hahm, H. (1993). *The development of the private sector in a small economy in transition.* World

Bank Discussion Papers, East Asia and Pacific Region Series, 223. World Bank, Washington D.C.

Hamm, S. (2007). The trouble with India. *Business Week*. March 19, 48-58.

Hall, E.T. (1976). How cultures collide. *Psychology Today, 5*(9), 66-97.

Hofstede, G. (1991). *Cultures and organizations: The software of the mind*. London: McGraw-Hill.

Innovation Briefing 07-06: Open innovation. (2007). Retrieved March, 2007 from http://www.innovaro.com/inno_updates/Innovation%20Briefing%2007-06.pdf

Jareszelski, D., Dehoff, K., & Bordia, R. (2006). *Smart spenders: The global innovation 1000*. strategy+business. Retrieved December 15, 2006, from http://www.strategybusines.com/press/article/064057?gko=c3340-1

Katz, D., & Kahn, R. L. (1966). *The social psychology of organizations*. New York: Wiley.

Laurence, P. R., & Lorsch, J. W. (1967). *Organization and environment*. Cambridge: Harvard University Press.

Mahatra, Y. Role of information technology in managing organizational change and organizational interdependence. http://www.brint.com/papers/change/

"Malaysia's Super Corridor" (1999). Special report, *The Washington Times*, April 28.

Melo, M., Denizer, C., & Gelb, A. (1996). Patterns of transition from planned to market economy. *World Bank Economic Review, 10*(3), 397-424.

Narula, R. N. (2003). *Globalization and technology: Interdependence, innovation systems, and industrial policy*. Cambridge: Polity Press.

Prahalad, C. K. (2005). *The fortune at the bottom of the pyramid*. Upper Saddle River, NJ: Wharton School Press.

Rawson, R. (2007). Overdose: How excessive government regulation stifles pharmaceutical innovation. *Journal of the American Medical Association, 297*(2), 646-647.

Sclove, R. S. (1999). *Position Paper, The loka institute*. Retrieved December 5, 2006, from http://www.loka.org/idt/intro.htm#1.%20%20Democratizing%20Technology:%20Historical%20&%20Theoretical%20Background

St. Michael's Guild. The barber-surgeon. Retrieved December 10, 2006 from http://www.st-mike.org/medicine/bs.html.

Tarso, L. (2001). *Innovation in the making*. Copenhagen: Business School Press.

Technology definition. Retrieved December 15, 2006 from http://en.wikipedia.org/wiki/Portal:Technology.

Trompenaars, F., & Hampden-Turner, C. (1998). *Riding the waves of culture: Understanding diversity in global business*. New York: McGraw-Hill.

Vara, V., & Chao, L. *eBay to leave China*. Wall Street Journal. December 19, 2006; Page A3

Vest., C.M. (1999) Science, innovation in technology: Reflections on change Retrieved December 10, 2006 from http://www.aaas.org/spp/rd/yrbk00/Part8.pdf)

Von Eringen, Y., & Waarts, E. (2003). *A multi-country study of ERP systems: The effect of national culture*. Erasmus Institute of Management. Retrieved December 10, 2006, from https://ep.eur.nl/bitstream/1765/280/1/erimrs20030310111626.pdf)

KEY TERMS

Concatenation: The co-evolution of innovation, internationalization, and technology both independently and interdependently.

Culture: A pattern of thought, speech, action, and artifacts, which distinguishes one group or clan from another. Cultures emerge from deeply held values, which, in turn, are based on assumptions about the meaning of life, nature, and humanity. Cultures are learned and evolved over generations and permeate the society they characterize to such a level that it may be completely unaware that there are other ways of thinking.

Environment (of the organization): Is that set of organizations, institutions and factors outside the organization which, directly or indirectly, affect its existence, its success and its evolution.

Innovation: The process of creating something new, which has a significant result—whether within or outside of some prior context.

Maelstrom: An intersection of vortices which, when positioned uniquely in the earth's topography, create a massive downward spiral, drawing water, objects, men and materials into the seemingly bottomless hole at its center.

Technology: Solutions for real human problems by the development and application of tools, machines, materials, goods, or information in the form of skills, knowledge, processes, blueprints, plans, diagrams, models, formulae, tables, engineering designs, specifications, manuals, or instructions.

The Seven Dimensions

Communication Dimension: A characterization of the manner in which nationals typically express themselves or the cultural uniquenesses related to such self expression.

Competitive Dimension: That aspect of a country's environment that offers the challenge of unexpected or unique alternatives to a given product or service. Further, the competitive dimension may also refer to competition among nations to attract foreign investment.

Economic Dimension: Refers to the those national characteristics pertaining to the exchange of goods and services. Economics may be the source of risk for entry.

Legal and Regulatory Dimension: That set of rules and laws that govern human and organizational interaction within a given nation. Such rules or laws may be either opaque (difficult to see) or transparent (easily accessible) to the outside world. The consistency or inconsistency of the application of law may lead to risk of entry.

Political Dimension: Refers to that aspect of a nation's environment that speaks to the manner in which it organizes and structures the conduct of its national affairs. Politics may be the source of risk for national entry.

Socio-Cultural Dimension: Refers to that learned set of values, beliefs, practices, and artifacts that distinguish one nation from another.

Technological Dimension: Refers to the relative sophistication of hardware, software and human talent that a given country may provide for technological innovation. Further, it pertains to the technological infrastructure and other infrastructure elements (such as electricity) supporting it.

Chapter XXIII
Disruptions in Global Industries Caused by Controversial Technologies:
The Case of Lead–Free Soldering in Electronics

Roman Boutellier
ETH Zurich, Switzerland

Andreas Biedermann
ETH Zurich, Switzerland

ABSTRACT

In this chapter, the raise of a business phenomenon is introduced and illustrated with the case of the ban of lead-bearing solders in electronics manufacturing: The disruptions caused by controversial technologies. Technologies are praised initially as problem solvers and frequently evolve into problem causers themselves. Affected companies are facing the threat of technological obsolescence and fundamental change processes. A framework of the social environment and the value chain helps the management to better understand the relevant mechanisms. Using the case of lead-bearing solders, the chapter illustrates the far-reaching consequences of the forced phase-out of these alloys, which have been used since the beginning of industrial electronics production. Lead bearing solders are one example of many technologies, which are candidates to become controversial. Increased awareness of side effects, globalization, and intensified use of single technologies indicate that this management task will gain momentum in the electronics industry and others.

INTRODUCTION

Already, one year after the discovery of x-rays in 1885, reports about people losing their hair after having been exposed to a high dose of x-rays occurred; other early researchers reported skin injuries (Gee et al., 2001, p. 31; Radiologie.de, 2006). Despite these adverse effects, x-rays have been successfully applied in various fields such as medicine or material analysis. Also for other technologies, early warnings about side effects of their application were known since their market introduction, but they were not taken serious or the merits of the application surmounted the possible drawbacks. Such technologies are the use of asbestos as an insulation material (D'Agostino & Wilson, 1993, p. 186) or the application of Bisphenol A as a plasticizer (Cook, Dodds, & Hewett, 1933; Hentges, 2003). But not all of these early warnings prove to be of relevance: The most prominent examples of exaggerated precaution towards a new technology are the fears of adverse health effects on the travelers caused by the unnatural high traveling speed at the introduction of railways during industrialization.

The application of technologies will always be accompanied by assumptions of possible side effects. If these side effects are not accepted anymore, the technology is endangered of being banned. A recent example of such a process is the European restriction of the use of lead in electronics manufacturing, which caused big efforts to the affected companies and generated technological and regulatory uncertainty. Other materials were affected and future regulations are expected. Due to the global interweavement of the electronics industry, the European ban has led to a global phase-out of lead bearing electronics.

To master such controversial technologies successfully, companies need to understand the relevant social mechanisms and the interweavement of the value chain. Therefore, this chapter starts with the introduction of a framework that helps the management to understand these rela-tionships. Afterwards, the framework is applied to the case of lead-bearing electronics.

FRAMEWORK FOR THE DESCRIPTION OF CONTROVERSIAL TECHNOLOGIES

Many decision processes in the environment of a controversial technology are less technologically driven, they are ill defined problems and thus driven by power and politics. According to Haller (1999, p. 79), the activities and decisions of one social group do affect other social groups. To create an understanding of the overall mechanisms, a basic understanding of the involved actors is needed.

The Framework

Pistorius and Utterback distinguish four different areas that influence the technological environment of a company: Technology-related, raw material, market and political developments (1995, p. 220). Having the technology user in the middle, the framework takes these four possible influences into account. It consists of two main areas: Society and the value creation chain (see Figure 1).

Changes in public acceptance and new regulations do not happen overnight. There are long evolutionary processes going on that can be identified and monitored (Liebl, 1991, p. 34). As Maguire has identified in the case of the insecticide DDT, social discourses about a controversial technology can significantly influence their future (Maguire, 2004, p. 129). Especially in the public discourse, different pictures of realities are constructed that are accepted by actors. Research in the field of scientific uncertainty stresses the importance of such considerations as well (Shrader-Frechette, 1996, p. 12). As Barnett and Breakwell show in the case of the 1995 oral contraceptive pill scare, the approach of the social amplification of risk emphasizes the importance of social mechanisms

Figure 1. Research framework

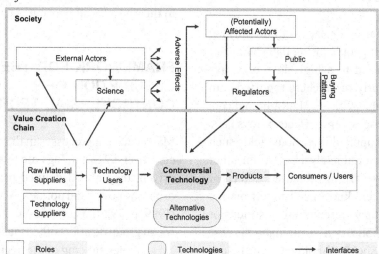

Figure 2. Results of scientific studies about the question whether low-dose effects of Bisphenol A are dangerous (vom Saal et al., 2005, p. 31)

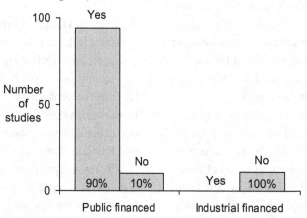

in the public risk discourse (2003, p. 302) and in particular the role of "stations of amplification" (Pidgeon & Beattie, 1998, p. 306). Since adverse effects are typically considered as risks, these amplification mechanisms are important to understand the social behavior towards potential adverse effects.

In the following paragraph, the social environment of controversial technologies is briefly outlined.

Science

For many decades, the prevailing understanding was that science had the "monopoly on truth in society" (Weingart, 1998, p. 869). Therefore, society addresses questions about adverse effects typically by scientific studies, but the results of such epidemiological studies or laboratory experiments are far from being certain (Foster, Bernstein, & Huber, 1993, p. 3; Mills, 1993, p.

92). In contrast, outputs of scientific studies are always uncertain and conditional (Zehr, 1999, p. 3) and therefore, scientific consensus often cannot be reached for many years. Examples are the cases of dioxin or Bisphenol A (Friedman, 1999; vom Saal & Hughes, 2005) (see Figure 2). Recent events indicate that rules of media attention are adapted by some scientists in order to bypass peer review mechanisms (Weingart, 1998, p. 872). In the public, scientific uncertainty is often neglected (Stocking, 1999, p. 24), which leads to misinterpretation of the research outputs. Scientifically unfounded reactions can result. The misinterpretation of the research results of a study concerning the toxicity of Acrylamid is a recent example thereof (Rögener, 2004).

Public

Intensive research has been undertaken in the last decades to gain an understanding of the social perception of risks and the resulting reactions. Pidgeon et al. (1998) provide an overview thereof. The importance of the public is at least known since the public outcry concerning the application of certain chemicals in the 1960s (Anastas & Warner, 2000, p. 2; Carson, 1962). Public and scientific risk assessments apply different logics.

As Slovic shows, ranking of risk varies greatly by laypeople and experts (Slovic, 1987, p. 281). In order to analyze public behavior towards a controversial technology, technocratic and populist dimensions have to be considered (Pidgeon et al., 1998, p. 308).

Regulators

Governments dispose of a variety of different means to influence the development and application of a technology, as Figure 3 shows. Since the 1960s, massive improvements in the regulatory assessment of technologies have been realized (Simonis, Bröchler, & Sundermann, 1999, p. 13). While at the beginning, technology assessment has been applied as a corrective mean after adverse effects have already manifested, regulators have recently started to influence potentially controversial technologies already in the early development phases (Rophol, 1999, p. 83; Sundermann, 1999, p. 119).

To cope with the increasing speed of the technological change, regulators apply a strategy known as the precautionary principle, which legitimates regulations even before a presumed adverse effect has been empirically proven. Early roots of the precautionary approach can be identified as soon

Figure 3. Continuum of degrees and types of government intervention (Allenby, 1999, p. 210)

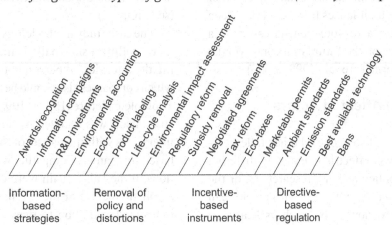

433

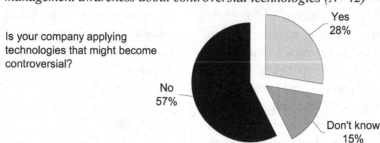

Figure 4. Lack of management awareness about controversial technologies (N=42)

as 1854. Nowadays, it is widely applied in international treaties as well as in national law (Gee et al., 2001, p. 11). Its application is not without controversy: Industry and politicians claim hidden intentions of precautionary regulations mainly in terms of protectionism (Kogan, 2003, p. 3). The increasing number of regulatory constraints that are motivated by adverse effects of technologies will aggravate the need to follow and influence developments in this area (Bernauer & Ruloff, 1999, p. 113).

External Actors

Amongst others, environmental activists, attorneys or insurance companies play an important role in the social environment of controversial technologies (Braun & Wield, 1994, p. 265). Even though these external actors are typically not directly affected by adverse effects they are interested in influencing the behavior of other actors. Dangerous alliances like the one between environmentalist and protectionists can have a strong influence on the future of a controversial technology (Bernauer et al., 1999, p. 113).

(Potentially) Affected Actors

The perspective of someone who has fallen victim to an adverse effect is completely different to the one of policy makers, researchers, or the public (Foster et al., 1993, p. 14). Persons can be affected in various ways such as health or material damages. Often, these people do not notice by themselves that they are affected, as the case of long-term exposure to chemicals shows (Kuran & Sunstein, 1999, p. 717). They have to rely on scientific analysis and other information sources. Psychological factors play a crucial role (MacGregor & Fleming, 1996).

RESEARCH METHODOLOGY

The research focuses on the mechanisms triggered when a technology becomes controversial until it is phased out. In addition, the question of how a company can operate in such an uncertain situation is approached. Since such processes usually last for several decades, no longitudinal studies are available and the research therefore focuses on current examples that industry is dealing with. An industry survey indicated a lack of management awareness about controversial technologies (see Figure 4).

The case study methodology which is referred to as "rolling a snowball" is most suitable: Asking the interviewed person at the end of the talk which companies else should be interviewed to get a complete picture (Bijker, 1995, p. 46). The case study itself was realized by a series of 40 open interviews with specialists of Swiss and German based companies. Companies with different positions in the value chain were chosen to provide a holistic picture of the mechanisms within the industry. In addition to these interviews of directly involved people, literature research and 12 expert interviews have been conducted to develop explanations for some of the findings on a more comprehensive and as well technical basis. Due to business confidentiality and uncertain legislative situation concerning the use of lead-bearing solders in electronic components, companies are not named. Since companies are in an uncertain legal situation, only little can be found in literature about managerial action. Research was difficult to carry out for the same reason. Technical aspects are well covered in literature.

MECHANISMS IN THE SOCIAL ENVIRONMENT OF LEAD-BEARING ELECTRONICS

As many other controversial technologies, *lead-bearing solders* follow a life cycle that constitutes of six phases (Figure 5): At the beginning, many different technologies are available until one dominant design elaborates. After intense use of the dominant technology, late effects are detected due to accumulated knowledge and residues.

Figure 5. Five phases in the life cycle of a controversial technology : Lead-bearing electronics

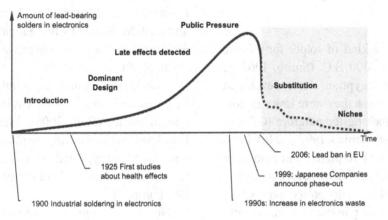

Figure 6. Social environment in the framework

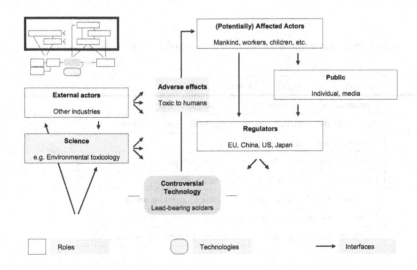

Public pressure evolves causing regulators and industry to phase-out the technology. Due to a lack of suitable substitutions and a dependency of the technology, the phase-out process is realized gradually. At the end, very few highly specialized applications are still allowed for the controversial technology. As the history of lead-bearing solders shows, such a life cycle can last more than one century.

In the following paragraphs, we describe the elements of the social environment of the lead-bearing soldering technology (see Figure 6).

Adverse Effects: Effects of Lead-Bearing Soldering in Electronic Equipment

Lead was used as a kind of solder for joining copper as early as 3000 B.C. (Smith, 1967, p. 165) Romans and Egyptians have developed lead-tin solders because they were lower in cost and had a lower melting temperature (Gibson, Choi, Bieler, & Subramanian, 1997, p. 246). Lead has been used as a white pigment in paints for more than 2000 years and in more recent history, lead has been used as a rust protection coating and in special types of glassware. Furthermore, lead compounds are added as antiknock agent in gasoline (NZZaSo, 2004). The rapid increase

of electronic waste at the end of the last century has given rise to concerns about late effects of lead-bearing solders in electronics when deposed in solid waste landfills (Turbini, Munie, Bernier, Gamalski, & Bergman, 2001, p. 4).

Science: Understanding of Lead-Bearing Solders as a Threat To Health

Hippocrates described lead colic already in 370 B. C. The effects of heavy metals on the environment have been systematically studied since the 1920s (Smrchek & Zeeman, 1998, p. 26). Shortly after the start of the manufacturing of leaded gasoline some plant workers became psychotic and died. Motivated by these incidents researchers started to investigate the causes (Needleman, 2000, p. 20).

In 1933, studies brought to light that lead can be found very widely in the environment and in human bodies (Bolt, 2005). Measurements of lead-levels in blood during the phase-out of leaded gasoline have suggested that the lead in gasoline was a main source for lead in human organisms (see Figure 8).

Nowadays, there are a high number of studies that describe a variety of different adverse health effects of lead. Amongst others, lead poisoning

Figure 7. Milestones in the development of lead-bearing solders as a controversial technology

3000 B.C.	Lead bearing solders applied to join materials
app. 370 B.C.	Hippocrates describes adverse effect of lead (lead colic)
1900	Advent of radio communication gives rise to electronics soldering
1920s	First studies about health effects of lead
Until 1990s	Lead bearing solders are the prevailing solder alloys
1990s	US legislation initiative to ban lead (not realized)
1996	European Union formulates strategy to reduce hazardous waste
1999	Japanese Companies roadmap the phase-out of lead soldering
2006	European Union broadly bans the use of lead-bearing solders in electronics

Figure 8. Use of lead in gasoline and mean blood levels of lead (Sexton, Needham, & Prikle, 2004, p. 44)

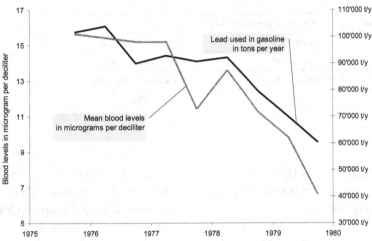

Figure 9. Blood level defining lead poisoning (Sexton et al., 2004, p. 44)

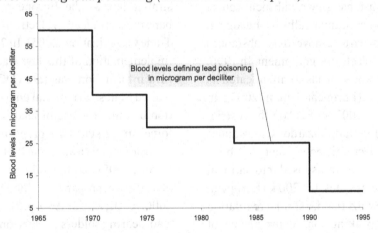

may result in neurological and reproduction-toxic effects. Furthermore, lead is considered as a possible carcinogenic to humans (Bolt, 2005). As Figure 9 shows, the threshold of lead poisoning diagnosis has been decreased over time. While the health effect of lead are well known scientific evidence about the late effects of lead-bearing electronic components in landfills is not yet available (Abtew & Selvaduray, 2000, p. 101).

Public: Perception of the Adverse Effects of Lead-Bearing Solders

The toxicity of lead is well known in public. Topics like lead-free gasoline or lead poisoning of famous art painters or children are of some interest in public. In contrast, very few news articles about contamination resulting from lead-bearing solders in electronic equipment were published. The public is even unaware of the ongoing big transition to lead-free solders in the electronics

Figure 10. Uncertainty about the deadline for the phase-out of lead-bearing solders; Final phase-out date: 1ˢᵗ July 2006

Year of statement	Predicted phase-out date	
1997	1ˢᵗ January 2002	Vianco, 1997, p. 47
2000	1ˢᵗ January 2004	Abtew et al., 2000, p. 101
2000	1ˢᵗ January 2008	Laeutenschuetz, 2000
2002	1ˢᵗ July 2006	NZZ, 2002

manufacturing industry. None of the interviewed companies got into contact with journalists because of lead-bearing solders.

Regulators: European Ban Of Lead Triggers Global Transition

Since electronic waste has grown with the advent of consumer electronics dramatically, the European Union has emphasized to remove toxic substances out of electric and electronic equipment. In 1996, the European Commission has communicated its intentions to do so (European Union, 2003). In 2003, the directive 2002/95/EG "on the restriction of the use of certain hazardous substances in electrical and electronic equipment" has been published and had to be transposed into national law of the member states by 2004 (European Union, 2003). In Switzerland, a similar regulation exists. Broadly speaking, one consequence of these regulatory measures is that the marketing of new electronic equipment for many applications is banned from the European Market after mid 2006. Due to the global interweavement of the electronics value chains, the European phase-out forces a big part of the global manufacturers to convert their products to meet lead-free requirements. Up to now, different temporary exemptions (European Union, 2003, 2005a) have been included in the directive (e.g., brass, medical devices) and several application areas are not covered at all (e.g., automotive). Reviews of these exemptions are planned to be carried out every four years

(European Union, 2003). Only in August 2005, the tolerable contamination of lead in electronics has been defined (European Union, 2005b). In addition, there has been confusion about the exact date of the phase-out of lead-bearing solders in the European markets:

People's Republic of China will enforce a similar law as the European directive, which bans the use of lead in electronics, as well (World Trade Organization, 2005). In 2006, the intended implementation of this law was not defined and firm information was rare (DCA, 2006). In the United States, no national environmental regulation banning the use of lead in electronics is in force, single states are preparing corresponding environmental laws (Abtew et al., 2000, p. 101; Arrow, 2005) and federal laws to reduce the use of lead are in preparation since 1991 (Abtew et al., 2000, p. 101; ZVEI, 1999, p. 8). In Japan, no ban of lead-bearing solders in electronics is enforced or planned up to date (Klee, 2005, p. 2). Due to other reasons, Japanese multinational electronics manufacturers have started to phase-out lead-bearing solders already at the end of the 1990s (Fukuda, Pecht, Fukuda, & Fukuda, 2003, p. 616).

External Actors: Charges of Protectionism Offending WTO Agreement

Industries outside Europe claim that banning lead-bearing solders from electronics would build-up technical barriers to trade which might be a breach of the corresponding agreement within the World Trade Organization (Kogan, 2003, p. 13; ZVEI, 1999, p. 8). This conflict has not yet been solved.

CONSEQUENCES IN THE ELECTRONICS VALUE CREATION CHAIN

The developments in the last years have given rise to the substitution of lead-bearing solders in the electronics industry. Though different regulations apply, many exemptions exist and due to the high uncertainty within the industry the phase-out activities are not synchronized which results in many challenges for the companies. Within this chapter, we outline the major groups of the market participants and give a brief overview of their particular phase-out situation in the value chain. Figure 11 shows a simplified value creation chain of the electronics industry.

The changeover to lead-free soldering processes has triggered a cascade of changes in the electronics value chain. To give an impression of the complexity of this change processes, some of the consequences for the different market participants are illustrated in the following paragraphs.

Controversial Technology: Diffusion of Lead as a Soldering Compound into the Industry

The electronics revolution has been ushered by the advent of wireless radio communication at the end of the nineteenth century. At that time, soldering has been recognized as an ideal joining for assuring electrical conductivity (Vianco, 1997, p. 46). In modern electronics, solder joints fulfill different basic functionalities beyond electronic conductance between electronic elements and printed circuit boards, as for example the mechanical mounting of components (especially smaller ones). Increasing power consumption per volume has resulted in the use of the solder joints as heat conductors for the cooling of some elements (Rahn, Diehm, & Beske, 1995, p. 19). Figure 12 illustrates a typical application of solder joints in electronics.

In the modern electronics industry, lead-tin solders allow a reliable and well-known joint of

Figure 11. Value creation chain in the framework: Simplified value creation chain in the electronics industry

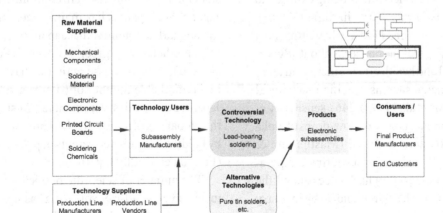

Figure 12. Solder joints can be found in all electronic product (example: surface mounted device-SMD)

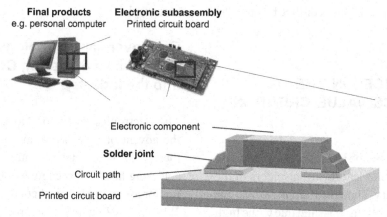

elements (NZZaSo, 2004). Until the mid 1990s, this metallic system was the prevailing technology for soldering. Modern prevalence of lead-tin solders (especially the eutectic 63Sn-37Pb solder) is due to the resource related factors such as availability and cost of lead and tin as well as to path-dependent factors such as the large established manufacturing base and the extensive experience with tin and lead (Gibson et al., 1997, p. 246).

Alternative Technologies: Intensive Research since the 1990s

Electronics are applied in a range of different ambiances: Aircraft electronics being exposed to temperatures as low as -40°C in flight (Vianco, 1997, p. 47) and as high as +140°C when sitting next to the engine. Besides the concerns about adverse environmental and health effects, increased technical requirements such as specific mechanical strength (Gibson et al., 1997, p. 246), sensitivity of electronic components towards low-doses of alpha radiation of contaminated lead (Mastipuram & Wee, 2004, p. 70) and higher operating temperatures (Rahn, 2004, p. 109) have necessitated the quest for alternative lead-free solders by industry already before public pressure started to mount.

Therefore, lead-free solders have been researched on for several years.

In the US, the first joint industrial research started in 1992 to search systematically for lead-free solder alloys (ZVEI, 1999, p. 9). European companies have started research in lead-free soldering processes in the second half of the 1990s (Vincent et al., 1999). The main focus of these activities was on the technological feasibility, quality and reliability. In 1999, the Japan Electronics and Information Technology Industries Association (JEITA) published a roadmap according to which Japanese companies will gradually phase-out the use of lead-bearing solders. This voluntary self-commitment of the Japanese companies has mainly been motivated by the market potential that Japanese companies have predicted for "green products" (Fukuda et al., 2003, p. 616). These activities have resulted in a remarkable number of patents generated by Japanese companies. For example, Matsushita lead the global lead-free intellectual property activity by holding 43 lead-free patents or patents pending (Fukuda et al., 2003, p. 617).

The number of scientific publications related to the topic of lead-free soldering has significantly grown since the end of the 1990s.

Figure 13. Increase of the number of scientific articles related to the lead-free soldering since the late 1990s (Data: Web of Science, 2006)

Figure 14. Manufacturing line for electronic subassemblies: Wave soldering

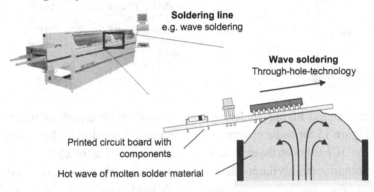

Technology Users: Manufacturers of Subassemblies

Economies of scale, globalization, and standardization have changed the electronics manufacturing industry. Many companies have outsourced their electronics manufacturing lines to subcontractors that mount the electronic components on the printed circuit boards and do the quality testing of these subassemblies. This trend has given rise to a number of highly specialized global manufacturing companies that do not market their own products but produce a variety of electronic subassemblies for a number of different final product manufacturers. A manufacturer of electronic assemblies typically manages several ten thousands of different product masters in his enterprise planning system.

The manufacturers of the electronic subassemblies are heavily affected by the technological substitution. Not only do they have to guarantee the quality and reliability of their products that are newly manufactured in lead-free processes but they often are forced to provide lead-bearing and lead-free solder processes in parallel. This is due to the fact that some of their customers still demand the old, mastered and trusted solder technology (e.g., aviation, military, medical technologies). For many such subassembly manufacturers, this means a new segmentation of their customers which leads to a drop of the economies of scale because they have to run additional manufacturing lines. Though manufacturing line suppliers offer special machines to rapidly switch from lead-free to lead-bearing, additional costs are generated due to additional changeover times.

Figure 15. Melting temperatures of solders (Grossmann, 2004, p. 9); Actual soldering temperatures are higher

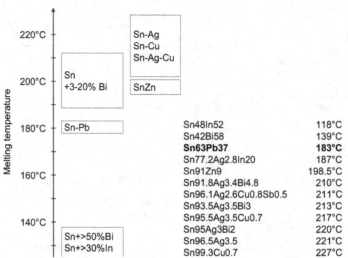

Lead-free solders demand higher soldering temperatures. (See Figure 15 for some examples of melting temperatures.) Changes on the installed manufacturing base comprise mainly the purchasing of new equipment either for higher temperature (reflow soldering) or soldering equipment that resists to the more aggressive solder alloys (wave soldering).

Apart from the higher soldering temperature, other important changes in the soldering processes are necessary: Due to more aggressive chemical characteristics of the lead-free solders, small amounts of metals or other materials of the circuit board or the components might be elutriated and contaminate the tank of molten solder of wave soldering machines. This leads to a loss in quality and reliability (Grossmann, 2005, p. 43). In addition, due to the lower wetting performance of the solders the soldering process has to be protected by a shielding gas, typically nitrogen.

Initial fears of some manufacturers of the impossibility to mount lead-free together with lead-bearing devices have not been proven to be true. Therefore, many logistical nightmares were avoided. Subassembly manufacturers might have

several ten thousands of different components to manage. It would have been a very demanding task to synchronize the changeover of all the-several hundred-components of a printed circuit board. In addition, the timing of the use of the components in stock would have been nearly impossible.

In production, the mixture of lead-bearing and lead-free components has to be controlled. Though often a mixture would be technically feasible thanks to mixed-mounting of lead-free and lead-bearing components, regulations in some countries do not allow the use of lead-bearing components anymore.

Lead-free components sometimes do not show identical performance or other characteristics (e.g., shape) as their lead-bearing components. In addition, not all of the used components will be available as a lead-free-soldering version forcing manufacturers to use new components.

All components have to be analyzed for their future availability as lead-free or lead-bearing versions, which cause an immense workload for the corresponding departments. Substitution of these components leads to a temporary doubling of stock that can result in a substantial increase in fixed capital.

Most electronics industries have very demanding quality standards, including a recertification of the products after any changes in the manufacturing process. In practice, this means a recertification of the bigger part of all the products. This work is usually done periodically, depending on the introduction of new products or processes. Due to the phase-out of lead-bearing solders, many recertifications have to be done within a short period of time.

Consumers and Users: Product Manufacturers and End Customers

Electronic subassemblies are used in a plurality of products such as cars, pocket calculators, greeting cards, light bulbs, manufacturing systems, and medical devices. Correspondingly, the product manufacturers are situated in different industries and the product requirements vary widely. Typically, the subassemblies are integrated into final products by mechanical joining processes. Due to the different work sharing models with the subassembly manufacturers, the final product manufacturers are affected in different ways. Normally, they try to outsource the problem on their subcontractors by just ordering their products "lead-free" to have no problems in sales.

Depending on the specific situation, product manufacturers have to deal with a lot of queries from their customers for a confirmation of their phase-out dates. Sometimes the requested information cannot be given because the request is too specific and would require unreasonable clarification activities. Despite the administrative efforts to deal with these queries, strategic questions may arise due to business confidentiality considerations.

Lead-bearing soldered parts are usually still needed even after the phase-out because new spare products might not be compatible or because of special customer requirements. Manufacturers of final products have to ensure the availability of such spare parts by placing an all-time need into stock or by ensuring the ability to re-manufacture these subassemblies. Manufacturers sometimes encounter high depreciation of obsolete leaded inventory in stock.

Despite the rougher environments and increased requirements caused by the changes in the manufacturing process, the established design rules for the layout of printed circuit boards do not have to be changed substantially. In the "lead era," a breach with these design rules did only seldom result in quality problems of the whole subassembly. Now, this has changed due to the more narrow tolerances in the production process. Therefore, poor board design can cause quality problems (Grossmann, 2005, p. 49). Since changes in the design of printed circuit boards, required new templates for production, such redesigns can cause high costs of adoption.

On the one hand, some product manufacturers of final products still do their subassembly manufacturing in-house. This gives them the freedom to synchronize the change of their soldering processes which preservers the economies of scale. On the other hand, some manufacturers of final products are influenced by their customers, again because they have strict requirements for the quality of their products. This is typically true in industries that are not affected by any regulatory need to phase-out lead-bearing solders at this moment.

Usually, final product users do not notice any change of the product at all. Even though in Japan, companies claim that lead-free electronics are a competitive advantage in consumer electronics, at least in Switzerland's cell phone or computer market, lead-free is not considered to be a purchase criterion at all. The situation seems to be similar or even more striking in industrial electronics, where customers sometimes even try to postpone the shift to lead-free soldered products due to missing trust in the new technology: "Never change a running system" seems to be the maxim.

Raw Material Suppliers: Manufacturers of Components, Printed Circuit Boards and Others

Like boards, electronic components are exposed to a higher temperature during the soldering process, as well. Since the previous temperatures had already stressed the components to the limit, old components were not usable within the new process. Basically, the old plastic compounds do not withstand the higher process temperature. Melting or deformation of the components or even explosion of the components due to absorbed humidity can be observed. New compounds have to be found that endure the lead-free soldering. The connections of the leads of the components that are soldered need to be adopted in order to be compatible with the new soldering alloys.

Sales figures of lead-bearing solders have already decreased. In the lead-era, there has only been one prevailing family of solder alloys, namely the tin-lead system. No alternative solder can fulfill all the requirements that lead-bearing solders fulfill (e.g., price, operation temperature or mechanical strength). Today, different families of solders are applied for specific applications which automatically lead to a segmentation of the market for soldering alloys (Rahn, 2004, p. 65).

Fluxers are chemicals that are deposed on boards prior to soldering to increase the joining of the surfaces. During usage of the product, ingredients of the fluxers react with new lead-free solder alloys resulting in a higher tendency of the solders to substrate moisture from the air leading to an increased danger of corrosion and therefore lowering the expected lifetime of the electronic part.

The printed circuit boards themselves have to be changed, as well. This is mainly due to the higher temperatures during the soldering process, changed chemical properties of the applied agents and other requirement on the surface to guarantee appropriate solder joints. The prevailing finishing technique (hot air solder leveling, HASL) has to

be replaced by alternative surfaces. Different alternatives exist and have already been applied due to other technical reasons years before the advent of the lead-free requirement. Their handling and their long-term behavior is known (Rahn, 2004, p. 39). Other effects like delaminating caused by the higher temperatures during soldering have not yet been proven to be of big concern.

Technology Suppliers: Vendors and Manufacturers of Soldering Equipment

Adoption in the soldering equipment has been driven by different changes in the production process that were triggered by the shift to lead-free soldering. The most striking ones were higher soldering temperatures, more aggressive soldering materials and gas-shielded soldering processes (Rahn, 2004, p. 51). In general, these adoptions of the soldering equipment triggered the development of new products by the vendors of the soldering equipment and increased the sales. Since the new equipment can in general be used for lead-free as well as lead-bearing soldering, no new segmentation of the market can be observed. Some manufacturers have developed production lines that can rapidly switch between lead-bearing and lead-free alloys.

Dealers of Electronic Components

Standardization and globalization has given rise to business-to-business dealers of electronic components. On the one hand, these dealers distribute the physical goods; on the other hand, they serve as an information platform between manufacturer of components and manufacturers of subassemblies or products. Since many manufacturers source their components through a dealer, the role of these dealers in the technological change to lead-free solders has become critical. Not only do they have to double their number of stock places but also have an immense workload in updating their data management systems. In addition, brokering occurs where dealers buy the rare lead-free products and sell them at higher prices. The same happens with dealers stocking old, lead-bearing materials in order to sell them at a rather high price within some years when the installed manufacturing base for leaded components has been converted to a lead-free basis.

CONCLUSION: MANAGERIAL CHALLENGES WITH CONTROVERSIAL TECHNOLOGIES

From our research in the electronics industry, we can identify a set of basic principles for a good management of controversial technologies.

Be Aware of the Different Possibilities to Phase in a Technology outside your Company

Controversial technologies usually need several decades to diffuse into the products and processes of companies. The whole value chain has to be considered. The term phase-in therefore does not only mean the planned introduction of a new technology by the company itself but includes changes by customers and suppliers, as well.

Phase-in on the customer side means the emergence of a new and unforeseen application mode of the own products. Customer monitoring is crucial because technologies usually become regulated or controversial in relation to their application. Due to the high number of changes in the whole value chain a company cannot be aware of all these developments. Unknown phase-in happens.

Phase-in of new technologies through suppliers is usually handled by product change notifications or prequalification where any changes in the products have to be approved by the customer. Due to complexity not all changes can be covered. Therefore, implicit introduction of technologies has to be taken into account. A residual uncertainty is unavoidable.

Analyze Long-Term Reliability of Alternatives in Long-Term Studies

Some companies have identified the looming demand for lead-free products very early. Typically, these companies started with a rough assessment of the own situation and also with first research projects in the technical feasibility of certain alternatives. At the end of the 1990s, the German "Zentralverband Elektrotechnik- und Elektronikindustrie" has called industry's atten-

Figure 16. Different possibilities to phase in a technology

	supplier	manufacturer	customer
known to the company **Phase-In**	Approved Change	Classical Phase-In	Anticipated Use of the Product
unknown to the company	Implicit Introduction	Unconscious Application	Unconscious Use

Technology User

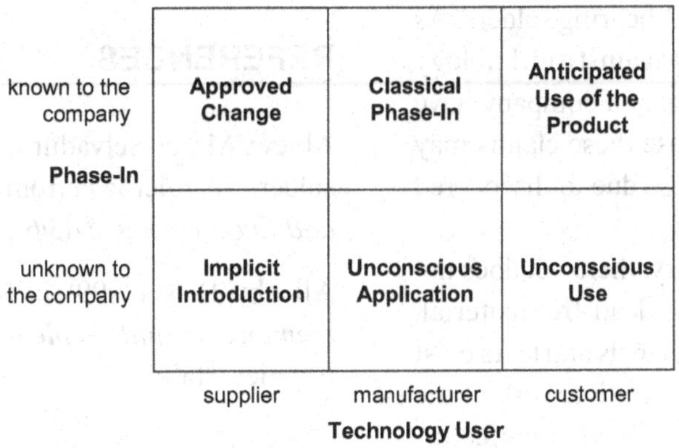

Disruptions in Global Industries Caused by Controversial Technologies

tion to the potential issue of long-term reliability and the necessity of starting tests to ensure the future functionality of the products (ZVEI, 1999, p. 41).

The most common long-term reliability issues of lead-free solders include spontaneous growth of shortage-causing dendrites from the solder joints (whiskers) and spontaneous decomposition of solder joints at very deep temperatures (tin pest). Lead has been added to the solder alloys to prevent these long-term effects.

Different views on the relevance of several long-term reliability issues exist. Long-term effects can only be truly understood by real empirical long-term studies, not through models and artificial aging. Artificial aging of components may give some hints about the relevance of certain long-term effects but they often cannot provide the necessary certainty concerning the behavior of the components in real use.

Companies are urged to conduct long-term studies about long-term reliability of new technologies that have to be applied, emphasizing their specific modes of applications. The earlier they start the less uncertainty they will have to manage.

Realize the Claims Even Outside your Main Business and Cultivate External Communication

Knowledge about the toxicity of lead that has been gained during the debate of leaded gasoline is also applicable in the case of lead-bearing solders. As this case shows, even claims against a technology outside of the main business of a company have to be taken seriously, because these claims may spill over to the own business due to discovered application of the technology.

In the electronics industry, there yet does not exist any common labeling of lead-free material. A huge diversity of stickers, labels and texts exist that produce a lot of administrative work in the goods receiving departments. Some manufactur-

ers do not label their products at all. Not only the labeling itself varies from manufacturer to manufacture but also the term "lead-free" is interpreted differently. Sometimes, "lead-free" is used as a synonym for "conform to regulations."

As practitioners of the industry know, whenever people who are unfamiliar with the business tell one what to do, a suboptimal solution will result (Bigelow, 2005, p. 14). Since important decisions about the future of a controversial technology are made by non-experts, communicating the relevant aspects of the business situation to laymen becomes an important capability.

Accept the Complexity

A big part of knowledge, norms, and quality standards in industrial soldering of electronic components that have evolved in the last decades is still valid but the details need adoption. New quality standards have to be developed (IPC, 2005). A well introduced and historically developed technology cannot be changed easily; too many unknown interdependencies exist. The phase-out of a technology, therefore, has always to be seen as an evolving project where new challenges are identified during the change-over itself. Especially in electronics manufacturing companies are currently facing different tasks to phase out many different technologies. Current examples are volatile organic compounds (VOCs) or halogens that are used in electronics manufacturing.

REFERENCES

Abtew, M., & Selvaduray, G. (2000). Lead-free solders in microelectronics. *Materials Science and Engineering, 27*(5/6), 95.

Allenby, B. R. (1999). *Industrial ecology: Policy framework and implementation*. NJ: AT&T, Prentice-Hall.

Anastas, P. T., & Warner, J. C. (2000). *Green chemistry: Theory and practice.* Oxford: Oxford University Press.

Arrow. (2005). *US Environmental Proposals and Legislation.* Retrieved November 16, 2005, from http://www.arrow.com/green/legislation/us.html

Barnett, J., & Breakwell, G. M. (2003). The social amplification of risk and the hazard sequence: The October 1995 oral contraceptive pill scare. *Health, Risk & Society, 5*(3), 301.

Bernauer, T., & Ruloff, D. (1999). *Handel und Umwelt: Zur Frage der Kompatibilität internationaler Regime.* Opladen: Westdeutscher Verlag.

Bigelow, P. (2005). Keep it simple, stupid! *Printed Circuit Design & Manufacture*(August), 14.

Bijker, W. E. (1995). *Of bicycles, bakelites, and bulbs: Towards a theory of sociotechnical change.* Boston: Massachusetts Institute of Technology.

Bolt, H. M. (2005). Lead. In *Ullmann's Encyclopedia of Industrial Chemistry*: Wiley-VCH Verlag GmbH & Co. KGaA.

Braun, E., & Wield, D. (1994). Regulation as a means for the social-control of technology. *Technology Analysis & Strategic Management, 6*(3), 259.

Carson, R. L. (1962). *Der stumme Frühling.* München: Biederstein.

Cook, J. W., Dodds, E. C., & Hewett, C. L. (1933). A synthetic oestrus-exciting compound. *Nature, January 14, 1933*, 56.

D'Agostino, R. J., & Wilson, R. (1993). Asbestos: The hazard, the risk, and public policy. In K. R. Foster, D. E. Bernstein & P. W. Huber (Eds.), *Phantom risk: Scientific interference and the law.* London: The MIT Press.

DCA. (2006). *China RoHS: DCA overview and insights.* Retrieved February 1, 2006, from http://www.designchainassociates.com/chinarohs.html

European Union. (2003). Directive 2002/95/EC of the European Parliament and of the Council of 27 January 2003 on the restriction of the use of certain hazardous substances in electrical and electronic equipment. *Official Journal of the European Union, L 37*, 19.

European Union. (2005a). Entscheidung der Kommission vom 13. Oktober 2005 zur Änderung des Anhangs der Richtlinie 2002/95/EG des Europäischen Parlaments und des Rates zur Beschränkung der Verwendung bestimmter gefährlicher Stoffe in Elektro- und Elektronikgeräten zwecks Anpassung an den technischen Fortschritt. *Official Journal of the European Union, L 271*, 48.

European Union. (2005b). Entscheidung der Kommission vom 18. August 2005 zur Änderung des Anhangs der Richtlinie 2002/95/EG des Europäischen Parlaments und des Rates zwecks Festlegung von Konzentrationshöchstwerten für bestimmte gefährliche Stoffe in Elektro- und Elektronikgeräten. *Official Journal of the European Union, L 214*, 65.

Foster, K. R., Bernstein, D. E., & Huber, P. W. (1993). A scientific perspective. In K. R. Foster, D. E. Bernstein, & P. W. Huber (Eds.), *Phantom risk: Scientific interference and the law.* London: The MIT Press.

Friedman, S. M. (1999). The never-ending story of Dioxin. In S. M. Friedman, S. Dunwoody, & C. L. Rogers (Eds.), *Communication uncertainty: Media coverage and new and controversial science* (pp. 113). New Jersey, London: Lawrence Erlbaum Associates Publishers.

Fukuda, Y., Pecht, M. G. P., Fukuda, K., & Fukuda, S. (2003). Lead-free soldering in the Japanese electronics industry. *IEEE Transactions on components and packaging technologies, 26*(3), 616.

Gee, D., MacGarvin, M., Stirling, A., Keys, J., Wynne, B., & Guedes Vaz, S. (2001). *Late lessons from early warnings: The precautionary principle 1896-2000*. Copenhagen: European Environment Agency.

Gibson, A. W., Choi, S., Bieler, T. R., & Subramanian, K. N. (1997, 1997-05-05). *Environmental concerns and materials issues in manufactured solder joints*. Paper presented at the IEEE International Symposium on Electronics and the Environment.

Grossmann, G. (2004). Beifreies Löten: Technik ist bereit. *Bulletin SEV/VSE*(17), 9.

Grossmann, G. (2005). *WEEE & RohS: Technologische Aspekte*. Paper presented at the Seminar "Wer hat Angst vor WEEE/RoHS," Dübendorf.

Haller, M. (1999). Erübrigt sich angesichts der Globalisierung der Risiko-Dialog? In P. Gomez, G. Müller-Stewens & J. Rüegg-Stürm (Eds.), *Entwicklungsperspektiven einer integrierten Managementlehre* (pp. 73). Bern, Stuttgart, Wien: Paul Haupt.

Hentges, S. G. (2003). *Bisphenol A-A fact sheet*: American Plastics Council.

IPC. (2005). *Acceptability of electronic assemblies: Rev. D 2/05*. Retrieved February 22, 2006, from http://www.ipc.org/4.0_Knowledge/4.1_Standards/revstat1.htm

Klee, B. (2005). *Stoffverbote: EU-Richtlinie 2002/95/EG -RoHS*.

Kogan, L. A. (2003). *Looking behind the curtain: The growth of trade barriers that ignore sound science: Executive Summary*. Washington: National Foreign Trade Council, Inc.

Kuran, T., & Sunstein, C. R. (1999). Availability cascades and risk regulation. *Stanford Law Review, 51*(4), 683.

Laeutenschuetz, R. (2000, 2000-06-14). EU kämpft gegen den wachsenden Abfallberg: Rich-tlinienentwuerfe zur Entsorgung von Elektronikschrott. *Neue Zürcher Zeitung*, p. 23.

Liebl, F. (1991). *Schwache Signale und Künstliche Intelligenz im strategischen Issue Management*. Frankfurt am Main, Bern, etc.: Lang.

MacGregor, D. G., & Fleming, R. (1996). Risk perception and symptom reporting. *Risk Analysis, 16*(6), 773-783.

Maguire, S. (2004). The co-evolution of technology and discourse: a study of substitution processes for the insecticide DDT. *Organization Studies, 25*(1), 113.

Mastipuram, R., & Wee, E. (2004). Soft errors' impact on system reliability. *EDN, 49*(20), 69.

Mills, J. L. (1993). Spermicides and birth defects. In K. R. Foster, D. E. Bernstein, & P. W. Huber (Eds.), *Phantom risk: Scientific interference and the law*. London: The MIT Press.

Needleman, H. L. (2000). The removal of lead from gasoline: Historical and personal reflections. *Environmental Research, 84*(1), 20.

NZZ. (2002, 2002-04-11). Elektroschrott wird rücknahmepflichtig. *Neue Zürcher Zeitung*, p. 19.

NZZaSo. (2004, 2004-09-14). Ökologische Elektrogeräte. *NZZ am Sonntag*.

Pidgeon, N. F., & Beattie, J. (1998). The psychology of risk and uncertainty. In P. Calow (Ed.), *Handbook of environmental risk assessment and management* (pp. 289). London: Blackwell Science.

Pistorius, C. W. I., & Utterback, J. M. (1995). The death knells of mature technologies. *Technological Forecasting and Social Change, 50*(3), 133-151(19).

Radiologie.de. (2006). Die Geschichte der Radiologie: Curagita AG.

Rahn, A. (2004). *Bleifrei Löten: Ein Leitfaden für die Praxis*. Bad Saulgau: Eugen G. Leuze Verlag.

Rahn, A., Diehm, R., & Beske, E. (1995). Bleifreie Lote? *productronic*(2), 19.

Rögener, W. (2004, 23. September 2004). Acrylamid nicht entlastet: Chemiker geben voreilig Entwarnung vor dem Plastik im Essen. *Süddeutsche Zeitung*, p. 9.

Rophol, G. (1999). Innovative Technikbewertung. In S. Bröchler, G. Simonis, & K. Sundermann (Eds.), *Handbuch Technikfolgenabschätzung* (Vol. 1, pp. 83ff). Berlin: edition sigma.

Sexton, K., Needham, L. L., & Prikle, J. L. (2004). Human biomonitoring of environmental chemicals. *American Scientist, 92*(1), 38.

Shrader-Frechette, K. (1996). Methodological rules for four classes of scientific uncertainty. In J. Lemons (Ed.), *Scientific uncertainty and environmental problem solving* (pp. 12). Cambridge: Blackwell Science.

Simonis, G., Bröchler, S., & Sundermann, K. (1999). *Handbuch Technikfolgenabschätzung* (Vol. 1). Berlin: edition sigma.

Slovic, P. (1987). Perception of risk. *Science, 236*(4799), 280.

Smith, C. S. (1967). Metallurgy in the seventeenth an eighteenth centuries. In M. Kranzberg & C. W. J. Pursell (Eds.), *Technology in Western Civilisation: The emergence of modern industrial society. Earliest Times to 1900* (pp. 142). New York, London, Toronto: Oxford University Press.

Smrchek, J. C., & Zeeman, M. G. (1998). Assessing risks to ecological systems from chemicals. In P. Calow (Ed.), *Handbook of environmental risk assessment and management* (pp. 24). London: Blackwell Science.

Stocking, S. H. (1999). How journalists deal with scientific uncertainty. In S. M. Friedman, S. Dun-woody, & C. L. Rogers (Eds.), *Communication uncertainty: media coverage and new and controversial science* (pp. 113). New Jersey, London: Lawrence Erlbaum Associates Publishers.

Sundermann, K. (1999). Constructive technology assessment. In S. Bröchler, G. Simonis, & K. Sundermann (Eds.), *Handbuch Technikfolgenabschätzung* (Vol. 1, pp. 119). Berlin: edition sigma.

Turbini, L. J., Munie, G., C., Bernier, D., Gamalski, J., & Bergman, D. W. (2001). Examining the environmental impact of lead-free soldering alternatives. *IEEE Transactions on Electronics Packaging Manufacturing, 24*(1), 4.

Vianco, P. T. (1997). Solder alloys: A look at the past, present, and future. *Welding Journal*(March), 45.

Vincent, J. H., Harrison, M. R., Langeveld, P., de Kluizenaar, E. E., Steen, H. A. H., Warwick, M., et al. (1999). *Improved design life and environmentally aware manufacturing of electronics assemblies by lead-free soldering: IDEALS*: Marconi Materials Technology (UK).

vom Saal, F. S., & Hughes, C. (2005). An extensive new literature concerning low-dose effects of Bisphenol A shows the need for a new risk assessment. *Environmental Health Perspectives, 113*(8).

Weingart, P. (1998). Science and the media. *Research Policy, 27*(8), 869-879.

World Trade Organization. (2005). *Notification G/TBT/N/CHN/140*: Comittee on Technical Barriers to Trade.

Zehr, S. C. (1999). Scientists' Representations of Uncertainty. In S. M. Friedman, S. Dunwoody & C. L. Rogers (Eds.), *Communication uncertainty: Media coverage and new and controversial science* (pp. 3). New Jersey, London: Lawrence Erlbaum Associates Publishers.

ZVEI. (1999). *Bleifreies Löten: Materialien, Komponenten, Prozesse.* Frankfurt am Main: Zentralverband Elektrotechnik- und Elektronikindustrie e.V.

Compilation of References

Aarts, E. (2004). Ambient intelligence: A multimedia perspective. *IEEE Multimedia*, 12-19.

Abouzeedan, A., & Busler, M. (2005). ASPEM as the new topographic analysis tool for small and medium-sized enterprises (SMEs) performance models utilization. *Journal of International Entrepreneurship, 3*(1), p. 53.

Abtew, M., & Selvaduray, G. (2000). Lead-free solders in microelectronics. *Materials Science and Engineering, 27*(5/6), 95.

Abuznaid, S. (2006). Islam & management—what can be learned. *Thunderbird International Business Review, 48*(1), 125-140.

Adair, J. (1990). *The challenge of innovation*. London: Kogan Page.

Adam, A. (2005). Delegating and distributing morality: Can we inscribe privacy protection in a machine? *Ethics and Information Technology, 7*(4), 233-242.

Adam, E. E. (1992). Quality improvement as an operations strategy. *Journal of Industrial Management and Data Systems, 92*(4), 3-12.

Afuha, A., & Tucci, C. L. (2001). *Internet business models and strategies, text, and cases*. New York: McGraw-Hill.

Agre, P. E. (1999). *Rethinking networks and communities in wired societies*. University of California. Retrieved 2002, from http://dlis.gseis.ucla.edu/people/pagre/asis.html

Ahire, S. L., & Golhar, D. Y. (1996). Quality management in large vs small firms. *Journal of Small Business Management, 34*(2), p. 1.

AIM. (2005). IST-2001-52222: *Acceleration of innovative ideas to market*. Project public report, EC.

Ajzen, I. (1985). From intentions to actions: A theory of planned behaviour. In J. Kuhl & J. Beckmann (Eds.), *Action-control: From cognition to behaviour*. Heidelberg: Springer Verlag.

Ajzen, I., & Fishbein, M. (1980). *Understanding attitudes and predicting social behavior*. Englewood Cliffs, NJ: Prentice-Hall.

Akao, Y. (2004). *QFD-Quality Function Deployment*. Productivity Press.

Al'tshuller, G. S., Shulyak, L., & Rodman, S. (1999). *The innovation algorithm*. Worcester, MA: Technical Innovation Center.

Albers, J. A., & Brewer, S. (2003). Knowledge management and the innovation process: The eco-innovation model. *Journal of Knowledge Management Practice*, June. Retrieved January, 2007, from http://www.tlainc.com/articl52.htm

Alcaniz, M. (2005). New technologies for ambient intelligence. In G. Riva, F. Vatalaro, F. Davide, & M. Alcaniz (Eds.), *Ambient intelligence: the evolution of technology, communication, and cognition towards the future of human-computer interaction*. IOS Press.

Aldrich, H. E. (1999). *Organizations evolving*. London: Sage.

Aldrich, H., & Zimmer, C. (1986). Entrepreneurship through social networks. In D. Sexton & R. Smilor (Eds.), *The art and science of entrepreneurship*. New York: Ballinger.

Alexander, S. (2001). E-learning developments and experiences. *Education + Training, 43*(4/5), 240-248.

Ali, A. J. (2005). *Islamic perspectives on management & organizations.* Glos: Edward Elgar Publishing Limited.

Ali, I. (2003). *A performance measurement framework for a small and medium enterprise.* Unpublished thesis, University of Alberta, Canada.

Allenby, B. R. (1999). *Industrial ecology: Policy framework and implementation.* NJ: AT&T, Prentice-Hall.

Allenby, B. R. (1999). *Industrial ecology: Policy framework and implementation.* NJ: AT&T, Prentice-Hall.

Alsharif, M. M. (2005). *Sahih Muslim: The Authentic Hadiths of Muslim* (Imam Muslim Bin Hajaj Bin Naysaburi). Garden Grove, CA: Dar Al Kotob & Jarir Bookstore.

Altshuller, G. (1988). *Creativity as an exact science.* New York: Gordon and Breach Science Publishers.

Alvesson, M., & Willmott, H. (1996). *Making sense of management: A critical approach.* London: Sage Publications.

Amabile, T. M. (1983). *The social psychology of creativity.* Berlin, Heidelberg, New York: Springer.

Amabile, T. M. (1996). *Creativity in context.* Boulder, CO: Westview Press.

Amabile, T. M., Barsade, S. G., Mueller, J. S., & Staw, B. M. (2005). Affect and creativity at work. *Administrative Science Quarterly, 50*(3), 367-403.

Amar, D. A. (2004). Motivating knowledge workers to innovate: A model integrating motivation dynamics and antecedents. *European Journal of Innovation Management, 7*(2), 89-101.

Amit, R., & Zott, C. (2001). Value creation in e-business. *Strategic Management Journal, 22*(6/7), 493-520.

Anastas, P. T., & Warner, J. C. (2000). *Green chemistry: Theory and practice.* Oxford: Oxford University Press.

Andrianopoulos, C. (2001). Determinants of organizational creativity: A literature review. *Management Decision, 39*(10), 834-840.

Anelli, M. (2005). *What is chaos theory?* Ufdbparam (online) Retrieved August 6, 2005, from http://www.ufdbparam.info/spip/article.php3?id_article=2

Angele, J., & Nierlich, A. (2003). *Semantic business integration—speed up your processes.* Ontoprise Whitepaper Series

Aram, J. D., & Cowan, S. S. (1990). Strategic planning for increased profit in the small business. *Long Range Planning, 23*(6), 63-70.

Argyris, C., & Schon, D. A. (1978). *Organisational learning: A theory of action perspective.* Reading, MA: Addison-Wesley.

Armstrong, K. (2000). *Islam: A short history.* New York: Random House.

Arrow. (2005). *US Environmental Proposals and Legislation.* Retrieved November 16, 2005, from http://www.arrow.com/green/legislation/us.html

Arrow. (2005). *US Environmental Proposals and Legislation.* Retrieved November 16, 2005, from http://www.arrow.com/green/legislation/us.html

Arteaga, J. (2005). *Adaptive management system overview.* Retrieved December 30, 2006, from http://senseandrespond.com/downloads/S_R_AMS_Overview_JArteaga_6-28-2005

Arthur Andersen & National Small Business United (1998). *Survey of Small and Medium-sized Businesses.* Report, November. (pp.19-20).

Arvan, A. (1988). Those fabulous Japanese banks. *Bankers Monthly, 105*(1), 29-35.

Asif, S., & Sargeant, A. (2000). Modelling internal communications in the financial services sector. *European Journal of marketing, 34,* 299-318.

Atherton, A.., & Hannon, P. D. (2000). Innovation processes and the small business: A conceptual analysis. *International Journal of Business Performance Management, 2*(4), 276-292.

Atkinson. C. (1997). The total team way. *National Society for Quality through Teamwork (NSQT), 7*(3),32-34, Salisbury, England.

Auditor-General. (2003). Review of Sydney Water's customer information and billing system. *Auditor-General's Report to Parliament 2003* (Volume One). Retrieved June 20, 2007, from http://www.audit.nsw.gov.au/publications/reports/financial/2003/vol1/SpecialRevSydneyWaterCIBS.pdf

Australian Bankers' Association. (2004). *Code of banking practice.* Sydney NSW, Australia.

Australian National Audit Office. (2007). *Audit Report no 24 2006-07, Customs' Cargo Management Re-engineering Project.* Canberra, Australia: Australian National Audit Office.

Australian National Training Authority. (2004). *Meat safety toolbox.* Australian Flexible Learning Framework, Commonwealth of Australia. Retrieved November 17, 2006, from http://toolboxes.flexiblelearning.net.au/series4/414.htm#desc

Australian Pharmaceutical Industries. (2006). Australian Pharmaceutical Industries and Its Controlled Entities ABN 57 000 004 320 *Annual Report,* 30 April 2006.

Autio, E., & Sapienza, H. J. (2000). Comparing process and born global perspectives in the international growth of technology-based new firms. In W. D. Bygrave, C. G. Brush, P. Davidsson, J. O. Fiet, P. G. Greene, R. T. Harrison, M. Lerner, G. D. Meyer, J. Sohl & A. Zacharakis (Eds.), *Frontiers of Entrepreneurship Research.* (pp. 413-424). Babson College, Centre for Entrepreneurial Studies.

Autio, E., Sapienza, H. J., & Almeida, J. G. (2000). Effects of age at entry, knowledge intensity, and imitability on international growth. *Academy of Management Journal, 43*(5), 090-924.

Automotive SIG. (2005). *Automotive SPICE Process Reference Model,* release V4.3, http://www.automotivespice.com/AutomotiveSPICE_PRM

Avkiran, N. (1997). Models of retail performance for bank branches: Predicting the level of key business drivers, *International Journal of Bank Marketing, 15*(6).

Azmi, S. (2002). Islamic economics. New Delhi: Good word Books Pvt Ltd.

Bachman, R., & Lane, C. (1998). T*rust within & between organizations: Conceptual issues & empirical applications.* Oxford: Oxford University Press.

Backhaus, W., Bolesta, M., Creed, A., Ross, J., & Stewart, J. (2005, July 9-12). Faculty collaboration in teaching global business. MBA Teaching Process: A Case Analysis of Collaborative Communication Applied as a Teaching Preparation Resource in a module of the Online MBA at University of Maryland University College. *Proceedings of the Academy of International Business.* Quebec: Canada.

Badiru, A., Chen. J., & Jen. J. (1992). IEs help transform industrial productivity and quality in Taiwan. *Industrial Engineering, 24*(6), 53-55.

Bailey, K. D. (1973). Monothetic and polythetic typologies and their relation to conceptualization, measurement, and scaling. *American Sociological Review, 38*(1), 18-33.

Bailey, K. D. (1994). *Typologies and taxonomies: An introduction to classification techniques* (Vol. 07-102). Thousand Oaks, CA: Sage Publications.

Baker, K. (1986). Dilemmas at a distance. *Assessment & Evaluation in Higher Education, 11*(3), 219-230.

Balzert, H. (2000). *Lehrbuch der Softwaretechnik.* Spektrum. In R. G. Cooper (1990). Stage-gate systems: A new tool for managing new products. *Business Horizons, 33*(3), 44-54.

Barad, M., & Kayis, B. (1994). Quality teams as improvement support systems (ISS): An Australian perspective. *Management Decision, 32*(6), 49-57.

Barnes, M., Coulton, L., Dickinson, T., Dransfield, S., Field, J., & Fisher, N. (1998). *A new approach to performance measurement for small to medium enterprises.* Paper presented to Conference Proceedings Performance Measurement - Theory and practice conference, Cambridge.

Barnett, J., & Breakwell, G. M. (2003). The social amplification of risk and the hazard sequence: The October 1995 oral contraceptive pill scare. *Health, Risk & Society, 5*(3), 301.

Basilevsky, A. (1994). *Statistical factor analysis and related methods: Theory and applications.* New York: John Wiley.

Basili, V. R. & Rombach, H. (1988). The TAME project: Towards improvement-oriented software environments. *IEEE Transactions on IEEE Transactions on Software Engineering, 14*(6), 758-773.

Bassetti, P. (2003). *Innovation, social risk, and political responsibility*. London: Public Lecture at the London School of Economics, 14.5.2003.

Bastmeijer, K, & Roura, R. (2004). Regulating antarctic tourism and the precautionary principle. *The American Journal of International Law, 98*(4), 763-781.

Battellino, R. (2000). *Deregulation*. Paper presented at the Australian Finance and Capital Markets Conference, The Westin Hotel, Sydney, Australia.

Bauer, M., & Aarts, B. (2000). Corpus construction: A principle for qualitative data collection. In M. Bauer & G. Gaskell (Eds.), *Qualitative researching with text, image and sound: A practical handbook*. London: Sage Publications.

Baumol, W. J. (1993). *Entrepreneurship, management and the structure of payoffs*. Cambridge MA: MIT.

Beaver, G., & Prince, C. (2004). Management, strategy, and policy in the UK small business sector: a critical review. *Journal of Small Business and Enterprise Development, 11*(1), 34-49.

Beaver, G., & Ross, E.C. (2000). Enterprise in recession: The role and context of strategy. *International Journal of Entrepreneurship and Innovation, 1*(1), 23-31.

Beck, K. (2003). *Extreme programming*. Boston: Addison-Wesley.

Beekun, R. I., & Badawi, J. (2004). *Leadership-An Islamic perspective*. Beltsville, Maryland: Amana Publications.

Behzadnia, A. A., & Denny, S. (1981). *To the commander in chief from Imam Ali to Malik-e-Ashter*. Houston, TX: Free Islamic Literature.

Belbin, M. (1981). *Management teams: Why they succeed or fail*. London: Butterworth-Heinemann.

Bell, G., & McNamara, J. F. (1991). *McHigh-Tech ventures: The guide for entrepreneurial success*. New York: Perseus Books Publishing L.L.C.

Bell, J. (1995). The internationalisation of small computer software firms: A further challenge to "stage" theories. *European Journal of Marketing, 29*(8), 60-75.

Bennett, R., & Gabriel, H. (1999). Organizational factors and knowledge management within large marketing departments: An empirical study. *Journal of knowledge management, 3*(3), 212-225.

Bentley T, Page, S., & Laird, S. (2000). Safety in New Zealand's adventure tourism industry: The client accident experience of adventure tourism operators. *Journal of Travel Medicine, 7*(5), 239-246.

Berge, Z. L. (1998). Differences in teamwork between post-secondary classrooms and the workplace. *Education and Training, 40*(1), 194-201.

Berger, P. L., & Luckmann, T. (1966). *The social construction of reality: A treatise in the sociology of knowledge*. Harmondsworth: Penguin, 1967

Berger, S. (2000). Globalization and politics. *Annual Review of Political Science 3*, 43-62.

Bergson, H. (1911/1983). *Creative evolution* (A. Mitchell, Trans.). Lanham, MD: University Press of America.

Bergum, V. (1998). *Relational ethics. What is it?* In Touch. 1(2). Retrieved September 29, 2006, from http://www.phen.ab.ca/materials/intouch/vol1/intouch1-02.html

Bergum, V., & Dossetor, J. (2005). *Relational ethics, the full meaning of respect*. Hagerstown, MD: University Publishing Group.

Berk, J., & Berk, S. (1995). *Total quality management, implementing continuous improvement*. Kuala Lumpur, Malaysia: S. Abdul Majeed & Co. in Association with Sterling Publishing Company,Inc.

Berlin Communiqué. (2003). *Realising the European higher education area*. Communiqué of the Conference of Ministers responsible for Higher Education in Berlin on 19 September 2003. Retrieved February 10, 2007, from http://www.dfes.gov.uk/bologna/uploads/documents/Berlin_Communique1.pdf

Bermus, P., & Fox. M. (2005). *Knowledge sharing in the integrated enterprise, interoperability strategies for enterprise architect*. New York: Springer.

Bernauer, T., & Ruloff, D. (1999). *Handel und Umwelt: Zur Frage der Kompatibilität internationaler Regime*. Opladen: Westdeutscher Verlag.

Bernstel, J. B. (2002). Teaming with possibilities. *ABA Bank Marketing, Washington, 34*(3), 14-12.

Berry, M. (1998). Strategic planning in small high tech companies. *Long Range Planning, 31*(3), 455-466.

Bhatt, G., & Emdad, A. (2001). An analysis of the virtual value chain in electronic commerce. *Logistics Information Management, 14*(1), 78-85.

Bigelow, P. (2005). Keep it simple, stupid! *Printed Circuit Design & Manufacture*(August), 14.

Biggs, J. (2003). *Teaching for quality learning at university* (2nd ed.). Buckingham: Open University Press.

Bijker, W. E. (1995). *Of bicycles, bakelites, and bulbs: Towards a theory of sociotechnical change.* Boston: Massachusetts Institute of Technology.

Bird, B. (1989). *Entrepreneurial behaviour.* Glenview, IL: Scott Foresman & Company.

Bjornenak, T. (1997). Diffusion and accounting: The case of ABC in Norway. *Management Accounting Research, 8*(1), 3-17.

Blackler, F. (1995). Knowledge, knowledge work and organizations: An overview and interpretation. *Organization Science, 16*(6), 1021-1046.

Blackman, C. (2004). Stumbling along or grave new world? *Towards Europe's Information Society Foresight, 6*(5), 261-270.

Blake, A., & Mann, D. (2000). *Making knowledge tangible.* CMC and DuVersity, September 2000.

Blascovich, J., & Goffre, J. (2003). *Unlocking value from e-supply management.* A. T. Kearney Technology Watch. Executive Agenda. Third Quarter, 2003. Retrieved January 8, 2007, from http://www.atkearney.com/shared_res/pdf/EA63_unlocking_S.pdf

Boehm, B. W. (1988). A spiral model of software development and enhancement. *IEEE Computers, 21*(5), 61-72.

Bogue, R. (1989). *Deleuze and Guattari.* London: Routledge.

Bolman, L. G., & Deal, T. E. (1997). *Reframing organizations: Artistry, choice & leadership.* San Francisco: Jossey-Bass.

Bologna Declaration. (1999). *Joint declaration of the European Ministers of Education.* Retrieved February 10, 2007, from http://www.dfes.gov.uk/bologna/uploads/documents/BOLOGNA_DECLARATION1.pdf

Bolt, H. M. (2005). Lead. In *Ullmann's Encyclopedia of Industrial Chemistry*: Wiley-VCH Verlag GmbH & Co. KGaA.

Bolton Committee. (1971). *Report of the Committee of Enquiry on Small Firms* (Cmnd 4811) London: HMSO.

Bolton, J. E. (1971). *Small firms: Report of the committee of inquiry on small firms.* London: Her Majesty's Stationery Office.

Book, L. Y. (2001). Strategic management. In *Management in Malaysia.* Kuala Lumpur: Malaysian Institute of Management.

Bordo, M. D. (2002) Globalization in historical perspective, *Business Economics, 11*(January), 20-30.

Borgatti, S., & Everett, M. (2000). Models of core/periphery structures. *Social Networks, 21*(4), 375-395.

Bouchikhi, H. (1993). A constructive framework for understanding entrepreneurship performance. *Organisational Studies, 14*(4), 549-570.

Boyd, N., & Vozikis, G. (1994). The influence of self-efficacy on the development of entrepreneurial intentions and actions. *Entrepreneurship Theory and Practice, 18*(4), 63-77.

Bradach, J. L., & Eccles, R. G. (1989). Price, authority & trust: From ideal types to plural forms. *Annual Review of Sociology, 15*(1), 97-118.

Bradley, S., & Nolan, R. (1998). *Sense & respond: Capturing value in the network era.* Boston, MA: Harvard Business School Press.

Brain, M. (2001). *How cells work.* Retrieved December 30, 2006, from http://science.howstuffworks.com/cell7.htm

Braun, E., & Wield, D. (1994). Regulation as a means for the social-control of technology. *Technology Analysis & Strategic Management, 6*(3), 259.

Brazil, K., Serdella, A. (2005). *Next generation extended enterprise.* Juniper Networks, USA.

Breen, B. (2004). Living in Dell time. *Fast Company, 11*(88), 86, November 2004.

Brey, P. (2005). Freedom and privacy in ambient intelligence. *Ethics and Information Technology, 7*(3), 157-166.

Bringle, R. G., Games, R., & Malloy, E. A. (1999). *Colleges and universities as citizens.* Boston: Allyn & Bacon.

Brockhaus, R. H., & Horwitz, P. S. (1986). The psychology of the entrepreneur. In D. Sexton & R. Smilor (Eds.), *The art and science of entrepreneurship.* New York: Ballinger.

Broersma, M. (2005). *EU rejects controversial software patents proposal.* Enterprise Apps. Retrieved from http://www.eweek.com/article2/0,1895,1834392,00.asp

Brown, J. S., & Duguid, P. (1991). Organizational learning and communities-of-practice: Toward a unified view of working, learning, and innovation. *Organization Science, 2*(1), 40-57.

Brown, J. S., & Duguid, P. (2001). Knowledge and organization: A social-practice perspective. *Organization Science, 12*(2), 198-213.

Brown, J. S., Collins, A., & Duguid, S. (1989). Situated cognition and the culture of learning. *Educational Researcher, 18*(1), 32-42.

Brown, S. D., & Lunt, P. (2002). A genealogy of the social identity tradition: Deleuze and Guattari and social psychology. *British Journal of Social Psychology, 41*(1), 1-23.

Brown, S., & Blackmon, K. (2005). Aligning manufacturing strategy and business-level competitive strategy in new competitive environments: the case for strategic resonance. *Journal of Management Studies, 42*(4), 793-815.

Brown, S., & Eisenhardt, K. M. (1998). *Competing on the edge.* Boston, MA: Harvard Business School Press.

Browne, J., Sackett, P. J., & Wortmann, J. C. (1995). Future manufacturing systems—Towards the Extended Enterprise. *Computers in Industry.*

Brush, C. G., & Vanderwerf, P. A. (1992). A comparison of methods and sources for obtaining estimates of new venture performance. *Journal of Business Venturing, 7*(2), 157-70.

Bryant, L. R. (2000). *The Transcendental Empiricism of Gilles Deleuze* (unpublished manuscript). Chicago: Loyola University of Chicago.

Brynjolfsson, E., & Smith, J. (2000). Frictionless commerce? A comparison of Internet and conventional retailers. *Management Science, 46*(4), 563-585.

Buckingham, M. (2006). Engaging generation Y: An interview with Marcus Buckingham. *ASTD*, August, *60*(8), 27-30.

Burgel, O., & Murray, G. C. (2000). The international market entry choices of start-yup companies in high-technology industries. *Journal of International Marketing, 8*(2), 33-62.

Burlton, R. (2001). *Business process management: Profiting from process.* Indianapolis, IN: Sams Publishing.

Burns, T., & Stalker, G. M. (1994). *The management of innovation*, Tavistock, 1961, 3rd Ed, Oxford University Press, Oxford.

Burton, T. T., & Shaw, T. E. (2005). *Building the lean extended enterprise through adaptive supply chain networks.* LAI (Lean Aeronautics Imitative).

Busby, J. S., & Fan, I. S. (1993). The extended manufacturing enterprise: Its nature and its needs. *International Journal of Technology Management*, Special Issue on Manufacturing Technology: Diffusion, Implementation and Management.

Byers, S. (2000). *"Knowledge 2000"—Conference on the Knowledge Driven Economy.* Department of Trade and Industry. Retrieved February 12, 2002, from http://www.dti.gov.uk/knowledge2000/byers.htm

Cai, S., Jun, M., & Yang, Z. (2006). The impact of interorganizational Internet communication on purchasing performance: A study of Chinese manufacturing firms. *The Journal of Supply chain Management, 42*(3), 16-29

Caldeira, M. M., & Ward, J. M. (2003). Using resource-based theory to interpret the successful adoption and use of information systems and technology in manufacturing small and medium-sized enterprises. *European Journal of Information Systems, 12*(2), 127-141.

Caldwell, T. (2006). Social networking technologies. *Information World Review, 230*, 26.

Caldwell, T. (2006). Who shares, wins. *Information World Review, 230,* 26.

Camarinha-Matos, L., & Afsarmanesh, H. (2004). *Collaborative networked organizations—A research agenda for emerging business models.* UK: Kluwer Academic Publishers

Campbell, J. (2000). Using Internet technology to support flexible learning in business education. *Information Technology and Management, 1*(1), 351-362.

Campos, A. R., da Silva, R., & Stokic, D. (2004). Integrated approach for innovation and problem solving in dynamic virtual enterprises. *Proceedings of the INDIN 04,* Berlin.

Cantu, C. (1997). *Virtual teams.* Retrieved July 26, 2006, from www.workteams.unt.edu/literature/paper-ccantu.html

Carley, K. M., & Hill, V. (2001). Structural change and learning within organization. In A. Lomi & E. R. Larsen (Eds.), *Dynamics of organizations: Computational modeling and organizational thoeries* (pp. 63-92). Live Oak: MIT Press/AAAI Press.

Carnegie Mellon Software Engineering Institute. (2006). *CMMI® for Development, Version 1.2.* Pittsburgh, USA.

Carneiro, A. (2000). How does knowledge management influence innovation and competitiveness? *Journal of Knowledge Management, 4*(2), 87-98.

Carrier, C., Raymond, L., & Eltaief, A. (2004). Cyberentrepreneurship: A multiple case study. *International Journal of Entrepreneurial Behaviour and Research, 10*(5), 349-363.

Carroll, J. M. (1989). *Interfacing thought: Cognitive aspects of human-computer interaction.* MA: The MIT Press.

Carson, R. L. (1962). *Der stumme Frühling.* München: Biederstein.

Carson, R. L. (1962). *Der stumme Frühling.* München: Biederstein.

Caruso, D., & Cecere, L., & O'Marah, K. (2004). *Demand-driven supply networks.* Retrieved December 30, 2006, from http://www.amrresearch.com/Content/View.asp?pmillid=17647

Casal, C. R., Burgelman, J. C., & Bohlin, E. (2004). Prospects beyond 3G. *Info, 6*(6), 359-362.

Caskey, K. R. (1995). *Co-operative distributed simulation and optimization in extended enterprise.* IFIP WG5.7 Conference Proceedings.

Cassia, L., Fattore, M., & Paleari, S. (2006). *Entrepreneurial strategy.* Cheltenham: Edward Elgar.

Castells, M. (1996). *The rise of the network society.* Malden, MA: Blackwell.

Castells, M. (1996/97). *The information age: Economy, society, and culture.* Oxford: Blackwell.

Cetinkunt, S. (2006). *Mechatronics.* John Wiley & Sons.

Chakrabarti, S., Joshi, M., Punera, K., & Pennock, D. (2002). The structure of broad topics on the Web. In D. Lassner, D. De Roure, & A. Iyengar (Eds.), *Proceedings of the 11th International World Wide Web Conference* (251-262), New York: ACM Press.

Chan, C., Pearson, C., & Entrekin, L. (2003). Examining the effects of internal and external team learning on team performance. *Team Performance Management: An International Journal, 9*(7/8), 174-181.

Chandler, G. N., & Hanks, S. H. (1993). Measuring the performance of emerging businesses: A validation study. *Journal of Business Venturing, 8*(5), 391-408.

Chandy, M. (2005). *Event servers for sense and respond applications.* Retrieved December 30, 2006, from http://senseandrespond.com/downloads/iSPHERES_S_R_WEBCAST.ppt

Chatterton, P., & Goddard, J. (2000). The response of higher education institutions to regional needs. *European Journal of Education, 35*(4), 475-496.

Chay, Y. (1993). Social support, individual differences, and wellbeing: A study of small business entrepreneurs and employees. *Journal of Occupational and Organizational Psychology, 66*(1), 285-302.

Chell, E. (2000). Towards researching the "opportunistic entrepreneur": A social constructionist approach and research agenda. *European Journal of Work and Organizational Psychology, 1 March 2000*(1), 63-80.

Chen, L., Haney S., Pandzik, A., Spigarelli, J., & Jesseman, C. (2003). Small business Internet commerce: A case study. *Information Resources Management Journal, 16*(3), 17-42.

Chen, S. (2003). Strategic decision-making by e-commerce entrepreneurs. *International Journal of Management and Decision Making, 4*(2/3), 133-142.

Chen, S. (2005). *Strategic management of e-business* (2nd ed.). Chichester: John Wiley and Sons.

Chen, S., Magoulas, G., & Dimakopoulos, D. (2005). A flexible interface design for Web directories to accommodate different cognitive styles. *Journal of the American Society For Information Science And Technology, 56*(1), 70-83.

Chesbrough, H. (1999). *The role of the institutional environment on the organizational impact of innovation.* Harvard Business School. Retrieved December, 2006, from http://smealsearch2.psu.edu/cache/papers/Business/1419/http:zSzzSzemlab.berkeley.eduzSzuserszSzbhhallzSzchesbrough.pdf/the-role-of-the.pdf/

Chesbrough, H. (2003). *Open innovation: The new imperative for creating and profiting from technology.* Harvard Business School Publishing Corporation.

Chesbrough, H., & Rosenbloom, R. S. (2004). The role of the business model in capturing value from innovation. *Industrial and Corporate Change, 11*(3), 529-555. Retrieved December 30, 2006, from icc.oxfordjournals.org/cgi/content/abstract/11/3/529

Chiou, J., & Shen, C. (2006). The effects of satisfaction, opportunism, and asset specificity on consumers' loyalty intention toward internet portal sites. *International Journal of Service Industry Management, 17*(1), 7-22.

Chou, T., Hsu, L. Yeh, Y., & Ho, C. (2005). Towards a framework of the performance evaluation of SMEs' industry portals. *Industrial Management and Data Systems, 105*(4), 527-544.

Christensen, C. M. (1997). *The innovator's dilemma: When new technologies cause great firms to fail.* Boston: Harvard Business School Press.

Chun, C. W. (2001). *Environmental scanning as information seeking and organizational learning.* Information Research, 7. October. Retrieved December, 2006, from http://informationr.net/ir/7-1/infres71.html

Chung, K. S., Hossain, L., & Davis, J. (2005). *Social networks and ICT correlates to individual performance.* Paper presented at the Applications of Social Network Analysis Conference, University of Zurich

Church, R. L., Zimmerman, D. L., Bargerstock, B. A., & Kenney, P. A. (2003). Measuring scholarly outreach at Michigan State University: Definition, challenges, tools. *Journal of Higher Education Outreach and Engagement, 8*(1), 141-152.

Churchill, N. C., & Lewis, V. L. (1983). The five stages of small business growth. *Harvard Business Review, 61*(3), 2-11.

Cigolini, R., Cozzi, M., & Perona, M. (2004). A new framework for supply chain management. *International Journal of Operations and Production Management, 24*(1), 27-41

Clancey, W. J. (1994). Situated cognition: How representations are created and given meaning. In R. Lewis & P. Mendelsohn (Eds.), *Lessons from learning* (pp. 231-242). Amsterdam: North Holland.

Clark, B. (2001). The entrepreneurial university: New foundations of collegiality, autonomy, and achievement. *Higher Education Management, 13*(2), 9-24.

Clark, K. B., & Fujimoto, T. (1991). *Product development performance.* Boston: Harvard Business School Press.

Cobbenhagen, J. (2000). Successful innovation—towards a new theory for the management of small and medium-sized enterprises. Cheltenham, UK: Edward Elgar.

Cochrane, T. (2006, December 3-6). Learning with wireless mobile devices and social software. *Proceedings of the 23rd Annual Conference of the Australasian Society for Computers in Learning in Tertiary Education. "Who's Learning? Whose Technology?"* Sydney: Australia.

Coffey, J., & Hoffman, R. (2002). A knowledge modeling approach to institutional memory preservation. *The Journal of Knowledge Management, 7*(3), 38-49.

Cohen, S., & Brand, R. (1993). *Total quality management in government (USA).* A practical guide for real world. The Jossey-Brass Publication administration series.

Colebrook, C. (2002). *Understanding Deleuze.* Crows Nest, Australia: Allen & Unwin.

Collins, J. (2001). *Good to great.* New York: Harper Business.

Collis, J., & Hussey, R. (2003). *Business research: A practical guide for undergraduates and postgraduate students* (2nd ed.). Palgrave Macmillan: Creative Print and Design.

Colombo, M. S., & Delmastro, M. (2001). Technology-based entrepreneurs: Does the internet make a difference. *Small Business Economics, 16*(3), 177-190.

Connaughton, S. L., & Daly, J. A. (2004). Identification with leader. A comparison of perceptions of identification among geographically dispersed and co-located teams. *Corporate Communications: An International Journal, 9*(2), 89-103.

Conner, M., & Finnemore, P. (2003). Living in the new age: Using collaborative digital technology to deliver health care improvement. *International Journal of Health Care Quality Assurance, 16*(2), 77-86.

Conner, M., & Finnemore, P. (2003). Living in the new age: Using collaborative digital technology to deliver health care improvement. *International Journal of Health care Quality Assurance, 16*(2), 77-86.

Conti, B., & Kleiner, B .H. (1997). How to increase teamwork in organizations. *Training for Quality, 5*(1), 26-29.

Cook, J. W., Dodds, E. C., & Hewett, C. L. (1933). A synthetic oestrus-exciting compound. *Nature, January 14, 1933,* 56.

Coopey, J., Keegan, O., & Emler, N. (1998). Managers' innovations and the structuration of organizations. *Journal of Management Studies, 35*(3), 263-284.

Coppola, N. W., Hiltz, S. R., & Rotter, N. G. (2004). Building trust in virtual teams. *IEEE Transactions on Professional Communication, 47*(2).

Cottrill, K. (1998). Reinventing innovation. *Journal of Business Strategy, 19*(2), 47-51.

Courtney, H., Kirkland, J., & Viguerie, P. (1997). Strategy under uncertainty. *Harvard Business Review, 75*(6), 66-79.

Covey, R. S. (1989). *The 7 habits of highly effective people: Powerful lessons in personal change.* New York: Free Press—A division of Simon and Schuster, Inc.

Coviello, N. E., & Munro, H. J. (1995). Growing the entrepreneurial firm: Networking for international market development. *European Journal of Marketing, 29*(7), 49-61.

Covin, J. G., & Slevin, D. P. (1989). Strategic management of small firms in hostile and benign environments. *Strategic Management Journal, 10*(1), 75–87.

Cowan, R. A. (1984). *Teleconferencing: Maximising human potential.* Preston Publication.

Coyne, K. P. (1986). Sustainable competitive advantage—What it is and what it isn't. *Business Horizons, 29*(January-February), 54-61.

Crabb, H. C. (1997). *The virtual engineer: 21st century product development.* Society of Manufacturing.

Creed, A., Ross, J., Stewart, J., Bolesta, M., Hladik, M., & Backhaus, W. (2006, December 13-15). Tapping global human resources in an MBA teaching team: Insights with implications for management education worldwide. *Proceedings of Australian and New Zealand Academy of Management 2006 Conference.* Management: Pragmatism, Philosophy, Priorities. Rock Hampton: Australia.

Creswell, J. W. (1998). *Qualitative inquiry and research design: Choosing among five traditions.* California: SAGE Publications, Inc.

Croom, S. (2001). *Supply chain management in the e-business era—An investigations into supply chain strategies, practices, and progress in e-business adoption.* BT/Warwick Business School, SC Associates, Coventry.

Croom, S. (2005). The impact of e-business on supply chain management: An empirical study of key developments. *International Journal of Operations & Production Management, 25*(1), 55-73.

Cross, R., & Parker, A. (2004). *The hidden power of social networks.* Boston, MA: Harvard Business School Press.

Cumby, J., & Conrod, J. (2001). Non-financial performance measures in the Canadian biotechnology industry. *Journal of Intellectual Capital, 2*(3), 261.

Curran, J., & Blackburn, R. (2001). *Researching the small enterprise*. London: Sage.

Czech Statistical Department Report #9605-04. (2004) Retrieved December 16, 2006 from http://www.liberec. czso.cz/eng/edicniplan.nsf/publ/9605-04-2002_2003.

D'Agostino, R. J., & Wilson, R. (1993). Asbestos: The hazard, the risk, and public policy. In K. R. Foster, D. E. Bernstein & P. W. Huber (Eds.), *Phantom risk: Scientific interference and the law*. London: The MIT Press.

D'Aveni, R. A. (1994). *Hyper-competition: Managing the dynamics of strategic Maneuvering*. New York: Free Press.

Daniel, E. (2003). An exploration of the inside-out model: E-commerce integration in UK SMEs. *Journal of Small Business and Enterprise Development, 10*(3), 233-249.

Daniel, E., Wilson, H., & Myers, A. (2002). Adoption of e-commerce by SMEs in the UK: Toward a stage model. *International Small Business Journal, 20*(3), 253-270.

Davenport, T. H. (1993). *Process innovation: Reengineering work through information technology*. Boston: Harvard Business School Press.

Davenport, T. H., & Prusack, L. (1998). *Working knowledge: How organizations manage what they know*. Boston: Harvard Business School Press.

Davis, E. W., & Spekman, R. E. (2003). The extended enterprise: Gaining competitive advantage through collaborative supply chains. *Financial Times Prentice Hall*.

Davis, G. B. (2002). Anytime/anyplace computing and the future of knowledge work. *Communications of the ACM, 45*(12), 67-73.

Davis, G., Wilt, C., Dillon, P., & Fishbein, B. (1997). *Extended product responsibility: A new principle for product-oriented pollution prevention*. The University of Tennessee. The Gordon Institute, INFORM.

Davis, K. (2002). *Organizational behaviour-human behaviour at work*. New York: McGraw-Hill.

Dawson, P., & Patrickson (1991). Total quality management in the Australian Banking sector. *International Journal of Quality and Reliability Management, 8*(5).

Day, R. (2001). Totality and representation: A history of knowledge management through European documentation, critical modernity, and post-fordism. *Journal of the American Society for Information Science and Technology, 52*(9), 725-735.

DCA. (2006). *China RoHS: DCA overview and insights*. Retrieved February 1, 2006, from http://www.design-chainassociates.com/chinarohs.html

De Berranger, P., Tucker, D., & Jones, L. (2001). Internet diffusion in creative micro-businesses: Identifying change-agent characteristics as critical success factors. *Journal of Organizational Computing and Electronic Commerce, 11*(3), 197-214.

De Boer, L., Harink, J., & Heijboer, G. (2002). A conceptual model for assessing the impact of electronic procurement. *European Journal of Purchasing and Supply Management, 8*(1), 25-33.

Deaux, K., & Philogène, G. (2001). *Representations of the social*. Oxford: Blackwells Publishers Inc.

De-Graft Aikins, A. (2004). *Social representations of diabetes in Ghana: Reconstructing self, society, and culture*. Unpublished Thesis, London School of Economics and Political Science, London.

DeLanda, M. (1998). *Deleuze and the open-ended becoming of the World*. Paper presented at the Chaos/ Control: Complexity Conference, Bielefeld, Germany.

Deleuze, G. (1968). *Différence et répétition*. Paris: Presses Universitaires de France.

Deleuze, G. (1983). *Kant's critical philosophy: The doctrine of the faculties*. London: The Athlone Press.

Deleuze, G. (1995). *Negotiations*. New York: Columbia University Press.

Deleuze, G., & Guattari, F. (1987a). *Anti-Oedipus: Capitalism and schizophrenia* (translation). New York: Viking Press.

Deleuze, G., & Guattari, F. (1987b). *A thousand plateaus: Capitalism and schizophrenia*. London: Athlone Press.

Deleuze, G., & Parnet, C. (1987). *Dialogues* (H. Tomlinson & B. Habberjam, Trans.). London: The Athlone Press.

Deloitte Research. (2006). *China and India: The reality beyond the hype.* May. Retrieved January 5, 2007, from http://www.deloitte.com/dtt/research/0,1015,sid=2318&cid=117814,00.html

Denbigh, A. (2003). The *Teleworking handbook, the essential guide to working from where you want* (4th ed.). London, UK: A & C Black.

Deresky, H. (2004). *International management-managing across borders & cultures.* NJ: Prentice Hall.

Dess, G. G., & Picken, J. C. (1999). Creating competitive (dis)advantage: Learning from Food Lion's freefall. *Academy of management Executive, 13*(3), 97-111.

Dewey, J. (1963). *Experience and education.* London: Collier Books.

Diamante, T., & London, M. (2002). Expansive leadership in the age of digital technology. *Journal of Management Development, 21*(6), 404-416.

Diaz, F., & Rodriguez, A. (2003). Locus of control, nAch and values of community entrepreneurs. *Social Behavior & Personality: An International Journal, 31*(8), 739-748.

Dickson, P. R. (1992). Toward a general theory of competitive rationality. *Journal of Marketing, 56*(January), 69-83.

Diegel, O., Bright, G., & Potgieter, J. (2004). Bluetooth ubiquitous networks: Seamlessly integrating humans and machines. *Assembly Automation, 24*(2), 168-176.

Dieke, P. (2003). Tourism in Africa's economic development: Policy implications. *Management Decision, 41*(3), 287-295.

Dillon, P. (2004). Trajectories and tensions in the theory of information and communication technology in education. *British Journal of Educational Studies, 52*(2), 138-150.

DiMaggio, P. J., & Powell, W. (1983). The iron cage revisited: Institutional isomorphism and collective rationality in organizational behavior. *American Sociological Review, 48*(April), 147-160.

Dirks, K., & Ferrin, D. (2002). The role of trust in organizational settings. *Organization Science, 12*(4), 450-467.

Dirks, K., & Ferrin, D. (2002). Trust in leadership: Meta-analytic findings & implications for research & practice. *Journal of Applied Psychology, 87*(4), 611-628.

Dobson, P., & Starkey, K. (1993). *The strategic management blueprint.* Oxford: Blackwells.

Dodd, S. D., & Anderson, A. R. (2001). Understanding the entreprise culture: paradigm, paradox and policy. *International Journal of Entrepreneurship and Innovation, 2*(1), 13-27.

Dodgson, M., Gann, D., & Salter, A. (2005). *Think, play, do: Technology, innovation, and organization.* New York: Oxford University Press.

Dolan, C., & Humphrey, J. (2001). Governance and trade in fresh vegetables: The impact of UK supermarkets on the African horticultural industry. *Journal of Development Studies 37*(2), 147-76.

Donovan, M. R. (n.d.). *Supply chain management: Transforming with an e-strategy.* Supply chain management (pp. 176-180). Touch Briefings. Retrieved February, 5, 2007, from http://www.touchbriefings.com/pdf/977/supplychain4.pdf

Doran, D. (2003). Supply chain implications of modularisation. *International Journal of Operations and Production Management, 23*(3), 316-326.

Downes, L. (2004). First empower all the lawyers. *Harvard Business Review, 82*(12), 19.

Drennan, J., Kennedy, J., & Pisarksi, A. (2005). Factors affecting student attitudes toward flexible online learning in management education. *Journal of Educational Research, 98*(6), 331-340.

Drew, S., & Coulson-Thomas, C. (1997). Transformation through teamwork: The path to the new organisation? *Team Performance Management, 3*(3), 162-178.

Drucker, P. F. (2003). *The essential Drucker: The best of sixty years of Peter Drucker's essential writings on management.* HarperCollins.

Drury, D. H., & Farhoomand, A. (1999). Knowledge worker constraints in the productive use of information technology. *Computer Personnel, 19/20*(4/1), 21-42.

DTI. (2000). *A new future for communications—Summary of proposals.* Department of Trade and Industry.

Retrieved November 15, 2001, from www.communicationswhitepaper.gov.uk

DTI. (2002). *DTI Data Internet Scoping Study—Section One (the Outsider's View)*. London: Department of Trade and Industry.

Ducatel, K., Bogdanowicz, M., Scapolo, F., Leijten, J., & Burgelman, J. C. (2001). *Scenarios for ambient intelligence in 2010* (ISTAG 2001 Final Report). IPTS, Seville: ISTAG.

Duffy, G., & Dale, B. (2002). E-commerce processes: A study of criticality. *Industrial Management and Data Systems, 102*(8), 432-441.

Duffy, J., & Tod, M. (2004). *The extended enterprise: Eliminating the barriers.* CIO Magazine. Retrieved from http://www2.cio.com/analyst/report2118.html

Duguid, P. (2005). The art of knowing: social and tacit dimensions of knowledge and the limitations of the community of practice. *The Information Society, 21*(2), 109-118.

Duncan, E., & Elliot, G. (2002). Customer service quality and financial performance among Australian retail financial institutions. *Journal of Financial Services Marketing, 7*(1)25-38.

Duncombe, R. A., & Molla, A. (2006). E-commerce development in developing countries: Profiling change agents for SMEs. *International Journal for Entrepreneurship and Innovation, 7*(3), 185-196.

Duncombe, R. A., Heeks, R. B. Abraham, S., & Lal, N. (2005). *E-commerce for small enterprise development: A handbook for enterprise support agencies in India*. Retrieved December 12, 2006, from http://www.ecomm4dev.org

Duveen, G. (2000). Introduction: The power of ideas. In G. Duveen & S. Moscovici (Eds.), *Social representations: Explorations in social psychology*. Cambridge: Polity Press.

Dwyer, S., Mesak, H., & Hsu, M. (2005). An exploratory examination of the influence of national culture on cross-national product diffusion. *Journal of International Marketing, 13*(2), 48-69.

Dyer, J. H. (2000). *Collaborative advantage: Winning through extended enterprise supplier networks*. Oxford University Press.

Dynes, S., Breschbühl, H., & Johnson, M. (2005). *Information security in the extended enterprise*.

Eccles, R. G. (1991). The performance measurement manifesto. *Harvard Business Review, 69*(1), 131-137.

Edwards, A., & Wilson, J. R. (2004). *Implementing virtual teams: A guide to organizational and human factors*. Aldershot/Hants: Gower Publishing Limited.

Ehrlenspiel, K. (2003). *Integrierte Produktentwicklung*. München, Germany: Hanser.

Eisenhardt, K. M., & Brown, S. L. (1998). Time pacing: Competing in markets that won't stand still. *Harvard Business Review, 76*(2), 59-69.

Eisenhardt, K. M., & Brown, S. L. (1999). Patching—restitching business portfolios in dynamic markets. *Harvard Business Review, 77*(3), 72-82.

Eisner, S. (2005). Managing generation Y. *SAM Advanced Management Journal, 70*(4), 4-15.

Ellis, L. (1997). *Evaluation of R&D processes: Effectiveness through measurements*. London: Artech House Publishers

Ellis, L. W., & Curtis, C. C. (1995). Measuring customer satisfaction. *Research Technology Management, 38*(5), 45-48.

Elovici, Y., Glezer, C., & Shapira, B. (2005). Enhancing customer privacy while searching for products and services on the World Wide Web. *Internet Research, 15*(4), 378-399.

Elsammani, Z. A., Hackney, R., & Scown, P. (2004). SMEs adoption and implementation process of Websites in the presence of change agents. In N. A. Y. Al-Qirim (Ed.), *Electronic commerce in small to medium-sized enterprises: Frameworks, issues, and implications*. London: Idea Group Publishing.

Emiliani, P. L., & Stephanidis, C. (2005). Universal access to ambient intelligence environment: Opportunities and challenges for people with disabilities. *IBM Systems Journal, 44*(3), 605-619.

Escriba-Moreno, M. A., & Canet-Giner, M. T. (2006). The combined use of quality management programs and work teams. A comparative analysis of its impact in the organizational structure. *Team Performance Management, 12*(5/6), 162-181.

Etzkowitz, H., & Leydesdorff, L. (2000). The dynamics of innovation: From national systems and "mode 2" to a Triple Helix of university-industry-government relations. *Research Policy, 29* (2), 109-123.

European Industrial Research Management Association. (1995). *Evaluation of R&D Projects*, EIRMA Paris, Working group reports, Report No. 47.

European Union. (2003). Directive 2002/95/EC of the European Parliament and of the Council of 27 January 2003 on the restriction of the use of certain hazardous substances in electrical and electronic equipment. *Official Journal of the European Union, L 37*, 19.

European Union. (2005). Entscheidung der Kommission vom 13. Oktober 2005 zur Änderung des Anhangs der Richtlinie 2002/95/EG des Europäischen Parlaments und des Rates zur Beschränkung der Verwendung bestimmter gefährlicher Stoffe in Elektro- und Elektronikgeräten zwecks Anpassung an den technischen Fortschritt. *Official Journal of the European Union, L 271*, 48.

European Union. (2005). Entscheidung der Kommission vom 18. August 2005 zur Änderung des Anhangs der Richtlinie 2002/95/EG des Europäischen Parlaments und des Rates zwecks Festlegung von Konzentrationshöchstwerten für bestimmte gefährliche Stoffe in Elektro- und Elektronikgeräten. *Official Journal of the European Union, L 214*, 65.

Eurostat. (2006). *Internet usage in the EU25*. News release.

Evans, D., & Volery, T. (2001). Online business development services for entrepreneurs: An exploratory study. *Entrepreneurship & Regional Development, 13*(1), 333-350.

Evans, P., & Wurster, T. S. (1999). *Blown to bits: How the new economics of information transforms strategy*. Boston: Harvard Business School Publishing.

Farid, J. A. (2006). *Blue screen of death: A Desi, s misadventure in the land of opportunity*. Karachi: Alchemy Technologies.

Farr, R. M. (1996). *The roots of modern social psychology, 1872-1954*. Oxford: Blackwell Publishers.

Faye, M., McArthur, J., Sachs, J., & Snow, T. (2004). The challenges facing landlocked developing countries. *Journal of Human Development, 5*(1), 31-68.

Feldmüller, D., Frick, A., & Grau, N. (2006). *Welche Kompetenzen benötigt das IT-Projektmanagement?* Paper presented at interPM conference, Glashütten, Germany.

Fenwick. (2003). Innovation: Examining workplace learning in new enterprises. *Journal of Workplace Learning, 15*(3), 123-132.

Ferdig, R. E., & Roehler, L. R. (2004). Student uptake in electronic discussions: Examining online discourse in literacy preservice classrooms. *Journal of Research on Technology in Education, 36*(2), 119-136.

Fernandez, M., Gomez-Perez, A., & Juristo, N. (1997). METHONTOLOGY—From ontological art towards ontological engineering. *In Proceedings in the AAAI97 Spring Symposium Series on Ontology Engineering (pp. 33-40)*. Stanford, USA

Fiet, J. O. (2001). The theoretical side of teaching entrepreneurship. *Journal of Business Venturing, 16*(1), 1-24.

Filion, L. J. (2003). *From entrepreneurship to entreprenology*. HEC, The University of Montreal Business School. Retrieved 2003, from http://www.sbaer.uca.edu/Research/1997/ICSB/97ics006.htm

FINHEEC. (2006). *Audits of quality assurance systems of Finnish higher education institutions*. Audit Manual for 2005-2007. Publications of the Finnish Higher Education Evaluation Council 4:2006. Retrieved February 10, 2007, from http://www.kka.fi/pdf/julkaisut/KKA_406.pdf

Fitz-Enz, J. (2001). *How to measure human resource management*. McGraw-Hill.

Fitzgerald, L. A. (2002). Chaos—the lens that transcends. *Journal of Organisational Change Management, 15*(4), 339-358.

Fjeldstad, O. D., & Haanaes, K. (2001). Strategy tradeoffs in the knowledge and network economy. *Business Strategy Review, 12*(1), 1-10.

Flavian, C., & Guinaliu, M. (2006). Consumer trust, perceived security, and privacy policy: Three basic elements of loyalty to a Web site. *Industrial Management and Data Systems, 106*(5), 601-620.

Flick, U. (1992). Triangulation revisited: Strategy of validation or alternative? *Journal for the theory of Social Behaviour, 22*(2), 175 -197.

Flick, U. (1998). Everyday knowledge in social psychology. In U. Flick (Ed.), *The psychology of the social*. Cambridge, UK, New York, NY: Cambridge University Press.

Florida, R. (2002). *The rise of the creative class: And how it's transforming work, leisure, community, and everyday life*. New York: Basic.

Florida, R. (2005). *The flight of the creative class: The new global competition for talent*. New York: Harper Collins.

Font, X., Tapper, R., & Cochrane, J. (2006). Competitive strategy in a global industry: Tourism. *Handbook of Business Strategy, 7*(1), 51-55.

Forrester Research. (1998). *Growth spiral in online retail sales will generate $108 billion in revenues by 2003*. Retrieved November 19, 2006, from http://www.forrester.com

Forsyth, T. (1997). Environmental responsibility and business regulation: The case of sustainable tourism. *The Geographic Journal, 163*(3), 270-280.

Foster, K. R., Bernstein, D. E., & Huber, P. W. (1993). A scientific perspective. In K. R. Foster, D. E. Bernstein, & P. W. Huber (Eds.), *Phantom risk: Scientific interference and the law*. London: The MIT Press.

FPC. (2001). *Guidelines on privacy in the private health sector*. Australia: Office of the Federal Privacy Commissioner.

French, S. J., Kelly, S. J., & Harrison, J. L. (2004). The role of strategic planning in the performance of small, professional service firms—a research note. *Journal of Management Development, 23*(9), 765-776.

Friedewald, M., & Da Costa, O. (2003). *Science and technology roadmapping: Ambient intelligence in everyday life (AmI@Life)*. Seville, Spain: JRC-IPTS/ESTO.

Friedlob, G. T., Schleifer, L. L. F., & Plewa, F. J. J. (2002). *Essentials of corporate performance measurement*. New York: John Wiley & Sons.

Friedman, S. M. (1999). The never-ending story of Dioxin. In S. M. Friedman, S. Dunwoody, & C. L. Rogers (Eds.), *Communication uncertainty: Media coverage and new and controversial science* (pp. 113). New Jersey, London: Lawrence Erlbaum Associates Publishers.

Friscia, T., O'Marah, K., & Souza, J. (2004). *The AMR research supply chain top 25 and the new trillion dollar opportunity*. Retrieved January 8, 2007, from http://www.i2cis.ru/pdf/The_AMR_Research_Supply_Chain_Top_25.pdf

Fukuda, Y., Pecht, M. G. P., Fukuda, K., & Fukuda, S. (2003). Lead-free soldering in the Japanese electronics industry. *IEEE Transactions on components and packaging technologies, 26*(3), 616.

Fukuyama, F. (1995). *Trust-the social virtues & the creation of prosperity*. London: Hamish Hamilton.

Gadde, L., & Hakkansson, H. (2001). *Supply network strategies*. John Wiley & Sons.

Galloway, E. C. (1971). Evaluating R&D performance—Keep it simple. *Research Management, 14*(2), 50-58.

Galloway, L. (2005). Internet business and e-commerce. In D. Deakins & M. Freel (Eds.), *Entrepreneurship and small firms*, (pp.139-156). Maidenhead: McGraw-Hill.

Gambetta, D. (1988). Can we trust. In D. Gambetta (Ed.), *Trust-making & breaking of cooperative relations*. Oxford: Blackwell.

Gandy, A., & Chapman C. S. (1997). *Information technology and financial services, the new partnership*. The Chartered Institute of Bankers. Chicago: Glenlake Publishing Company Ltd.

Gans, J. S., & Stern, S. (2003). The product market and the market for "ideas": Commercialisation strategies for technology entrepreneurs. *Research Policy, 32*(2), 333-350.

Garavan, T. N., & O' Cinneide, B. (1994). Entrepreneurship education and training programmes: A review and evaluation—Part 1. *Journal of European Industrial Training, 18*(8), 3-12.

Garcia-Dastugue, S. J., & Lambert, D. M. (2003). Internet-enabled coordination in the supply chain. *Industrial Marketing Management, 32*(3), 251-263.

Gardner, R. A. (2004). *The process-focused organization*. Milwaukee, WI: ASQ Quality Press.

Garengo, P., Biazzo, S., & Bititci, U. S. (2005). Performance measurement systems in SMEs: A review for a research agenda. *International Journal of Management Reviews, 7*(1), 25.

Garfinkel, H. (1967). *Studies in ethno methodology.* Englewood Cliffs, NJ: Prentice-Hall.

Gartner Group. (2002). *Gartner Says 20 Percent of Corporate IT Budgets Wasted Globally in 2001 on Inefficient Information Communication Technology Spending.* Gartner Group Press Release, Egham, UK, 14 March 2002. Retrieved March 15, 2007, from http://www.gartner.com/5_about/press_releases/2002_03/pr20020314a.jsp

Gartner, W. (1985). A conceptual framework for describing the phenomenon of new venture creation. *Academy of Management Review, 10*(1), 696-706.

Gartner's (1989). Who is an entrepreneur? is the wrong question. *American Journal of Small Business, 12*(3), 11-32.

Gaskell, G., & Bauer, M. (2000). Towards public accountability: Beyond sampling, reliability and validity. In M. Bauer & G. Gaskell (Eds.), *Qualitative researching with text, image and sound: A practical handbook.* London: Sage Publications.

Gassmann, O. (2006). Innovation und Risiko - zwei Seiten einer Medaille. In O. Gassmann & C. Kobe (Ed.), *Management von Innovation und Risiko.* Berlin, Germany: Springer.

Gausemeier, J., Hahn, A., Kespohl, H. D., & Seifert, L. (2006). *Vernetzte Produktentwicklung.* München, Germany: Hanser.

Gee, D., MacGarvin, M., Stirling, A., Keys, J., Wynne, B., & Guedes Vaz, S. (2001). *Late lessons from early warnings: The precautionary principle 1896-2000.* Copenhagen: European Environment Agency.

Genero, M., Piattini, M., & Calero, C. (2005). *Metrics for software conceptual models.* Imperial College Press.

George, M. L., Rowlands, D., Price, M., & Maxley, J. (2005). *The Lean Six Sigma Pocket. 60 Toolbook. A quick reference guide to nearly 100 tools for improving process, quality, speed and complexity.* Mc Graw-Hill.

Georgellis, Y., Joyce, P., & Woods, A. (2000). Entrepreneurial action, innovation, and business performance. *Journal of Small Business Development, 1*(1), 7-17.

Gergen, K. (1999). *An invitation to social construction.* Beverly Hills, CA: Sage.

Gibb, A. (1993). The enterprise culture and education. *Entrepreneurship Theory & Practice, 11*(3), 11-34.

Gibb, A. (2006). *[Internet] entrepreneurship: Unique solutions for unique environments is it possible to achieve this with the existing paradigm?* Background paper to the plenary presentation to the International Council for Small Business World Conference June 2006, Melbourne. Returned July 2006, from http://www.icsb2006.org/docs/Allan_Gibb-Plenary_Paper_ICSB2006.pdf

Gibb, A. A. (1995). Learning skills for all: The key to success in small business development. *International Council for Small Business (ICSB) 40th World Conference Proceedings,* Sydney.

Gibb, A. A. (1996). Entrepreneurship and small business management: Can we afford to neglect them in the twenty-first century business school? *British Journal of Management, 7*(4), 309-321.

Gibb, A., & Scott, M. (1985). Strategic awareness, personal commitment, and the process of planning in the small business. *Journal of Management Studies, 22*(6), 597-624.

Gibson, A. W., Choi, S., Bieler, T. R., & Subramanian, K. N. (1997, 1997-05-05). *Environmental concerns and materials issues in manufactured solder joints.* Paper presented at the IEEE International Symposium on Electronics and the Environment.

Gibson, B., & Cassar, G. (2005). Longitudinal analysis of relationships between planning and performance in small firms. *Small Business Economics, 25*(3), 207-222.

Gil, F., Rico, R., Alcover, C. M., & Barrasa, A. (2005). Change-oriented leadership, satisfaction, and performance in work groups. Effects of team climate and group potency. *Journal of Managerial Psychology, 20*(3), 312-328.

Gill, S. K., & Cormican, K. (2006). *Support ambient intelligence solutions for small to medium size enterprises: Typologies and taxonomies for developers.* Paper presented at the 12th International Conference on Concurrent Enterprising.

Gillespie, A. (2004). *Returning surplus: Constructing the architecture of intersubjectivity.* Unpublished Thesis, University of Cambridge, Cambridge.

Giménez, C., & Lourenço, H. R. (2004). *e-supply chain management: Review, implications, and directions for future research*. IET Working Paper # 17 October 2004. Retrieved January 8, 2007, from http://www.ietcat.org/htmls04/cat/publicacions/wpaper/IET%20working%20paper%20017.pdf

Giunipero, L., Dawley, D., & Anthony, W. (1999). The impact of tacit knowledge on purchasing decisions. *Journal of Supply Chain Management*. Tempe; Winter (electronic).

Glassop, L. I. (2002). The organization benefits of teams. *Human Relations, 55*(2), 225-249.

Global Reporting Initiative. (2006). *A common framework for sustainability reporting*. Retrieved November 14, 2006, from http://www.globalreporting.org/Home

Gloet, M., & Terziovski, M. (2004). Exploring the relationship between knowledge management practices and innovation performance. *Journal of Manufacturing Technology Management, 15*(5), 402-409.

Glover, D., Miller, D., Averis, D., & Door, V. (2005). The interactive whiteboard: A literature survey technology. *Pedagogy and Education, 14*(2), 155-170.

Goh, M. (2000). Quality circles: Journey of an Asian enterprise. *The International Journal of Quality & Reliability Management, 17*(7), 784-793.

Gómez-Pérez, A., Fernández, M. & Juristo, N. (1997). METHONTOLOGY: From ontological art towards ontological engineering. In Proceedings from AAAI Spring Symp. Series, (pp. 33-40). Menlo Park, CA. AAAI Press.

Gough, H. (1981). Studies of the Myers-Briggs type indicator in a personality assessment research institute. The *4th National Conference on the Myers-Briggs Type Indicator,* Stanford University, July 1981, CA.

Gould, D. (1997). *Virtual organisation*. Retrieved July 26, 2006, from www.seanet.com/~daveg/ltv.htm

Gould, D. (2006). *Virtual teams*. Retrieved July 26, 2006, from www.seanet.com/~daveg/vrteams.htm

GPM Deutsche Gesellschaft für Projektmanagement e.V., P. C. G. D. (2004). *Studie zur Effizienz von Projekten in Unternehmen.*

Graeff, T., & Harmon, S. (2002). Collecting and using personal data: Consumers' awareness and concerns. *Journal of Consumer Marketing, 19*(4), 302-318.

Gray, C. (1998). *Entreprise and culture*. London: Routledge.

Greenspan, A. (2004). *"Globalization and innovation" Speech to the Federal Reserve Bank*. Chicago. Retrieved December 15, 2006, from http://www.techlawjournal.com/home/newsbriefs/2004/05b.asp

Greenwood, F. (1992). Continuous improvements to meet customer expectations. *Journal of Systems Management, 43*(2), 13-15.

Greve, H. R., & Taylor, A. (2000). Innovations as catalysts for organizational change: Shifts in organizational cognition and search. *Administrative Science Quarterly, 45*(March), 54-80.

Grewal, R., Comer, J. M., & Metha, R. (2001). An investigation into the antecedents of organisational participation in business-business electronic markets. *Journal of Marketing, 65*(3), 17-34.

Griffin, A., &. Page, A. L. (1995). The PDMA success measurement project: Recommended measures for product development success and failure. *Journal of Product Innovation Management, 13*(6), 478-496.

Griggs, H. E. (2002). Strategic planning system characteristics and organisational effectiveness in Australian small-scale firms. *Irish Journal of Management, 23*(1), 23-53.

Griliches, Z. (1990). Patent statistics as economic indicators: A survey. *Journal of Economic Literature, 28*(4), 1661-1707.

Gross, M. (2001). *Travels to the Nanoworld*. Jackson, TN: Perseus Book Group.

Grossmann, G. (2004). Beifreies Löten: Technik ist bereit. *Bulletin SEV/VSE*(17), 9.

Grossmann, G. (2005). *WEEE & RohS: Technologische Aspekte*. Paper presented at the Seminar "Wer hat Angst vor WEEE/RohS," Dübendorf.

Gruber, T. R. (1993). A translation approach to portable ontologies. *Knowledge Acquisition. 5*(2), 199-220.

Gruninger, M., & Uschold (1996). Ontologies: Principles, methods, and applications. *Knowledge Engineering Review, 11*(2).

Gunasekara, C. (2004). The third role of Australian universities in human capital formation. *Journal of Higher Education Policy and Management, 26*(3), 329-343.

Gupta, D. (2005). *EPL Server 5.1 Released by iSpheres.* Retrieved December 30, 2006, from http://www.ebizq.net/news/5826.html

Haavind, S. (2006). Book review of learning together online: Research on asynchronous learning networks. *Journal of Interactive Online Learning, 5*(2), 217-223.

Haeckel, S. (1999). *Adaptive enterprise: Creating and leading sense-and-respond organizations.* Boston, MA: Harvard Business School Press.

Haeckel, S. (2005). Becoming a sense and respond organization. Retrieved December 30, 2006, from http://senseandrespond.com/downloads/iSPHERES_S_R_WEBCAST.ppt

Hagel, J., & Singer, M. (1999). Unbundling the corporation. *Harvard Business Review, March-April 1999.*

Hahm, H. (1993). *The development of the private sector in a small economy in transition.* World Bank Discussion Papers, East Asia and Pacific Region Series, 223. World Bank, Washington D.C.

Hahn, A., Hausmann, K., Preis, S., & Strickmann, J. (2006). Ein Konzept für das Entwicklungscontrolling auf PLM-Basis. *HMD Praxis der Wirtschaftsinformatik 249.*

Hair Jr., J. F., Anderson, R. E., Tatham, R. L., & Black, W. C. (1998). *Multivariate data analysis.* (5th ed.). NJ: Prentice-Hall.

Hall, E.T. (1976). How cultures collide. *Psychology Today, 5*(9), 66-97.

Hall, R. (1993). A Framework linking intangible resources and capabilities to sustainable competitive advantage. *Strategic Management Journal, 14*(8), 607-618.

Hallberg, B. (2005). *Networking: A beginner's guide* (4th ed.). Emeryville, CA: The McGraw-Hill Companies, Inc.

Hallberg, B. A. (2003). *Networking: A beginner's guide* (3rd ed.). McGraw-Hill/Osborne.

Haller, M. (1999). Erübrigt sich angesichts der Globalisierung der Risiko-Dialog? In P. Gomez, G. Müller-Stewens & J. Rüegg-Stürm (Eds.), *Entwicklungsperspektiven einer integrierten Managementlehre* (pp. 73). Bern, Stuttgart, Wien: Paul Haupt.

Hamel, G. (2002). *Leading the revolution.* Boston: Harvard Business School Press.

Hamel, G. (2003). Innovation as a Deep Capability. *Leader to Leader, Winter*(27), 19-24.

Hamel, G. (2006). The why, what, and how of management innovation. *Harvard Business Review, Feb. 1, 2006,* 1-5.

Hamel, G. (2006, November). *Continuous management innovations.* Speech presented at the Fortune Innovation Forum, New York, NY, November.

Hamel, G., & Prahalad, C. K. (1989). Strategic intent. *Harvard Business Review, 67,* 63-76.

Hamid, W. A. (1995). *Companions of the Prophet.* Leicester: Kitaboon.

Hamm, S. (2007). The trouble with India. *Business Week.* March 19, 48-58.

Hammer, M. (2001). *The agenda.* New York: Crown Business.

Hammer, M., & Champy, J. (1993). *Reengineering the corporation: A manifesto for business revolution.* New York: HarperBusiness.

Handfield, R. B., & Nichols, E. L. (2003). *Supply chain redesign: Transforming supply chains into integrated supply systems.* NJ: Financial Times Prentice Hall.

Hannafey, F. T. (2003). Entrepreneurship and ethics: A literature review. *Journal of Business Ethics, 46*(2), 99-110.

Hannay, M., & Newvine, T. (2006). Perceptions of distance learning: A comparison of online and traditional learning. *Journal of Online Learning and Teaching, 2*(1), 1-11.

Hannon, P. (2005). The journey from student to entrepreneur: A review of existing research into graduate entrepreneurship. *Intent Conference July 2005*, School of Management, University of Surrey: London.

Hanti, S., & Kairisto-Mertanen, L. (2006). Making students learn about entrepreneurship through real life company assignments. *EFMD 36ᵗʰ EISB Conference Proceedings on Embedding Entrepreneurship Education in Europe: Evaluating Effective Policy and Practice at the Institutional, Regional and National Levels*, September 2006, Southampton.

Harding, R. (2002). *Global entrepreneurship monitor (GEM)—United Kingdom 2002*. London: London Business School.

Harmuth, U. (2003). *Erfolgsfaktoren für Projekte*. Unpublished master thesis, University of Wuppertal, Germany.

Harrington, L. (1995). Taking Integration to the next level, *Transportation and Distribution*.

Harvard Business School. (2004). *Creating teams with an edge: The complete skill set to build powerful and influential teams*. Boston: Harvard Business School Press.

Harveston, P. D. (2000). *Synoptic versus incremental internationalisation: An examination of born global and gradual globalising firms*. Unpublished doctoral dissertation, The University of Memphis.

Harvey, L., & Green, D. (1993). Defining quality. *Assessment and Evaluation in Higher Education, 18*(1), 9-34.

Haskell, D. (2005). *What is extended product responsibility?* NZ2000 Plastics, Otaki, New Zealand.

Haskins, J. S. (2002). e-teamwork: Using an intranet to your advantage. *AFP exchange*, Bethesda, *22*(1), 62-67.

Hauser, J. R. (1996). *Metrics to value R&D: An annotated bibliography*. Cambridge, MA: Marketing Science Institute Working Paper.

Hauser, J. R., & Zettelmayer, F. (1997). Metrics to evaluate R,D&E. *Research Technology Management, 40*(4), 32-38.

Hayes, F. (2004). *Chaos is back*. November 08, 2004. Retrieved March 7, 2007, from http://www.computerworld.com/managementtopics/management/project/story/0,10801,97283,00.html

Hegel, G. W. F. (1807). *Phenomenology of spirit* (A. V. Miller, Trans.). Oxford: Clarendon Press (1977).

Hegel, G. W. F. (1830). The encyclopedia of the philosophical sciences (Part 1). The science of logic. In W. Wallace (Ed.), *The logic of Hegel*. London: Oxford University Press (1873).

Heisig, U., & Littek, W. (1995). Trust as a basis of work organization. In W. Littek, & T. Charles (Ed.), *The new division of work*, (pp.17-56). Berlin: De Gruyter.

Hellenschmidt, M., & Kirste, T. (2004, November 8-11). A generic topology for ambient intelligence. Paper presented at the Ambient Intelligence: The 2ⁿᵈ European Symposium, EUSAI Eindhoven, The Netherlands.

Hensley, R. L., & Dobie, K. (2005). *Assessing readiness for six sigma in a service setting*. Managing Service Quality, Vol.15. No.1. Greensboro, USA: North Carolina A & T state University, Department of Business Administration.

Hentges, S. G. (2003). *Bisphenol A-A fact sheet*: American Plastics Council.

Hernández-Ramos, P. (2004). Web logs and online discussions as tools to promote reflective practice. *The Journal of Interactive Online Learning, 3*(1), 1-16.

Hersey, P., Blanchard, K. H., & Johnson, D. E. (2006). *Management of organizational behaviour: Leading human resource*. New Jersey: Prentice Hall.

Hill T., Etienne, N., & Trotter, D. (2006). Small-scale, nature-based tourism as a pro-poor development intervention: Two examples in Kwazulu-Natal, South Africa. *Singapore Journal of Tropical Geography, 27*(2), 163-175.

Hill, G. (2006). *The Lean CRM-Toyota Story*. Retrieved December 30, 2006, from

Hiltz, S. R., & Goldman, R. (2005). *Learning together online: Research on asynchrous learning networks*. NJ: Lawrence Erlbaum Associates.

Hlupic, V., Pouloudi, A., & Rzevski, G. (2002). Towards an integrated approach to knowledge management: "Hard," "soft" and "abstract' issues." *Knowledge and Process Management, 9*(2), 90-102.

Ho, L., & Lin, G. (2004). Critical success factor framework for the implementation of integrated-enterprise systems in the manufacturing environment. *International Journal of Production Research, 42*(17), 3731-42.

Hochman, S., (2007). *Value chain complexity, Part 1: What is it, why it matters.* AMR Research. Retrieved February 8, from http://www.amrresearch.com/Content/View.asp?pmillid=20248

Hofstadter, D. R. (1980). Gödel, Escher, Bach : An eternal golden braid (1st ed.). Harmondsworth: Penguin Books Ltd.

Hofstede, G. (1991). *Cultures and organizations: The software of the mind.* London: McGraw-Hill.

Hofstede, G. (2003). *Culture's consequences: Comparing values behaviors institutions & organizations across nations.* California: Sage Publications Inc.

Holcombe, R. G. (1999). Equilibrium versus the invisible hand. *Review of Austrian Economics, 12*(2), 227-243.

Holmes, D., Hughes, K., & Julian, R. (2003). *Australian sociology: A changing society.* Sydney: Pearson.

Holton, G. (1978). *The scientific imagination: Case studies.* Cambridge: Cambridge University Press.

Holton, J. (2001). Building trust and collaboration in a virtual team. *Team Performance Management, 7*(3/4), 36-47.

Hooper, N. (2005). The Australian Financial Review newspaper, pp.1 & 17.

Horsch, J. (2003). *Innovations- und Projektmanagement.* Wiesbaden, Germany: Gabler.

Horvath, J. (2002). *Making friends with Big Brother?* [Electronic Version]. Telepolis. Retrieved December 6, 2005.

Hoshmand, L. T., & Polkinghorne, D. E. (1992). Redefining the science-practice relationship and professional training. *American Psychologist, January*, 55-66.

Hosmer, L. T. (1995). Trust-the connecting link between organizational theory & philosphical ethics. *Academy of Management Review, 20*(2), 379-403.

Hostager, T. J., Neil, T. C., Decker, R. L., & Lorentz, R. D. (1998). Seeing environmental opportunities: Effects of intrapreneurial ability, efficacy, motivation, and desirability. *Journal of Organisational Change Management, 11*(1), 11-26.

Howell, J. M. (2005). The right stuff: Identifying and developing effective champions of innovation. *The Academy of Management Executive, 19*(2), 108-119.

Hsieh, C., Lai, F., & Shi, W. (2006). Information orientation and its impacts on information asymmetry and e-business adoption: Evidence from China's international trading industry. *Industrial Management and Data Systems, 106*(6), 825-840.

Huber, G. P. (1991). Organisational learning: The contributing processes and the literatures. *Organisation Science, 2*(1), 88-115.

Hudson, M., Smart, A., & Bourne, M. (2001). Theory and practice in SME performance measurement systems. *International Journal of Operations & Production Management, 21*(8), 1096.

Huff, S. L., Michael Maher, P., & Munro, M. C. (2006). Information technology and the board of directors: Is there an IT attention deficit? *MIS Quarterly Executive, 5*(2), [electronic version]. Retrieved January 10, 2007, from http: www.misque.org/V0502-03.pdf

Hunt, I., Pereira Klen, A., & Zhang, J. (1997). Cross border enterprises: Virtual or extended! *ISIP '97 OE/IFIP/IEEE International Conference on Integrated and Sustainable Industrial Production*, Lisboa, Portugal.

Hutley, P. S. B., & Russell, P. A. (2005). *An introduction to the Financial Services Reform Act, 2001* (3rd ed). Australia: LexisNexis Butterworths.

Hvolby, H. H., & Thorstenson, A. (2000, April). Performance measurement in small and medium-sized enterprises. *The 3rd Conference on "Stimulating Manufacturing Excellence in Small and Medium Enterprises."* Coventry, UK.

Hwang, L., & Lockwood. A. (2006). Understanding the challenges of implementing best practices in hospitality and tourism SMEs. *Benchmarking: An International Journal, 13*(3), 337-354.

Iacovou, C. L., Benbasat, I., & Dexter, A. A. (1995). Electronic data interchange and small organisations: Adoption and impact of technology. *MIS Quarterly, 19*(4), 465-485.

Ibbotson, F., & Fahy, M. (2004). The impact of e-commerce on small Irish firms. *International Journal of Services Technology and Management, 5*(4), 317-332.

Ibrahim, A. B., & Soufani, K. (2002). Entrepreneurship education and training in Canada: A critical assessment. *Education + Training*, 44(8/9): 421-430.

IEEE. (1998). *IEEE Standard for a Software Quality Metrics Methodolog Institute of Electrical and Electronics Engineers*.

Igbaria, M., & Tan, M. (2002). *The virtual workplace*. Tel Aviv University and Claremont Graduate University and National University of Singapore: IDEA Group Publishing.

Ingram, H., Richard, T., Scheuing, E., & Armistead. (1997). A systems model of effective teamwork. *The TQM magazine*, 9(2), 118-127.

Inland Revenue. (1998). *Chapter 1—Encouraging the growth of e-commerce. Electronic Commerce: The UKs Taxation Agenda*. Retrieved November 19, 2006, from http://www.inlandrevenue.gov.uk/taxagenda/ecom1.htm

Innovation Briefing 07-06: Open innovation. (2007). Retrieved March, 2007 from http://www.innovaro.com/inno_updates/Innovation%20Briefing%2007-06.pdf

Institute of Quality Assurance (IQA-bulletin). (March 2005-April 2006). *Quality world*. Grosvenor Crescent, London: Friary Press.

IPC. (2005). *Acceptability of electronic assemblies: Rev. D 2/05*. Retrieved February 22, 2006, from http://www.ipc.org/4.0_Knowledge/4.1_Standards/revstat1.htm

Iqbal, M. (2006). Bang e Dara. Lahore: Iqbal Academy.

ISTAG. (2000). Recommendations of the IST Advisory Group for Workprogramme 2001 and beyond "implementing the vision": ISTAG.

IT Governance Institute. (2007). *Board briefing on IT governance*. Retrieved March 7, 2007, from www.itgi.org.

ITEA. (2003). *The Ambience Project*. Retrieved September 21, 09, 2005, from http://www.extra.research.philips.com/euprojects/ambience

Jack, S. & Anderson, A. (1999). Entrepreneurship education within the enterprise culture: Producing reflective practitioners. *International Journal of Entrepreneurial Behaviour and Research*, 5(3), 110-125.

Jacko, J. A., & Sears, A. (2003). *The human-computer interaction handbook: Fundamentals, evolving technologies, and emerging applications*. Mahwah, NJ: Lawrence Erlbaum Associates Publishers.

Jackson, M. C. (2000). *Systems approaches to management*. New York, London: Kluwer Academic/Plenum.

Jacobson, I., Booch, G., & Rumbaugh, J. (1999). *The unified software development process*. Boston: Addison-Wesley.

Jaffe, A. B. (1986). Technological opportunity and spillovers of R&D: Evidence for firms patents, profits, and market value. *American Economic Review*, 76(5), 984-1001.

James, R. (1991). Quality service in banking: how to turn good intentions into reality. *Hoosier Banker*, Indianapolis, 74(11), 43.

Jania, T. (2004). *Änderungsmanagement auf Basis eines integrierten Prozess- und Produktdatenmodells mit dem Ziel einer durchgängigen Komplexitätsbewertung*. Doctoral Dissertation, University of Padeborn, Germany.

Jareszelski, D., Dehoff, K., & Bordia, R. (2006). *Smart spenders: The global innovation 1000*. strategy+business. Retrieved December 15, 2006, from http://www.strategy-busines.com/press/article/064057?gko=c3340-1

Jarvis, R., Curran, J., Kitching, J., & Lightfoot, G. (2000). The use of quantitative and qualitative criteria in the measurement of performance in small firms. *Journal of Small Business and Enterprise Development*, 7(2), 123-34.

Javalgi, R., & Ramsey, R. (2001). Strategic issues of e-commerce as an alternative global distribution system. *International Marketing Review*, 18(4), 376-391.

Jayson, S. (2007). *Generation Y's goal? Wealth and fame*. USA Today. January 10, 2007. Retrieved February 7, 2007, from http://www.usatoday.com/news/nation/2007-01-09-gen-y-cover_x.htm

Jelassi, T., & Leenen, S. (2003). An e-commerce sales model for manufacturing companies: A conceptual framework and a European example. *European Management Journal*, 2(1), 38-47.

Jenne, F. (2001). *PDM-basiertes Entwicklungsmonitoring*. Doctoral Dissertation, University of Karlsuhe, Gemany.

Jenning, J. (May 6, 2006). Accountancy toes the online approach. Accounting and Finance.

Johanson M. *White Paper: Sharing Product Data Through Life in the Extended Enterprise –the share-A-space™ solution.* Eurostep Commercial Solutions AB, Sweden.

Johnson, G., & Scholes, K. (2002). *Exploring corporate strategy: Text and cases.* Cambridge: Prentice Hall.

Jones, C., Hecker, R., & Holland, P. (2003). Small firm Internet adoption: Opportunities forgone, a journey not begun. *Journal of Small Business and Enterprise Development, 10*(3), 287-297.

Jones, P., Muir, E., & Benyon-Davies, P. (2004). An evaluation of inhibitors to e-commerce and e-business growth. In G. Packham, C. Miller, & B. Thomas (Eds.), *The phenomenon of small business growth* (pp. 117-137) Monograph 5. Pontypridd: The Welsh Enterprise Institute, University of Glamorgan.

Jorgensen, B. (2003). Baby boomers, generation X and generation Y? *Foresight, 4*(5), 41-49.

Jungkurz, R. M. (2005). *PDM-basierte Überwachung komplexer Entwicklungsprojekte.* Doctoral Disseration, Technical University of München, Germany.

Jutla, D., Bodorik, P., & Dhaliqal, J. (2002). Supporting the e-business readiness of small and medium sized enterprises: Approaches and metrics. *Internet Research: Electronic Networking Applications and Policy, 12*(2), 139-164.

Kahn, K. B. (2004). *PDMA handbook of new product development.* New York: John Wiley & Sons.

Kanter, R. M. (1997). *Rosabeth Moss Kanter on the frontiers of management.* Boston: Harvard Business Press.

Kanuka, H., & Anderson, T. (1998). Online social interchange, discord, and knowledge construction. *Journal of Distance Education.* ICAAP. Retrieved December 16, 2006, from http://cade.athabascau.ca/vol13.1/kanuka.html

Kaplan, R. S., & Norton, D. P. (1992). The balanced scorecard - measures that drive performance. *Harvard Business Review*, January-February, 71-9.

Kaplan, R. S., & Norton, D. P. (1996). *The balanced scorecard: Translating strategy into action.* Boston: Harvard Business School Press.

Kaplan, R. S., & Norton, D. P. (2001). *The strategy-focused organization: How balanced scorecard companies thrive in the new business environment.* Boston: Harvard Business School Press.

Katz, D., & Kahn, R. L. (1966). *The social psychology of organizations.* New York: Wiley.

Kearins, K., Luke, B., & Corner, P., (2004). What constitutes successful entrepreneurship? An analysis of recent Australian awards experiences. *Journal of Australian and New Zealand Academy of Management, 10*(1), 41-55.

Keen, P. (2004). *Business process management is not workflow automation.* Retrieved December 30, 2006, from http://www.peterkeen.com/recent/articles/index.htm

Keen, P. (2004*). Knowledge mobilization.* Presentation at The Millennium Technology Conference. Helsinki, Finland.

Keen, P. (2004). *What exactly is a business process?* Retrieved December 30, 2006, from http://www.peterkeen.com/recent/articles/index.htm

Keen, P. (2005). *Organizational transformation through business models.* Retrieved December 30, 2006, from http://www.peterkeen.com/recent/articles/index.htm.

Keen, P., & Sol, H. (2005). *Coordination by design: Chapter one.* Retrieved December 30, 2006, from http://www.peterkeen.com/forthcoming/publications.htm

Kehoe, D. F., & Boughton, N. J. (1998). DOMAIN: Dynamic operations management across the Internet. *Proceedings of the International Federation for Information Processing Working Group 5.7 (IFIPWG5.7,)* (pp. 421-30). Kluwer Academic Publishers, Dordrecht .

Kehoe, D. F., & Boughton, N. J. (2001). New paradigms in planning and control across manufacturing supply chains: The utilisation of Internet technologies. *International Journal of Operations and Production Management, 21*(5/6), 582-593.

Kehoe, D. F., & Boughton, N. J. (2001). New paradigms in planning and control across manufacturing supply chains—The utilisation of Internet technologies. *International Journal of Operations & Productions Management 21*(5/6), 582-593.

Kehoe, D. F., & Boughton, N. J. (2001). Internet based supply chain management—A classification of approaches to manufacturing planning and control. *International Journal of Operations & Production Management, 21*(4), 516-524.

Kellert, S. H. (1993). *In the wake of chaos: Unpredictable order in dynamical systems*. Chicago: University of Chicago Press.

Kelly, S., & Allison, M. A. (1998). *The complexity advantage*. New York: McGraw-Hill.

Kent, T. (2005). Leadership and emotions in health care organisations. *Journal of Health Organisation and Management, 20*(1), 49-66.

Kern, W. (1993). Forschung und Entwicklung. In U. Arentzen & E. Winter (Ed.), *Gabler Wirtschaftslexikon,* Wiesbaden, Germany: Gabler.

Kettunen, J. (2004). Bridge building to the future of Finnish polytechnics. *Journal of Higher Education Outreach and Engagement, 9*(2), 43-57.

Kettunen, J. (2004). The strategic evaluation of regional development in higher education. *Assessment & Evaluation in Higher Education, 29*(3), 357-368.

Kettunen, J. (2006). Strategic planning of regional development in higher education. *Baltic Journal of Management, 1*(3), 259-269.

Kettunen, J. (2006). Strategies for the cooperation of educational institutions and companies in mechanical engineering. *International Journal of Educational Management, 20*(1), 19-28.

Kettunen, J., & Kantola, I. (2005). Management information system based on the balanced scorecard. *Campus-Wide Information Systems, 22*(5), 263-274.

Kettunen, J., & Kantola, M. (2006). Strategies for virtual learning and e-entrepreneurship. In F. Zhao (Ed.), *Entrepreneurship and innovations in e-business: An integrative perspective* (pp. 107-123). Hershey, PA: Idea Group Publishing.

Khoshafian, S., & Buckiewicz, M. (1995). *Introduction to groupware, workflow, and workgroup computing*. John Wiley and Sons, Inc.

Kickul, J., & Walters, J. (2002). Recognising new opportunities and innovations: The role of strategic orientation and proactivity in internet firms. *International Journal of Entrepreneurial Behaviour and Research, 8*(6), 292-308.

Kidd, A. (1994). *The marks are on the knowledge worker.* Paper presented at the Conference on Human Factors in Computer Systems.

Kim, E., Nam, D., & Stimpert, J. L. (2004). The applicability of **Porter's generic strategies** in the digital age: Assumptions, conjectures, and suggestions. *Journal of Management, 30*(5), 569-589.

Kimball, L. (1997). *Managing virtual teams.* Text of speech given by Kimball, L for Team Strategies Conference, Toronto Canada, 1997. Retrieved July 26, 2006, from http://www.groupjazz.com/pdf/vteams-toronto.pdf

Kimble, C., Li, F., & Barlow, A. (2000). *Effective virtual teams through communities of practice. management science. Theory method & practice*. Strathclyde Business School. Research Paper No. 2000/9. Retrieved July 26, 2006, from http://dissertation.martinaspeli.net/papers/communities-of-practice/kimble-et-al-2000-effective-virtual-teams-through-communities-of-practice

King, D., Lee, J., Warkentin, M., & Chung, H. (2002). *Electronic commerce: A managerial perspective*. Upper Saddle River, NJ: Pearson Education International.

King, J. L., Gurbaxani, V., Kraemer, K. L., MacFarlan, F. W., Raman, K. S., & Yap, C. S. (1994). Institutional factors in information technology innovation. *Information Systems Research, 5*(2), 139-169.

King, M. (2006). MBAs decline into mediocrity. The Montreal Gazette. Friday, November 24.

King, W. R. (2007). IT strategy and innovation: The IT deniers versus a portfolio of IT role. *Information Systems Management, 24*(2), 197-200, Boston: Spring 2007.

Kinnunen, J. (2001). Korkeakoulujen alueellisen vaikuttavuuden arviointi (Evaluation of the regional impact of higher education institutions). Finnish Higher Education Evaluation Council Publications 5:2001. Helsinki: Edita.

Kippenberger, T. (1999). Is this chaos, at least in theory? *The Antidote, 4*(2), 64-66.

Kirby, D. (2003). *Entrepreneurship*. London: McGraw-Hill Publishing.

Kirchhoff, U., Kuczynski, A., & Stokic, D. (2005). *Set-up and maintenance of ontologies for innovation support in extended enterprises*. Int J Adv Manuf Technol, Published online: 12 October 2005

Kiritsis, D., Bufardi, A., & Xirouchakis, P. (2003). Research issues on product lifecycle management and information tracking using smart embedded systems. *Advanced Engineering Informatics, 17*(3-4), 189-202.

Kirton, M. (2001). Adaptors and innovators: Why new initiatives get blocked. In J. Henry (Ed.), *Creative management* (2nd ed, pp. 169-180). London: Cromwell Press Ltd.

Kirzner, I. M. (1973). *Competition and entrepreneurship*. Chicago, IL: University of Chicago Press.

Kivistö, J. (2005). The government-higher education institution relationship: Theoretical considerations from the perspective of agent theory. *Tertiary Education and Management, 11*(1), 1-17.

Klee, B. (2005). *Stoffverbote: EU-Richtlinie 2002/95/EG -RoHS*.

Knight, G. A., & Cavusgil (1996). The born global firm: A challenge to traditional internationalisation theory. In S. T. Cavusgil & T. K. Madsen (Eds.), *Export internationalising research—enrichment and challenges. Advances in International Marketing* (Vol. 8, pp. 11-26). NY: JAI Press Inc.

Knol, W. H. C., & Stroken, J. H. M. (2001). The diffusion and adoption of information technology in small- and medium-sized enterprises through IT scenarios. *Technology Analysis & Strategic Management, 13*(2), 227-245.

Knox, S., & Maklan, S. (2005). Case study-guarentee trust bank of Nigeria: Building a trusted brand in financial services. *Thunderbird International Business Review, 47*(6), 737-756

Kock, N. (2005). *Business process improvement through e-collaboration: Knowledge sharing through the use of virtual groups*. Hershey, PA: Idea Group Publishing.

Kogan, L. A. (2003). *Looking behind the curtain: The growth of trade barriers that ignore sound science: Executive Summary*. Washington: National Foreign Trade Council, Inc.

Kogure, M. (1998). *TQC in Japanese corporations-its review and a new way of development*. Tokyo: Nikkagiren.

Koh, C., Prybutok, V., Ryan, S., & Ibragimova, B. (2006). The importance of strategic readiness in an emerging e-government environment. *Business Process Management Journal, 12*(1), 22-33.

Kohnhauser, V. (1999). Use of TRIZ in the Development Process. *Triz Journal, June 1999*.

Kolb, D. (1984). Experiential learning: Experience as a source of learning and development. NJ: Prentice-Hall.

Kolb, D. (2000). Learning places: Building dwelling thinking online. *Journal of Philosophy of Education, 34*(1), 121-133.

Kollmann, T. (1998). The information triple jump as the measure of success in electronic commerce. *Electronic Markets, 8*(4), 44-49.

Kollmann, T. (2001). Measuring the acceptance of electronic marketplaces. *Journal of Computer Mediated Communication, 6*(2).

Kollmann, T. (2004). Attitude, adoption, or acceptance?—measuring the market success of telecommunication and multimedia technology. *International Journal of Business Performance Management, 6*(2), 133-52.

Kollmann, T. (2006). What is e-entrepreneurship?—fundamentals of company founding in the net economy. *International Journal of Technology Management, 33*(4), 322-340.

Kollmann, T., & Häsel, M. (2006). *Cross-channel cooperation: The bundling of online and offline business models*. Wiesbaden: DUV.

Kollmann, T., & Kuckertz, A. (2006). Investor relations for start-ups: An analysis of venture capital investors' communicative needs. *International Journal of Technology Management, 34*(1/2), 47-62.

Koska, D. K., & Romano, J. D. (1988). *Profile 21 issues and implications, countdown to the future: The manufacturing engineer in the 21st Century*. Dearborn, MI: Society of Manufacturing Engineers.

Kostoff, R., & Block, J. (2005). Factor matrix text filtering and clustering. *Journal of the American Society for Information Science and Technology, 56*(9), 946-968.

Koza, J. (2004). What is genetic programming? Retrieved December 30, 2006, from http://www.genetic-programming.com/

KPMG. (2005). *Global IT project management survey—How committed are you?* Retrieved March 7, 2007, from http://www.kpmg.com.au/aci/issues.htm#105

Kramer, R. M., & Tyler, T. R. (1996). *Trust in organizations*. London: Sage Publications.

Krebbs, V. (2005). Social network analysis software and services for organizations and their consultants. Retrieved June 20 2005, from http://www.orgnet.com

Kristiansen, S., & Ryen, A. (2002). Enacting their business environments: Asian entrepreneurs in East Africa. *African & Asian Studies, 1*(3), 165-186.

Krovi, R., Chandra, A., & Rajagopalan, B. (2003). Information flow parameters for managing organisational processes. *Communications of the ACM, 46*(2) ,77-82.

Kuan, K. K. Y., & Chau, P. Y. K. (2001). A perception-based model for EDI adoption in small businesses using a technology-organization-environment framework. *Information & Management, 38*(8), 507-521.

Kühule H, Wagenhaus G (2005) *Extended Enterprise Architectures (E2A)-Towards a powerful Mode of Production*. Otto-von-Guericke-University Magdeburg.

Kuran, T., & Sunstein, C. R. (1999). Availability cascades and risk regulation. *Stanford Law Review, 51*(4), 683.

Laeutenschuetz, R. (2000, 2000-06-14). EU kämpft gegen den wachsenden Abfallberg: Richtlinienentwuerfe zur Entsorgung von Elektronikschrott. *Neue Zürcher Zeitung*, p. 23.

Laitinen, E. K. (2002). A dynamic performance measurement system: Evidence from small Finnish technology companies. *Scandinavian Journal of Management, 18*(1), 65-99.

Lal, K. (2003). E-business and export behaviour: Evidence from Indian firms. *World Development, 32*(3), 505-517.

Lambert, D. M., Cooper, M. C., & Pagh, J. D. (1998). Supply chain management: Implementation issues and research opportunities. *The International Journal of Logistics Management, 9*(2), 1-17.

Lancioni, R. A., Smith, M. F., & Oliva, T. A. (2000). The role of the Internet in supply chain management. *Industrial Marketing Management, 29*(1),45-56.

Landesberg, P. (1999). In the beginning, there were Deming and Duran. *The Journal for Quality and Participation*, Cincinnati, *22*(6), 59-60.

Langfred, C. W. (2004). Too much of a good thing: The negative effects of high trust & autonomy in self-managing teams. *Academy of Management Journal, 47*(3), 385-399.

Large, A., Beheshti, J., & Cole, C. (2002). Information architecture for the Web: The IA matrix approach to designing children's portals. *Journal of the American Society For Information Science And Technology, 53*(10), 831-838.

Laserna, C. (1990). Lessons in milking and math. In J. Ross & V. Bergum (Eds.), *Through the looking glass, children, and health promotion*. Ottawa: Canadian Pubic Health Association.

Lash, S. (2000). *Silicon alleys: Networks of virtual objects*. Paper presented at the Virtual Society? Get Real! Conference, 4-5th May, Said Business School, University of Oxford, Hertfordshire, UK.

Laurence, P. R., & Lorsch, J. W. (1967). *Organization and environment*. Cambridge: Harvard University Press.

Lave, J., & Wenger E. (1991). *Situated learning: Legitimate peripheral participation*. Cambridge UK: Cambridge University Press.

Lave, J., & Wenger, E. (1991). *Situated learning: Legitimate peripheral participation*. Cambridge: Cambridge University Press.

Law, R., & Hsu, C. (2005). Customers' perceptions on the importance of hotel Web site dimensions and attributes. *International Journal of Contemporary Hospitality Management, 17*(6), 493-503.

Lee, C. (2001). An analytical framework for evaluating *e-commerce* business Models. *Internet Research: Electronic Networking Applications and Policy, 11*(4), 349-359.

Lee, G., & Lin, H. (2005). Customer perceptions of e-service quality in online shopping. *International Journal of Retail and Distribution Management, 33*(2), 161-176.

Leitch, C. & Harrison, R. (1999). A process model for entrepreneurship education and development. *International Journal of Entrepreneurial Behaviour and Research, 5*(3), 83-102.

Leonard, D., & Sensiper, S. (1998). The role of tacit knowledge in group innovation. *California Management Review, 40*(3) (electronic).

Levy, A., Rajaraman, & Ordille, K. (1996). Querying heterogeneous information sources using source descriptions. *Proceedings of the 22nd VLDB Conference.*

Lewicki, R. J., & Bunker, B. B. (1996). Developing & maintaining trust in working relationships. In R. M. Kramer, & T. R. Tyler (Ed.), *Trust in organizations: Frontiers of theory & research*,(pp. 114-139). Thousand Oaks, CA: Sage Publications.

Lewis, R., & Cockrill, A. (2002). Going global—remaining local: The impact of e-commerce on small retail firms in Wales. *International Journal of Information Management, June, 22*, 195-209.

Liebl, F. (1991). *Schwache Signale und Künstliche Intelligenz im strategischen Issue Management.* Frankfurt am Main, Bern, etc.: Lang.

Liebl, F. (1991). *Schwache Signale und Künstliche Intelligenz im strategischen Issue Management.* Frankfurt am Main, Bern, etc.: Lang.

Lightner, N. J., Yenisey, M. M., Ozok, A. A., & Salvendy, G. (2002). Shopping behaviour and preferences in e-commerce of Turkish and American University Students: Implications from cross-cultural design. *Behaviour & Information Technology, 21*(6), 373-385.

Liker, J. (2004). *The Toyota way.* New York: McGraw-Hill Corporation.

Limerick, D., & Cunnington, B. (1993). *Managing the new organisation.* Chatswood: Business & Professional Publishing.

Lindwer, M., Marculescu, D., Basten, T., Zimmermann, R., Marculescu, R., Jung, S., et al. (2003). *Ambient intelligence vision and achievement: Linking abstract ideas to real-world concepts.* Paper presented at the Design, Automation, and Test in Europe Conference and Exhibition.

Little, A. D. (2004). *Innovation Excellence Studie 2004.*

Liuhanen, A. M. (2005). University evaluations and different evaluation approaches: A Finnish perspective. *Tertiary Education and Management, 11*(3), 259-268.

Loi, D., & Dillon, P. (2006). Adaptive educational environments as creative spaces. *Cambridge Journal of Education, 36*(3), 363-381.

Lorenz, E. H. (1988). Neither friends nor strangers: informal networks of subcontracting in French industry. In D. Gambetta, D. (Ed), *Trust making & breaking of cooperative relations,* (pp. 194-210). Oxford: Blackwell.

Lu, J., & Lu, Z. (2004). Development, distribution, and evaluation of online tourism services in China. *Electronic Commerce Research, 4*(3), 221-239.

Luciw, R. (2004). *RBC extends bank hours.* Retrieved June 20, 2007, from http://www.theglobeandmail.com

Lumpkin, G. T. (1998). *Do new entrant firms have an entrepreneurial orientation?* Paper presented at the annual meeting of the Academy of Management, San Diego, CA.

Lumpkin, G. T., & Dess, G. G. (1996). Clarifying the entrepreneurial orientation construct and linking it to performance. *Academy of Management Review, 21*(1), 135-172.

Lumpkin, G. T., & Dess, G. G. (2004). E-business strategies and internet business models: How the Internet adds value. *Organizational Dynamics, 33*(2), 161-173.

Lyles, M. A., Baird, I. S., Orris, J. B., & Kuratko, D. F. (1993). Formalised planning in small business: increasing strategic choices. *Journal of Small Business Management, 31*(2), 38-50.

Lynn, R. (1969). Personality characteristics of a group of entrepreneurs. *Occupational Psychology, 43*(2), 151-152.

Macey, J. R. (2006). Commercial banking and democracy: The illusive quest for deregulation. *Yale Journal on Regulation, 23*(1).New Haven: Yale University, School of Law.

Macfarlane, D. (2000). Unis urged to join the e-revolution, *The Australian*, November 22, p.38.

MacGregor, D. G., & Fleming, R. (1996). Risk perception and symptom reporting. *Risk Analysis, 16*(6), 773-783.

Madsen, T. K., & Servais, P. (1997). The internationalisation of born globals: An evolutionary process? *International Business Review, 6*(6), 561-583.

Madsen, T. K., Rasmussen, E. S., & Servais, P. (2000). Differences and similarities between born globals and other types of exporters. In A. Yaprak & J. Tutek (Eds.), *Globalisation, the multinational form and emerging economies, Advances in International Marketing* (pp. 247-265). Amsterdam: JAI/Elsevier Inc.

Maguire, S. (2004). The co-evolution of technology and discourse: a study of substitution processes for the insecticide DDT. *Organization Studies, 25*(1), 113.

Maguire, S. (2004). The co-evolution of technology and discourse: a study of substitution processes for the insecticide DDT. *Organization Studies, 25*(1), 113.

Mahatra, Y. Role of information technology in managing organizational change and organizational interdependence. http://www.brint.com/papers/change/

"Malaysia's Super Corridor" (1999). Special report, *The Washington Times*, April 28.

Mamis, R. A. (1989). Global start-up. *Inc.*, Aug. 38-47.

Mandl-Striegnitz, P., & Lichter, H. (1999). Defizite im Software-Projektmanagement – Erfahrungen aus einer industriellen Studie. *Informatik / Informatique* 5, 4-9.

Mandviwalla, M. (1993*). The world of collaborative tools*. Paper presented at the People and Computers VIII Conference (HCI'93), Computer and Information Sciences, Temple University, Philadelphia, USA.

Mann, C., & Gotz, K. (2006). *Borderless business: Managing the far-flung enterprise*. West Port, CT: Praeger.

Mannion, R., Davies, H., & Marshall, M. N. (2005). Cultural characteristics of "high" and "low" performing hospitals. *Journal of Health Organisation and Management, 19*(6), 431-439.

Margerison, C. J. (2002). *Team leadership, A guide to success with team management systems*. UK: Thomson.

Marková, I. (2000). The individual and society in psychological theory. *Theory & Psychology, 10*(1), 107-116.

Marková, I. (2003). *Dialogicality and social representations—The dynamics of mind*. Cambridge: Cambridge University Press.

Marlow, M., Stanley, K., & Connors, S. (2005). Collegiality, collaboration and Kuleana: Complexity in a professional development school. *Education, 25*(4), 557-568.

Martin, C. (2005). From high maintenance to high productivity: What managers need to know about generation Y. *Industrial and Commercial Training, 37*(1), 39-44.

Martino, J. P. (1995). *R&D project selection*. New York: John Wiley & Sons.

Maskell, B. H. (1991). *Performance measurement for world class manufacturing: A model for American companies (corporate leadership)*. Productivity Press.

Mason-Jones, R., & Towill, D. R. (1997). Information enrichment: Designing the supply chain for competitive advantage. *Supply chain Management, 2*(4), 137-48.

Mason-Jones, R., Naylor, B., & Towill, D. R. (2000). Engineering the leagile supply chain. *International Journal of Agile Management Systems, 2*(1), 54-67.

Massie, J. (1987). *Essentials of management*. NJ: Prentice-Hall.

Massumi, B. (1992). *A user guide to capitalism and schizophrenia: Deviations from Deleuze and Guattari*. Cambridge: The MIT Press.

Mastipuram, R., & Wee, E. (2004). Soft errors' impact on system reliability. *EDN, 49*(20), 69.

Mastny, L. (2002). *Ecotourism* trap. *Foreign Policy, 42*(133), 94-96.

Masurel, E., & Smit, H. P. (2000). Planning behavior of small firms in Central Vietnam. *Journal of Small Business Management, 38*(2), 95-102.

Matlay, H. (2004). E-entrepreneurship and small e-business development: Towards a comparative research agenda. *Journal of Small Business and Enterprise Development, 11*(3), 408-414.

Mc Hugh, M., & O'Gorman, B., (2006). Enterprise education does make a difference. *EFMD 36ᵗʰ EISB Conference Proceedings on Embedding Entrepreneurship Education in Europe: Evaluating Effective Policy and Practice at the Institutional, Regional and National Levels*, September 2006, Southampton.

McAdam, R. (2000). Quality models in an SME context: A critical perspective using a grounded approach. *The International Journal of Quality & Reliability Management, 17*(3), 305.

McClelland, D. (1987). Characteristics of successful entrepreneur. *The Journal of Creative Behavior, 21*(3), 219-233.

McClelland, D. C. (1961). *The achieving society*. NJ: D.Van Nostrand.

McCracken, S. (2001). *Banking and financial institutional law*. Published in association with the Australasian Institute of banking and Finance. Sydney: Thomson legal and Regulatory Limited trading as Lawbook Co.

McCue, S. (1999). Small firms and the Internet: Force or farce? In *Proceedings of the International Trade Forum* (pp. 27-29).Geneva,.

McDavid, H., & Ramajeesingh, D. (2003). The state and tourism: A Caribbean perspective. *International Journal of Contemporary Hospitality Management, 15*(3), 180-183.

McDougall, P. P., & Oviatt, B. M. (1996). New venture internationalisation, strategic change, and performance: A follow-up study. *Journal of Business Venturing, 11*(1), 23-40.

McGowan, P., Durkin, M., Allen, M., Dougan, C., & Nixon, S. (2001). Developing competencies in the entrepreneurial small firm for use of the Internet in the management of customer relationships. *Journal of European Industrial Training, 25*(2/3//4), 126-136.

McGrath, M. E., & Romeri, M. N. (1994). The R&D effectiveness index: A metric for product development performance. *Insight, 5*(3), 1-12.

McGrath, M.E. & Iansiti, M. (1998). Envisioning IT-enabled innovation. *PRTM Insight Magazine.*

McIsaac, M. S. (2002). Online learning from an international perspective. *Journal of Education Media International, 39*(1), 17-21.

McLaughlin, H., & Thorpe, R. (1993). Action learning: A paradigm in emergence: The problems facing a challenge to traditional management education and development. *British Journal of Management, 4*(1), 19-27.

McLeod, R., & Winsor, B. (2003). *Entrepreneurship case studies: 3M*. Scottish Institute for Enterprise and Napier University Edinburgh. Retrieved from http://www.sie.ac.uk/UserFiles/File/3m.pdf

McMurray, A. J., & Dorai, R. (2003). Workplace innovation scale: A new method for measuring innovation in the workplace. The *5ᵗʰ European Conference on Organizational Knowledge, Learning and Capabilities (OKLC 2003)*. Barcelona, Spain April.

McMurray, A. J., Cross, J., & Caponecchia, C. (2007, August 3-8). *Business continuity plan practices within the risk management profession*. Presented at the Academy of Management Meeting, Philadelphia, Pennsylvania.

McMurray, A. J., Pace, R. W., & Scott, D. (2004). *Research: A commonsense approach*. Melbourne: Thomson Learning Social Science Press.

McShane, S., & Von Glinow, M. (2005). *Organizational behavior* (3ʳᵈ ed.). New York: McGraw Hill.

Mechlin, G. F., & Berg, D. (1980). Evaluating research—ROI is not enough. *Harvard Business Review, 58*(5), 93-99.

Meggginson, D. (1996). Planned and emergent learning—consequences for development. *Management Learning, 27*(4), 411-428.

Mehling, H. (1998). Survey says: E-commerce is crucial to success—Small businesses are eager to sell wares on the Web. *Computer Reseller News*, May 4, 787.

Melo, M., Denizer, C., & Gelb, A. (1996). Patterns of transition from planned to market economy. *World Bank Economic Review, 10*(3), 397-424.

Menczer, F. (2004). Lexical and semantic clustering by Web links. *Journal of the American Society for Information Science and Technology, 55*(14), 1261-1269.

Merton, R. K. (1957). *Social theory and social structure*. Glencoe, IL: The Free Press.

Meyer, C. (2001). The second generation of speed. *Harvard Business Review, 79*(4), 24-26.

Meyer, C., & Davis, S. (2003). *It's alive: The coming convergence of information, biology, and business*. New York: Crown Publishing.

Meyer, J. W., & Scott, W. R. (1992). *Organizational environment: Ritual and rationality*. Newbury Park: Sage Publications.

Meyerson, D., Weick, K. E., & Kramer, R. M. (1996). Swift trust & temporary groups. In R. M. Kramer, & T. R. Tyler (Ed.), *Trust in organizations: Frontiers of theory & research* (pp. 166-195). Thousand Oaks, CA: Sage Publications.

Mezias, S. J., & Kuperman, J. (2001). The community dynamics of entrepreneurship: The birth of the American film industry, 1895-1929. *Journal of Business Venturing, 16*(3), 209-233.

Michigan State University. (1993). *The defining dimension of university outreach*. Report of the provost's committee on university outreach. Retrieved October 11, 2006, from http://www.msu.edu/unit/outreach/missiondefinition.html

Miles, R. E., & Snow, C.C. (1978). *Organizational strategy, structure, and process*. New York: McGraw-Hill.

Miller, G. A., Galanter, E., & Pribram, K. A. (1986). *Plans and the structure of behavior*. Adams Bannister Cox Pubs.

Miller, J. (2006). Catching generation Y. *CMA Management*, April, 13-14.

Miller, R. (1992). The Influence of primary task on R&D laboratory evaluation: A comparative bibliometric analysis. *R&D Management, 22*(1), 3-15.

Miller, W., & Langdon, M. (1999). *Fourth generation R&D: Managing knowledge, technology, and innovation*. Canada: John Wiley & Sons Inc.

Mills, J. L. (1993). Spermicides and birth defects. In K. R. Foster, D. E. Bernstein, & P. W. Huber (Eds.), *Phantom risk: Scientific interference and the law*. London: The MIT Press.

Mills, J., Platts, K., Bourne, M., & Richards, H. (2002). *Competing through competences*. Cambridge, UK: Cambridge University Press.

Mink, G., Mink, P., & Owen, K. (1987). *Groups at work, Techniques in training and performance development series*. Englewood Cliffs, NJ: Educational technology Publications.

Mintzberg, H. (1990). The design school: Reconsidering the basic premises of strategic management. *Strategic Management Journal, 11*(3), 171-195.

Mintzberg, H. (1991). The innovative organization. *The Strategy Process: Concepts, Contexts, Cases*. 2nd Edn, Prentice Hall, Englewood Cliffs, NJ, pp. 731-746.

Mintzberg, H. (1994). *The rise and fall of strategic planning*. New York: Free Press.

Mintzberg, H., & Waters, J. (1982). Tracking strategies in an entrepreneurial firm. *Academy of Management Journal, 25*(3), 465-499.

Mintzberg, H., Ahlstrand, B., & Lampel, J. (1998). *Strategy Safari: A guided tour through the wilds of strategic management*. Hemel Hempstead: Prentice Hall Europe.

Mintzberg, H., Quinn, J. B., & Ghoshal, S. (1998). *The strategy process* (Revised European Edition). London: Prentice Hall.

Mirchandani, D. A., & Motwani, J. (2001). Understanding small business electronic commerce adoption: An empirical analysis. *Journal of Computer Information Systems, 41*(3), 70-74.

Mishra, A. (1996). Organizational response to crises—The centrality of trust. In R. M. Kramer & T. R. Tyler (Ed.), *Trust in organizations: Frontiers of theory & research*, (pp. 261-287). Thousand Oaks, CA: Sage Publications.

Mitchell, R. (1999). Quality circles in the U.S: Rediscovering our roots. *The Journal for Quality and Participation, 22*(6), 24-28.

Molla, A., & Licker, P. (2005). Perceived e-readiness factors in e-commerce adoption: An empirical investigation in a developing country. *International Journal of*

Electronic Commerce, 10(1), 83-110.

Molla, A., Heeks, R., & Balcells, I. (2006). Adding clicks to bricks: A case study of e-commerce adoption by a Catalan small retailer. *European Journal of Information Systems, 15*(4), 424-438.

Moncrief, M. (April 12, 2006). Banking reporter, The Age business newspaper.

Monczka, R., & Morgan, J. (2000, January 13). Competitive supply strategies for the 21st Century *Purchasing* , 48-59

Mondragon, A. E. C., Lyons, A. C., Michaelides, Z., & Kehoe, D. F. (2006). Automotive supply chain models and technologies: A review of some latest developments. *Journal of Enterprise Information Management, 19*(5), 551-562

Moon, M., & Norris, D. (2005). Does managerial orientation matter? The adoption of reinventing government and e-government at the municipal level. *Information Systems Journal, 15*(1), 43-60.

Moore, C. F. (1986). Understanding entrepreneurial behaviour. In J. A. Pearce & R. B. J. Robinson (Eds.), *Academy of management best papers proceedings.* Chicago: Forty-sixth Annual Meeting of the Academy of Management.

Morino, M. (1999). *Netpreneurs: A new breed of entrepreneur.* Ewing Marion Kauffman Foundation [online]. Retrieved from http://eventuring.kauffman. org/Resources/Resources.aspx?id=33588

Morville, P. (2005). *Ambient findability* (1st ed.). Sebastopol, CA: O'Reilly.

Moscovici, S. (1961/1976). *La psychanalyse, Son Image et son Public.* Paris: Presses Universitaires de France.

Moscovici, S. (1984). Introduction: le domaine de la psychologie sociale. In S. Moscovici (Ed.), *Psychologie Sociale.* Paris: Presses Universitaires de France.

Moscovici, S. (1984). The phenomenon of social representations. In R. Farr & S. Moscovici (Eds.), *Social representations.* Cambridge: Cambridge University Press.

Moscovici, S. (1988). Notes towards a description of social representations. *European Journal of Social Psychology, 18*(3), 211-250.

Moscovici, S. (2000). *Social representations: Explorations in social psychology.* Cambridge: Polity Press.

Moscovici, S. (2001). Why a theory of social representations? In K. Deaux & G. Philogène (Eds.), *Representations of the social.* Oxford: Blackwells Publishers Inc.

Moscovici, S., & Marková, I. (2000). Ideas and their development: A dialogue between Serge Moscovici and Ivana Marková. In S. Moscovici (Ed.), *Social representations: Explorations in social psychology.* Cambridge: Polity Press.

Moscovici, S., & Vignaux, G. (2000). The concept of themata. In G. Duveen (Ed.), *Social representations: Explorations in social psychology.* Cambridge: Polity Press.

Moutinho, L., & Phillips, P. A. (2002). The impact of strategic planning on the competitiveness performance and effectiveness of bank branches: A neural network analysis. *International Journal of Marketing, 20*(3), 102-110.

Mulhaney, A., Sheehan, J., & Hughes, J. (2004). Using ISO9000 to drive continual improvement in a SME. *The TQM Magazine, 16*(5), 325.

Munoz, M. (2005). Executive insights on globalization: implications for hospitality managers in emerging locations. *International Journal of Contemporary Hospitality Management, 17*(4), 365-371.

Nandwa, J. (1990). Oral literature as a tool for children's education in Africa. In J. Ross & V. Bergum (Eds.), *Through the looking glass, children, and health promotion.* Ottawa: Canadian Pubic Health Association.

Narula, R. N. (2003). *Globalization and technology: Interdependence, innovation systems, and industrial policy.* Cambridge: Polity Press.

Naylor, J. B., Naim, M. M., & Berry, D. (1999). Leagality: Integrating the lean and agile manufacturing paradigm in the total supply chain. *International Journal of Production Economics, 63*(1-2), 107-118.

Needleman, H. L. (2000). The removal of lead from gasoline: Historical and personal reflections. *Environmental*

Research, 84(1), 20.

Neely, A. (2002). *Business performance measurement.* Cambridge University Press.

Neto, F. (2003). A new approach to sustainable tourism development: Moving beyond environmental protection. *Natural Resources Forum, 27*(1), 212-222.

Ng, H. I., Pan, Y. G., & Wilson, T. D. (1998). Business use of the world wide Web: A report on further investigations. *International Journal of Information Management, 18*(5), 291-314.

Nonaka, I., & Nishiguchi, T. (2001). Conclusion: Social, technical, and evolutionary dimensions of knowledge creation. In I. Nonaka & T. Nishiguchi (Eds.), *Knowledge emergence: Social, technical, and evolutionary dimensions of knowledge creation.* Oxford: Oxford University Press.

Nonaka, I., & Takeuchi, H. (1995). *The knowledge-creating company.* New York: Oxford University Press.

Nonaki, I. & Nichiguchi, T. (2001). *Knowledge emergence: Social, technical, and evolutionary dimensions of knowledge creation.* Oxford University Press.

Norm A., & Yuan, Y. (2000). Managing business-to-business relationships throughout the *e-commerce* procurement life cycle. *Internet Research: Electronic Networking Applications and Policy, 10*(5), 385-395.

Norris, G., Hurley, J., Hartley, K., Dunleavy, J., & Balls, J. (2000). *E-business and ERP–transforming the enterprise.* PriceWaterhouseCoopers John Wiley & Sons Inc.

Noy, N., & McGuiness, D. (2001). *Ontology development 101—A guide to creating your first ontology.* Stanford University.

Numetrics Management Systems. (2000). *Measuring IC and ASIC design productivity.* White Paper submitted to the Fabless Semiconductor Association (FAB), Santa Clara, CA.

Nurmi, R. (1996). Teamwork and team leadership. *Team performance management: An International Journal, 2*(1), 9-13, MCB University Press.

NZZ. (2002, 2002-04-11). Elektroschrott wird rücknahmepflichtig. *Neue Zürcher Zeitung,* p. 19.

NZZaSo. (2004, 2004-09-14). Ökologische Elektrogeräte. *NZZ am Sonntag.*

O'Gorman, C. (2000). Strategy and the small firm. In S. Carter & D. Jones-Evans (Eds.), *Enterprise and small business: Principles, practice, and policy* (Vol. 16, pp. 179-208). London: Macmillan.

O'Marah, K. (2006). *AMR research releases second annual supply chain top 25.* Retrieved December 30, 2006, from http://www.amrresearch.com/Content/View. asp?pmillid=18895

O'Neill, H., & Sackett, P. J. (1994). *The extended manufacturing enterprise paradigm.* Management Decision.

Oblinger, D., & Oblinger, J. (2005). Educating the net generation. A new EDUCAUSE e-book. Retrieved February 16, 2007, from http://www.educause.edu/content. asp?PAGE_ID=5989&bhcp=1

OECD. (1993). *The measurement of scientific and technical activities.* OECD Publishing.

OECD. (2005). *Oslo manual.* OECD Publishing.

Olsen, M. (1968). *The process of social organization.* Holt, NY: Rinehart & Winston.

Opportunity Wales. (2007). *On-line guides—the ecommerce ladder.* Retrieved March 6, 2007, from http://www. opportunitywales.co.uk

Oviatt, B. M., & McDougall, P. (1994). Toward a theory of international new ventures. *Journal of International Business Studies, 25*(1), 45-64.

Oviatt, B. M., & McDougall, P. (1995). Global start-ups: Entrepreneurs on a worldwide stage. *Academy of Management Executive, 9*(2), 30-43.

Oviatt, B. M., & McDougall, P. P. (1997). Challenges for internationalisation process theory: the case of international new ventures. *Management International Review, 37*(2) (Special Issue), 85-99.

Oxford English Dictionary. (2005). *Compact Oxford English Dictionary.* Retrieved December 1, 2005, from http://www.askoxford.com/?view=uk

Ozer, M. (2005). Fuzzy c-means clustering and Internet portals: a case study. *European Journal of Operational Research, 164*(3), 696-714.

Pallot, M., Salminen, V., Pillai, B., & Kulvant, B. (2004).

Business semantics: The magic instrument enabling plug & play collaboration? *ICE 2004, International Conference on Concurrent Engineering*, Sevilla, June 14-16.

Parnell, J. A., & Wright, P. (1993). Generic strategy and performance: An empirical test of the Miles and Snow typology. *British Journal of Management, 4*(1), 29-36.

Pascale, R., Millemann, M., & Gioja, L. (2000). *Surfing the edge of chaos*. New York: Crown Business.

Paul, D. L., & McDaniel, R. R. (2004). A field study of the effect of interpersonal trust on virtual collaborative relationship performance. *MIS Quarterly, 28*(2), 183-228.

PDM Implementor Forum. (2002). *Usage guide for the STEP PDM Schema V1.2.* Retrieved from http://www.prostep.org

Peck, S. (1993). *A world waiting to be born: Civility rediscovered*. New York: Bantam Books.

Perez-Prado, A., & Thirunarayanan, M. O. (2002). A qualitative comparison of online and classroom-based sections of a course: Exploring student perspectives. *Journal of Education Media International, 39*(2), 195-202.

Perry, S. C. (2001). The relationship between written business plans and the failure of small businesses in the US. *Journal of Small Business Management, 39*(3), 201-208.

Peters, T. J. (1997). *The circle of innovation*. London: Hodder and Stoughton.

Pflughoeft, K. A., Ramamurthy, K., Soofi, E. S., Yasai-Ardekani, M., & Fatemah, M. (2003). Multiple conceptualizations of small business Web use and benefit. *Decision Sciences, 34*(3), 467-513.

Phan, D. D. (2003). E-business development for competitive advantages: a case study. *Information and Management, 40*(6), 581-590

Piattini, M., Genero, M., Poels, G., & Nelson, J. (2005). Towards a framework for conceptual modelling quality. In C. Genero/Piattini (Ed.), *Metrics for software conceptual models*. London, UK: Imperial College Press.

Pidgeon, N. F., & Beattie, J. (1998). The psychology of risk and uncertainty. In P. Calow (Ed.), *Handbook of environmental risk assessment and management* (pp. 289). London: Blackwell Science.

Pisano, G. P. (2006). *Science business: The promise, the reality, and the future of biotech*. Boston, MA: Harvard Business Press.

Pistorius, C. W. I., & Utterback, J. M. (1995). The death knells of mature technologies. *Technological Forecasting and Social Change, 50*(3), 133-151(19).

Pittard, V. (2004). Evidence for e-learning policy. *Technology, Pedagogy, and Education, 13*(2), 181-194.

Plaschka, G. & Welsch, P. (2005). Emerging structures in entrepreneurship education: Curricular designs and strategies. In R. van der Hrost, D., S. ing-Kauannui, & S. Duffy (Eds.), *Keystones of entrepreneurship knowledge*, (pp. 322-338). Blackwell Publishing.

Platonova, E. A., Hernandez, S. R., Shewchuk, R. M., & Leddy, K. M. (2006). Study of the relationship between organisational culture and organisational outcomes using hierarchical linear modelling methodology. *Quality Management in Health Care, 15*(3), 200-210.

Poirier, C. (n.d.). *Beyond supply chain to the networked enterprise*. From CSC Research Services. Retrieved September 20, 2006, from http://uk.country.csc.com/en/kl/uploads/196_1.pdf

Polkinghorne, D. (1988). *Narrative knowing and the human sciences*. New York: SUNY Press.

Poon, S., & Swatman, P. M. C. (1999). An exploratory study of small business Internet commerce issues. *Information and Management, 35*(1), 9-18.

Porter, M. (1990). *The competitive advantage of nations*. London: MacMillan.

Porter, M. (1998). *On competition*. Boston: Harvard Business School Press.

Porter, M. E. (1980). *Competitive strategy*. New York: The Free Press.

Porter, M. E. (1985). *Competitive advantage: Creating and sustaining superior performance*. New York: The Free Press.

Porter, M. E. (2001, March). Strategy and the Internet. *Harvard Business Review* pp. 63-78

Porter, M. E., & Millar, V. E. (1985). How information gives you competitive advantage. *Harvard Business Review, 63*(4), 149-160.

Postman, N. (1985). *Amusing ourselves to death: public discourse in the age of show business*. New York: Viking.

Potter, B. (2005). RFID: Misunderstood or untrustworthy? *Network Security, 2005*(4), 17-18.

Prahalad, C. K. (2005). *The fortune at the bottom of the pyramid*. Upper Saddle River, NJ: Wharton School Press.

Preece, J., Rogers, Y., Sharp, H., Benyon, D., Holland, S., & Carey, T. (1994). *Human-computer interaction*. Essex, London: Pearson Education Limited.

Prensky, M. (2001a). *Digital natives, digital immigrants*. On the Horizon, 9(5), 1-2. Retrieved February 7, 2007, from http://www.marcprensky.com/writing/Prensky%20-%20Digital%20Natives,%20Digital%20Immigrants%20-%20Part1.pdf

Prensky, M. (2001b). *Digital natives, digital immigrants, Part II: Do they really think differently?* On the Horizon, 9(6), 1-2. Retrieved December 16, 2006, from http://www.marcprensky.com/writing/Prensky%20%20Digital%20Natives,%20Digital%20Immigrants%20-%20Part2.pdf

Prescott, M. B., & Conger, S. A. (1995). Information technology innovations: A classification by it locus of impact and research approach. *Data Base Advances, 26*(2-3), 20-41.

Priskin, J. (2003). Issues and opportunities in planning and managing nature-based tourism in the Central Coast Region of Western Australia. *Australian Geographical Studies, 41*(3), 270-286.

PRO:NED. (2007). *Non-Executive Directors' Survey Report 2007*. IBM:NSW.

Puhretmair, F., & Woess, W. (2001). XML-based integration of GIS and heterogeneous tourism information systems. *Lecture Notes in Computer Science, 2068, 346*. Heidelberg: Springer Publishing.

Puhretmair, F., Rumetshofer, H., & Schaumlechner, E. (2002). Extended decision- making in tourism information systems. *Lecture Notes in Computer Science, 2455, 57*. Heidelberg: Springer Publishing.

Pyötsiä, J. (2001). Innovation management in network economy. *186JP IAMOT Conference*, Lausanne, 19-22

March 2001.

Quah, D. (2003). *Creativity and knowledge: Managing and respecting intellectual assets in the 21st Century - Clifford Barclay Memorial Lecture*. London School of Economics. Retrieved from http://econ.lse.ac.uk/staff/dquah

Quality Systems. (1996). Quality Control Circle hand Book, Singapore.

Quayle, M. (2001, May). *E-commerce: The challenge for Welsh small and medium size enterprises*. Paper presented at Business Week in Wales Lecture (pp. 1-14) Cardiff: Cardiff International Arena.

Quinn, J. B. (1985). Managing innovation: Controlled chaos. *Harvard Business Review, 63*(3), 73-84.

Quinton, S., & Harridge-March, S. (2003). Strategic interactive marketing of wine—a case of evolution. *Marketing Intelligence and Planning, 21*(6), 357-363.

Qutb, M. (1997). *Bhrantir Berazale Islam*. (Translated by Razzaq, A.A. Islam-The Misunderstood Religion). Dhaka: Dhunik Prokashani.

Rabelo, R., & Camarinha-Matos, L. (1996). Towards agile scheduling in extended enterprise. In L. M. Camarinha-Matos, H. & Afsarmanesh (Eds.), *Proceedings of BASYS'96: Balanced Automation Systems II—Implementation Challenges for Anthropocentric Manufacturing*. Chapman & Hall.

Radiologie.de. (2006). Die Geschichte der Radiologie: Curagita AG.

Rae, D. (2004). Entrepreneurial learning: A practical model from the creative industries. *Education + Training, 46*(8/9), 492-500.

Rahman, S. U. (2001). A comparative study of TQM practice and organisational performance of SMEs with and without ISO 9000 certification. *International Journal of Quality & Reliability Management, 18*(1), 35-49.

Rahn, A. (2004). *Bleifrei Löten: Ein Leitfaden für die Praxis*. Bad Saulgau: Eugen G. Leuze Verlag.

Rahn, A., Diehm, R., & Beske, E. (1995). Bleifreie Lote? *productronic*(2), 19.

Rai, A, Patnayakuni, R., & Patnayakuni, N. (2006). Firm performance impacts of digitally enabled supply chain integration capabilities. *MIS Quarterly, 30*(2), 225-240

Raisinghani, M. S., Benoit, A., Ding, J., Gomez, M., Gupta, K., Gusila, V., et al. (2004). Ambient intelligence: Changing forms of human computer interaction and their social implications. *Journal of Digital Information, 5*(4).

Rajagopalan, N., & Spreitzer, G. M. (1997). Toward a theory of strategic change: A multi-lens perspective and integrative framework. *Academy of Management Review, 22*(1), 48-79.

Ramona, N. C., & Fjermestad. (2006). *Collaborative project management: Challenges and opportunities for virtual teams and projects in e-collaboration.* USA: Oklama State University and New Jersey Institute of technology.

Ramsden, P. (2003). *Learning to teach in higher education.* London: RoutledgeFalmer.

Rasmussen, E. S., & Madsen, T. K. (2002). *The born global concept.* Paper presented in the 28th EIBA Conference, Athens, Greece.

Rawson, R. (2007). Overdose: How excessive government regulation stifles pharmaceutical innovation. *Journal of the American Medical Association, 297*(2), 646-647.

Ray, D. M. (1989). Strategic *implications of entrepreneurial ventures "born international": Four case studies.* Paper presented at the Frontiers in Entrepreneurship Research, Babson-Kauffman Entrepreneurial Research Conference (BKERC).

Raymond, L. (2001). Determinants of Web site implementation in small businesses. *Internet Research, 11*(5), 411-423.

Rayport, J. F., & Jaworski, B. J. (2002). *Introduction to e-commerce.* Boston: McGraw-Hill.

Rayport, J., & Jaworski, F. (2000). *E-Commerce.* New York: McGraw-Hill/Irwin.

Reeves, B., & Nass, C. (1996). *The media equation: How people treat computers, television, and new media like real people and places.* Cambridge: Cambridge University Press.

Rennie, M. (1993). Global competitiveness: Born global. *McKinsey Quarterly, 4*, 45-52.

Rheingold, H. (1994). *The virtual community—Finding connection in a computerized world.* London: Secker & Warburg.

Rialp-Criado, A., Rialp-Criado, J., & Knight, G. A. (2002). *The phenomenon of international new ventures, global start-ups, and born-globals: What do we know after a decade (1993-2002) of exhaustive scientific inquiry?* Working Paper, Department d'Economia de l'Empresa, Universitat Autònoma de Barcelon, Barcelona.

Ricchiuto, J. (2005). *Appreciative leadership, building sustainable organizations.* Cleveland: Designing life books.

Rich, P. (1992). The organizational taxonomy: Definitions and design. *The Academy of Management Review, 17*(4), 758-781.

Rich, P. (1992). The organizational taxonomy: Definitions and design. *The Academy of Management Review, 17*(4), 758-781.

Richards, D., & Busch, P. (2003). Acquiring and applying contextualised tacit knowledge. *Journal of Information and Knowledge Management, 2*(2), 179-190.

Richardson, M. L., & Gurtner, W. H. (1999). Contemporary organisational strategies for enhancing value in health care. *International Journal of Health Care Quality Assurance, 12*(5), 183-189.

Ring, P. S., & Van De Ven, A. H. (1992). Structuring cooperative relationships between organizations. *Strategic Management Journal, 13*(7), 483-498.

Riva, G. (2005). The psychology of ambient intelligence: Activity, situation, and presence. In G. Riva, F. Vatalaro, F. Davide, & M. Alcaniz (Eds.), *Ambient intelligence: The evolution of technology, communication, and cognition towards the future of human-computer interaction.* IOS Press.

Riva, G., Vatalaro, F., Davide, F., & Alcaniz, M. (2005). *Ambient intelligence: The evolution of technology, communication, and cognition towards the future of human-computer interaction.* IOS Press.

Robbins, S. P., Millett, B., & Waters-Marsh, T. (2004). *Organisational behaviour* (4th ed.). Pearson, Prentice Hall, Frenchs Forest, NSW.

Roberts, B. (1988). Managing invention and innovation. *Research Technology Management, 31*(1), 1-19.

Roberts, C. (2006). Retaining tomorrow's technician …. the generation Y worker is accustomed to instant gratification. *Fleet Equipment*, July, *32*(7), 11.

Roberts, E. B., & Senturia, T. A. (1996). Globalising the emerging high-technology company. *Industrial Marketing Management, 25*(6), 491-506.

Robinson, R. B., & Pearce, J. A. (1984). Research thrusts in small firm strategic-planning. *Academy of Management Review, 9*(1), 128-137.

Roffe, I. (1999). Innovation and creativity in organizations: A review of the implications for training and development. *Journal of European Industrial Training, 23*(4/5), 224-237.

Rögener, W. (2004, 23. September 2004). Acrylamid nicht entlastet: Chemiker geben voreilig Entwarnung vor dem Plastik im Essen. *Süddeutsche Zeitung*, p. 9.

Rogers, E. M. (1995). *Diffusion of innovation* (4th ed.). New York: The Free Press.

Rooijmans, J., Aerts, H., & van Genuchten, M. (1996). Software quality in consumer electronics products. *Software, IEEE, 13*(1), 55-6455-6455-64.

Rophol, G. (1999). Innovative Technikbewertung. In S. Bröchler, G. Simonis, & K. Sundermann (Eds.), *Handbuch Technikfolgenabschätzung* (Vol. 1, pp. 83ff). Berlin: edition sigma.

Rose, D., Efram, D., Gervais, M. C., Joffe, H., Jovchelovitch, S., & Morant, N. J. (1995). Questioning consensus in social representations theory. *Papers on Social Representations, 4*(2), 1-6.

Rugendyke, B., & Son, N. (2005). Conservation costs: Nature-based tourism as development at Cuc Phuong National Park, Vietnam. *Asia Pacific Viewpoint, 46*(2), 185-200.

Ruhnka, J. C., & Young, J. E. (1987). A venture capital model of the development process for new ventures. *Journal of Business Venturing 2*(2), 167-184.

Ruppel, C. (2006). An information systems perspective of supply chain tool compatibility: The roles of technol-ogy fit and relationships. *Business Process Management Journal, 10*(3), 311-324.

Russo, A. (2001). *Five myths about entrepreneurs: Understanding how businesses start and grow.* Washington DC: National Commission on Entrepreneurship.

Ryan, G., & Valverde, M. (2006). Waiting in line for online services: A qualitative study of the user's perspective. *Information Systems Journal, 16*(2), 181-211.

Saarenketo, S. (2002). *Born globals—internationalisation of small and medium-sized knowledge-intensive firms.* Unpublished doctoral dissertation, Lappeenranta University of Technology, Finland.

Saari, S. (2006). Mistä korkeakoulujen laatukäsite ja laatu määrittyy? *Hallinnon tutkimus, 2*, 54-62.

Sabel, C. (1992). Studied trust-building new forms of cooperation in a volatile economy. In F. Pyke, & W. Segenberger (Ed.), *Industrial districts & local economic regeneration,* (pp. 215-250). Geneva: IILS.

Sadowski, B. M., Maitland, C., & van Douyer, J. (2002). Strategic use of the Internet by small-and medium-sized companies: An exploratory study. *Information Economics and Policy, 14*(1), 75-93.

Sako, M. (1992). *Prices quality & trust-interfirm relations in Britain & Japan.* Cambridge: Cambridge University Press.

Sanchez, R. (1995). Strategic flexibility and product competition. *Strategic Management Journal, 16*(Special Issue), 135-159.

Saparito, P. A., Chen, C. C., & Sapienza, H. J. (2004). The role of relational trust in bank-small firm relationships. *Academy of Management Journal, 47*(3), 400-410.

Sapienza, H. J., & Grimm, C. M. (1997). Founder characteristics, start-up process, and strategy/structure variables as predictors of shartline railroad performance. *Entrepreneurship Theory and Practice*, vol. Fall, 5-24.

Sawaguchi, M. (2001). Study of effective new product development activities through combination of patterns of evolution of technological systems and VE. *Triz Journal. March 2001.*

Schacter, J., & Fagnano, C. (1999). Does computer technology improve student learning and achievement? How, when, and under what condition? *Journal of Educational Computing Research, 20*(4), 329-343.

Schaefer, O. M. (2002). *Performance measures in value management.* Berlin, Germany: Erich Schmidt Verlag.

Schaper, M., & Volery, T. (2003). *Entrepreneurship and small business: A Pacific Rim perspective.* Brisbane: John Wiley.

Scheer, A. (1998). *Wirtschaftsinformatik.* Berlin, Germany: Springer.

Schekkerman, J. (2004). *Another View at Extended Enterprise Architecture Viewpoints.* Institute For Enterprise Architecture Developemets.

Schumpeter, J. (1934). *The theory of economic development.* Cambridge, MA: Harvard University Press.

Schumpeter, J. A. (1911). *The theory of economic development: An inquiry into profits, capital, credit, interest and the business cycle.* 1934 translation. Cambridge, MA: Harvard University Press.

Schumpeter, J. A. (1947). The creative response in economic history. *Journal of Economic History, 7*(2), 149-159.

Schutte, F., & van der Sijde, P. (2000). *The university and its region.* Enschede: Twente University Press.

Schwandt, T. (1998). Constructivist, interpretivist approaches to human inquiry. In N. Denzin & Y. Lincoln (Eds.), *The landscape of qualitative research.* Beverly Hills, CA: Sage.

Schweizer, T. S. (2004). *An individual psychology of novelty seeking, creativity, and innovation.* RIM Ph.D. Series, 48.

Sclove, R. S. (1999). *Position Paper, The loka institute.* Retrieved December 5, 2006, from http://www.loka.org/idt/intro.htm#1.%20%20Democratizing%20Technology:%20Historical%20&%20Theoretical%20Background

Scott, G., & Walter, Z. (2003). DELPHI findings about Internet systems problems, with implications for other technologies. *Technology Analysis and Strategic Management, 15*(1), 103-115.

Scott, M., & Bruce, R. (1987). Five stages of growth in small business. *Long Range Planning, 20*(3), 45-52.

SCUP. (2004). *Trends in higher education: November Ed. Society for College and University Planning.* Ann Arbor, MI.

Sellitto, C., Wenn, A., & Burgess, S (2003). A review of the websites of small Australian wineries: Motivations, goals, and success. *Information Technology and Management, 4*(2-3), 215-232.

Senge, P. (1990). *The fifth discipline: The art and practice of the learning organization.* New York: Doubleday.

Sensiper, S. (2000). Making the case online Harvard business school multimedia. *Information, Communication, and Society, 3*(4), 616-621.

Servais, P., & Rasmussen, E. S. (2000, November). *Different types of international new ventures.* Paper presented at the Academy of International Business (AIB) Annual Meeting (pp. 1-27). Phoenix, AZ, USA.

Sexton, K., Needham, L. L., & Prikle, J. L. (2004). Human biomonitoring of environmental chemicals. *American Scientist, 92*(1), 38.

Shane, S. (2000). Prior knowledge and the discovery of entrepreneurial opportunities. *Organization Science, 11*(4), 448-469.

Shapiro, J. C. (1997). The impact of a TQM intervention on teamwork: A longitudinal assessment. *Team performance management, University of Oxford, 3*(3), 150-161.

Sharifi, H., Kehoe D.F., Hopkins J. (2006). A classification and selection model of e-marketplaces for better alignment of supply chains. *Journal of Enterprise Information Management 19*(5), 483-503.

Shiels, H., McIvor, R., & O'Reilly, D. (2003). Understanding the implications of ICT adoption: Insights from SMEs. *Logistics Information Management, 16*(5), 312-326.

Short, J., & Venkatraman, N. (1992). *Beyond business process redesign: Redefining Baxter's business network.* Sloan Management Review, *34*(1), Fall 1992

Shrader, C. B., Mulford, C. L., & Blackburn, V. L. (1989). Strategic and operational planning, uncertainty, and performance in small firms. *Journal of Small Business Management, 27*(4), 45-60.

Shrader-Frechette, K. (1996). Methodological rules for

four classes of scientific uncertainty. In J. Lemons (Ed.), *Scientific uncertainty and environmental problem solving* (pp. 12). Cambridge: Blackwell Science.

Shuell, T. J., & Farber, S. L. (2001). Students perceptions of technology use in college courses. *Journal of Educational Computing Research, 24*(2), 119-138.

SIBIS. (2002). *Towards the information society in Europe and the US: SIBIS Benchmarking Highlights 2002.* Bonn: Emipirca.

Siddique, K. (1998). *Political dimensions of Seerah.* London & Toronto: ICIT.

Silverman, D. (2001). *Interpreting qualitative data, methods for analysing talk, text, and interaction.* USA: Sage Publication.

Silverthorne, S. (2006). *Science Business: What Happened to Biotech? Q&A with Gary Pisano.* Harvard Business School Working Knowledge. Retrieved December 30, 2006 from http://hbswk.hbs.edu/item/5503.html

Simon, S., & Schuster. (2004). *The seven and eight habits of highly effective people.* Covey-Principle Centered Leadership Programme.

Simonis, G., Bröchler, S., & Sundermann, K. (1999). *Handbuch Technikfolgenabschätzung* (Vol. 1). Berlin: edition sigma.

Simonis, G., Bröchler, S., & Sundermann, K. (1999). *Handbuch Technikfolgenabschätzung* (Vol. 1). Berlin: edition sigma.

Simons, J. (1999). States chafe as Web shopper ignore sales taxes. *The Wall Street Journal*, January 26, p.B1.

Simonton, D. K. (1981). Creativity in western civilization: Intrinsic and extrinsic causes *American Anthropologist, New Series, 83*(3), 628-630.

Singapore Technologies Automobile. (1996). *Business improvement handbook* (5th ed.). Singapore: Singapore Technologies.

Singh, G., O'Donoghue, J., & Betts, C. (2002). A UK study into the potential effects of virtual education: Does online learning spell an end for on-campus learning? *Behaviour & Information Technology, 21*(3), 223-229.

Singh, M. (2005, November 23-25). *Business to employee (B2E) e-management.* Proceedings of the 6th International We-B (Working for E-Business) Conference, Melbourne, Australia.

Slater, S. F., & Narver, J. C. (1995). Market orientation and the learning organization. *Journal of Marketing, 59*(July), 63-74.

Slovic, P. (1987). Perception of risk. *Science, 236*(4799), 280.

Small Business Service. (2004). *A government action plan for small business: Making the UK the best place in the world to start and grow a small business—The evidence base.* London: Department of Trade and Industry.

Small, P. (2000). *The entrepreneurial Web: E-commerce tools for the new breed of Internet trader.* London: FT.com.

Smircich, L. (1983). Concepts of culture and organizational analysis. *Adminstrative Science Quarterly, 28*(3), 339-358.

Smith, C. S. (1967). Metallurgy in the seventeenth an eighteenth centuries. In M. Kranzberg & C. W. J. Pursell (Eds.), *Technology in Western Civilisation: The emergence of modern industrial society. Earliest Times to 1900* (pp. 142). New York, London, Toronto: Oxford University Press.

Smith, H. (2006). *Process innovation.* Retrieved December 30, 2006, from http://www.bptrends.com/publicationfiles02%2D06%20COL%20Proc%20Innovation%20P%2DTREZ%20Smith%2Epdf

Smith, H., & Fingar, P. (2002). *Business process management: The third wave.* Tampa, FL: Meghan-Kiffer Press.

Smith, J., & Webster, L. (2000). The knowledge economy and SMEs: A survey of skills requirements. *Business Information Review, 17*(3), September, 138-146.

Smith, R. (2005). Working with difference in online collaborative groups. *Adult Education Quarterly, 55*(3), 182-199.

Smrchek, J. C., & Zeeman, M. G. (1998). Assessing risks to ecological systems from chemicals. In P. Calow (Ed.), *Handbook of environmental risk assessment and management* (pp. 24). London: Blackwell Science.

Smyth, M., & Ibbotson, P. (2001). *Internet connectivity in Ireland.* Joint report by the Bank of Ireland and the University of Ulster. Retrieved March 6, 2007, from www.bankofireland.co.uk/whats_new/item.php?whatsnew_id=8

Snee, R. D., Kelleher, K. H., & Reynard, S. (1997). *Improving team effectiveness* (Report No. 156). New York: CQPI, University of Wisconsin.

Snowden, D. (2002). Just in time knowledge management. *KM Review, 5*(5), 14-17.

Snowden, D. (2002). Narrative patterns: Uses of story in the third age of knowledge management *Journal of Information and Knowledge Management, 00,* 1-5.

Snowden, D. (2005). From atomism to networks in social systems. *The Learning Organization, Special Issue "Knowledge Sharing," 12*(6), 552-562.

So, W., Wong, T., & Sculli, D. (2005). Factors affecting intentions to purchase via the internet. *Industrial Management and Data Systems, 105*(9), 1225-1244.

Soliman, F., & Youssef, M. A. (2003). Internet-based e-commerce and its impact on manufacturing and business operations. *Industrial Management and Data Systems, 103*(8), 546-552.

Sommer, S. S. (2002). *A practical guide to behavioural research: Tools and techniques* (5th ed). New York: University of California.

Sommerville, I. (2004). *Software engineering (international computer science series).* Addison Wesley.

Sørensen, C., & Gibson, D. (2004). Ubiquitous visions and opaque realities: Professionals talking about mobile technologies. *Info, 6*(3), 188-196.

Sorice, M., Shafer, C., & Ditton, R. (2006). Managing endangered species within the use preservation paradox: The Florida manatee (trichechus manatus latirostis) as a tourism attraction. *Environmental Management, 37*(1), 69-83.

Sorli, M. (1999). Innovación en el Diseño de Productos. *Forum Calidad Journal.*

Sorli, M., Mendikoa, I., Barbero, J. I., & Carrillo, A. (2006). *Distributed product design and manufactur-*

ing based on KBE. Computer Supported Cooperative Work in Design II; Lecture Notes in Computer Science 3865. Springer-Verlag Berlin Heidelberg, 2006, ISSN 0302-9743.

Sorli, M., Stokic, D., Gorostiza, A., & Campos, A. (2006). *Managing product/process knowledge in the concurrent/simultaneous enterprise environment.* Robotics and Computer Integrated Manufacturing. Elsevier (2006) p. 399–408. Volume 22, October-December 2006. ISSN 0736-5845.

Sorli, M., Stokic, D., Gorostiza, A., & Campos., A. (2006). Fostering innovation in practice through TRIZ-based CAI tool. *International Journal of Computer Applications in Technology (IJCAT),* special issue on Computer Aided Innovation (CAI).

Sparkes, A., & Thomas, B. (2001). The use of the Internet as a critical success factor for the marketing of Welsh agri-food SMEs in the twenty-first century. *British Food Journal, 103*(5), 331-337.

Spradley, J. P. (1980). *Participant observation.* USA: Thomson Learning Academic Resource Centre.

Spyros, V., & Christos, C., (2006). Entrepreneurial education and training in the tertiary level institutions of Greece. *EFMD 36th EISB Conference Proceedings on Embedding Entrepreneurship Education in Europe: Evaluating Effective Policy and Practice at the Institutional, Regional and National Levels,* September 2006, Southampton.

St. Michael's Guild. The barber-surgeon. Retrieved December 10, 2006 from http://www.st-mike.org/medicine/bs.html.

Stacey, R. D. (2000). *Strategic management & organisational dynamics—the challenge of complexity* (3rd ed.). London: Financial Times/ Prentice Hall.

Staff. (2003, July 1). *Process industry products, services to reach $786 billion by 2010.* Control Engineering. Retrieved September 20, 2006, from http://www.manufacturing.net/ctl/article/CA307757.html?text=process+industry+products%2C+services+to+reach+%24786+billion+by+2010&spacedesc=news

Stalk Jr., G. (1988). Time—The next source of competitive advantage. *Harvard Business Review, 66*(4), 28-60.

Stamatis, D. H. (2003). *Six-Sigma for financial profes-*

sionals. NJ: John Wiley and sons, Inc

Standards Australia. (2005). *AS8015-2005—Australian Standard for Corporate Governance of Information and Communication Technology*. Sydney.

Standing, C., Vasudavan, T., & Borbely, S. (1998). Re-engineering travel agencies with the world wide web. *Electronic Markets, 8*(4), 40-43.

Standish Group. (1994). *The CHAOS Report*. Retrieved March 7, 2007, from http://www.standishgroup.com/sample_research/chaos_1994_1.php

Steinberg, A. (2005). *Emergent knowledge dynamics in innovation: Exploring e-business entrepreneurship after the dotcom crash*. Unpublished thesis, London School of Economics and Political Science, University of London.

Steinberg, A. (2006). Exploring Rhizomic becomings in post dotcom-crash networks: A Deleuzian approach to emergent knowledge dynamics. In F. Zhao (Ed.), *Entrepreneurship and innovation in e-business: An integrative perspective*. Hershey, PA: Idea Group Inc.

Steiss, A. W. (2003). *Strategic management for public and nonprofit organisations*. New York: Marcel Dekker.

Stephens, P. R. (2000). *Small business and high performance management practices*. Unpublished doctoral dissertation, The University of Cincinnati.

Sternberg, R., Wagner, R., Williams, W., & Horvath, J. (1995). Testing common sense. *American psychologist, 50*(11), 912-927.

Stevenson, H. H., & Gumpert, D. E. (1985). The heart of entrepreneurship. *Harvard Business Review, 63*(2), 85-94.

Stockdale, R., & Standing, C. (2004). Benefits and barriers of electronic marketplace participation: An SME perspective. *The Journal of Enterprise Information Management, 17*(4), 301-311.

Stocking, S. H. (1999). How journalists deal with scientific uncertainty. In S. M. Friedman, S. Dunwoody, & C. L. Rogers (Eds.), *Communication uncertainty: media coverage and new and controversial science* (pp. 113). New Jersey, London: Lawrence Erlbaum Associates Publishers.

Stokic, D. (2006). *A New Collaborative Working Environment for Concurrent Engineering in Manufacturing Industry*. Proc. CE 2006, 13th ISPE International Conference on Concurrent Engineering, Juan-les-Pins, France.

Storey, D. (1982). *Entrepreneurship and the new firm*. New York: Praeger.

Straub, D. (1997). The effect of culture on IT diffusion: E-mail and fax in Japan and the US. *Information Systems Research, 5*(1), 23-47.

Strickmann, J., & Hahn, A. (2007). *Integrierte Wissensbasis für Projektcontrolling und Änderungsmanagement*. Paper presented at the 4th Conference on Professional Knowledge Management – Experiences and Visions, Potsdam, Germany

Sullivan, R., (2000). Entrepreneurial learning and mentoring. *International Journal of Entrepreneurial Behaviour & Research, 6*(3), 160-172.

Sundermann, K. (1999). Constructive technology assessment. In S. Bröchler, G. Simonis, & K. Sundermann (Eds.), *Handbuch Technikfolgenabschätzung* (Vol. 1, pp. 119). Berlin: edition sigma.

Swade, D. (2000). The cogwheel brain: Charles Babbage and the quest to build the first computer (1st ed.). London: Little, Brown and Company.

Swan, J., & Newell, S. (2000). *Linking knowledge management and innovation*. Paper presented at the European Conference on Information Systems (pp. 591-598). ECIS, Vienna.

Swanson, E. B. (1994). Information systems innovation among organizations. *Management Science, 40*(9), 1069-1092.

Swayne, C., & Tucker, W. (1973). *The effective entrepreneur*. Morristown, NJ: General Learning Press.

Szakonyi, R. (1990). 101 tips for managing R&D more effectively - I. *Research Technology Management, 33*(4), 31-36.

Szgeo, O., & Andersen, B. *Modeling the Extended Enterprise: A comparison of Different Modeling Approaches*.

Tagliaferri, L. E. (1982). As quality circles fade, a bank

tries top-down teamwork. *American Bankers Association, ABA Banking Journal, 74*(7), 98.

Tammela, J., & Salminen, V. (2006). *Modeling business innovation collaboration in open infrastructure.* In K. D. Thoben, K. S. Pawar, & S. Terzi (Ed.), *ICE 2006, 12ᵗʰ International Conference on Concurrent Enterprising,* Milan, Italy 26-28 June 2006: Innovative products and services through collaborative networks (pp. 283-290). Nottingham: Centre for Concurrent Enterprise Nottingham University Business School.

Tarso, L. (2001). *Innovation in the making.* Copenhagen: Business School Press.

Tassabehji, R. (2003). *Applying e-commerce in business.* London: Sage Publications.

Tassabehji, R., Taylor, W. A., Beach, R., & Wood, A. (2006). Reverse e-auctions: An exploratory study. *International Journal of Operations and Production Management, 26*(2), 166-184.

Tassabehji, R., Wallace, J., & Tsoularis, T. (2006). Reverse e-auctions: Introducing agility to organisations. *International Journal of Agile Systems and Management 1*(4), 407-421.

Tatnall, A., & Davey, B. (2003). ICT and training: A proposal for an ecological model of innovation. *Education Technology and Society, 6*(1), 14-17.

Taylor, M., & Murphy, A. (2004). SMEs and e-business. *Journal of Small Business and Enterprise Development, 11*(3), 280-289.

Technology definition. Retrieved December 15, 2006 from http://en.wikipedia.org/wiki/Portal:Technology.

Teece, D. J. (2002). *Managing intellectual capital* (pp. 183). Oxford: Oxford University Press.

Teece, D., Pisano, G., & Shuen, A. (1997). Dynamic capabilities and strategic management. *Strategic Management Journal, 18*(7), 509-533.

Teo Siew Chin, S., & Williams, J. B. (2006). A theoretical framework for effective online course design. *MERLOT Journal of Online Learning and Teaching, 2*(1), 12-21.

Terlep, S. (2007). T*oyota overtakes GM.* Retrieved January 30, 2007, from http://www.toyotaweekly.com/index.php?categoryid=1&p2_articleid=5

Terninko J, Zlotin B. & Zusman A (1996). *Step by Step TRIZ. Creating Innovative Solution Concepts.* Responsible Management Inc.

Terziovski, M., Sohal, A., & Moss, S. (1999). Longitudinal analysis of quality management practices in Australian organizations. *Total Quality Management, 10*(6), 915-926.

The Standish Group (1994). *The CHAOS Report.* West Yarmouth.

The Weekend Australian Financial Review. (2006). *CBA ushers in the people era.* 2006. pp.13. Retrieved April 1-2, 2006, from http:// www.afr.com

Thomas, J. B., Watts Sussman, S., & Henderson, J. C. (2001). Understanding "strategic learning": Linking organizational learning, knowledge management, and sensemaking. *Organization Science, 12*(3), 331-45.

Thomas, R., & Thomas, H. (2006). Micro politics and micro firms: A case study of tourism policy formation and change. *Journal of Small Business and Enterprise Development, 13*(1), 100-114.

Thompson, J., & Martin, F. (2005). *Strategic management, awareness, & change.* London: Thomson Learning.

Thompson, L., Arlanda, E., & Robbins, S. (2000). *Tools for teams: Building effective teams in the workplace.* Needham Heights, Pearson Education, Inc.

Thompson, V. A. (1965). Bureaucracy and innovation. *Administrative Science Quarterly, 10*(1), 1-20.

Thorp, J. (2005, September 7). Meeting the challenge for IT-enabled change: A strategic governance approach. *Presented at the Committee for Economic Development of Australia (CEDA) Luncheon.* Melbourne, Australia.

Timm, P. R., & Jones, C. G. (2005). *Technology and customer service: Profitable relationship building.* NJ: Pearson Education, Inc, Pearson Prentice Hall.

Titus, S., & Brochner, J. (2005). Managing information flows in construction supply chains. *Construction Innovation. 5,* 71-82.

Toomey, M. (2005). *A catastrophe in governance of IT: Australian customs integrated cargo system.* Melbourne,

Australia: Infonomics Pty. Ltd.

Toomey, M. (2006). Achieving business sustainability: Director's perceptions of information technology investment, corporate, monitoring, and governance. *Infonomics Newsletter Report.*

Toomey, M. (2007, August 13-25). Achieving business sustainability: Director's perceptions of information technology investment, corporate monitoring, and governance. *Presented at itSMF Australia National Conference, Melbourne, Australia.*

Tranfield, D., Parry, I., Wilson, S., Smith, S., & Foster, M. (1998). Teamworked organizational engineering: Getting the most out of teamworking. *Management decision, 36*(6), MCB University Press.

Treacy, M., & Wiersema, F. (1995). *The discipline of market leaders: Choose your customers, narrow your focus, dominate your market.* Reading, MA: Addison-Wesley Pub. Co.

Trompenaars, F., & Hampden-Turner, C. (1998). *Riding the waves of culture: Understanding diversity in global business.* New York: McGraw-Hill.

Tsaih, R., & Lin, W. (2006). The process-wide information organism approach for the business process analysis. *Industrial Management and Data Systems, 106*(4), 509-522.

Tucker, D., & Jones, L. D. (2000). Virtual organisation: The new competitive arena of the global entrepreneur. *Management Case Quarterly, 3*(2), 29-33.

Turbini, L. J., Munie, G., C., Bernier, D., Gamalski, J., & Bergman, D. W. (2001). Examining the environmental impact of lead-free soldering alternatives. *IEEE Transactions on Electronics Packaging Manufacturing, 24*(1), 4.

Turvey, N. K., & Neal, A. (2001). *High performance work practices and business success. Evidence from Australian Enterprises. Results of the 2001 National Survey.* The University of Queensland (QUT), Centre for Human Factors and Applied Cognitive Psychology, Centre for Organizational Psychology and Centre for strategic management.

Tyree, A. (2005). *Banking law in Australia* (5th ed.). NSW:

Centrum Printing. LexisNexis Butterworths

UMUC. (2004). Graduate program information. University of Maryland University College. Retrieved February 14, 2007, from http://umuc.edu/grad/mba/mba_information.shtml

UN-ECE. (1996). *Small and medium-sized enterprises in countries in transition: Government policy, legislation, statistics, support institutions.* United Nations Economic Commission for Europe. Retrieved June 14, 2007, from http://www.unece.org/indust/sme/review96.htm

United States Department of Commerce (USDoC). (1998). *The emerging digital economy.* Washington, DC.

Valsiner, J. (1998). *The guided mind.* Cambridge, MA: Harvard University Press.

Van Alstyne, M., & Brynjolfsson, E. (2005). Global village or cyber-balkans? Modeling and measuring the integration of electronic communities. *Management Science, 51*(6), 851-868.

Van de Ven, A. H., Angle, H., & Poole, M. S. (2000). *Research on the management of innovation: The Minnesota studies.* New York: Oxford University Press, August, 2000 (paperback) Originally printed 1989.

Van der Velde, L. N. J., & Meijer, B. R. (2003). A system approach to supply chain design with a multinational for colorant and coatings. Retrieved September 20, 2006, from http://www.ifm.eng.cam.ac.uk/mcn/pdf_files/part6_5.pdf

Van Eck, R. (2006). Digital game-based learning: It's not just the digital natives who are restless. *EDUCAUSE Review, 41*(2), 16-30.

Van Ketel, M., & Nelson, T.D. (1998). *E-commerce.* Retrieved May 18, 2006, from http://www.whatis.com/

Van Yperen, N. W. (2003). Task interest and actual performance: The moderating effects of assigned and adopted purpose goals. *Journal of Personality and Social Psychology, 85*(6), 1006-1015.

Vara, V., & Chao, L. *eBay to leave China.* Wall Street Journal. December 19, 2006; Page A3

Varela, F., Thompson, E., & Rosch, E. (1991). *The em-*

bodied mind: Cognitive science and human experience. Cambridge, MA: MIT Press.

VDI. (1993). *VDI-Richtlinie 2221: Methodik zum Entwickeln und Konstruieren technischer Systeme und Produkte.* Düsseldorf, Germany: VDI.

Venkataraman, N. (1989). The concept of fit in strategy research: Toward verbal and statistical correspondence. *Academy of Management Review, 14*(3), 423-444.

Venkataraman, S., & Sarasvathy, S. D. (2001). Strategy and entrepreneurship: Outlines of an untold story. In M. A. Hitt, R. E. Freeman & J. S. Harrison (Eds.), *Handbook of Strategic Management,* (pp. 650-668). Oxford: Blackwell Publishers.

Verma, H. (2005). Enhancing export competitiveness of Indian SMEs through ICT. *Technology Exports, 11*(3), Jan-Mar 2005.

Vest., C.M. (1999) Science, innovation in technology: Reflections on change Retrieved December 10, 2006 from http://www.aaas.org/spp/rd/yrbk00/Part8.pdf)

Vianco, P. T. (1997). Solder alloys: A look at the past, present, and future. *Welding Journal*(March), 45.

Vincent, J. H., Harrison, M. R., Langeveld, P., de Kluizenaar, E. E., Steen, H. A. H., Warwick, M., et al. (1999). *Improved design life and environmentally aware manufacturing of electronics assemblies by lead-free soldering: IDEALS*: Marconi Materials Technology (UK).

vom Saal, F. S., & Hughes, C. (2005). An extensive new literature concerning low-dose effects of Bisphenol A shows the need for a new risk assessment. *Environmental Health Perspectives, 113*(8).

Von Eringen, Y., & Waarts, E. (2003). *A multi-country study of ERP systems: The effect of national culture.* Erasmus Institute of Management. Retrieved December 10, 2006, from https://ep.eur.nl/bitstream/1765/280/1/er-imrs20030310111626.pdf)

von Goeler, K. (1998). *Internet commerce by degrees: Small business early adopters.* Retrieved November 8, 2006, from http://instat.com

von Hippel, E. (1988). *The sources of innovation.* Oxford University Press.

Waddell, D., Singh, M., & Musa, A. (2006). Entrepreneurial opportunities on the Internet. In F. Zhao (Ed.), *Entrepreneurship and innovations in e-business: An integrative perspective* (pp. 179-199). Hershey, PA: Idea Group Publishing.

Wagner, R., & Sternberg, R. (1985). Practical intelligence in real world pursuits: The role of tacit knowledge. *Journal of personality and social psychology, 49*(2), 436-458.

Wagner, W. (1994). Fields of research and socio-genesis of social representation: A discussion of criteria and diagostics. *Social Science Information, 33*(2), 199-228.

Wailgum, T. (2006). *Integration liberation.* CIO Magazine. October 15, 2006. Retrieved January 15, 2007, from http://www.cio.com/archive/101506/integration.html

Wakkee, I., van der Sijde, P., & Kirwan, P. (2003). *An empirical exploration of the global startup concept in an entrepreneurship context.* Working Paper. Holland: GS Leuven.

Wallace, J., Tsoularis, T., & Tassabehji, R., (2006). Internet technology and stochastic automata to improve supply chain agility. *International Journal of Agile Systems and Management, 1*(4), 346-359.

Wallgren, L., & Hanse, J. (2007). Job characteristics, motivators and stress among technology consultants: A structural equation modeling approach. *International Journal of Industrial Engineers, 37*(1), 51-59.

Walter, A., Auer, M., & Gemünden, H. G. (2002). The impact of personality, competence, and activities of academic entrepreneurs on technology transfer success. *International Journal of Entrepreneurship and Innovation Management, 2*(2/3), 268-289.

Wang, C. K., & Ang, B. L. (2004). Determinants of venture performance in Singapore. *Journal of Small Business Management, 42*(4), 347.

Watkins, J. (2005). *Gen Y knocking at the door of ownership.* The Washington Times. November 18, 2005. Retrieved February 7, 2007, from http://www.washtimes.com/fhg/20051117-083543-6983r.htm

Webb, P., Pollard, C., & Ridley, G. (2006). Attempting to define IT governance: Wisdom or folly? *Proceedings of the 39th Hawaii International Conference on System Sciences.* Retrieved April 26, 2007, from http://ieeexplore.ieee.org/iel5/10548/33368/01579684.

pdf?arnumber=1579684

Webber, A. M. (1999). New math for a new economy. *Fast company,* I *31*, 214. Retrieved on May 21, 2006, from http://www.fastcompany.com/magazine/31/lev.html

Weiber, R., & Kollmann, T. (1998). Competitive advantages in virtual markets—perspectives of "information-based-marketing" in cyberspace. *European Journal of Marketing, 32*(7/8), 603-615.

Weick, K. E. (2002). Puzzles in organizational learning: An exercise in disciplined imagination. *British Journal of Management, 13*(S2), S7-S15.

Weick, K. E., & Sutcliffe, K. M. (2001). *Managing the unexpected.* New York: Jossey-Bass.

Weill, P., & Ross, J. (2004). *IT governance: How top performers manage IT decision rights for superior results.* Boston: Harvard Business School Press.

Weingart, P. (1998). Science and the media. *Research Policy, 27*(8), 869-879.

Weiser, M. (1993, October 1993). Ubiquitous computing. *IEEE Computer,* 71-72.

Weiser, M. (1999, 9-12 May 1999). *How computers will be used differently in the next twenty years.* Paper presented at the Symposium on Security and Privacy Oakland, CA, USA.

Weisser, S. O. (2005). *Believing in yourself as classroom culture.* Retrieved November 25, 2006, from http://www.aaup.org/publications/Academe/2005/05jf/05jfweis.htm

Weissman, D. (2000). *A social ontology.* New Haven, CT: Yale University Press.

Wenger, E. (1998). *Communities of practice: Learning, meaning, and identity.* Cambridge: Cambridge University Press.

West, M.,Tjosvold, D., & Smith, K. (2005). *The essential of Teamworking, International Perspectives.* West Sussex: John Wiley and Sons Ltd.

Whang, S. (2005). *Sense and respond—The next generation business model.* Retrieved December 30, 2006, http://www.gsb.stanford.edu/news/research/sup-plychain_whang_senserespond.shtml

Wheatley, B., & Greer, E. (1995). Interactive television: A new delivery system for a traditional reading course. *Journal of Technology and Teacher Education, 3*(4), 343-351.

Wheelen, T. L., & Hunger, J. D. (1999). *Strategic management and business policy* (6th ed.). New York: Addison-Wesley.

Whinston, A., Barua, A., Shutter, J., Wilson, B., & Pinnell, J. (2001). *Measuring the Internet economy.* Cisco Systems & University of Texas. Retrieved July 18, 2001, from www.internetindicators.com

Whiting, R. (2006, November 6). BPM gets smarter with a little help from BI. *Information Week,* November 6, 2006.

Wickramasinghe, L., Amarasin, R., & Alahakon, L. (2004). A hybrid intelligent multiagent system for e-business. *Computational Intelligence, 20*(4), 603-623.

Wildemann, H. (2006). *Innovationen.* München: TCW.

Wildemann, H. (2006). *Innovationscontrolling, Leitfaden zur Selektion, Planung, Steuerung und Erfolgsmessung von F&E-Projekten.* München, Germany: TCW.

Williams, T. (2002). *Modeling complex projects.* Chichester, UK: John Wiley & Sons.

Williams, V., & Phillips B. D. (1999). *E-commerce: Small businesses venture online.* Report, Office of Advocacy, US Small Business Administration, Washington, DC. Retrieved July 1, 2006, from http://www.sba.gov/advo/stats/e_comm.pdf

Williamson, O. E. (1993). Calculativeness, trust, & economic organization. *Journal of Law & Economics, 34*(1), 453-502.

Wimmer, M., & Holler, U. (2003). Applying a holistic approach to develop user-friendly customer-oriented e-government portal interfaces. *Lecture Notes in Computer Science, 2615,* 167-178. Heidelberg: Springer Publishing.

Wittel, A. (2001). Toward network sociality. *Theory, Culture & Society, 18*(6), 51-76.

Woess, W., & Dunzendorfer, A. (2002). Homogeneous

EDI between Web-based tourism information systems. *Lecture Notes in Computer Science, 2455*(1), 183. Heidelberg: Springer Publishing.

Wolff, M. (1999). *Burn rate: How i survived the gold rush years on the Internet.* London: Orion.

Wood, M., & Ferlie, E. (2003). Journeying from Hippocrates with Bergson and Deleuze. *Organization Studies, 24*(1), 47-68

Woodhouse, D. (1999). Quality and quality assurance. In J. Knight & H. de Wit (Eds.), *Quality and internationalisation in higher education* (pp. 29-44). Paris: OECD.

World Tourism Organization (WTO). (2006). *Tourism highlights: 2006.* Madrid: WTO.

World Trade Organization. (2005). *Notification G/TBT/N/CHN/140*: Comittee on Technical Barriers to Trade.

Wright, D. (2005). The dark side of ambient intelligence. *Info, 7*(6), 33-51.

Wright, W. F., Smith, R., Jesser, R., & Stupeck, M. (1999). Information technology, process reengineering and performance measurement: A balanced scorecard analysis of Compaq Computer Corporation. *Communications of AIS (Association for Innovation System), 1*(8), 1-61.
Wu, J., & Chang, Y. (2005). Towards understanding members' interactivity, trust, and flow in online travel community. *Industrial management and Data Systems, 105*(7), 937-954.

Yankee Group (YG). (1998). Yankee Group finds small and business market missing the Internet commerce opportunity: Market Unsatisfied with current Internet solution provider offerings, *YG Communication*, November 17. Retrieved from http://www.yankeegroup.com

Yap, C. S., Soh, C. P. P., & Raman, K. S. (1992). Information systems success factors in small business. *Omega—International Journal of Management Science, 20*(5/6), 597-609.

Yasin, M., Alavi, J., Sobral, F., & Lisboa, J. (2003). Realities, threats, and opportunities facing the Portuguese tourism industry. *International Journal of Contemporary Hospitality Management, 15*(4), 221-225.

Yavas, U., & Romanova, N. (2005). Assessing performance of multi-hospital organisations: A measurement approach. *International Journal of Health Care Quality Assurance, 18*(3), 193-203.

Yeh, E., Smith, C., Jennings, C., & Castro, N. (2006). Team building: A 3-dimensional teamwork model. *Team Performance Management, 12*(5/6), 192-197.

Yin, K.R. (2008). *Case stydy research: Design and methods.* Sage, CA.

Yin, R. K. (1994). *Case study research: Design and methods* (2nd ed.). London: Sage.

Yousaf, A. A. (1989). *Holy Quran: Text, translation & commentary.* Beltville, MD: Amana Corporation.

Yukongdi, V. (2001). Teams and total quality management. A comparison between Australia and Thailand. *The International Journal of Quality and Reliability Management, 18*(4), 387.

Zaheer, A., & Venkatraman, N. (1995). Relational governance as an interorganizational strategy: An empirical test of the role of trust in economic exchange. *Strategic Management Journal, 16*(5), 373-392.

Zahira, S. A., Ireland, R. D., & Hitt, M. A. (2000). International expansion by new firms: International diversity, mode of entry, technological learning and performance. *Academy of Management Journal, 43*(5), 925-950.

Zaltman, G., Duncan, R., & Holbek, J. (1973). *Innovations and organizations.* New York: John Wiley.
Zampetakis, L. A., & Moustakis, V. (2006). Linking creativity with entrepreneurial intentions: A structural approach. *The International Entrepreneurship and Management Journal, 2*(3), 413-428.

Zank, G. M., & Vokurka, R. J. (2003). The Internet: Motivations, deterrents, and impact on supply chain relationships. *S.A.M. Advanced Management Journal, 68*(2), 33-40.

Zehr, S. C. (1999). Scientists' Representations of Uncertainty. In S. M. Friedman, S. Dunwoody & C. L. Rogers (Eds.), *Communication uncertainty: Media coverage and new and controversial science* (pp. 3). New Jersey, London: Lawrence Erlbaum Associates Publishers.

Zehr, S. C. (1999). Scientists' Representations of Uncertainty. In S. M. Friedman, S. Dunwoody & C. L. Rogers

(Eds.), *Communication uncertainty: Media coverage and new and controversial science* (pp. 3). New Jersey, London: Lawrence Erlbaum Associates Publishers.

Zetie, S. (2002). The quality circle approach to knowledge management. *Managerial Auditing Journal, 17*(6), 317-321.

Zettelmeyer, F., & Hauser, J. R. (1995). *Metrics to evaluate R&D groups: Phase I, qualitative interviews," Working Paper #125-95.* Cambridge, MA.

Zhao, F. (2006). *Maximize business profits through e-partnerships.* Hershey, PA: IRM Press.

Zlotin B. & Zusman A. (1999). Managing Innovation Knowledge. *Triz Journal.*

Zucker, L. G. (1986). Production of trust – International source of economic structure 1840-1920. *Research in Organizational Behaviour, 8*(1), 53-111.

Zutshi, A., Zutshi, S., & Sohal, A (2006). How e-entrepreneurs operate in the context of open source software. In F. Zhao (Ed.), *Entrepreneurship and innovations in e-business: An integrative perspective* (pp. 62-88). Hershey, PA: Idea Group Publishing.

ZVEI. (1999). *Bleifreies Löten: Materialien, Komponenten, Prozesse.* Frankfurt am Main: Zentralverband Elektrotechnik- und Elektronikindustrie e.V.

Zwass, V. (2003). Electronic commerce and organizational innovation: Aspects and opportunities. *International Journal of Electronic Commerce, 7*(3), 7-37.

About the Contributors

Fang Zhao is senior lecturer and also senior supervisor of Doctor of Business Administration (DBA) and PhD at the School of Management, RMIT University, Australia. She has recently published two research books (300 pages each) in the areas of e-business management, and around 50 refereed research works internationally in the areas of innovation and entrepreneurship, knowledge management, performance measurement, TQM, etc. She has won a number of research grants and funding including an Australian Research Council grant. She is holding two posts of Visiting Professor of Management in two prestigious universities in China. Zhao is the founding editor-in-chief of the *International Journal of e-Business Management,* which is a refereed international journal published by RMIT University Publishing Press.

* * *

Shamsuddin Ahmed is professor of operations management at the Bang College of Business, Kazakhstan Institute of Management Economics and Strategic Research. He is also an adjunct faculty at the Edith Cowan University, Australia. Outside academia, he worked in industries and gained experiences as system analyst and chief executive industrial engineer. In such capacities, he commissioned and managed a manufacturing industry. He authored research books published by American Society of Mechanical Engineers, USA and published extensively in operations management and information systems areas. His research areas are process management, hospital service simulations, statistical model building, neural network computations, etc.

Francis Amagoh is an assistant professor of public administration at Kazakhstan Institute of Management, Economics, and Strategic Research (KIMEP). He received his PhD in public administration (concentration in public financial management) and an MBA (management and finance) from Virginia Commonwealth University, Richmond Virginia, USA. He has worked as a structural engineer, project engineer, and senior project engineer at the Virginia Department of Transportation, and North Carolina Department of Transportation in the United States. His research interests include municipal finance, public policy, and business administration.

Andreas Biedermann is scientific assistant of Prof. Dr. Roman Boutellier. His research focuses on the field of the management of controversial technologies, whereof lead-bearing solders are a typical example. Biedermann studied industrial engineering and management at the ETH in Zurich. His major subjects were information systems, technology, and innovation management and mechanical engineering. Biedermann works in innovation management consultancy and new business development. He gained work experience at several multinational companies and SMEs from various industries.

Roman Boutellier is an ordinary professor for technology and innovation management at the Department for Management, Technology, and economics (D-MTEC) at the Swiss Federal Institute of Technology (ETH) in Zurich and Titular Professor at the University of St. Gallen (HSG). From 1981 to 1993, Boutellier worked in a number of capacities at Kern AG (as of 1987, Leica AG). He taught as a professor of Business Management at the University of St. Gallen (CH) between 1993 and 1998. From 1999 to 2004, he was CEO and Delegate to the Board of SIG Holding AG (CH). Boutellier is a member of the board of directors of several large-scale Swiss enterprises.

Peter Busch is a lecturer in the Department of Computing at Macquarie University. Having studied geography at the University of Adelaide and then undertaken a masters degree in Librarianship at Monash University, Busch undertook studies in computing at the University of Tasmania. He then became an associate lecturer in the Department of Computer Science and thereafter the School of Information Systems at the University of Tasmania. He has completed his PhD under the supervision of the late C.N.G. "Kit" Dampney at Macquarie University, examining the knowledge management implications of tacit knowledge diffusion in the IT organisational domain. His areas of teaching include databases and information systems. His research area focuses on knowledge management.

Kathryn Cormican lectures in the Faculty of Engineering at the National University of Ireland, Galway. Her research interests lie in the areas of enterprise integration and technology management. Kathryn leads a number of funded research projects in these areas. She has published widely at international conferences and peer reviewed journals. Kathryn also works with many leading organisations helping them to design, develop, and deploy new processes and systems.

Andrew Creed is currently a lecturer at Deakin University with research interests in e-learning technologies in the field of management education. Creed is an author of multimedia learning objects and supplements for management textbook with publishers including Wiley and Prentice-Hall. He was an instructional designer, writer, and project manager for online industrial training toolboxes in the fields of food and meat processing, and office administration. Creed is also a research assistant in the online MBA program at University of Maryland University College and has been a consultant and mentor to hundreds of start-up entrepreneurs via the Australian federal government's new enterprise incentive scheme.

Richard Duncombe is lecturer in information systems and development at the Institute for Development Policy and Management (IDPM) at the University of Manchester in the UK. He holds a PhD in development administration and management from the University of Manchester, and an MSc from the Science Policy Research Unit at the University of Sussex. Duncombe's research interests include information systems, e-commerce, and small enterprise development in developing countries. He has undertaken contract research for the World Bank Macro-economics Division and UNIDO and has produced technical reports and manuals for the Commonwealth Telecommunications Organisation (CTO) and the UK Department for International Development (DFID).

Simrn Kaur Gill is a master's research student in the Faculty of Engineering at the National University of Ireland, Galway. Her research interests lie in the areas of innovation, project, and knowledge management. She has been actively involved in a European Union research project in the area of ambient intelligence, manufacturing, and project management.

Laura Galloway is a lecturer in entrepreneurship in the School of Management and Languages at Heriot-Watt University. She has held research posts at the University of Strathclyde and the University of Paisley. Her research interests include studying the impacts of entrepreneurship education, and internet-based entrepreneurial start-ups and growth. She has published papers on small firms, enterprise, and entrepreneurship in a number of journals.

Mary De Gori graduated as a physiotherapist from the University of Melbourne in 1995. Her clinical career has seen her practice in both acute and subacute care with children, adults, and the ageing. She has several physiotherapy and health care related publications, conference presentations, and posters. De Gori has a keen interest in leadership, change management, and health care innovation. She has worked more recently in the area of project management within health care and is currently the manager for quality and safety at a metropolitan health service in Victoria. De Gori is currently completing her masters in business leadership at RMIT University.

Axel Hahn has been a full professor for business engineering in the Department of Computer Science at the University of Oldenburg since 2002. Previously, he was managing director of myview technologies, a software company for product information management systems. Research interests are R&D Management and interoperability especially in logistics.

Stefan Häusler studied computer science at the University of Oldenburg. Since his master thesis in 2006, he is employed in the R&D division Embedded Hardware/Software Systems at the OFFIS Institute for Information Technology in Oldenburg. He is involved in research projects that aim to improve the efficiency and productivity of product development in the semiconductor and automotive industry. In this context his research activities are focused on the employment of semantic web technologies for domain modelling and information integration.

Kevin Hausmann is employed by the OFFIS institute since 2006. He received a bachelor degree (BSc) and masters degree (Dipl.-Inform) at the University of Oldenburg, Germany. He is experienced in research project work, both in national and international contexts. His participation in the InterOP NoE allowed the establishment of his far ranging network of research colleagues. Kevin's main interests are interoperability of information systems, software development, and usage of ontologies in complex information systems. He has been leading several successful development projects, in particular Permeter, see http://www.permeter.de.

Cecilia Hegarty is a teaching fellow in entrepreneurship with the Northern Ireland Centre for Entrepreneurship (NICENT) at University of Ulster. Her pioneering all-island research investigated entrepreneurial development processes in Northern Ireland and the Republic of Ireland. Cecilia has consulted on different projects including EU Framework projects. She has published widely in the field of entrepreneurship, business and rural tourism and her most recent book is "*Sources of Funding for Irish Entrepreneurs*." Her research interests include entrepreneurship education, family firms, small business development, and entrepreneurial networking practices.

William Keogh is professor and the head of the Department of Management and enterprise coordinator at Heriot-Watt University, Edinburgh. He has been leading teaching and research activities in the area of Science and Technology, seeking to widen access to enterprise teaching across the University. His main research interest lies in the strategic use of knowledge in innovative, entrepreneurial technology-based small firms. He is currently a member of a number of journal editorial boards including the *International Small Business Journal* (ISBJ), *Small Business and Enterprise Development,* and the *Journal of Strategic Change*. He is an external examiner for entrepreneurship at a number of British universities and is a director of the Institute for Small Business and Entrepreneurship (ISBE).

Suryadeo Kissoon is a PhD candidate in quality management at RMIT University. He is a holder of a master degree in business administration with about 15 years' practical working experience in general management at executive level. He has also been working in a major Australian banking organization and other Australian organizations. He received five nominations and quality awards nationally and internationally as operations manager. He has been working as a management consultant and been lecturing for nearly ten years in fields of HRM, quality management, financial management, strategic management, and production/operation management.

Tobias Kollmann received his doctorate in 1997 with a thesis on the acceptance of innovative telecommunication and multimedia systems. In 1997, he moved into the industry and co-founded autoscout24, the largest used car electronic trading platform in Europe. In October 2001, he became a professor for e-business at the University of Kiel, Germany. Since 2005, he has been holding the chair of e-business and e-entrepreneurship at the University of Duisburg-Essen, Germany, where he focuses particularly on questions of business venturing and business development in the field of the Net Economy.

Adela J. McMurray is associate professor and the director of entrepreneurship at RMIT School of Management and has both academic and industrial experience gained through her business, research and consulting activities in both manufacturing and service industries. Her work in the area of culture and cultural diversity, innovation and learning is recognised internationally resulting in over 60 refereed publications. She has attracted over $3.5 million in research and industry funding and is the recipient of three Australian Research Council grants. She reviews for the Academy of Management and is the International Entrepreneurship Chair for ANZIBA.

Christopher Miller is a principal lecturer in small business management at the University of Glamorgan Business School. His main teaching areas are small business, strategy, enterprise, business start up, small business, and general business. Research interests are in the areas of Construction management and culture, small business management, sustainability and growth, technology diffusion, supplemental instruction, and innovative learning. Current research activity concerns barriers to technology diffusion, small business management, reduction costs for construction organisations, supply chain harmonisation in construction, and innovative learning through supplemental instruction.

Alemayehu Molla is senior lecturer in information systems at the School of Business Information Technology, RMIT University, Australia. He holds a PhD and MSc in information systems, BA in business management, and a diploma in computer science. Molla's research interests include B2B e-business, information systems outsourcing and success, ERP and culture, and ICTs and socio-economic development. His work has appeared in journals such as the *European Journal of Information Systems, The International Journal of Electronic Commerce, Information & Management, Electronic Commerce Research, Journal of Internet Banking and Commerce, International Journal of Entrepreneurship and Innovation, Journal of Information Technology Management, Information Technologies and International Development, Journal of IT for Development*, and *Electronic Journal of Information Systems in Developing Countries.*

Gary Packham is deputy head for the Department of Enterprise and Economic Development at the University of Glamorgan Business School. He was academic delivery manager for E-College Wales, between 2004-2005, which was an ESF funded project. He was project manager for the Wales Fast Growth Fifty project between 1999-2000. Research interests are in the areas of small business management, strategic decision-making and small firms, small business growth, construction management, technology diffusion, student centred learning, and innovative learning techniques. Current research activity concerns strategic decision-making and small business growth, barriers to technology diffusion, small business management, and enterprise education.

James Perotti is currently teaching in the MBA program of the Rochester Institute of Technology's College of Business as a distinguished lecturer in MIS. He retired from Ohio University as the O'Bleness professor of MIS in 2001. Prior to serving in Ohio University's business college, he was associate provost for budget and planning. He has published two books and numerous articles on issues in information technology and management.

Valerie S. Perotti is distinguished lecturer of management at Rochester Institute of Technology and professor emeritus of management at Ohio University where she held a variety of teaching and administrative offices. Perotti has managed, worked, or taught in many different nations including Canada, France, Holland, Hong Kong, Jamaica, Malaysia, Norway, Singapore, and the United Kingdom. She continues to do active research and publication in both learning innovation and global business. In addition, she maintains a small private consulting practice focused on issues related to management, organizational structure, and international business.

Debbie Richards is currently an associate professor in the computing department at Macquarie University in Sydney. She has been interested in expertise and knowledge management from a theoretical and practical point of view since the early 80s. This was initially inspired by her work in industry with experts from various commercial and retail domains and explored further in her masters and PhD theses, following completion of a bachelor of business. While much of Debbie's research is within the field of artificial intelligence she is keen to develop systems that people are able to use and which make a difference to practice in industry. Turning the ideas of creative people into innovative solutions is part of achieving this goal and the first step is identifying these people, which is the aim of the reported work.

Jane Ross has expertise in areas of international business, organizational, and educational experience and has taught face to face and online globally including in Asia Pacific, Europe, and USA. She has a background of working in public, private, and nongovernmental organizations. She has also served on many organizational boards, including the Board of Governors for St. Stephen's College at the University of Alberta campus, Edmonton, Canada. Since 2000, Ross has been with the Graduate School of Science & Technology, University of Maryland University College where she serves as professor and director of MBA and executive programs.

Muhammad Mohtsham Saeed is working as a research assistant at Centre for Strategic Management and Leadership, University of Innsbruck, Austria. Previously he has worked for National Telecommunication Corporation, United Bank Limited, and Bank Alfalah in Pakistan. His last assignment was as incharge of a general banking unit. He has been brilliant throughout his academic record and has obtained a number of Awards/Gold Medals/Distinctions etc in the process. His research interests include Servant Leadership, Islamic Management Systems, Islamic Leadership Styles, and Cross Cultural Comparisons. Presently he is working on development of a strategic management model for Islamic World.

John Sanders is a lecturer in strategic management in the School of Management and Languages at Heriot-Watt University. Previously he held a lecturing position at Massey University, New Zealand, and taught International Business and General Management courses. His research efforts focus on organisational alignment.

Geoff Simmons is a lecturer in e-marketing/food marketing at the School of Marketing, Entrepreneurship, and Society within the University of Ulster. This role involves developing a food marketing competency within the school with a particular research focus on the adoption of e-marketing applications and an increase in the marketing orientation within the SME dominated agri-food sector. He is actively involved in research which is focussing on the determinants of Web site adoption for marketing by SME agri-food companies. His current international contact network, in relation to agri-food marketing and e-marketing, includes collaborations with the Centre for Food Marketing at St. Josephs University in Philadelphia, the University of Otago in New Zealand, and the National Food Centre in Dublin.

Alexandra Steinberg is assistant professor of management and human resources at the EM Lyon Business School. She is member of the editorial advisory and review board of the *International Journal of e-Business Management*. She earned her PhD in organisational social psychology at the London School of Economics and Political Science in the UK, where she is also a guest lecturer. Over the past decade, Alexandra has worked as a management consultant both in Europe and overseas, focusing on strategic change and communication management in large-scale IT-system transformation programmes. She has worked with Siemens Business Services in Germany and most recently with IBM Global Business Services in London (UK).

Ing. Dragan Stokic gained a PhD in electrical engineering from the University of Belgrade (1980). Stokic has more than 30 years experience in industrial and research projects on the knowledge management, intelligent control of robots, modelling, and control of flexible manufacturing systems. Stokic is the author and co-author of more than 150 papers, more than 80 of them on KM, robot control, modelling and application, on process improvements in manufacturing enterprises. Stokic is also a co-author of three monographs and two textbooks on robotics systems, published by Springer-Verlag, Berlin.

Jan Strickmann studied information systems at the University of Muenster, focusing on process management in development organizations. He has worked at the OFFIS Institute for Information Technology and the Department of Information Systems in Oldenburg. His research interests include the interoperability of project and product data management, engineering performance measurement, and the application of semantic Web technology to model and control the domain of engineering projects. His research projects are motivated by and applied in automotive development organizations, both for major suppliers and OEMs

Jari Tammela is managing director of Spiral Business Services Corp that is providing consulting services for network business. He is also working as project manager in Lappeenranta University of Technology, where he is coordinating industrial research projects Life Cycle Business (LCB) and Modelling of business concepts in innovation commercialization (LIIMA) funded by TEKES. Tammela has 16 years of experience in manufacturing industry from Metso Automation including product development, engineering, marketing, and system/business development. He has a master's degree from Helsinki University of Technology, Department of Mechanical Engineering, where he is carrying on his doctoral studies.

Rana Tassabehji was awarded a master's degree in computing, and an MBA and a PhD in Internet security. She worked for several years as a consultant in the UK IT sector and as an International Business consultant, before returning to university. She currently specialises in e-business and IT at the University of Bradford. Her research interests are in e-supply chains, e-auctions, Internet security, and e-government where she has published her research in international journals and presented at international conferences She is also a subject referee for several international journals.

Brychan Thomas is senior research fellow in small business and innovation at the Welsh Enterprise Institute at the University of Glamorgan Business School. His main research interests lie in innovation and small business, SMEs and technology transfer networks, technology transfer and Internet adoption in the agri-food industry, etc. As such he has been involved with a number of projects examining technology transfer and small firms in Wales, as well as the development of the communication of science and the role of innovation within science and innovation centres. He has produced over 230 publications in the area of science communication, innovation and small business policy and is on the Editorial Advisory and Review Board of the *International Journal of E-Business Management* and the Editorial Advisory Board of International Management Journals.

Mark Toomey is a principal member of the Standards Australia team, which created AS8015 and continues this work through participation in an ISO/IEC Study Group leading to forthcoming publication of ISO standards in IT Governance. He is the author of "*The Director's IT Compass*" and several papers on IT Governance and IT failures, and regularly speaks to diverse audiences on corporate governance of IT. His company, Infonomics, specialises in helping corporate leaders understand and improve their organization's IT Governance. Mark commenced his IT consulting career in 1977, and has focused on governance of IT since 2000.

Anastasios Tsoularis received a degree in physics, a master's degree in operational research, and a PhD in cybernetics. He worked in the electricity supply industry in the UK prior to returning to university. Currently, he is a lecturer in mathematical sciences at Massey University in New Zealand. His research interests are in mathematical and computational modelling in management, engineering and the sciences. He is a reviewer for several international journals and has published refereed articles in a variety of science, engineering, and mathematics journals.

James Wallace obtained a degree in Mathematics and theoretical physics, a master's degree in electrical engineering and a Ph.D. in statistics. He worked in the energy utilities industries in the UK before returning to university and currently lectures in statistics and research methods at the University of Bradford. His research interests are in the application of mathematical and statistical approaches to modelling and analysis in management, engineering, and the sciences. He is a reviewer for several international journals and has published in management, engineering, science, and mathematics journals.

Donglin Wu is currently a PhD student in the School of Management, RMIT University, Australia. He has many years' work experience in the area of performance measurement and strategy research in hi-technology companies. His research interests are in the areas of performance measurement in hi-technology industry, small business, and the enterprise competitive intelligence system.

Ambika Zutshi is currently a lecturer at Deakin University, Australia. Her qualifications include a bachelor's degree in environmental sciences, a masters' degree in environmental management, and PhD. Her current research is focused in the area of triple bottom line reporting, role of stakeholders in the environmental management systems (EMS), business ethics and supply chain management. She has articles accepted for publication in journals such as *Business Process Management Journal, Managerial Auditing Journal, Management of Environmental Quality: An International Journal, Australian Accounting Review, and Alternative Law Journal and the International Journal of Environmental and Sustainable Development.*

Index

lead-free solders 442
lead-levels in blood 436
lead colic 436
lead compounds 436
leadership, in Islam 295
lead poisoning diagnosis 437
learning, defined 330
learning process 345
local area network (LAN) 6

M

manufacturing environment 1
Microsoft Corporation 278
Microsoft ESC 286
mobile phone security (MPS) 112
Motorola 300
multi-modality 7
multi-national organizations (MNCs) 419

N

national environments 417
national environments, seven dimensions of 420
newsgroups 193
New South Wales (NSW) 402
Northern Alliance Hospital Admission Risk Program (HARP) 189

O

online learning 346, 347
opportunity recognition 406
organisational culture 196
organizational performance measurement (OPM) 82
organizational process performance (OPP) 383
organization for economic co-operation and development (OECD) 383

P

performance, definition of 125
performance measurement 376
performance measurement (PM) 79
performance measurement techniques 377
Permeter Workflow 391
personal area network (PAN) 5
portal design, metric for 45
portal function 42
portal navigation tool design 45
portal navigation tool design, correlation analysis 51
Porter's generic strategies 164

product data management-systems (PDM) 382
product development 376

Q

quality assurance, in higher education 281
quality function deployment (QFD) 386

R

radio frequency identification (RFID) 10
realization stage of innovation 406
regional development, in quality assurance 281
rhizomic network analysis (RNA) 224, 226

S

semantic infrastructure 23, 28, 29
sense and respond (S&R) 368
Sense Interpret Decide Act (SIDA) 368
small- and medium-sized enterprises (SMEs) 101
small- and medium-sized firms (SMEs) 80
Small- and medium-size enterprises (SMEs) 122
Small- and medium-size enterprises (SMEs), innovations in 122
small- and middle-sized firms (SMEs) 79
SME motivation, three types of 127
social knowledge, construction of 228
social network 234
SparkNet 287
SPICE 383
Spot Runner 166
strategic awareness, definition of 157
supply chain innovations 361
supply chain management (SCM) 365
supply chain management technologies, three 182
supply network, information nodes 183
supply network partners, degree of integration 183

T

tacit knowledge measurement 396
technical system boundaries 31
technology, definition of 416
teleconferencing 193
triangulation 73
trust, in Islam 295
trust-based Islamic leadership model 294, 296
Turku University of Applied Sciences (TUAS) 278
turmoil, and business market opportunities 159

U

ubiquitous communication 5